Flyfisher's Guide to™

NEW ENGLAND

MAINE, NEW HAMPSHIRE, VERMONT, MASSACHUSETTS

LOU ZAMBELLO

Fishing Titles Available from Wilderness Adventures Press, Inc.™

Flyfishers Guide to™

Flyfisher's Guide to Alaska
Flyfisher's Guide to Arizona
Flyfisher's Guide to the Big Apple
Flyfisher's Guide to California
Flyfisher's Guide to Chesapeake Bay
Flyfisher's Guide to Colorado
Flyfisher's Guide to Colorado's
 Lost Lakes and Secret Places
Flyfisher's Guide to Connecticut
Flyfisher's Guide to Eastern Trophy Tailwaters
Flyfisher's Guide to the Florida Keys
Flyfisher's Guide to Freshwater Florida
Flyfisher's Guide to Idaho
Flyfisher's Guide to Mexico
Flyfisher's Guide to Montana
Flyfisher's Guide to Michigan
Flyfisher's Guide to Minnesota
Flyfisher's Guide to Missouri & Arkansas
Flyfisher's Guide to Nevada
Flyfisher's Guide to the New England Coast
Flyfisher's Guide to New Mexico
Flyfisher's Guide to New York
Flyfisher's Guide to the Northeast Coast
Flyfisher's Guide to New England
Flyfisher's Guide to Oregon
Flyfisher's Guide to Saltwater Florida
Flyfisher's Guide to Tennessee
Flyfisher's Guide to Texas
Flyfisher's Guide to the Texas Gulf Coast
Flyfisher's Guide to Utah
Flyfisher's Guide to Virginia
Flyfisher's Guide to Washington
Flyfisher's Guide to Western Washington Lakes
Flyfisher's Guide to Wisconsin & Iowa
Flyfisher's Guide to Wyoming
Flyfisher's Guide to Yellowstone National Park

On the Fly Guide to™

On the Fly Guide to the Northern Rockies

Best Fishing Waters™ Books

California's Best Fishing Waters
Colorado's Best Fishing Waters
Idaho's Best Fishing Waters
Montana's Best Fishing Waters
Oregon's Best Fishing Waters
Washington's Best Fishing Waters

Micro SD Cards with GPS Waypoints

Montana's Fishing GPS Maps
Colorado's Fishing GPS Maps
Washington's Fishing GPS Maps

Anglers Guide to™

Complete Anglers Guide to Oregon
Angler's Guide to the West Coast
Saltwater Angler's Guide to Southern California

Field Guide to™

Field Guide to Fishing Knots

Fly Tying

Go-To Flies™

Flyfishing Adventures™

Montana

Trout Adventures™

North America

Flyfishing Northern New England's Seasons

INCLUDING GPS

Flyfisher's Guide to™
NEW ENGLAND
MAINE, NEW HAMPSHIRE, VERMONT, MASSACHUSETTS

Lou Zambello

Flyfisher's Guide to™ Series

Wilderness
Adventures
Press, Inc.™

Belgrade, Montana

Published by Wilderness Adventures Press, Inc.™
45 Buckskin Rd
Belgrade, MT 59715
866-400-2012
Website: www.wildadvpress.com
email: books@wildadvpress.com

Printed in South Korea

ISBN: 978-1-940239-07-1

Table of Contents

Dedication

To my mother Kathy, who instilled in me early on my sense of adventure, and who still inspires me every day to enjoy life to the fullest and never stop learning.

Acknowledgements

A book of this type, covering so many waters across four states and many thousands of square miles, would not be possible without the knowledge and wisdom of many people. I couldn't possibly have first-hand knowledge of every locale, even if I fished New England for a dozen lifetimes. Fortunately, during my travels and flyfishing experiences, wonderful people openly shared their insights about home waters including fishing suggestions, maps and directions, hatch information, and photographs.

For Massachusetts, I would like to thank Charlie Shadan, owner of the fine Evening Sun Fly Shop (www.eveningsunflyshop.com), Brian Lynch of Pheasant Tail Tours (www.pheasanttailtours.com), Harry Desmond of Berkshire Rivers Flyfishing (www.berkshireflyfishing.com), the wonderful folks at the Cape Cod Chapter of Trout Unlimited (and for sharing with me their beloved Quashnet River).

For Vermont, angler Mark Allen, angler and friend Ben Sturtevant, Marty Oakland, owner of the Quill Gordon Bed and Breakfast (www.quillgordon.com), Dave Durovich, a very knowledgeable northern Vermont guide(davedurovich@gmail.com), and the two Brians of Vermont's Stream and Brook Guide Service (www.streamandbrook.com).

For New Hampshire, anglers Ray Gagnon and Philip Trasatti, Steve Heinz, Lisa Savard – former owner of the Cabins at Lopstick (www.cabinsatlopstick.com), and Sean Smith from Three Rivers Stocking Association (www.threeriversstocking.com).

For Maine, the Sebago Lake Chapter of Trout Unlimited, but in particular Steve Heinz and Tenley Bennett of Fish River Lodge (www.fishriverlodge.com), Ben Rioux of Mainely Flycastings and Quigley's Outdoors, Brett Damm of Rangeley Region Sport (Fly) Shop, Jeff McEvoy, owner of Weatherbys, Jane Brophy of Red River Lodge, Joe and Sue from Matagamon Campground, all of the columnists of the *Maine Sportsman* including Jim Andrews, William Clunie, Tom Seymour and David Van Wie, author of *The Confluence* (stories from the Dartmouth Grant). I would be remiss if I didn't give a shout out to Tim Shaw for his fabulous photos. Also, Jeff Kaine and Mike Gerald for their knowledge of the Moosehead area.

I would also like to thank members of my family including my mother, Kathy; Lindsey, Erika, Mary, Gwynn, Brian Whalen, Gwenne Oberg, and Ken Zambello for, at various times, acting as photographers, subjects, tour guides and road crew.

And a special acknowledgement to **John Boland**, *long-time fisheries biologist and eventual director of all things fisheries and wildlife related at the Maine Department of Inland Fisheries and Wildlife. I have known John for 30 years and his contributions to Maine fisheries are incalculable and his infusion of knowledge into this book substantial.*

And finally, a shout out to Josh, Blanche, and Chuck of Wilderness Adventures Press for their hard work on all matters pertaining to the book.

How to Use this Book

The challenge with writing of a book of this type is how to structure the information so it is most useful to the fisherman or fisherwoman, what to leave in and leave out, and how to best communicate the location of the various waters so they can be easily found. That being said, trade-offs always exist. Readers have disparate interests and plan differently, so one approach doesn't fit all and the size of the book has to balance comprehensiveness with readability and economics. Hopefully, my approach works for most people.

WATERS COVERED

This guidebook covers (at varying degrees of specificity) 650 rivers and streams and 500 lakes and ponds found within 200,000 square miles; more than anyone could fish in a lifetime. And yet many – and I am sure, wonderful – waters are not mentioned in this book. What is included are the best and most popular (not always the same thing) fisheries as judged by me, my fishing acquaintances, guides, and other writers. Also covered are lesser known waters that we have fished (some for many years) and thoroughly enjoyed. I have also spent the past several years criss-crossing most of New England (apologies to Rhode Island and Connecticut) discovering and exploring waters that were unknown up to that point. There is no doubt that I missed some intriguing and productive waters. But part of angling fun is to find and explore your own secret spots, so maybe it is a good idea not to catalog and systematically write about every possibility and to leave some uncertainty out there.

One of the reasons I wrote this book is that, while flyfishing participation in New England has remained level at best, anglers continue to complain about crowded conditions. Part of this phenomenon is due to the fact that everybody seems to be gravitating towards the same blue-ribbon waters. The speculation is that people today have less free time to explore and tend to gravitate towards the known. A number of recent books ("50 Best...", "25 Blue-ribbon...", "Trophy tailwaters...") encourage that behavior. So, certain waters experience crowding while other good options hardly see an angler. I marvel when I leave a crowded pool on the Rapid River, and then drive to a river that offers really outstanding fishing and never see a soul. I hope that this guidebook provides multiple options and ideas so readers can find their own, relatively uncrowded special places in addition to popular waters that we know and still love.

CONTENT

Guidebooks like this one have been around for a long time, but the Internet and smart devices have changed travel planning. Until recently, guidebooks contained basic facts: state information, tourism interests, lodging and travel resources, fish species identification, angling rules and laws, etc. Little of this information needs to be in a guidebook anymore because it can be found online very quickly. Therefore it is not included as part of this book. What anglers desire in a guidebook, I've found, is not basic facts, but compiled and thoroughly vetted information that they trust, along with some key websites for further information.

At the end of each geographical section is additional information geared to anglers with special interests: beginners, anglers with special limitations, and vacationers. These specialized suggestions do not appear in other guidebooks that I know of.

Beginner anglers are interested in fishing spots where they have a reasonable chance of success and are good locations to learn this fascinating new sport. These locations should also have relatively straightforward access, easy wading with room for backcasts, and fish that don't require very technical approaches. There are suggestions of waters that are good for beginners at the end of each section.

This book also includes easy-access options. Anglers that appreciate easy-access options include folks with disabilities, older fishers with less balance or strength, and parents that might fish with small children. Any angling places that can be visited with small children usually means parents get more fishing time in than they might otherwise, and that is a good thing.

Flyfishers are so time-crunched these days. Often carving out even a couple of weekends or one week of fishing time per year is a tall order. And therefore, these anglers want can't-miss options (or as close to can't miss as you can get when one is talking about flyfishing). I am contacted regularly by readers pleading for specific weekend or one-week vacation flyfishing recommendations, and so a number of them are included in this book. Obviously, many more vacation possibilities exist, but those listed I can personally vouch for.

This author firmly believes that when it comes to getting a feel for whether you want to try fishing unfamiliar water, a picture is worth a thousand words and sometimes a video is worth a hundred photos. So this book is filled with dozens of photos that show what many of the rivers, streams, and lakes look like. Word descriptors don't always do an adequate job, particularly when a "stream" in one part of New England might be far larger than a "river" in another area. Another example: Some ponds are larger than many lakes. An accompanying website is planned that will contain additional photographs and videos. Go to www.mainelyflyfishing.com or www.wildadvpress.com for the specific website address or search for it using keywords *Flyfisher's Guide to New England.*

DIRECTIONS AND LOCATIONS

Navigation is being revolutionized every year with technology. USGS topographical maps and old Rand McNally Road Maps have been replaced with *Delorme Atlas and Gazetteers* (both paper and digital), which are in turn being replaced with GPS capability in most automobiles and smart phones. Google Maps, Google Earth, and similar products or apps allow anyone to zoom in and see remarkably fine features on the most remote places on Earth. Each reader can choose what navigational aid (or combination) with which he or she feels most comfortable, including:

- All major waters have detailed individual maps right in the book for handy reference.
- Street and road references are often described for those utilizing street maps.
- For specific spots that are hard to find, GPS references are included in parentheses in a simple (positive-latitude, negative-longitude) format. Simply enter them directly into the Google or Bing search box, or your GPS device. NOTE: Bing is preferrable to Google, as Google will often take you to the *road* nearest the searched location, rather than the precise spot.

Remember, many rural or remote areas of New England have spotty cell phone coverage at best. GPS units always seem to run out of power at the most inconvenient times. Remote fishing camps may not have electricity or web-access. Computers fail. Cell phones fall in the water. Therefore, it is prudent to have multiple electronic and non-electronic navigational aids at your disposal. Nothing is more frustrating than wasting valuable fishing time because you are lost. In my travels across New England, I used GPS, Delorme Atlases, and supplemental maps and needed all of them at certain times.

THE REALITIES

The natural world changes in real time so the reality is that as soon as this book was published, it was obsolete. Fisheries improve or diminish. New species are introduced by "bucket biologists". Laws and regulations change. Logging activities, wind storms, and floods change the landscape. All this means that it pays to use this guide as a reference, but then do further research on your own to confirm access roads and points, current regulations, and fishing facts. Please e-mail me with any questions you have or if you experience something different than what is in the book, because I will be doing updates from time to time.

FLYFISHING NORTHERN NEW ENGLAND'S SEASONS

This guidebook is by its very nature, more of a where-to-go book than a how-to primer. Yet obviously, flyfishing success is based not just on where an angler fishes, but what fishing strategies and tactics he or she utilizes. Not many how-to flyfishing books exist that focus specifically on New England – which is why you should look for my first book, *Flyfishing Northern New England's Seasons.*

Central New England Hatch Chart

Insect	J	F	M	A	M	J	J	A	S	O	N	D	Fly Patterns
Midges			●	●	●	●	●	●	●	●			Griffith's Gnat #16-22,, Parachute Adams #16-22, Hatching Midge #18-22, Twisted Midge #16-20, Brassie #16-20, Zebra Midge #16-22
Early dark stoneflies			●										Black Klinkhammer #10-14
Misc. stoneflies					●	●	●						Stimulator #6-16, Swanson Stone #6-10, Yellow Sally nymph #2-6, Sim's Stone #10-12
Blue-winged olives				●	●	●	●		●	●			BWO Thorax #16-20, Pheasant Tail #16-20
Caddis				●	●	●	●	●	●				Elk Hair Caddis #8-18, X-caddis #12-16, Puterbaugh Caddis #16-18, Goddard Caddis #12-16, EZ Caddis #12-18, Emergent Sparkle Pupa #12-18
Light Cahills						●	●						Light Cahill #12-16, White Miller #14-16, Pheasant Tail #12-16
Quill Gordons				●									Hornberg Dry #10-14, Gray Klinkhammer #8-12
Hendrickson/Red quills				●									Adams Klinkhammer #12-16, Hornberg Dry #10-14, Copper John #12-16, Nemes Wet Fly #10-16
Gray fox/March browns					●								Parachute Adams #12-16, Klinkhammer #8-12, Parachute Hare's Ear #10-16, Hornberg Dry #12-16, Hare's Ear #10-14
Sulphurs					●	●							CDC Sulphur Comparadun #16-18, Hare's Ear #16-18
Dragonflies and Damselflies						●	●	●					Mini-muddler #6-10, Whitlock's Dragonfly #4-8, Whitlock Spent Blue Damsel #6
Green drakes/brown drakes						●							Lawson Paradrake #8-12, Wulff #8-12, Grizzly Wulff #10-12, Quigley Green Drake Cripple #10, Hare's Ear #6-10
Hexagenia							●						Parachute Hex #6-8, Grizzly or Kennebago Wulff #6-10, Royal Wulff #6-10, Black Wulff #6-10 (after dark), Maple Syrup #6-8
Leadwing coachman								●	●				Leadwing Coachman wet fly #10-12, Zug Bug and Prince Nymph #10-14, Gray Wulff #10-14, Parachute Adams #10-14
Tricos								●	●				Trico Spinner #18-24
Ants							●	●					Black Foam Ant #10-14, Black Fly Ant #10-14, Black Puterbaugh Caddis #12-18, Royal Wulff #14-20 (trust me on this one)
Beetles/Grasshoppers/Crickets								●	●	●			Parachute Hopper #8-14, Dave's Hopper #6-8, Letort Cricket #8-14, Foam Beetle #12-18
Leeches				●	●	●	●	●	●	●			Marabou Leech (black) #6-10, Black, brown, or olive Woolly Bugger #4-10
Minnows/baitfish			●	●	●	●	●	●	●	●	●		Marabou Ghost #4-10, Gartside Soft-hackle Gray Ghost #4-8, Baby Brook Trout #4-8, Wood Special #4-8, Kennebago Smelt 6-10, Montreal Floosie 6-10

Northern New England Hatch Chart

Insect	J	F	M	A	M	J	J	A	S	O	N	D	Fly Patterns
Midges, tricos, and miniature flies			▬	▬	▬	▬	▬	▬	▬	▬			Griffith's Gnat #16-22,, Parachute Adams #16-22, Hatching Midge #18-22, Twisted Midge #16-20, Brassie #16-20, Zebra Midge #16-22
Stoneflies				▬	▬	▬	▬						Black Klinkhammer #10-14, Stimulator #6-16, Swanson Stone #6-10, Yellow Sally nymph #2-6, Sim's Stone #10-12
Blue-winged olives					▬	▬	▬		▬	▬			BWO Thorax #16-20, Pheasant Tail #16-20
Caddis						▬	▬	▬	▬				Elk Hair Caddis #8-18, X-caddis #12-16, Puterbaugh Caddis #16-18, Goddard Caddis #12-16, EZ Caddis #12-18, Emergent Sparkle Pupa #12-18
Hendrickson					▬								Adams Klinkhammer #12-16, Hornberg Dry #10-14, Copper John #12-16, Nemes Wet Fly #10-16
Light Cahills						▬	▬						Light Cahill #12-16
Gray fox/March brown						▬							Parachute Adams #12-16, Klinkhammer #8-12, Parachute Hare's Ear #10-16, Hornberg Dry #12-16, Hare's Ear #10-14
Dragonflies/Damselflies							▬	▬	▬				Mini-muddler #6-10, Whitlock's Dragonfly #4-8, Whitlock Spent Blue Damsel #6
Green drakes/Brown drakes						▬							Lawson Paradrake #8-12, Wulff #8-12, Grizzly Wulff #10-12, Quigley Green Drake Cripple #10, Hare's Ear #6-10
Hexagenia							▬						Parachute Hex #6-8, Grizzly or Kennebago Wulff #6-10, Royal Wulff #6-10, Black Wulff #6-10 (after dark), Maple Syrup #6-8
Leadwing coachman								▬					Leadwing Coachman wet fly #10-12, Zug Bug and Prince Nymph #10-14, Gray Wulff #10-14, Parachute Adams #10-14
White fly (ephoron)								▬					Lawson Paradrake #8-12, Wulff #8-12, Grizzly Wulff #10-12, Quigley Green Drake Cripple #10, Hare's Ear #6-10
Ants							▬	▬	▬	▬			Black Foam Ant #10-14, Black Fly Ant #10-14, Black Puterbaugh Caddis #12-18, Royal Wulff #14-20 (trust me on this one)
Beetles/Grasshoppers/Crickets							▬	▬	▬	▬			Parachute Hopper #8-14, Dave's Hopper #6-8, Letort Cricket #8-14, Foam Beetle #12-18
Fish roe		▬	▬										Sucker Spawn #8-12, Glo-bugs #8-12
Leeches					▬	▬	▬	▬	▬	▬			Marabou Leech (black) #6-10, Black, brown, or olive Woolly Bugger #4-10
Minnows/baitfish				▬	▬	▬	▬	▬	▬	▬			Marabou Ghost #4-10, Gartside Soft-hackle Gray Ghost #4-8, Baby Brook Trout #4-8, Wood Special #4-8, Kennebago Smelt 6-10, Montreal Floosie 6-10

Flyfisher's Guide to New England Locator Map

1. Nashua River
2. Nissitissit River
3. Squannacook River
4. Wachusett Reservoir
5. Quinapoxet River
6. Stillwater River
7. Cape Cod Kettle Ponds
8. Quashnet River
9. Red Brook
10. Ipswich River
11. Westfield River
12. Fort River
13. Swift River
14. Quabbin Reservoir
15. Quabog River
16. Mill River
17. Millers River
18. Ware River
19. Deerfield River
20. Hoosic River
21. Housatonic River
22. Farmington River
23. Walloomsac River
24. Battenkill River
25. Mettawee River
26. Poultney River
27. Castleton River
28. Upper Otter Creek
29. Ottauquechee River
30. Black River
31. Williams River
32. Saxtons River
33. West River
34. Furnace Brook
35. Neshobe River
36. Middlebury River
37. New Haven River
38. Lower Otter Creek
39. White River

40. Ompompanoosuc River
41. Waits River
42. Wells River
43. Winooski River
44. Lamoille River
45. Missisquoi River
46. Upper Connecticut River
47. Clyde River
48. Willoughby River
49. Black River
50. Lake Champlain
51. Hampton River Estuary
52. Great Bay
53. Lamprey River
54. Isinglass River
55. Berry Brook
56. Cocheco River
57. Exeter River
58. Stonehouse Pond
59. Hoyt's Pond
60. Ashuelot River
61. Cold River
62. Contoocook River
63. Merrimack River
64. Pemigewasset River
65. Souhegan River
66. Sugar River
67. Upper Pemigewasset River
68. East Branch of the Pemi
69. Newfound River
70. Swift River
71. Lake Winnipesaukee
72. Androscoggin River
73. Upper Connecticut River
74. Big / Little Diamond Ponds
75. Back Lake
76. Christine Lake
77. Lake Francis
78. Connecticut Lakes

79. Crooked River
80. Presumpscot River
81. Royal River
82. Mousam River
83. Sebago Lake
84. Lower Kennebec River
85. Ducktrap River
86. St. George River
87. Damariscotta Lake
88. Cupsuptic River
89. Magalloway River
90. Kennebago River
91. Upper Dam
92. Rapid River
93. Androscoggin River
94. Rangeley Lake
95. Mooselookmeguntic Lake
96. Richardson Lakes
97. Kennebago Lake
98. Aziscohos Lake
99. Kennebec River
100. Moose River
101. Dead River
102. Roach River
103. W. Branch Penobscot River
104. E. Branch Penobscot River
105. Upper Kennebec River
106. Lower Moose River
107. Moosehead Lake
108. Baxter State Park
109. Machias River
110. Acadia National Park
111. West Grand Lake
112. Grand Lake Stream
113. St. Croix River
114. Allagash River
115. Fish River Chain
116. St. John River
117. Deboullie Mountain Region

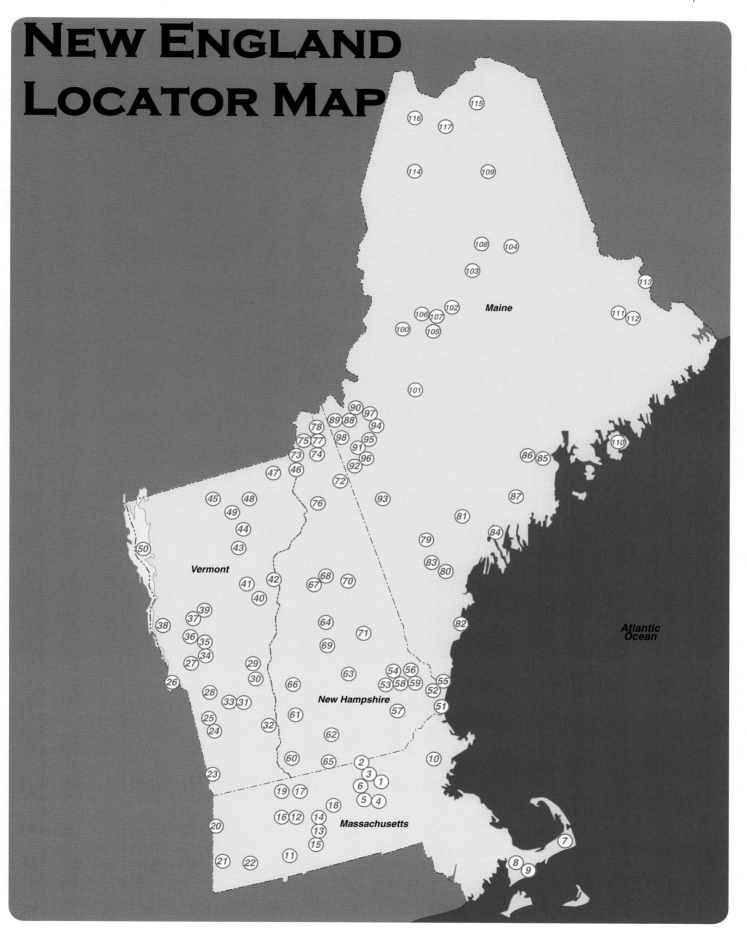

NEW ENGLAND LOCATOR MAP

Massachusetts

Massachusetts offers a surprising variety of flyfishing opportunities for a state that is only one-third the size of Maine. Some of the diversity is in habitats: from clear, cold, Berkshire brooks filled with small wild brook trout to the mighty Connecticut River with myriad fish species that drains a major portion of New England, and even Cape Cod kettle-hole ponds that are stocked with quick-growing rainbows that can be caught to the sounds of crashing surf. Coastal options for stripers abound as well; the *Flyfishers Guide to the New England Coast* by Tom Keer covers the options in great detail for the coast of Massachusetts as well as other New England states.

The quality of the water varies as well, from the relatively pure waters of the Swift River to the PCB and mercury-tainted waters of the industrially impacted Millers and Nashua Rivers. The Federal Water Pollution Control Act and the Clean Air Act and their ammendments have provided landmark legislation that has measurably improved water quality in Massachusetts waters. The state has additionally removed dams, set minimum-flow guidelines, and assisted with other clean-up activities. Despite these advances, much work remains to protect the water and watersheds of this heavily populated state.

The settings vary too, from the near wilderness forests surrounding Quabbin Reservoir to aging mill cities trying

Nymphing the Westfield River in the Chesterfield Gorge.

to reinvent themselves, to classic small towns with restored New England architecture in the form of 300-year-old farms and shipbuilders' mansions.

While historically, native brook trout and Atlantic salmon were found throughout Massachusetts, hundreds of years of dam building, water pollution, and habitat destruction have reduced the self-sustaining native brookie populations to a fraction of their former territory. The Atlantic salmon is holding on for dear life in the Connecticut River. Thus, while there are some wild salmonids, and certainly hold-overs (hatchery fish that survive longer than the season in which they were stocked), much of the flyfishing in Massachusetts relies on regular stocking from

the Massachusetts Department of Fish and Game.

That dependency is a mixed bag. Certainly the stocked fish are healthy (for the most part), well-proportioned, and seem to adapt well to their new natural environments. Over 700,000 trout are stocked annually in March, April, May, and October and most are over 12 inches in length.

But stocking timing, techniques, and quantities are based on a variety of economic and political factors, and not necessarily what is best for the anglers or the fishery. Massachusetts sometimes stocks too many fish in some rivers, or too late in the season in others. Often stocked fish do not move far from where they were stocked and stay concentrated in only a few watershed locations. Sometimes stocked fish compete with wild fish to their detriment.

Massachusetts is home to a large number of avid flyfishers. They travel throughout New England to enjoy their avocation. They are also as loyal to their local Massachusetts waters as they are to the Boston Red Sox. There are a number of active Trout Unlimited Chapters in Massachusetts, and these chapters and other anglers volunteer countless hours to improve their local waters by raising money to purchase and protect the river corridors, pass protective regulations, and even to assist the stocking process by bucket-brigading stocked fish to different sections of their home rivers. Without them, flyfishing in Massachusetts would not be as rewarding as it is today.

Anglers that live in Vermont, New Hampshire, and Maine usually travel north when they want to fish waters outside their immediate areas. Let me remind those folks that early or late in the year, when your favorite northern waters are too cold to fish well or may even be frozen, consider traveling south to Massachusetts, where the fishing starts early and continues until later in the year.

For the purposes of this book, I am dividing up Massachusetts into three sections: eastern, central, and western. Each area has its own unique characteristics. The western waters run down the spine of the eroded and ancient Berkshire Hills in the most rural part of the state. The central watersheds have been the engines that have historically driven major industries and agriculture in the state, often paying the environmental price for that burden. Eastern Massachusetts rivers and streams flow through the most heavily populated part of a state. This region is home to nine million people, yet boasts surprisingly productive flyfishing.

Public access to Massachusetts waters are governed by laws that have existed for hundreds of years. It can all be summarized thusly: As long as anglers access the river at a public spot, then they are free to fish Massachusetts water if they stay below the high-water mark, regardless of whether or not it goes through private land (including when the river bottom is owned). So basically, stay below the high-water mark and access from public entries and you should be within your rights.

Fishing regulations are very straightforward. Fishing is open year round and only a handful of catch-and-release artificial-lures-only areas exist, indicated with the appropriate waters.

Eastern Massachusetts

In eastern Massachusetts, several geographies can be found with a number of flyfishing options close to each other. These are the Nashua River area, the Wachusett Reservoir area, and Cape Cod.

One important additional note about flyfishing eastern Massachusetts: This area has one of the highest infection rates for Lyme disease in the country. Please take precautions if you are hiking the area without waders. Tuck your pants inside your socks, spray insect repellant around your ankles, and check yourself for ticks at the end of the day. These simple precautions will largely prevent infection.

Rising rainbows on a mid-October evening at Walden Pond.

NISSITISSIT RIVER

This popular tributary is a very "pleasant" river to fish, although that is not a word as exciting as other adjectives that you might read in flyfishing magazines such as brawling, spring creek, blizzard hatches, and ten-mile riffle. But there is nothing wrong with spending a nice evening taking a short trail walk through mature woodlands to reach an easily-fished river, and casting to several rising fish.

The Nissitissit River runs 3.5 miles from the New Hampshire border to its confluence with the Nashua River in the small town of East Pepperell. This is not big water, and the Nissitissit is more a stream than a river. It is an easy cast from bank to bank. This is well-loved water with local townspeople and fishermen who have protected the river corridors so they remain in a natural state, with occasional towering white pines, frequent wild flowers, and little development. A catch-and-release section (one of the few in the state) runs from the state line to the Prescott Street Bridge, a distance of almost two miles. The Nissitissit State Wildlife Management Area borders nearly this entire section.

Like many other similar Massachusetts rivers and streams, the Nissitissit has an annual cycle that is important to the serious angler. It is stocked in the spring with browns and rainbows, and local volunteers assist and spread the fish out throughout the river. Fish acclimate quickly and rise to a fairly typical progression of seasonal hatches, starting in March with a heavy hatch of early brown/black stoneflies. Some of the more effective dry flies are black quill imitations, Quill Gordons, Hendricksons, and Light Cahills. Subsurface options to try are wet flies that approximate what is hatching, such as Prince Nymphs, Pheasant Tails, and Gold-ribbed Hare's Ears, sizes 10 to 20.

As spring turns to summer, fish quickly become more educated, water gets lower and warmer, and fishing becomes more technical and difficult. Long leaders, 6x or 7x tippets, and delicate, drag-free presentations are a must. Some fish do hold over, but many anglers rely on the stocking trucks that arrive in the fall, usually in October. The additional trout stocked provide excellent fishing for the

An early-spring angler nymphs a deep pocket on the Nissitissit River.

NISSITISSIT RIVER

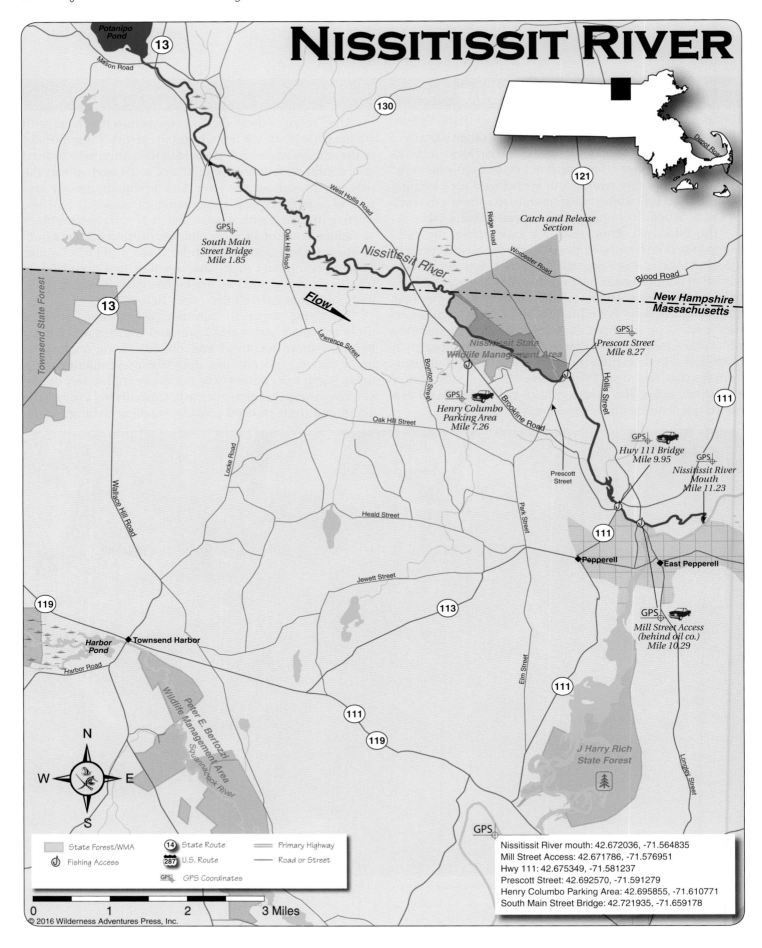

Potanipo Pond

13

Mason Road

130

West Hollis Road

GPS
South Main
Street Bridge
Mile 1.85

Oak Hill Road

Nissitissit River

Catch and Release
Section

121

Ridge Road

Worcester Road

Blood Road

New Hampshire
Massachusetts

Townsend State Forest

13

Flow

Lawrence Street

Nissitissit State
Wildlife Management Area

Prescott Street
Mile 8.27

GPS

111

Boynton Street

GPS
Henry Columbo
Parking Area
Mile 7.26

Brookline Road

Hollis Street

GPS
Hwy 111 Bridge
Mile 9.95

GPS
Nissitissit River
Mouth
Mile 11.23

Oak Hill Street

Prescott
Street

Locke Road

Heald Street

Park Street

J

111
Pepperell

East Pepperell

Wallace Hill Road

Jewett Street

113

GPS
Mill Street Access
(behind oil co.)
Mile 10.29

119

Elm Street

111

Harbor Pond
Townsend Harbor

Harbor Road

Peter E. Bertozzi
Wildlife Management Area

Squannacook River

111

119

J Harry Rich
State Forest

Longley Street

N
W E
S

GPS

Depot Road

Legend

State Forest/WMA	14	State Route		Primary Highway
Fishing Access	287	U.S. Route		Road or Street
	GPS	GPS Coordinates		

Nissitissit River mouth: 42.672036, -71.564835
Mill Street Access: 42.671786, -71.576951
Hwy 111: 42.675349, -71.581237
Prescott Street: 42.692570, -71.591279
Henry Columbo Parking Area: 42.695855, -71.610771
South Main Street Bridge: 42.721935, -71.659178

0   1   2   3 Miles

© 2016 Wilderness Adventures Press, Inc.

rest of the year. I can personally attest to the fact that fish hold over all winter, because I have fished to a small pod of risers in early spring before stocking. I will also reveal that the trout are tough because I didn't fool one before my casts put them down. Educated holdovers can often be fooled with small wet flies or CDC emergers fished in the film.

There are a number of convenient access points. From Brookline Street is the well-marked "Henry Columbo Parking Area". A well-maintained trail leads you to the river in the middle of the catch-and-release section after about a five-minute walk. A short distance downstream is a big "S" bend with deeper water and downed trees that is excellent holding water. The Prescott Road bridge (42.692540,-71.591310), the Route 111 bridge (42.674346,-71.580934), and the Mill Street bridge all provide additional access. Even though the lower, more developed stretch is general law and open to all types of fishing, it can still fish well, particularly off-season.

The town of East Pepperell is five minutes from the river and a good base of operations – the building on the corner of Groton Street and Main Street contains the Evening Sun Fly Shop, a diner/café, an auto-supply store, and a liquor store. Why would an angler need anything else?

Nashua River

Historically, this was a much polluted river but it has been cleaned up to the point that fishing opportunities now exist, despite certain longer-lived pollutants still being present. This river is best fished from a canoe, kayak, or small boat although there are wading opportunities in certain areas. The Nashua is primarily a slow-moving, warmwater fishery with a good population of smallmouth bass that are a hoot to catch on a fly rod. Although the state does not stock trout in the Nashua River, there are trout to be caught, particularly in the spring and fall at the mouths of its cooler and well-stocked tributaries such as Mulpus Brook and the Nissitissit and the Squannacook Rivers. Trout will drop down from the tributaries if the water gets too warm or low, or move back up in the fall. In the spring, suckers move from the Nashua River to the tribs to spawn, usually in the first riffle water. A

small egg pattern of pale yellow will fool the trout that have come to feast.

One good wading area is both upstream and downstream of the old covered bridge on Groton Street, just north of the town of East Pepperell near the mouth of the Nissitissit River.

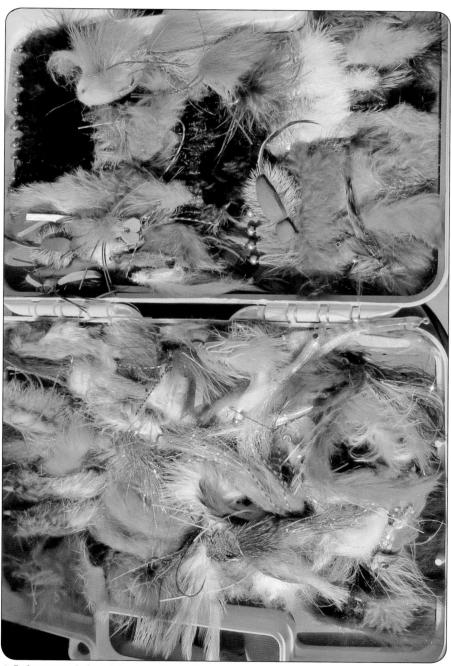

A fly box crowded with bass and large trout patterns.

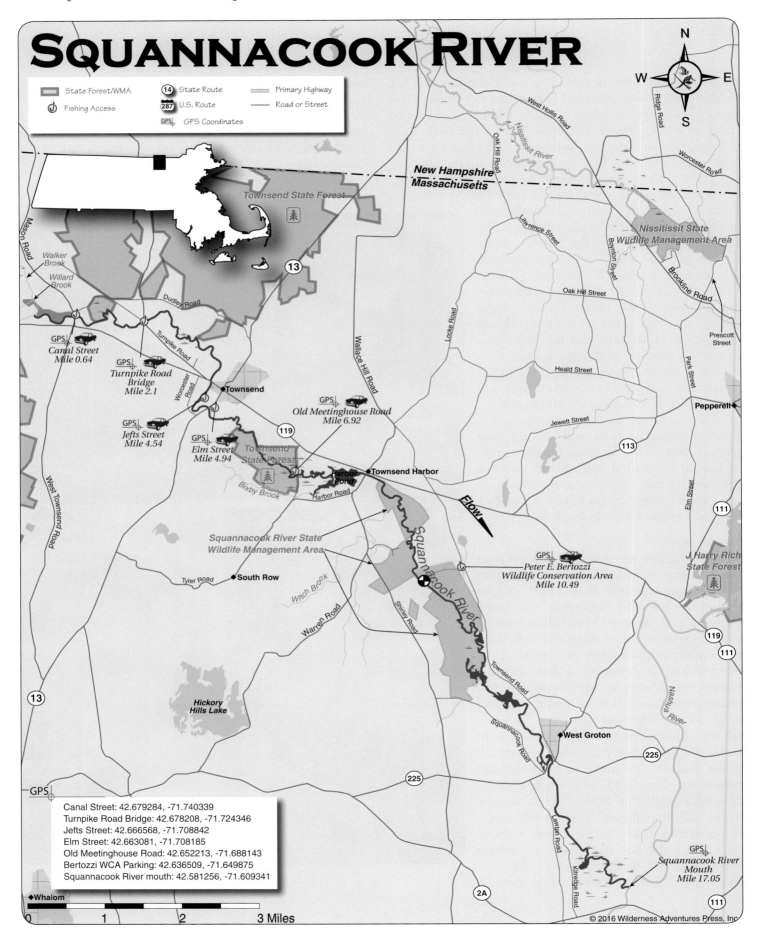

SQUANNACOOK RIVER

State Forest/WMA

Fishing Access

14 State Route

287 U.S. Route

GPS GPS Coordinates

Primary Highway

Road or Street

New Hampshire
Massachusetts

Townsend State Forest

Nissitissit State
Wildlife Management Area

Walker Brook

Willard Brook

Dudley Road

GPS
Canal Street
Mile 0.64

GPS
Turnpike Road
Bridge
Mile 2.1

Townsend

GPS
Old Meetinghouse Road
Mile 6.92

GPS
Jefts Street
Mile 4.54

GPS
Elm Street
Mile 4.94

Townsend
State Forest

119

Townsend Harbor

Harbor Pond

Bixby Brook

Harbor Road

Squannacook River State
Wildlife Management Area

Tyler Road

South Row

Wnch Brook

Warren Road

Shirley Road

Squannacook River

Flow

GPS
Peter E. Bertozzi
Wildlife Conservation Area
Mile 10.49

J. Harry Rich
State Forest

West Townsend Road

Hickory
Hills Lake

Townsend Road

West Groton

Squannacook Road

225

Nashua River

13

225

2A

Lawton Road

Kitredge Road

GPS
Squannacook River
Mouth
Mile 17.05

111

Whalom

GPS
Canal Street: 42.679284, -71.740339
Turnpike Road Bridge: 42.678208, -71.724346
Jefts Street: 42.666568, -71.708842
Elm Street: 42.663081, -71.708185
Old Meetinghouse Road: 42.652213, -71.688143
Bertozzi WCA Parking: 42.636509, -71.649875
Squannacook River mouth: 42.581256, -71.609341

0   1   2   3 Miles

© 2016 Wilderness Adventures Press, Inc

SQUANNACOOK RIVER

The Squannacook River is considered by some to be one of the best trout streams in Massachusetts. It is a close neighbor of the Nissitissit and is similar in many ways. It is about the same size, has similar stocking schedules, and it has also been protected and watched over by its angler friends. The Squannacook offers a variety of water types as it flows 14 miles from its source before it enters the Nashua River. Large pools, wide and slow runs, and quicker riffles and pocket water are among the options that can be fished with a variety of approaches. Anglers can choose the type of water that they prefer.

Water can get low during drought periods (often in late summer and early fall) and fishing can get difficult. Fish do hold over all summer. I have fished here in early autumn and caught brook trout, rainbow trout, and spooked what looked to be a good-sized brown trout holding in water that was about six inches deep. October stocking, rains, and cooler temperatures rejuvenate the fishing later in the year.

While most of the stocking is done at the obvious road-access points, these areas get fished heavily as well. It pays to walk 100 or 200 yards from these spots before you start fishing. You will find a better fishing experience and a better chance at some larger and unpressured fish.

Much of the river corridor has been protected in the form of state forest and wildlife management areas and despite steady fishing pressure, it is possible to hike to more secluded areas. One of the more popular sections is the Peter E. Bertozzi Wildlife Management Area (aka Wildlife Conservation Area, 42.639120,-71.650555). A ten-minute walk from a large parking lot leads to the river. Downstream are swifter and rockier runs, while upstream are larger, slower pools and languid currents that curl around downed trees. This slow-water section is a favorite of skilled anglers who enjoy the technical challenge of stalking a solitary trout rising in a difficult spot, and enticing a take with a 7x tippet. In the faster water downstream, nymphing and drifting a small streamer will pay dividends for the less experienced angler.

The following are a number of good access points as you move upstream from the Bertozzi WMA:

- Upstream from the town of Townsend Harbor, take MA 119, then take a left and go south on the dirt Old Meetinghouse Road. Park behind the Sterlite factory and hike behind it to the river.
- Elm Street dead-ends directly downstream from the MA 13 bridge in Townsend. Park there and it is a short walk down a path to the river (42.663014,-71.708316).
- Just upstream off of Jefts Street is a short dirt road that will take you to an old railroad trestle by an old dam(42.666498,-71.709033). Fish downstream.
- Go west on MA 119 from Townsend Center and take a right on Turnpike Road. In about one mile, a bridge crosses the river and you can work your way upstream or downstream.
- Farther west on MA 119, take a right on Canal Street. There is a parking area east of the Canal Street bridge and a productive pool just below a dam immediately downstream from the bridge (42.679161,71.740380).

You can also fish the smaller tributary streams that form the Squannacook for stocked and wild brook trout. Try Trapfall, Willard, Locke, Walker, Mason, Witch, and Bixby Brooks.

Stream Facts: Nissitissit and Squannacook

Season and Regulations
Massachusetts has no closed fishing season. General Massachusetts law is a three-fish limit but there is a two-mile stretch of catch-and-release only on the Nissitissit.

Game Fish
Stocked rainbows, brown trout, and brook trout both spring and fall with hold-over fish and the occasional stream-bred brook trout.

Tackle
Three- or 4-weight rods are as big as you want to go. Fish can become wary and educated so sometimes a long leader tapering to 7x is helpful for fooling the more difficult fish.

Flies
If there is not obvious surface activity, prospect with a small Gray Ghost, Wood Special, Zug Bug, size 16 Mini-muddler, or size 8 to 10 Woolly Buggers in a variety of colors.

If fish are rising, match the hatch. Small black stonefly imitations are important early in the season with small black caddis imitations such as a size 16 Puterbaugh Caddis a close-enough choice.

Fly Shops and Other Suppliers
This is a suburban area so there are several stores within half an hour. Evening Sun Fly Shop (55 Groton Street, Pepperell / 978-433-4910 / www.eveningsunflyshop.com) is close by and highly recommended for flyfishing gear.

LOWER LEFT: Autumn on the Squannacook.
UPPER RIGHT: The lower Quinapoxet River joining Wachusett Reservoir under the Route 140 triple-arched bridge.

WACHUSETT RESERVOIR

Highly restrictive regulations make it difficult to fish this body of water, but lack of access also means that its fish are not often caught and can reach some impressive sizes. You cannot boat or wade the reservoir. The only way you can fish is from shore and that isn't always easy if brush and trees grow right to the shoreline.

Most of New England's game fish are found in the Wachusett Reservoir, a few reaching state-record sizes including lake trout, smallmouth bass (8 pounds), rainbow trout (13 pounds, 13 ounces) brown trout (19 pounds, 10 ounces) and landlocked salmon (10 pounds, 2 ounces). Yikes! The landlocked salmon and brown trout are wild and stream bred while the rainbows are stocked in rivers and make their way down to the lake.

So, how do you maximize shoreline fishing success if you are flyfishers? Access is easy because Wachusett is encircled with highways: MA 140, 70, and 110. Find the access gates and hike on down to the "Chu" on existing trails. Spring and fall seasons bring the fish into shallow shoreline water. You must find a shoreline that is free from brush or trees so that you can manage a back cast. If you have a spey rod and have mastered that art, then by all means bring it; the places you can cast and the water you can cover will greatly increase. Although casting is more difficult into the wind, the windward shore usually fishes better because wind traps food in the shallows and game fish follow.

Your best odds of success is casting streamer patterns. In the spring, try smelt imitations such as Gray and Black Ghosts, Joe's and Jerry's Smelts, or your own favorite. The new marabou versions with coneheads or flashy synthetic materials may work better than the old standards, although these fish don't see many flies so it may not matter. During other seasons, try black-nose dace, yellow perch, or baby trout imitations.

Another way to catch the big reservoir salmonids is to intercept them when they enter the inlet rivers to spawn or chase baitfish. Timing is critical because it takes the right combination of increased water flow and seasonal weather changes to draw fish into the tribs.

Wachusett Reservoir hosts lake trout, smallmouth bass, brown trout, landlocked salmon and rainbow trout.

QUINAPOXET RIVER

There are two draws to the Quinapoxet River, affectionately called "The Quinnie" by its anglers. The first is the aforementioned large reservoir fish that enter the lower part of this river to spawn in the fall. The second is the stocked, hold-over, and wild fish that inhabit the upper reaches of this watershed.

The Lower River

A sediment dam (42.385852,-71.802436) separates the lower from the upper river. Lake-run fish cannot go over the dam so their progress is stopped and fishing for these trophies takes place from the dam to the reservoir. This stretch of river is governed by the same rules as the Wachusett Reservoir – no wading or boating, and a fishing season from April 1 to November 30. There is no fishing immediately below the power outlet (it is clearly marked.)

The water flows can vary here unexpectedly because sometimes water from Quabbin Reservoir can be diverted via an aqueduct through the lower river. With only 1,500 feet of fishing from dam to reservoir, it can get crowded with spin fishers and bait casters, as well as flyfishers. This can be combat fishing at its finest. But several weeks after ice-out when the predatory fish are chasing smelt, and in late October and early November when falling water temperatures and increased flows from fall storms draw reservoir salmonids into the lower river, the size of the trout and salmon make the effort well worth it.

Access is off MA 140 to Thomas Road and then to the River Road. You will see cars parked when you arrive at the entry points to the river.

The Upper River

The upper Quinapoxet River is located in Holden and is both an oasis of natural beauty and a quality fishing experience in the midst of a thickly-settled environment, ten miles north of Worcester. Because the Metropolitan District Commission owns the river corridor for the river's entire seven miles from its origin at the Quinapoxet Reservoir, the Quinapoxet is surrounded by hemlock and hardwood forest. The water is a classic mix of rocky runs, small plunge pools, riffles emptying into larger pools, and pocket water. The upper stretches have more sand and gravel and less rocks and boulders.

Native brook trout, wild browns, and stocked rainbows provide the fishing opportunities. Although the Quinnie is designated a river, this is small-stream fishing to be sure. A quiet approach, small rods, and delicate presentations are a must because these fish are not easy to fool. Plenty of fishing pressure because of the metropolitan area nearby and easy access makes for surviving fish that are very educated. While the state stocks rainbows several times a year, many of the holdover and wild fish are nocturnal or take up residence in feeder creeks or less accessible areas. With the number of anglers, this river's fishing would be greatly improved if Massachusetts would enact a catch-and-release section.

All major eastern hatches of mayflies take place along with regular stonefly and caddis emergences. When water is high, try searching with small Muddlers, Hornbergs, or wet flies. When the water drops, choose your favorite mayfly or caddisfly searching pattern and look for active fish. Adams, March Brown, White Miller, and black-, tan-,

The middle section of the Quinapoxet during early autumn's lower flows.

or olive-bodied Puterbaugh Caddis, all in sizes 12 to 16, are good options. In the summer or early fall, it pays to be on the water at dusk or later.

There is excellent access with a paved bike/walking trail that parallels the river closely from its mouth off Thomas Road from Route 140 (42.385852,-71.802436) to the River Road, several miles upstream. If you enjoying biking, this trail allows you to pedal along, stop at likely spots, and then continue cycling to new spots. You can cover miles of territory this way.

From the MDC building by the Oakdale Dam, another non-vehicular paved road continues upstream on the south bank of the river until it approaches the Route 190 bridge overpass high above. As you walk or bike this road, you will find that sometimes the river is close, and other times out of sight. It is never very far away, however, so at any point you can walk through the woods to the river and find the bankside trail.

You can find other entry points farther upstream. Take Manning Road and find the parking area by Trout Brook, a major cold water feeder creek that helps support the river (42.383673,-71.836867). Take the trail by the brook downstream to its confluence with the Quinnie and you can fish upstream and downstream by following a good trail. You can also wade across and access the paved bike trail on the other side.

Several miles farther upstream off of Wachusetts Road is Mill Street, which crosses the Quinnie. You can park there and walk up or downstream on a good trail to access more of the upper river. This is smaller water so stealth is critical to success.

STILLWATER RIVER

This small river near the Quinnie has a variety of water types and is stocked in the spring with rainbows. Your highest percentage play for catching these stockers is to fish from any of the MA 140 road access points in April and May. This road parallels the river and crosses it several times. The Stillwater gets pretty low and warm during the summer and the fishing tapers off.

The Stillwater's claim to fame is not the put-and-take part of the fishery but the trophy trout and salmon from the Wachusett Reservoir that enter the Stillwater in the spring and fall. These fish are blocked from accessing much of the Quinapoxet by its dam, but they have free run for over six miles up the Stillwater. Landlocked salmon up to five pounds or larger and several species of trout that can be measured in pounds show up in the spring chasing smelt, and in the fall to spawn or feed on eggs. When a combination of shorter days, cooler temperatures, and an increased flush of water from fall rains occurs, landlocked salmon will run up miles of river looking for spawning sites. Natural reproduction in the Stillwater for salmon means that all of the fish returning to the river were born there a number of years before.

Timing and location is critical. In the spring, the smelt run several weeks after ice-out and won't travel too far upriver. Concentrate your fishing close to the reservoir and cast into the larger and deeper pools (try Muddy Road 42.411055, -71.790635). You want to fish on the bottom so a sinking leader, sink-tip or sinking line is recommended. In the fall, try to be on the river from mid-October or early November, after a rainfall of at least three-quarters of an inch. You can fish the same pools you fished in the spring but you can also try farther upriver. It will take a few days for the salmon to swim into the upper parts of the river.

How do you find landlocks farther upstream? Choose an access point, walk, and scout the river. Look for nervous water or a wake that indicates that a good-size fish has been spooked. Salmon like relatively shallow areas with pea- to marble-sized gravel and moderate current to spawn. They will hold in deeper pools immediately adjacent to these areas.

Fish streamers in both spring and fall. In the spring, choose your favorite smelt imitation including the classic Black Ghost, Gray Ghost, or a Winnipesauke Smelt. In the fall, brown trout and salmon will get aggressive and hit streamers that have yellow accents. Try some of the newest generation of streamers including Gartside Soft-hackle Marabou patterns, John Barr's Meat Whistles, or articulated streamers. If you can find or can tie tungsten cone-head versions that will sink rapidly, so much the better. You will want to fish with at least a 7-weight rod, and an 8 would be better. Heavy leaders (3x and stronger) are a must. Don't forget your camera; you might hook the fish of the year.

Crowley Road Bridge access on the upper Stillwater River.

CAPE COD KETTLE PONDS

When the last Laurentide ice sheet receded from the Massachusetts area 18,000 years ago, it left huge glacial deposits of sand, rock, and gravel (sometimes called outwash) that became Cape Cod, Martha's Vineyard, and Nantucket. Sometimes, the outwash was deposited around and over an ice block. When the ice block melted away, the outwash collapsed to form a hole or kettle. Some of these holes filled with water and became the kettle ponds of today.

A number of kettle ponds are scattered throughout Cape Cod, ranging from a smallish 25 acres to significantly larger. Because of the influence of the nearby ocean, the ponds stay cooler than you might expect in the summer and warmer than typical inland ponds in the winter. The larger ponds might not freeze over for more than a few weeks during warmer winters. Because there is no closed fishing season in Massachusetts, you can sometime flyfish these ponds every month of the year.

The kettle ponds fishing regulations are general law for the most part so all types of fishing are allowed including ice fishing. There is no natural reproduction, so the fishery is maintained by annual stockings of brookies, rainbows, browns, and even tiger trout. Tiger trout are a cross between a brown and brookie and if you have never caught one, several ponds offer that opportunity. Most waters are stocked both spring and fall. Which trout species goes in what pond varies, but generally, the larger ponds receive the most brown trout. Because these ponds do not receive heavy fishing pressure and due to their plentiful food sources of insects, minnows, and other forage (particularly those ponds that have an outlet to the ocean and receive ocean-source baitfish), there are a fair number of hold-over fish that can grow fairly large.

Many of the ponds have regulations prohibiting gasoline-powered motors. All these ponds have road access but not necessarily a boat ramp, so they are best fished by small hand-carried boats or float tubes. Some of the ponds do fish fairly well from shore with firm, sandy bottoms and moderate drop-offs.

Most of the kettle ponds fish well spring, summer, and fall and anglers can cast sinking lines with streamers that imitate baitfish, or can match the hatch with dry flies or emergers. The larger Hexagenia mayflies emerge during June evenings in many of the ponds, and some anglers keep watch in order to be there when the surface is covered with bugs that can be measured in inches instead of millimeters. Some of the ponds receive their fair share of swimmers and boaters, so fishing early or late in the day is the sensible way to go.

Local flyfishers rave about the fall fishing when tremendous midge hatches occur and hold-over trout rise to the surface, providing dry-fly fishing from early October all the way to the beginning of December. Fishing pressure and other pond usage is light, and other than perhaps one other bait caster, you might have the pond to yourself.

If you find yourself on Cape Cod semi-regularly, I suggest trying a number of different ponds to develop your own favorites. Every angler that fishes the Cape seems to develop their own personal preference depending on where they are coming from, whether they are "big brown" hunters on the larger ponds, or prefer the intimacy of smaller waters.

Smaller ponds have the advantage of being calmer when the sea breeze is blowing. Hathaway, Goose, Goude, and Schoolhouse Ponds are all around 25 acres and are perfect for float-tube fishing, although Goose Pond can be windy. Hathaway, Goude, and Schoolhouse Ponds (all in Chatham) are very similar (although Schoolhouse is more developed) and can be waded along the shoreline in hip boots. They all have prolific midge hatches and your best approach because of the crystal clear water is to use 15-foot leaders tapering to 7x. One of my favorite midge patterns is the Twisted Midge.

Larger ponds such as Peters Pond (in Sandwich), Gull Pond (in Wellfleet) and Hamlin Pond (in Barnstable) receive good stockings of brown trout. Gull Pond is a large kettle pond of 100 acres that is over 60 feet deep with sea-run herring that spawn in its waters, which makes juvenile herring a major food source for the several trout and bass species here. Zonkers that imitate juvenile herring are a good choice in the fall. These ponds also have a variety of warmwater species to cast to as the water warms. Peters Pond does have a good boat ramp, so there is more boat traffic there in the summer.

Twisted Midge

Hook: Tiemco TMC 100, size 22
Thread: Black 8/0 Unithread
Extended Body: Black or golden olive Montana Fly Company midge body thread
Wing: Gray Medallion sheeting
Hackle: Grizzly saddle hackle
Thorax: Peacock herl

Nineteen-hundred-acre Nickerson State Park features a natural Cape habitat of sandy soil and scrub pines with several kettle ponds in close proximity including Big Cliff, Little Cliff, Flax, and Higgins Ponds. All Cape Cod ponds seem to grow leeches in a multitude of sizes and colors. Try sparsely-tied Woolly Buggers in black, brown, orange, red, and purple to imitate the varied leech population and fish on the bottom with sink-tip lines. These waters also have profuse midge activity in the colder months, best matched by size 20 to 24 Griffith Gnats or other midge imitations.

Most of the fishing in the summer is at dusk or after. Big Cliff has a good Hexagenia emergence in late June and does allow outboard motors.

For a complete listing of ponds (with maps) for southeast Massachusetts, go to the Massachusetts Fish and Wildlife website: www.mass.gov/eea/agencies/dfg/dfw/, and under their destinations tab, click on Pond Maps. The direct link is: www.mass.gov/eea/agencies/dfg/dfw/maps-destinations/state-pond-maps.html. Not all of the ponds listed will be kettle ponds.

Quashnet River

Historically, Cape Cod was home to a native sea-run brook trout population that lived in small streams and rivers that had an outlet to the sea. Population growth, pollution, and agricultural development in the form of cranberry bogs almost eliminated these fish from Cape Cod.

The Quashnet River is a great example of how committed volunteers can bring back endangered native fish populations. For over 35 years, Trout Unlimited members (most recently the Cape Cod Chapter of Trout Unlimited) have worked on restoring this river. It was once a destination trout stream for native brook trout before it was dammed by cranberry growers. Today this river is free-flowing once again and is populated with hundreds of native trout that move freely from this stream to the ocean and either back again or to other nearby streams. Trout tagging and tracking research has verified the movement of these stream-born trout.

Fishing is allowed on the Quashnet, but please protect this restored resource by using only barbless flies, handle the fish as little as possible, and quickly release all that you

ABOVE: A solar panel powers a tagged fish sensor to record fish movements on the Quashnet River. Photo courtesy Cape Cod Trout Unlimited.
LEFT: A December Big Cliff Pond rainbow with ice rimming the pond. Photo courtesy Dave Burkitt.

catch. The brook trout will move in and out of the river and the ocean based on water temperatures, rain events, and availability of food. Generally, the trout will be in the river in the early spring, through the summer and fall, and move back into the ocean during the winter. For best results, fish downstream and subsurface with a variety of small streamers and wet flies during the early spring and late fall seasons. You can tell if the brook trout you catch has been in the ocean recently because it will have a distinctive silvery sheen overlaying its classic brook trout colorations

A typical Cape Cod kettle pond. Photo courtesy Dave Burkitt.

Red Brook

Another option if you want to catch a salter brook trout is Red Brook, which can be found in the western (widest) part of Cape Cod just east of Wareham, inside the Theodore Lyman Reserve. Named for water tinted red by the iron-rich soil near its source, Red Brook is a 4.5-mile, spring-fed, coldwater stream that empties into Buttermilk Bay and is home to native sea-run brook trout. Flyfishing is allowed but is catch and release only.

Most fishers concentrate their efforts at the various old bridge and flume sites upstream and from the marsh near the mouth of Red Brook. For more information see http://www.thetrustees.org/places-to-visit/southeast-ma/lyman-reserve. For more information about the restoration of sea-run brook trout, go to the Sea Run Brook Trout Coalintion website at www.searunbrookie.org.

Cape Cod Stream Facts

Regulations

Massachusetts has no closed fishing season and general law covers most of Cape Cod waters. Most kettle ponds have some restrictions on motorized boats and a few have different fishing regulations. Please check the rule book before fishing each pond.

Game Fish

In the ponds, coldwater fish include rainbow trout, brown trout, brook trout, and tiger trout. Warmwater game fish are also found in most ponds including smallmouth, largemouth bass, and pickerel.

A few of the coastal streams have native salter brook trout.

Tackle

I would bring two different fly rods to the kettle ponds. The first would be a 5- or 6-weight rod rigged with full-sink or sink-tip line and a 7-foot 3x leader to fish streamers near the bottom. The second rod would be a 4- or 5-weight with a 9- to 12-foot leader tapering to 6x or 7x to fish the surface when small mayflies, flying ants, or the prolific midges are emerging and fish are rising.

Fly Shop

Black Eel Outfitters,
708 Main Street Route 6A
Dennis, MA 02638
508-619-7681

Other Options

Ipswich River

This 34-mile river runs through the northern Boston suburbs from Wilmington to Ipswich before entering Ipswich Bay near Cranes Beach. I spent my boyhood in Hamilton and as I explored along the banks of both this river and one of its feeders, the Miles River, my love for all things riverine was first kindled. The Ipswich River drains a large wetland system fed by bogs and springs that keep the water cooler than you might expect, even during the summer. Stocked and holdover trout live throughout the river, holding in areas that provide cover, food, and temperatures to their liking. Much of the water does not look like classic trout water but instead is slow-moving and meandering with a calm surface, but the fish are there. This river contains stocked rainbows, brook trout, and brown trout, along with some larger holdovers and some streamborn fish. The state stocks in the spring from access points such as road bridges.

Finding the trout and even reaching them is a challenge because much of the surrounding area is boggy with thickets and brambles (what we used to call "prickers"). Since you can't build in a wetland area, the immediate areas around this river are less developed than you might think, and wildlife use this river as a travel corridor. My brother, who lives along this river, has seen everything including deer, beavers, otters, coyotes, foxes, eagles, and herons, just to name a few species. A small kayak or canoe is probably the best bet for fishing from certain access points, and if you prospect for trout and other warmwater fish while you canoe along, you will enjoy the journey as much as the fishing. According to Massachusetts law, all boaters must wear life jackets between October 15 and May 15 to prevent accidents in cold-water seasons from hypothermia.

Here are a few access points that I recommend. Ipswich River Park in North Reading offers easy access, parking, a picnic area, and a grassy expanse to throw a Frisbee or kick a soccer ball, if flyfishing for you is frequently a family affair where other activity options are helpful. In the park, the river widens into a small pond and look for the open, sandy shoreline where you can practice casting without worrying about snagging trees or grass, if you are new to the sport. Trout stay active here into the summer. I watched someone land a nice rainbow during the middle of the afternoon on August 1. You can walk up and down the river from the park and find some nice water. Turn south on Central Street off MA 62, cross the river, and the park is immediately on your left (42.572152,-71.087499).

Other good access points are Endicott Street in North Reading, MA 114 in Middleton (where there is a small boat launch), Peabody Street and East Street (also in Middleton), Salem Road near the fairgrounds and the Newburyport Turnpike in Topsfield, the Massachusetts Audubon Ipswich River Wildlife Sanctuary (also In Topsfield), and at Foote Brothers Canoe and Kayak Rental in Ipswich (www.footebrotherscanoe.com).

During the spring, a small dark mayfly about a size 14 that some call a black quill, can be found in abundance. A classic Quill Gordon tie is a "near-enough" imitation, as is a gray Hornberg. Another fly to try is a Parachute Adams. Under-the-surface fare should include Hare's Ears, Zug Bugs, Prince Nymphs, Gray Ghosts, Mickey Finns, and leech patterns.

Close by the Ipswich River, very near my childhood town of Hamilton, is Pleasant Pond, a 40-acre pond with a

Kayaking the Ipswich River near Bradley Palmer State Park.

The Charles River just upstream from the Watertown Dam. Photo courtesy Mary Zambello.

surprising depth of over 40 feet. The shoreline is a mix of homes and steep banks with towering pines. There is a boat ramp at the end of Pleasant Road off of US 1A in Wenham, and another small parking lot where you can carry a kayak or canoe down off of Lake Drive.

This pond is highly productive with holdover brook trout reaching three pounds or better. Local anglers troll the western shore in the spring. As the waters warm, fish rise to small mayflies best imitated by a Hornberg, Black Quill, or Adams sizes 12 to 16. Later in the season, late evening fishing with tiny midge patterns is possible. Some dense weedy areas provide good surface popper action for largemouth bass and chain pickerel.

Urban Options

Maybe it's just me, but when I find myself in a city, I enjoy finding decent fishing in urban settings. It's nice to get a little fishing in without fighting the exiting weekend traffic and taking the time to get out of town.

Both Walden and Jamaica Ponds are "kettles", similar to their Cape Cod cousins, and are deep, clear-water ponds that stay relatively cool for much of the year. The good news is that they are both heavily stocked with trout and some survive the fishing pressure for quite some time. The bad news is that you will be sharing these ponds with quite a few other people.

Jamaica Pond is in Boston and can be reached by taking the MBTA subway. Encircling the pond is a paved trail that everybody uses for fitness activities. Watch your back casts if you try to fish during your lunch break. Try to arrive at first light or fish in less-than-ideal weather if you want to avoid the Powerbait anglers. This pond is stocked heavily in both spring and fall with rainbows. As the water warms, some good-sized largemouth bass can be landed on bass poppers or large Woolly Buggers.

Before you fish Walden Pond in Concord, refresh your memory by reading a little Henry David Thoreau or some passages from his book *Walden*, an account of the two years he lived there, starting in 1845. The best way to fish this pond is to wade the shoreline until you get away from the majority of the tourists and swimmers. Look for rising ("midging") rainbow trout in the spring and fall. Last year in the middle of October as the light faded – but not so completely that I couldn't still enjoy the vibrant colors of the shoreline maples – I had pods of rising rainbows all to myself.

I would also be remiss if I didn't mention the Charles River, which for hundreds of years was more a polluted sewer than a river. Environmental regulations and other clean-up efforts have been effective and thousands of people now boat on, fish in, and picnic near the Charles. This is a warmwater fishery for the most part, but flyfishing for panfish, bass, and carp can be quite fun. It is 40 miles long with plenty of shore and boating options, and I will mention just one spot as an example. In downtown Watertown, the Charles flows through conservation land and is tree lined on both banks. By an old dam, one always finds fishers, mostly of the feathered variety: great blue herons and the rarely seen night herons that are almost always perched on rocks, waiting for fish to get pulled over the dam. The water is clear and smells fresh. Flyfishing both above and below the dam can be excellent for many species including sunfish, bass, and carp (42.366001,-71.188754).

Eastern Massachusetts Planning Considerations

Nearby Hub Cities and Towns

- Pepperell (www.eveningsunflyshop.com)
- Worcester (www.worcesterchamber.org, www.thelowerforty.com)
- Sandwich (www.sandwichchamber.com)
- Barnstable (www.hyannis.com/visitors, www.saltyflycapecod.com)

Easy Access Options

- The Quinapoxet River has a short, level, wide trail from River Road (off of Thomas Street) that skirts the side of the MDC power station fence, and leads down to the water. Slightly downstream is a fishing platform for handicapped anglers (42.387035,-71.801337). It is a little high above the water for the best flyfishing but workable if someone else can land any fish caught.
- Ipswich River Park in North Reading has a paved parking lot, and a short walk over mowed grass leads to a wide and sandy beach on the Ipswich River (42.572152,-71.087499).
- The Mill Street Bridge over the Nissitissit River has a parking lot right next to it that is just a couple of steps to the water. It is an open law area but there are still plenty of fish.

The fishing platform on the lower Quinapoxet River.

Suggested Beginner Options

- Ipswich River Park in North Reading (42.572152,-71.087499) has a wide sandy beach with plenty of back-cast room and space on either side to practice casting and retrieving your fly line. This is a pond-like part of the river, so the current is extremely slow, but the fish cruise around there. The last time I visited, I ended up giving an impromptu casting lesson to a beginner trying to master fly casting.
- Try the Nissitissit River but check with the Evening Sun Fly Shop first. Tell Charlie, the owner, that you are a beginner and he will let you know the best place to try based on the day that you will be fishing. He might even take you himself for a few hours, or pair you up with someone else.

Vacation Suggestions

Weekend Getaway

- Plan to fish the Wachusett Reservoir's inlet rivers on the first weekend in November, which is usually the peak of the spawning run for big landlocks. If it is a cooler or rainier October, you might choose a late October weekend instead. Try to first hit several different locations on the lower Quinapoxet and the Stillwater to determine where most of the fish might be and then concentrate efforts there for the rest of the weekend. Plenty of accommodations and restaurants can be found in nearby Worcester, but the Wachusett area is easy to reach from any town north of the Massachusetts Pike and in the Route 495 vicinity.

One-week Vacation

- Take a relaxing week-long vacation to Cape Cod during the first week of November. The touristas will have vacated the area, traffic will be light, and you will have the kettle ponds and salter streams to yourself (as well as the beaches). Try a pond or two every day and take the rest of the time to explore the Cape's museums, antique stores, restaurants, beaches, parks, and its general charm at a leisurely pace. Not everything will still be open, so check ahead of time. The weather is usually still reasonable and the leaves may still have some color. The towns of either Sandwich or Barnstable are close to a cluster of ponds and several lodging and dining options should still be open.

Easy access, plenty of casting room and stocked trout make Ipswich River Park a good beginner destination. Photo courtesy Ken Zambello.

Central Massachusetts

Central Massachusetts encompasses several large watersheds. The Westfield and all of its branches empty into the Connecticut from the west, as does the Manhan River and two different Mill Rivers. The Chicopee River watershed including the vast Quabbin Reservoir and its tributaries, all flow into the Connecticut River from the east.

While the Chicopee River and a few of its tributaries are too industrialized, dammed, and warm in the summer to offer consistent salmonid angling, other rivers provide fine flyfishing opportunities. North of the Chicopee River confluence, the Millers River flows almost due west from Worcester County before it meets the Connecticut River at Millers Falls. Other smaller west-flowing tributaries in central Massachusetts also add their waters to the mighty Connecticut.

The history of central Massachusetts rivers is similar to other moving waters in the state. Originally great fisheries, these rivers were severely damaged by industrial pollution before staging a comeback over the last thirty years. While some issues remain — residual pollutants (including PCB), dams that block fish passage, and warm summer water temperatures because trees have been replaced by commercial and residential development — fishing is good again. The fisheries are maintained by stocking but hold-overs are common and some wild fish are present too. While most of the fisheries are well worth trying if you are in the area; there are a few, such as the Westfield, Millers, and Swift Rivers that should be destinations for out-of-state anglers.

The rivers of central Massachusetts will be presented geographically, roughly from west to east. It is important to note the size of these rivers, because while almost any moving water in the state is called a "river", they vary dramatically in size. For example, the Millers River is 100 times the size of the West Branch of the Swift River.

Flyfishers testing their skills at the "Y" pool on the Swift River. Photo courtesy Dave Talmanson.

WESTFIELD RIVER

The Westfield River system has such a wide variety of fishing options that one could fish it every day for a year and never get bored. Some of the system is freestone, subject to the vagrancies of the weather, while other parts are dam controlled. There are wild, stocked, and holdover brookies, brown trout, and rainbow trout that range from several inches to many pounds depending upon where you are fishing. The topography ranges from concrete bridges and other structures in high-developed areas, to undeveloped woodlands, and even a deep gorge. Three major river branches exist, each with distinctive characteristics, and a mainstem. The three branches are typical mountain streams with a mix of pocket waters, runs, and riffles, and are the only rivers in Massachusetts federally designated as wild and scenic waters.

Mainstem

Don't overlook this water on your way to the upper river branches. You can find sections surrounded by lush and towering trees, with gin-clear water flowing over cobblestones on long glides, the smooth surface marked by the rings of rising rainbows; like a poor man's New Zealand. There are obvious pull-offs along MA 20 from Huntington to Westfield, a distance of about 18 miles. Check out different spots and fish the type of water that you like the look of and also that fits the water conditions. Deep pools, glides, runs, and pocket water are all available; some right next to the road, with other areas out of view. During low or moderate flows, the river is very wadeable in most sections.

Anglers vie for both stocked and holdover browns and rainbows with some wall-hangers possible, as long as a local company continues to stock hundreds of 3- to 8-pound fish.

Some popular spots are as follows:
- Roughly three miles upstream from Westfield, look for a Fisheries and Wildlife sign that points to river access where you can then work your way either upstream or downstream.
- The pull-offs near B G Sporting Goods store.
- Under the I-90 Turnpike bridge (there is public access).
- The pools below the Tekoa Golf Course.

Salmonids in the mainstem dine from a wide and varied menu, from the standard succession of mayfly hatches, to strong caddis hatches, and including meatier fares such as dace, shiners, and crayfish. The water treatment plants that return clean and nutrient-rich water to the river are probably responsible for the rich aquatic life. Fish with whatever methods you prefer, but if you want to target the larger fish, big meaty steamers will increase your odds. If you like to dry-fly fish, check out a succession of spots until you see rising fish. If rises are sparse, a sink-tip line with a small silvery streamer featuring a little pink or red usually fools the rainbows. Even though these are stocked fish, they acclimate quickly and can get quite snooty. Watch the rise forms to see if they are eating below-surface emergers; the last time I fished the Westfield, the only pattern that worked was a small soft-hackle wet fly, fished subsurface.

East Branch Westfield River

The East Branch of the Westfield is the largest of the branches, receives most of the fishing attention, and perhaps has the highest productivity. The upper headwater sections can be fished by following MA 9 to River Road. There are plenty of pull-offs with folks often enjoying the river for bathing and boating, but fishable pocket water is easily found. The five miles below the community of Swift River flows through mostly conservation land to the MA 143 Bridge. This is the so-called "Pork Belly" section of the river and is, for some, a favorite section because of holdover trout and not much fishing pressure. If you are canoeing (which is a great idea if water flows are adequate) make sure you take out above the bridge, before the river enters the Chesterfield Gorge.

Chesterfield Gorge

Fishing in the Chesterfield Gorge is an experience that I heartily recommend. In this totally natural setting, the East Branch runs clear over cobbles, rocks, and boulders – offering endless runs, pocket water, plunge pools, and wide runs. This is not a steep gorge with cliffs down to the water. Wading is fairly easy as long as you maintain your footing on the rocky bottom. Browns, rainbows, and brookies rise to well-presented dry flies or nymphs when conditions are right. A normal day (flows between 300 and 500 cubic feet per second- cfs - and cool water temps) might bring a dozen trout to hand for the experienced flyfisher.

From the MA 143 Bridge (42.403429,-72.876540), look for signs to the Chesterfield Gorge (head south on Ireland Street) and after several miles and a left hand turn on River Road, find a small parking lot (42.393299,-72.880226). From there, you can hike along the East Branch and experience seven miles of remote fishing that is catch and release, artificials only. The River Road (blocked for vehicle access after one mile) offers easy walking down the west bank of the river. If you have a four-wheel drive high-clearance vehicle, you can drive the additional mile on River Road

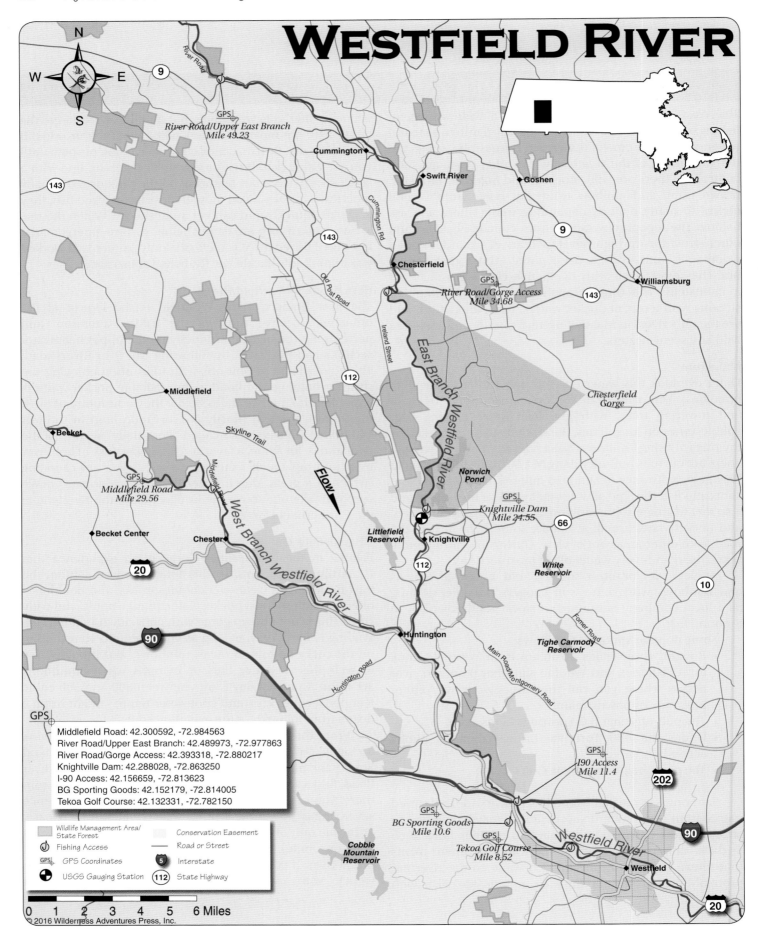

WESTFIELD RIVER

N
W — E
S

Cummington

Swift River

Goshen

River Road/Upper East Branch
Mile 49.23

Chesterfield

River Road/Gorge Access
Mile 34.68

Williamsburg

Chesterfield Gorge

Middlefield

East Branch Westfield River

Norwich Pond

Skyline Trail

Middlefield Road
Mile 29.56

Becket

Knightville Dam
Mile 24.55

Becket Center

Knightville

Chester

White Reservoir

West Branch Westfield River

Littlefield Reservoir

Flow

Huntington

Tighe Carmody Reservoir

Foster Road

Main Road Montgomery Road

Huntington Road

I90 Access
Mile 11.4

GPS
Middlefield Road: 42.300592, -72.984563
River Road/Upper East Branch: 42.489973, -72.977863
River Road/Gorge Access: 42.393318, -72.880217
Knightville Dam: 42.288028, -72.863250
I-90 Access: 42.156659, -72.813623
BG Sporting Goods: 42.152179, -72.814005
Tekoa Golf Course: 42.132331, -72.782150

BG Sporting Goods
Mile 10.6

Tekoa Golf Course
Mile 8.52

Cobble Mountain Reservoir

Westfield River

Westfield

Wildlife Management Area/ State Forest
Fishing Access
GPS Coordinates
USGS Gauging Station
Conservation Easement
Road or Street
Interstate
State Highway

0 1 2 3 4 5 6 Miles

© 2016 Wilderness Adventures Press, Inc.

to the gate, and save yourself some walking. This is also an excellent mountain-biking track if you want to bike to some of the more remote water. Good fishing for stocked, holdover, and wild trout continues throughout the entire gorge, but of course the farther you walk away from the parking areas on either end, the less people you see and the less pressured the fish will be. On the other hand, the stocking truck can't drive past the gate, so the concentration of fish might be higher closer to the parking lot. Most pools hold fish, and between the parking lot and the gate are a number of turnouts and small parking areas close to good holding water. Several pools that are well-publicized and deservedly so are:

- Two-mile Pool that lies, not surprisingly, at the two-mile sign on the dirt road.

- Les's Pool, which can be found one-quarter of a mile below the gate and is bordered by a cliff on one side. It is best fished by crossing the river above and holds fish all year because of its size and cool water.
- At about mile 3 is the old mill site, and then one-half mile farther is the inner gorge.
- About a mile upstream from the lower gate is the renowned Rainbow Pool.

The temperatures in the gorge section can get high because of the rocky ledges and large boulders that hold heat. If you visit this area during the summer, either fish at dawn or after dark, or try the area below the Knightville Dam (the water stays cooler because of its bottom-release characteristics.) If you try fishing at night, utilize dark or

Charlie Shadan, owner of Evening Sun Fly Shop, plays a nice rainbow on the mainstem of the Westfield.

black flies that have some bulk to them and retrieve slowly. My favorite is a black Wulff in a size 6 to 10. Remember, even though you have trouble seeing a black fly against the black surface of the water, the fish are looking up at a lighter sky, so for them, the silhouette of a black fly is more easily seen.

Caddis are prolific on the East Branch with black, brown, and green species in various sizes along with sporadic mayfly hatches. Nymphing along the bottom with cased caddis nymph imitations is a good option, as is casting weighted black-nose dace or dragonfly nymph imitations. By late May, large black stoneflies can be found blundering around the water and a black Kaufmann's Stimulator can draw confident strikes.

In the fall, the water is low and gin-clear but the foliage magnificent, and careful fishing with larger streamers such as Zoo Cougars, large yellow/brown marabou streamers, and Woolly Buggers, just might yield bigger trout on the pre-spawn prowl.

West Branch Westfield River

The West Branch of the Westfield is best fished from US 20 and the Middlefield Road. A trail down the far bank and a railroad bed on the near side allows you to move up and down river easily. The 13.8 miles from Beckett Center to the Huntington town line is federally designated as *Wild and Scenic*. This branch is not dammed and runs clear and cold all year. The stocked and wild trout are smaller, but at certain times, larger trout from the mainstem of the Westfield will travel upstream to escape high-roiled water, high summer water temperatures, or to spawn. When this occurs, you might be surprised at the size of the trout you catch in this small water.

Presentation and stealth matters more than the exact fly pattern. Approach in a manner such that you are not easily seen by the fish, and try to limit false-casting. Try to land just the leader and tippet in the water.

Fort River

If you do find yourself in Amherst – the home of five colleges – the most convenient river to fish is the Fort River, which runs right through the center of town. Several coldwater brooks merge east of Amherst to form the river that then runs through town, neighboring South Hadley, and then into the Connecticut River. If you follow Main Street in Amherst due east, it becomes Pelham Road and that route provides good access to the upper river and its tributaries, all of which are stocked and hold fish. The lower reaches are accessed from the MA 9 bridge (42.364184, -72.489949), Southeast Street (42.357176, -72.504565), and MA 47 in Hadley. I know the lower river has large holdover brown trout because I have seen them when playing golf with my father at the Hickory Ridge Golf Course.

Stream Facts: Westfield River

Season
Open year round but fishes best between April and November. It is catch and release only in the Chesterfield Gorge.

Fish
Stocked brook trout, brown trout, and rainbow trout (some up to five pounds in the mainstem), holdovers, and wild brook and brown trout in the upper reaches.

River Characteristic
The three branches of the Westfield River are designated as Wild and Scenic. The upper sections of the three branches offer small-stream fishing to trout resting in tiny plunge pools. Farther downstream, each branch offers tree-lined freestone river fishing to small runs, pools, and pocket water, everything wadeable. The water is crystal clear and cool. The West Branch is freestone all the way to the Mainstem; the other branches have dams prior to reaching the mainstem. The tailwater below the Knightville Dam is moderated by the dam and can be fished all year. The mainstem flows through more urban areas with its accompanying traffic noise, but the water remains clear and fast-flowing. There are deep runs and pools that are too deep to wade across. State land along the river upstream from Westfield guarantees good angler access for 18 miles.

Equipment
A 4-weight rod with a 9-foot tapered leader to 5x will serve well for most of the branches. In the mainstem, a 5-weight rod will provide more distance. Sinking leaders or a sink-tip line will allow the angler to sink streamers into the deeper spots during higher flows.

Flies
Depending on the season and where the angler is fishing, almost every fly in your vest could be a good fly to try. It pays to be observant. Match the hatch when you can. In the smaller and faster sections, cast attractors that float well and can be seen (Hornbergs, caddis imitations, Royal Wulffs). In deeper runs and pools, retrieve streamers on a sink-tip line. To target browns, try bulky streamers with black, brown, and yellow colors featured. For rainbows, white streamers with red or pink highlights can be effective. If nymphing is your thing, then standard patterns such as Copper Johns, Pheasant Tails, Prince Nymphs, and stonefly imitations in sizes 12 to 18 will usually suffice.

SWIFT RIVER

The Swift River, like the Deerfield River to the west, is a true tailwater fishery with water drawn from 70 feet below the surface of the monster Quabbin Reservoir. The Swift's temperature never falls below 40 or above 60 degrees, making it a rare year-round, catch-and-release, flyfishing opportunity in Massachusetts. For those readers that have fished the spring creeks of Montana, there are elements of similarity here. This is small, shallow water – more stream than river – and although it doesn't have the luxurious weed growth of the western spring creeks, stalking large trout in gin-clear water offers the same experience.

This river is well-stocked with rainbows, brook trout, and brown trout, and sometimes landlocked salmon wash over the spillway. The fish hold over and become very educated and finicky since most of their food sources are small. The name of the game, particularly in the winter is tiny flies and very fine tippets. Anglers fishing this stream usually have an attitude of "we are all in this together" and share what they know about fly patterns and fishing techniques.

Close to Windsor Dam, the famous Y pool and surrounding water attracts many fishers who ply the waters with tiny dry flies year round. Big fish can be spotted cruising around boulders in the crystal-clear water. One access is through the Quabbin Reservoir main gate, past the visitor's center, across the dam, and then a right-hand turn to a parking and picnic area. My entrance of choice is from a small parking lot on MA 9 (42.273620,-72.337846), where a recently improved trail runs through a red pine forest and parallels the river as you walk upstream. This is a cool place to fish (literally and figuratively), even on the hottest summer days. It is only a ten-minute walk to the Y pool and you can look for trout all along the way. While this water was channelized years ago, the observant angler will spot holding water amongst the downed timber and slightly deeper runs and holes caused by an incoming stream and some bank structure.

Below the bridge, regulations change to artificial lures only from July 1 to December 31, with general regulations the remainder of the year. Pools become deeper in this section with overgrown banks and downed wood making it more difficult to fly cast. A canoe or switch rod can be very useful in this section. Access is from River Road on the east bank and Enoch Sanford Road and East Street on the west bank. Notable features include a small parking area on East Sanford Street and another off of River Road, where you can park and fish this section of stream, which is wadeable when flows are lower. Also, look for a big pool immediately below a private house on the stream that you can access from the other side. Farther downstream, the Hatchery Pool is heavily fished, but always has trout in it. Etiquette varies here from respectful sharing of space to bait-slinging hogs.

A beautiful Swift River brown salmonid. What do you think: Landlocked salmon or brown trout? Photo courtesy Dave Talmanson.

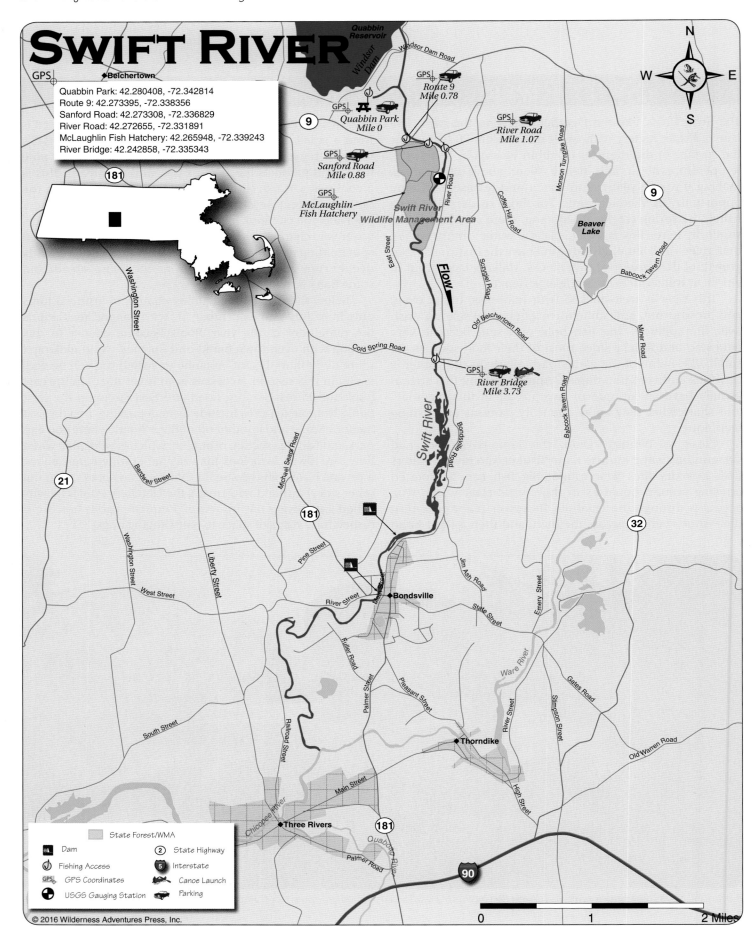

SWIFT RIVER

Quabbin Reservoir

Windsor Dam

GPS ◆ Belchertown

Quabbin Park: 42.280408, -72.342814
Route 9: 42.273395, -72.338356
Sanford Road: 42.273308, -72.336829
River Road: 42.272655, -72.331891
McLaughlin Fish Hatchery: 42.265948, -72.339243
River Bridge: 42.242858, -72.335343

Windsor Dam Road

GPS Route 9 Mile 0.78

⑨

GPS Quabbin Park Mile 0

GPS River Road Mile 1.07

Monson Turnpike Road

⑨

GPS Sanford Road Mile 0.88

GPS McLaughlin Fish Hatchery

Swift River Wildlife Management Area

River Road

Cottey Hill Road

Beaver Lake

Babcock Tavern Road

181

Washington Street

East Street

FLOW

Sczygiel Road

Old Belchertown Road

Cold Spring Road

GPS River Bridge Mile 3.73

Miner Road

21

Bardwell Street

Michael Sears Road

Swift River

Bondsville Road

Babcock Tavern Road

32

181

Pine Street

West Street

Washington Street

Liberty Street

Jim Ash Road

Emery Street

River Street

Bondsville

South Street

Railroad Street

Fuller Road

Palmer Street

Pleasant Street

Main Street

State Street

Ware River

River Street

Stimpson Street

Gates Road

◆ Thorndike

Old Warren Road

High Street

Chicopee River

◆ Three Rivers

181

Quaboag River

Palmer Road

90

	State Forest/WMA		
Dam		②	State Highway
Fishing Access		⑤	Interstate
GPS	GPS Coordinates		Canoe Launch
USGS Gauging Station			Parking

© 2016 Wilderness Adventures Press, Inc.

0   1   2 Miles

The upper reaches of the West Branch flow through mountain laurel bushes.

The so-called River Bridge parking area (42.273620,-72.337846) is another entry point and is a good place to launch a canoe and fish upstream where weed growth is less. Farther downstream, the outflows from the two Bondsville Dams can produce good fishing as well, although this more urban area is not as ascetically pleasing as the upper river.

Both holdover and stocked fish will move up and down the Swift River. If you don't see signs of life in one section, move to other parts of the river. Newly stocked fish can be caught on a variety of flies: streamers, nymphs, or attractor dries, but they quickly smarten up. Above the bridge, all of the natural insects are tiny because of the cold water, so size 20 and smaller midge imitations and tiny sulphur or blue-winged olive patterns (either emerger or nymphs) usually carry the day. Below the bridge, small caddis work, and farther downstream, a variety of mayfly imitations may work, although blue-winged olives are the most consistently available. In the spring, suckers will run up to at least Cody Lane and as far as the lower section of the Hatchery Pool to spawn. The trout will sometimes take advantage and become keyed into sucker spawn, so try small, pale, yellow-yarn eggs.

West Branch Swift River

The West Branch of the Swift River is stream-sized and flows through natural woodland that is protected within the Quabbin Reservoir watershed (east of MA 202). This is the inlet to the West Arm of the reservoir and is open when the reservoir is open, generally from mid-April to mid-October depending on ice-out. West of Route 202 is public land and the river is open to fishing year round.

This river offers two types of flyfishing. The first is for landlocked salmon that ascend this stream shortly after ice-out, chasing the spawning rainbow smelt, and again in the fall, looking for spawning territory of their own. Salmon will generally move higher up the stream on their spawning runs, which occurs when a good rainstorm raises the level of the river. So even when Quabbin Reservoir, its lands, and that part of the river closes (east of Route 202) in the fall, salmon can sometimes be found and fished to farther upstream, where the water stays open for fishing.

Spring salmon flies should generally be smelt-imitation streamers such as the Black Ghost, Gray Ghost, or any of the other old standbys. In the fall, streamers with some yellow or orange tempt aggressive salmon. Be warned, this is not easy fishing, the water is crystal clear and not very deep. The salmon spook easily.

For most of the year, this is a brook trout stream for both stocked, holdover, and wild trout, with the wild trout found upstream from MA 202. To enjoy this fishing, you must be the type of angler that enjoys fishing in tight quarters. Above 202, enjoy the hiking, scenery, wildlife, and wildflowers that you will see, and when you find a small pool more than ankle deep, it will often hold at least one small, wild brookie.

The West Branch can be located from Route 202 on the Shutesbury-New Salem Line. There is a small parking area just north of the stream and a faint anglers' path on the right side of the river (as you face downstream). To access farther upstream, turn west on Cooleyville Road just north of the river. Bear left, and after you cross the river, take your next right on a dirt road that shortly ends at a locked gate (42.465582,-72.387786). A fifteen-minute walk will take you to within sight of the river. You will also cross a tributary and you may want to fish downstream from that point because the tiny stream increases in size.

A word of warning for this river, the entire Quabbin Reservoir area, and most of the wetlands of Massachusetts: Be diligent as it relates to deer ticks and Lyme disease. Wet areas and a high density of deer make for high tick infestations. They are particularly active in spring and fall when we fishermen and women are out and about. This writer wears waders whenever possible or keeps pant legs tucked inside his socks and sprayed with DEET. Remember at the end of the day to check (or have a very close friend check) your skin for ticks, especially lower legs, crotch, and under your belt. As long as you remove ticks within 24 hours, the risk of Lyme disease is very low.

East Branch Swift River

The East Branch of the Swift River flows out of the Popple Camp State Forest Wildlife Management Area and empties into Quabbin's East Arm. This is a coldwater fertile stream with good hatches that tumbles along through magnificent mature forest. The bottom is a mix of small gravel, larger rocks, and fallen logs; and the water, while clear, is tannin stained. Stocked and holdover rainbows and brook trout, and some wild brook trout, hold in this river all year long. Landlocked salmon do not run up this branch in the fall because a dam at the confluence blocks access for the fish.

This is a delightful river to fish because the sides of the streams are mostly free of underbrush, useful trails run alongside much of it, and it is larger water than the West Branch. Try prospecting with a Hornberg, a Mini-muddler, or Baby Brook Trout streamer, and move quickly from run to run until you locate active fish. Look for hatches to match, starting with midges and small caddis in the early spring.

To find the East Branch, take MA 32A north from Hardwick Center toward Petersham (or MA 32 from Route 2, and then south on MA 32A) and look for the river running under the road. You can fish here or choose from several other good access points. Beyond the bridge, turn right onto Glen Valley Road until you reach a closed bridge over the river (42.443426,-72.187243). Park and go upstream or down. Another good option is the bridge on Quaker Drive off of MA 32 (42.470581,-72.161682). You can also reach the river by heading east on East Street from the Petersham town center for about a mile. By the way, the center of Petersham is worth seeing because of the interesting and classic architecture of many of its houses, as well as its cute town store.

A final access point is farther downstream where MA 32 crosses the river just below miniscule Connor Pond. The section of river right below the dam is stocked as is the pond itself. It is easy to put a small canoe in the pond and cast for rising trout and then fish the stream right below.

The Glen Valley Road Bridge (closed) over the East Branch of the Swift River.

QUABBIN RESERVOIR

This man-made lake encompasses some 25,000 acres and its entire watershed is protected from development, making it a wilderness oasis in southern New England with loons, eagles, and even moose. Although there was much screwing around in the past by stocking all sorts of different fish species, Quabbin is now pretty much a lake trout and landlocked salmon fishery. Please check the Massachusetts Law Book for all of Quabbin Reservoir's regulations, boat type and horsepower restrictions, and a closed season that varies based on ice-out.

Just like they do in northern New England salmonid lakes, most Quabbin anglers troll, but casting for landlocked salmon is possible and productive. In the spring, resident rainbow smelt school near the feeder streams and gravel shoals to spawn and the landlocks concentrate in those areas as well. Quabbin has a West Arm and an East Arm. To fish the West Arm, anchor and cast near any feeder streams, particularly the West Branch of the Swift, which enters at the very top of the West Arm. You may want to land the boat (if you can) and walk up the West Branch to cast into its lower pools.

Smelt also utilize the feeder streams in the East Arm as well as shallow shoals to spawn, and the salmon school there as well. Any traditional smelt-imitating streamer will garner strikes, but for casting, the more lifelike marabou or rabbit-fur streamers work better than hair-winged or feathered imitations. If the salmon are unwilling to go to the surface to eat, cast a sink-tip line with a weighted streamer to achieve a retrieve closer to the bottom.

Right before the season closes in the fall, salmon will congregate at the mouths of the West Branch and East Branch of the Swift in preparation for running up the rivers to spawn, and can be caught by casters again.

Quabog River

East of Springfield and south of Quabbin Reservoir lies the Quabog River. It is a fertile stream with a variety of insects and some strong hatches that start earlier here than other Massachusetts waters. Hendrickson's emerge in great quantities as early as late April, followed by a variety of midges, caddis, and mayflies.

Access is good from US 20 in Palmer, and the prime area runs 12 miles along MA 67 to West Warren. The fishing experience here is enhanced by the natural setting, as there is very little development and the river runs through mature forest. Directly downstream from West Warren, the river is bouldery with rapids, and if you can cast to the current seams, you will find success. Be careful wading this section.

Areas where an angler can reach the river are too numerous to mention and you can fish almost anywhere up and down the river. Most early-season anglers fish the obvious access points after the stocking truck has departed. Two undeveloped roadside parks can be identified by their concrete blockades designed to prevent folks from driving down to the river's edge (42.182991,-72.264239 / 42.192986,-72.264419). This section is characterized by wide riffles and runs, with much of the water knee deep or lower. The river can be waded here, but be certain of your footing because it is difficult to see the bottom because of the dark-colored water. A wading staff is very helpful. This section cries out to be fished with a dry fly, dry-dropper combination, or a classic wet-fly swing.

For the best success catching stocked and holdover trout, fish areas away from the popular parking areas. Sometimes the road is high above the river, and I would guess those parts are less fished. This river would greatly benefit from a catch-and-release section.

Farther downstream, one prime spot is the pool under the US 20 bridge just east of where US 20 meets MA 67. You can then walk upstream or downstream to fish some nice pools. Watch for the no parking signs and

A lakeside view of Quabbin Reservoir's Windsor Dam.

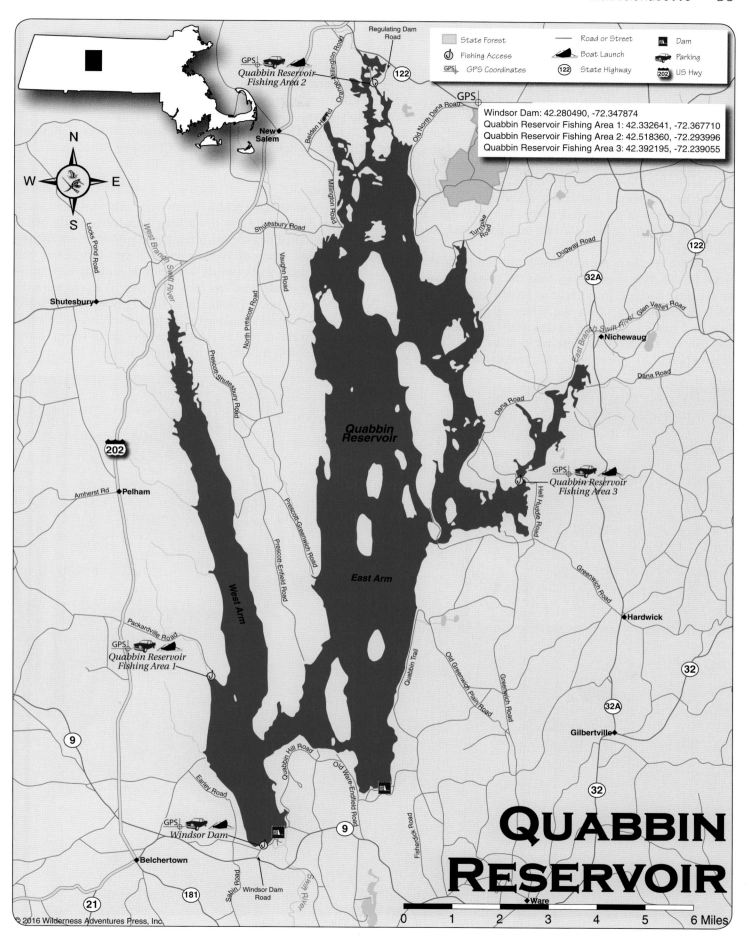

State Forest
Fishing Access
GPS Coordinates
Road or Street
Boat Launch
State Highway
Dam
Parking
US Hwy

Windsor Dam: 42.280490, -72.347874
Quabbin Reservoir Fishing Area 1: 42.332641, -72.367710
Quabbin Reservoir Fishing Area 2: 42.518360, -72.293996
Quabbin Reservoir Fishing Area 3: 42.392195, -72.239055

Regulating Dam Road

GPS
Quabbin Reservoir
Fishing Area 2

New Salem

Belden Hill

Orange-Millington Road

Old North Dana Road

GPS

122

122

Turnpike Road

Dugway Road

32A

Glen Valley Road

East Branch Swift River

Nichewaug

Dana Road

West Branch Swift River

Locks Pond Road

Shutesbury Road

Shutesbury

Vaughn Road

North Prescott Road

Prescott-Shutesbury Road

202

Amherst Rd

Pelham

Prescott-Greenwich Road

Prescott-Enfield Road

Quabbin
Reservoir

Dana Road

GPS
Quabbin Reservoir
Fishing Area 3

Hell Huddle Road

West Arm

East Arm

Greenwich Road

Hardwick

Packardville Road

GPS
Quabbin Reservoir
Fishing Area 1

32

Quabbin Trail

Old Greenwich Plain Road

Greenwich Road

32A

Gilbertville

Earley Road

Quabbin Hill Road

Old Ware-Enfield Road

9

Fisherdick Road

32

9

GPS
Windsor Dam

Belchertown

Sabin Road

Windsor Dam Road

Swift River

181

21

Ware

QUABBIN RESERVOIR

0 1 2 3 4 5 6 Miles

© 2016 Wilderness Adventures Press, Inc.

park elsewhere. For a more secluded experience, travel farther east and find Fenton Road. Within a quarter of a mile, there is a grassy old road off to the right (42.141205,-72.282003). Park on the side of Fenton Road and walk down. It follows the river for a mile and is less fished than other sections. Look for short side trails to the river's edge.

The lower Quabog River, from MA 32 downstream, is not as heavily fished but it is stocked and hold-over fish reside in some of its deeper pools. Three bridges provide access in this more heavily industrialized and residental section.

Recent stockers are not fussy, but the trout that have been in the river a while key into the predominant insect at the time and it is important to roughly match the hatch. With multiple insects on the water at the same time (a masking hatch), it is not always easy to figure out what the fish are feeding on. Patterns in sizes 12 to 18 that are close enough to a number of the natural insects are good searching patterns, including the Hornberg, Tapply's Near Nuff, Parachute Adams, Puterbaugh Caddis, Klinkhammers (in various colors), and the traditional Adams.

Some Quabog tributaries are also stocked: Blosgett Mill Brook, School Street Brook, Chicopee Brook, and Coys Brook.

Mill River

There are actually two Mill Rivers in central Massachusetts, but the river that I am describing here runs along MA 9 from Williamsburg to Northhampton, with the best fishing starting just south of Williamsburg. If you are clever, you will find many entry points from public parking lots, small parks, side roads, and bridges. This river is freestone with shaded runs, pocket water, and small pools. It is stocked well and is a pleasant place to fish for a few hours if you find yourself in the area. The water does get quite warm in the summer, so it is mostly just a spring fishery.

UPPER LEFT: Low summertime flows on the Mill River at the Route 9 Bridge, which provides access.
MAIN IMAGE: The author fishing the Quabog from one of the roadside parking areas.

MILLERS RIVER

The Millers River has a devoted following of anglers that consider it one of the best rivers to fish in Massachusetts, and the best brown trout fishery. It shares a history with other Massachusetts rivers in that it was historically considered one of the best fisheries in southern New England until the 1930s when the effects of the local manufacturing industry took a heavy toll. With many of those issues resolved starting in the 70s, it is fishing well again for stocked rainbows and stocked and holdover brown trout.

The Millers is by far the largest river of all of the Connecticut River's eastern tributaries, flowing west from a series of lakes in northern Worcester County before emptying into the Connecticut River after over 40 miles. It offers quality trout fishing in many areas, some settled, and some remote. Parts of this river run through town centers while the sections in between maintain a more natural feel. You could fish this river every day for an entire year and never fish the same section twice.

This is a fertile freestone river with healthy insect hatches along its length but also prone to high water or drought conditions because it is not dam-regulated. Because of residual PCB and mercury contamination, the entire lower Millers River is defacto catch and release for all but recently stocked fish, but two official catch-and-release sections exist. The first one is called the Bears Den section and runs from the railroad trestle just downstream from the South Ralston bridge to the old Starret Factory Dam location in Athol.

To reach the South Ralston bridge, take MA 202 North from US 2 and turn left on MA 68 until you reach the river. Find the parking area to the right and you can fish this heavily-stocked section up to the dam. The last time I visited, I watched a man pull up three large rainbows in short order from under the bridge.

To reach the catch-and-release section, cross the bridge, bear left and, after a short distance, you will notice an old blocked bridge crossing the river by a restaurant and a general store. Fish downstream and when you reach a railroad trestle crossing the river, you will be at the beginning of the catch-and-release section. The land surrounding the river here is protected and has remained undeveloped. A hiking trail runs the length of the river downstream and a little walking will give you some solitude to fish the fast water of this part of the river.

A railroad track with multiple trestles allows quicker walking to the catch-and-release section and access to the other side of the river. I don't know about you, but I have nightmares about getting stuck on trestles with on-coming trains. However, these trestles are wide enough to have a trail on one side, and train traffic is light. I have actually never heard a train while I have fished the Millers.

Many anglers prefer the middle of the Bears Den Catch-and-Release Section with its reasonable wading and good numbers of browns (some are stocked at this location). From the general store in the village of South Royalston, continue on MA 68 a short distance and take a left at a fork in the road. Head uphill and take the first left (Gulf Road). This road will turn into a dirt road shortly. Follow the power lines that hug the road as they take a left (a mile or so). Follow this dirt road until you see a red cottage. Parking is next to the Trout Unlimited kiosk on the right (42.624084,-72.180561). You are a long stone's throw from the middle of this catch-and-release section. The lower end of this special regulation area can be reached by taking Main Street in Athol, turning into Green Street, and traveling to the end.

The other catch-and-release area (the so-called Wendell Depot section) runs from the town of Orange at the Wendell Depot Road bridge to the breached Erwin Center dam about 2.5 miles downstream. Park at the Wendell Depot Road bridge and walk downstream along the south bank on a dirt road that runs through a wildlife management area. To reach it, travel west on US 2 past Exit 14, cross the Millers River and take the next left. Bear left and continue back to the river, and take a right over the Wendell Depot bridge. The parking area to the left is quite obvious (42.59748,-72.358738), and you can walk down to the river and start fishing.

Another good section to fish outside of the two

Joe Heineman of Wakefield, Rhode Island casts to the middle part of the Bears Den catch-and-release section of the Millers River. The walking trail is to the left of this photograph and the Medondez Pool is visible upstream.

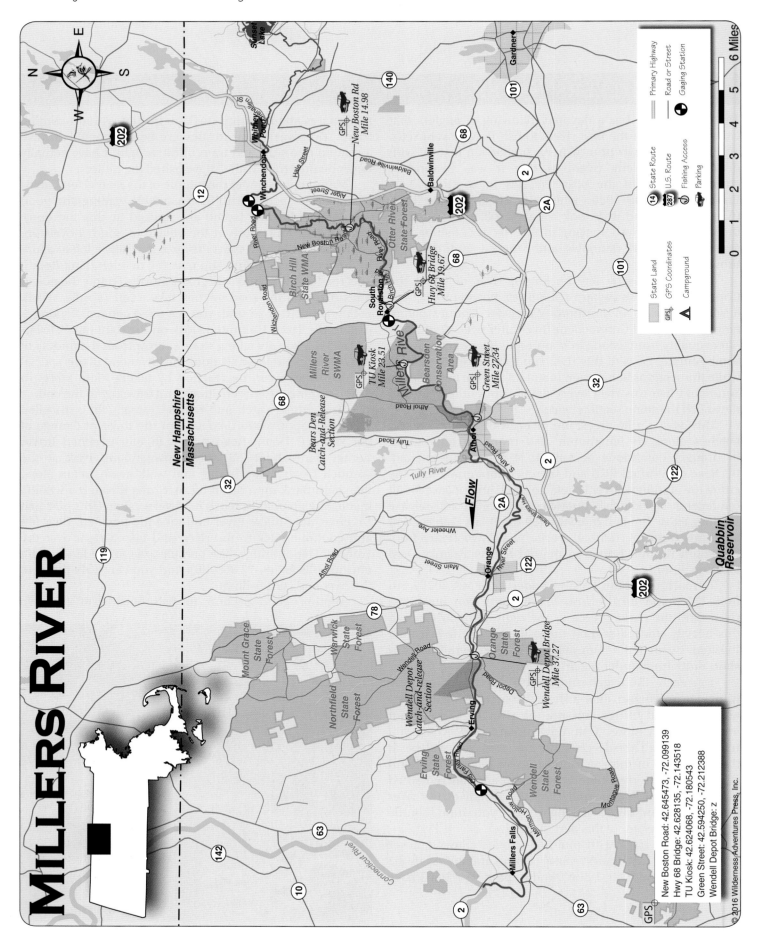

MILLERS RIVER

New Boston Road: 42.645473, -72.099139
Hwy 68 Bridge: 42.628135, -72.143518
TU Kiosk: 42.624068, -72.180543
Green Street: 42.594250, -72.212388
Wendell Depot Bridge: z

catch-and-release areas is in the Birch Hill Wildllife Management Area in Winchendon.

The best fishing occurs in the spring when flow diminishes after snow melt and early season storms. Rainbows and brown trout are stocked in areas with good access and the fish are uneducated. After mid-June the fishing changes; it is still productive but becomes more difficult as the target becomes hold-over browns. During the warm weather months, the best fishing is early in the morning and late in the evening in deep pools that have cooling springs or tributaries. Find such spots at sundown and you will be rewarded with rising browns. From July through October, fish continue to rise in certain spots on the river.

The Millers is a fertile river and has good hatches of mayflies, caddisflies, and stoneflies. Mayfly species include Hendricksons, March browns (early May through June), sulphurs, and a variety of drakes (Ephemerella species). Yellow,

Beautfiul riffles and runs of the lower catch-and-release section, from Depot Bridge.

brown and grey drakes are available all summer. In the fall, the mayflies are smaller (sizes 20 to 24). Additional food sources include abundant bait fish, aquatic worms and leeches, as well as terrestrial insects at certain times, including flying ants (often in September).

The Millers has a variety of water types and when water temperatures are moderate, the fish can be anywhere. It pays to match your techniques and fly patterns with the water you are fishing. For riffles and pocket water, try high-stick nymphing on a short line with any brown-bodied nymph, sized to match the naturals. Move slowly and probe all of the likely spots. In deeper runs with structure such as boulders and rocks, try a sink-tip line with weighted Woolly Buggers (olive or black), Conehead Marabou steamers, or large nymphs – either drifted naturally with the current or retrieved actively.

For fishing the larger pools, observation will often help determine how to fish them. If you don't see fish rising, start at the faster water at the head of the pool and swing wet flies down and across. Then creep leech patterns and Mini-Muddlers along the bottom. If you are fortunate enough to see fish rising, your best chance of success is to fish upstream to the rising fish, being careful not to line them with your casts. Parachute, Comaradun, or Emerger styles that sit down in the water will trigger the most strikes. Carry sizes 14 to 20 with brown, light yellow, or olive bodies

and you will successfully match most events. If trout are rising to something you can't see, and ignoring your dry flies, then they are often taking emergers. Try fishing small nymphs in or just under the surface film.

Another key to successfully fishing the Millers, particularly later in the year, is to plan your fishing approaches carefully. Don't just hop into the water where most fly casters go. Each feature is best fished from one side or the other. Look for where the deeper water or channel is and try to fish it from the other side, taking into account room for a backcast. Railroad trestles provide crossing points and depending on water levels, look for shallower areas where one can wade across.

For more information on the Millers, call or visit Charlie Shadan at the Evening Sun Fly Shop (www.eveningsunflyshop.com) or look up Ken Elmer (http://millersriverflyfishingforum.blogspot.com) who guides in the area. Ken has fished the river for over 25 years and has documented its prime pools and access points.

The Tully River is the main tributary of the Miller's River and its confluence is just west of Athol Center. This river consists of a west branch, an east branch, and a mainstem that is very short. The stream has stocked browns and rainbows with some fish holding over, and plenty of easy access. There are rumors of native brookies in the headwaters.

Millers River Stream Facts

Season
Fishing is allowed all year. Best fishing is late April through early June. Fishing in the summer is limited to early in the morning and at dusk.

River Characteristics
This is a large river by Massachusetts standards and careful wading is required especially during higher flows. Deep runs, deep pools, riffles, and large pockets can all be found, so fish the types of water that you like to fish. In the summer, the brown trout will concentrate in the larger and deeper water.

Waterflow
At the South Royalston gauge, normal river flows are around 100cfs. Wading and good fishing is optimized at flows between 50 and 200cfs.

Species
Mostly rainbow and brown trout

Tackle
This is a larger river, so for casting and mending dry flies or nymphs, bring at least a 9.5-foot, 5-weight rod with a floating line. For probing deeper pools and runs, it pays to have another reel with a fast-sink, sink-tip line or fast-sink leader.

Flies
For dry-fly action, carry a full assortment of parachute, Comparadun, or emerger styles. Carry sizes 14 to 20 with brown, light yellow, or olive bodies and you will successfully match most hatches. For nymphing, use brown, black, and olive Pheasant Tails, Copper Johns and Hare's Ears in sizes 14 to 20. For probing the bottom with sink-tip line, use black and brown Woolly Buggers, leech patterns, and Muddlers (including mini-sizes). Rainbows will often take white streamers with a red or pink collar or tail.

Access
For Wendell Depot Catch-and-Release Area, park at the Wendell Depot bridge and walk downstream along the south bank on a dirt road that runs through a Wildlife Management Area. To get there, travel west on US 2 past Exit 14, cross the Millers River and take the next left. Bear left and continue back to the river, and take a right over the Wendell Depot bridge.

For the start of the Bear's Den C&R section, start at the South Royalston General Store, cross over the old bridge (closed to cars) and follow the path along the railroad tracks downstream to the trestle (about a half mile). For the middle of the Bear's Den C&R section, start at the general store, continue on MA 68 a short distance and take a left at a fork in the road. Take the first left (Gulf Road), and follow the power lines that hug the road and follow them as they take a left (a mile or so). Follow this dirt road until you see a red cottage.

Ware River
This river can be accessed from MA 32 traveling north from Route 9 in Palmer or traveling south from Route 2. This good-sized river warms significantly in the summer, so the best fishing is in the spring after it is stocked with brook and brown trout, although some browns may hold over in deep holes with some incoming colder water.

The trout fishing section is generally between Barre Plains and Ware. Perhaps because I am a sucker for old-fashioned New England charm, I like to fish in the fast water both upstream and downstream from the covered bridge at the end of Bridge Road in downtown Gilbertville (42.310307,-72.212472). Of course, the river here is typical northern New England freestone riffle, run, and pool water, so perhaps I feel right at home.

Another area to try is in the vicinity of Hartwick, where Hartwick Road crosses the river and another old road juts out just upstream. The river here is more of a meadow type of water with undercut banks, and slow, deep pools with eddies. Several deep pools can be found both upstream and downstream from the bridge.

Farther downriver, anglers who have kids to entertain like to try their luck right inside the park in Ware where the river is dammed to create a small pond.

The covered bridge over the Ware River in Gilbertville.
A small pool right below the bridge often yields a trout or two.

CENTRAL MASSACHUSETTS PLANNING CONSIDERATIONS

Nearby Hub Cities and Towns

- Amherst: (www.amherstarea.com)
- Springfield: (www.myonlinechamber.com)
- Athol: (www.northquabbinchamber.com)

Easy Access Options

In central Massachusetts, many easy access options exist because of the frequent river bridge crossings or major roads following the course of many rivers. The following are a few suggestions, but there are many more options that you can discover for yourself if you study Google maps or the *Massachusetts Delorme Atlas*.

- Any of the road crossings of the East Branch of the Swift provide access with just a few steps down a gradual bank. Try MA 32, MA32A, Quaker Road, and Glen Valley Road bridges.
- One of the Quabog River parking areas (42.192986,-72.264419) offers a very short walk through a level grassy park to the river. An open area near the bank allows for easy back casts.
- The Irving Road Bridge parking area offers a two-minute walk down a dirt road and grassy field to fish nice pocket water on the Millers River under the MA 2 bridge (42.597506, -72.358797).
- Enjoy the scenery of the old covered bridge in Gilbertville over the Ware River, and it is but 20 steps down a gradual grassy slope to fish the good water under the bridge (42.310307, -72.212472).
- The mainstem of the Westfield River is just a short walk or a quick descent down a roadside bank from any number of pull-offs on MA Route 20.

Suggested Beginner Options

If you are a beginner, generally your best chance of success is to fish the area streams and rivers after the waters have been freshly stocked. Find out when the stocking trucks have made their rounds, wait several days to a week for the stockers to get acclimated, and then go fishing. Try the following spots:

- The East Branch of the Swift where MA 32 crosses the river (42.460929,-72.164137). Try the shoreline of the pond or the river immediately below the dam. You will find plenty of backcast room. Launch a canoe to cover more water throughout the pond.
- The midpoint access of the Millers River Bears Den C&R section from mid-May to mid-June. Watch how other anglers are fishing and ask questions. Find a spot where you can safely wade out a little and leave yourself a clear back cast.
- Fish upstream and downstream from the covered bridge in Gilbertville. This is fast-moving pocket water so anglers don't need to worry about long casts or perfect drifts. Flip a small streamer such as a Wood Special or cast a Hornberg short distances into likely holding water, retrieving slowly against or perpendicular to the current.

A good mid-winter brookie from the easily accessible Swift River below Quabbin Dam. Photo courtesy Dave Talmanson.

A pretty brookie that took a Wood Special just downstream from the Gilbertville Covered Bridge on the Ware River.

Vacation Suggestions

Weekend Getaway

- Take a weekend and fish the Millers from mid-May to mid-June. The lodging options range from quaint Bed and Breakfasts to 1950s style motels off of MA 2. Try each of the two catch-and-release sections – one day each.
- Another option if you want to try your hand at technical dry-fly fishing for bigger fish is to wait until a July weekend. Fish the Swift River during the bright and hot part of the day and then take the hour drive up to the Millers towards evenings and fish the evening hatch on the Millers when the bigger holdover browns come out to play.
- If you get winter fever, pick a weekend when the weather is reasonable and spend it fishing the Swift River's Y Pool. This is technical fishing with tiny flies, but you will enjoy the comradarie with the other crazies out fishing with you and you might land a trophy. It is a decent alternative to sitting at home reading flyfishing magazines.

One-week Vacation

In May or June, fish the destination fisheries of central Massachusetts. Perhaps you find yourself in the area attending graduation at any of the many fine schools located in Amherst. Steal away from the Lord Jeff Inn and do some fishing, or arrive several days before the graduation ceremonies. Non-fishing family members can go to Old Sturbridge Village or sightsee around Quabbin Reservoir. You might allocate your time this way:

- A day fishing the Chesterfield Gorge – spectacular scenery and good fishing on the west branch of the Westfield River.
- Don't neglect the mainstem of the Westfield. It will take an entire day to fish a number of different sections from the convenient pull-offs.
- Several days on the Millers, fishing different sections.
- A day testing your technical skills on the Swift.
- Take your 3-weight, hiking boots, and a handful of flies and try the simplicity of small stream fishing by hiking and casting along the forested sections of the east and west branches of the Swift River.

Western Massachusetts

Western Massachusetts is dominated by the Berkshire Hills, which are part of the Appalachian Mountain Chain that includes Vermont's Green and New Hampshire's White Mountains to the north. Because the Berkshires run generally north and south, streams and rivers that flow from the western slopes either run south into Connecticut, or in the case of the Hoosic watershed, run north into the Hudson River. Streams that have their origins on the eastern slopes end up flowing east, many entering the Deerfield River, and then joining the Connecticut River in northern Massachusetts.

Brian from Pheasant Tail Tours holding a nice western Massachusetts rainbow trout.

DEERFIELD RIVER

The Deerfield River may be the most well-known flyfishing river in Massachusetts and is certainly the most classic with miles of pools, riffles, glides, and runs over a rocky bottom and through mostly wooded countryside. When you drift the Deerfield, it is as close to a western fishing experience as you can get in Massachusetts.

The Deerfield River's headwaters are in the Green Mountains of Vermont, from which it flows southward into the Sherman Reservoir at the Massachusetts border and into the Berkshire Hills before being briefly captured by the Bear Swamp Generating Facility Lower Reservoir created by the Fife Brook Dam. From there it completes its 70-mile journey by flowing south and then east through a narrow valley and past several minor impoundments, before joining the Connecticut River in Greenfield.

The Deerfield River is paralleled for much of its way by MA 2, which follows the course of the original Mohawk Trail, a footpath traveled by Native Americans to trade and interact with other tribes. A bronze statue of a Mohawk Indian just off the banks of the river in Charlemont pays homage to that history.

Because its source is the bottom-release Fife Brook Dam, the Massachusetts portion of the Deerfield stays cold for most of its length and provides good conditions for trout the entire year. Successful spawning is limited so the fishery is maintained by stocking; although fish do hold over with some browns growing large enough to be measured in pounds instead of inches. Despite the good water conditions, trout do not hold over as often as you might think because of high harvest rates and some mortality in the winter. Fortunately, the state stocks this river weekly and heavily with rainbows, brookies, and brown trout in the 12-inch class. In fact, if you fish often enough, you will get to see the

hatchery truck on overpasses, dropping fish several stories into the water.

Occasionally, wild brookies, browns, and rainbows can be caught. In fact one guide told me that when Hurricane Irene's flood waters poured down the Deerfield in 2011, decades of sediment and pollutants were flushed down the river, yielding increased spawning habitat. Since then, the numbers of river-born fish are increasing. The Deerfield has the potential to be a really great fishery if regulations and anglers' behavior changed so that more fish caught were then released.

The key to successfully fishing the Deerfield is understanding the daily water flow fluctuations because of scheduled dam releases. At low flows, the river is easily waded with defined pools and runs. At higher flows, the river's current strengthens appreciably and it is more easily floated. Floating also lets you fish water where shore access is difficult. Generally flows are low in the morning, ramp up towards the middle of the day for three to eight hours, and then decline again. Of course, rainfall the previous month has a bearing on flows as well. The range can be from 125 to 800cfs during a single day, so it is critical if you are wading

UPPER RIGHT: What might be New England's biggest brown trout was recently landed in the Deerfield. Photo courtesy Brian Lynch, Pheasant Tail Tours.
MAIN IMAGE: The bouldery section below Zoar Picnic Area.

DEERFIELD RIVER

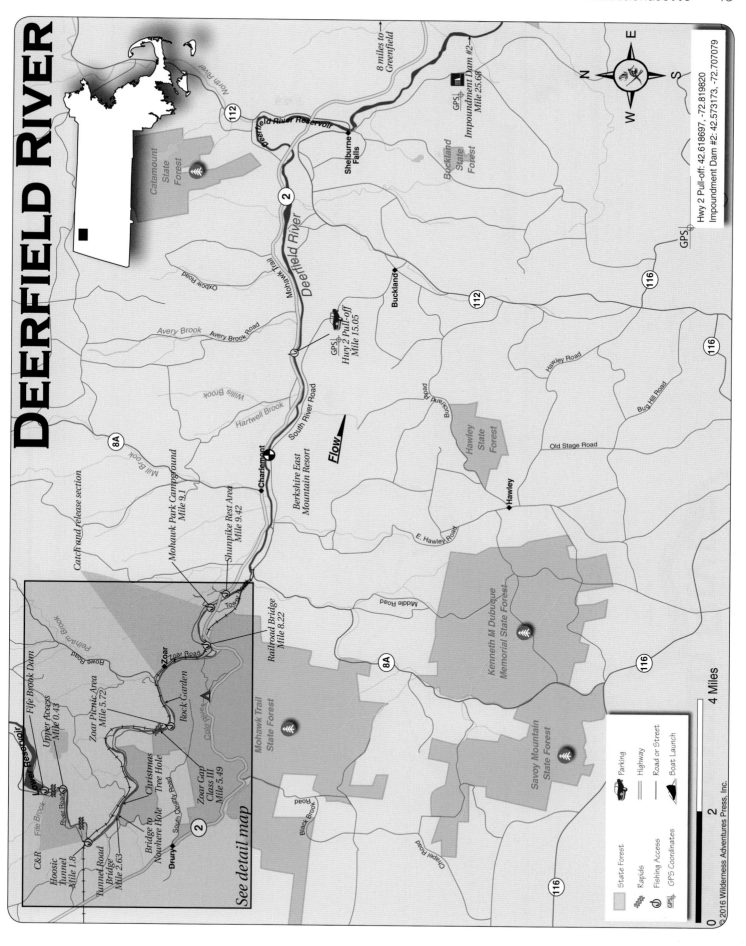

North River

Catamount State Forest

112

8 miles to Greenfield

Deerfield River Reservoir

Shelburne Falls

2

GPS
Impoundment Dam #2
Mile 25.68

Buckland State Forest

Mohawk Trail

Deerfield River

Buckland

112

GPS

116

Oxbow Road

Avery Brook

Avery Brook Road

GPS
Hwy 2 Pull-off
Mile 15.05

116

Willis Brook

Hartwell Brook

South River Road

Flow

Berkshire East Mountain Resort

Hawley Road

Bug Hill Road

Buckland Road

Hawley State Forest

Old Stage Road

8A

Mill Brook

Charlemont

Hawley

Mohawk Park Campground
Mile 9.1

Shunpike Rest Area
Mile 9.42

E. Hawley Road

116

Railroad Bridge
Mile 8.22

Middle Road

Kenneth M Dubuque Memorial State Forest

116

Mohawk Trail State Forest

8A

Zoar Road

Cold River

Savoy Mountain State Forest

Chapel Road

Black Brook Road

2

See detail map

Pelham Brook

Rowe Road

Fife Brook Dam

Upper Access
Mile 0.43

Zoar Picnic Area
Mile 5.72

Zoar

Rock Garden

Christmas Tree Hole

Zoar Gap
Class III
Mile 5.49

Bridge to Nowhere Hole

South County Road

Lower Reservoir

C&R

Fife Brook

River Road

Hoosic Tunnel
Mile 1.8

Tunnel Road Bridge
Mile 2.63

Drury

2

Catch and release section

Legend

	State Forest
	Rapids
	Fishing Access
GPS	GPS Coordinates

Parking
Highway
Road or Street
Boat Launch

0   2   4 Miles

© 2016 Wilderness Adventures Press, Inc.

Hwy 2 Pull-off: 42.618697, -72.819820
Impoundment Dam #2: 42.573173, -72.707079

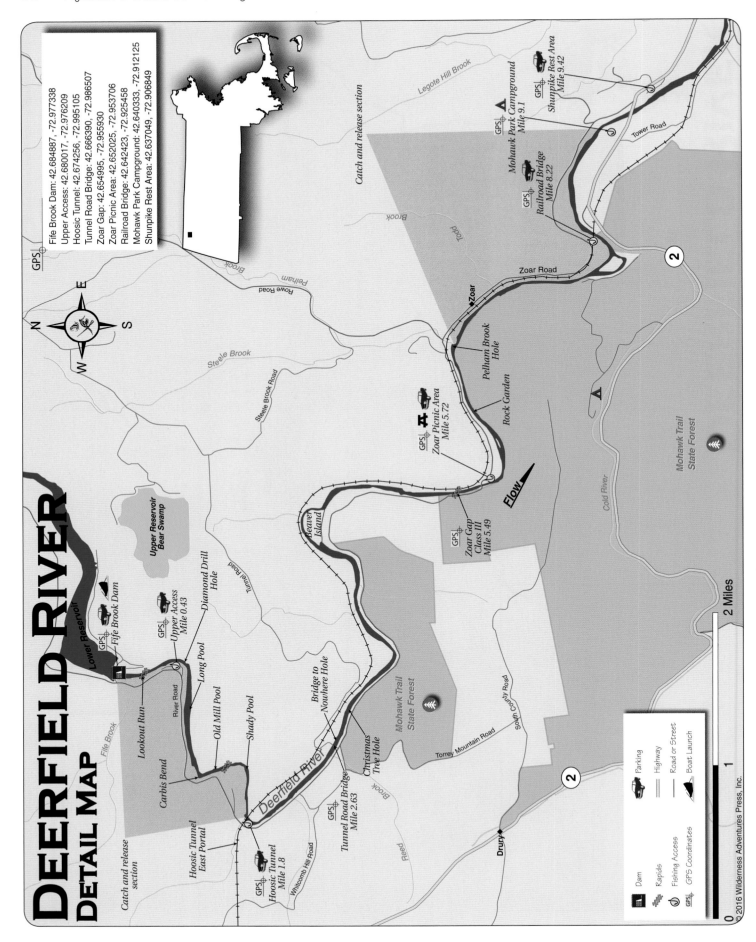

DEERFIELD RIVER
DETAIL MAP

Fife Brook Dam: 42.684887, -72.97338
Upper Access: 42.680017, -72.976209
Hoosic Tunnel: 42.674256, -72.995105
Tunnel Road Bridge: 42.666390, -72.986507
Zoar Gap: 42.654995, -72.955930
Zoar Picnic Area: 42.652025, -72.953706
Railroad Bridge: 42.642423, -72.925458
Mohawk Park Campground: 42.640333, -72.912125
Shunpike Rest Area: 42.637049, -72.906849

Catch and release section

Lower Reservoir
Upper Reservoir
Bear Swamp

Fife Brook Dam
Fife Brook

Lookout Run
River Road
Carbis Bend
Long Pool
Diamond Drill Hole
Old Mill Pool
Shady Pool
Upper Access Mile 0.43

Hoosic Tunnel East Portal
Hoosic Tunnel Mile 1.8
Whitcomb Hill Road
Tunnel Road

Bridge to Nowhere Hole
Beaver Island
Christmas Tree Hole
Tunnel Road Bridge Mile 2.63

Deerfield River

Mohawk Trail State Forest

Torrey Mountain Road
South County Road
Reed Brook

Drury

Steele Brook
Steele Brook Road

Pelham Brook
Rowe Road

Zoar Picnic Area Mile 5.72
Zoar

Zoar Gap Class III Mile 5.49
Flow
Rock Garden
Pelham Brook Hole

Zoar Road

Cold River

Mohawk Trail State Forest

Legote Hill Brook
Todd Brook

Mohawk Park Campground Mile 9.1
Railroad Bridge Mile 8.22
Shunpike Rest Area Mile 9.42
Tower Road

2

2

Catch and release section

Legend
- Dam
- Rapids
- Fishing Access
- GPS Coordinates
- Parking
- Highway
- Road or Street
- Boat Launch

0   1   2 Miles

©2016 Wilderness Adventures Press, Inc.

to stay alert, and if you notice the water is rising, get to shore quickly. If you find yourself on the opposite shore to where you began your day, you can cross the river on the railroad trestle bridge.

If you prefer wading, one tactic is to fish early in the day up by the Fife Brook Dam before the flows increase. When they start releasing water, get in your car and drive farther downstream, and you will have several hours before the higher flows reach you. Then drive back up to the dam and start fishing again when the flows drop.

If you are floating the river, wait until the flows increase before starting. There will be a flotilla of rafters, tubers, and kayakers during the warmer months, particularly on weekends and holidays, so either get started right when the flows increase, or wait until the hoards move through. If you prefer to have someone else do the rowing, there are a number of excellent guides that offer float trips. I floated with Brian Lynch of Pheasant Tail Tours (www. pheasanttailtours) and he was excellent.

Travel along the Deerfield River from MA 2, which follows the river upstream from Greenfield. Continue to

More rainbows splash into the Deerfield River.

follow the river from Zoar Road by bearing right just before the Mohawk Campground. Zoar Road becomes River Road and continues to follow the river upstream.

The Deerfield has a number of distinct segments with different fishing characteristics, including two catch-and-release zones. The upper catch-and-release section runs from the Fife Brook Dam (42.684887,-72.977338) to the Hoosic Tunnel Railroad Trestle (42.674256,-72.995105), a distance of 1.5 miles. This section is easily fished from the River Road, which has frequent pull-outs and paths to the water, often to popular and named pools, such as the Diamond Drill Hole.

Another popular segment a few miles downstream is the Zoar Picnic Area (42.652025,-72.953706) which provides a convenient launch point for water craft. It is not a catch-and-release section, but increasing structure in the form of larger rocks, boulders, and the occasional lodged deadfall, make it an interesting place to fish. I can still picture the large brown trout that appeared from under a sunken log to slash at my large marabou streamer before disappearing again. This section can be accessed by Zoar Road or just walking downstream from the picnic area.

The lower catch-and-release section starts a mile from Zoar Picnic Area, at the mouth of Pelham Brook and continues for a mile to the Mohawk Park Campground. My favorite spots on this section are the pool where the brook enters the river, and then farther down, a deep pool by a shallow riffle.

From Charlemont to Shelbourne Falls, the river flattens out, slows down, shallows up, and warms. More warmwater species appear such as smallmouth bass, but the fishing can still be excellent, particularly early and late in the day. MA 2 parallels this section, so there are frequent spots to park and fish. Look for ledges, boulders, or river bends that create good holding water.

From Impoundment Dam #2 in Shelbourne to Greenfield, the river flows unimpeded all the way to the Connecticut River, a distance of eight miles. Public access points are limited to the Stillwater and Bardwell's Ferry Bridges (the canoe float between them is about five miles). As the water quality has improved, more trout have moved downriver and both browns and rainbows can be caught in this section.

To target the largest fish, fish the deepest pools with sinking line and Muddlers, stonefly nymphs, and Woolly Buggers in various colors. Even shad that have made their way all the way up the Connecticut River from Long Island Sound can be found in late spring to early summer. If you think you spot a school of shad, and you left your pink Shad Darts at home, cast the largest Wood Special pattern that you can find, along with a little weight to sink it. You may find out how fun it is to catch shad on a fly rod.

Patterns and Tactics

Early in the year, particularly when there are higher flows, the action will be subsurface. Sink-tip lines, weighted leaders, and coneheads will sink the flies to the bottom where the flows are slower. Mend to slow the rate of drift and at the end, let your streamer dangle downstream for a bit. Any marabou streamer or Woolly Bugger in green, grey, or white should be effective. When Brian from Pheasant Tail Tours is floating the river in the spring, he prefers a green Crystal Bugger with a little flash.

Later in the year, as the water drops and warms, hatches will commence and matching them will improve results. I remember one glorious, robin's-egg blue sky afternoon in May, when I fished an upper-section pool that seemed fishless until March browns started emerging. As if from nowhere, feisty rainbows appeared to slash at the emerging bugs. Every drag-free drift with a March brown imitation paid off with a fish. Imitations that were less than perfect or dragged even slightly were ignored.

At other times of the year, matching the hatch requires caddis, blue-winged olive, Light Cahill, sulphur, and chironomid imitations. Golden stones also emerge sporadically spring and fall and keep fish looking up for large flies, such as size 6 or 8 yellow Stimulators.

During low flows in late summer and early autumn, successful anglers reduce tippet sizes and fish tiny flies, smaller than size 20. In late October and November, when the bigger browns are in pre-spawn mode, meaty brown and yellow streamers (perhaps with an egg dropper) may yield some truly memorable fish.

When the Deerfield River fishing guides put their rafts away for the day, where and how do they fish? Most go after big browns. I have seen cell phone photos that look like they were taken in New Zealand or Patagonia.

If you are so inclined, do what they do. Fish during the early spring or particularly in late autumn, when the beasties are more active. Concentrate on the pools immediately below any of the Deerfield's Vermont or Massachusetts dams, or any of the deepest pools. Fish from dusk until midnight using the biggest, ugliest streamers you can find (use a stout tippet). Another time to try for poundage is the transition period when the waters are rising from a dam release. Browns become active in the biggest pools to grab insects and small fish that are being swept downstream in the sudden torrent.

I was fishing one day when the water started to rise around me. I grabbed a rod with sinking line and a small Muddler Minnow and cast into the nearby deep pool and immediately hooked up with a large brown that I fought for quite some time before the hook pulled free. On the next cast, I immediately hooked up again with a fish that seemed much smaller than the first. That brown measured a full 16 inches, so I can only imagine how big the first fish was.

DEERFIELD RIVER STREAM FACTS

Seasons
Year round

Flows
Vary greatly during the day. Morning and evening generally around 125cfs, midday up to 800cfs.

River Characteristics
This is a relatively large river by Massachusetts standards and has every type of water including deep pools, runs, riffles, and pockets. As water flows change, one river location can yield all of those. A deep run and pool at high flows can become riffle and pocket water under lower flows.

Fish
Stocked rainbows, browns, holdover rainbows and browns, some wild browns and brookies.

Tackle

Nine-foot 6-weight (during high flows) or 9-foot 4-weight (during low flows) rods, floating and sink-tip lines, 3x to 6x tippets.

Flies

For subsurface fishing, Woolly Buggers and Crystal Buggers in green, brown, and black; small Muddlers, marabou streamers in white, gray, and yellow; for the bigger browns, the largest, gnarliest rabbit-fur streamers that you can find. For surface action, Hendrickson or March brown imitations, Klinkhammers to match whatever is emerging, Elk Hair and Puterbaugh Caddis patterns, and a variety of smaller midge and blue-winged olive patterns such as small San Juan worms and Zebra midges.

Guides

Pheasant Tail Tours (www.pheasanttailtours.com), Harrison Anglers (www. harrisonanglers.com), Berkshire Rivers Flyfishing (www.berkshireriversflyfishing.com).

Tributaries of the Deerfield

Many of the Deerfield tributaries offer good fishing for hand-sized stream-born trout as well as stockers.

The Green River (not to be confused with another Green River in far western Massachusetts) is a wonderful river to fish. The color of the water is a greenish-blue in the deep pools and its course takes it through a deep gorge before its confluence with the Deerfield. This small river strongly reminds me of my time fishing small creeks in the Idaho mountains for native cutthroat. Of course the fish here are wild brook trout and stocked rainbows. The last time I fished it, you could still see the damage from Hurricane Irene, with huge piles of uprooted trees and debris from houses that were literally washed into the stream.

Access is from MA 2. Take Colrain Road to River Road that becomes dirt for a while but parallels the river through the small town of West Layden, before reaching the Vermont border.

Other tribs to try (from west to east) include Cold River, Willis Brook, Avery Brook, North River, and Sluice Brook.

A deep ledge pool on the Green River.

Hoosic River

In extreme northwest Massachusetts, the Hoosic River flows around Mount Greylock, the highest peak in the state, and under a walking bridge The Hoosic is another Massachusetts river that has been channeled, polluted, and generally abused over the past several hundred years. Water quality is greatly improved, although the continued presence of PCBs in the mainstem limits the swimming and fish-eating options on the river.

With a mix of habitats, you can find wild and stocked brown, brook, and rainbow trout year round, with a small, but catchable population of holdover browns and rainbows up to 24 inches. Hatches of caddisflies and mayflies such as sulphurs occur regularly. Successful anglers fish caddis imitations in sizes 14 to 18 and caddis and mayfly emergers work better than traditional dry flies. Nymphing probably gives you the highest chance of success because recent severe flooding has reduced the quality of the hatches.

Local anglers are fishing this river year round, and a YouTube video shows anglers successfully nymphing the Hoosic for browns right next to MA 2 from a drift boat in early January.

The North and South Branches run cooler in the summer, are not polluted with PCBs, and are stocked by the state with rainbows and brown trout. Access to the South Branch is from MA 8, and the best fishing on the mainstem is downstream from the Cheshire Reservoir to the town of Adams, because the water runs colder than in other sections. Cheshire Reservoir itself is a good bass, pike, and pickerel lake.

Berkshire Outfitters is the primary source of both flyfishing gear and information in this part of the state and their shop is on 169 Grove Street in Adams, on MA 8, right alongside the river. An angler can literally fish across the road from their store. Harry Desmond of Berkshire Rivers Flyfishing (www.berkshireriversflyfishing.com) is very knowledgeable about flyfishing the Hoosic, Housatonic, and Farmington Rivers in Massachusetts in case you are interested in guided trips.

Housatonic River

The upper river in Massachusetts is not as well-known as its southern part in Connecticut. Nevertheless, the upper Housatonic travels 36 miles through the beautiful hills and pastoral settings of the Berkshires, and the fishing improves every year. Access is good with MA 7 and MA 20 paralleling the river south of Pittsfield, forage and hatches are more than adequate, and trout migrate in and out of the tribs (where they are stocked) and hold over. Some large browns are caught every year. Because of lingering pollution such as PCBs, keeping fish to eat is discouraged, and that keeps

Abby from Kismet Outfitters and happy client with handsome Hoosic River brown. Photo courtesy Kismet Outfitters.

A Housatonic brown trout. Photo courtesy Berkshire Rivers Flyfishing.

fishing pressure down. During hot or drought summers, the trout do suffer from thermal stress. Two catch-and-release areas are now stocked. The first section runs from the MA 20 bridge in Lee, six miles to the Willow Mill Dam in South Lee. There are a number of large pools in this section separated by shallow riffles. A variety of fish species are caught here including stocked and holdover brown trout, fallfish, and bass. Farther downstream, pike are also present and guided trips are being offered for those who want to try catching these toothy predators.

The second catch-and-release section (Glendale Reach) stretches from the Glendale bridge off of MA 183 and continues for a mile to the railroad bridge (42.275628,-73.359545). But I wouldn't limit myself to the catch-and-release sections, as regulations are pretty restrictive for the entire main branch of the river. Wherever water quickens into riffles, runs, and pocket water that flows into large pools, trout are probably present.

South of Great Barrington, the Housatonic flows through farmlands and mature woodlands with public access off East Sheffield Street, which parallels the river. The river is a little silty here but can be waded. A small boat access at Brush Hill Road is convenient for canoes or kayaks, with many paddling back upstream at the end of the trip, back to the put-in point.

Don't neglect a main tributary of the Housatonic River – the Konkapot River – which might just be my favorite river name in all of New England. Just say it a few times in a row and see if you don't start smiling. Off of MA 57, find the small town of Mill River (42.112836,-73.267714) and Clayton Mill River Road, and you will also find easy access to the river. It is a pretty little stream with good water quality and a healthy population of wild and stocked trout, flowing through a largely unspoiled rural countryside. The fishing is easier earlier in the spring. As the water drops during the summer, the fish become increasingly spooky.

The Housatonic has the standard hatches that you might find in the Catskills and you can't go wrong by fishing the usual imitations at the appropriate times, although many anglers find success by nymphing Pheasant Tails and Hare's Ears of the appropriate sizes.

Farmington River

Like its cousin, the Housatonic, the Massachusetts stretch of the Farmington River is not nearly the fishery that it is in Connecticut (after it is cooled by two bottom-release dams). The Massachusetts Farmington (also referred to as the West Branch of the Farmington) is primarily a put-and-take fishery in the springtime, before lower and warmer water temperatures, and predation from trout fishers, take a large toll on the fish. Still, it is a pleasure to fish in the spring because it has easy access (MA 8 parallels the river), is easily waded, doesn't receive much fishing pressure, and is heavily stocked. The trout take the usual progression of mayfly and caddisfly imitations as spring commences. The half mile of river before it empties into Otis Reservoir may be the most productive stretch, probably because the reservoir provides some thermal protection.

The Farmington has two tributaries, the Buck and Clam Rivers (two more great names) that join together and then enter the Farmington above Colebrook Reservoir. Find these two remote mountain streams via side roads off of MA 57. Expect small native brookies that will strike any reasonably presented Adams, Hornberg, or Royal Wulff (if they don't spook first).

Stillwaters of Western Massachusetts

The ponds and small lakes of western Massachusetts share many of the same characteristics and are typically modest in size, generally under 300 acres. They have an array of both coldwater and warmwater fish species. The trout are generally stocked and many (but not all) of the waters are under general law. Check the Massachusetts rule book for the latest regulations. Flyfishing for the coldwater species tends to be best in the spring until the water warms, at which time flyfishing for bass, pickerel and other warmwater species takes over. The following are your options:

- In the town of Lee: Goose Pond is considered a premium coldwater pond managed for salmonids with a size and numbers limit on brown trout; Laurel Lake is one of the better known trout fisheries in the region. Trolling streamers or casting flies appropriate for lakes such as shiner imitations, dragonfly or damselfly nymphs can be effective.
- In the town of Monterey: Lake Buel has a paved boat launch and is heavily stocked with trout that then hold near the two deep holes on the north and south bays of the pond or on the windward side; Lake Garfield can only be fished by boat; trout fishing can be very good because of limited fishing pressure.
- In the town of Otis: Big Benton Pond is a trout fishery that holds up well because of its limited access – by boat only, down a muddy and poor road.
- In Pittsfield: Onota Lake is a 600-acre lake that is stocked heavily but managed for trophy brown trout with a one-fish 15-inches-or-greater limit; Lake Pontoosuc and its two feeder streams are heavily stocked and most of the fishing is by boat only.

Western Massachusetts Planning Considerations

Nearby Hub Cities and Towns

- Greenfield (www.mohawktrail.com, www.deerfieldattractions.com)
- Adams : (www.explorenorthadams.com, www.berkshireoutfitters.com)

Easy Access Options

- Zoar Picnic Area (42.652025,-72.953706) on the Deerfield River. Park the car, grab a picnic table, and make your way to the water which curves around the entire area. It is a few steps to the river at high water flows, and fish are available right in front of you.

Suggested Beginner Options

- Hire a guide and float the Deerfield during the spring time when casting streamers downstream and to the banks will no doubt yield at least a few fish regardless of your expertise.

Vacation Suggestions

Weekend Getaway
- Fish the Deerfield watershed during the spring or fall. I would avoid peak summer weekends. On Saturday, float the upper river with a guide. On Sunday, go back and wade your favorite sections and fish them again. Remember, you fished those sections during high flows when you were floating the river. The same water will look very different when you are wading them under lower flows. Another option for Sunday is to fish the Green River.

One-week Vacation

- Take your significant other or entire family and vacation in the Berkshires for a week in late June or September. Listen to music at Tanglewood, visit art galleries and museums, go antiquing, or hike part of the Appalachian Trail. Stay at quaint "bed and breakfasts" and eat in a variety of good local restaurants. In between all of these leisure activities, get some flyfishing in. I usually find a 50/50 split between fishing and non-fishing activities maintains relationship or family harmony, particularly if that ratio is negotiated upfront. Explore the western slope of the Berkshires as you fish the Housatonic or Konkapot Rivers from rural secondary roads. Try the Hoosic, south of Adams. Take at least one day to float the Deerfield. Assemble your 3-weight rod and choose a smaller tributary of either the Deerfield or the Housatonic, and try to find a few of the small native brook trout that reside there. At the end of the week, you will be tired, but probably content.

A feisty rainbow puts a good bend in Mike Hyde's rod just downstream from the Deerfield's Fife Brook Dam.

When flyfishing in Vermont, an angler doesn't have to "rough it". Tourism is a major Vermont industry and most parts of Vermont have maintained a quaint New England flavor, while at the same time offering a full array of excellent lodging and eating options to make visitors comfortable and happy. The angler can take his or her pick of hotels, motels, country inns, and of course the famous Vermont bed and breakfasts. Restaurants for every taste are usually nearby, often with fine chefs cooking with natural and local ingredients. This is the state to take your significant others on the fishing trip with you, even if they aren't anglers. An enjoyable time will be had by all, regardless.

Another advantage to Vermont is that waters are not crowded, especially compared to the other New England states. Generally, you can find entire sections of river or stream to yourself. The fishing is diverse, from huge Lake Champlain with over a dozen catchable fish species including pike and bowfin to small mountain brooks with miniature wild brookies.

The ancient, rounded Green Mountains provide the topography that determines the course of rivers and streams and the placement of ponds and lakes. The streams drain the mountains to the west into Lake Champlain or the Hudson River and to the east into the Connecticut River Valley.

Guide Dave Durovich fishes the Lamoille River.

At higher elevations, wild brook trout swim in the headwaters and beaver ponds. Deeper lakes hold landlocked salmon and togue. Rivers such as the Battenkill, Winooski, Lamoille, and Missisquoi are home to rainbow trout and brown trout. Otter Creek may produce bigger pike than any water of its size in the northeastern United States.

Not that Vermont waters don't have issues. Major floods from inundating rain events have caused major stream and river habitat damage. The scouring of floods, and conversely low water and high temperatures in the summer, have made natural reproduction and maintaining coldwater fish populations a challenge without annual stocking. Many lakes are threatened with nutrification or invasive species. Nonetheless, the fishing in Vermont is hugely underrated in my humble opinion.

In general, Vermont's rivers and streams are open to trout fishing from the second weekend in April through the last Sunday in October. A few stretches of a handful of streams have catch-and-release or other special regulations. Check the rulebook for specifics. Vermont's laws support the rights of anglers to fish, walk, portage, or float through any navigable river or stream below the high water mark. As long as the water is reached through public access or with the permission of one landowner, the angler should be fine.

If the reader has bypassed Vermont in favor of more publicized waters in Maine or northern New Hampshire and found those waters over-hyped or crowded, I encourage a trip or two to Vermont.

Southern Vermont

You will discover old New England as you cross the Massachusetts or New York border and enter the southwest corner of Vermont. The mills and factories of North Bennington operate with eternal rhythm. Narrow streets lined by the look-alike homes of the workers parallel railroads and river passages.

On the outskirts of town, you'll pass the massive, groomed lawns bearing the pillared homes of the "old families". Stone framed entrances, long driveways, and lanes replace the streets. The landscape is entirely manicured and groomed. Many of these impressive homes have Revolutionary War era construction dates. Roadside historical markers describe such things as, "George Washington slept here in...," or "Daniel Webster spoke...." There is a deep sense of history as you gaze upon the hills and lawns of southern Vermont.

Rivers and streams wander lazily through the valleys and farmlands of southwestern Vermont: the Walloomsac near North Bennington, the famous Battenkill passing through Manchester and Arlington, the beautiful Mettawee, the Poultney and Castleton Rivers, and the headwaters of Otter Creek share their history with the landscape.

In southeastern Vermont, the east-facing slopes of the Green Mountains have their own history. The transportation offered by the Connecticut River encouraged industrial and commercial development from Brattleboro north to Springfield. The healing spring waters near Brattleboro and Woodstock attracted wealthy patrons from around the country as tourists and settlers. Mills – once hydro-powered – and factories mix with the federal and Greek revival residential styles in southwest Vermont's villages to create what, to many visitors, is a classic New England setting.

The most popular Vermont tourist area lies in the state's southeast corner. From the city of Brattleboro near the Massachusetts border, north to White River Junction, the Connecticut River forms the border that Vermont shares with New Hampshire. Five beautiful trout streams: the Ottauquechee, the Black, the West, the Saxtons, and the Williams Rivers, flow out of the Green Mountains into the Connecticut River, sharing their beauty with the landscape, covered bridges, inns, and antique shops that attract visitors from all over.

Flyfishers coming to southeastern Vermont will find rivers holding warmwater species, mostly bass and pike, near their mouths at the Connecticut River. Upstream are found brown trout, rainbows, and wild brook trout.

The Burt Henry Covered Bridge over the Walloomsac River creates a classic southern Vermont scene.

BATTENKILL

The promise of fishing over selective brown trout on the legendary Battenkill (sometimes written as Batten Kill) draws flyfishers each season from all over the world. They come to fish the one-time homewaters of Charles Orvis, John Atherton, and Lee Wulff. The Battenkill is the most famous of Vermont's rivers and, until recently, the most heavily fished. Anglers have written extensively about this river for over 100 years, including *The Battenkill* (1993) by John Merwin.

Maintained and managed for decades as a wild fishery without stocking, the Battenkill has had a reputation as one of the top trout rivers in the East. The East and West Branches join in Manchester to form the mainstem. From there, it slowly flows through the concealed back side of the exclusive country clubs and estates of Manchester's lower village, through brushy pastures and farmland along VT 7A through the town of Sunderland and on to the village of Arlington, where it turns sharply to the west for a nine-mile journey to the New York border.

Access may be gained in the lower village of Manchester by turning east on Union Street off VT 7A by the mall of the Equinox Inn. There are several unmarked pull-off areas near the two bridges (43.132207,-73.079231) and along Richville Road and River Road (43.123659,-73.085496), which eventually return to 7A. Through this area, the Battenkill is mostly pocket water of medium depth with some undercut banks and pools. As you continue south, the river deepens and meanders lazily through fields with good cover. The banks are steep and holes, undercutting the sides, are deep.

There is a marked Vermont Fish and Wildlife public access at the river crossing in the town of Sunderland on Route 7A (43.097346,-73.141436). A quarter-mile down the road, turn east on Dunham Road and backtrack upriver to Sunderland Station. There are a couple of good pull-offs with river access near the railroad tracks along this dirt road.

Access to the Battenkill is limited as it continues south behind a very conveniently located campground on the river, named "Camping on the Battenkill". It continues behind a residential area and golf course before entering Arlington, where it turns abruptly west toward New York state. There are both marked and unmarked access points along VT 313 and on River Road, which parallels the Battenkill to the south.

The easy access and water quality have made this section of river one of the most popular fishing areas in Vermont. It is also a very popular recreational float for canoeists and tubers. In fact, to have consistent success with the larger brown trout, it requires a specific strategy to combat the water traffic because wary browns disappear when boaters appear overhead. The best course of action is to get up early and fish the upstream section of the river before the canoeists and kayakers start their excursions. When boat traffic commences, drive down river and continue fishing until the floating hordes catch up with you. In that way, you can get some quality fishing time over unspooked trout.

In general, the Battenkill may be classified as a spring creek, receiving much of its icy waters from beneath the

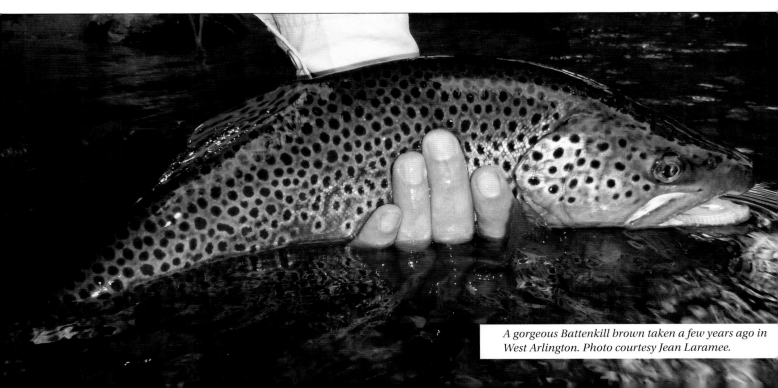

A gorgeous Battenkill brown taken a few years ago in West Arlington. Photo courtesy Jean Laramee.

BATTENKILL

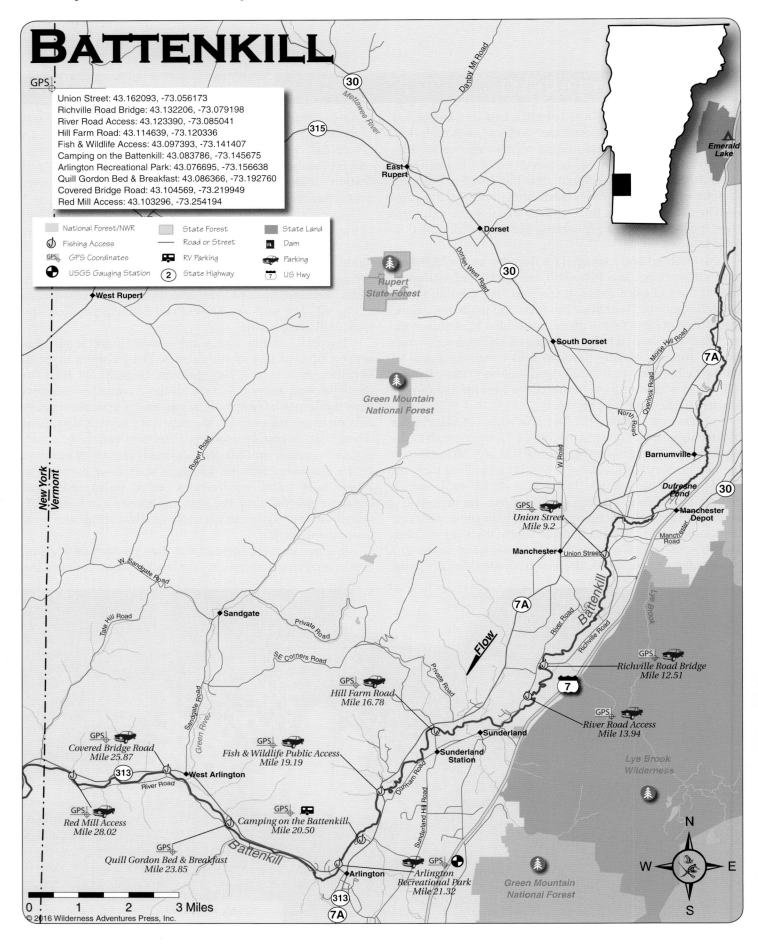

GPS

Union Street: 43.162093, -73.056173
Richville Road Bridge: 43.132206, -73.079198
River Road Access: 43.123390, -73.085041
Hill Farm Road: 43.114639, -73.120336
Fish & Wildlife Access: 43.097393, -73.141407
Camping on the Battenkill: 43.083786, -73.145675
Arlington Recreational Park: 43.076695, -73.156638
Quill Gordon Bed & Breakfast: 43.086366, -73.192760
Covered Bridge Road: 43.104569, -73.219949
Red Mill Access: 43.103296, -73.254194

National Forest/NWR
Fishing Access
GPS Coordinates
USGS Gauging Station
State Forest
Road or Street
RV Parking
State Highway
State Land
Dam
Parking
US Hwy

Emerald Lake

West Rupert
East Rupert
Dorset
South Dorset
Barnumville
Dufresne Pond
Manchester Depot

Rupert State Forest

Green Mountain National Forest

Manchester
Union Street
Union Street Mile 9.2

Richville Road Bridge Mile 12.51
River Road Access Mile 13.94

Sandgate

Hill Farm Road Mile 16.78

Flow

Sunderland
Sunderland Station

Lye Brook Wilderness

Covered Bridge Road Mile 25.87
Fish & Wildlife Public Access Mile 19.19

West Arlington
River Road

Red Mill Access Mile 28.02
Camping on the Battenkill Mile 20.50

Quill Gordon Bed & Breakfast Mile 23.85

Battenkill

Arlington

Arlington Recreational Park Mile 21.32

Green Mountain National Forest

New York / Vermont

Mettawee River

Danby Mt Road
Dorset West Road
Morse Hill Road
Overlook Road
North Road
W Road

Rupert Road
W. Sandgate Road
Tate Hill Road
Sandgate Road
Green River
SE Corners Road
Private Road
Durham Road
Sunderland Hill Road
River Road

0   1   2   3 Miles

N
W   E
S

riverbed. It offers a rich habitat for wild trout. Consequently, Vermont has managed the river without stocking since the 1970s. Wild brook trout can average from 8 to 11 inches, and brown trout may range up to 16 or 17 inches.

Unfortunately, the Battenkill has become more of a memory of its former days when prolific hatches brought scores of wild trout to the surface. Merwin, in his book, *The Battenkill*, puts it this way: "It's a lovely river that's now more rich with angling tradition than with trout."

Studies over the last 20 years have shown a marked decline in the numbers and size of the trout in this river. One of the reasons for the decline, according to experts, is the lack of cover and holding water for larger fish. Efforts to improve river structure may be having a positive impact as the fishery seems to be slowly improving lately, although nowhere close to its former glory. The Battenkill Watershed Alliance continues to add logs, trees, and large boulders in the river for trout cover, as well as planted trees along the banks in order to keep the trout population growing.

In 2007, didymo, or rock snot, was discovered in the Battenkill. Didymo quickly forms into a massive mat of goopy algae, making fishing difficult and making it harder for fish to feed. It is easily spread via boats, waders, and boots, so be sure to either dry out your gear or clean it thoroughly before entering another river. It's the reason the felt-sole ban went into effect.

In spite of these troubles, the Battenkill still draws devotees to its challenging currents and trout. Perhaps the history and scenery of this quintessential eastern trout river makes up for the frequent one- or two-trout days. Brown trout and brookies in this river are wild and sophisticated. The riverbanks are steep and undercut, making an approach to a fish rising close to shore almost impossible. Its hatches are legendary. Mayflies, from quill Gordons and blue quills to Hendricksons, pop from the river's surface film and float downstream like miniature sailboats during early spring afternoons. Later in the day, evening caddis, sulphurs, and drakes appear. In the heat of summer, waters remain cool and trout feed on various terrestrials that stumble into the water from the riverbanks and proceed to struggle, enticing the waiting predator. During August and September on

Consistent success with the Battenkill's larger brown trout requires a specific strategy, as the big ones often disappear when boaters appear. Photo courtesy Jean Laramee.

the Battenkill, tiny mayflies, tricos, and blue-winged olives make their way to the fish's table. In fact, tricos provide the most consistent hatch all year and are best imitated by size 20 parachute imitations.

Fishing techniques should not be limited to classic dry-fly fishing. Recently, anglers are having quite a bit of success for good-sized browns using very meaty streamers as described in Kelly Galoup's book, *Modern Streamers for Trophy Trout*. Articulated streamers and such patterns as the Zoo Cougar, Meat Whistle, and others are hooking 20-inch-plus trout during spring's high water, late October's pre-spawning season, and at first and last light of any day. Large Conehead Soft-hackle Marabou streamers with lots of yellow are also effective.

The Manchester-Arlington area is one of Vermont's major tourist centers. Inns, historical sites, shops, museums, and breathtaking scenery bring visitors from all over the world. Manchester is the home of the Orvis Company and where Orvis fly rods are built. The American Museum of Flyfishing has treasures to share and will stir your imagination of bygone eras of flyfishing. Arlington was the home of Norman Rockwell, and the area's splendor and character of local life inspired his work. The West Arlington Covered Bridge is yet another attraction. The Battenkill itself remains a treasure and a major draw. If we continue to show an interest by visiting this once-great river and contributing to organizations such as Trout Unlimited, the Battenkill may once again be the jewel of flyfishing streams in northern New England.

The Battenkill's season runs from the second Saturday in April through October 31. Since 2000, regulations limit all fishing to catch and release only on the Vermont portion of the Battenkill from the base of Dufresne Pond Dam in Manchester to the New York state line. This regulation is in response to the marked decline in wild brown trout over the last few decades.

A number of tributaries to the Battenkill are well worth fishing. The Green River starts in Sandgate/Beartown at the bases of Bear Mountain and Mother Myrick Mountain and parallels Sandgate Road before crossing VT 313 and emptying into the Battenkill. This is small water and stealth is critical. The Green has good mayfly hatches in mid- to late May, but stays cold and fishes well all summer for small brookies. There are also some good browns that range from 10 to 18 inches, mostly Battenkill browns that run up the tributary to spawn in the fall and overwinter and stay the next year.

Mad Tom Brook flows down the slopes of Mount Tabor and joins the Battenkill's headwaters just north of East Dorset. Expect to find both brookies and browns in its five miles of riffles and runs.

Roaring Branch is readily accessible from a Forest Service Road that follows it and has colorful hand-sized wild brook trout.

The West Branch Battenkill starts on the north slopes of Bear Mountain and flows for nine miles before its confluence with the mainstem near Manchester. This is mostly brook trout water.

Stream Facts: Battenkill River

Season
Mid-April through October with some tributaries closed in October.

Location
Dorset, Manchester, and Arlington, Vermont.

Species
Brown trout with brook trout in the tributaries.

Equipment
Three- to 6-weight rods, floating line, 9-foot leaders, 4x to 7x tippet.

Fly Patterns
Red Quills, Light Cahills, Parachute Trico, CDC Caddis, Pheasant Tail and bead-head Pheasant Tail nymphs, Prince Nymph, Zebra Midge nymph, Mini-muddler; and yellow Soft-hackle Marabou streamer, and black or brown Woolly Buggers (in September and October).

Fly Shops
Orvis Retail Store (4382 Main Street, Manchester, Vermont / 802-366-9134 / www.orvis.com), The Reel Angler (302 Depot St, Manchester Center / 802-0362-0883 / www.thereelangler.com)

Walloomsac River

From the mountains east of Bennington, the Walloomsac River flows for 25 miles within Vermont before it enters New York State, where it joins the Hoosic River. Access is gained from VT 7A and 87A that parallel the river between Bennington and North Bennington (if you park near a local business, first ask permission from the owner). This section of river is quite fertile, supporting a healthy base for regularly stocked as well as abundant holdover brown trout, rainbows, and brookies. The average length is 8 to 14 inches, with many holdovers over 18 inches caught every year.

Caddis and stoneflies are the dominant aquatic insects, with regular mayfly hatches occurring throughout the summer.

The upper reaches of the Walloomsac are largely unproductive as trout waters. Tributaries, including Furnace Brook and Paran Creek, however, are good nursery habitat and hold healthy numbers of wild trout. Downstream, the river broadens and flows over gravel bars, through cutbanks under low-hanging trees, and into many deep pools. Three covered bridges cross the Walloomsac in the seven miles between the villages of Bennington and North Bennington.

The Walloomsac's season runs from the second Saturday in April through October 31, with no special regulations.

METTAWEE RIVER

Four of the six Vermont rivers that are managed as wild trout streams (no stocking) are in the southwestern part of the state. The Battenkill, Mettawee, Poultney, and Castleton Rivers support wild brook trout, brown trout, and in the Mettawee, rainbow trout. The waters of these streams have a high dissolved mineral content and are nurtured by many underground springs. Trout thrive in this habitat, and there is significant reproduction in the upper reaches and tributaries.

The Mettawee flows 17 miles within the borders of Vermont, from the hills in the town of Dorset to the New York state line west of Granville. One of the loveliest of Vermont trout streams, it slowly meanders through farm fields and woods, paralleling VT 30.

Because it is an entirely different watershed, it can be fishable even if the Battenkill is blown out.

The upper river above Dorset is best reached from Lower Hollow Road. It is narrow here, so typical small-stream fishing tactics are in order: wade wet, use a small rod, and fish dry flies such as small Royal Wulffs, Humpies, and Elk Hair Caddis. Look for slightly deeper water such as glides and small pools. Between the villages of East Rupert and North Rupert, there is a Vermont Fish and Wildlife public access (43.293270,-73.140475). Much of the Mettawee flows through dairy farms, and some farmers will grant permission to fish if you ask. As you continue north along Route 30, several bridges cross the Mettawee, creating unmarked access points. The water is crystal clear, the bottom is easy to wade, and there is good stream cover keeping water temperatures cool on even the hottest of summer days.

The West Pawlet cutoff joins VT 153 where the river bears away from VT 30. A natural waterfall creates a local swimming hole. This holds large rainbows if you fish it early, before the swimmers arrive. Much of the area around the falls is posted. Downstream and as the river continues to twist and turn, there are some fine runs and deep holes. The bridge where Route 153 crosses the river offers several parking spots and you can fish the pool under the bridge and also wade quite a distance upriver (43.373139,-73.230198). Try a dry fly and nymph dropper combination. Grasshopper imitations are the ticket later in the year.

Early season caddisflies give way to Hendricksons, stoneflies, and Cahills as temperatures warm in May, June, and into July. The stoneflies are a smaller yellow species. The Cahill and *Potamanthus* hatches of midsummer can bring even the most selective trout to the surface. The old faithful Cream Variant remains a successful pattern.

Early mornings in August bring out tricos and, as fall begins to color the valley, blue-winged olives make an appearance. Each river's unique character comes from the hatches, particularly the trico hatch, which is timed differently on each river. It is possible to follow the trico hatch from the Castleton in the early morning, then onto the Mettawee, and finally the Battenkill and cast to rising fish continuously all morning. When you stop at a bridge to check out the river, don't forget to inspect resident spider webs for the insect du jour.

The Mettawee's season consists of the second Saturday in April through October 31. From the downstream edge of the Rt 153 bridge in Pawlet, upstream (approximately 16 miles) to the downstream edge of the first bridge on Dorset Hollow Road (including its tributary, Flower Brook, upstream to the downstream edge of the Rt 30 bridge in Pawlet): trout between 10 and 14 inches must be released. Also in this section, there is a two-trout limit with only one greater than 14 inches.

Streamside marsh marigolds are early bloomers that flower about the same time as trout get active.

Poultney River

The west-facing slope of Tinmouth Mountain, near the village of Middletown, spawns the headwaters of the Poultney River. The river runs approximately 40 miles west and then north through the towns of Poultney and Fair Haven. It defines the New York/Vermont border for several miles and eventually flows into the Lake Champlain Canal near Whitehall, New York. New York state has river jurisdiction along the border. Residents of Vermont with current fishing licenses are able to fish this stretch of the Poultney. Nonresidents are required to purchase a New York state fishing license.

The Poultney is a wild-trout stream, and its upper flow contains high quality spawning and nursery habitat for brook and brown trout. The brook trout are wild and small – a good one is 12 inches. Browns average 10 to 14 inches, with the occasional one of 18 inches or more caught each year below Carver's Falls.

It is also stocked annually with several thousand eight-inch brook trout. Downstream from the village of Poultney, the cover is sparse and flow diminishes. This section of river, except for the area just below Carver's Falls, three miles east of Fair Haven, holds no significant population of trout.

There is a three-mile section of quality water between the villages of Poultney and East Poultney. It begins near the falls just west of Poultney at the New York state line off the bypass on Route 22A where VT 140 begins. Access is made near the bridge by the falls (43.526359,-73.246790) and at several unmarked pull-offs as you continue upstream along Route 140 (43.526694,-73.199252). Pocket water tumbling from narrow gorges and fertile tributaries makes this section of the Poultney excellent wild-brook-trout water.

The best flies are small beadhead nymphs fished up into pockets, and dries such as Hornbergs and Bivisibles. The deeper pools hold brown trout averaging 10 to 14 inches. Early in the season, fish Woolly Buggers deep and slow through pools. Later, watch for caddis and fish beadheads and emergers.

In general, the season runs from the second Saturday in April through October 31. From Lake Champlain to Carver's Falls in the town of West Haven, angling for brook

A wild Poultney River brook trout holding next to the cover of the bank.

trout, rainbows, and brown trout is open all year. The limit is three-fish in total, with a 12-inch length rule.

Castleton River

Castleton River is a tributary of the Poultney and flows from the marshes in Whipple Hollow in the town of West Rutland for 20 miles until it joins the Poultney west of Fair Haven. The waters of the Castleton are cooled by springs welling up in the riverbed along its length, from the headwaters to the outflow of Lake Bomoseen. The constant cool temperatures and rich mineral content of its waters have made this an important wild trout resource.

Flyfishing on the Castleton River has always been a challenge. Access is limited due to posted land. In the small village of Hydeville on VT 4A, turn south on Blissville Road to a bridge and small pull-off area (43.600202,-73.232688). The land on the south bank is posted, but access can be made on the opposite side. Once you've gained access, the fun really begins. The river is slow and the bottom deep with mud. Alders and brush canopy the river as it twists and turns. Access can also be made east of Castleton Corners, where the train tracks cross the river and Route 4A. Be patient – a hike through the brush and mud can pay off with the sight of a rising 16-inch wild brown trout.

Early in the season, the Castleton River plays host to a strong population of Hendrickson mayflies. As the season continues, other mayflies such as March browns, sulphurs, tricos, and blue-winged olives make their presence known. Midges seem to be around constantly, and there is some caddis activity.

This is a wild-trout fishery managed by the state of Vermont without stocking. It has a strong population of brook trout in the upper stretch of the river between the villages of West Rutland and Hydeville. Brook trout of 12 inches aren't uncommon, and browns reach 17 or 18 inches. Below the outflow of Lake Bomoseen in Hydeville, the water is generally unsuitable for trout, as warmer waters skimmed off the surface of the lake enter the river, making water temperatures uncomfortable for trout. Downstream from the village of Castleton, the river bottom is covered with silt and mud. Upstream, the current runs more swiftly, and there is good spawning habitat.

The second Saturday in April through October 31 comprises the season on Castleton River and general regulations apply.

Upper Otter Creek

Otter Creek is a long river by Vermont standards, flowing 100 miles north from its source in Emerald Lake near the village of East Dorset to Lake Champlain, east of Vergennes. The nature of the river ranges from cold brook trout water to slow, warm water that holds smallmouth bass and some good-sized northern pike.

The upper 10 miles or so of Otter Creek has productive trout waters as it parallels US 7 from the villages of Danby to Rutland. There are numerous access points at the bridges that cross the creek. The area known as Danby Swamp has a history of better-than-average brook trout numbers. Fishing the swamp area is best done by canoe. Access is gained by a short carry from pull-offs along the highway. This swampy area is loaded with insect life. Swimming nymph patterns, large Hornbergs on summer evenings, and caddis imitations are flies of choice.

From the railroad bridge in the village of Danby to the #10 bridge on the Forest Road in Mount Tabor, the state allows a two-fish limit for brook trout, rainbows, and brown trout. Otter Creek is refreshed at this point by the Big Branch. This is a beautiful little tributary holding brook trout in its tumbling upper waters and rainbows, browns, and brookies below the Long Trail crossing. A U.S. Forest Service road (10) follows the Big Branch for much of its course. The best way to fish this is to tie on your go-to attractor dry fly such as a Wulff or Hornberg, and work quickly upstream, hitting all of the likely pockets and current lines. Where Big Branch joins the Otter, brown trout gather in the deeper holes that are shaded by the deep banks and streamside cover. This is a challenging stretch of water with access limited to pull-offs near bridges and thickly covered, deep cutbanks. But, as with many quality waters, the effort can be worthwhile.

Farther north, two tributaries, Mill River in Clarendon and Cold River in the village of North Clarendon, enter Otter Creek. The mouths of these rivers create a small but suitable habitat for trout. The Mill River's headwaters offer excellent wild brookie fishing. Try fishing soft-hackle patterns into the pockets as you work upstream.

Otter Creek receives regular stockings of brook and brown trout. Fish average 8 to 14 inches, with numbers supplemented by the state with the occasional introduction of trophy-sized fish. As the Otter proceeds north of Danby, the flow slows and heats up as it passes through open fields and pastures. There is some cooling provided by tributaries, but trout fishing becomes less productive as you travel north. There are good numbers of warmwater species, such as smallmouth bass and northern pike, throughout the lower section.

Upper Otter Creek's season extends from the second Saturday in April through October 31. From the railroad bridge in the village of Danby to Forest Road #10 bridge in Mount Tabor, the total creel limit of brook, brown, and rainbow trout is two.

OTTAUQUECHEE RIVER

The Ottauquechee, from its mountain headwaters in the town of Sherburne, flows southeast for 38 miles toward the Connecticut River. Its journey begins as a tiny brook trout stream studded with boulders and jump pools that are shaded and cooled by an awning of overhanging tree branches. Fishing access is good along VT 4 at the several unmarked pull-off areas and side road river crossings. Along with brook trout, the upper stretch of the Ottauquechee offers good flyfishing for wild and stocked rainbows.

Both the Ottauquechee and Route 4 were severely impacted in 2011 by Hurricane Irene. The road completely collapsed in several places, while rampaging flood waters altered the river's course, banks, and features. In order to repair the road as quickly as possible, the river in places was channelized with artificial riprap banks. Still other parts of the river have huge fallen trees along its course. Flood waters widened and shallowed the river channel in spots as well. Nature (and man) is slowly repairing the damage, and the trout remain, although good trout habitat has been reduced in the upper river.

Near the village of West Bridgewater, the Ottauquechee bends more to the east, passing the "mill-turned-mall" in the village of Bridgewater, and then through the quaint and lovely village of Woodstock. If there is a more picturesque town in New England, I haven't seen it. The river is stocked in town and trout can sometimes be seen rising as one crosses Woodstock's covered bridge (43.624598,-72.520157).

Access continues to be good along VT 4 as one heads downstream. The river is fed by several small streams and widens and deepens into waters that favor brown trout as well as rainbows. There is less cover along the river through this stretch, so it's best to fish before and after the high sun. As water temperatures rise in the summer, look for active fish near the mouths of tributaries. Elk Hair Caddis and stonefly patterns, along with attractors like Adams and Wulffs, work well.

Below Woodstock, three dams control the power of the river before it charges through Quechee Gorge. The shear rock walls of the gorge drop 165 feet down to the river. Two trails start at the highway bridge on Route 4 spanning the gorge (43.637378,-72.407374). The trail along the west rim goes upstream about a half-mile and provides access to the Ottauquechee where it enters the canyon. From the bridge, the trail on the east rim slopes down, again for about a half-mile, meeting the river at the lower end of the gorge. This is not a tough walk, as the wide and level gravel trail slopes gradually.

Anglers should be cautious when fishing in and around the gorge. The dam, upstream at Deweys Mills, regulates the flow of the river through the gorge, and at the sound of an alarm, the water can rise rapidly. The river passes through

A wild brook trout caught on the upper Ottauquechee River.

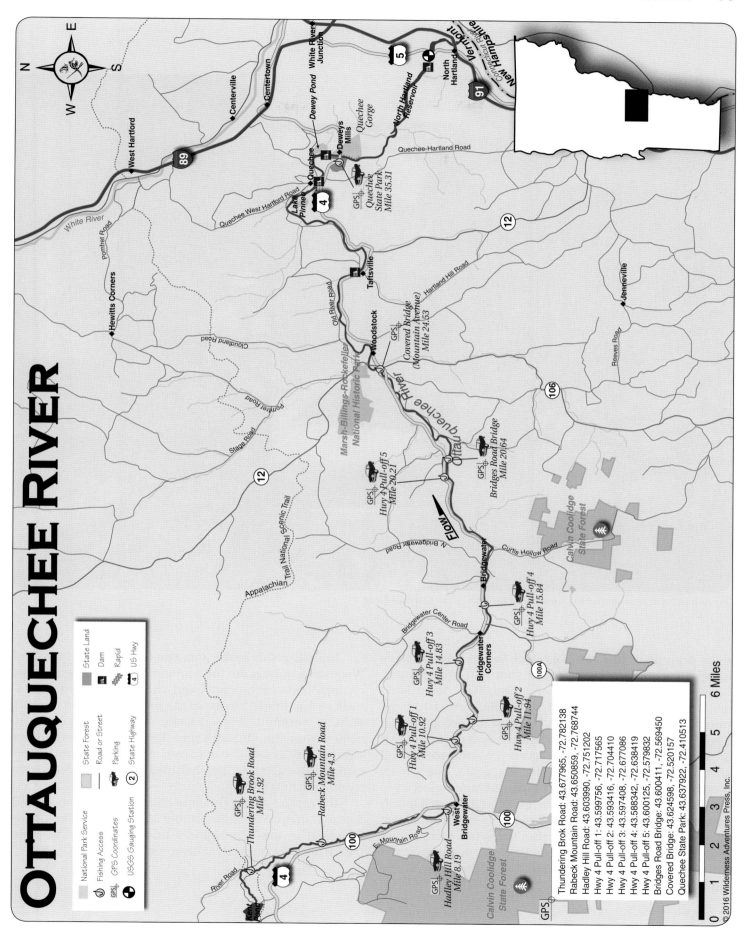

OTTAUQUECHEE RIVER

Legend

- National Park Service
- Fishing Access
- GPS — GPS Coordinates
- ② USGS Gauging Station
- State Land
- State Forest
- Road or Street
- State Highway
- Dam
- Rapid
- ④ US Hwy
- Parking

Thundering Brok Road: 43.677965, -72.782138
Rabeck Mountain Road: 43.650859, -72.768744
Hadley Hill Road: 43.603990, -72.751202
Hwy 4 Pull-off 1: 43.599756, -72.717565
Hwy 4 Pull-off 2: 43.593416, -72.704410
Hwy 4 Pull-off 3: 43.597408, -72.677086
Hwy 4 Pull-off 4: 43.588342, -72.638419
Hwy 4 Pull-off 5: 43.600125, -72.579832
Bridges Road Bridge: 43.600411, -72.569450
Covered Bridge: 43.624598, -72.520157
Quechee State Park: 43.637922, -72.410513

0 1 2 3 4 5 6 Miles

© 2016 Wilderness Adventures Press, Inc.

Thundering Brook Road
Mile 1.92

Rabeck Mountain Road
Mile 4.3

Hadley Hill Road
Mile 8.19

Kent Pond

River Road

E. Mountain Road

West Bridgewater

Calvin Coolidge State Forest

Hwy 4 Pull-off 1
Mile 10.92

Hwy 4 Pull-off 2
Mile 11.94

Bridgewater Corners

Bridgewater Center Road

Hwy 4 Pull-off 3
Mile 14.83

Hwy 4 Pull-off 4
Mile 15.84

Curtis Hollow Road

Bridgewater

N Bridgewater Road

Calvin Coolidge State Forest

FLOW

Hwy 4 Pull-off 5
Mile 20.21

Bridges Road Bridge
Mile 20.64

Ottauquechee River

Appalachian Trail National Scenic Trail

Stage Road

Pomfret Road

Cloudland Road

Marsh-Billings-Rockefeller National Historic Park

Old River Road

Covered Bridge
(Mountain Avenue)
Mile 24.53

Woodstock

Taftsville

Reeves Road

Jenneville

Hartland Hill Road

106

12

Lake Pinneo

Quechee West Hartford Road

Quechee

Quechee-Hartland Road

Deweys Mills

Quechee Gorge

Quechee State Park
Mile 35.31

Dewey Pond

North Hartland Reservoir

White River Junction

North Hartland

Centerville

Centertown

West Hartford

White River

Pomfret Road

Hewitts Corners

Connecticut River

Vermont

New Hampshire

5

89

91

4

100

100A

12

The author retrieving a weighted streamer at the base of the Quechee Gorge.

some deep pools that can hold large brown trout. The key is to utilize enough weight to get your fly to the bottom. Conehead Marabou streamers, weighted articulated rabbit-fur streamers, weighted Woolly Buggers, and large stonefly nymphs are required to interest the predators that might lurk here. To be honest, while it is really fun to fish the deep, clear, runs in the lower gorge, I have never hooked anything other than yellow perch. Then again, I have been skunked in some of the best trout streams in America!

The Ottauquechee below the gorge to the river's fourth dam in the village of North Hartland is not trout water. There are, however, some opportunities to fish for rainbows coming out of the Connecticut River in the spring and autumn below the North Hartland dam, but this is very unpredictable.

Tourists gather in the area around Quechee Gorge and Woodstock throughout the summer season. There are inns, campgrounds, restaurants, and shops all along Route 4. Visitors find this to be one of the most scenic and popular parts of Vermont. A good share of this region's beauty comes from the Ottauquechee River as it passes under covered bridges and carves out farm valleys and deep canyons along its way. The flyfishing is good and deserves a try on your next visit.

The season on the Ottauquechee runs from the second Saturday in April through October 31. From the river mouth upstream to the first highway bridge crossing the river, please refer to Connecticut River regulations.

BLACK RIVER

More than any other river in southeastern Vermont, the Black River is a destination fishery for out-of-state anglers, and it is not a mystery why. This water is really fun to flyfish.

I vividly remember spotting a rise in a 10-foot run that wasn't more than two feet deep, at the tail end of a long and shallow riffle. An upstream cast from my knees landed the fly at the head of the run. As the size 16 Adams Klinkhammer floated with the current, I watched a large butter-belly brown trout rise off the bottom, turn 180 degrees, and follow the fly downstream for several feet before slurping it down. I wish I had had my camera to photograph this perfect 18-inch specimen of *salmo trutta*.

There are several distinct sections of the Black. The upper reaches and tributaries as they come out of Coolidge State Forest above the village of Plymouth are beautiful brook trout waters. Route 100 follows the river south through the village of Plymouth Union. Pull-offs along the main highway and several hiking trails in the state forest provide access to small feeder streams.

As the Black continues on its 40-mile journey to the Connecticut River, several dams, including those at Amherst Lake, Echo Lake and Lake Rescue, stifle and warm its flow. Amherst and Echo offer fishing for lake trout and fairly-good-sized rainbows. These small lakes are sheltered and stay calm, making them excellent choices for small boats, kayaks, or canoes. Each has a public boat access – Echo Lake's is right off VT 100. Lake Rescue is primarily a bass fishery, and in the spring you can catch these fish right from the dam or the shore by the road.

Near the village of Ludlow, the Black swings east and passes below Okemo Mountain, parallel to VT 131. Downstream, some of the best fishing is found in the section from the village of Cavendish to Amsden, eight miles of river that the state regularly stocks with brown trout, rainbows, and brookies. The fish are widely dispersed and there are obvious pull-off areas and other entry points to the river. Due to the liberal fishing regulations, many of the stockers are caught quickly by the wormers and hardware chuckers.

The so-called trophy section of the river attracts flyfishers from all over New England to the four miles of water in the town of Weathersfield (between Howard Hill Bridge and the Downers Village covered bridge – 43.398206,-72.522361). The creel limit is two fish of either species. What's more – the state stocks trophy fish here that range from 16 to 20 inches. While there are limited holdovers, my experience clearly illustrates that some trout

A happy Mark Allen poses for a photograph before releasing a nice rainbow back into the upper part of the trophy section.

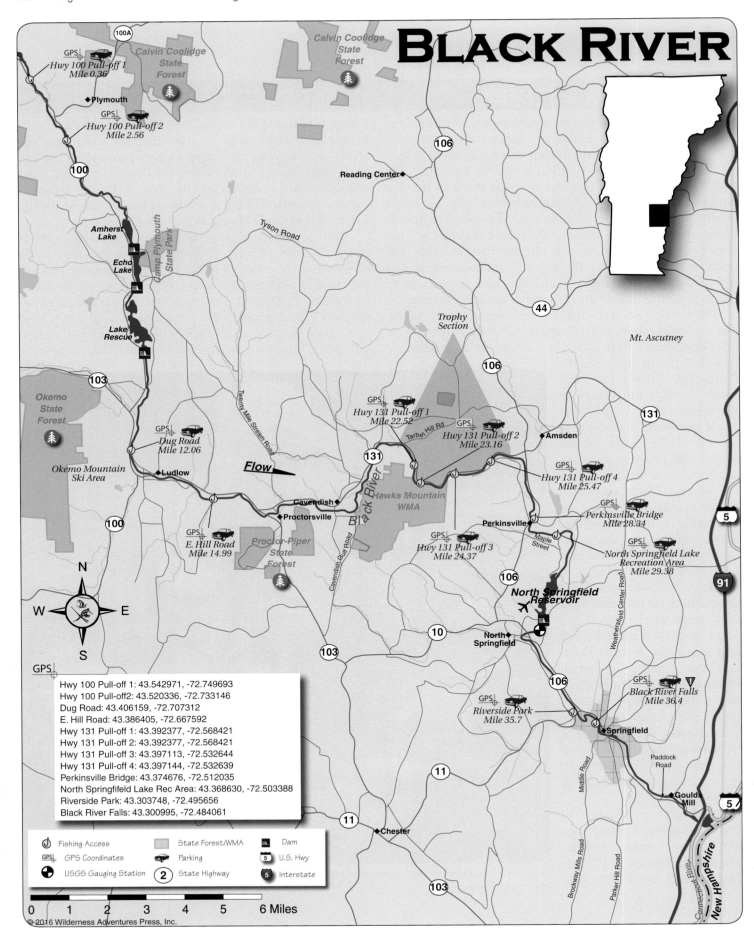

BLACK RIVER

Hwy 100 Pull-off 1
Mile 0.36

Hwy 100 Pull-off 2
Mile 2.56

Calvin Coolidge
State
Forest

Calvin Coolidge
State
Forest

Plymouth

Reading Center

Amherst
Lake

Echo
Lake

Tyson Road

Lake
Rescue

Trophy
Section

Mt. Ascutney

Okemo
State
Forest

Dug Road
Mile 12.06

Hwy 131 Pull-off 1
Mile 22.52

Tarbel Hill Rd

Hwy 131 Pull-off 2
Mile 23.16

Amsden

Okemo Mountain
Ski Area

Ludlow

Flow

Hwy 131 Pull-off 4
Mile 25.47

Cavendish

Proctorsville

Hawks Mountain
WMA

Perkinsville Bridge
Mile 28.34

E. Hill Road
Mile 14.99

Proctor-Piper
State
Forest

Perkinsville

North Springfield Lake
Recreation Area
Mile 29.38

Hwy 131 Pull-off 3
Mile 24.37

Maple
Street

North Springfield
Reservoir

North
Springfield

Black River Falls
Mile 36.4

Riverside Park
Mile 35.7

Springfield

Paddock
Road

N
W E
S

GPS
Hwy 100 Pull-off 1: 43.542971, -72.749693
Hwy 100 Pull-off2: 43.520336, -72.733146
Dug Road: 43.406159, -72.707312
E. Hill Road: 43.386405, -72.667592
Hwy 131 Pull-off 1: 43.392377, -72.568421
Hwy 131 Pull-off 2: 43.392377, -72.568421
Hwy 131 Pull-off 3: 43.397113, -72.532644
Hwy 131 Pull-off 4: 43.397144, -72.532639
Perkinsville Bridge: 43.374676, -72.512035
North Springfifeld Lake Rec Area: 43.368630, -72.503388
Riverside Park: 43.303748, -72.495656
Black River Falls: 43.300995, -72.484061

Chester

Goulds
Mill

New Hampshire

Fishing Access
GPS Coordinates
USGS Gauging Station
State Forest/WMA
Parking
State Highway
Dam
U.S. Hwy
Interstate

0 1 2 3 4 5 6 Miles

© 2016 Wilderness Adventures Press, Inc.

do survive for some time. Flyfishers dominate this stretch and most practice catch and release.

Good access points abound along VT 131 through the trophy section. For the first few miles, the river gradient is gradual with long riffles, shallow runs, and some deeper pools. Then the drop increases and the Black contains deeper runs and pocket water around large boulders.

The Black River still has an unpredictable flow caused by the demands of the upriver power dams but overall, the trout habitat is stable. As with all rivers in this part of Vermont, anglers will notice for quite some time the damage wreaked by Hurricane Irene. Route 131 required massive repairs, and the river channel had to be redirected back to its original course in places. Large gravel bars remain in spots.

Trout that are not caught immediately become cautionary and adapt quickly to existing food sources. Caddis and stonefly imitations work well throughout the season. In the faster water section, choose patterns that will float well despite the currents. Fluctuating water levels limit regular hatches of mayflies. Attractor patterns, such as small Royal Wulffs and Adams, do work well, however. Under low-water conditions or for experienced fish, downsize your patterns. Try size 20 midge pupa patterns or small soft hackles drifted in the film. In warmer months, the downstream banks of the small tributaries hold active trout.

The Black River's season extends from the second Saturday in April through October 31. From the river mouth upstream to the Interstate 91 bridge, please refer to Connecticut River regulations. From the Interstate 91 bridge upstream to Gould's Mill Site in the town of Springfield, there is an artificials-only, catch-and-release winter season from October 31 to the Friday before the second Saturday in April.

The author met Wendy Lichtensteiger as she was plying the lower part of the Black River's trophy section. See her beautiful wood carvings at www.wendylichtensteiger.com.

downstream pools. Summertime water temperatures regularly reach in excess of 80 degrees in the main river. That is one of the reasons efforts to try to restore Atlantic salmon in this river (and others) has been stopped. The water temperatures are just too warm.

A flood-control project dam at Ball Mountain and one forming Townsend Lake have limited flooding and created two short tailwater fisheries. The river stretch just below both dams stays cooler and more aerated, providing some good flyfishing for brown trout throughout the season.

The mainstem of the river parallels VT 100 south from the village of Weston. Route 100 joins VT 30 in the village of Ransomville and escorts the West all the way to the river's mouth in Brattleboro. It is the upper reaches of the West River's tributaries and small feeder brooks that offer the best flyfishing opportunities. You'll find some lovely wild brook trout in the headwaters of some of these brooks and in the lower sections, some nice, small browns. It's a way to enjoy some solitude and a few fish. You can reach these somewhat more remote areas from either Route 100 or Route 30 on the several maintained and unimproved back roads that follow the brooks back up into the Green Mountains. There are some excellent hiking trails in Jamaica State Park and Townshend State Park that give access to some of these smaller streams as well as to the two tailwater sections of the West.

Anglers fish the Townshend Dam tailwater daily in the spring and fall and never really know what fish species they might catch. In the spring it could be a big brown, a five-pound smallmouth, or the day I was there, a walleye over two feet long. Holdover brown trout also migrate to the dam in the autumn as they become active pre-spawn. There aren't that many of them but there is always a chance to catch one. A local park ranger told me that a few big browns also migrate to the Rock River, a tributary that enters the West a few miles upstream from Brattleboro. A few have been caught in the large pool at the confluence of the two rivers (42.948045,-72.641079).

A short distance downstream of the dam at Townsend, the West River broadens and becomes a slower moving, warmwater river. This section is wide open, with gravelly runs and long, slow glides. There is good fishing for smallmouth bass in this lower stretch of river. Access is easy along the highway, making it a popular area for canoeists and tubers.

Insect hatches on the main river are sporadic, probably because of the severe scouring the riverbed experiences during spates and runoff, though there are caddisflies and stoneflies throughout the river system. In the smaller brooks, fish small attractor patterns such as Adams, Wulffs, and Humpies. Also try small, weighted Hare's Ears fished up into the pockets. Fish the popular tailwater areas early and late in the day. Brown trout of up to 15 inches might be fooled by a small midge pattern drifted in the right feeding lane. Otherwise, try beadhead nymphs, caddis emergers, and Woolly Buggers.

Regulations allow fishing from the second Saturday in April through October 31. From the VT 5 bridge at Brattleboro to the river mouth, refer to Connecticut River regulations. From the US 5 bridge upstream to Townshend Dam, near Townshend, there is a winter, artificials-only, catch-and-release season from the November 1 to the Friday before the second Saturday in April.

The Townshend Dam tailwater by Townshend State Park.

STILLWATERS OF SOUTHERN VERMONT

There are two beautiful brook trout ponds east of Arlington, known as Stratton Pond (43.104441, -72.967927) and Bourn Pond (43.105318, -73.003198). Drive up Kelly Stand Road for a little over six miles to Forest Road 70. This road that leads to the foot trails is unpaved and can be impassible during wet seasons and intersects the Appalachian and Long Trails near a memorial to Daniel Webster. There is a parking area for about four to five cars, and the trail to the ponds is well marked. Kelly Stand Road was closed after being damaged by Hurricane Irene, but hopefully will be reopened by the time you read this book, although there is a longer alternate route in. Both of these remote mountain ponds are shallow with densely vegetated banks, and are best fished from shore. Good flies include dragonfly and damselfly imitations.

Gale Meadows Pond is off of VT 30 near the village of Bondville, east of Manchester. It is regularly stocked with rainbow trout. There is good public access and a boat ramp.

Amherst Lake and Echo Lake are right along VT 100 north of the village of Ludlow. Amherst holds rainbow and lake trout. Echo is stocked with rainbows. As the water warms, they are bass fisheries as well. Both have State Fish and Wildlife public access areas and boat launches. They're busy lakes during the summer months, so you might want to schedule yourself for the early or late season. Good midge hatches during the fall can produce large rainbows. Camp Plymouth State Park is close by and offers convenient camping facilities. For more information, see the Black River write-up earlier in this section.

Lake Ninevah is reached from Dublin Road, which runs west from the south end of Echo Lake. It is stocked with rainbow trout and has a public boat ramp.

Stradding the border between Vermont and New York lies Harriman Reservoir, a large coldwater impoundment that hosts rainbow trout, large brown trout, and lake trout. Its north shore is near the village of Wilmington, along VT 9, convenient to two public boat launches. There is a third public access area at the south end of the reservoir, near the village of Whitingham, on VT 100.

Echo Lake on a calm day with rainbows rising. Camp Plymouth State Park can be seen on the opposite shore.

SOUTHERN VERMONT PLANNING CONSIDERATIONS

Hub Cities

- Manchester (www.manchestervermont.net)
- Bennington (www.bennington.com)
- Brattleboro (brattleborochamber.org/visit-us)
- Wilmington (http://wilmingtonvermont.us/about/visit-wilmington/)

Easy Access Options

- The Black River trophy stretch has numerous and obvious pull-offs that require only a few steps to reach the water. While some access points require working your way down a steep bank, others are more benign, needing only a few steps down to reach water level. The river can be fished from the bank with adequate backcast space. The river by the pull-outs is obviously fished heavily, but the trout move around and, since most anglers are practicing catch and release, there are always fish to be caught.
- Covered bridges are numerous in Vermont and almost all provide good river access. I indicate a number of options in this book, but there are many other covered bridges as well. I find fishing under covered bridges a quintessential New England experience and the reality is that much stocking also takes place right there so the fishing can be good. Some of the banks are a little steep to reach the water, but there is almost always a well-worn path, and you can choose an access point that you feel comfortable with. Just remember that your capabilities must include going back up the bank from the water, not just descending.

This covered bridge marks the end of the Black River trophy section.

Suggested Beginner Options

- The Black River is stocked heavily with lots of obvious access points. Most spots have more than adequate room for backcasting. Other flyfishers are usually trying their luck here and one can learn from observation and asking questions, which most anglers are happy to answer. The sooner you fish the area after the stocking trucks depart, the easier the fish will be to fool.

- The headwaters of numerous rivers and streams start in the beautiful Green Mountain National Forest of Vermont. Since it is public land, there is 100 percent public access. Choose several streams that are paralleled by Forest Service roads and you won't have to hike far. Small native brook trout in these streams are not hard to fool. Walk up the stream along the bank with a good pair of hiking boots, fish an easy-to-see dry fly such as a small Royal Wulff or a large foam ant, and take short casts to the deeper pockets or plunge pools. The strike will be obvious and most fish will hook themselves. There is no more fun way to learn the basics of the sport.

- In Southwest Vermont, the Walloomsac River flows right through Bennington with easy access points. Try fishing at the Burt Henry Covered Bridge, off of the River Road and VT 67A. The river is stocked heavily here. A convenient parking lot, ready access to the river, easy wading, and plenty of backcast room all support a beginners efforts. Just upstream, try below the dam on Murphy Road. Park in the lot and follow the obvious trail downstream for more places to fish.

Vacation Options

Weekend Getaway

- If your significant other is not a flyfisher and has either never accompanied you on a weekend fishing trip, or did but was not satisfied with the experience, this is the weekend that you insist that he or she comes along. Book a room at one of the inns in Woodstock, make reservations for each evening at one of the fine restaurants, spend part of each day with each other relaxing or walking the quaint streets, and spend the rest of the time fishing the Ottauquechee River, while your partner bikes, shops or visits whatever tourist attraction suits their fancy.

- On second thought, even if your partner is also an avid flyfisher, enjoy a weekend in Woodstock, and adjust the schedule to include a little more fishing.

- Take a weekend to fish the Black River in late May to early July. The trophy section has enough water types – from fast, boulder-filled pocketwater to languid pools – so you will never be bored. Or if you want to diversify the experience, take one day on the Black and one day fishing the White River, a short drive to the north.

- Spend a weekend at the Quill Gordon Bed and Breakfast (www.quillgordon.com) right on the banks of the Battenkill. The owner, Marty Oakland, is an experienced guide and can tell you when to visit and what strategies and tactics maximize your chances for fishing success.

One-week Vacation

- Enjoy a leisurely vacation through southern Vermont. Take your bikes, books, and art supplies for exercise, reading, and painting. Visit the quaint towns of Woodstock, Quechee, Grafton, and others. Walk through as many covered bridges as you can find. And of course as you sightsee, do some flyfishing on the Black, Ottauquechee, Williams, and Saxton Rivers. This should not be a dawn-to-dusk fishing-only expedition. Flyfishing should be part of the entire rural Vermont experience.

Central Vermont

The rivers of central Vermont flow west from the Green Mountains into Otter Creek and east into the Connecticut River. Visitors seeking the home of poet Robert Frost or the spectacular autumn colors on display through the mountains of central Vermont can also take advantage of some of Vermont's finest trout streams. Otter Creek finishes its 100-mile journey north to Lake Champlain by picking up four major tributaries: Furnace Brook, the Neshobe River, the Middlebury River, and the New Haven River. From the eastern slope of the Green Mountains, the Wells and Waits Rivers, the Ompompanoosuc River, and White River flow to meet their fate in the mighty Connecticut River.

The Green Mountains offer numerous tiny creeks and headwaters to explore, complete with beaver ponds and other water features that hold native brookies bigger than you might expect.

Anglers plying larger rivers in central Vermont often must share the waterways with kayakers during the middle of the day.

LOWER OTTER CREEK

Lower Otter Creek has gained a well-deserved reputation as one of the best northern pike fisheries in New England. Many other species can be caught as well, but if you want to tangle with an aggressive predator that can reach over 40 inches, then lower Otter Creek is for you.

Lower Otter Creek crawls for nearly 70 miles from the city of Rutland to the river mouth at Lake Champlain near Vergennes. All the water from Rutland to Lake Champlain holds pike from 24 to 36 inches with larger specimens possible. The best way to fish this water is by a small boat that can be schlepped up and down muddy banks and portaged around the frequent falls, log jams, and dams. One recommended stretch is from Proctor Falls below Rutland to Middlebury Falls, a 30-mile section of big-pike water that can be accessed by a number of covered bridges and other small crossing roads.

Other sections that fish well for pike are the 15 miles between Middebury and Vergennes Falls, and then the seven miles from there to Lake Champlain (this section is governed by lake fishing regulations). Otter Creek is open to fishing year round from Center Falls in Rutland all the way to the lake.

To improve your pike fishing success, target the deeper runs and pools along with weeds and structure. While a floating line is adequate most of the time, a sink-tip line can help sink the fly in the deeper spots. An 8-weight rod with heavy mono or a bite tippet is required for these toothy denizens. Pick out some large pike flies from your favorite online or local fly shop. Red/white or yellow/brown combinations are all you will probably need. Cover water quickly, looking for active pike, and keep moving. If you do get a follow or miss a strike, then take a little more time and vary fly color or speed of retrieve to encourage another strike.

Trout and bass fishing is also possible on the lower Otter, but there is little cooling cover through the farmland and low swampy areas of the Otter Creek Valley. The only relief the river gets is the aeration from the five dams that interrupt the flow and the refreshing waters of its four coldwater tributaries.

The most productive trout water available in the lower section of Otter Creek, from the city of Rutland to its mouth at Lake Champlain, is between the two dams near the mouth of the New Haven. This short section of river holds rainbow and brown trout in the more aerated waters below Beldens Dam. At Beldens Dam, fish both sides of the river by traversing a narrow pedestrian bridge over the falls. From the confluence of the New Haven, the water warms and becomes an excellent smallmouth bass fishery. You can reach this section of Otter Creek by turning west off US 7 on the Beldens Dam Road or from River Bend Campground. There is an area to launch a canoe by the Clickety Clack Bridge near the Huntington Falls Dam, downstream of both Beldens Dam and the campground. It's an easy paddle upstream, and the smallmouth fishing can be exciting. Always bring a pike outfit with you, however.

Otter Creek is a very fertile piece of water. Caddisflies in all sizes and colors hatch near Beldens Dam and the

Brian Cadoret's Go-Pro selfie with a 45-inch pike caught on lower Otter Creek. He was casting an 8-weight from Rock River Rods, and a locally tied fly named the Lug Slayer. Photo courtesy Vermont Stream and Brook Guide Service.

LOWER OTTER CREEK

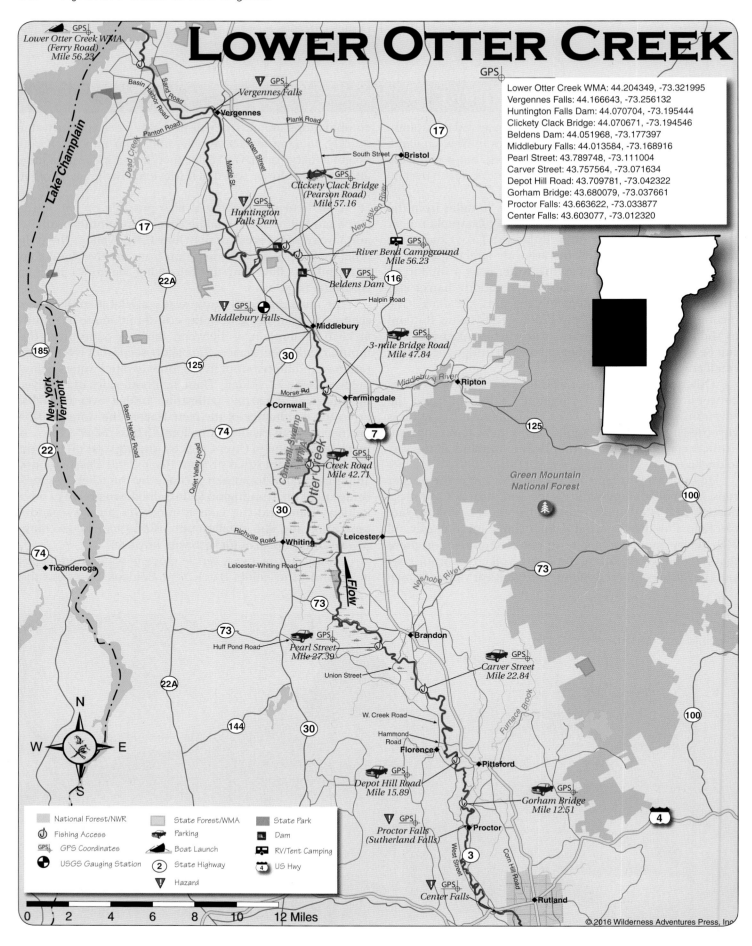

Lower Otter Creek WMA (Ferry Road) Mile 56.23

Vergennes Falls

Clickety Clack Bridge (Pearson Road) Mile 57.16

Huntington Falls Dam

River Bend Campground Mile 56.23

Beldens Dam

Middlebury Falls

3-mile Bridge Road Mile 47.84

Creek Road Mile 42.71

Pearl Street Mile 27.39

Carver Street Mile 22.84

Depot Hill Road Mile 15.89

Gorham Bridge Mile 12.51

Proctor Falls (Sutherland Falls)

Center Falls

Lower Otter Creek WMA: 44.204349, -73.321995
Vergennes Falls: 44.166643, -73.256132
Huntington Falls Dam: 44.070704, -73.195444
Clickety Clack Bridge: 44.070671, -73.194546
Beldens Dam: 44.051968, -73.177397
Middlebury Falls: 44.013584, -73.168916
Pearl Street: 43.789748, -73.111004
Carver Street: 43.757564, -73.071634
Depot Hill Road: 43.709781, -73.042322
Gorham Bridge: 43.680079, -73.037661
Proctor Falls: 43.663622, -73.033877
Center Falls: 43.603077, -73.012320

Lake Champlain

New York / Vermont

Green Mountain National Forest

Flow

Legend:
National Forest/NWR
Fishing Access
GPS Coordinates
USGS Gauging Station
State Forest/WMA
Parking
Boat Launch
State Highway
Hazard
State Park
Dam
RV/Tent Camping
US Hwy

Places: Bristol, Vergennes, Middlebury, Cornwall, Farmingdale, Ripton, Whiting, Leicester, Brandon, Florence, Pittsford, Proctor, Rutland, Ticonderoga

0 2 4 6 8 10 12 Miles

© 2016 Wilderness Adventures Press, Inc.

campground through May and June. As the summer warms up, you'll find sulphurs and Cahills. August and September bring *Isonychia* and blue-winged olives. Fishing a Woolly Bugger or a streamer could result in the tackle-shattering strike of a three-pound smallmouth.

From here, Otter Creek makes slow, winding progress over another two dams through the city of Vergennes and on to Lake Champlain. There are stories of some landlocked salmon and steelhead running from the lake in the spring and fall as far as the dam in Vergennes. All in all, the run of salmonids from the lake seems insignificant.

The physical characteristics of the four lower Otter Creek tributaries (Furnace Brook, Neshobe River, Middlebury River, and New Haven River) are quite similar. All flow west out of the Green Mountains. Their headwaters are steep and rocky and hold good populations of wild and stocked brook trout. As these rivers descend, the flows slow down and become a series of riffles and deep corner pools holding rainbow and brown trout. Brookies in these streams are generally small, averaging 7 or 8 inches. Rainbows and browns average 8 to 12 inches. Occasionally, a fish in excess of 16 inches is caught.

The season for these tributaries is the second Saturday in April through October 31, with no special regulations.

Furnace Brook

If you prefer to fish away from crowds of other anglers amidst beautiful scenery, then this is yet another good central Vermont option that will meet that objective. High above the village of Pittsford, Furnace Brook tumbles down through boulders and gorges, abruptly flattening out through farmland and floodplain to where it enters Otter Creek. It is managed by the Department of Fish and Wildlife as a wild-trout fishery without supplemental stocking and is home to brook trout, rainbows, and browns. The natural spawning areas and nursery waters have been enhanced by habitat improvement programs through modest grants and the volunteer labors of the Green Mountain Fly Tyers Club, which is located in Rutland.

There is a federal fish hatchery on Furnace Brook in the small crossroads town of Holden. Brown trout escaping from this hatchery in the 1950s helped establish a population in the lower section of the river. Now, the hatchery raises landlocked salmon for Lake Champlain.

Furnace Brook crosses US 7 on the south side of the village of Pittsford, about eight miles north of Rutland. Furnace Brook Road follows the river upstream crossing the river in Grangerville. Between this crossing and the hatchery, a hike into the gorge from one of the unmarked roadside pull-offs offers the flyfisher challenging pocket-water fishing for rainbow and brook trout. The water stays cool and aerated throughout the summer. Beadhead nymphs and stonefly patterns fished up into the pools work well. Dries, such as small caddis, or attractor patterns such as Humpies and Wulffs, will often catch a wild, 12-inch rainbow off guard.

Downstream from Pittsford, Elm Street follows Furnace Brook and crosses it with a lovely covered bridge (43.690360,-73.028576) near the confluence with Otter Creek. This stretch of river is dominated by brown trout and offers good spring and early summer hatches. Here also is the mouth of Sugar Hollow Brook, a small tributary of Furnace Brook. At one time, the alder-covered waters of Sugar Hollow held a wealth of the most beautiful wild brook trout in the state. Sadly, development along this little stream over the past four decades has taken its toll and used up a great deal of the resources available to the fish. Many people miss this brook.

In the fall, larger brown trout move into Furnace Brook from Otter Creek, and anglers fishing large streamers with some yellow accents can tie into a surprisingly large brownie.

Neshobe River

The Neshobe rises out of the foothills of the Green Mountains in the town of Goshen. It follows VT 73, eventually crossing US 7 in the village of Brandon and finally enters Otter Creek. It is a healthy stream, supporting three varieties of trout. Rainbow and brook trout populate the stretch of river above Brandon; the waters below hold more brown trout. Much of the land near the upper river is private and posted against trespassing, making access difficult. There are a few unmarked pull-offs along Route 73 near the golf course that afford modest access.

The swift-moving, cold waters of the upper Neshobe are perfect breeding areas for caddisflies and stoneflies. Fish move in and out of Otter Creek into the lower Neshobe to feed. Here, you might try swimming nymphs and streamers fished in the slower waters and deeper pools. In the fall, larger browns will move into the Neshobe looking for spawning areas.

Middlebury River

Just a stone's throw from the Long Trail where it passes Middlebury Gap, you'll find Pleiad Lake, the source of the South Branch of the Middlebury River. The title of this lake is somewhat misleading. Pleiad is not much more than five acres, but it does hold brook trout. The South Branch runs parallel to VT 125 toward the village of Ripton, where it joins the Middle Branch and forms the Middlebury River. A third stream, the North Branch, joins the river two miles farther down. This is a good area if your family is fishing with you.

There is ample access along VT 125 and several nice picnic areas where you can take a break for lunch.

The Middlebury River is a lovely mountain stream that sings through gorges, running cold and clear toward Otter Creek in the valley below. Its cold waters make it a real treasure in midsummer when other rivers warm to uncomfortable temperatures. Wild brook trout are found throughout the upper stretches and tributaries. Although the trout are generally small, if you like fishing little, pristine waters, these fish are a worthy reward.

The river enters a deep gorge that extends two miles downstream from the village of Ripton. Sheer rock walls, boulders, and bottomless pools make this area safe water for rainbow and brook trout from 10 to 16 inches. Although a safe haven for trout, the gorge is treacherous wading for anglers. It is about 150 feet deep, making access very difficult. A bridge just east of the village of East Middlebury is the easiest and safest point to enter the gorge (43.969896,-73.085643). There is not much room to cast. Roll casting dries or quick-sinking nymphs cast up into the pocket water is the best approach. Use attractor patterns such as Wulffs and Hare's Ear nymphs. With all of east-central Vermont's waters, sometimes if the trout are sluggish or the water a little high, try size 8 small steamers such as a Mickey Finn, Baby Brook Trout, Wood Special, or small olive or black Woolly Buggers.

West of East Middlebury, particularly after the Middlebury River crosses US 7, the flow slows and holds more brown trout. Access is possible from several unmarked pull-offs along Three Mile Bridge Road that runs east from Route 7. Although unmarked, these pull-offs are obvious and easily located.

New Haven River

The New Haven River is a lovely trout stream that flows off the western slope of the Green Mountains of central Vermont. It offers some of the best scenery in the area and other anglers are scarce. From its headwaters in South Lincoln, the New Haven travels almost 30 miles to where it joins Otter Creek just north of the village of Middlebury. The upper river and its main tributary, Baldwin Creek, are classic brook trout waters. Downstream from Bartlett's Falls in Bristol, you'll find browns, rainbows, and brookies, particularly browns.

Lincoln Gap Road follows the New Haven as it twists and turns around boulders, creating swift runs and deep pools. There are some unmarked parking areas, but be prepared to hike and climb over some boulders to get to the river. The trout aren't very selective in the upper section. Hornbergs, Adams, and other attractor dries, and small nymphs will be all you'll need. The river becomes larger as it approaches Bartlett's Falls. This is a popular summer swimming and sunning area, and there are a number of roadside pull-offs (44.128336,-73.049090).

Baldwin Creek joins the New Haven River where the Lincoln Gap Road meets Routes 17 and 116. There is good access to the river along the highway and as you leave the village of Bristol on Lower Notch and Carlstrom Roads. The river becomes somewhat more remote through this section and receives less angling pressure. Recent flooding has made some changes to the stream through this section. However, it is still a productive area to fish. In fact, all of the rivers and streams in central Vermont have been severely impacted by several 100-year flooding events punctuated by Hurricane Irene. Visitors will see the eroded banks, downed trees, widened stream channels, and reconstructed roads and bridges. Man and nature are slowly repairing the damage year by year.

River Road joins VT 116 near a bridge and follows the New Haven to US 7. The mouth of the New Haven where it joins Otter Creek is less than a mile downstream and is accessible near the Dog Team Tavern or the River Bend Campground. There is a small parking fee at the campground.

Anglers will find more brown trout like this 22-inch beast in the Middlebury River. Photo courtesy of Vermont Stream and Brook Guide Service.

WHITE RIVER

In the heart of the Green Mountains above Granville Gulf, the White River has its humble beginnings. Rising as a small brook trout stream, it gathers water from dozens of brooks and other larger tributaries to become one of the finest trout rivers in northern New England.

The White River and its relatively large tributaries drain a huge area of central Vermont. The headwaters are fast-flowing and well-shaded brook trout waters. Downstream, the river opens up into gravelly runs and then deepens and carves out deep corner pools and runs. The river flows over large gravel and broken ledge rock as it turns east. From the village of Bethel, downstream, the gradient decreases and the water temperatures begin to rise. Ledges are now more pronounced and the bottom more silty.

Historically, the White River was a major spawning area for Atlantic salmon. The series of dams built on the Connecticut River during the latter part of the 19th century terminated the salmon migration by blocking access to upstream spawning water. The White River, however, was spared and has remained healthy and vital, albeit without Atlantics. The White is one of the most beautiful rivers in the Northeast. It shares the character and the moods of a wild and free Atlantic salmon river.

Uninhibited by dams, the White River flows 57 miles southeast from the town of Granville through the villages of Hancock, Rochester, and Bethel to the villages of Royalton, Sharon, and Hartford, where it finally joins the Connecticut River near White River Junction.

This is a large river system, so let me cover it section by section starting from its origins. The White River is a freestone stream, and its headwaters and cold tributaries provide steady flows of clean, cold water to the mainstem, offering excellent spawning and nursery habitat. Wild brook trout can be found in the upper stretches of the river where the water passes under the cover of green forests, tumbling over rocks into small pools and riffles. The Hancock and West Branches join the White near the village of Rochester. Here, wild and stocked rainbows – which make up the bulk of the river's trout population – and some brown trout share

A classic White River ledge pool.

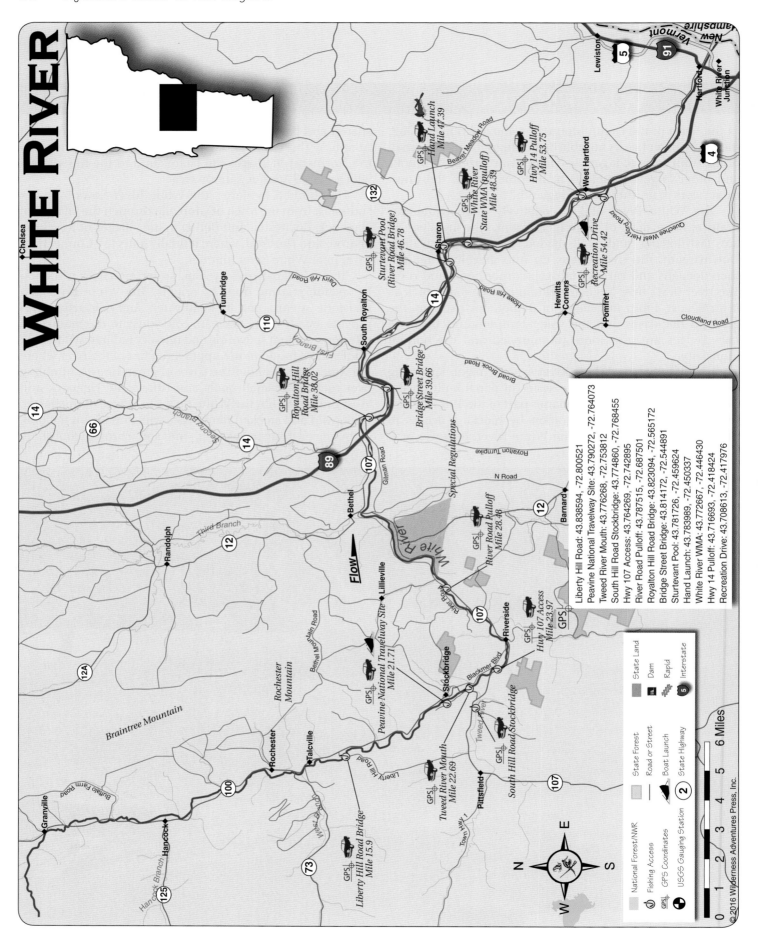

WHITE RIVER

Chelsea

FLOW

White River

Hand Launch
Mile 47.39

Huey 14 Pulloff
Mile 53.75

White River
State WMA (pulloff)
Mile 48.39

Recreation Drive
Mile 54.42

Sturtevant Pool
(River Road Bridge)
Mile 46.78

Royalton Hill
Road Bridge
Mile 38.02

Bridge Street Bridge
Mile 39.66

Special Regulations

River Road Pulloff
Mile 28.48

Hwy 107 Access
Mile 23.97

Peavine National Travelway Site
Mile 21.71

Tweed River Mouth
Mile 22.69

South Hill Road/Stockbridge

Liberty Hill Road Bridge
Mile 15.9

Lewiston

Hartford

White River
Junction

West Hartford

Sharon

South Royalton

Tunbridge

Bethel

Lillieville

Stockbridge

Riverside

Rochester

Talcville

Pittsfield

Hancock

Granville

Randolph

Hewitts
Corners

Pomfret

Barnard

Beaver Meadow Road

Howe Hill Road

Broad Brook Road

Royalton Turnpike

N Road

Dairy Hill Road

Gilman Road

River Road

Blackmer Blvd

Bethel Mountain Road

Liberty Hill Road

Buffalo Farm Road

Quechee West Hartford Road

Cloudland Road

Rochester Mountain

Braintree Mountain

First Branch

Second Branch

Third Branch

Hancock Branch

Town Hwy 1

Liberty Hill Road: 43.838594, -72.800521
Peavine National Travelway Site: 43.790272, -72.764073
Tweed River Mouth: 43.776268, -72.753812
South Hill Road Stockbridge: 43.774860, -72.768455
Hwy 107 Access: 43.764269, -72.742895
River Road Pulloff: 43.787515, -72.687501
Royalton Hill Road Bridge: 43.823094, -72.565172
Bridge Street Bridge: 43.814172, -72.544891
Sturtevant Pool: 43.781726, -72.459624
Hand Launch: 43.783989, -72.450337
White River WMA: 43.772667, -72.446430
Hwy 14 Pulloff: 43.716693, -72.418424
Recreation Drive: 43.708613, -72.417976

Legend

National Forest/NWR

State Land

State Forest

Dam

Rapid

Road or Street

Fishing Access

Boat Launch

GPS Coordinates

State Highway

USGS Gauging Station

Interstate

0 1 2 3 4 5 6 Miles

©2016 Wilderness Adventures Press, Inc.

the water. Some surprisingly large trout are caught in this section at times, mostly likely lower river fish that have moved upstream to find cooler water, food, or spawning territory. The White River in this area is similar to a large stream with the beginning of some deeper runs and pools. Prolific small caddis emerge in May – shake any bankside branches to see dozens of the little guys energetically try to find new shelter.

There are several unmarked highway public access areas along VT 100 as the White River winds south of Rochester. Another good access spot is the Liberty Hill Road Bridge (43.838594,-72.800521). Park in a small dirt parking area after crossing the bridge, and fish the run above the bridge where a small stream cascades into the river. Lodging is available at the Liberty Hill Farm just up the road.

Route 100 curves sharply west and crosses the river in the village of Stockbridge. After the bridge, turn north to enter the Peavine National Travelway Site. This area provides excellent access. Other access sites include an area near the mouth of the Tweed River on VT 100 and on Blackmer Boulevard, a small road between Routes 100 and 107.

Near the junction of Routes 100 and 107, the Tweed River meets the White as it bends sharply to the east (43.776268,-72.753812). The river, from the mouth of the Tweed to the village of Bethel where the Third Branch enters, offers some quality flyfishing opportunities. The trout habitat in this area is a combination of classic freestone and deep ledge pools. Access is readily available along Route 107 at marked and unmarked public access areas. Local roads on the north bank of the river also offer entry points. The Vermont Department of Fish and Wildlife has designated a 3.3-mile section of river in this stretch as a special regulation area. From Lillieville Brook, which enters the White on the north bank near Gaysville, downstream to just below the junction of Cleveland Brook, fishing is with artificial flies and lures only, and all trout under 18 inches must be released. The daily limit is one fish.

Spring on the White River brings large hatches of caddisflies. Stonefly nymph patterns work throughout the season, and as the weather warms in July and August, stoneflies hatch at dusk. The mayfly hatches of mid- and late summer are the most anticipated by flyfishers. The *Potamanthus* bring many good fish to the surface in the slower pools just before and after dark during July and August. If you're an early riser, you'll find tricos emerging between 6:30 and 7:30am from July through September. The White also gives rise to *Isonychia* bicolor during the late season. Patterns with peacock herl as the major body

ingredient, such as the Zug Bug, Prince Nymph, and Leadwing Coachman, are effective wet flies. Dry patterns include the Gray Wulff and Dun Variant. Autumn is also time to enjoy some good blue-winged olive fishing.

There is a little green stonefly that you'll see sporadically hatching in the late afternoon in pocket water on the White during the summer. A larger-than-usual Henryville Special can sometimes be just the ticket.

From the village of Bethel, the White River flows south to the Second and First Branches as it runs along VT 14 and Interstate 89. The best access is from Route 14. I-89 is not as intrusive as you might think. It is mostly out of sight and earshot, and takes all of the cross-state traffic so that VT 14 and its small towns can remain quiet and peaceful.

The White River is larger and deeper through this section, making it popular with canoeists and patient anglers seeking larger browns and rainbows. Between North Royalton and Sharon, there are cross-river ledges and islands that create large, deep, aquamarine pools with significant eddies. While the state still stocks this section with cookie-cutter rainbows, there is a growing recognition that wild fish numbers are increasing, including large holdover browns and rainbows, so less trout are being stocked every year. The patient angler, working the deeper runs and pools with fast-sink line and large streamers will be rewarded with trout that rival those caught in the major western rivers.

There are dry-fly opportunities as well, at certain times. Significant summer midge hatches arise throughout this stretch of river, particularly where it flows from the village of Royalton to the village of South Royalton. Observant anglers may see larger browns and rainbows sipping on midges and evening blizzard caddis hatches in the many ledge pools between Royalton and the village of Sharon. One productive spot, the so-called Sturtevant Pool, is just upstream of the Sharon bridge (43.781675,-72.459606) that joins VT 14 with the River Road. Cross the river on the bridge, park along the road, and you will see the pool created by a short ledge. In the evening large rainbows rise, although an occasional smallmouth bass may surprise you as well.

If you want to explore this part of the river by watercraft, there is one small boat launch near Sharon and another downstream about five miles at a picnic area off Westfield Road and Route 14 near the village of West Hartford (take the bridge in town over the river). Other access areas are dispersed along the highway, so an angler should plan on some hiking. This is a popular area for swimmers and tubers, so the best fishing times in the summer are early morning and late evening. As you continue down the

White, you'll also have the opportunity to cast flies for some very nice smallmouth bass.

The branches of the White River are noteworthy. The cool waters of the Hancock and West Branches offer the angler some opportunities to catch small, wild rainbows and brook trout. The Hancock Branch tumbles down the mountain from Texas Fall near Middlebury Gap on VT 125. The West Branch picks up Brandon Brook, a good brook trout stream in its own right, and flows along VT 73 from Brandon Gap to the village of Rochester. Both of these tributaries have good cover and cool temperatures throughout the season. The Tweed River, which follows VT 100 north from above the village of Pittsfield, is known to have excellent spawning habitat for rainbows. It is a cool, fast-flowing stream with many shallow riffles and pockets of crystal-clear water that make for difficult fishing,

because the fish are sensitive to any disturbance. South Hill Road in Stockbridge is one good access point (43.774860,-72.768455).

The Third Branch runs parallel to VT 12 from the village of East Granville through Randolph and into the village of Bethel. The best fishing is for brook trout in the upper reaches. The lower section can offer some brown trout fishing in the slower, deeper runs. The Second Branch runs south along VT 14 from above the village of Braintree to where it meets the White River in the village of Randolph. Access is limited in the upper stretch, and there has been significant stream bank erosion. There is some good fishing for rainbows and browns near the mouth of the Second Branch.

The First Branch offers the best fishing of all the branches. As it crisscrosses Route 110 from the village

The Tweed River, a White River tributary, is so clear that it can be difficult to tell where the water ends and the dry bankside gravel begins.

of Chelsea to the village of Tunbridge, there are several bridges. This section offers good fishing for rainbows and browns in its long riffles and deep ledge pools. As the river approaches the mouth near the village of South Royalton, the water warms and trout fishing becomes more limited.

Seasons and special regulations for the White River include:

- Second Saturday in April through October 31.
- From the river mouth upstream to the Route 5, Bridge Street bridge in the town of Hartford, refer to Connecticut River Regulations.
- From the Route 5, Bridge Street bridge, town of Hartford, upstream to the VT 107 bridge, village of Bethel, there is a winter, artificials-only, catch-and-release season from November 1 to the Friday before the second Saturday in April.

- From the Route 5, Bridge Street bridge, town of Hartford, upstream to the Route 107 bridge, village of Bethel, the season is year round for largemouth and smallmouth bass, with a daily limit of five.
- From Cleveland Brook, in the town of Bethel, upstream to Lillieville Brook in the town of Stockbridge, angling is restricted to artificials; there is a length limit of 18 inches and a creel limit of one fish.

Stream Facts: White River

Season
From the VT 107 bridge in Bethel to its Connecticut River confluence, the season is year round but from November to March it is artificial catch and release only. The rest of the river is general law and is open from second weekend in April to the end of October.

Species
Wild brook trout, rainbow trout, and brown trout; stocked rainbow and brown trout; smallmouth bass.

River Characteristics
This is a large river by Vermont standards, traveling 55 miles, draining 700 square miles, and carrying an impressive flow of water in its lower reaches. Between its headwaters, major tributaries, and lower mainstem, the White River contains just about every kind of fishable water there is. Travel up and down the river and its tributaries and you will find pocket water, plunge pools, shallow riffles, deep runs, bend pools, and lower down, very deep and green-tinted ledge pools with heavy current and sweeping backeddies.

Hatches
Sporadic hatches of mayflies, caddis, and stoneflies throughout the year. From late May through August, heavy hatches of caddisflies can occur during the evening. Abundant baitfish and crayfish make streamer fishing a good option.

Tackle
A 9-foot 5-weight rod with a floating line tapering to 5x will serve most of the time. If fishing to a smaller blue-winged olive hatch, perhaps a 4-weight is better. For streamer fishing, a 6-weight with fast sinking full-sink line is best to reach the bottom of the deeper pools when the current is strong. Match the hatch for the most part, and when fishing streamers, try weighted Woolly Bugger, sculpin, and Soft-hackle Smelt patterns.

OMPOMPANOOSUC RIVER

The Ompompanoosuc River has its headwaters in the hills above the village of Vershire. The river runs south along VT 113, picking up water from a tributary flowing out of Lake Fairlee, and from its main source, the West Branch, which joins the river about two miles south of the village of Thetford Center. There is a large, flood-control dam at Union Village from which the Ompompanoosuc makes a short run to its mouth at the Connecticut River.

High water temperatures limit fishing in the upper river in summer, although below the covered bridge in Thetford Center (43.832212,-72.252507) is a series of small falls that add oxygen and cools the water. I fished below the bridge in very late June and caught small native brookies with a water temperature of only 64 degrees. There are clear trails that lead to the river from the bridge.

The West Branch, which flows from South Strafford along Route 132, does offer wild and stocked brook trout fishing. Park on the side of VT 132 where there are no houses, and a short walk through the woods will put you on the West Branch. There is also a side road off of VT 132 that parallels the river and you can also walk in from Tucker Hill Road. There are usually a few anglers trying their luck on the West Branch during spring weekends. Above the Union Village Dam, where the river flows through the Federal Forest Management Area, the state of Vermont regularly stocks rainbow and brown trout. Fish, holding over in the deeper pools can average 13 or 14 inches. The road upstream from the dam is closed to vehicular traffic, so walking or biking is required to reach this section. There is excellent access to the river below the dam from the recreation and picnic area just outside Union Village (43.790198,-72.256575). There is a large and turbulent pool where the river exits below the dam.

At Union Village, the river changes character with slower runs and deeper pools for stocked as well as holdover trout. Asking private homeowners for permission to fish from their property opens up more water in this area. The lower river quickly turns into a warmwater fishery. The river setback and backwaters near the mouth are best fished from a boat or canoe. As with all the rivers that flow into the Connecticut River, the Ompompanoosuc offers excellent flyfishing for smallmouth bass near the river mouth.

There are no special regulations for the Ompompanoosuc River, and its seasons are:

- Second Saturday in April through October 31.
- From the river mouth upstream to the US 5 bridge in the town of Norwich, refer to Connecticut River regulations.
- From the Route 5 bridge in Norwich upstream to the dam in Union Village, there is a winter artificials-only, catch-and-release season from November 1 to the Friday before the second Saturday in April. Largemouth and smallmouth bass are open year round, with a daily limit of five.

The upper Ompomanoosuc River below the covered bridge on Tucker Hill Road.

Waits River

The Waits River begins as a small brook trout stream in the high mountains of Groton State Forest. The river flows southeast through the town of Orange, picking up VT 25 near the village of West Topsham. The trees, which most years begin to show autumn colors in late August, provide a protective canopy over the river. This upper stretch of river holds a good population of wild and stocked brown trout and rainbow trout, as well as some brookies. A short walk through the woods provides access from roadside pull-offs (44.102651,-72.319648). Farther downstream, bridges provide access as well as a pull-off across the road next to a cemetery.

As you follow the Waits downstream along Route 25 toward the village of East Corinth, water temperatures rise and trout fishing diminishes. The river becomes broad and shallow with a gravel-covered bed, especially from where the South Branch joins the Waits to the high dam in the village of Bradford.

Wells River

The Wells River rises out of the hills and ponds of Groton State Forest. The upper reaches are generally warm and unremarkable as trout waters. Its main artery, the South Branch, which flows out of Noyes Pond, is a fine little brook trout stream. Its shaded waters remain cool all season long, and the steep runs and pockets provide good trout habitat. Brook trout abound from the pond all the way to its confluence with the mainstem. The brookies are a decent size for such as small stream, ranging up to 10 inches with a few larger. The Wells is not a large river. Light tackle and a quiet approach are the best tools. Fish a dry fly in every deeper pocket or plunge pool. Orange seems to be a good color on this stream so try small orange Stimulators, Elk Hair Caddis, or Goddard Caddis with an orange body. If the trout seem finicky, attach a small nymph as a dropper on your dry fly. Access is easy as US 302 follows the river closely.

The South Branch of the Wells River features many plunge pools, often with a brookie in residence.

The South Branch meets the mainstem of the Wells a few hundred yards east of the intersection of Routes 232 and 302. US 302 follows the river the rest of its 20-mile course to its mouth at the Connecticut River in the village of Wells River.

From the mouth of the South Branch, downstream to the village of South Ryegate, the Wells River is home to both brown trout and brookies. The banks are undercut and the runs are deep and cool. River access is along Route 302 and off the side roads and river crossings. The banks become overgrown and a canoe might be the best option lower down.

The river continues in graceful meanders through valley fields and then over some steep ledges to a dam in the village of Boltonville. There is river access to the water below the dam from a dirt road on the north bank of the river after you cross the dam. Avoid obvious private property and No Trespassing signs. You can also reach the river from a rail trail that follows the south bank (44.170467,-72.099458). Walk until the very steep and high bank diminishes to where you can walk down.

Downstream from the overpass of Interstate 91 there is a State Fish and Wildlife access area near a very nice stretch of water.

With no special regulations, Wells River seasons include:

- Second Saturday in April through October 31.
- From the river mouth upstream to the US 302 bridge in the village of Wells River, refer to Connecticut River regulations.

STILLWATERS OF CENTRAL VERMONT

Most ponds and lakes in Vermont support a wide variety of cold and warmwater species. If you plan on fishing these waters in May, June, early July, or October, any number of species are catchable on a fly rod. It pays to come prepared with a variety of fly rods and fly-line types. Take a 5-weight with both floating lines and fast-sink lines for trout (if they aren't rising, try dredging the bottom with leech imitations or Woolly Buggers). For bass, cast a 6-weight bass rod with a floating line and a box of bass poppers or Gartside Gurglers.

Catching pike on a fly rod is a high-adrenaline activity, if you have never tried it. Fish a 7-weight with a clear intermediate line and large colorful streamers alongside shoreline weeds and vegetation. Later in the year as pike move into deeper water, use a slow-sink line and fish deeper weed beds along drop-offs.

Cedar Lake, some know it as Monkton Pond, and Winona Lake, alias Bristol Pond, are two excellent warmwater ponds less than 20 miles from the city of Burlington. From Burlington, Route 116 South passes through Hinesburg where you can pick up Silver Street and head south to Monkton Ridge, then Monkton Road and Cedar Lake. The lake supports smallmouth as well as largemouth bass and panfish. There is a State Fish and Wildlife public boat access on the north shore.

Winona Lake, just north of the village of Bristol on VT 116, has a good reputation for bass as well as some good-sized northern pike. There is a public access and boat ramp at the north end of the lake. Winona is a fairly shallow lake with a healthy population of aquatic plant life, making it difficult if not impossible for your float tube.

Pleiad Lake is a small brook trout pond near the Long Trail, where it passes over Middlebury Gap, near the village of Ripton. Access to the pond is a short hike south

MAIN IMAGE: Heading out to fish the evening rise on Noyes Pond.
UPPER LEFT: Tee-hee.

from VT 125. There is primitive camping available nearby on the Long Trail.

South of Middlebury, off US 7 near the village of Salisbury, is Lake Dunmore. It is a good-sized lake with a mixed cold and warmwater habitat that supports bass and northern pike, as well as lake trout, rainbows, and landlocked salmon. There is a boat launch on the west shore; and on the east shore an excellent campground at Branbury State Park.

Silver Lake is on a high ridge east of Lake Dunmore. It is a beautiful lake that receives regular stockings of rainbow and brown trout. The north end is shallow, having a silt-covered bottom that gives rise to good insect hatches in May and June. Silver Lake is accessible by foot on a trail that starts just across the road from Branbury State Park (43.905734,-73.066473). The trail is about a mile long and uphill all the way. Primitive camping is available at the lake.

Sugar Hill Reservoir is located at Goshen Dam, east of Silver Lake. Access to this brook trout pond is by a foot trail (43.905606, -73.016641) off the Goshen-Ripton Road. Take VT 73 east out of Brandon for five miles to the junction of the Ripton-Goshen Road (Forest Road 32). Turn right onto Forest Road 32 and travel in a northerly direction a distance of about 3.2 miles to the junction with a gravel road on the right (43.905606,-73.016641). Turn right onto the gravel road and travel easterly about 0.75 of a mile to a parking lot at the end of the road. A gated ramp at the parking area is available to launch canoes and kayaks.

A number of years ago, *Outdoor Life* published an article on the outstanding northern pike fishing available in eastern Vermont. In addition to the southernmost end of Lake Champlain, Lakes Bomoseen and Hortonia were named in this article as top northern pike waters. Both still deserve that recognition. Glen Lake also has a growing pike reputation.

In recent years, Lake Bomoseen has gained a reputation as a coldwater fishery, producing some very large brown trout weighing up to eight pounds. Both Lake Bomoseen and Lake Hortonia are easily accessible from VT 30 south of the village of Middlebury.

Just east of Lake Hortonia is Sunset Lake, a deep, coldwater lake supporting rainbow and lake trout. It is part of a flood-control project and although water levels

A happy angler on Sunset Lake's floating bridge, holding a large stocked rainbow trout before taking it home for dinner.

fluctuate, its average maximum depth is in excess of 100 feet. Sunset Lake is located east of the village of Benson off VT 144.

Glen Lake lies near the western shore of Lake Bomoseen not far from Bomoseen State Park. It is a cold, clear lake that supports rainbow trout. Every species seems to grow large in this lake, it is also known for its lunker pike and large bluegills.

Near the eastern border of central Vermont off of I-93, you will find 39-acre Noyes Pond, considered to be one of Vermont's finest wild brook trout fisheries. This is the only public, flyfishing-only pond in Vermont and its shoreline is undeveloped and pristine because it lies within the Groton State Forest. This pond is part of Seyon (Noyes spelled backwards) Lodge State Park and has been managed by the State of Vermont as a wild trout fishery with no stocking for over 20 years. In the park, you can rent small row boats for an hour, a half day, or a full day at reasonable prices. You must fish from their boats as outside boats are not allowed, and casting from shore is also not permitted for some reason. You can stay overnight at the lakeside lodge, which can accommodate up to 16 people.

People try to time their visits for a very prolific giant mayfly (*Hexagenia limbata*) emergence during June but even without hexes, caddis hatches bring fish up in the evening. Best fishing is from the far side of the pond, but trout can be found anywhere.

The excellent fishing is not the only draw at Noyes Pond. The setting is quietly beautiful. You might hear the whistle of a peregrine soaring on the wind currents high overhead, or see a loon dive beneath the surface of the pond, holding its breath for what seems an impossible amount of time. Or a moose, wading in the weeds at the shallow west end of the pond, may lift its head to passively observe you as you silently drift on this lovely pond.

To find Noyes Pond, take Exit 17 off of I-93 and travel up VT 302. Shortly after the intersection of VT 232 look for Seyon Pond Road on your right and follow it to the end.

Nearby is Ticklenaked Pond, a short drive from Boltonville Road from the Boltonville Dam. Frankly, the fishing isn't special although there are good numbers of smallmouth bass, and it has Eurasian milfoil so you have to be careful to clean your boat if you put a boat in. I just included it because I love the name. No, it does not derive from some hippy commune but instead is a corruption of a difficult-to-pronounce Native American name.

Chittenden Reservoir is an impoundment, reclaimed in the mid-1970s, that supports brook trout, rainbow trout, brown trout, and landlocked salmon. It is located in the Green Mountain National Forest near the village of Chittenden, about eight miles north of the city of Rutland. There is public fishing access and a boat launch on the south end adjacent to the spillway.

If you like to combine backpacking and flyfishing, there are footpaths that lead to the Long Trail, about a mile east of Chittenden Reservoir. If you are interested in a longer trek on the Long Trail, then there are a number of other access points. From the Long Trail, it is a short hike to the two brook trout ponds: North Pond (43.748290,-72.886540) and South Pond. There is primitive camping on the trail.

East of the city of Rutland and not far from the Killington Mountain Ski Resort, are Colton Pond and Kent Pond. Kent Pond is north on VT 100, less than a mile from the bottom of the Killington access road. The pond supports rainbow and brook trout and has a public fishing access area and boat launch. Excellent camping facilities can be found nearby at Gifford Woods State Park. Colton Pond is a brook trout pond and is located just two miles farther up Route 100.

To the north and east of the Killington area, the famous "Floating Bridge" spans the narrows of a second Sunset Lake (this one located in the village of Brookfield) and is worth a visit. It is midway between those two I-89 exits, so choose your exit based on whether you traveling south or north on I-89.

The eighth version of this bridge was completed and opened for traffic in the spring of 2015 (44.042660,-72.605097). It uses the Army Corp of Engineers' latest technology and is very stable. Driving over it, you wouldn't know it is floating, but it is fun to do, nonetheless. Sunset Lake is very deep for its size (over 60 feet, thus the need for a floating bridge) and is stocked with standard-sized as well as trophy-sized rainbow trout. It also produces lunker smallmouth bass and pickerel. The new bridge has wide pedestrian walkways on either side, perfect to fish from. Powerbait chuckers and fly casters share the bridge and by all reports, do equally well with flyfishers taking fish from the surface. This small lake can also be fished by canoe or float tube. Many trout are taken along the shore where a small stream cascades over a dam in the village proper.

The town of Brookfield is a cute little town with dirt roads, an old fashion country inn, and a fine restaurant – well worth a visit on its own.

MAIN IMAGE: A high-elevation and aging beaver pond, but still full of trout.
UPPER RIGHT: A typical beaver-pond brook trout.

Rood Pond is located north of the village of Brookfield by continuing up the dirt main street of the village, bearing east until you intersect with Rood Pond Road. From the north, Rood Pond Road intersects with VT 64, two miles west of the village of Williamstown. This small pond is picturesque with little development and receives regular stockings of brook trout It has a reputation for nice evening hatches of insects. There is a well-maintained public access and boat launch (44.078014,-72.588354) with a nearby casting platform that can be easily reached by anyone in a wheelchair or with other limitations.

Green Mountain Beaver Ponds

This section would not be complete if I didn't write a little bit about beaver ponds. The Green Mountains of Vermont and the White Mountains of New Hampshire hold dozens, if not hundreds of small creeks, streams, and river headwaters. Hundreds of miles of pristine mountain waters shelter small, if not tiny, native brookies. When a beaver dams up one of these small waters and a beaver pond is created, habitat for trout improves because the deeper water provides more shelter and food sources. Brook trout grow bigger and more numerous. Beaver ponds are temporary and transitory. They form, get washed out by heavy rainstorms, or silt-in and become marshes or swamps. But sometimes, for a golden three to five years, an adventuresome angler can discover an unfished beaver pond filled with 6- to 12-inch brook trout. I encourage you to tramp up watersheds, explore the headwaters, and discover your own beaver ponds. They are special places to fish and see the abundant wildlife that call their unique ecosystems home.

CENTRAL VERMONT PLANNING CONSIDERATIONS

Hub Cities

- Rutland (www.rutlandvermont.com)
- Middlebury (www.midvermont.com)
- White River Junction (www.uppervalleychamber.com)
- Woodstock (www.woodstockvt.com

Easy Access Options

- Sunset Lake in Brookfield has a floating bridge with wide pedestrian walkways on either side. It is wheelchair accessible and provides flyfishing opportunities across the entire width of the lake with depths from 5 to 60 feet.
- Just up the road, is Rood Pond with a wheelchair accessible casting platform (44.078014,-72.588354). The water is relatively shallow near the casting platform, so lengthy casts would be required, or fishing in the early morning or late evening when trout move into shallower water to feed. With Rood Pond and Sunset Lake close to another, Historic Brookfield with its lodging options and fine dining is a good base of operations for anglers who prefer easy access options.

Suggested Beginner Options

One of the best ways for beginners to hone their flyfishing skills is to fish small mountain streams. It is very straightforward: a pair of boots and shorts, a floating line, and a small box of attractor dry flies (Hornbergs, Puterbaugh Caddis, and Royal Wulffs) with perhaps a few nymphs is all that you need. Make short casts to deeper pockets, plunge pools, or corner banks. If you don't get an eager strike after half a dozen casts, move on to the next spot. Eventually, eager native trout will attack your fly. And you probably won't see more than a few other anglers. Central Vermont offers lots of options.

- In east-central Vermont, two good options are the South Branch of the Wells River and the upper Waits River.
- In west-central Vermont, try any of the tributaries of Upper Otter Creek: the Middlebury River, Furnace Brook, the Neshobe River, and the New Haven River.

Vacation Options

Weekend Getaway

- Brookfield is a nice option for a quiet romantic weekend with flyfishing opportunities at Sunset Lake and Rood Pond. Historic Brookfield is a living look back to historic rural New England and beautiful country farms are just a short bike ride away on dirt roads. Green Trails Country Inn (www.greentrailsinn.com) offers lodging options near or on the lake where you can relax or take a short walk to fish off the bridge. Widely recognized Ariel's Restaurant offers fine dining near the bridge.
- Spend a June or early July weekend at Seyon Lodge in Seyon Lodge State Park. There are a variety of outdoor activities to enjoy in the Groton State Forest including hiking, bird-watching, and photography, but the central focus will be fishing Noyes Pond for native squaretails, particularly during the evening rise. During the day, one can fish the nearby South Branch of the Wells River or the Waits River.

One-week Vacation

- One can explore the villages and waters of central Vermont for at least a week and never feel like the experiences are repetitive. The month of July offers morning and evening hatches, but most rivers are still cool enough to fish well. Several days can be spent fishing the White River, from its smaller tributaries to its larger ledge pools. One strategy is to fish the larger pools between Royalton and Sharon in the early morning and late evening and then explore the tribs or upper reaches during the day. Stay in the quaint and funky town of South Royalton or at a real working farm at Liberty Hill Farm, right on the upper White River.
- Then head west and fish any of the tributaries of Otter Creek for small native brookies in the Green Mountains or stocked rainbows farther downstream. Hike the famous Long Trail for a day or two. Stay in the college town of Middlebury or camp out in any of the numerous campgrounds in the area.

A Brookfield bed and breakfast.

Northern Vermont

Northern Vermont offers a surprising diversity of fishing opportunities as well as other recreational, cultural, and tourism diversions.

Northwest Vermont is the population and development center of the state and also the location of Lake Champlain – the unofficial sixth Great Lake. Three main river systems drain the northwest slope of Vermont into Lake Champlain: the Winooski, the Lamoille, and the Missisquoi. The business and population centers of Burlington and Saint Albans make these rivers and their tributaries very accessible to visiting flyfishers. Everything is here, from wild brook trout, trophy brown trout, and rainbow trout to landlocked salmon and steelhead.

Lake Champlain alone offers almost every type of fishing imaginable including trolling or casting for coldwater species, taking part in international fishing derbies and BASS Top 100 Tournaments, stalking large northern pike in the spring, and catching rare species such as bowfin.

Burlington, the home of the University of Vermont, is an energetic small city right on the shore of Lake Champlain, and is one of the best places in New England to live or visit.

The Green Mountains occupy the center of the state and are the source of many of Vermont's rivers from the multitude of small tributaries that arise from the flanks of the mountains. Rivers such as the Middlebury, Barton, and Nulhegan have their origins here. The Green Mountains are geologically old, and minerals are all but spent. In the winter, anchor ice chokes the rivers and just as quickly turns into spate that can scour the streambed of most life. Caddis and stoneflies have hardened themselves to these conditions and are the predominant food source in the northern streams.

Northeast Vermont, called the Northeast Kingdom, is bordered by the Connecticut River to the east and the Green Mountains to the west. Tourists seeking remote places to ski, hike, camp, or just "to peep" come to this part of Vermont throughout the year. Some come to fish for the large lake trout of Lakes Seymour and Willoughby, the historic spring run of rainbow trout in the Willoughby River, the autumn run of salmon up the Clyde, or native brookies in a multitude of smaller mountain trout streams. The Connecticut River offers the opportunity to take drift boat floats for trophy salmonids.

The Northeast Kingdom is mostly forest and small dirt-road villages with a total population of only 70,000 and two towns: Newport and St. Johnsbury.

Classic small-town Vermont scenery.

WINOOSKI RIVER

The Winooski River flows west and north from the hills of Cabot to its mouth near the city of Burlington at Lake Champlain. For 90 miles, the Winooski carries the waters of more than 1,000 square miles of watershed. Its varied habitat is home to wild brook, rainbow, and brown trout. Smallmouth bass, salmon, and steelhead reside in the lower river where they migrate from Lake Champlain. There is little overall fishing pressure on this river. Anglers from more crowded areas will be flabbergasted at how many good runs and pools with eager trout they will have completely to themselves. The last time I fished this area, it was a prime early July weekend, and river flow, clarity, and temperatures where excellent. Yet, there was not another angler to be seen the entire two days.

The Winooski River and its tributaries, along with the Lamoille River and its tributaries, offer miles and miles of water to explore. If you want to shorten your learning curve, consider hiring a flyfishing guide for a day. I can recommend Dave Durovich, a local guide who has fished this area his entire life. You can find Dave through the website: www.streamandbrook.com.

The Winooski River is a freestone stream with its flow interrupted by seven dams. Levels fluctuate without warning, and the water can color up after a summer storm and remain high for a week. Water temperatures fluctuate quite dramatically from a springtime temperature at runoff of the middle 30s and 40s to summertime temperatures of as high as 85 degrees. Although temperatures approach dangerous limits for trout, enough cooling waters enter the mainstem to provide habitat throughout the river's length. Caddisflies are the predominant aquatic insect, with a fair representation of mayflies as well.

Brown trout are stocked regularly and average 8 to 14 inches with larger fish in the range of four to five pounds caught each year. Rainbow trout downstream of Bolton Dam are wild and average 6 to 13 inches with many in the 18-inch range. Brook trout are found in the upper section of the river.

Seasons and regulations for the Winooski River vary by section and species. Please study the rule book before venturing out.

Montpelier, the state's capital city, is the portal to the upper Winooski. The river's beginnings are fragile. Water temperatures run high for trout species and beaver activity has choked the river's flow, making life pretty tough for the brookies and small browns in this section of river. Consequently, the fishing can be a challenge.

Farther downstream, access is along US 2 where pull-offs come close to the river or off side roads that cross the river. You'll find a freestone stream with pocket water and many twists and turns. The best way to fish this stretch is to cover some ground. A favorite short river section of mine is downstream from the ballfield in Plainfield. Access from Recreational Field Road.

The author with a nice Winooski rainbow.

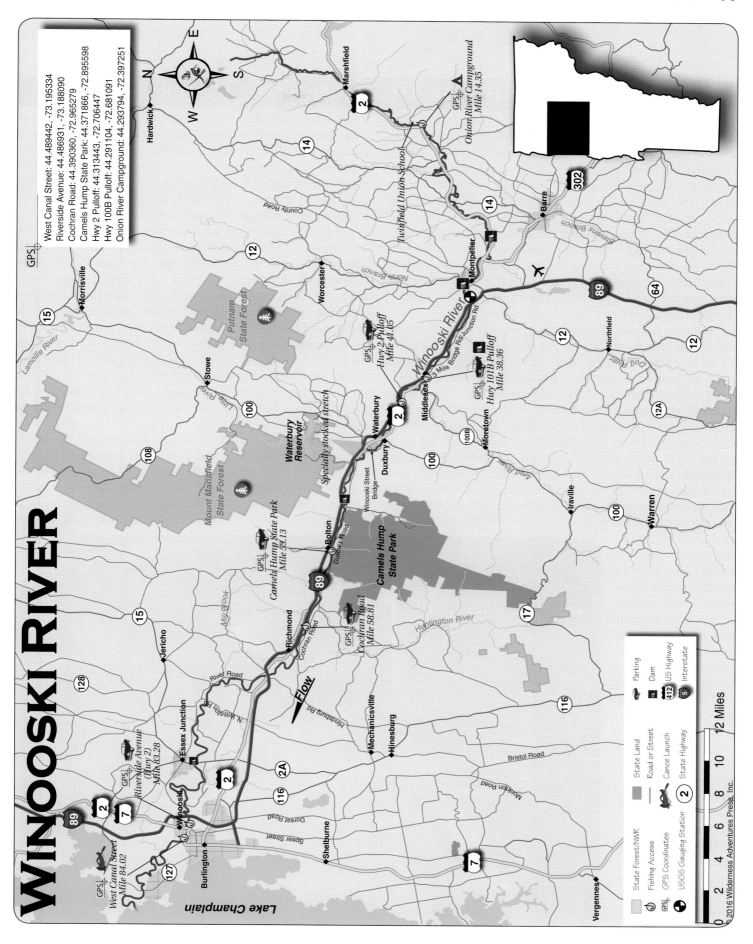

WINOOSKI RIVER

West Canal Street: 44.489442, -73.195334
Riverside Avenue: 44.486931, -73.188090
Cochran Road: 44.390360, -72.965279
Camels Hump State Park: 44.371866, -72.895598
Hwy 2 Pulloff: 44.313443, -72.706447
Hwy 100B Pulloff: 44.291104, -72.681091
Onion River Campground: 44.293794, -72.397251

Lake Champlain

Burlington

Vergennes

Shelburne

Hinesburg

Mechanicsville

Richmond

Jericho

Essex Junction

Winooski

West Canal Street
Mile 84.02

Riverside Avenue
(Hwy 2)
Mile 83.28

Stowe

Morrisville

Hardwick

Marshfield

Worcester

Waterbury

Waterbury
Reservoir

Putnam
State Forest

Mount Mansfield
State Forest

Lamoille River

Little River

Mill Brook

Camels Hump
State Park

Camels Hump State Park
Mile 33.13

Cochran Road
Mile 58.81

Bolton

Duxbury

Middlesex

Montpelier

Barre

Moretown

Northfield

Warren

Iraville

Specially stocked stretch

Huntington River

Mad River

Dog River

North Branch

Stevens Branch

Winooski River

Twinfield Union School

Onion River Campground
Mile 14.35

3 Mile Bridge Rd/Junction Rd

Hwy 2 Pulloff
Mile 41.05

Hwy 101B Pulloff
Mile 38.36

Winooski Street
Bridge

Duxbury Road

Cochran Road

Flow

River Road

N Williston Rd

Hindsburg Rd

Dorset Road

Spear Street

Bristol Road

Monkton Road

County Road

Flow

Legend

State Forest/NWR
Fishing Access
GPS Coordinates
USGS Gauging Station

State Land
Road or Street
Canoe Launch

Parking
Dam
US Highway
Interstate

0 2 4 6 8 10 12 Miles

©2016 Wilderness Adventures Press, Inc.

BRANCHES OF THE WINOOSKI RIVER

The North Branch Winooski follows VT 12 from above Worcester to its mouth near Montpelier. Brown trout are predominant below the Wrightsville Dam. Above Wrightsville Reservoir, one is more likely to encounter brook trout. There are plenty of access points where the road runs close to the river or where bridges cross. The upper stretch flows through wetlands and conifers that look more like Maine than Vermont. The North Branch then continues through mixed farmland and small house lots. Remember, once you access the river, you can walk along its shore below the high-water mark regardless of whether the land on either side is private or posted. The North Branch is a delightful size to fish with a light 3-weight rod.

Stevens Branch and Jailhouse Branch (where legend has it that Elvis fished) are in the Barre area running along VT 62 and US 302. These are good wild rainbow and brook trout waters and are therefore not stocked by the state.

The lower Winooski, flowing north from Montpelier to Burlington, is the most heavily fished water in the area. Following US 2 from the dam in Middlesex into the village of Waterbury, there are several unmarked pull-off areas giving good river access although the banks are steep. Although warm water from the reservoir behind the dam has an adverse effect during the summer, the Mad River that enters the Winooski just downstream from Middlesex, adds cooler flows. The river is larger through this section and has boulders that break up the river current. Runs and pools are more rapid and deep. This is good holding water for browns and larger rainbows throughout the season.

The state manages a specially stocked stretch of river that runs from the US 2 bridge in Waterbury to the railroad bridge just north of town. Access can be made either from behind the state hospital in town or from River Road, which parallels the river along the southwest bank. Here, the Winooski is flatter and its bottom is made up of small gravel, silt, and cut ledge. Fishing pressure is constant at times, and there are no restrictions on bait or other angling techniques. Early morning and evening hours tend to be the best times to fish this stretch of river, where there is a chance for a large brown or rainbow.

The Winooski River gets another cool drink from the outflow of the Waterbury Reservoir dam through the Little River in the town of Waterbury and from the Bolton Dam in the town of Bolton. The river from Bolton Dam to the village of Richmond is very productive. River Road follows the Winooski closely, giving anglers good access to its many runs and deep pools. You find River Road where the bridge crosses the river in Jonesville, just east of Richmond on Route 2, or from the east side of town in Waterbury off Route 100 South. The banks are steep but wading is fairly forgiving. Pay attention to changes in flow – water can be released from the dams without warning, creating strong currents.

Caddisfly and stonefly imitations work consistently throughout the season. The first really important mayfly hatches on this portion of the river are the sulphurs and Cahills in late May. You will probably see some blue quills and Hendricksons earlier, but the water's usually so cold the fish show little interest. In midsummer at dusk, a large

Rural Vermont bridge over the North Branch of the Winooski River.

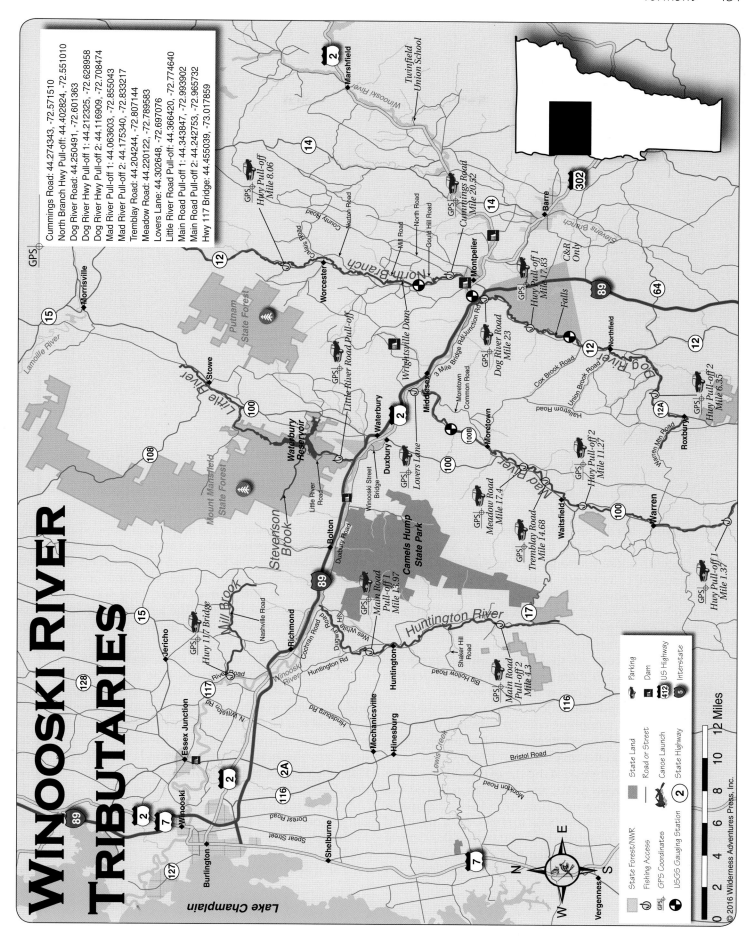

WINOOSKI RIVER
TRIBUTARIES

Cummings Road: 44.274343, -72.571510
North Branch Hwy Pull-off: 44.402824, -72.551010
Dog River Road: 44.250491, -72.601363
Dog River Hwy Pull-off 1: 44.212325, -72.628958
Dog River Hwy Pull-off 2: 44.116909, -72.708474
Mad River Pull-off 1: 44.063603, -72.855043
Mad River Pull-off 2: 44.175340, -72.833217
Tremblay Road: 44.204244, -72.807144
Meadow Road: 44.220122, -72.789583
Lovers Lane: 44.302648, -72.697076
Little River Road Pull-off: 44.366420, -72.774640
Main Road Pull-off 1: 44.343847, -72.993902
Main Road Pull-off 2: 44.242753, -72.965732
Hwy 117 Bridge: 44.455039, -73.017859

Lake Champlain

Legend
State Forest/NWR
Fishing Access
GPS Coordinates
USGS Gauging Station

State Land
Road or Street
Canoe Launch
State Highway

Parking
Dam
US Highway
Interstate

0 2 4 6 8 10 12 Miles

© 2016 Wilderness Adventures Press, Inc.

The clear waters and lack of cover on the Dog River lead to spooky trout.

yellow mayfly called the golden drake *(Potamanthus)* emerges. The first indication that this hatch is occurring is the watchful cedar waxwings taking flight and diving for this mouthful of an insect. There is little chance for the trout to get at the adult after the birds have had their way, so the hatch is best fished with swimming nymph (sizes 8 and 10) or emerger patterns. Fall can provide some good blue-winged olive (sizes 16 to 20) fishing.

Generally, because of the sparse fishing pressure, the fish are not picky. If there are no fish rising, a generic beadhead Hare's Ear, Copper John or Prince Nymph works fine. A strike indicator allows you to cast farther, but short-line high-stick nymphing with no indicator will catch plenty of fish. To tempt larger denizens of the deeper water, cast meaty streamers on a sink-tip line.

In the village of Winooski at the site of the old falls is the Salmon Hole. For many years, the dam that replaced the falls was a barrier to fish migrating from Lake Champlain to spawn (44.488648,-73.187432). In 1993, as a result of licensing conditions negotiated by members of the Central Vermont Chapter of Trout Unlimited and the Vermont Department of Fish and Wildlife, a trap truck facility with a fish elevator was constructed at the dam. Supervised jointly by hydroelectric personnel and state and federal fish and wildlife biologists, this facility allows spawning steelhead and landlocked salmon to be captured and trucked upstream above the dams, where they have access to tributaries and native waters. The farthest upstream access for these migrant species is the Bolton Dam in the town of Bolton.

Fishing in the Salmon Hole area is closed from mid-March through the first of June to protect spawning walleyes that also arrive from the lake. After this period, and especially in autumn, fishing for lake-run salmon and steelhead can be exciting. Streamer patterns that represent smelt or small nymphs, fished on the swing or dead-drifted deep, are the most effective methods of fishing Salmon Hole. Fish all the water. During the day, salmon will move out of the fast water and into the depths.

Access to Salmon Hole is gained from either the Burlington side, off Riverside Avenue (US 2) or, in Winooski, by the fish trap or at the canoe access on West Canal Street. Wading can be challenging because the river bottom is typical of areas below city dams. Rocks and concrete blocks with rebar protruding are a hazard to wading, but make good flow diversions for holding fish. Also, watch out for unannounced changes in flow levels.

There are other varieties of fish that reside in and around Salmon Hole, such as smallmouth bass, the occasional lake trout, perch, pike, and pickerel. So if you're in the Burlington area with a little time to kill, cast a fly in the Winooski River at Salmon Hole.

Dog River

From its headwaters in Roxbury north to its confluence with the Winooski River in Montpelier, the Dog River slowly winds its way through valley fields and farmland. The Dog River valley is extremely scenic and well worth visiting, including the town of Northfield Falls, known for its covered bridges.

The Dog River has a good population of wild brook, brown, and rainbow trout managed by the state without stocking as a wild trout fishery. Access is along VT 12 and 12A. One mile south of I-89 is a dirt road with a small parking area (44.250491,-72.601363). Farther south, walking the train tracks gives additional access. Finally, the Dog River Natural Area in the town of North Berlin has a trail along the river. In other spots there is quite a bit of posted land, so please be courteous and ask permission – most landowners are very willing to allow anglers access to the river as long as they ask first.

As with most wild trout fisheries, a slow, cautious approach is advised; the water is very clear and the fish spook easily. Every fish caught on this river is earned, and yet is a favorite among some local guides. There can be a good Hendrickson hatch on the Dog River sometime towards the middle of May, although the trout don't always respond to it initially. Later, small nymphs, midge patterns, and terrestrials do well. In mid-August, tricos hatch at dawn. Fishing spinner falls right at dark is another good strategy. In October, pre-spawn brown trout can become aggressive and fishing articulated streamers or similar meaty offerings can yield trophy butter-bellies.

Due to a decline in fish numbers in the early 2000s, the state imposed catch-and-release regulations on certain sections of the river. This includes the section between Northfield Falls in Northfield and the Junction Road Bridge in Montpelier. This rule change seems to have had a beneficial effect and it hopefully will be renewed well into the future.

Mad River

The next major tributary of the lower Winooski is the Mad River. The Mad's headwaters are found to the south in Granville Gulf. The river flows north along Route 100 and 100B for about 25 miles through the scenic ski area villages of Warren and Waitsfield. Mad River is a classic beauty. Its course makes deep cuts in ledge rock, creating waterfalls and deep, cold pools. The upper reaches hold wild brook trout in tumbling pocket water while below, in the more defined runs and pools, there are rainbows and browns. Numerous roadside pull-offs or picnic areas on Route 100 and 100B provide access to water, sometimes requiring a short walk through the woods.

This river stays cool even during the summer, particularly just downstream from where smaller tributaries join. Mill Brook in Fayston is worth fishing in its own right for wild brookies (use VT 17 for access).

The stretch of the Winooski just downstream from the Mad River confluence, where there is a small island, is worth checking out. Fish the deeper runs on both sides of the island. Wading in the gravel is straightforward here and access is from Lovers Lane off of US 2 (44.302648,-72.697076). This is a river that deserves a visit; so take the time to check it out.

Take the same flies you used on the Winooski and Dog Rivers to the Mad. As summer begins, terrestrials become increasingly important because the dairy farm fields along the river are just filled with grasshoppers, crickets, ants, and beetles. Early in the season, fish smaller versions and then increase the size as the naturals themselves mature. To avoid swimmers and kayakers, it pays to get on the river early or late in the day – this holds true for most Vermont Rivers. Also keep an eye out for Vermont's relatively abundant bicyclists. I can't tell you how often I have been driving, looking at the nearby river, and almost didn't see cyclists nearby.

Little River

Below the village of Waterbury, the Little River enters the Winooski. As the 60-degree-or-cooler outflow of the Waterbury Reservoir, it is the cooling source of the Winooski where it flows past the village of Richmond. In summer heat, browns and rainbows will seek shelter in and around the Little River, providing good fishing opportunities. The Little River runs quite high at times due to power releases surging and cutting through the clay and ledge that line its bottom. During these times, the river is not really fishable. When generating stops, the river slows down by a factor of ten, and flyfishing is easier for the trout holding in its now small quiet pools. If you enjoy fishing small water, this is the river for you. Try drifting small nymphs on a 3-weight rod in the faster current tongues, or seams against rock banks or fallen timber. If action is slow, try stripping the nymph across likely holding spots. To fish the river, park anywhere along Little River Road, a dirt road off of US 2.

"Hunt the little mad dog north" is a handy ditty that will help an angler remember the order of the Winooski tributaries: Huntington, Little, Mad, Dog, and the North Branch.

Waterbury Reservoir

You should not overlook the waters of Waterbury Reservoir, which holds smallmouth bass, brown trout, and rainbows, and even some brookies. Trolling with flies in spring after ice-out and casting at the mouth of Stevenson Brook could produce a lively, fat rainbow. Waterbury Reservoir is considered a trophy smallmouth bass fishery. It offers great early summer and autumn fly-casting action from a canoe along the shore. Smallies will generally be found in 10 feet of water or less and will hit surface flies and poppers, as long as surface water temperatures stay below 70 degrees. Try yellow Gartside Gurglers. In mid-summer, they move out into deeper water structures such as submerged boulders or rocky ridges, and sink-tip lines with sinking leech or crayfish-imitating streamers become more effective. As water cools in September, the bass move back towards shore to fatten up before the ice arrives. The campground at Little River State Park is excellent and provides access to much of the area.

Huntington River

The Huntington River enters the Winooski at Jonesville. It is a beautiful trout stream, flowing out of the foothills near Camel's Hump through farm fields and meadows until it crashes into a gorge 0.75 of a mile from its mouth. The Huntington is a popular river, particularly in the area around the gorge. It is home to large browns and rainbows coming in and out of the Winooski. The Huntington River Gorge is best fished early in the season or later, and early in the day before swimmers and picnickers gather. Large stonefly patterns, Woolly Buggers, and streamers fished with patience can pay off with a large brown or rainbow on your line. Make sure to try the newest generation of large-fish streamers; conehead Gartside Soft-Hackle Marabous, or any of Kelly Galloup's creations. Upriver, small brown trout and brookies are found.

The last major tributary of the Winooski River is Mill Brook. It is accessible off VT 117 east of the village of Essex Junction. A good deal of the brook is posted. The upper portions of Mill Brook offer good brook trout pocket water with plenty of cover, while the lower section has brown trout and some rainbows that migrate out of the Winooski in spring. The mouth of Mill Brook fishes well at low water.

Lewis Creek

This small stream runs virtually uninhibited for 20 miles from its source in the foothills above Starksboro and into Lake Champlain. At its origin, the creek drops fast and is good brook trout water. Stocking programs to introduce steelhead have had a varied degree of success. The run of steelhead that everyone anticipates each year can occur anytime during the months of March and April, if at all. Years ago, we had a very dramatic thaw in January that coincided with the mouth not being totally frozen. The resulting heavy runoff caused an influx of steelhead that is still talked about. Flies for steelhead include egg patterns and small nymphs. If the water is a little off-color try bigger and brighter patterns. Fish them deep and slow. If an angler isn't hooking bottom occasionally then adding more split shot is advised.

Access is from US 7 where Lewis Creek passes under the highway in North Ferrisburg, about 15 miles south of Burlington. Hollow Road follows the creek upstream for a way, or you can find access from Starksboro along VT 116. Lewis Creek below North Ferrisburg is good smallmouth water in May and June. Flycasting Woolly Buggers or yellow marabou streamers can reward an angler with a fat, leaping smallmouth bass in heavy current. This is not trout fishing, so be prepared with a stout rod and 2x tippet

Guide Dave Durovich selecting a fly on the Little River.

Lamoille River

Near Caspian Lake in the town of Greensboro, the Lamoille River receives its first waters from the mountains. As it begins its 85-mile journey toward Lake Champlain, the upper Lamoille to Hardwick is a classic brook trout stream, covered by alders, and contains a series of bends and pocket water. As the river turns toward the west, it widens and courses through pastures and farms. Continued flooding has silted many of the pools and straightened out runs. Water temperatures run dangerously high in the summer. However, the colder waters of the tributaries make the main river tolerable to trout throughout most the season. Silt has taken its toll on the insects, and hatches have been sparse in recent years. There is good caddis activity throughout the season and an occasional blue-winged olive hatch in the fall.

Don't get the wrong impression, though. The Lamoille is a great river to fish – pressure is low and the fish delightfully naïve. There are plenty of spots where the river quickens over ledges or rocks and cool seeps and tributaries keep the water at the temperatures trout prefer. In these areas trout are plentiful. At some point during the summer, the water does warm into the 70s and trout fishing needs to take a haitus until autumn. Heavy rain also can raise and muddy the river, requiring a break in the action. It pays to monitor the river closely so that fishing can be timed for optimal conditions.

The upper stretch of the Lamoille from above Greensboro Bend downstream along VT 16 to Hardwick is accessible by several unmarked pull-off areas and bridges as it flows through woods, farms, and small settlements. With a little hiking and bushwhacking, an angler can have a quiet, enjoyable day stalking brook trout. Small nymphs fished upstream into the pockets and searching patterns, such as Royal Wulffs, Puterbaugh Caddis, and Hornbergs, are good bets.

The river broadens along VT 15 as it flows between Hardwick and Morrisville. Brown trout and rainbows begin to dominate the river in this area. The Green River's cooling waters where it enters the Lamoille have a great influence on the quality of water, making this a productive stretch of river to fish. In general, however, this part of the river has taken a beating in recent years – floods and decreased flows from development have caused a downturn in the numbers of fish available. Unfortunately, this is a story often repeated recently for many of Vermont's rivers and streams.

There is good fishing to be had around the village of Wolcott. Access the river directly from VT 15 or cross the river on School Street and find the somewhat overgrown rail trail that parallels the opposite bank (44.544125,-72.459113).

On the other hand, groups such as the Lamoille River Anglers Association and their work to reinforce stream banks and aggressive state stocking programs are aiding the Lamoille's recovery.

The Lower Lamoille begins below the impoundment called

The upper Lamoille River.

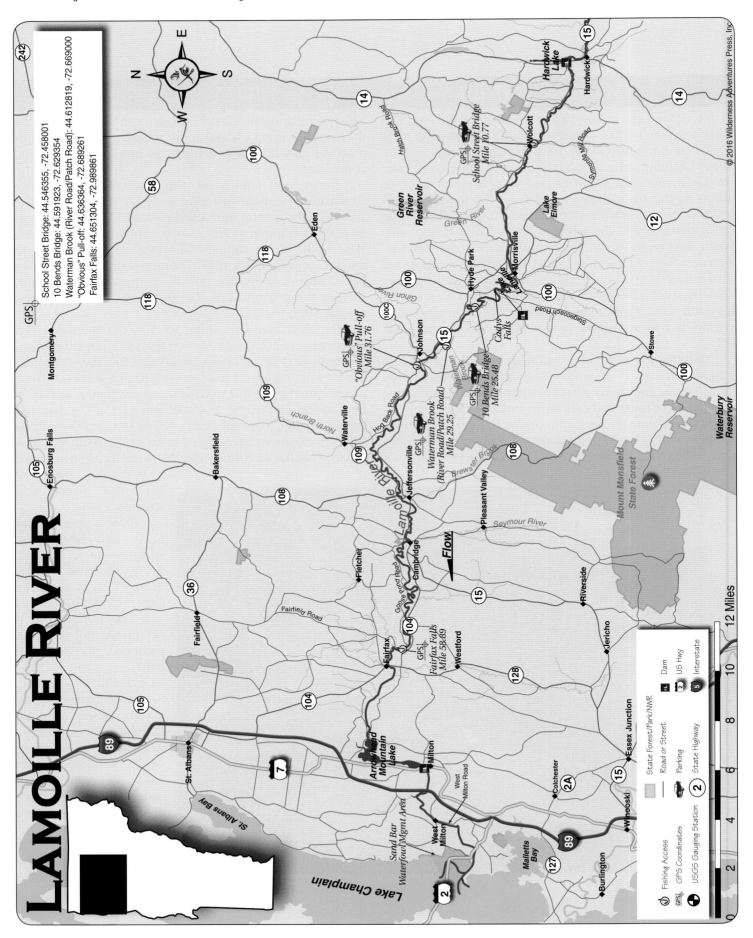

LAMOILLE RIVER

School Street Bridge: 44.546355, -72.458001
10 Bends Bridge: 44.591923, -72.629354
Waterman Brook (River Road/Patch Road): 44.612819, -72.669000
"Obvious" Pull-off: 44.636364, -72.689261
Fairfax Falls: 44.651304, -72.989861

© 2016 Wilderness Adventures Press, Inc.

Lake Lamoille in Morrisville at Cadys Falls. A privately managed catch-and-release area, known as "Ten Bends", starts there and winds slowly through Hyde Park to just upstream from the village of Johnson. Access to Ten Bends is at the farmhouse on a side road off VT 15 near the high school to the west of Hyde Park. You're asked to register there and to report your catch at the end of the day. This is good dry-fly water throughout the season. The water does heat up during the summer, making early mornings and evenings the best times to fish. The river bottom is silty and provides habitat

Looking downstream on the middle section of the Lamoille River.

for drake mayflies and other burrowing aquatic life forms. Swimming nymphs and large mayfly patterns should be tried just at dark on hot summer nights. Emerger patterns will tempt trout that have seen too many traditional patterns. A Quigley Cripple or Klinkhammer pattern in the appropriate size and color is sometimes the solution to a difficult fish. Blue-winged olives are the best bet in the fall, and caddisflies appear consistently throughout the season.

Downstream from Ten Bends, the Lamoille picks up speed as it rounds a bend near Waterman Branch, a small tributary. For three miles, the river becomes a quality fishery for rainbows and browns. The flow cuts under the ledge rock creating deep, swirling pools. As the river approaches the village of Johnson, it courses through a small canyon and eventually receives a cool drink from the water of the Gihon River that enters from the north bank. All in all, this is a beautiful area and deserves a day or two of your flyfishing time.

Access can be gained on either side of the river. From VT 15, there is an obvious pull-off close to the riverbank just to the west of Johnson. There are several pull-offs providing access to the south side of the river near where Waterman Brook enters the Lamoille. Wading is easy here – you can

cross (with care) in many areas above and below the big holes in this stretch of river. I think this is a particularly nice piece of water for the less experienced angler to have an enjoyable day of fishing. It's also a section of river from which, with a little patience and persistence, a large, yellow-bellied brown trout might be coaxed.

Beadhead nymphs, such as Hare's Ears, Copper Johns, and Prince Nymphs can be effective. Early in the morning, try running a big, weighted Woolly Bugger or crayfish pattern slowly through a big back eddy, such as the one below Dog's Head Falls. There are caddisflies throughout the season, and in autumn look for blue-winged olives.

The river from Johnson to Cambridge along Route 15 and via Hogback Road on the north side can be fished either on foot or by canoe. The North Branch Lamoille, Brewster, and Seymour Rivers cool off the mainstem of the Lamoille and provide good holding water for trout. The river warms as it passes from Cambridge to Fairfax along VT 104. Below the falls at Fairfax Dam, the state stocks large rainbows and browns usually ranging from 13 to 18 inches, for a regulated put-and-take fishery. There is good smallmouth fishing below this run, where the river eventually dumps into an impoundment known as Arrowhead Lake.

At West Milton, the outflow of Peterson Dam is the lowest stretch of the Lamoille River where it passes into

Lake Champlain. As in the Winooski River to the south, runs of landlocked salmon and steelhead have made this section of river important. Access is limited to the area below the dam and a couple of pull-offs on West Milton Road. The season is closed to fishing in the spring until the first of June. After that and in the fall, you should try your luck with streamers and small nymphs. The fishing season and other regulations vary by section and species; please consult the most recent regulations before fishing the Lamoille.

Brown and rainbow trout are stocked throughout the river and average 9 to 16 inches. There is some natural rainbow reproduction and a limited population of wild fish, especially in the Johnson area. Larger browns and rainbows are stocked in the special regulation section in Fairfax.

Lamoille River Tributaries

Between Wolcott and Morrisville is the first of the Lamoille River's main tributaries, the Green River. Coming out of Green River Reservoir, this alder-covered canyon is a coldwater sanctuary for some nice-sized brown trout. Rainbows and brook trout also call the Green their home, especially in the heat of summer when temperatures in the Lamoille often reach the uncomfortable mid-70s. Access on this 2.5-mile river is limited to walking in from VT 15 near the mouth (44.573098,-72.516589, look for a used car lot). The going is tough and the fish are skittish. For the more adventurous flyfisher, the Green River can be a fun day.

The Gihon River, a tributary that enters in the village of Johnson, is a lovely stream with wild brookies and colorful brown trout. Covered bridges cross the river in classic Vermont style, following its course out of Lake Eden along VT 100 and 100C for about 14 miles. There are several pull-offs and side roads making the Gihon relatively accessible. Temperatures remain cool and cover is good. Fish with small nymphs or attractor dries, such as small yellow or red Humpies or small Wulffs.

The North Branch Lamoille is a major tributary that extends from Belvidere Pond and running beside VT 109 to where it enters the main river in Jeffersonville. The North Branch is a pretty good fishery

due, in part, to heavy stocking. But there are plenty of wild fish in the upper reaches of the stream. In the lower part of this river, there is little streamside cover, but deep holding pools shelter brown trout. There are unmarked pull-offs providing access along Route 109.

Rainbows and brookies can be found all along the upper flows. Jaynes Covered Bridge (44.712200,-72.756276) is a good access point to fish up or downstream. If you walk upstream, you will find virtually unfished pocket water where energetic trout will attack any bushy dry fly you throw.

On the south side of the Lamoille in Jeffersonville, the Brewster River joins the main river after its run off Sterling Mountain along VT 108. Wild brook trout can be found in this little stream. In its lower reaches, one will find spawning browns and rainbows in the fall and spring.

Don't forget to pack your float tube and make the mile hike north on the Long Trail at Smuggler's Notch off Route 108 to Sterling Pond, Vermont's highest brook trout pond. Wading is possible from the west end, but you can't beat a lazy float in a high eastern mountain pond while casting dry flies for sipping brook trout.

The Seymour River flows into the Lamoille in the village of Cambridge. This small stream, which tends to have low summer flows, can hold browns in the 8- to 15-inch range. There's been a lot of residential development in this area, and unfortunately, access is limited.

The North Branch of the Lamoille from the Jaynesville Covered Bridge.

MISSISQUOI RIVER

The visiting fly angler seeking trout in the most northeastern part of Vermont should make visiting the Missisquoi River a priority. Its headwaters drain the Lowell Mountains as Burgess Branch and East Branch join to form the main river in the village of Lowell. From here, the Missisquoi winds north for 15 miles, where it makes a sudden 14-mile tour through Sutton, Quebec. The river returns to its natal Vermont at East Richford and journeys south and east for another 45 miles to its confluence with Lake Champlain in Swanton.

The Missisquoi River runs an almost circular course of 80 miles. The river winds through fields and farmland and has been subject to agricultural runoff and severe floods. The temperatures warm dramatically in the summer and, were it not for the major tributaries – Trout River and Tyler Branch – trout fishing would be limited.

The upper section of the Missisquoi, from Lowell to Westfield and paralleling VT 100, holds brook trout. Wild fish are supplemented with stockings. The small upper tributaries are good breeding areas for natives. Brookies run from 6 to 10 inches. It's not uncommon for the cautious fly caster to break the 12-inch barrier. You'll find some sulphur and blue-winged-olive activity. Fish terrestrials where fields abut the river. As the river winds through fields and farms, the banks are undercut and the riverbed tends to be made up of medium-sized gravel. Small feeder streams are good brook trout nurseries.

Spring comes later in the northern part of Vermont than lower New England. The waters are cold and snow will be in the woods into May. Brook trout chase small streamers and nymphs, fished slowly early in the season. As temperatures warm, caddis will become active as well as small midges and terrestrials. Try big, weighted Woolly Buggers and crayfish patterns for browns.

Summer evenings are pleasant times to flyfish on the upper Missisquoi. The Hornberg is my favorite pattern for this part of the river. Fished in all sizes, it can represent a caddis or a large, struggling mayfly on the surface. Fished as a wet fly, the Hornberg looks like a small, tempting minnow.

From Westfield downstream, the Missisquoi becomes a mixed brook trout and brown trout fishery. There is good brown trout fishing from Big Falls to North Troy. Large browns are reported to come from the base of the falls each year.

Access to the river can be gained where it crosses at the town line on the north edge of Lowell. The river sweeps back from the road about a quarter of a mile, and the hike can be worth the effort. Just east of the intersection of VT 100 and 101 in Troy, a secondary road follows the Missisquoi downstream past a covered bridge and on to Big Falls.

Below Westfield there is a mix of brown and brook trout. Browns average 8 to 14 inches. Larger ones are caught each year below Big Falls and farther down near Richford and the tributaries, Trout River in East Berkshire, and Tyler Branch in Enosburg Falls.

The middle stretch of the Missisquoi begins where the river returns to Vermont at East Richford and continues on to below the village of Enosburg Falls, where the Tyler Branch enters. Rainbow trout have a small showing around the Tyler Branch downstream from Enosburg Falls and in the Tyler Branch itself.

It is an open river, coursing through farmlands and pastures. Agricultural runoff and lack of cover cause the temperatures to rise the farther you go downstream. The cooling waters of the two main tributaries – the Trout River in East Berkshire and the Tyler Branch in Enosberg Falls – help maintain good conditions for brown trout throughout this section.

There are several pull-offs from VT 105 as it parallels the river and the old bed of the Central Vermont Railroad. The river's flow is a good blend of runs and deep pools, gravel bottom in the rapids, and more silt in the long, deeper glides. This produces fairly abundant aquatic insect

Smallmouth bass generally prefer small surface poppers.

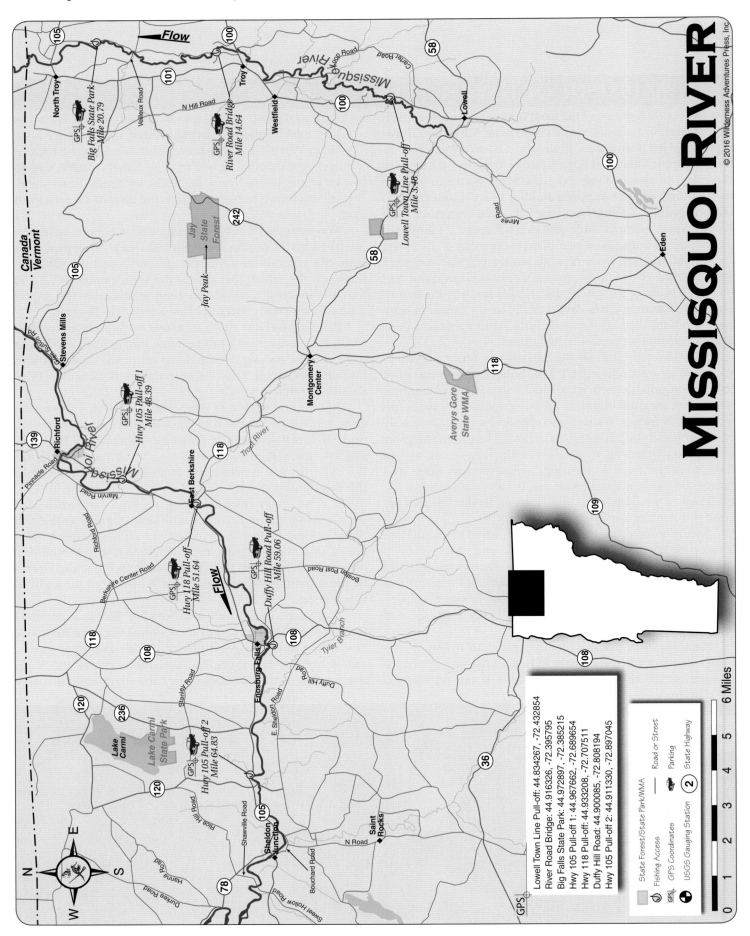

MISSISQUOI RIVER

Lowell Town Line Pull-off: 44.834267, -72.432854
River Road Bridge: 44.916326, -72.395795
Big Falls State Park: 44.972897, -72.385215
Hwy 105 Pull-off 1: 44.967662, -72.689654
Hwy 118 Pull-off: 44.933208, -72.707511
Duffy Hill Road: 44.900085, -72.808194
Hwy 105 Pull-off 2: 44.911330, -72.897045

State Forest/State Park/WMA
Fishing Access
GPS Coordinates
USGS Gauging Station

Road or Street
Parking
State Highway

0 1 2 3 4 5 6 Miles

© 2016 Wilderness Adventures Press, Inc

Big Falls State Park - Mile 20.79
River Road Bridge Mile 14.64
Lowell Town Line Pull-off Mile 3.48
Huffy Hill Road Pull-off Mile 59.06
Huey 118 Pull-off Mile 51.64
Huey 105 Pull-off 2 Mile 64.83
Hwy 105 Pull-off 1 Mile 48.39

Jay State Forest
Averys Gore State WMA
Lake Carmi State Park

North Troy
Troy
Westfield
Lowell
Eden
Stevens Mills
Richford
East Berkshire
Montgomery Center
Enosburg Falls
Sheldon Junction
Saint Rocks

Canada
Vermont

Jay Peak
Trout River
Missisquoi River
Tyler Branch

N Hill Road
Velleux Road
Carter Road
Mines Road
Glen Sutton Rd
Pinnacle Road
Marvin Road
Richford Road
Berkshire Center Road
Boston Post Road
Duffy Hill Road
E. Sheldon Road
Stanley Road
Rice Hill Road
Shawville Road
N Road
Bouchard Road
Sweet Hollow Road
Hanna Road
Durkee Road

The Tyler Branch holds the only significant rainbow trout population in the Missisquoi River system.

life, and where the stream touches pastures, good terrestrial activity.

The waters of the Missisquoi warm up quite a bit as the season progresses; however, there are pockets of cold water all the way down to Sheldon Springs where, while casting for smallmouths, you might pick up a big brown. The lowest section of the Missisquoi River doesn't really hold much interest for flyfishers pursuing trout. The waters below North Sheldon, however, have a good population of smallmouth bass. Fishing poppers on summer evenings amidst the big boulders between Sheldon Springs and Enosburg for smallmouths can be a lot of fun. Vary the size and color of your poppers until you find the combination that works best. Then you may fish the rest of the month with the exact same one.

Salmon restoration efforts from Lake Champlain to the dam in Swanton have had little return.

Missisquoi River Branches

From its small beginnings on the towering Jay Peak and Hazon's Notch, the Trout River flows from Montgomery Center for seven miles along VT 118 to East Berkshire. This area has been devastated by major floods in recent years, and many of the river bends have been straightened and pools filled in with silt (stop me if you have heard this story before). The Trout River has a good reputation as a brown trout nursery, and large fish come up out of the Missisquoi in the autumn to spawn. This is a river to keep an eye on in the years to come. Mother Nature has a way of healing her injured.

The Tyler Branch is the second important tributary that nurtures the Missisquoi. Its cold waters enter the mainstem downstream about two miles from the falls in Enosberg Falls. This area holds the only significant amount of rainbow trout in the whole river system. Also, in its upper waters, the Tyler Branch has some nice brook trout fishing. Access is off the back road to East Sheldon on the south side of the Missisquoi.

The Missisquoi's seasons are as follows:

- Second Saturday in April to October 31.
- From Lake Champlain to 850 feet below Swanton Dam in Swanton: open all year (Lake Champlain regulations).
- From 850 feet below dam to Swanton Dam: open all year except closed to fishing March 16 through the Friday before the first Saturday in May.
- From the top of the Swanton Dam in the Village of Swanton downstream approximately 850 feet to the water treatment plant on the west side of the river and downstream approximately 850 feet to the upstream end of the cement breakwater on the east side of the river: closed to fishing March 16 through May 31.
- From the downstream edge of Kane Road (TH-3) bridge upstream (approximately 5.7 miles) to the top of the Enosburg Falls Dam in Enosburg Falls: Daily limit of no more than two trout.

UPPER CONNECTICUT RIVER

The upper Connecticut River, from Beecher Falls near the Canadian border, downstream about 35 miles to the mouth of Paul Stream in the town of Bloomfield, is one of the finest trout streams in the Northeast. Brook trout, rainbows, and brown trout thrive, often growing to trophy proportions.

The river section that forms the Vermont/New Hampshire border belongs to and is managed by the state of New Hampshire. Through an agreement between New Hampshire and Vermont, resident license holders from either state may fish the Connecticut River. Others must purchase a nonresident New Hampshire fishing license. The state of New Hampshire has established a special regulations area for catch and release from the bridge that spans the Connecticut between the village of Bloomfield, Vermont and North Stratford, New Hampshire, upstream about 2.5 miles to Lyman Falls.

In Vermont, VT 102 parallels the Connecticut River. There is plenty of access from unmarked pull-off areas and river crossings. There is a bridge near the village of Colebrook, New Hampshire as well as the Columbia Covered Bridge (44.852960,-71.551252) near Lemington, Vermont and the bridge in the village of Bloomfield, Vermont. Floating the Connecticut, either by canoe, drift boat, or inflatable, is a good way to reach the more remote stretches of water. The river, however, is quite easily waded in sections and fishes well from shore.

The water runs fast and clear as the Connecticut enters Vermont. Upstream, cool tributaries and the outflow of Murphy Dam in the town of Pittsburg, New Hampshire refresh the mainstem of the upper Connecticut. Flow levels fluctuate from dam releases, but the changes are not extreme. Healthy water temperatures, in the range of 55 to 65 degrees, and an abundant food supply provide a rich habitat for resident trout. This habitat is maintained all year by continued cold water from upriver dam releases and from the minor feeder streams and three larger tributaries: the Nulhegan River, Paul Stream, and the Passumpsic River.

The dam in the village of Beecher Falls briefly interrupts the flow, but the pocket water below the dam is very fishable. It seems that each spring, the local newspaper features the picture of a young resident proudly holding a huge brown trout caught in the run below Beecher Falls. Pocket water and deep corner pools alternate with long, slow runs as the river winds through a beautiful valley of farms and woods. Some of the larger pools have silt bottoms.

Regulations allow fishing in the Connecticut River and its tributaries up to the first highway crossing from the first of January. Don't get too excited, though. It's pretty cold that time of year, although there can be a mild respite during a "January thaw". If conditions are right and you're sick of jigging for perch through the ice, a winter's day flyfishing on the Connecticut could be just what the doctor ordered. You'll have to run your fly slowly and deeply through the pools. Try Woolly Buggers and egg patterns such as the Thor, a known favorite of coldwater brown trout.

Spring comes late in northeast Vermont. It is well into the month of May when water levels recede from spring runoff. If spring has been particularly warm, there may be some early dry-flyfishing on the upper Connecticut during an afternoon hatch of small black caddis or Hendricksons. For the most part though, early fishing is limited to casting sinking or sink-tip lines with streamers and Woolly Buggers.

June brings warm, sunny days and clouds of caddisflies. Beadhead nymph patterns, Deep Sparkle Pupae, and emergers are effective. During the heat of the day, look carefully for fish sipping midges in the fast water at the head of pools and in the scum lines of back eddies. A tiny, size 18 or 20, Peacock Herl-and-Partridge Soft Hackle will work on even the most finicky trout.

When most other waters are too warm or low to fish well, Connecticut's trout are usually willing. July and August are a great time to float the river between Canaan and Colebrook. Several take-out alternatives on the New Hampshire side can be chosen from along the way, since flow and the fishing will determine how far you float in a day. I sometimes paddle my kayak upstream from a put-in location and then float back to my car. The Cabins at Lopstick (www.cabinsatlopstick.com) offers excellent guided trips on the Connecticut River, even if you don't stay with them.

The water stays cool enough so the fish stay active even on warm summer days. When the sun is on the water, the most productive float-trip tactic is to cast Woolly Buggers on sink-tip lines with a trailer fly such as a caddis pupa or Pheasant Tail. Hook-ups in the deep runs are usually

Brook trout, rainbows, and brown trout thrive in the Upper Connecticut, often growing to trophy proportions.

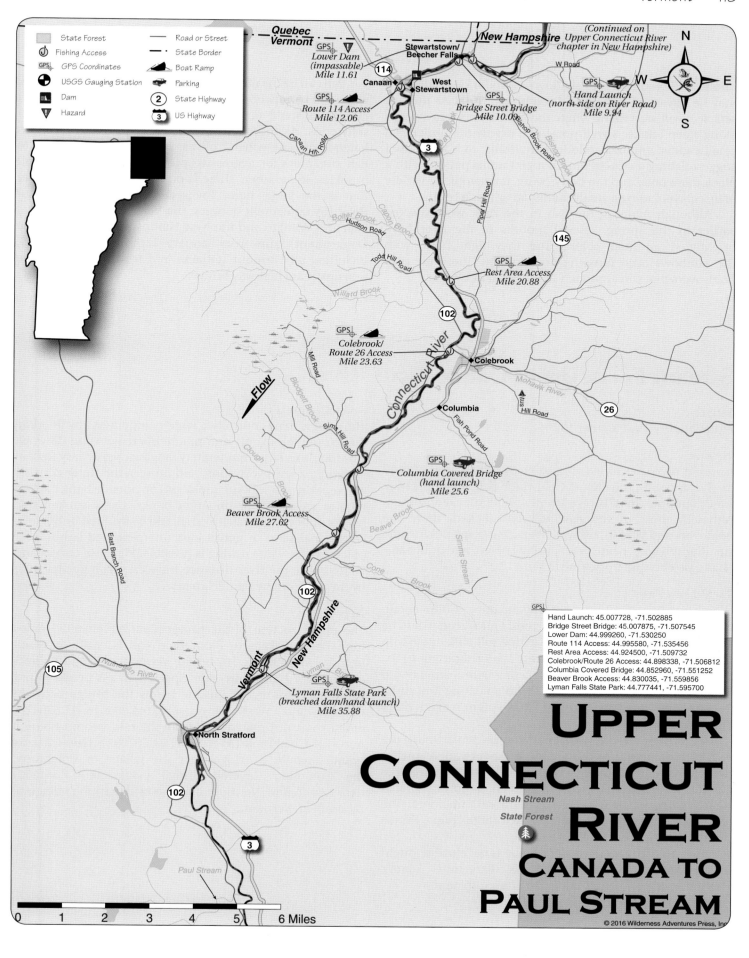

State Forest
Fishing Access
GPS Coordinates
USGS Gauging Station
Dam
Hazard

Road or Street
State Border
Boat Ramp
Parking
State Highway
US Highway

Quebec
Vermont
New Hampshire

(Continued on
Upper Connecticut River
chapter in New Hampshire)

Stewartstown/
Beecher Falls

Lower Dam
(impassable)
Mile 11.61

114

Canaan

West
Stewartstown

Hand Launch
(north side on River Road)
Mile 9.94

Route 114 Access
Mile 12.06

Bridge Street Bridge
Mile 10.09

3

145

Rest Area Access
Mile 20.88

102

Colebrook/
Route 26 Access
Mile 23.63

Connecticut River

Colebrook

Mohawk River

Flow

Columbia

26

Columbia Covered Bridge
(hand launch)
Mile 25.6

Beaver Brook Access
Mile 27.62

102

Vermont
New Hampshire

105

Hand Launch: 45.007728, -71.502885
Bridge Street Bridge: 45.007875, -71.507545
Lower Dam: 44.999260, -71.530250
Route 114 Access: 44.995580, -71.535456
Rest Area Access: 44.924500, -71.509732
Colebrook/Route 26 Access: 44.898338, -71.506812
Columbia Covered Bridge: 44.852960, -71.551252
Beaver Brook Access: 44.830035, -71.559856
Lyman Falls State Park: 44.777441, -71.595700

Lyman Falls State Park
(breached dam/hand launch)
Mile 35.88

North Stratford

102

3

UPPER
CONNECTICUT
RIVER
CANADA TO
PAUL STREAM

Nash Stream

State Forest

Paul Stream

0   1   2   3   4   5   6 Miles

© 2016 Wilderness Adventures Press, Inc

rainbows. If you cast into shadows or under deadfalls, you may be rewarded by a good-sized brown trout. As the sun sets, fish will start rising where the primary current sweeps along steep banks. A well-presented dry fly that imitates a small caddis, ant, or beetle usually results in a hook-up. I suggest fishing a size-16 Puterbaugh Caddis pattern with a black-foam body and tan down-wing. It resembles a variety of insects including a small caddis, an ant, or a beetle.

Although many of the fish in the river were stocked earlier in the spring, several months in the river have brightened up their colors, and they fight hard, with the rainbows even jumping occasionally. There are also hold-overs that can approach 18 inches, if not larger.

Fall can be the nicest time to fish the upper Connecticut, when the hardwood leaves are changing color. Golden tamaracks stand out against the evergreens in groves of softwoods. As the river cools, a warm sun will bring on hatches of blue-winged olives. It is also a good time to fish streamers for aggressive pre-spawn brown trout and brookies. Remember: There is no such thing as a streamer that is too large, here. The season on the Connecticut River (by agreement between the Vermont Department of Fish and Wildlife and the New Hampshire Fish and Game Department) runs from January 1 through October 15, including all Vermont setbacks and tributaries up to the first upstream highway bridge.

Stream Facts: Upper Connecticut River

Season
From January 1 to October 15.

Species
It would be easier to list what species of fish aren't found in the upper Connecticut! Coldwater fish include brook trout, rainbow trout, brown trout, and landlocked salmon. Although most of the fish will be stocked, there are holdovers and wild fish as well. Warmwater species include smallmouth bass, white perch, yellow perch, and bullheads. Shad also show up from time to time.

Tackle and Flies
Whether you are floating or wading the upper Connecticut, it is most efficient to carry two fly rods. One fly rod would be a 9- or 9.5-foot 5-weight, rigged with a full-sink or sink-tip line, or sinking leader with a short leader tapering to 3x. Fish this rod when you are prospecting with a streamer. If working to rising fish, a 4-weight with a floating line and a 9-foot leader tapering to 5x will allow you to make a more delicate presentation.

If no rising fish are visible and you are prospecting, the best combination is to fish a large streamer with a smaller nymph or wet fly tied on the bend of the streamer hook as a trailer. The guides utilize brown, green, or gray conehead Woolly Buggers, or Soft-Hackle Marabou streamers. The trailer pattern can be a green or brown caddis pupa, Prince Nymph, or a soft-hackled wet fly.

For rising fish, match the hatch. Generic "close-enough" flies including Puterbaugh Caddis, Parachute Adams, Hornberg, and Elk-Hair Caddis are often sufficient.

River Characteristics
The river is dam-controlled, which moderates any flooding due to rainfall events and maintains reasonable flows all summer. This large, moderately flowing river is easy to float with only a few tricky spots and most of the water consists of deep runs, slow bend pools, and an outside bank current next to steep dirt or undercut banks. Large sunken tree trunks offer cover for fish and should be avoided by boaters. Occasional sand or gravel bars or rip-rapped banks offer places where wade fishing is possible. Plenty of curves and bends make the river distance traveled much greater than by traveling on the parallel roads.

Access
The upper section of the Connecticut stretches 35 miles from Beecher Falls to Bloomfield and is easily accessed from Vermont Route 102 on the Vermont side and Route 3 on the New Hampshire side. Specific access points to put in trailered watercraft include below the bridge between Canaan and West Stewartson (44.995616,-71.535416) and a short dirt road across from the rest area on Route 3 north of Colebrook (44.922607,-71.507092). Other access points include a bridge near the village of Colebrook, the Columbia Covered Bridge (44.852960,-71.551252) near Lemington, Vermont and the bridge in the village of Bloomfield, Vermont.

Tributaries of the Upper Connecticut River

The Nulhegan River and its tannin-stained branches – the North, Yellow, Black, and East Branches – drain a huge area of bogs and woods in the extreme northeast corner of Vermont. This is paper company land where hundreds of miles of logging roads zigzag through the woods and over the streams, providing access. Moose, white-tailed deer, black bear, ruffed grouse, and spruce grouse range freely in this remote wilderness. Brook trout, both wild and stocked, populate the headwaters and upper reaches of the Nulhegan's tributaries. Resident brown trout can be found in the lower river, sometimes augmented from seasonal migrants from the Connecticut River.

The mainstem of the Nulhegan is 15 miles long and parallels VT 105 about two miles east of the village of Island Pond to the village of Bloomfield. The upper reach of the Nulhegan, like its tributaries, runs flat and deep with overhanging banks. It passes through a gorge near the junction of the Black Branch and continues as mixed pocket water, runs, and pools to the mouth. Wild trout are present but become increasingly rare in this river system as one heads downstream. The result has been the initiation of a more aggressive stocking program by the state fish and wildlife department.

Paul Stream joins the Connecticut River about 6.5 miles south of the village of Bloomfield. It is primarily a brook trout stream, draining a large area near Ferdinand Bog northwest of Maidstone Lake. Paul Stream is noteworthy in that, in addition to brook trout and browns in the lower reaches, it hosts a small run of rainbow trout from the Connecticut River. Access to Paul Stream is along the Maidstone Lake dirt access road that runs parallel to the river toward Maidstone State Park.

The southernmost tributary of the upper Connecticut River is the Passumpsic River. The West and East Branches begin in the high, northeast ridges and bogs above the city of St. Johnsbury and join to form the mainstem of the Passumpsic a few miles north of the village of Lyndonville. The upper reaches run cool and clear and offer good habitat for wild brook trout and browns. Access to the East Branch is from VT 114 between Lyndonville and the village of Island Pond. The West Branch runs parallel to US 5. One excellent stretch of the West Branch is best accessed from the Hayden Crossing Bridge (44.628783,-71.966504) off of Burke Hollow Road or US 5 (the bridge itself is closed to traffic). The West Branch here flows through fields and wetlands and contains abundant brookies and browns of all sizes. Try nymphing the larger plunge or deeper bend pools with a Pheasant Tail nymph or Copper John. Casting is not required; "dangling" is more effective. The Passumpsic River passes underneath several classic Vermont covered bridges near Lyndonville, making for good photo opportunities.

Water temperatures in the lower Passumpsic, downstream of Lyndonville, run uncomfortably warm in the summer. But you will find some pockets of cold water that hold trout near tributaries.

The Moose River is a 25-mile long tributary of the Passumpsic. It rises high in the mountains near the town of East Haven and, with several feeder streams, flows into Victory Bog, which is primarily public land owned by the state. The upper river section and bog area is abundant with wildlife. The waters are deep and dark from the rich forests and soils that surround the river. Moose River supports both wild and stocked brook trout and, as you proceed downstream below the town of Victory, brown trout share the stream. Access to Moose River, where it passes through the Victory Basin Wildlife Management Area north of US 2, is best gained by canoe at a parking lot (44.527901, -71.816594). Don't forget to bring your bug dope.

Farther downstream along Victory (sometimes referred to as River) Road, the Moose River becomes rockier and easy to wade, with good access from the road or from the bridge where the road crosses the river before it reaches US 2 (44.527901, -71.816594).

The covered bridge on the Passumpsic River (44.553721, -71.969459) upstream from Lyndon, Vermont.

CLYDE RIVER

When anglers throughout New England head up to northern Vermont to fish in the spring and the fall, most head for the Clyde River in the hope of hooking up with a trophy landlocked salmon, or perhaps a large rainbow heading upstream from Lake Memphremagog. The lower river is the historic spawning waters of the Memphremagog strain of landlocked salmon.

Since the 1930s, anglers from near and far came to the lakeside city of Newport to match wits with the salmon that enter the mouth of the Clyde, chasing smelt in the spring and making their spawning beds in the fall. Tales of tackle breakers weighing in excess of 12 pounds were not uncommon. In season, the hotels and inns were full and the riverbanks would be lined with anglers. Large steelhead, brown trout, and walleye were also caught. In 1957, dams built for generating electric power dealt the salmon runs an almost fatal blow by destroying most of the available spawning areas. Efforts to stock salmon met with limited success through the years that followed, and another glorious chapter of fishing history almost ended.

There were some older anglers, such as Warren "Jersey" Drown, who remembered the bygone days and told the young ones, David and Francis Smith, Gary Ward, Richard Nelson, and other passionate anglers, of the legendary salmon runs. These champions, who became known as the "Heroes of the Clyde", joined forces with Trout Unlimited and went up against the power companies and even against some of their fellow Vermonters who had been tempted by greed and power. The struggle was long and costly. At last, on May 1, 1994, just two days after the combined voices of the state of Vermont, Trout Unlimited, and the U.S. Fish and Wildlife Service called for the removal of the dam, an act of God (a flood caused by heavy rain), broke the Newport #11 Dam and set the Clyde River free. Today, efforts continue to improve the river with plans to restore the old river channel.

The river is once again offering good landlocked fishing, especially in the fall. While a few old-timers reminisce about the 90s when they claim the fish were bigger and more plentiful (including walleyes up to eight pounds), don't think for a second that there aren't good-sized salmon to be caught. The last time I was there, I watched a salmon of at least six pounds rolling on the surface as he sipped tiny mayflies from the surface, and fish three pounds or better are common.

The entire Clyde River is 34 miles in length, flowing north from the outflow of Island Pond to Lake Memphremagog.

The lower Clyde, from the mouth to the Great Bay Hydro Dam below Clyde Pond, is a couple miles in length and is a suburban setting with small houses lining the access roads. Take Route 191 from I-91 in Newport. At the first stoplight, take a right on Western Avenue. You will see the bridge over the river. Take Clyde Street before the bridge and you will immediately see a dirt parking area on your left. This road provides good river access as does the Clyde Street bridge and frequent pull-offs. You can also park at the dam and fish downstream, although fishing is prohibited right below the dam itself. The lowest stretch of water, upstream from the Western Avenue bridge is a long, slow run and fish can be difficult to fool. Farther upstream, the water consists of two deep pools (Halfmoon and Pumphouse) separated by shallower runs. As you continue farther upstream to the dam, the gradient increases and most of the fishing is in smaller pools and pocket water. A wading staff is helpful as the walking is more difficult as you navigate the rocks. All of the water fishes well, but certain stretches fish better at different water flows. It pays to move around to find active fish.

Many anglers chuck streamers, but there are a fair number of nymphers as well, and in the slower water I have watched really nice salmon sip blue-winged olives from the surface in October. Obviously, in the spring when the salmon are chasing smelt and other baitfish, standard smelt imitations would be my first choice. In the spring when rainbows are spawning, egg patterns can also be effective. From October 1 to October 31, angling is restricted to artificial lures and flies only, and all landlocked salmon must be immediately released. The Clyde River's season is the second Saturday in April (below the Clyde Street Bridge) or May 11 (above the bridge) through October 31.

The upper Clyde also offers anglers many pleasant opportunities. It begins as a brook trout stream moving lazily through marshes and alder-crowned channels from its source, the outflow of Island Pond. The upper reaches, between the villages of Island Pond and East Charleston, support wild and stocked brown trout as well as brookies. The river runs slowly, removed from roadways by swamps and marshlands. It is fished easily from a canoe.

The river follows VT 105 on its journey north. Seymour Lake and Echo Lake offer their cold, out-flowing water to the Clyde near the village of East Charleston. The river's gradient increases near the mouth of the outflow of Echo Lake and picks up speed, forming pocket water and more riffles and pools. Much of this stretch of river holds rainbow trout and some landlocked salmon, especially in the run from the dam that forms Charleston Pond to Salem Lake. Below the lake, the waters warm up and you'll find smallmouth bass moving in from Clyde Pond.

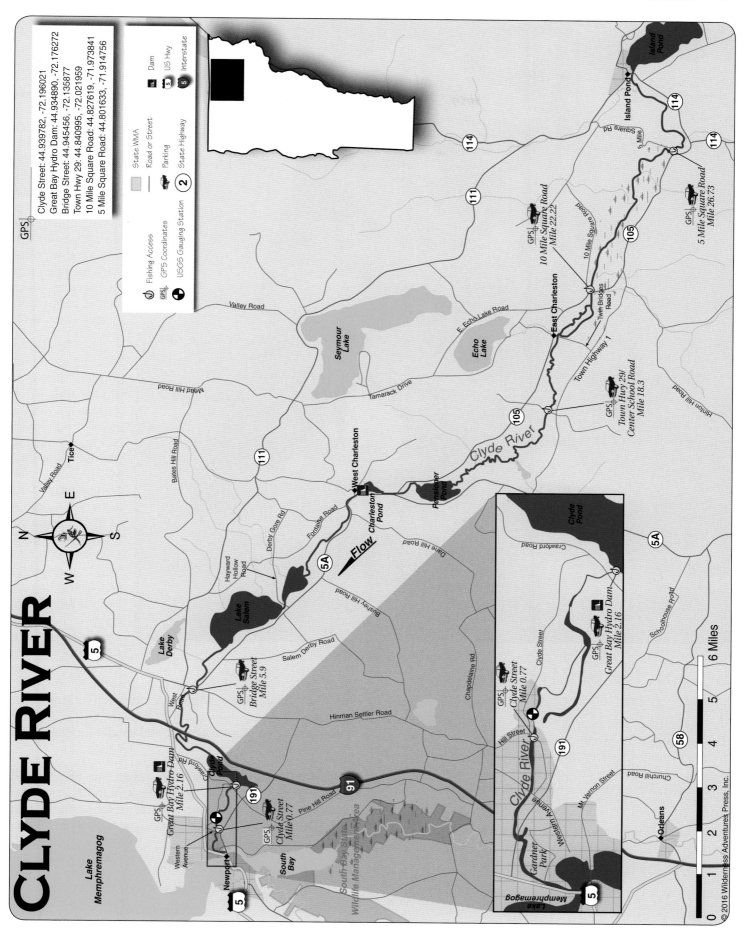

CLYDE RIVER

Lake Memphremagog

GPS
Clyde Street: 44.939782, -72.19021
Great Bay Hydro Dam: 44.934890, -72.176272
Bridge Street: 44.945456, -72.135877
Town Hwy 29: 44.840995, -72.021959
10 Mile Square Road: 44.827619, -71.973841
5 Mile Square Road: 44.801633, -71.914756

Fishing Access
GPS GPS Coordinates
USGS Gauging Station

State WMA
Road or Street
Parking
State Highway

Dam
US Hwy
Interstate

Great Bay Hydro Dam Mile 2.16

GPS Clyde Street Mile 0.77

Newport

South Bay

South Bay State Wildlife Management Area

Western Avenue

Crawford Rd

Clyde Pond

Lake Derby

Lake Salem

West Barnet

GPS Bridge Street Mile 5.9

Salem Derby Road

Hinman Settler Road

Pine Hill Road

Hayward Hollow Road

Bushey Hill Road

Derby Gore Rd

Fontaine Road

Flow

Charleston Pond

West Charleston

Pensioner Pond

Dane Hill Road

Clyde River

Valley Road

Bates Hill Road

Mead Hill Road

Seymour Lake

Tamarack Drive

Echo Lake

E. Echo Lake Road

Tice

Valley Road

East Charleston

10 Mile Square Road

GPS 10 Mile Square Road Mile 22.22

Twin Bridges Road

Town Highway 1

GPS Town Hwy 29/ Center School Road Mile 18.3

Hinton Hill Road

5 Mile Square Road

GPS 5 Mile Square Road Mile 26.73

5 Mile Square Rd

Island Pond

Crawford Road

Clyde Pond

Schoolhouse Road

Chapdelaine Rd

Hill Street

Mt Vernon Street

Western Avenue

Gardner Park

Clyde River

Lake Memphremagog

Great Bay Hydro Dam Mile 2.16

GPS Clyde Street Mile 0.77

Churchill Road

Oceans

0 1 2 3 4 5 6 Miles

© 2016 Wilderness Adventures Press, Inc.

A nice-sized lower Clyde River landlocked salmon caught in mid-October. Photo courtesy David Moore.

Stream Facts: Clyde River

Season

The Clyde River's season is the second Saturday in April (below the Clyde Street Bridge) or May 11 (above the bridge) through October 31. From October 1 to October 31, angling is restricted to artificial lures and flies only, and all landlocked salmon must be immediately released.

Species

Landlocked salmon and rainbow trout in the spring. Salmon in the fall. Rainbows can be up to four pounds, landlocked salmon will be three to six pounds.

Flows

The river is dam-controlled, which moderates the flows somewhat. Fishing is best when a rain raises the river flow and stimulates the fish to move into the river from the lake. Try to time your fishing trip for several days after a major rain event.

Tackle and Flies

The large and powerful fish that run up this river require a little more rod than you might usually wield. Nine-foot 6-weight or 7-weight rods with leaders tapering to 3x are required or you will break off some good fish. In the spring, fish feed on smelt and rainbow-trout eggs, so smelt-imitating streamers and egg patterns are the way to go. In the fall, try streamers such as the Black Ghost, Gray Ghost, and Mickey Finn, nymphs such as stoneflies, Hare's Ears, Copper Johns, and if you see fish rising, try small wet flies, Parachute Adams, and small Muddlers.

Access

Almost the entire lower river is wadable or easy to fish from the bank. Clyde River Road offers pull-offs at regular intervals between the Western Avenue bridge and the Great Bay Hydro Dam. The lower Clyde is a five-minute drive from Exit 27 on Interstate 91.

Barton River

Barton River is a 22-mile long trout stream flowing north from the marshes above the village of Glover to its mouth in Lake Memphremagog's South Bay, near the city of Newport. The headwaters and small feeder streams upriver (south) from Glover hold wild and hatchery brook trout. The water is cold and crystal clear. There are healthy, reproducing populations of rainbow and brown trout in the reach of river from Glover to the village of Orleans. One good access point is an official Vermont Fisheries access parking lot on VT 16 north of Glover (look for the sign). Although the waters below Orleans are generally too warm to support resident trout, this stretch of river is a passageway for spawning Memphremagog rainbows in the spring and brown trout in the fall.

The flow of the river is relatively slow as it rises, but soon quickens into lovely pocket water. There is good cover on the banks, and water temperatures in the upper reaches stay cool. Downstream, the runs begin to stretch out and pools deepen. The Barton runs slower and warmer from the mouth of the Willoughby to South Bay. Marked and unmarked river access areas are found along US 5 and VT 16. The Barton is an excellent river, but it is overshadowed by its major tributary, the Willoughby River – one of Vermont's best-known and loved streams. The season for the Barton is the second Saturday in April through October 31. Please note postings on streambanks.

Willoughby River

While the Clyde River has its "heroes", Willoughby River has its "guardians". Each year on opening day of trout season, no matter what the weather, you'll see them standing shoulder to shoulder on riverbanks and in the cold water, casting for migratory rainbow trout. For decades, fish and anglers have both stacked up below the falls in Orleans. The anglers are waiting for the fish, and fish are waiting for that inevitable rise in water that will allow them access to the upstream spawning grounds. Each year the fish return. In some years, the rainbows are plentiful and in other years, "it's not as good as it was in the good ol' days". Not that it matters. Each year, before first light on opening day, the "Guardians of the Willoughby" will take their positions on the river.

The rainbow trout that return from Lake Memphremagog to the Willoughby River are big, strong fish averaging two to four pounds. They enter the river in early April, with the run peaking the first or second week of May. Post-spawn fish return downstream throughout the month of June. This is one of the best opportunities to fish the Willoughby with a fly. Rainbows are hungry after they've completed spawning and greedily chase nymphs and minnows on their way back to the lake. Dead-drifting a streamer through the abundant pocket water can produce a bone-jarring strike and subsequent loss of all control as a two- or three-pound wild rainbow lets loose its full power.

A young angler tries his luck in the Barton River from the Vermont Fisheries Access on Route 16.

Access to the Willoughby below the falls in Orleans is straightforward. From I-91, take the Orleans exit and proceed through the town on VT 58. Take a left on East Road and cross a bridge over the river. There's a parking lot just across the bridge (44.812478,-72.193682) with a sign signifying the Germain A. Choiniere Willoughby River Access Area, and stairs that lead to well-worn trails to the river.

Seasoned anglers on the Willoughby know that a full complement of sophisticated flyfishing gear is not the measure of success when it comes to catching spawning rainbows. All you really need is a 5- or 6-weight Shakespeare Wonder Rod, to which is hung a Pflueger Medalist loaded with monofilament. Terminal tackle consists of a three-way swivel from which some split shot dangles and a leader section of 2-pound test. The fly of choice for many is Spring's Wiggler, a Michigan steelhead pattern, or any of a variety of egg patterns. One rule of thumb is that the clearer and lower the water, the smaller the egg pattern should be. With higher or slightly off-color water, fish an egg pattern with a bit more sparkle to it.

There is a local pattern called the Willoughby Seducer. But if you don't want to use underseat foam from the cushion of a Chevy pickup, McFly Foam in the McCheese color is an excellent substitute.

Rainbow trout stack up each spring below these falls outside of Orleans.

Above the falls, the Willoughby flows down from its source, the outflow of one of the most beautiful lakes in the world, Lake Willoughby. Vermont Route 58 follows the river all the way to Orleans. Alders shade the upper reach. There are long, protected shallow runs over a fine gravel bottom, providing excellent spawning area. The mid-river section is a mix of pocket water and corner pools. Below the hills in Orleans, the river slows down and joins the Barton.

There are pull-offs along Route 58 giving access to the river. One needs to be aware of river sections that are posted during spawning times. In addition to rainbows, the Willoughby has a strong population of brook trout in its upper reaches.

The season for the Willoughby River is the second Saturday in April through October 31. Fishing is closed from the second Saturday in April to June 1 on the Willoughby from Whetstone in Evansville downstream to the mouth of Brownington Branch and the stretch between the Orleans/Brownington Road bridge to the top of the natural falls. Please note postings on streambanks.

Black River

Contributing to the beauty and richness of Vermont's Northeast Kingdom is that beautiful trout stream, the Black River. It slowly flows out of the hills and bogs, surrounding the secluded village of Craftsbury Commons. As beautiful as it may be in its gracefully meandering headwaters, the Black begins as only a marginal brook trout stream. Logging near the upper river section has had a negative effect on water quality, and high water temperatures are common in the summer. As the river continues along VT 14 through the villages of Albany and Irasburg, the water quality improves and so does the fishing. The stream runs cool and is broken up with long stretches of pocket water and many deep, corner pools. This is good habitat for the wild and hatchery brown trout and brookies that call this section of river home. I have seen some photos of impossibly large brook trout from locals who have explored this river and know where to go.

Rainbow trout begin to show up in the Black River downstream from the mouth of Lords Creek, near Irasburg. Lake-run rainbows in the spring and brown trout in the fall enter the lower Black from Lake Memphremagog. The Black has excellent spawning habitat, and you'll find lovely, little wild rainbows in the river near the village of Coventry; plus you might happen upon large resident adult brown trout.

Stoneflies and caddisflies are the dominant aquatic insects in the Black River. There is access to quality water along VT 14 and in Irasburg off Old Dump Road. In Coventry, the stretch of river below the falls, near the site of the old covered bridge, and then farther downstream, fishes well. Be careful, the trail down to the falls is steep.

The Black River's season runs from the second Saturday in April through October 31; check regulations for specific spring river section closures.

Waterfall on the Black River in Coventry.

STILLWATERS OF NORTHERN VERMONT

Lake Champlain

Trolling flies for trout and landlocked salmon in coldwater lakes and ponds is a grand flyfishing tradition in the Northeast. There are still a few who "pull" flies with wire or lead coreline. Many troll flies behind metal dodgers and flashers, using downriggers to reach feeding fish at various water depths. In the spring and fall, changing water temperatures attract baitfish in bays, coves, shallow shoreline areas, and at river mouths. It is not uncommon to see flocks of frantic gulls, diving and picking up injured smelt driven to the surface by salmon feeding in a frenzy. A streamer, trolled or cast under feeding gulls, can often result in that anticipated interaction between you and a bright, landlocked salmon: a tightening of your line followed by a tightening of all your muscles, climaxed by the fish's silver leap.

Lake Champlain has become a main attraction for local and visiting anglers seeking early- and late-season lake trout and landlocked salmon flyfishing opportunities. As a bonus, there are football-sized brown trout, out-of-control steelhead, and an array of warmwater species that will take your fly. The U.S. Fish and Wildlife Service, along with agencies from New York, Vermont, and the Province of Quebec, continue to work cooperatively to maintain and improve Lake Champlain's water quality. The positive impact of a salmon and lake trout restoration program that began over 30 years ago and the success of the program to control the sea lamprey infestation in Lake Champlain, has resulted in a coldwater fishery that keeps getting better and better.

Lake Champlain is one of the gems of the Northeast. Many people have lobbied for it to be classified as our nation's sixth Great Lake. Yet it is very much a great lake. Lake Champlain is 136 miles long and surrounded by mountains: the Green Mountains of Vermont to the east and New York State's Adirondack Mountains to the west. Its jagged shoreline forms almost two-thirds of Vermont's western border and the northeast border of New York. Actually, the official boundary between New York and Vermont is a line that divides the lake essentially in half. In the north near the lake's outflow (the Richelieu River in Quebec), Lake Champlain is bejeweled by the Champlain Islands. Causeways and bridges along US 2 connect these islands, once home to very productive dairy farms. The body of water between these islands and the mainland of Vermont is known as the Inland Sea. Continuing south toward the city of Burlington, one finds Malletts Bay and Shelburne Bay at the lake's widest point. From here, Lake Champlain begins to narrow as you continue toward the village of Charlotte, where there is a ferry crossing. There are two more ferries that join Vermont and New York, one at Burlington and the other to Plattsburg, New York, from

A Lake Champlain bowfin landed by Brian Cadoret from his Jack Big Rig kayak. Photo courtesy Brian Cadoret.

the Champlain Islands. In addition, there is a highway bridge spanning the lake at the village of Port Henry, New York. Many convenient Vermont Department of Fish and Wildlife access areas as well as Perkins Pier in Burlington are available, with limited services, as early or late in the season as ice permits.

Trolling for trout and salmon in early spring and late fall is not only rewarding because of the fish you'll catch, but for the undisturbed beauty that Lake Champlain offers at those times of year. Techniques and flies vary. To have the most fun trolling, use an 8.5-foot 8-weight fiberglass fly rod, a Pflueger Medalist reel (they don't freeze up in subzero temperatures) and sinking line. The Cortland Line Company makes a 50-foot, level, 8-weight, sinking line just for this type of fishing. L.L. Beans offers fly rods, reels, and leaders specifically for trolling. The leader need not be tapered; a 10- or 12-foot length of your favorite 8-pound test mono will do nicely. There are dozens of trolling streamer patterns that imitate Lake Champlain's resident smelt and shiners. Excellent books for patterns are Joseph Bates Jr.'s *Streamers and Bucktails*, Stewart & Leeman's *Trolling Flies for Trout and Salmon*, Donald A Wilson's *Smelt Fly Patterns*, and Mike Martinek's little volume *Streamers: Fly Patterns for Trolling and Casting*.

There is some shore fishing for landlocks, particularly in the spring. Popular areas include the causeways and bridges on Route 2 through the Champlain Islands. A current builds in these channels, and salmon will chase baitfish and their fly imitations.

Coldwater species are not the only draw when it comes to flyfishing in Lake Champlain. There are largemouth and smallmouth bass, northern pike, and an abundance of panfish. In spring, when water temperatures approach the mid-50s, northerns will cruise in the shallows and in the weeds near shore. An angler with a fly can wade and stalk this magnificent game fish, as one would fish the flats of some island paradise. The area near Sandbar State Park off Route 2 as you cross into the Champlain Islands is easily accessible by canoe or boat. There are rental boats available at Apple Tree Bay Resort. Also try wading the shoreline area of Maquam Shore and Missisquoi Bay near the village of Swanton for both bass and pike.

If you are interested in trying something truly unique, try flyfishing for bowfin and longnose gar – prehistoric fish that live in the lake and reach impressive sizes. These fish live in choked, weedy backwaters and require specialized flyfishing techniques. For example, a hook cannot penetrate the bony, teeth-filled mouth of a gar, so a gar "fly" is a short length of frayed nylon boat rope that literally gets tangled in the gar's teeth when they strike. I suggest hiring a guide that specializes in this type of fishing. You can find them on the web along with videos that show what such fishing is all about (www.streamandbrook.com).

Lake Champlain is open to fishing all year. Please check the Vermont fishing regulations for all of general fishing rules and guidelines.

Northern Vermont's Inland Lakes

There are 11 major inland lakes in northern Vermont that offer first-rate fishing for trout and landlocked salmon. Trolling streamers and bucktails is the most popular method of angling in these cold, deep bodies of water. However, the early summer emergence of the large mayflies, *Hexagenia limbata* (referred to as the Hex), in the shallows of several of these lakes brings on a frenzy of feeding fish and provides some excellent fly-casting opportunities.

Lake Memphremagog

Vermont and Canada share Lake Memphremagog, the largest of Vermont's inland lakes. The lake supports rainbow trout, brown trout, and brookies, as well as lake trout and landlocked salmon. Fish have uninhibited access to spawning areas in the lake's tributaries: the Clyde, Johns, Barton/Willoughby, and Black Rivers, where seasonal runs

Lake Memphremagog.

of trout and salmon are legendary. There is some concern that the lake is beginning to suffer the eutrophication effects of agricultural runoff due to the continued use of liquid manure by some of the farmers along the its tributaries. Hopefully, the ecology will stabilize and not put this outstanding fishery at risk.

The city of Newport, off I-91, is the lake's port city and offers access and a full array of services to the visiting angler.

Lake Willoughby

The village of Westmore on US 5A is situated on the eastern shore of Lake Willoughby. It is a beautiful alpine lake, and its blue waters fill a long, narrow crack between the Green Mountains. Cliffs that are the backdrop to soaring ravens and peregrine falcons plunge into the lake's western side to a water depth in excess of 300 feet. These cold, deep waters are home to some of the largest and oldest lake trout in the Northeast. In addition, Lake Willoughby supports impressive rainbow and brown trout. Just stop into any local gas station or country store and look at the photos on the walls or tables.

Lake Seymour

Vermont Route 111, near the village of Morgan, runs along the north and east shorelines of Lake Seymour. For years, Lake Seymour was the destination for anglers from all over New England seeking lake trout, especially during the ice-fishing season. Lake Seymour also supports brook trout, brown trout, and landlocked salmon. Trolling smelt patterns in spring, soon after ice-out, can be very productive. In early July, the large mayfly hatches and fish will return to the shallows. There is a State Department of Fish and Wildlife access near the beach area in the village of Morgan Center.

Echo Lake

Echo Lake is a small lake connected to Lake Seymour by an out-flowing stream. Echo supports brook trout and rainbows as well as lake trout and landlocked salmon. Access is near the village of East Charleston off VT 105. Anglers tend to fish Echo, Willoughby, or Seymour based on the species they are targeting – one lake fishes better one year for one salmonid species and then the next year it changes. In 2015, Echo Lake yielded large and plentiful lake trout. Local anglers troll green or chartruese streamers as a first choice, but look for rising fish when the lakes are calm then switch to casting rods.

Crystal Lake

Crystal Lake is located south of the village of Barton near US 5. This is another of northern Vermont's great lake trout fisheries. Each year anglers land lakers weighing in excess of 16 pounds.

Shadow Lake

Off Route 16, about three miles south of the village of Glover, is Shadow Lake. Dropping off to a water depth of almost 140 feet, Shadow's cold waters support brook trout, browns, and lake trout.

MAIN IMAGE: Lake Seymour.
UPPER LEFT: Lake Willoughby's southern shore.

ABOVE: The boat launch at Echo Lake off of West Echo Lake Road.
RIGHT: Local favorite lake-trout trolling streamers.

Caspian Lake

North of the village of Hardwick, off Route 16 near the village of Greensboro, is Caspian Lake. The lake's shoreline slopes down from surrounding meadows and is lined with old family cottages and camps. Caspian supports both lake trout and rainbows that are particularly vulnerable to the fly during both ice-out and during the Hex hatch of early summer.

Great Averill Lake

Great Averill Lake lies in the northeast corner of Vermont, less than two miles from the Canadian border. It is a small, deep lake offering lake trout and landlocked salmon. In close proximity are two ponds worth mentioning: Little Averill Lake – a rainbow and lake trout pond – and Forest Lake, which supports browns. All three lakes have good access near the village of Averill.

Island Pond and Spectacle Pond

Island Pond and its close neighbor, Spectacle Pond, are located off VT 105 in the village of Island Pond. Brighten State Park, a very convenient camping and recreation area, provides access to both lakes. Island Pond holds large brown trout (the state record came from Island Pond several years ago), rainbows, and brook trout. Spectacle is primarily a brown trout pond.

Maidstone Lake

Maidstone Lake occupies the westernmost ridge before Vermont slips into the Connecticut River Valley. It is a deep-water lake, supporting both lake trout and rainbows. A good entry point and a very nice campground can be found at Maidstone State Park, a short distance from VT 102, south of the village of Bloomfield.

Waterbury Reservoir

Waterbury Reservoir is an impoundment formed by a dam on the Little River, a major tributary of the Winooski River (see Little River description earlier in this section). Since the reservoir was drained in 1985, the Vermont Department of Fish and Wildlife has stocked the reservoir with brown trout and rainbows. The smallmouth bass fishing in Waterbury Reservoir is excellent and an added bonus. The nearby Little River State Park is a convenient and excellent campground. Waterbury Reservoir is easily accessible from Interstate 89 at Exit 10 near the village of Waterbury, only 26 miles from Burlington.

Ponds of Northern Vermont

Northern Vermont is blessed with an abundance of small lakes and ponds. Some are near highways with well-maintained boat ramps, while others are miles back, reached only by traveling over abandoned logging roads or foot trails. The Vermont Fish and Wildlife Department manages the majority of ponds as coldwater fisheries with regular stockings of brown trout, rainbows, brook trout, lake trout, and landlocked salmon. In addition, there are several warmwater ponds in northern Vermont that offer anglers an opportunity to catch large and smallmouth bass, pickerel, or northern pike on a fly. Whatever your choice, northern Vermont has many ponds that offer flyfishing opportunities.

Shelburne Pond

Shelburne Pond, Colchester Pond, and Indian Brook Reservoir are three ponds within a short drive from Burlington. Shelburne Pond lies to the south, off US 7, about three miles from the village of Shelburne. It is a warmwater fishery, supporting large and smallmouth bass, walleye, and northern pike. Shelburne Pond suffers the eutrophication effects of agricultural runoff and warm summertime temperatures. During some years, weeds choke the water, resulting in fish mortality. It is however, a lovely pond. The banks are a combination of marsh and woodlands, perfect habitat for waterfowl and wild turkeys. The Vermont Department of Fish and Wildlife's efforts to reclaim and restock the pond have had positive results, and the fishery has been coming back.

Colchester Pond

Colchester Pond, north of Burlington near the village of Colchester, is managed for the public as a natural area by the Winooski Valley Park District. It is an excellent warmwater fishery with bass and some larger northern pike. There is parking and a canoe access and, for anglers using float tubes, a trail that follows much of the shoreline.

Indian Brook Reservoir

Indian Brook Reservoir is about two miles off VT 15 near the village of Essex Center. It is managed by the town of Essex, which charges a modest use fee in the summer. The pond is a mixed warm and coldwater fishery, supporting bass, panfish, and stocked brown trout and rainbows. There is parking and a convenient canoe launch. All power watercraft are prohibited.

Sterling Pond

High above the Lamoille River Valley and the ski slopes of the resort town of Stowe is beautiful Sterling Pond. This is Vermont's highest elevation trout pond and is accessible by foot from the Long Trail. There is a parking area (44.539574,-72.791251) where Route 108 passes through Smuggler's Notch between the village of Jeffersonville and Stowe. Sterling Pond is about an hour's hike north, up the well-maintained trail. It is a brook trout pond and receives annual stockings by the State Department of Fish and Wildlife. Flyfishing along the shore is best from the shallow areas on the west and south sides. A float tube gives an angler good access to the entire pond. There is a full-service campsite nearby at Smugglers Notch State Park, and primitive camping is available at the pond.

Green River Reservoir

Green River Reservoir is a recent addition to Vermont's state park program. This impoundment of the Green River, a tributary of the Lamoille, is about six miles from VT 15, northeast of the village of Morrisville. It is a warmwater fishery supporting bass, pan fish, pickerel, and northern pike. Canoe rentals are available in Morrisville and Stowe.

Zach Woods Pond

Zack Woods Pond is one of several small trout ponds near the Green River Reservoir. It is accessible from Garfield Road outside the village of Morrisville on VT 15. Do not try to access from the east on Zack Woods Road because it is a Jeep trail only (as I found out and had to back up a quarter mile – not fun). Zack Woods is a deep pond supporting stocked and some very nice holdover brook trout. Insect hatches are generally infrequent. However, fishing streamers and small wet flies soon after ice-out can be productive.

Lake Elmore

Anglers can put a small boat in Lake Elmore at several locations including Elmore State Park (a short carry from Beach Road or the parking lot) and even from where Elmore Brook flows out on VT 12 (44.541305,-72.524362). Lake Elmore receives regular stockings of brook trout.

The author fishing for Long Pond's brookies.

Long Pond

Long Pond is a deep, coldwater pond that supports brook trout as well as a remnant population of lake trout. There is a trailered boat access on Long Pond Road (44.756342,-72.020152), six miles from its intersection with VT 5A, near the village of Westmore on Lake Willoughby. This sheltered small pond can also be fished by kayak or even float tube, although the best fishing is at the far end of the pond from the road. The outlet stream that gurgles along the road (Mill Brook) has plenty of small wild brook trout.

Newark Pond, Bald Hill Pond, and Jobs Pond

To the east are Newark Pond, Bald Hill Pond, and Jobs Pond. All have convenient boat access areas and receive annual stockings of brook trout.

Lewis Pond

East of the village of Island Pond on VT 105, there is a railroad crossing known as Wenlock Crossing. The dirt road immediately on the north side of this crossing is Lewis Pond Road (44.776416,-71.748697), one of several maintained logging roads that crisscross this remote area of Vermont's Northeast Kingdom. Lewis Pond is in about 20 miles, so check your gas gauge before you leave. There actually is a boat access. It is a lovely brook trout pond in an area rich with wildlife. Chances are good that you'll see a moose before your day's fishing is done.

South American Pond

South American Pond is reached by foot on a trail that begins on the logging road (named South American Pond Road on Google Maps) south of Wenlock Crossing. It is a coldwater pond and supports brook trout. As with so many brook trout ponds, the fishing is at its best when the bugs are at their worst.

Holland Pond

Holland Pond is only a few miles from the Canadian border north of the village of Morgan near Seymour Lake. It supports brook trout as well as rainbow trout.

May Pond, Bean Pond, Vail Pond, Marl Pond, and Duck Pond

There are several beautiful trout ponds in the hills that separate Lake Willoughby and Crystal Lake near the village of Barton. May Pond, which offers good brook trout fishing, is easily accessible from May Pond Road that bears south from VT 16 north of Barton. There is a good boat launch, and you'll no doubt see May Pond's resident pair of loons during your visit. South of Barton and Crystal Lake, right on US 5, is Bean Pond. For the adventurous, nearby are three ponds – Vail, Marl, and Duck – that can only be reached by foot trails off unimproved logging roads. Vail Pond receives annual stockings of rainbow trout, while the others support brook trout.

Marshfield Dam

Marshfield Dam, whose outflow makes up some of the headwaters of the Winooski River, is located on US 2, east of the village of Marshfield. This is a mixed cold and warmwater fishery, supporting bass as well as brown trout. The view of Camel's Hump to the west, clear across the state, is dramatic, as is the undeveloped shoreline.

Peacham Pond

A road that parallels the reservoir's eastern shore will take you to Peacham Pond. This deepwater pond supports brown trout. Try trolling a "Nine-three" tied with a pale blue feather. There is a well-maintained boat launch and public access.

Groton State Forest Ponds

Groton State Forest, which lies about 20 miles east of the Barre/Montpelier area, holds several additional other good flyfishing ponds. This rich wildlife area offers several campgrounds, miles of trails, and access to some of the finest stillwater fishing in Vermont. The south entrance to Groton State Forest is off VT 302 east of Barre, near its junction with the south end of VT 232. From the north, follow US 2 east from Montpelier to where Route 232 joins, about two miles from the village of Marshfield.

As you enter Groton State Forest from the north, Osmore Pond is located adjacent to the New Discovery State Park and Campground. It is a brook trout pond, best fished from a canoe or float tube. The parking area for the short foot trail to Kettle Pond is about two miles farther down Route 232. It is a mixed warm and coldwater pond, supporting smallmouth bass in the shallower east end and rainbows in the deeper sections.

Both Groton Lake and Ricker Pond are warmwater fisheries supporting bass and panfish. Each offers excellent camping facilities and access to other state forest areas.

Martins and Levi Ponds are best reached from the east, from the village of Peacham. Both ponds receive annual stockings of brook trout. Martins Pond has a boat and public access off Green Bay Road, west of Peacham. Levi Pond can be reached by foot on an old logging road south of Martins Pond.

Noyes Pond is perhaps the most well-known brook trout pond in north-central Vermont. It is located just 20 miles east of Barre on the southern edge of Groton State Forest. The detailed write up for this pond is in the central Vermont stillwater section.

Northern Vermont Planning Considerations

Nearby Hub Cities and Towns

- Burlington (www.vermont.org, www.flyrodshop.com)
- Montpelier (http://www.montpelier-vt.org/)
- Island Pond (www.islandpondchamber.org, www.islandpond.com/fishhuntsupply/)
- Newport (www.vtnorthcountry.org)
- St. Johnsbury (www.nekchamber.com)

Easy Access Options

- The Clyde River has excellent access from the parking area by the Western Avenue bridge (44.939753,-72.196042). A very short walk over level ground and mowed grass brings you to the river. I believe this could be managed in a wheelchair. You can walk along the bank and fish without wading for 100 yards on a level grassy field. In the spring and fall, the fishing can be darn good there as well.

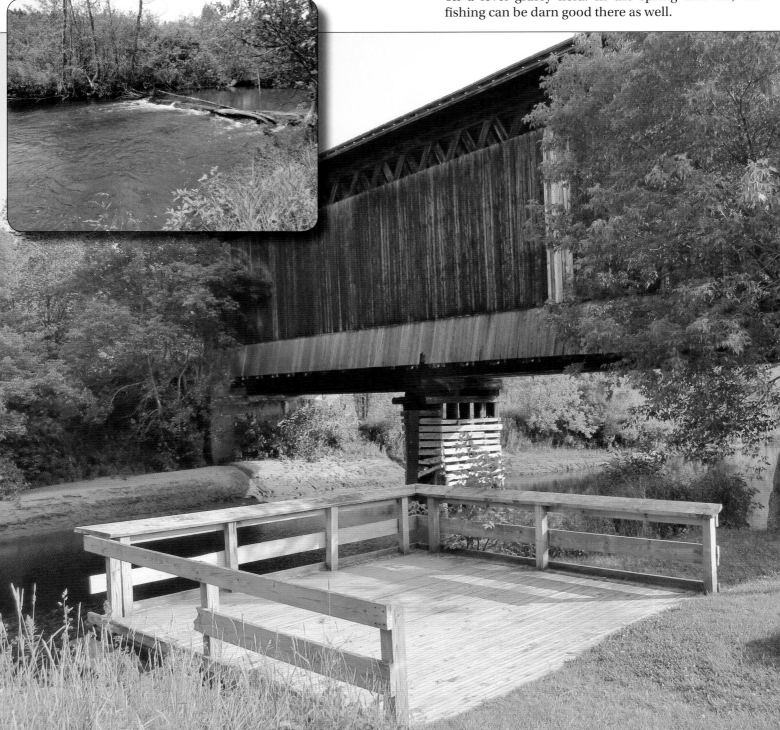

- The Germain A. Choiniere Willoughby River Access Area is a convenient way to access the river. If you can navigate some shallow metal stairs next to the bridge and a short sandy trail that leads to the river, then you will be able to take your place along other anglers trying for those nice spring rainbows. Park in the parking area across East Street (44.812478,-72.193682).
- The Lamoille River between Hartwick and Wolcott features a small park by the Fisher Covered Railroad Bridge. There is a handicapped accessible casting platform on the edge of the parking lot (44.532506,-72.427675) where one can make a short cast into a deep run that should hold fish, at least for parts of the year.

Suggested Beginner Options

- Hire a guide and float the Connecticut River. Your guide will manipulate the boat such that even modest casting ability will suffice to put your fly in front of fish. This is not technical fishing and you will have a reasonable chance of success, particularly with the lessons that you will receive along the way. Lopstick Cabins has excellent guides.
- Fish the Moose River during June anywhere along the River Road between US 2 and the Victory Bog Management Area. Choose a section visible from the road where the water flows amongst numerous rocks and boulders that create a mixture of pockets, runs, and small pools. Tie on a small Muddler, Hornberg, or Elk Hair Caddis and with short casts, travel up or downstream, trying each little pocket. Don't spend too much time fishing one small pool. Keep moving.
- Try dangling a nymph in the West Branch of the Passumpsic River. The West Branch is best accessed from the Hayden Crossing Bridge (44.628783,-71.966504) in Burke. Walk downstream from the bridge along the bank and dangle a nymph in any deeper pool, pocket, or bend and just wait to feel a grab from a waiting brook or brown trout.

MAIN IMAGE: The Lamoille River casting platform by the old covered railroad bridge. UPPER LEFT: The West Branch of the Passumpsic River. The author hooked six trout on six casts standing on the grassy bank.

Vacation Suggestions

Weekend Getaway

- Pick a weekend in mid-October and fish the lower Clyde River for landlocked salmon. Fishing is best after a rain event raises the flow, so if you can stay flexible and time your trip for after a rain, you will increase your odds. During this time of year in northern Vermont, foliage can still be colorful and the temperature is still reasonable. Newport is the closest place to stay, but St. Johnsbury is only 45 minutes away and is a very interesting town with a number of good restaurants and a natural history museum/ planetarium that will provide a non-fishing companion with hours of enjoyment.

One-week Vacation

- If you enjoy and are experienced with small watercraft – be it a drift boat, kayak, or canoe – spend a week in late June or early July in the Northeast Kingdom of Vermont and float different sections of the Connecticut River. It will take several days and you will want to repeat your favorite stretch of water. Since the river changes from year to year, ask local guides for the latest information about flows, access points, and any hazards. They usually don't hesitate to assist.
- Another option is to hire a guide for the first day to float one river section and ask a lot of questions so you can venture out yourself later in the week. You will also want to take a day or two and wade any of the Connecticut tributaries mentioned in this section.
- Derby and Newport offer a variety of lodging and restaurant options as well as other recreational alternatives, and are about an hour from the Connecticut River. There are other more rural lodging options in the small towns of Island Pond and North Stratford, which are on or near the river.
- Take a week in June or early July; stay in Stowe, Waterbury, or Montpelier; and explore the Winooski or Lamoille River systems. Options include quaint hotels, bed-and-breakfasts, and private residences through Airbnb.com. There are miles and miles of good trout water and you will have a good chance at catching both wild and stocked browns, rainbows, or brook trout. Best of all, you will most likely have the water to yourself. The only catch is that these watersheds are easily affected by either hot or rainy weather. It is best if one has some flexibility to move dates around while water conditions are monitored, particularly flow rates. But not everybody has that option.

The Granite State offers many opportunities for fly anglers.

You can fish for coastal striped bass on New Hampshire's southeast coast or stocked trout just inland in southern waters. In the far north, near the border of the Province of Quebec, Canada you'll find the hard-fighting landlocked salmon of the Connecticut Lakes Region. And in the state's center – the White Mountains – native brook trout swim in cool, crystal clear streams.

The New Hampshire Fish and Game Department manages a comprehensive fish stocking program in the streams, lakes, and ponds of the state. Large numbers of brook trout, brown trout, rainbows, and landlocked salmon, raised in the state's several fish hatcheries, are planted each year. As a result, several rivers have flyfishing-only sections, and the state manages 31 flyfishing-only ponds.

The New Hampshire trout and bass fishing season generally runs from January 1 through October 15. Designated Wild Trout Streams are open January 1 to Labor Day; designated Trout Ponds are open from the fourth Saturday in April to October 15; and Designated Wild Trout Ponds are open from the fourth Saturday in April through

Fish on at Perry Stream.
Photo courtesy of the Cabins at Lopstick.

Labor Day. Lake trout and/or salmon waters are open from January 1 to September 30.

The fishing season for landlocked salmon is from April 1 to September 30, except on Pleasant Lake near New London where it doesn't open until the fourth Saturday in April. Nonresident fishing licenses are available for one-day, three-day, or seven-day periods, as well as for the full season.

New Hampshire generally supports the right of anglers to fish, wade, boat, or portage any navigable river or stream as long as they stay below the high-water mark. Property owners have the right to manage their land as they see fit down to the low-water mark but cannot impede the ability of the angler or boater to move through. Any angler that can reach the water through a public access point or with the permission of one landowner can then fish the entire water, if they stay below the high-water mark.

New Hampshire's residents welcome visitors to share their state's beauty and recreational activities. Hospitality services are available in the major cities and towns, and there are full-service fly shops conveniently located throughout the state.

Southeastern/Coastal New Hampshire

COASTAL STRIPED BASS FLYFISHING

The New Hampshire coast offers excellent striper fishing. Of course like all striper fishing, the action depends on season, weather, tides, time of day, and shore and underwater structure. Some years the spring striper migration brings large number of fish, other years, not so much. The size of the stripers also varies year to year with schoolies (12- to 21-inch specimens) often dominating the catch, but large cow stripers (30- to 45-pounders) showing up at other times.

Most years, the stripers arrive sometime in mid-May and the fishing can be consistently good all the way into mid-July. If it is a warm summer, the fishing can slow down during August (except at night), and then will pick up again as the nights cool in September. Southward migrating stripers can keep the action hot until the first major cold spell in early November drops the water temperature and the stripers depart for warmer climes.

Anglers can choose the type of striper angling that they prefer among the following options:

- Wading out from the beaches and spey casting into wave troughs, cross currents, and around sand bars.
- Working the rocky shorelines, jetties, and other shoreline structures that stripers haunt during outgoing and incoming tides in order to trap disoriented baitfish, either on foot or by boat.
- With a larger boat, fishing the major river and offshore currents when diving birds, surfacing stripers, or boats with bent rods, show that predatory fish are on the prowl.
- Stalking stripers in the backwater estuaries and cuts from kayaks, paddleboards, and small boats. If you time it right, you can drift from the smaller channels out toward the ocean on an outgoing tide, have lunch or dinner during low tide, and wait for the tide to turn to drift back.

Certainly your odds increase by fishing at first light, last light, or at night. It's not just because stripers prefer low-light conditions. Fishing early or late in the day

An excited angler introduces a large striper to the camera. Photo courtesy of Sean Smith.

eliminates most recreational boating traffic, jet skis, swimmers, and the general commotion that spooks stripers and creates potential casting headaches. I once almost yanked a woman's swimsuit top off on a backcast, but that is a story for another time.

Fishing the oceanside after dark offers other rewards. I've seen anglers fish until dark and then leave. That's when the good fishing is just getting started.

New Hampshire sea-coast nights are often cooler than inland summer days and generally are more pleasant to fish. Stripers also seem less wary after nightfall, and haunt the shoreline to feed on baitfish, the occasional green crab, and small lobster.

The nighttime striper angler finds that the senses of hearing, smell, touch, and even taste are enhanced and enlivened to the point of creating a nighttime angling addiction. There are worse ways to spend a summer evening.

To prepare for a night of saltwater fishing along the coast, check the weather report for the threat of approaching storm fronts and the times of tidal exchanges. Though traditional surfcasting notions suggest fishing the first hour before high tide through the first hour after a flood tide, you can also do the opposite. The bottom of the tide, particularly the dead low, holds fish as well.

Flyfishing the nighttime surf involves assorted challenges. A good sense of the tidal exchange is necessary. Watch the shifting tide and fish only as long as you feel safe. Nights often require moving from one spot to another along the coast.

The after-dark surf can be dangerous. Rocky outcroppings are tough to negotiate. Crawling is as important as walking in some spots. Take your time and move slowly along with a small flashlight in hand or in mouth. Avoid shining the light directly into the water. It could spook fish. Set up on areas that have been scouted out previously, if possible.

Fly Tackle for Stripers

- Sheltered tidewaters can be fished with a 9-foot, 8-weight fly rod. An 8-weight line can handle small sand-eel patterns, and the light rod reduces the physical discomfort from repeated casts. Should the wind pick up, however, you may need a stouter rig.
- A 9- or 9.5-foot, 9-weight fly rod is a good bet for most beach casting and fishing in and around rocky outcroppings. Line weights can be increased for larger patterns and for fighting stiff breezes. Boat anglers may choose a 10- or 11-weight rod. Daytime stripers often hold in deeper water and feed on big

bait. A heavier rod will handle deep sinking lines and large flies.
- Basic striper reels should hold 200 yards of 20-pound test Dacron backing. Fly line choices include floating saltwater taper, intermediate sinking lines, and high-density sinktip lines. You want at least one spool with high-density sinking line that will drop your offering to the bottom despite heavy currents. In general, fishing near the bottom increases your odds of a hookup.
- Leaders can be easily tied while watching TV weather reports for the evening coastal conditions. Some fly anglers prefer intricate leaders and blood knot three sections of 40-, 30-, and 20-pound test. Others tie on a straight 8-foot section of 20-pound test monofilament. Both leader styles work.
- Traditional flies, such as Deceivers and Clouser Minnows, are proven offerings and work well. Chartreuse and white or gray and white color combinations in several different sizes will be adequate for most situations. Also try sand eel and crab patterns.

Regulations

New Hampshire's striper season is open year round. An angler may keep one fish per day, minimum size 28 inches (as of May 2015). Regulations change, so please refer to the current New Hampshire Fish and Game regulations for the most updated information.

Recommended Spots

Hampton River Estuary Access
US 1A follows the New Hampshire coastline from the Massachusetts border north to the city of Portsmouth. The highway spans the mouth of the Hampton River near the entrance to Hampton Beach State Park. From here, anglers have access to a jetty, the back portion of the estuary, and the beach itself. Fishing is not allowed from the bridge. There is a public boat launch on the north side of the bridge, and parking is available along the beach during the night and early mornings. Hampton Beach is a popular destination and highway traffic can be heavy.

Obviously, casting from the beach itself best be a very early morning or late evening proposition. Try wading out from the sandy shore along the banks of the Hampton River as it enters the ocean. The drop-off is gradual, wading is easy, current moderate, and stripers moving in and out are very reachable.

Casting for stripers at the Hampton River Estuary in the shadow of the Seabrook Nuclear Power Plant. Photo Courtesy Sean Smith.

If you are interested in a more secluded, back-to-nature experience, consider launching an ocean kayak deep into the estuary and paddling around, while moving farther in and out, driven by the tide. If you haven't tried this before, go with an experienced partner.

One good launch point is to take Depot Road from US 1 in Hampton Falls to its dead end (42.911690,-70.851727) – a good small boat launch will give you access to the "backwaters" of the estuary. If you launch on an outgoing tide, follow the tide out into the larger parts of the estuary, take a break during low tide, and then follow the rising tide back. Have a GPS (and know how to use it) and pay attention to landmarks, so you can get back to your launch point. If you get lost, no one may be around to help. Be careful, do not get stuck in the extreme shallow cuts during low tide. It is too mucky to walk out; you will have to wait until the tide returns to free the boat. If you don't have a boat, an angler can walk the railroad tracks from the end of Depot Road and reach some fishable water (walk the dirt road paralleling the tracks). Cast to deeper holes, or to the banks where there is flowing water and some evidence of bait fish or stripers slamming their prey.

Great Bay Access

Great Bay, west of the city of Portsmouth, is a large estuary formed by four rivers: the Oyster, Bellamy, Lamprey, and Piscataqua. A public fishing area is managed by the state of New Hampshire at the mouth of the bay at the General Sullivan Bridge off Routes US 4 and NH 16, north of Interstate 95 in Portsmouth. Tidal rips are extremely strong at the bridge, where the waters of Little Bay and the Piscataqua River mix. Fishing is best at slack tide. Just north of the I-95 bridge, across from the power plant against the Maine shoreline is a deep slot that frequently holds large fish. It is worth drifting through a few times with fast-sinking line.

In Portsmouth, several islands offer shoreline fishing for stripers when tidal currents sweep along their shorelines. From US 1B, try Goat, Shapleigh, Peirce, and Pine Tree Islands. You have to walk to Pine Tree Island from Peirce Island over a short causeway (no vehicles allowed), but there is a nice picnic area with all of the amenities and excellent shoreline rocks and other structure that hold stripers (43.076528,-70.747915).

Another option is Odiorne State Park, where a short walk or bicycle on a dirt road brings you to a massive rock jetty that extends 100 yards into Little Bay. Striper fishing can be good along its entire length but be cognizant of the tides and weather conditions. Getting washed off a jetty can ruin an otherwise good fishing day. Find the park off of US 1A across from Berry Brook bridge (43.048638,-70.727422)

One convenient place to put in a trailered boat is the boat launch on Peirce (yes, that is the way it is spelled) Island (43.074584,-70.747783). Find Peirce Island Road off of US 1B. Sometimes there are stripers right by the bridge, or you can go under the bridge and access the entire area. Cruise around and look for active birds or other anglers. The boat launch is also the home base for Rising Tide Anglers (www.risingtideanglers.com) if you prefer a guided trip.

Yet another rock jetty can be fished at Rye Harbor State Park (43.001600, -70.745057) where, on a fair day, the Isles of Shoals can be spotted just off shore.

I am told that the best striper fishing in all of Portsmouth is from the Navy Base on the Maine shoreline where deep drop-offs attract huge stripers feeding on schooling baitfish. Of course, anglers cannot fish on the Navy Base or even by boat towards the immediate shoreline. Oh well.

For further information about coastal fishing in New Hampshire, check out the *Flyfisher's Guide to the New England Coast* by Tom Keer.

LAMPREY RIVER

The Lamprey flows for 43 miles between Deerfield and Newmarket, where it empties into the Great Bay. It offers decent riffle water and many deep pools. Springtime whitewater conditions are brief, with slow-moving flows developing by summer. The river is lined by wooded, sandy stream banks as it flows through suburban developments as well as lush, green farmland. Tidal waters flow downstream through mudflats from NH 108 to Great Bay.

The best trout fishing is in the upper sections. NH 107 offers good access to the upper river in Deerfield and northern Raymond. Look for unmarked pullouts and bridges when looking for places to fish.

The state stocks the river in the spring and it receives heavy fishing pressure from local anglers casting lures, lobbing bait, and drifting fly patterns, especially in April and May. Expect company on springtime weekends and early evenings. Flyfishers frequent these waters, despite the fact that freshly stocked Lamprey River trout for a time seem to ignore their midge and early black stonefly offerings – so much for matching hatches.

Trout fresh from holding tanks always seem to nail Woolly Buggers with abandon, and olive Woolly Buggers work best. Stick with nymphs as you test these waters, preferably with a spot of color to attract attention. Selections should include the Bitch Creek (size 4 to 8), Pheasant Tail (size 12 to 20), and pink or red San Juan Worms. After the trout have been in the water for a week or two, they acclimate and start chasing natural food choices and fly patterns should match.

Water temperatures on the Lamprey get pretty warm in the summer. This can be a good time to try popping bugs for bass. The spring trout don't survive well so don't hesitate to take a few home for dinner in the spring if you are so inclined.

Don't let my description dissuade you from fishing the Lamprey. It is a beautiful river to fish in the spring as the leaves pop and wildflowers bloom. And the rainbows are eager and fun to catch. But most importantly, the autumn fishing can be special. The Three Rivers Stocking Organization is a private non-profit organization group that stocks the Lamprey (and three other rivers) with large, high quality (12- to 24-inch rainbows, brookies, and browns) in October and November. Stocking takes place from Wiswall Dam to Packers Falls, and the fish quickly acclimate and provide rewarding fishing all fall, winter, and spring. This organization relies on voluntary cash contributions from anglers to fund their stocking. If you would like to contribute, go to their website at www.threeriversstocking.org.

I know anglers that have a tradition to fish the river on Thanksgiving, Christmas, and New Year's. The trout do survive well into the spring. In fact, in late May of 2015, I ran into a flycaster fishing below Wiswall Dam that had just landed an 18-inch holdover rainbow on a midge pupa.

To protect the fall fishery, the Lamprey is catch and release from October 16 to the fourth Saturday in April (single hook and artificials only). The Lamprey trout season is year round.

In the town of Raymond, look for highway foot-access points near New Hampshire Fish and Game stream-stocking areas along NH 27. The Lee and Newmarket sections can be floated by canoe or waded. Popular locations are found at Wadley Falls and Lee Hook Road in Lee, and downriver at Wiswall Dam and Packers Falls in Durham.

An intrepid angler lands a winter rainbow on the Lamprey River. Photo Courtesy Sean Smith.

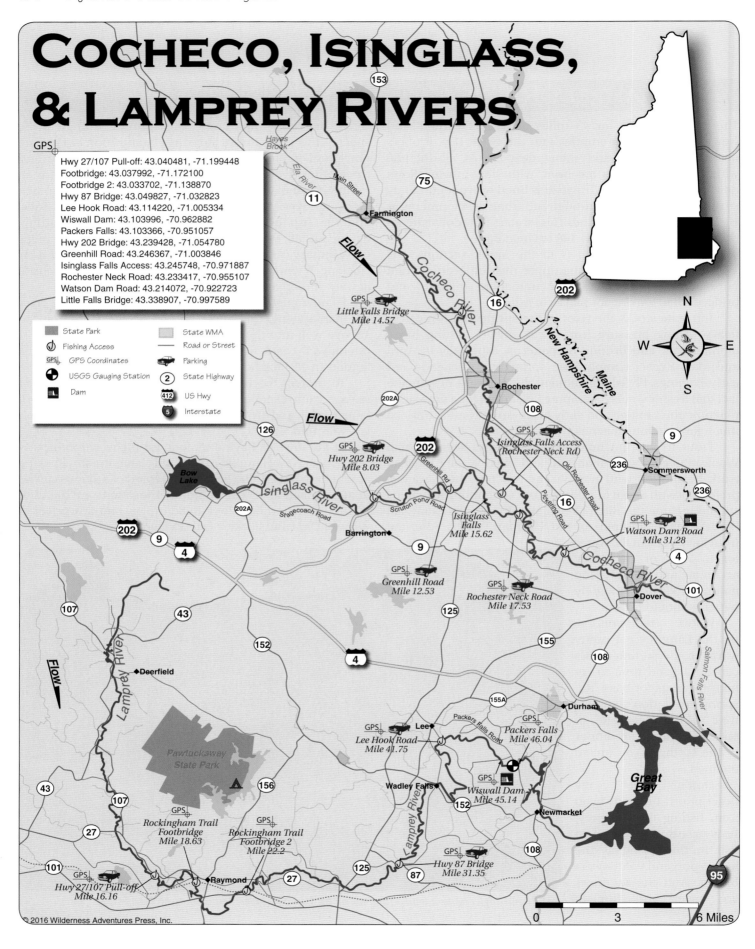

COCHECO, ISINGLASS, & LAMPREY RIVERS

Hwy 27/107 Pull-off: 43.040481, -71.199448
Footbridge: 43.037992, -71.172100
Footbridge 2: 43.033702, -71.138870
Hwy 87 Bridge: 43.049827, -71.032823
Lee Hook Road: 43.114220, -71.005334
Wiswall Dam: 43.103996, -70.962882
Packers Falls: 43.103366, -70.951057
Hwy 202 Bridge: 43.239428, -71.054780
Greenhill Road: 43.246367, -71.003846
Isinglass Falls Access: 43.245748, -70.971887
Rochester Neck Road: 43.233417, -70.955107
Watson Dam Road: 43.214072, -70.922723
Little Falls Bridge: 43.338907, -70.997589

State Park
Fishing Access
GPS GPS Coordinates
USGS Gauging Station
Dam

State WMA
Road or Street
Parking
2 State Highway
412 US Hwy
5 Interstate

Little Falls Bridge
Mile 14.57

Isinglass Falls Access
(Rochester Neck Rd)

Hwy 202 Bridge
Mile 8.03

Watson Dam Road
Mile 31.28

Isinglass
Falls
Mile 15.62

Greenhill Road
Mile 12.53

Rochester Neck Road
Mile 17.53

Hwy 27/107 Pull-off
Mile 16.16

Rockingham Trail
Footbridge
Mile 18.63

Rockingham Trail
Footbridge 2
Mile 22.2

Hwy 87 Bridge
Mile 31.35

Lee Hook Road
Mile 41.75

Packers Falls
Mile 46.04

Wiswall Dam
Mile 45.14

Farmington

Rochester

Sommersworth

Barrington

Dover

Deerfield

Pawtuckaway
State Park

Raymond

Lee

Wadley Falls

Durham

Newmarket

Great
Bay

Flow

Flow

Flow

Cocheco River
Isinglass River
Lamprey River
Salmon Falls River
Ela River
Hayes Brook
Bow Lake
New Hampshire
Maine

© 2016 Wilderness Adventures Press, Inc.

0   3   6 Miles

Wiswall Dam has a large parking lot (43.104702,-70.961335) off of Wiswall Road with good signage explaining the history of the location and obvious trails running along the river downstream. The area immediately below the dam is closed to fishing when the alewives are running and ascending the newly-built fish ladder.

Follow Wiswall Road downstream and then take a right on Packers Falls Road to find Packers Falls. Below Packers Falls is a very large pool where you will see trout rising, often just out of reach. Find Bennett Road for pool access (43.104827,-70.950899). A small canoe or kayak is a good solution to reaching those fish.

Isinglass River

Isinglass is another word for mica, the abundance of which makes rock at the Isinglass River sparkle. Running 14 miles from Strafford to Barrington, the Isinglass is made up of riffles, swift runs, and flatwater pools. Silt deposits line the bottom of deepwater pools, while slick rocks in runs will make you take your sweet time wading. Moderate springtime flows and April rains make wading difficult, but water levels drop quickly. This river falls to low levels by summer. Bow Lake in Strafford is the source of this coldwater fishery. From there, the Isinglass travels east to join the Cocheco River just south of Rochester.

Like the Lamprey River, warmer spring days see local and out-of-state flyfishers gravitating to the Isinglass River. This migration commences in late April after the stocking trucks have arrived. From late April through early June, the Isinglass offers some of the best trout fishing in this corner of the Granite State. Roadside pull-offs provide ample access. The river is regularly stocked with brookies, rainbows, and browns. The availability of specific species of trout at the various New Hampshire hatcheries determines the yearly stocking schedule. Most Isinglass River brook trout and rainbow trout come from the Powder Mill Hatchery in New Durham.

There are perhaps a few holdovers from year to year and a little natural reproduction, but not much.

The stocking program takes place during midweek, prior to the weekends. One sometimes gets the sense that phones ring all over Strafford County when stocking happens, as vehicles immediately arrive at the streams. Trout numbers are maintained at high counts through the Memorial Day weekend, making for several weeks of excellent flyfishing. Angling opportunities diminish as summer arrives and river water warms up.

The Three Rivers Stocking Organization also stocks this river at Isinglass Falls in mid-October, and the same regulations apply as they do on the Lamprey. It is catch and release from October 16 to the fourth Saturday in April (single hook and artificials only). The Isinglass trout season is year round.

Fish black stonefly nymphs (sizes 10 to 14) in April, but switch to black, olive, and tan Woolly Worms (sizes 8 to 12) if you strike out. Freshly planted trout seem to strike anything. Yellow, black, or olive Woolly Buggers (sizes 2 to 12) as well as white or black Marabou Muddlers (sizes 2 to 10) catch fish. Rainbows will take red or maroon San Juan Worms (sizes 8 to 12). As the fish settle down, Hornbergs fished deep can be effective.

My wife, Lindsey Rustad, fishing at the base of Isinglass Falls.

Ample roadside parking is available between the intersections of NH 126 and US 202 (43.242383,-71.082051) and downriver at the highway bridge near Scruton Pond Road. Park on the river side of the highway. This section is heavily stocked. Trout are also stocked in the river near Green Hill Road in Barrington. Fish downriver from Green Hill Road to NH 125.

One of my favorite sections to fish is Isinglass Falls (sometimes referred to as Lockes Mills Falls). To get there from NH 125, find Rochester Neck Road. After about a mile on the right, a parking lot provided by a local waste management company offers access to the trails in the Isinglass Recreational Area (43.245745,-70.971914). Most of the trails lead to the falls. The river from the pool at the base of the falls to around the next bend and on to the confluence of the Cocheco River is heavily shaded and features a series of riffles, pocket water, deep slots, and large pools where trout linger into the summer months, thanks to the oxygenation from the falls. Of course, the pool beneath the falls receives heavy fishing pressure, but that activity peeters out quickly as you walk downstream.

Cocheco River

The Cocheco River is accessible from NH 11 near the village of Farmington. The state stocks it with brook trout and browns in the spring, and the Three Rivers Stocking Association stocks it with its usual high quality, large trout in mid-October To protect these trout, the Cocheco has the same October to April regulations as the Lamprey and the Isinglass. The fish are stocked downstream of the Watson Road (Waldron) Dam (43.213675,-70.922186) and that portion of the stream is very popular with anglers because of its wooded banks and the numerous runs, pools, and pocket water that are fun to figure out and fish.

Recently stocked fish will respond to more flashy patterns before they settle down. A variety of food sources feed the trout and most anglers choose whatever type of fishing they prefer: nymphing, dry-fly fishing, wet-fly fishing, or casting small streamers. A good woody path parallels the river downstream from the dam on the south bank. Find Watson Road off of the Tolend Road from NH 9. Ela River and Hayes Brook are both tributaries of the Cocheco River and are regularly stocked with brook trout.

Berry Brook

A flyfishing experience is often measured by the difficulty of a particular quarry's acquisition, and sea-run brown trout certainly provide a challenge to flyfishers.

By October and November, most people turn their thoughts to wingshooting or deer hunting, and stash the fly rod away for the winter. Not everyone, though. When autumn arrives on the New Hampshire seacoast, ardent flyfishers, eager to continue angling beyond the trout days of summer, turn to the immediate coastline, specifically Berry Brook, just a short drive south of Portsmouth. Their quarry is the sea-run brown trout.

Historically, brown trout were stocked in Berry Brook, lived and fed in the estuary, and returned in late October and early November after rain events or strong flooding tides. Surviving fish were few, wary, and difficult to catch. In the 90s, studies showed it took over 30 hours of fishing on average to hook one fish. Because of the poor returns – most stocked brown trout probably became striper food – stocking is scheduled to stop in 2015. Still, if you are an angler looking for a little fishing activity in late autumn and who enjoys a challenge, perhaps you should give this fishery a try, at least for a few more years.

Fish the half-mile section from the wooden bridge on Route 1A to Brackett Road. Most anglers agree that the two hours before dead low tide and the two hours after the turn provide the best flyfishing opportunities. Others prefer the calm lull at full flood tide and some the dead low.

Fly selections here range from olive Woolly Buggers to the same sand-eel imitations that anglers toss at Granite State summertime stripers. Muddler Minnows, crab flies, a variety of streamers, and even traditional wet flies catch salters.

Two small, off-road parking spots are available at the Brackett Road bridge. Park at the gravel pull-off near the wooden Route 1A bridge, but leave room for small boat access to the water.

A holdover early-spring trout putting up quite a fight on the Cocheco near Watson Road's Waldron Dam.

Stream Facts: The Three Rivers Stocking Rivers
Isinglass, Cocheco, Lamprey and Exeter

River Distances
All of these rivers are close enough to be fished the same day, it takes perhaps up to one-half hour to travel from one to another.

Fish Species
Stocked brown trout, brook trout, and rainbow trout

Season
Special season: October 15 to fourth weekend in April, flyfishing only, barbless hooks, catch and release. Large rainbows are stocked in mid October.

River Characteristics
All these waters are best described as small rivers that can be cast across, and possess all water types including deep pools and impoundments, deep runs, riffles, small plunge pools, and pocket water.

Equipment
A standard 9-foot 5-weight rod will serve for most conditions. Those who nymph with tiny offerings might prefer a 10-foot nymphing rod. If fishing for the larger fish over the winter appeals to you, remember to dress warmly in layers, and use a wading staff. A dunking in the winter can range from inconvenient to dangerous.

Fly Patterns
Extremely varied, depending upon when the fish were stocked, the season, and any hatch activity. If fish seem fished over, try very small offerings, size 20 or smaller.

Exeter River
The Exeter River is a small river near the town of Exeter that is stocked in the spring by the state and may be further stocked in October starting in 2015 by the Three Rivers Stocking Association. Because this is a small stream, stocking is dependent on adequate water flow. One good stretch to fish runs from the Exeter Reservoir Dam on Cross Road to NH 111 (Kingston Road). Just take NH 111 west from Exeter and look for Cross Road after about four miles.

Almost all of the shoreline is private land but the local fishermen have done a good job of respecting the property and picking up litter, so most landowners support flyfishers fishing and patrolling their banks at the same time.

In this shallow stream, the trout will hold in any small pocket or run that offers slightly deeper water or cover.

EFT: An angler working a bankside un on the Exeter River.

IGHT: Woolly Buggers are favorites on e Exeter River.

Other Southeast New Hampshire Rivers and Streams

These rivers and streams, located in Strafford and Rockingham Counties, are stocked with trout on a regular basis. Most of these rivers are spate streams with the best angling in spring.

Salmon Falls River forms the border between the states of Maine and New Hampshire, flowing from Great East Lake into the Piscataqua River near Great Bay, north of Portsmouth. The stretch of river that runs along NH 125 between the villages of Milton and Rochester is regularly stocked with rainbows, brook trout, and browns. Branch River, a tributary of Salmon Falls River, flows through the village of Union. It receives regular stockings of brook trout and browns.

The Mad River, like its neighbor, the Cocheco River is accessible from NH 11 near the village of Farmington. The state stocks both streams with brook trout and browns. Ela River and Hayes Brook are both tributaries of the Cocheco River and are regularly stocked with brook trout.

Jones Brook is a small brook trout stream that runs out of the Jones Brook Wildlife Management Area east of the village of Union. There is an unimproved road off Kings Highway, a short distance from Middleton Corners that will get you to the brook.

Oyster River flows into Great Bay near Durham. It is stocked with browns, rainbows, and brookies. Little River flows out of Mendums Lake, located west of Durham off US 4. The state stocks brook trout in the stretch below the lake.

North River is another small brook trout stream in the town of Lee. It runs through the Nottingham State Forest along Route 152 near the village of Nottingham.

Bellamy River flows out of the Bellamy Reservoir and into Great Bay near the city of Dover. Access is available from NH 9. The state stocks the Bellamy with rainbow and brook trout.

STILLWATERS OF SOUTHEASTERN NEW HAMPSHIRE

The New Hampshire Fish and Wildlife Department manages a few southeastern stillwaters as flyfishing-only trout ponds. They are all located in Strafford County. Open season on flyfishing-only ponds runs from the fourth Saturday in April through October 15. The daily limit is five trout or five pounds, whichever limit is reached first.

Stonehouse Pond

This 14-acre pond receives moderate flyfishing pressure, with the heaviest coming on the New Hampshire trout pond opener, which is the fourth Saturday in April. And it's not just locals – some anglers come from quite a distance. A small boat or float tube allows an angler to cover more water than attempting to wade and cast through the shoreside tangles.

To reach Stonehouse Pond, take NH 9 and US 202 from Northwood for roughly three miles, then turn right at the sign for the pond. From the village of Barrington, drive out

This photo shows part of Bow Lake with its many islands and peninsulas.

of town until you reach the fork in the road at NH 126 and 9. Bear left on Route 9 and take this highway until you reach US 202. Turn left and proceed on Route 202 for about three miles. The sign for Stonehouse and the dirt (or muddy) road will be on your left (43.204904,-71.096659). Four-wheel drive is suggested, and it is often the only option.

Expect abundant brook trout numbers, with fish running from 9 to 11 inches in length.

Hoyt's Pond

Roughly an acre in size, Hoyt's is stocked with brook trout in April just before the Granite State trout-pond opener. Flyfishing remains steady through early June. After the weather warms, however, angling drops off dramatically.

Action-starved flyfishers gather at this fishery in the town of Madbury on opening day for the camaraderie as much as the angling. They swap stories and catch 9- to 10-inch hatchery brookies. Some first-timers might feel hemmed in by angler numbers. If so, it's probably best to stay away. Others, however, welcome the company, viewing Hoyt's Pond as a traditional stop during their day of trout angling in southeastern New Hampshire.

Catch and release isn't necessarily protocol. The daily limit is five fish or five pounds, whichever is reached first. Small nymphs retrieved slowly just off the muddy and stumpy bottom work best. Scuds are great.

Access is available from NH 108 between Durham and Dover. Drive north or south from either town, and then turn onto Freshet Road. Make an immediate left on the Hoyts Pond Road and look for the dirt road in the midst of the housing development. Fish and Game signs note the

location of the access area (43.160134,-70.899339). Parking is available at the end of the dirt road. From there, walk down the trail to the pond.

Barbadoes Pond

Barbadoes Pond, located in Madbury, is stocked with brook trout and rainbows and receives heavy pressure. Vehicles may park along Route 9 near the access trail. This 14-acre pond fishes best in April and May.

Bow Lake

Bow Lake (43.241644,-71.151705) has rainbows and browns, plus an assortment of warmwater game fish. It is located in the town of Strafford. This 1,160-acre pond often holds surprises — expect anything from four-pound rainbows to lunker smallmouth bass. Bow Lake is best fished before mid-June and after Labor Day. Because of its small size and numerous pennisulas and islands, it is always possible to find sheltered spots to fish out of the wind. Late September can be excellent for both largemouth bass and bronzebacks, especially on the rocky ledges near Bennett and Beech Islands. If you don't have access to a boat, the lake shore near the outlet dam can be easily fished by standing on the long granite retaining wall. There is plenty of room for a backcast, and the water is fairly deep. Trout and bass will take positions to intercept any food items being drawn by the current flowing through the dam outlet and can be fooled by a well presented meaty streamer with some articulation constructed of rabbit strips or marabou materials.

Bow Lake is the origin for the Isinglass River, and sometimes stocked trout will run up the river all the way to the bridge just below the dam. If the lake isn't producing, try walking down the river and trying your best small stream techniques.

Big Island Pond

Big Island Pond is a mixed warm and coldwater fishery. It is stocked with rainbows, browns, and brookies. This 510-acre pond is located west of Hampstead and has a campground on the northeast shore off NH 121. A boat access is located at Chase's Grove near NH 111 on the south shore.

Exeter Reservoir

Exeter Reservoir is the 20-acre impoundment of Dearborn Brook, located in the city of Exeter. It is stocked with rainbows and brook trout.

Lucas Pond

Lucas Pond is a 52-acre impoundment located off NH 43 south of the village of Northwood. It is stocked with brown trout, rainbows, brookies, and tiger trout.

South-central and Southwestern New Hampshire

Ashuelot River

Ashuelot River flows through both Cheshire and Sullivan Counties. Its source is Ashuelot Pond, a warmwater pond west of the village of Washington. It runs south, parallel to NH 10 and 12A, and through the city of Keene. Near the village of Winchester, the river swings west along NH 119 and joins the Connecticut River near the village of Hinsdale.

The river is stocked with rainbows and browns. Access is good at marked and unmarked roadside pull-off areas.

The South Branch of the Ashuelot River begins near the village of Troy and enters the mainstem south of Keene near the village of Swanzey. There is a flyfishing-only section on the South Branch between the Richmond Road Bridge in East Swanzey and the Marlborough Road Bridge in Troy from January 1 to October 15. There is a two-fish daily limit for brook trout.

Cold River

The Cold River begins north of the village of Acworth in Sullivan County. The river follows NH 123A and 123 through the villages of Alstead and Drewville and joins the Connecticut River in the village of Cold River in Cheshire County. The New Hampshire Fish and Game Department stocks the Cold River with brook trout, browns, and rainbows. In addition to the convenient access areas at highway pull-offs, there is a public canoe access on Route 123A near the village of South Acworth.

Contoocook River

The Contoocook River flows through both Merrimack and Hillsborough Counties. It begins north of the village of Peterborough, flows through the Powder Mill Pond impoundment near the village of Bennington, and on through the villages of Hillsborough and Henniker. The Contoocook eventually joins the Merrimack River north of Concord. There are dams at West Henniker and at the Hopkinton Flood Project near the village of West Hopkinton.

The state stocks the Contoocook River with brook trout, browns, and rainbows. Near the impoundments and in downstream sections there is good smallmouth bass fishing. The most consistent trout fishing is in the trophy section in West Henniker. This is a stretch that starts about one-half mile upstream from the mill dam in West Henniker and runs upstream about a mile that is restricted to flyfishing or the use of artificial, single-hooked lures only from January 1 to November 30. Brook trout need to be 12 inches in length, and the daily limit is two fish. This section and the access areas along Western Avenue are well marked.

Flyfishing stays productive longer in the fall in southern New Hampshire than more northern parts of New England. Photo courtesy Sean Smith.

Other fishing and canoe access areas are clearly marked along the highways that parallel the river.

Merrimack and Lower Pemigewasset Rivers

The Merrimack and Lower Pemigewasset Rivers create a single river system. The Pemigewasset has its beginnings near Franconia Notch in central New Hampshire. It flows south, parallel to US 3 and Interstate 93, through the villages of Lincoln and North Woodstock to Plymouth. A dam in the village of Bristol blocks the river's flow in the lower section downstream of Plymouth. From here, the Lower Pemigewasset enters a long flood plain within the Franklin Falls Dam Project. It merges with the Merrimack River at the dam north of the village of Franklin. From this point, the rivers continue south as one river, the Merrimack.

Since the elimination of the broodstock Atlantic salmon stocking program, this river system is no longer of great interest to flyfishers. Still, it is a fun river to canoe, kayak, or float, and by all means bring a fly rod along, cast to interesting spots, and see what you can catch. This river system holds largemouth and smallmouth bass, chain pickerel, yellow perch, bullhead, bluegill, carp, and an occasional trout that has migrated from its original stocking point in a tributary.

The Lower Pemigewasset River from Plymouth to Franklin is 28 miles; the Merrimack River from Franklin to Concord is 21 miles; from Concord to Manchester is 20 miles; and from Manchester to Nashua is 18.5 miles.

The river systems feature broad, flat-water sections with occasional drops, dams, and rapids running north to south through urban centers.

The Lower Pemigewasset has typical New England Class II-III rapids, with some portaging required. The Merrimack has slow-moving Class I-II rapids with some churning ledges and flow-restricting dams. Portaging by canoeists is necessary on some river sections. Merrimack anglers often fish by larger boat. The lower river from Manchester to Nashua can be fast moving early in the spring season. Use extreme caution when boating this section.

Access is available at the following:

- Eastman Falls Hydro Station, Franklin: By canoe, with parking for eight vehicles. Located off Route 3A. Owned by Public Service of New Hampshire.
- Winnipesaukee River, Franklin: Canoe access with public parking for five vehicles near Winnipesaukee River pumping station located off River Street.
- County Farm Access, Boscawen: Boat ramp available with public parking for 12 vehicles. Located off U.S. Route 3. Owned by the state, it provides access to the west side of the river.
- Sewalls Falls Multi-Use Recreation Area: North of the city of Concord and accessible from either Route 3 or I-93. A parking lot is located south of the main recreational facility at the end of 2nd Street after the Sewalls Falls Road turnoff from Route 3 on the west side of the river. This stretch of the Merrimack has a lot of good access. The current is relatively strong but the shoreline can be waded.
- New Hampshire Technical Institute Ramp, Concord: Boat ramp with parking for eight vehicles located off Fort Eddy Road. This is a state-owned access on the Merrimack's west side.
- Everett Arena Access, Concord: Boat ramp with parking for 12 or more vehicles. This east shore access off Loudon Road is city owned.
- Bow Steam Plant, Bow: Boat ramp with parking for about a dozen vehicles located off River Road. Owned and operated by Public Service of New Hampshire, it provides access to the river's west side.
- Lambert Park, Hooksett: Boat ramp available with ample parking for 30 or more vehicles located off Merrimack Street. This is a state-owned access on the river's eastern shore.
- Stark's Landing, Manchester: Boat ramp available with public parking. This city-owned access site is located off Granite Street on the river's east shore.
- Carthegina Island, Manchester: Eastern shore fishing off Riverdale Avenue, owned by the city.
- Bedford Riverfront Park: Canoe access and riverbank angling accessible from US 3, owned by the state and operated by the town.

Souhegan River

This waterway is the southernmost in the state, starting near the Massachusetts border and flowing north over 30 miles before its confluence with the Merrimack. Although it runs through populated areas, certain parts flow through very natural surroundings. The section from Greenfield to Wilton fishes best. It is stocked with the usual assortment of brook, brown, and rainbow trout. This freestone stream features a gravel bottom and several nice pools in the Greenfield area and then quickens its pace a bit and offers more riffles and runs as it moves towards Wilton. The river follows NH 31/101 for the most part, with obvious turn-offs and parking areas when the river moves closer to the road. The Interval Road also offers access. Some of the better spots are:

- "Shoreline Fishing" signage and parking (42.783472,-71.805274)
- Bridge access (42.791373,-71.795278)
- NH 31 new bridge parking lot and access by old bridge. Look for the angler paths on both sides of the river (42.834659,-71.750713).

SUGAR RIVER

The Sugar River flows west through wooded hills along NH 11 and 103 near the city of Claremont in Sullivan County, and good roadside access is available. The best fishing is around or upstream of Newport because the water stays cooler.

This river is heavily stocked with brown trout, rainbows, and brook trout. Some trout do hold over and grow to the 16-inch range or larger. The Sugar River's two major tributaries, the South Branch and the Croydon Branch (aka the North Branch, accessed from NH 10) are also stocked.

The section of river near the village of Kellyville, between the Kellyville Bridge and the Oak Street Bridge, is flyfishing only from January 1 to November 30, with a daily limit of two brook trout. This section is well marked and easily accessed by the Sugar River Rail Trail that closely follows the river. This trail is nine miles in length and features two covered bridges. One great way to fish this river is to bike along the trail with your fishing gear, and then stop and fish at promising locations.

The river is for the most part easily wadable in its upper reaches and anglers' paths follow the shoreline along difficult sections. The Sugar River contains a mixture of riffles and pocket water, as well as a few deeper runs and pools. Farther downstream along Chandler's Mills Road, the banks become very steep.

Local anglers drift stonefly nymphs early in the season because of the significant stonefly population in the river. Later on, popular nymphs include the standard Prince, Hare's Ear, Pheasant Tail, and Copper John. Caddis and stonefly imitations are the dry flies of choice, although the Sugar River has a good population of blue-winged olives. As summer approaches, ants, beetles, and other terrestrials become important options. Stocked trout, by that time, have become much more selective.

As with many southern New Hampshire rivers, the waters warm in the summer. Look for cooler tribs entering the river, deeper holes and runs, or fish early or late in the day. Mid-May to early July is the peak fishing period. This river drains Lake Sunapee and can rise significantly after a good rain. The fish will still be there and catchable but it requires sinking line and conehead streamers or tungsten beadhead nymphs in order to reach the bottom where the fish will be holding. Be careful when wading.

Some popular access points are:

- Corbin Covered Bridge off Corbin Road (43.390995,-72.194655)
- Start of flyfishing-only section off Oak Street (43.386565,-72.207672)
- End of flyfishing-only section off Route 11 and large parking area (43.362655,-72.225190).

The North Branch (aka Croydon Branch) and South Branch of the Sugar hold rainbows, brown trout, and brookies. The South Branch is accessible from NH 10 south of the village of Newport. The North Branch follows Route 10 around the village of Croydon north of Newport.

Rail trails that parallel flyfishing waters offer great access to miles of water if you like biking.

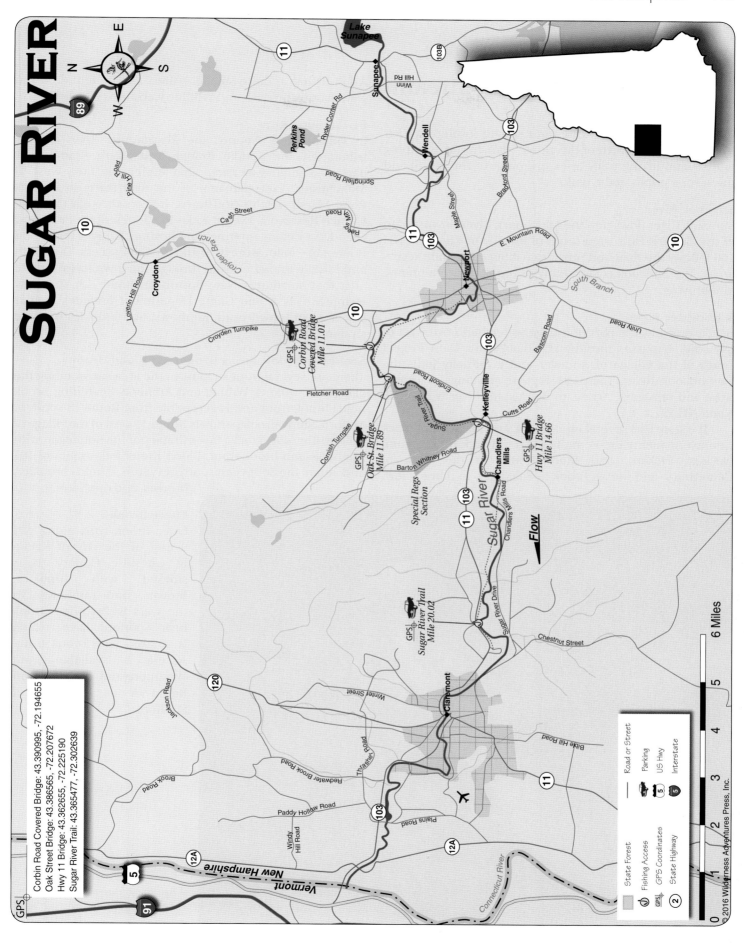

SUGAR RIVER

Corbin Road Covered Bridge: 43.390995, -72.194655
Oak Street Bridge: 43.386565, -72.207672
Hwy 11 Bridge: 43.362655, -72.225190
Sugar River Trail: 43.365477, -72.302639

Lake Sunapee

Perkins Pond

Pine Hill Road

Cash Street

Croydon Branch

Croydon

Loverin Hill Road

Croyden Turnpike

Ryder Corner Rd

Reed's Mill Road

Springfield Road

Sunapee

Winn Hill Rd

Wendell

Maple Street

Bradford Street

E. Mountain Road

South Branch

Unity Road

Bascom Road

Newport

GPS Corbin Road Covered Bridge Mile 11.01

Fletcher Road

Cornish Turnpike

GPS Oak St. Bridge Mile 11.89

Sugar River Trail

Endicott Road

Kelleyville

Cutts Road

Barton Whitney Road

Special Regs Section

Chandlers Mills

Chandlers Mills Road

GPS Hwy 11 Bridge Mile 14.66

Sugar River

Flow

GPS Sugar River Trail Mile 20.02

Sugar River Drive

Chestnut Street

Winter Street

Claremont

Thrasher Road

Redwater Brook Road

Jackson Road

Brook Road

Paddy Hollow Road

Windy Hill Road

Plains Road

Bible Hill Road

Connecticut River

Vermont New Hampshire

Legend

State Forest
Fishing Access
GPS Coordinates
State Highway

Road or Street
Parking
US Hwy
Interstate

0 1 2 3 4 5 6 Miles

© 2016 Wilderness Adventures Press, Inc.

Other Rivers and Small Streams

Bear Brook

Bear Brook is a small brook trout stream located in Bear Brook State Park north of the city of Manchester. Camping and several hiking trails are convenient to the brook and the several ponds in the park.

Suncook River

Suncook River flows into the Merrimack River downstream of the Garvins Falls Dam south of the city of Concord. NH 106 follows the river and provides fishing and canoe access areas. The Suncook is stocked with brook trout, rainbows, and browns.

Blackwater River

Blackwater River is part of a large watershed northwest of Concord. It passes through the Blackwater Dam Project south of the village of Andover and eventually joins the Contoocook River. There are regular stockings of brown trout and rainbows. Access to Blackwater River is from US 4 and NH 27.

The state lists several brook trout streams in Merrimack County: Academy Brook in the town of Loudon; Burnham, Hackett, Pickard, and Rum Brooks in the town of Canterbury; and Punch Brook in Salisbury, to name a few.

A full listing of these smaller waters can be found on the New Hampshire Fish and Wildlife website.

Piscataquog River

In Hillsborough County, the Piscataquog River and its tributaries, the Middle Branch and South Branch, are part of a large watershed that drains the area west of Manchester. The mainstem of the river starts in Perkins Pond Marsh west of Goffstown. It flows through the Lake Horace Reservoir, Everett Lake in Clough State Park, and Glen Lake before entering the Merrimack. River Road – off Route 114 – follows the river and provides access. The South and Middle Branches wind through the town forests in the area that surrounds New Boston on Route 13. The New Hampshire Fish and Game Department provides regular stockings of brown trout, rainbows, and brookies in these streams.

Spaulding Brook, Stony Brook, and Blood Brook

There are several trout streams in the area surrounding the villages of Milford, Wilton, and Amherst. Spaulding Brook holds brook trout and is accessible from Route 13 south of Milford. Stony Brook parallels Route 31 west of the village of Wilton. The state stocks this tributary of the Souhegan with rainbows and brook trout. Blood Brook follows Route 101 and enters the Souhegan south of Wilton. It holds brookies, browns, and rainbows.

Otter Brook

Otter Brook runs along NH 9 east of the city of Keene in Cheshire County. It is stocked with brookies, browns, and rainbows. To the west is Partridge Brook near Spofford Lake, which is stocked with brook trout. Access is available from Westmoreland Road off Route 9A near the village of Spofford.

A healthy southern New Hampshire rainbow trout.

SOUTH-CENTRAL AND SOUTHWESTERN NEW HAMPSHIRE STILLWATERS

Beaver Lake

Beaver Lake, in the town of Derry, covers 134 acres and is a nice two-tiered fishery: stocked with rainbows, browns, and brookies for the spring, and also holds warmwater species such as smallmouth, largemouth, and pickerel. A boat access is conveniently located off NH 102 north of Derry village. Take Pond Road a quarter-mile to the boat launch.

Massabesic Lake

Massabesic Lake, a large stillwater located east of the city of Manchester, supports a small population of resident brown trout and is also stocked with rainbows and brook trout. Its major attraction though, is a smallmouth bass fishery. This lake offers excellent smallmouth habitat because of its very irregular shape with its many fingers, rocky points, shoals, and islands. It is always possible to get out of the wind; a critical feature when you are flyfishing with surface poppers. During the late May spawning season, the bass will be right on shore and casts from a boat should literally hit water's edge. Post-spawn, while the water temperature remains below 70 degrees, the bass will move out from shore a little but will still hit poppers in over 6 to 10 feet of water, and even shallower at twilight or early morning. The best surface flyfishing smallmouth action always occurs between 5:00am and 8:00am, particularly as summer progresses.

Many convenient access areas are located around the lake, including a nice wide gravel ramp with parking for over 15 cars on NH 121 about a third of a mile south of Auburn town center.

Archery Pond

The south-central region of New Hampshire offers two flyfishing-only ponds. Archery Pond is a tiny one-acre pond located near Allentown, just southeast of Concord. It is located in Bear Brook State Park, off of Lower Road (43.138757,-71.347827). This pond is flyfishing only and no boats allowed – you can practically cast bank to bank. It is handicapped accessible with a paved way to the pond. The stocked trout get fished to and become extremely wary, but if you like to tangle with snooty, sophisticated trout, this might be a good option.

Stirrup Iron Pond

Stirrup Iron Pond is located in the town of Salisbury in Merrimack County. It is a two-acre pond stocked with brook trout averaging 9 to 10 inches in length. Access is off US 4 and NH 126 north of Salisbury. The road to the pond is unimproved and requires a 4-wheel drive vehicle.

Willard Pond

Willard Pond is Hillsborough County's single flyfishing-only pond. It is reached from Route 123 north of Hancock on Willard Pond Road (stay left at the fork). There is a dirt boat launch at the southern end of the pond (43.018638,-72.020505) The state stocks Willard with brook trout, brown trout, rainbows, and tiger trout – a brookie-brown trout hybrid.

This small but picturesque pond is partially located in the dePierrefeu Wildlife Sanctuary, which is owned by the New Hampshire Audubon Society, so no gas motors are

Massabesic Lake offers classic shoreline structure for smallmouth bass. Notice the bald eagle in the tree and the loons in the foreground.

allowed and the shoreline is undeveloped. Bald Mountain towers over the pond and adds to the scenery. Willard is a popular pond so you won't have it to yourself, but the fish are usually plentiful.

Chapman Pond

Chapman Pond is a flyfishing-only pond located about eight miles northwest of the village of Newport in Sullivan County. This remote, 20-acre pond is relatively shallow, so its trout are always reachable. Wading is difficult because of the muck bottom, so a boat or float tube is required. The state stocks Chapman with brook trout.

From the intersection of Route 9 and Center Street in East Sullivan, take Center Street for 2.3 miles, bear right at intersection, and then bear right at Gilsum Road. At 0.4 of a mile take a right on a dirt road, and after 0.7 of a mile another right onto the access road.

Center Pond

Located in the town of Nelson (follow Center Pond Road for 0.3 of a mile from the town center), Center Pond holds brook trout and rainbows. This is a small kettle-hole pond where motorboats are not allowed. Expect 9- to 10-inch brookies in this 20-acre stillwater.

Cold Spring Pond

Cold Spring Pond (43.099729, -72.151128) offers angling for brook trout and rainbows. It is located within the town of Stoddard.

Dublin Lake

Dublin Lake is a 239-acre brook trout and largemouth bass pond located in the village of Dublin. From the center of Dublin, Route 101 travels along the north side of the lake. Take Lake Road until you reach a good paved boat launch.

This is a deep, clear-water pond, and if you like to fish the evening rise, you won't be disturbed by fast-moving motorboats, because there is a speed limit after 4:00pm.

Sand Pond

Sand Pond is a clear-water body of water that is well stocked with brook trout and brown trout. Its topography shows many small holes and underwater "islands". It does have development on its western shore along with a paved boat ramp.

To find it, head north on Route 10 for three miles from Marlow and then take a right on Sand Pond Road. Stay right at the fork and after 0.3 of a mile, turn right and after half a mile, the boat ramp will be on your left.

SOUTHERN NEW HAMPSHIRE PLANNING CONSIDERATIONS

Hub Cities

- Portsmouth (www.portsmouthchamber.org)
- Durham (www.ci.durham.nh.us)
- Manchester (www.manchester-chamber.org)
- Keene (www.keenechapter.org)

Easy Access Options

- The Lamprey River below Wiswall Dam is easily accessible. A good parking lot leads to a short gradual downhill walk on a good trail to the Powerline Pool where trout are usually found. Enticing them to take your fly is another matter. Wading is easy and there is space for several anglers.
- The Bow Lake Dam is a very short walk from the nearby parking lot, and large granite blocks form the lake edge and make great casting platforms with plenty of backcast room to try your luck in the lake.
- Archery Pond in Bear Brook State Park, southeast of Concord (43.138757,-71.347827) is wheelchair accessible and, from the bank, one can almost cover all of this tiny pond. Catch and release insures that trout are usually present, but increasingly difficult to fool as the season progresses.
- Pine Tree Island offers the opportunity to fish for stripers from a wheelchair or walker. A casting platform makes this possible, although one has to be pushed or walk a short distance down a level road to reach the island. Fly casting is difficult because of the height of the platform above the water, so bring a good spinning rod as a backup.

Suggested Beginner Options

- The key to beginner success is to time your arrival at any of the rivers and streams mentioned here shortly after the stocking truck has arrived and the trout are plentiful and naïve. Try the Exeter River in Exeter just below the dam on Cross Street (42.970055,-71.000572). This is small moving water, so a cast isn't even really necessary, just flip your offering into the current, let the current take it downstream a bit and then retrieve it back. Try for water pockets that are a little deeper than surrounding flows. Any reasonable Woolly Bugger, Hornberg, or large nymph should work fine.

- Join one of the local Trout Unlimited chapters and attend the monthly meetings. During the meeting, volunteer that you are a beginner and ask if anyone would be willing to guide you to a few good nearby spots. My experience is that you will get plenty of offers. The three southern New Hampshire TU options are the Monadnock, Great Bay, and Merrimack Chapters.

Suggested Flyfishing Vacation Options

Weekend Getaway

Are you spending a weekend going to commencement ceremonies at the University of New Hampshire in Durham or Phillips Exeter Academy in Exeter?

- Escape for a few hours and fish the Lamprey (ten minutes away from Durham) or Exeter River (also ten minutes away from Exeter Center). Of course if you are a student, or you are visiting a student after October 15, try the fishing after the fall stocking program.
- Spend a weekend between mid-May and mid-July in Portsmouth: great downtown with places to stay, nightspots, good restaurants, and cute shops. Fish for stripers. Choose the type of fishing that appeals to you. Or mix it up. A day kayaking the Hampton River estuary and another day fishing the islands and piers around Portsmouth.
- During any winter weekend when the weather is forecast to be mild, cure your case of pent-up cabin/fishing fever by heading to the Isinglass, Lamprey River, or Cocheco River. These rivers offer up fish all year long. Some helpful hints are:
  - It is illegal to stand on the ice and fish, so you must find open water.
  - Try midge imitations or egg patterns.
  - Fish during the warmest part of the day. In the winter, getting on the water early is no advantage.
- Combine sightseeing, biking, and fishing all at the same time by riding the Sugar River Rail Trail outside of Newport. This picturesque 9.8-mile trail crosses numerous bridges over the Sugar River and its tributaries, including two historic covered railroad bridges. Stop and fish where it looks promising. A pack rod and a pared-down list of gear are required to combine fishing and biking. The trail has soft spots, so a mountain bike or any option with wider tires will minimize the time spent bogged down in sand. If combined with sightseeing in nearby towns or enjoying Lake Sunapee, an entire weekend of activity can ensue.

One-week Vacation

- Many families take a weeklong vacation in the Hampton Beach area to enjoy the ocean, the beautiful beach, and all of the family attractions in the area. (I find it a little too touristy but others enjoy all of the activity). If this fits the bill for your family and you take a vacation in the area, you can literally walk to good striper fishing locations on the Hampton River. The best times to fish are early in the morning and late in the evening, so you won't miss any of the family activities during the day. Of course, you might become a little sleep deprived!

I wouldn't actually recommend taking a week vacation specifically to fish southern New Hampshire rivers. Other destinations farther north offer more interesting flyfishing for that length of stay. However, if you find yourself in the Manchester, Portsmouth, or Boston area (only 1.5 hours away) for a week long business trip or conference, and you can escape for an afternoon or evening or two, then southern New Hampshire rivers and ponds are well worth fishing.

Portsmouth's Pine Tree Island casting platform.

Central New Hampshire

The central New Hampshire region includes Grafton, Belknap, and Carroll Counties, plus the White Mountain National Forest. A large part of this area is dominated by Mount Washington, the Presidential Mountain Range, and the Great Gulf Wilderness Area, all of which are the sources of dozens of small mountain streams that join to form major coldwater trout fisheries. Flyfishers have the opportunity to cast for native brook trout and, if you're as fortunate as Granite State angler Lance King, record-sized holdover rainbows.

I urge you to choose any of the almost countless small mountain streams with a light-weight fly rod and experience wild brook trout fishing at its finest – hand-sized brookies from water that you can almost jump across. Of course, there is nothing wrong with plying the larger rivers for bigger stocked and holdover brook, rainbow, or brown trout – healthy and colorful from the cold, clear water. The lakes and ponds offer trolling and casting for a variety of species often surrounded by mountain peaks on the horizon.

It should be noted that hatches in central New Hampshire (and other parts of glacially-scoured New England) are not like hatches in the Catskills, or perhaps, in the western United States. Hatches here tend to be sporadic and sparse, often with just a few insects flying around. Erratic weather means that some years certain hatches may not happen at all, or be early, or late. I think by now, you are probably getting the picture. Best to fish a relatively generic pattern that is "close-enough" in size and color to any number of species.

The Presidential Range.

UPPER PEMIGEWASSET RIVER

On September 16, 1996, Lance King of Franklin landed what proved to be a New Hampshire state record, a rainbow trout weighing 15 pounds, 7.2 ounces, while flyfishing in the Upper Pemigewasset River in the town of Bristol. His fly was a tandem Mickey Finn.

"The record fish was absolutely beautiful," said state fisheries biologist Don Miller at the time. "It had a big head, a bright pink stripe, and a caudal fin that was about nine inches wide; easily one of the nicest rainbows I've ever seen." King's rainbow, according to Miller, measured 35.5 inches long, with an 18.25-inch girth.

Word has it this record fish was one of a pair of late summer spawning rainbows spotted by King that day, and that the tandem streamer was the largest pattern he could find in his fly box. Hatchery rainbows are on a delayed photo-period program, which fools the fish. As a result, these rainbows spawn in the fall, or even in late summer and this would increase their aggressiveness to large streamers.

Stocked rainbows revert back to spring-spawning behavior in most cases, but perhaps not always.

Often, large fish are best tempted by large flies. My friend, Ray Gagnon, was fishing this river in the fall of 2014, when low water levels allowed anglers to reach deeper, faster flowing waters than they ordinarily could, and he landed two big, feisty rainbows on a large Conehead Gartside Soft-hackle Marabou Streamer with a yellow collar. This is a killer fly for large landlocked salmon, but clearly rainbows like it too.

The Upper Pemigewasset is a heavily stocked river, stretching 63 miles from its upper reaches in Franconia Notch south to Franklin, where it merges with the Merrimack River in the south-central part of the state. Access is convenient along I-93, the major connector for tourists traveling from southern New England to the White Mountains. Angling pressure can be high, particularly on weekends. The stretch between Lincoln and Plymouth that runs parallel to U.S. 3 and I-93 is a consistent springtime trout fishery. It is heavily stocked with brook and rainbow trout, with brown trout lightly mixed in. Additionally, fish drop down from Newfound Lake and other upstream sources. Rainbows from Newfound Lake have a distinctly different look when compared side by side with stocked rainbows. We catch both in the Pemi.

Access points to the upper Pemi include:

- A small pull-off from US 3 above North Woodstock near a sign for Woodwards Resort (44.036885,-71.686754). A short trail leads to the river and a beautiful wooded area, even though ski condos line the opposite bank. Ply the waters both above and below the easily spotted upstream dam.
- The first pool after the confluence with the Lost River and the East Branch (44.026167,-71.683943). Park behind a municipal building.
- A small parking area where the railroad crosses NH 175. Take a woods trail to the so-called Couch Pool, a large pool and beautiful spot downstream. The last time I visited, it looked like a road was being built so the area may change.
- A pull-off from NH 175 with a dirt road that parallels the river for a short distance (43.993771,-71.672862).
- A dirt road off to the left of NH 175 provides parking and the river here has lots of fishable water (43.981121,-71.677777).

Sections of the river are good float options in a canoe or kayak. One option is to put in near the NH 175 bridge north of Thornton, where a parking area leads to a rather

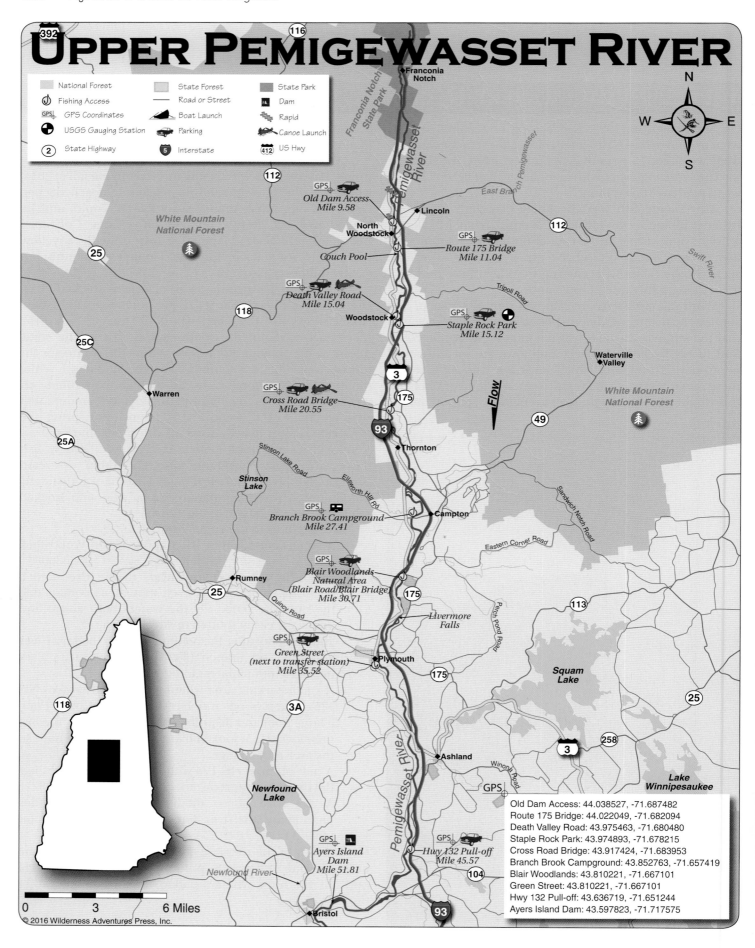

UPPER PEMIGEWASSET RIVER

Legend:
- National Forest
- Fishing Access
- GPS Coordinates
- USGS Gauging Station
- State Highway
- State Forest
- Road or Street
- Boat Launch
- Parking
- Interstate
- State Park
- Dam
- Rapid
- Canoe Launch
- US Hwy

Franconia Notch State Park

Franconia Notch

Pemigewasset River

Old Dam Access Mile 9.58

Lincoln

North Woodstock

Couch Pool

Route 175 Bridge Mile 11.04

East Branch Pemigewasset

Swift River

White Mountain National Forest

Death Valley Road Mile 15.04

Woodstock

Staple Rock Park Mile 15.12

Tripoli Road

Waterville Valley

White Mountain National Forest

Cross Road Bridge Mile 20.55

Flow

Thornton

Stinson Lake Road

Stinson Lake

Ellsworth Hill Rd

Branch Brook Campground Mile 27.41

Campton

Sandwich Notch Road

Eastern Corner Road

Rumney

Quincy Road

Blair Woodlands Natural Area (Blair Road/Blair Bridge) Mile 30.71

Livermore Falls

Perch Pond Road

Squam Lake

Green Street (next to transfer station) Mile 35.52

Plymouth

Newfound Lake

Pemigewasset River

Ashland

Winona Road

GPS

Lake Winnipesaukee

Newfound River

Ayers Island Dam Mile 51.81

Hwy 132 Pull-off Mile 45.57

Bristol

0   3   6 Miles

© 2016 Wilderness Adventures Press, Inc.

Old Dam Access: 44.038527, -71.687482
Route 175 Bridge: 44.022049, -71.682094
Death Valley Road: 43.975463, -71.680480
Staple Rock Park: 43.974893, -71.678215
Cross Road Bridge: 43.917424, -71.683953
Branch Brook Campground: 43.852763, -71.657419
Blair Woodlands: 43.810221, -71.667101
Green Street: 43.810221, -71.667101
Hwy 132 Pull-off: 43.636719, -71.651244
Ayers Island Dam: 43.597823, -71.717575

steep, but manageable launch area (Death Valley Road, 43.975463,-71.680480). A sizable parking lot and canoe/kayak boat launch are under the Cross Road bridge (43.917424,-71.683953). Take Robins Nest Road and then a left on an unpaved road that will take you right under the bridge.

North of Plymouth, the river is gentle and meandering until one reaches the Blair Covered Bridge (43.810340,-71.664767). It is a good idea to take out here if you are a less-than-experienced canoeist because farther downstream, there are long stretches of challenging whitewater. For wading anglers, a good point of entry is about a mile and a half south on US 3 with side-of-the-road parking right next to the river. Depending on water level, a number of runs, pocket water, and pools provide ample fishing opportunities.

Below the Ayes Island Dam, the river quickens and it is a nice stretch to fish complete with runs, chutes, and rapids. Look for several parking areas and access points around the town of Bristol including parking at the dam, the steel bridge, and a large parking area off of Coolidge Woods Road. The Pemigewasset between Bristol and Franklin, before it joins the Merrimack, does not receive as much angling pressure. The river is accessible from NH 3A.

Years ago, the Pemi was the victim of industrial pollutants. Higher water quality standards and controls have now returned the river to a productive sport fishery. Stocking efforts by New Hampshire Fish and Game have been aggressive. Of the thousands of fish stocked annually, good numbers of rainbows hold over. Some browns must hold over as well, because my friend Paul Gagnon, one early October evening just about dusk, caught a 22-inch brown trout (I doubt they are stocking them that size) just below Ayers Island Dam on a white conehad Zonker.

Don't get the impression, though, that this is an easy fishery. I have had some unproductive days on this river, and I have friends that fish this river regularly and tell me that slow days vastly out number good ones. It might have something to do with the fact that there is so much similar holding water that the fish spread out or move around a lot, and that the average number of fish within casting distance is not that high.

Rainbows will typically be found in the faster water emptying into major pools. Browns prefer structure such as islands, fallen timber, or slow, deep back-eddies. Brook trout prefer parts of the river that are protected from the main flow and have siltier bottoms. I was fishing the Pemi near Thornton and wading upstream when I came across the remains of a structure in the river. Large sunken wooden beams and rocks had created a downsteam eddy with a dark silty bottom. The area reminded me of a beaver dam pond that I like to fish for native brookies, and lo and behold, around those beams I landed half a dozen spirited brook trout on a Hornberg or Wood Special retrieved under the surface.

To cover as much water as possible, I prefer casting a variety of small streamers of all types. If you are targeting spawning rainbows, traditional bright orange and red steelhead patterns, such as the Skyomish Sunrise (sizes 2 to 8), Polar Shrimp (sizes 2 to 8), and single egg flies (sizes 2 to 10) are effective. Chuck large streamers if you want to try to catch larger fish. Conehead marabou steamers

The Pemigewasset River from the Route 175 bridge in Woodstock. Photo courtesy Lindsey Rustad.

The East Branch of the Pemi, upstream from Loon Mountain Ski Area.

with yellow, red, or pink accents, articulated rabbit-fur monstrosities, or large white Zonkers are all viable options. Today's flyfishing catalogs feature an expanded assortment of large streamers patterns tied with a variety of both natural and artificial fibers. Choose several that look fishy to you and try them out.

Regardless of its inconsistency of success, anglers love to fish the Pemigewasset with its easy access, bankside walking and wading, classic gravel and boulder pools and runs, unspoiled environs, and plentiful wildlife including ospreys and eagles. One word of warning though: Incredibly thick patches of poison ivy grow on the high banks (the kind you might walk through to get to the river) that get sunshine. Learn to recognize their distinctive leaves or better yet, put on the waders beside the car.

East Branch of the Pemi

This river starts in the White Mountains, picks up flow from a number of tributaries such as Franconia Brook, and flows 16 miles before its confluence with the mainstem. You can reach every part of the river because the Kangamangus Highway (NH 112) lies right next to the lower portion of the river and good forest service trails parallel the upper part below Franconia Falls and above the Lincoln Woods Visitors Center. Farther downstream, the East Branch flows right in front of Loon Mountain Ski Area and there are plenty of lodging, eating, and camping options nearby.

The huge boulders and countless rocks on this river create deep holes, pocket water, and a few pools that shelter stocked and native brook trout. The writer has a friend who caught a huge broodstock brook trout just downstream from the ski area, so perhaps trout run up the East Branch from Pemi's main branch. My first choice for flyfishing this river is to drift a big stonefly nymph fished among the rocks and crevasses along the bottom.

The East Branch can run high after a heavy rain, so it pays to check conditions ahead of time by contacting the Lincoln Woods Visitors Center or going on-line at www.americanwhitewater.org.

Newfound River

January 1, the traditional Granite State trout opener, finds flyfishers on the flyfishing-only section of the Newfound River that extends from West Shore Road to Crescent Street. Access is gained right below the Newfound Lake Dam (43.617338,-71.740645), at Crescent Street in Bristol, and at the Riverdale Road bridge. The river here offers good pocket water and then farther downstream is a good pool the locals call "the swimming hole".

The Newfound River is a beautiful stream but the major draw is that in late fall, winter, and early spring, fish drop down to the river from the lake. If you are there at the right time, you will catch gorgeous rainbows that look like Montana trout. Fishing during the low-light edges of the day is best for catching rainbows that run up to five pounds. There are a few landlocks and three- to four-pound lakers that will also drop down to the river from Newfound Lake.

During the colder months, the best patterns are small nymphs. The late Joe Conklin, a regular on these waters liked to fish size 14 to 18 beadhead Pheasant Tails, weighted black and olive Woolly Buggers, micro-egg patterns, and San Juan Worms in white, pink, or burgundy.

In the spring, the stocking truck arrives and stocked rainbows add to the existing fish. As the water warms, caddis patterns are the flies to cast on the Newfound. If there is no surface activity, fish a weighted green caddis pupa. In late June there is zebra caddis hatch, the same bug that is called an alder fly on the Rapid River. Imitations should be about a size 12 with a caddis body/wing configuration, a black body, and mottled wing. A drowned (wet fly) imitation can be dynamite in the faster water.

Nearby Newfound Lake holds angling opportunities as well.

"Newfound is one of our older lakes, with crystal-clear water that stays that way throughout the season," says fisheries biologist Miller. New Hampshire Fish and Game stocks thousands of rainbows and landlocked salmon in Newfound Lake in the spring when the water temperatures reach 44 degrees. The fishing can be difficult because of the clear water, but if one of the sporadic hatches occurs, the dry-fly fishing can be outstanding.

SWIFT RIVER

During the Ice Age, glaciers plowed through the White Mountains of central New Hampshire, leaving behind a rugged landscape filled with rivers, ponds, and small mountain streams. The Swift River is one of these beautiful glacial creations and it offers continuous riffles, runs, eddies, and pools. It flows along the Kangamangus Highway (NH 112) off the mountain of the same name. From there, the river twists and turns east and joins the Saco near the village of Conway.

Several small tributaries feed the 23-mile Swift River, including the Sabbaday, Downes, and Oliverian. These small feeder streams range from foot-deep trickles to deeper plunge pools, run cold and clear, and offer good angling throughout the season. Brook trout in these tributaries average six inches and should be released unharmed by using barbless hooks.

Native brookie populations are also found in the upper reaches of the mainstem of the Swift, but for the most part, the fishery is maintained by planted brook and rainbow trout for most of its length, and some brown trout closer to the Saco River. Winter anchor ice and the turbulent action around rocks make it difficult for hatchery trout to survive and create natural stocks.

Early-season flyfishers may find winter runoff and fast-rising water levels that make angling difficult. Conditions improve by late May. Swift River water levels and water temperatures dictate annual trout-stocking schedules. The New Hampshire Fish and Game stocking program begins when the water temperature is around 45 degrees. Water flows must be at a reasonable level for stocking to be successful.

June is usually the best month to fish the Swift. The fish are active and feeding, but the crush of tourists has yet to arrive. There will also be a mix of mayfly hatches, from light Cahills to March browns to blue-winged olives, but standard hatches are sporadic at best. For dry flies, carry a range of caddis imitation (Elk Hair, Goddard, and Puterbaugh) and standard mayfly patterns (Adams, Hornberg, Klinkhammer), sizes 12 to 20. Cast upstream into slower, placid pocket water in streamside eddies or boulder-protected pools. Try a weighted Gold-ribbed Hare's Ear or stonefly nymph (sized 8 to 16) in the faster, more turbulent water. Stay back if you can, as wild and stocked trout may not be selective, but can be skittish in skinny water.

The boulder-strewn Swift River is easily accessible from the Kangamangas Highway. Photo courtesy Lindsey Rustad.

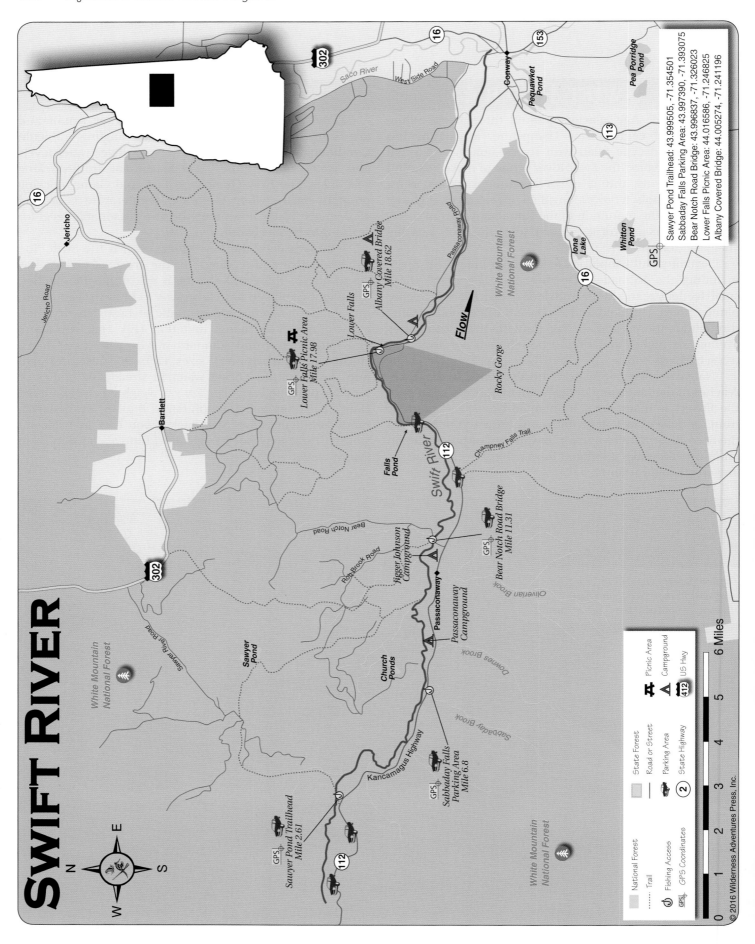

SWIFT RIVER

Sawyer Pond Trailhead: 43.999505, -71.354501
Sabbaday Falls Parking Area: 43.997390, -71.393075
Bear Notch Road Bridge: 43.996837, -71.326023
Lower Falls Picnic Area: 44.016586, -71.246825
Albany Covered Bridge: 44.005274, -71.241196

Lower Falls Picnic Area
Mile 17.98

Albany Covered Bridge
Mile 18.62

Lower Falls

Falls Pond

Swift River

Champney Falls Trail

Bear Notch Road Bridge
Mile 11.31

Oliverian Brook

Jigger Johnson Campground

Passaconaway Campground

Passaconaway

Bear Notch Road

Rob Brook Road

Church Ponds

Downes Brook

Sawyer Pond

Sabbaday Brook

Sabbaday Falls Parking Area
Mile 6.8

Kancamagus Highway

Sawyer Pond Trailhead
Mile 2.61

White Mountain National Forest

White Mountain National Forest

White Mountain National Forest

Sawyer River Road

Rocky Gorge

Flow

Jericho

Bartlett

Conway

Saco River

West Side Road

Passaconaway Road

Pequawket Pond

Pea Porridge Pond

Whitton Pond

Iona Lake

Jericho Road

Legend

National Forest
State Forest — Picnic Area
Trail
Road or Street — Campground
Parking Area
Fishing Access 2 State Highway
GPS Coordinates 412 US Hwy

0 1 2 3 4 5 6 Miles

© 2016 Wilderness Adventures Press, Inc.

During the summer, the river is popular with tourists. If you want a more secluded experience, stay away from the Rocky Gorge, Lower Falls, and Covered Bridge areas, but there is plenty of room for everyone in this pleasant mountain setting, and anglers will find plenty of places to park along the Kangamangus Highway. On the upper river, near the Sabbaday Falls Picnic Ground is a parking area for six to eight cars and a short walk to the river (43.997270,-71.387092). Another spot is the parking area for the Sawyer Pond Trailhead (43.999505,-71.354501). The river has a different character here with a sandy bottom, deep pools, beaver dams, and oxbows.

The Bear Notch Road bridge provides another river access point with a large pool immediately below the bridge (43.996837,-71.326023). The Rocky Gorge and Lower Falls part of the river is a steeper gradient with plunge pools and pocket water and is very popular with a large paved parking lot and picnic area (44.016586,-71.246825). To see the Albany Covered Bridge and fish downstream (a recommended choice during non-tourist times), find the paved parking area (44.005274,-71.241196).

Autumn is another great time to fish the Swift because the tourists diminish and the sugar maples and birches put on quite a show as their leaves begin to turn.

From the NH 113A bridge to the Route 113 bridge, the Swift River's season runs from January 1 to October 15, and is flyfishing only with a daily limit of two brook trout.

The river is 15 miles long from Passaconaway Campground to Conway. Take NH 16 north to Conway, then turn left on Route 112, the Kangamangus Highway. Staff at the Saco Ranger District Office located on the right after the turn, can fill you in on current river conditions. Call them at 603-447-5448.

Interstate 93 north to Lincoln will put you on this mountainous access highway from the west. NH 112 runs right through Lincoln's downtown area, then eastward along the Swift River toward the village of Conway.

Recreation passports are required for parking along the Kangamangus Highway and for any other vehicles left unattended in the White Mountain National Forest. For information, see the WMNF website (http://www.fs.usda.gov/detail/whitemountain/) or contact the office at 603-528-8721. Fees are used to maintain existing trails and WMNF facilities.

For those who like to camp, the Covered Bridge Campground near Albany is a convenient location with good fishing right there, particularly during midweek and before the tourists arrive in force in early July.

Mascoma River

The Mascoma River runs southwest from Cummings and Reservoir Ponds, north of the village of Canaan in the Mascoma River Wildlife Management Area. From Canaan, the river follows US 4 through Mascoma Lake and joins the Connecticut River near the village of West Lebanon after a total run of 34 miles. The flyfishing-only section runs from the Route 4 bridge to the Packard Hill covered bridge. There is a nice parking area at the covered bridge (43.639021,-72.222043). Anglers can hike or bike up and down the river on the Northern Rail Trail which follows along the north bank of the river, while the Mill Road Trail follows the south bank.

Another nearby option is a large parking lot for the Northern Rail Trail (and then a short walk to the river,

The Mascoma River downstream from Mascoma Lake. Photo courtesy of Phil Trasatti.

43.638001,-72.216824). There is also an entrance to the Mill Road Municipal Trail at a blinking light on US 4, opposite Route 4A (43.646007,-72.188549) however, recent bridge construction has messed with that entire area, as of early 2016.

Finally, the outflow of the dam at Mascoma Lake provides good trout habitat and excellent fishing opportunities for larger-sized fish until the water warms too much in the summer. If the Mascoma Lake dam released water from below the surface, this fishery would be greatly improved. In that respect and in appearance, the Mascoma is not too different from the Newfound River. Parking is available near the dam (43.649170,-72.182523).

Early in the season, the flow is deep and fast but is easily waded. The water is a mixture of long riffles, rapids, and deep pools. Caddis and stonefly patterns will work well. In the summer, water levels drop and fish gather in the deeper pools. Then, fishing with small emerger patterns and midges and a lot of patience are the only formula.

From the Route 4 bridge downstream to the Packard Hill covered bridge, the Mascoma is flyfishing only from January 1 through October 15. The daily limit in this regulated section is two brook trout. There is an unpaved road that parallels the river and provides parking and convenient access. In addition to brook trout, the state stocks the Mascoma with rainbows and browns.

The upper stretch of the Mascoma, above Canaan, offers fine fishing opportunities as well. The trout are smaller, but you have a chance to fish over more wild fish. There is a dirt road that parallels the river and provides parking and easy access.

Mad River

Mad River is the mainstem of the Waterville Valley watershed but is still easy to wade. It flows south from the village of Waterville Valley along NH 49, to the village of Campton, where it joins the Pemigewasset River. There are several pull-offs and parking areas along the highway, providing easy access. This is a relatively sterile stream that is scoured by ice and the spring run-off. This fishery is maintained with stocked brook trout and rainbows but there are small wild brook trout as well, particularly as you move upriver. This is a beautiful stream; the anglers that fish it always talk glowingly about how fun it is. It doesn't receive a lot of fishing pressure. Try high-floating dry flies such as Wulffs and Humpies.

Gale River

The Gale River is a fast-flowing, mountain brook trout stream that feeds the Ammonoosuc near the village of Franconia. NH 18 follows the river, and access is from the main highway and secondary roads near the river. There are plenty of access points. In Franconia proper, several bridges cross the river and the old iron furnace historical site (right on NH 18) park has a riverside trail (44.230110,-71.754527). The upper river can be fished from NH 142 and Gale River Road. The state regularly stocks wild brook trout in Franconia and Bethlehem.

This is a typical central New Hampshire freestone stream: clear water, great scenery, easy to wade under most conditions, but will flood after a good rainstorm. As with other New Hampshire mountain freestones, bushy dry flies that float well, perhaps with a Pheasant Tail dropper, are the way to go. Move quickly upriver and cast into every likely pocket, deeper run, or plunge pool as you go. The month with the most predictably good fishing is June or early July. The larger Gale River tributaries also hold good populations of small brook trout.

Beaver Brook, Coffin Brook, Hurd Brook, Post Office Brook, and Watson Brook are small brook trout streams in the town of Alton.

Merrymeeting River

Merrymeeting River flows into Lake Winnipesaukee at Alton Bay just north of the village of Alton. The section of river between the lower dam in Alton and the Route 11 bridge at Alton Bay is flyfishing only, all fish must be released, and fishing is restricted to the use of barbless hooks from January 1 to June 15 and also in October. Access is from NH 11.

As with most Winnipesaukee tributaries, timing is everything as it relates to hooking landlocked salmon. They migrate into the river chasing smelt in the spring and in October to begin their spawning run. Typically, smelt run shortly after ice-out and

your favorite smelt-imitation streamer should be your first choice. This river can get crowded and the salmon see many streamers. Try different colors, front-weighted patterns, or even floating options in order to show the fish something different.

Big River
Big River is a tributary of the Suncook River and flows between the villages of Strafford and Barnstead. The state stocks Big River with brook trout. The Suncook flows south from Barnstead along NH 28 through the village of Pittsfield and joins the Merrimack River near the village of Suncook. This river is heavily stocked with brook trout, rainbows, and brown trout.

Nighthawk Hollow Brook
Nighthawk Hollow Brook is a small brook trout stream that parallels Route 140 near the village of Gilmanton south of Laconia.

Gunstock Brook
Gunstock Brook flows into Lake Winnipesaukee at Sanders Bay east of Laconia off NH 11. The state stocks this brook with rainbows and brookies.

Winnipesaukee River
Winnipesaukee River runs parallel to US 3 and NH 11 and joins the Merrimack River below the Franklin Falls Dam in the village of Franklin. The state regularly stocks this stream with brown trout, rainbows, and brookies.

Salmon Brook
Salmon Brook lies north of Franklin, near NH 127 and Exit 22 of I-93. The state stocks this brook with rainbows and brook trout.

The Gale River just upstream from the old iron foundry building in Franconia.

ELLIS RIVER

Ellis River flows from the heights of Mount Washington along Route 16 through the village of Jackson. It joins the Saco River near the village of Glen. There are paved parking areas and road pull-offs where Route 16 passes close to the river. The upper river is smaller, but still holds small wild and larger stocked brook trout if you probe the deeper pools and pockets. In the town of Jackson, the river grows in size as several tributaries join the flow. There is a flyfishing-only section on the Ellis between the famous Honeymoon Covered Bridge in Jackson (44.141566,-71.186291) and the iron bridge in Glen. This section is well marked, and there is good access to the river. Other access points are at the Route 16 bridge (44.126919,-71.189058) and the Rt. 302 bridge (44.110199,-71.183726).

The New Hampshire Fish and Game Department regularly stocks the Ellis River with rainbows and brook trout and, because the river stays cool and due to the growing catch-and-release mentality, the river fishes well through the summer.

The Ellis is a small river with boulders, large rocks, and ledges creating all sorts of pockets, small pools, and runs that just cry out to be fished with a dry fly, or perhaps a dry fly and nymph dropper combination. Any reasonable caddis imitation or a small Royal Wulff usually does the trick. Hatches include green and tan caddis, gray drakes, and yellow Sally stoneflies. During late summer, flying ants become important and trying foam ant imitations in various colors and sizes is a high percentage play. Although they are raised in concrete pools, Ellis River trout quickly adapt and take on the beauty of their new surroundings. This river is a favorite of many flyfishers who travel several hours to fish it regularly. Wading ankle deep will allow you to reach every part of the river.

An angler fishes a promising run on the Ellis River below the Honeymoon Covered Bridge in Jackson.

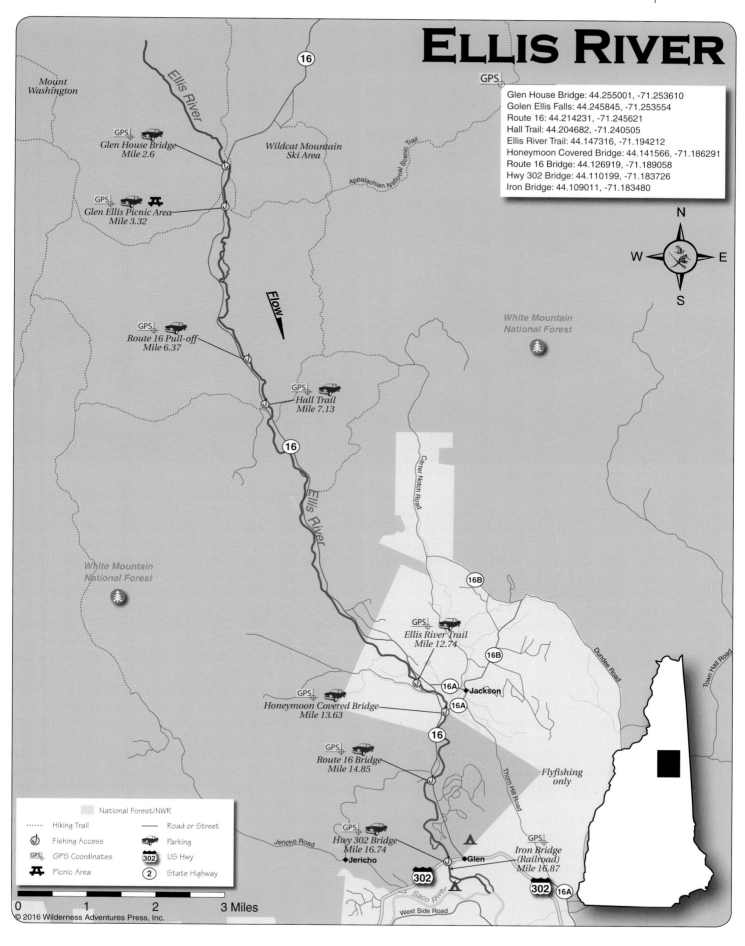

ELLIS RIVER

Mount Washington

Ellis River

Wildcat Mountain Ski Area

Appalachian National Scenic Trail

GPS

Glen House Bridge: 44.255001, -71.253610
Golen Ellis Falls: 44.245845, -71.253554
Route 16: 44.214231, -71.245621
Hall Trail: 44.204682, -71.240505
Ellis River Trail: 44.147316, -71.194212
Honeymoon Covered Bridge: 44.141566, -71.186291
Route 16 Bridge: 44.126919, -71.189058
Hwy 302 Bridge: 44.110199, -71.183726
Iron Bridge: 44.109011, -71.183480

GPS
Glen House Bridge
Mile 2.6

GPS
Glen Ellis Picnic Area
Mile 3.32

Flow

White Mountain National Forest

GPS
Route 16 Pull-off
Mile 6.37

GPS
Hall Trail
Mile 7.13

16

Ellis River

White Mountain National Forest

Carter Notch Road

16B

GPS
Ellis River Trail
Mile 12.74

16B

16A
◆ Jackson

Dundee Road

16A

GPS
Honeymoon Covered Bridge
Mile 13.63

16

Thorn Hill Road

Flyfishing only

Town Hall Road

GPS
Route 16 Bridge
Mile 14.85

Jericho Road

GPS
Hwy 302 Bridge
Mile 16.74

◆ Jericho

GPS
Iron Bridge
(Railroad)
Mile 16.87

◆ Glen

302

302   16A

West Side Road

Saco River

Legend

National Forest/NWR

····· Hiking Trail   Road or Street

🎣 Fishing Access   🚗 Parking

GPS GPS Coordinates   302 US Hwy

⛐ Picnic Area   2 State Highway

| 0 | 1 | 2 | 3 Miles |

© 2016 Wilderness Adventures Press, Inc.

A deep hole on the upper Saco River near Fourth Iron Bridge campsites.

Saco River

Saco River begins in Crawford Notch below Mount Washington at Saco Lake and holds stocked and holdover brookies, rainbows, and browns. In the lower river from Bartlett to the confluence of the Swift and Ellis Rivers, 18-inch and larger browns (and a few rainbows) are caught every year. From its origins to the Maine border, this river travels 33 miles through mostly pristine surroundings. If you're going to fly fish three rivers in Carroll County, start with the Swift along Route 112, then move over to the Saco, and then wet a line in the Ellis.

From Crawford Notch State Park dam up to Willey Pond, only children 12 and under can fish. A two-trout limit is in place, though anglers rarely keep fish. There are plenty of put-and-take stockers elsewhere on the river. You can park by the dam and walk downstream from there. Bigger fish can be caught when heavy rain washes fish over the dam. A flyfishing-only section has been established from the Lucy Brook sign downstream to the confluence of Artist Falls Brook.

From Crawford Notch to Bartlett, this is a wading river and there is plentiful access along Highway 302. A limited amount of hiking from the obvious parking spots will give you almost unlimited water to fish for brook and rainbow trout.

From mid-June through the Fourth of July, there is usually a caddis hatch. This is best matched with a range of larva, pupa, wet and dry patterns. When dry-fly fishing the Saco and the Ellis, one effective strategy is to fish "near 'nuff" patterns that look similar to the scattering of common mayflies that are usually present. Try traditional Adams, Parachute Adams, Parachute Hare's Ear, Hornberg, mosquitoes, or small Wulffs of various sizes. Gray drakes start emerging in late May and the spinner fall is important. Most successful anglers fish very early in the morning or late in the day when the recreational boaters are off the water because all of the activity can spook the fish in this gin-clear water. Later in the summer terrestrials such as grasshoppers, ants, and beetles are effective patterns.

Below Bartlett, a canoe or kayak will allow you to fish more water and enjoy a great float at the same time. The scenery in the fall is spectacular. In the section of the Saco from close to North Conway to the Maine border, experienced local anglers hook some good-sized holdover browns by fishing the deeper pools very early or very late in the evening with sinking leaders and large streamers; articulated, conehead Marabou Gray Ghost, large brown or black Woolly Buggers, Zonkers, or other rabbit-fur streamers work well.

Ossipee River

The Ossipee River is another New Hampshire river that crosses the border into Maine and then joins with the Saco. It starts at the outlet of Ossipee Lake. One good access point is from Route 153 bridge in Freedom (43.796301,-71.056282). You can walk upriver to the power station dam. In the spring, the fishing may be better above the dam than below for holdover rainbows. There is also a good pool about 200 yards downstream. The best way to fish this pool is from the island upstream.

As the water warms, this river becomes a great smallmouth bass fishery. Unlike the Saco River to the north, you can drift down this beautiful river in a canoe, catch a lot of bass, and not see too many other boaters. You can launch a canoe from a boat launch at the Route 25 bridge (43.791840,-71.033673). One possible take-out is at the Country Store near the state line (ask permission first). The river is fairly wide with a sandy bottom and one faster section that requires caution if the water is high.

Bearcamp River

Bearcamp River is stocked with brook trout, rainbows, and browns. Expect brookies upriver in the Sandwich area, a mix of browns and brook trout in Tamworth, and rainbows in the Ossipee River section. Most fish run in the 9- to 11-inch range. This river is worth fishing because certain sections have lots of boulders and other interesting structure, and access for most of the water is easy from NH 25 and 113. Most tributaries flowing into the Bearcamp River down from mountain slopes have wild brookies in them.

Swift River

There is another, much smaller fishery known as Swift River (this is not the Kancamangus Highway river but a tributary of the Bearcamp River) that flows in the Tamworth area just west of Lake Ossipee. Expect 9- to 14-inch brookies in the three-mile flyfishing-only stretch between the Route 113A bridge and the Route 113 bridge. There are small wild brookies as well, particularly farther upstream. This river is another favorite of small stream aficianados who compare it to the Mad River.

LEFT: The Ossipee River upstream from the NH 153 Bridge.
ABOVE: A bouldery section of the Bearcamp River.

Stream Facts: White Mountains Rivers (Upper Pemi, Swift, Mad, Saco, Ellis, and others)

Species
Wild brook trout, stocked (with a few holdovers) brook trout, brown trout, and rainbow trout

When
April to October, but prime time is mid-May to mid-October

River Characteristics
All these rivers are modest-sized freestone rivers that start on the flanks of the White Mountains, and run fast, cold, and clear for much of their length. Spring runoff scours these waterways, so native trout are small but stocked trout do well. Most of the fishing is into pocket water, small runs, and plunge pools. As these rivers enter valleys, they slow, widen, and warm. Wading is easier and brown trout become the most important species.

Gear
Three- to 5-weight rods, floating or clear intermediate lines with 7.5- to 9-foot leaders tapering from 3x to 6x. Also consider bringing a wading staff, waist-high waders, polarized sunglasses, sunblock and insect repellant, catch-and-release net, gps device or topo map, and water bottle.

Flies
Elk Hair Caddis, Goddard Caddis, CDC Caddis, Adams, Parachute Adams, Royal Wulff, RS2 emerger, red quill emerger, Klinkhammer Adams, beadhead Sparkle Caddis Pupa, beadhead soft-hackle caddis pupa, Gold-ribbed Hare's Ear, and beadhead Pheasant Tail.

Nearest Fly Shop
North Country Anglers, 2888 White Mountain Highway, North Conway / 603.356.6000 / www.northcountryangler.com

Salmon follow smelt from Lake Winnipesaukee into the Merrymeeting River. Photo courtesy Tim Shaw.

LAKE WINNIPESAUKEE

For many Granite State flyfishers, open water on Lake Winnipesaukee on the first of April signals the start of the New Hampshire landlocked-salmon fishing season. Alton Bay on the big lake gets some serious attention from die-hards. An open-water section the size of a football field usually appears by the April 1 opener. At least we hope it does. Some years the ice lingers and fishing doesn't get started until a week or two later. Alton Bay can be chilly on April Fool's Day while slowly trolling tandem streamers for salmon and rainbows. Suddenly, the sky-blue ceiling above can close up darkly and start snowing.

Lake Winnipesaukee covers 44,586 acres and has a maximum depth of 168 feet. Ice-out arrives in late April, though open water can be found in Alton Bay and near the docks and bridges around the lake by opening day (April 1). Hot spots include Weirs Beach, Long Island, and the shore near the town of Meredith. Early spring conditions can be blustery for boat anglers and canoeists trolling streamer flies. A slight chop on the water's surface, however, is often good.

As the ice leaves, smelt move into the bay and gather in the Merrymeeting River, where they eventually spawn.

Salmon follow these staging smelt. Flyfishers, with vests stuffed full of smelt patterns, follow the salmon. It's not just landlocks that get our attention – rainbows in Lake Winnipesaukee run large, and four-pounders are not uncommon during the ice-out season.

In the summer, trout and salmon move out of the rocky shallows toward deeper water. Angling for smallmouth bass and other warmwater game fish offer good warm-weather opportunities. Recreational boat traffic is heavy from Memorial Day through Labor Day. Flyfish for trout and salmon from early April through the month of May.

Though some enthusiastic flyfishers dutifully chase salmon right at ice-out, most Winni veterans like to wait until late April.

Many anglers prefer fishing the lake's southernmost end by boat. Traditional trolling with tandem streamers will yield a lot of landlocks in the turbulent water of the lake's windward shore. Big rainbows are also possible.

By Mother's Day weekend, angling becomes steady. Smelt patterns and traditional salmon flies are effective at this time of the year. Sheltered coves, including Alton Bay, continue to get major attention.

Anglers flyfish Alton Bay several ways. Some cast from the wooden docks located behind Alton Bait & Tackle, while others choose to troll the southwestern side of the bay. Small-boat anglers, defying the weather, fish the Alton Bay floating bandstand area at ice-out. Many rainbows and salmon have been caught around this landmark.

Useful patterns include anything yellow, the Barnes Special, Magog smelt, the Gray Ghost (sizes 2 to 12), Black Ghost (sizes 2 to 10), Black Nose Dace (sizes 2 to 10), Mickey Finn (sizes 6 to 12) and Grizzly King (sizes 6 to 12).

Lake Winnipesaukee's season runs from April 1 through September 30 and there are many specific regulations that are subject to change. Be sure to know the rules before you wet a line.

NH 11 or 28A will take you to the village of Alton Bay at the lake's southernmost tip. The Alton Bridge is just 40 miles from downtown Portsmouth via the Spaulding Turnpike.

Boat ramp access areas, both public and fee, are available around the lake on side roads. All major points on the lake have good access. You're never really far from a launch.

The Roberts Cove boat launch, accessible near the junction of Route 28 and Roberts Cove Road, is a good put-in location for salmon angling on the lake's southern shore. The Wolfeboro town launch on Wolfeboro Bay is convenient and relatively sheltered. The Alton Bay boat access is off Routes 11 and 28A.

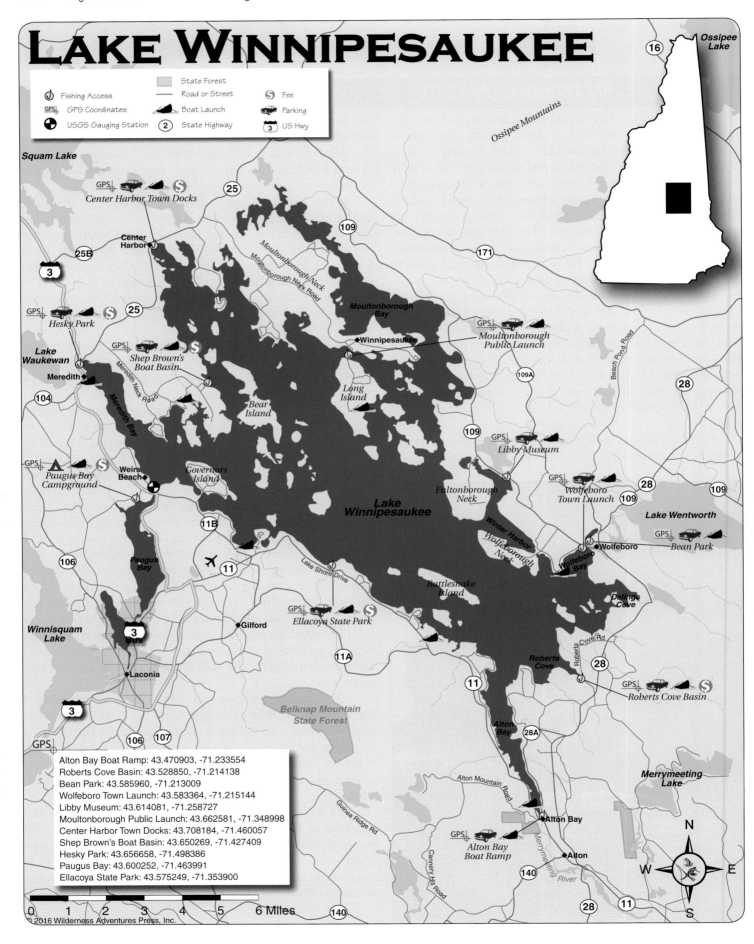

LAKE WINNIPESAUKEE

Legend:
- Fishing Access
- GPS Coordinates
- USGS Gauging Station
- State Forest
- Road or Street
- Boat Launch
- Fee
- Parking
- State Highway
- US Hwy

Ossipee Lake

Squam Lake

Ossipee Mountains

Center Harbor Town Docks

Center Harbor

Moultonborough Neck

Moultonborough Neck Road

Moultonborough Bay

Winnipesaukee

Moultonborough Public Launch

Hesky Park

Lake Waukewan

Meredith

Shep Brown's Boat Basin

Meredith Neck Road

Bear Island

Long Island

Meredith Bay

Libby Museum

Fultonborough Neck

Weirs Beach

Paugus Bay Campground

Governors Island

Lake Winnipesaukee

Winter Harbor

Wolfeborough Neck

Wolfeboro Town Launch

Lake Wentworth

Wolfeboro

Bean Park

Wolfeboro Bay

Paugus Bay

Gilford

Ellacoya State Park

Rattlesnake Island

Delings Cove

Lake Shore Drive

Winnisquam Lake

Laconia

Belknap Mountain State Forest

Roberts Cove

Roberts Cove Rd

Roberts Cove Basin

Alton Bay

Merrymeeting Lake

Alton Mountain Road

Guinea Ridge Rd

Cannery Hill Road

Alton Bay Boat Ramp

Alton

Merrymeeting River

Alton Bay Boat Ramp: 43.470903, -71.233554
Roberts Cove Basin: 43.528850, -71.214138
Bean Park: 43.585960, -71.213009
Wolfeboro Town Launch: 43.583364, -71.215144
Libby Museum: 43.614081, -71.258727
Moultonborough Public Launch: 43.662581, -71.348998
Center Harbor Town Docks: 43.708184, -71.460057
Shep Brown's Boat Basin: 43.650269, -71.427409
Hesky Park: 43.656658, -71.498386
Paugus Bay: 43.600252, -71.463991
Ellacoya State Park: 43.575249, -71.353900

0 1 2 3 4 5 6 Miles

© 2016 Wilderness Adventures Press, Inc.

N E S W

OTHER STILLWATERS OF CENTRAL NEW HAMPSHIRE

Horn Pond

East of Lake Winnipesaukee, but south of the White Mountains, is a number of ponds and lakes. Horn Pond contains brook trout, browns, rainbows, largemouth and smallmouth bass. It is located east of the village of Sanbornville on the Maine/New Hampshire border. This is one of those New Hampshire fisheries that offers both springtime angling for trout as well as bass-bugging in the summer. All three species of trout are stocked in this 435-acre pond.

Ossipee Lake

Ossipee Lake offers rainbow and salmon as well as largemouth and smallmouth bass fishing. It is located in the town of Ossipee. Ossipee Lake is 3,092 acres in size with easy access off NH 16 and 25. The lake is a mile down the Pine River from the boat ramp. The Deer Cove boat launch is located off Deer Cove Road. Ossipee Lake sees landlocked salmon and rainbows planted every year. The lake has a 61-foot maximum depth that provides cool waters through summer. Larger-sized rainbows are often caught, especially in the early season.

Shawtown Pond

Shawtown Pond (also known as Shaws Pond) is a flyfishing only, brook trout pond located in Freedom (43.824724, -71.112711) that is actively fished but also heavily stocked with some larger brookies. There is a slot limit, so trout between 13 and 18 inches must be released. To reach this pond, take Ossipee Lake Road east from the north shore of Ossipee Lake and take a left on Shawtown Road.

Silver Lake

Silver Lake, located in the town of Madison, holds rainbows, lake trout, and smallmouth bass. It covers 995 acres and is managed as a rainbow fishery. There is good smallmouth bass fishing in the northernmost section of the lake near Big Island. This lake is a favorite fishing locale for many New Hampshire anglers. A boat launch is located off NH 41 (2.7 miles from the intersection with Route 113) on the lake's western side.

Ossipee Lake looking north from the south shore.

White Pond

White Pond is stocked with brook and rainbow trout and is located in Ossipee near the Pine River State Forest. It covers a total of 47 acres, and anglers can expect 9- to 14-inch brook trout and rainbows. When the water warms up, the trout head for the three 30-foot-deep holes and flyfishing anglers should probe these holes with sinking line. If you think of the pond as an upside down face, the deep holes are where you would expect the eyes and mouth to be. This flyfishing-only stillwater is accessible from White Pond Road (43.696337,-71.077523).

White Lake

A brook-trout pond, White Lake is located within the town of Tamworth. It is stocked with brookies. This 120-acre, 40-feet-deep pond is flyfishing only, no motorboats allowed, and has no shoreline development because it is located inside the state park. There is a campground and a beach. Access is available in White Lake State Park off NH 16 near Silver and Ossipee Lakes.

Coldrain Pond, Club Pond, and Merrymeeting Lake

Located in northern Strafford County in eastern New Hampshire, the next three stillwaters are in the vicinity of the village of New Durham. Coldrain Pond offers 18 acres of flyfishing-only trout water. Not far from Alton Bay on Lake Winnipesaukee, flyfishers often stop here before heading northwest to the big lake. Access to this pond is made off Birch Hill Road in New Durham. A boat launch is available on the pond's southernmost shore. Club Pond holds planted brook trout and rainbows and covers 38 acres. Merrymeeting Lake is stocked with rainbows and salmon and is also located in the town of New Durham. Roughly the same size as Bow Lake in southeast New Hampshire, this clear and cold stillwater is accessible from Chesley Road near the dam. At the intersection of NH 11 and 28, take Route 11 east for three miles, turn left onto Depot Road, and then find Chesley Road. Trolled streamers work best on this 50-foot-deep lake.

MAIN IMAGE: Mascoma Lake with its historic Shaker Village in the foreground.
Photo courtesy Philip Trasatti.
UPPER LEFT: It is easy to get distracted by the stunning views while fishing in Franconia Notch.

Saltmarsh Pond

Other fisheries close to the big lake include Saltmarsh Pond, stocked with brook trout and rainbows. Located in the town of Gilford, this 34-acre stillwater can be accessed from NH 11A just west of Alton Bay. Expect company as this is a popular fishery.

Winnisquam Lake

Winnisquam Lake holds rainbows and landlocked salmon and is annually stocked with these species. This 4,264-acre lake is located in the town of Laconia and close to the Lake Winnipesaukee fishery. US 3 south of Meredith provides access to Winnisquam, which is a good second choice when Lake Winnipesaukee is crowded. Fishing is best during the month of May.

Waukewan Lake

Just north of Winnisquam Lake is Waukewan Lake, which holds rainbows as well as smallmouth bass. It is located in the town of Meredith, with highway access via US 3. There is a boat launch for this 912-acre lake in the village of Meredith. Although rainbow trout are stocked, this is primarily a bass fishery by summer.

Squam Lakes

Just north of Winnipesauke you will find Big and Little Squam Lakes, stocked with rainbows, lake trout, landlocked salmon, and with a resident population of smallmouth bass. These small lakes are located in the town of Holderness. Big Squam is 6,765 acres and Little Squam is 408 acres. Expect the usual run of nine-inch trout. Holdovers can be much larger. Bass bugging for smallmouths is excellent in the rocky shallows of these lakes, especially in the spring. Fishing is also good in early autumn after the recreational boat traffic subsides. There is a large boat ramp with lots of parking on the causeway between the two lakes off of NH 113.

Hall Ponds

Upper Hall Pond is a brook-trout pond located north of Squam Lake. Expect 9-to 11-inch brookies on this 24-acre flyfishing-only pond. It is accessible from NH 49, off Sandwich Notch Road (a relatively rough dirt road) and has a two-trout daily limit, with no fish between 12 and 16 inches, and only one over 16.

Middle Hall Pond holds brook trout and is located in the town of Sandwich. It is the smallest of the Hall Ponds at only five acres. Middle Pond is being developed as a brook-trout fishery by New Hampshire Fish and Game.

Lower Hall Pond also holds brook trout and is located in Sandwich. Again, this remote pond is a developing fishery, which should provide good flyfishing in the coming years.

Cole Pond

In far west-central New Hampshire is the town of Enfield with several flyfishing options. Cole Pond is a flyfishing-only pond stocked with brook trout. This 17-acre stillwater is located in the town of Enfield and is accessible by foot trail from Route 4A near the village of Fish Market.

Crystal Lake

Crystal Lake is a moderately developed 365-acre pond holding rainbows and smallmouth bass. It is located in the town of Enfield (and not to be confused with another Crystal Lake, just south of Lake Winnipesaukee). The lake is stocked with rainbows every year. While most anglers troll to catch the rainbows, these trout will rise in the sheltered coves when the lake is calm in the mornings and evenings. When conditions are right, fly casting to the risers is a real thrill. Also, try bass-bugs for Crystal Lake bronzebacks in June and early autumn. To reach Crystal Lake, take Exit 17 off of I-89, and then take US 4 and then 4A a total of seven miles to Crystal Lake Road. A right on Algonquin Road leads to a good boat launch.

Mascoma Lake

Mascoma Lake is heavily developed but the fishing can be quite good for a variety of coldwater species (brown and rainbow trout) and warmwater species (small and largemouth bass). There are boat ramps on both the north and south shores. Take Exit 17 off of I-89 and take US 4 East several miles. On the shore of this lake is an historic Shaker village that is worth visiting if you are a history buff or are curious about the Shakers.

Tewksbury Pond

Farther east on US 4 in the town of Grafton is Tewksbury Pond. This is a beautiful little pond with no motors allowed and is stocked with all three species of trout. A boat launch (43.606913,-71.966512) can be found near where Tunnel Road meets Route 4.

Joe Coffin Pond and Streeter Pond

The Franconia Notch area offers a number of stillwater flyfishing options. Joe Coffin Pond is located off NH 18 north of the village of Franconia (44.241568,-71.761302). This 10-acre pond is planted with rainbow trout. Red, orange, or burgundy colored micro-egg patterns are effective flies for these fish. Streeter Pond holds brook trout, rainbows, and browns and is located in the town of Sugar Hill. There is a New Hampshire Fish and Game boat access at the south end. This is a shallow, tannin-stained pond with some development, and is not one of my favorite ponds to fish. Find Streeter Pond Road off NH 18/116, north of Franconia Village (I-93 Exit 38).

Echo Lake

Echo Lake, located in Franconia Notch State Park, holds brook trout and covers 28 acres. This water offers one of the better flyfishing opportunities in central New Hampshire. Expect fish from 9 to 16 inches in length. Most of the brook trout run a pound or less, but there are plenty of them to keep you busy. To find it, follow signs to Cannon Mountain Ski Area. There is a good boat launch on the south shore and you can also wade that part of the sandy shoreline. This small water body is perfect for canoes, kayaks, or float tubes. You will enjoy the stunning views, but the constant noise from I-93 along one shoreline does subtract from the experience. Some folks slowly troll streamers, but trout will rise well into the summer. The last time I was there in early July, the surface temperature was only in the high 60s.

Profile Lake

Profile Lake is a flyfishing-only pond, managed for larger trout and is located just south of Echo Lake in Franconia Notch. In the recent past, what appeared to be a man's profile jutted out of the granite mountainside almost 1,200 feet above the lake. Dubbed "Old Man of the Mountains", this sight attracted camera-wielding tourists from all over until one day natural erosion and weathering caused much of his face to fall to the valley below. Now Profile Lake has just one attraction – its trout. There is a small-boat hand-launch point on the south shore (no motors allowed). To reach this lake, take Exit 34B off of I-93. This is a southbound-only exit. To access from the north, drive past it to the Cannon exit, then double back southbound until you find Exit 34B.

Brook trout in this flyfishing-only pond range from 12 to 16 inches. Those angling for the pan should note that there is a two-fish limit with only one over 16 inches. Profile is best flyfished from a canoe or float tube. Since the collapse of the main attraction, there are far fewer people stopping here. Last July, in the middle of the afternoon, I was the only one parked in the lot. The shoreline near the parking lot is sandy, gently sloping, and easy to wade out quite a distance to reach the deeper water. Trout will congregate near the outlet in both spring and fall. This is a very fun place to fish in a float tube despite the annoying sound of trucks downshifting on nearby I-93 traffic.

All ready to head out onto Profile Lake.

Lonesome Lake

Lonesome Lake is a remote hike-in pond located on the Appalachian Trail that can be hiked to from the Lafayette Campground in Franconia Notch, just south of Profile Lake. In fact, all of the above three lakes are easily reached from this well-maintained, stream-side, wooded campground with all of the amenities. The only downside, once again, is the traffic noise from the highway. A paved bike path connects the campground with both

Echo and Profile Lakes. The hike up to Lonesome Lake is roughly a mile in length and includes an elevation climb of 1,000 feet. Still, the climb is gradual over a well-built trail and it wouldn't be too much of a burden to take a float tube up.

Lonesome Lake itself is spectacular with mountain views all around and an AMC hut where one can stay overnight in bunk rooms with that same view from the front windows. Lonesome Lake is pond sized, stocked well, and fishing from shore is productive, especially from the outlet, where the dam and a wooden bridge provide good casting platforms. The outlet

Fall comes to Mirror Lake.

stream, Cascade Brook, is also full of small native brook trout and can be reached by the Appalachian Trail that parallels it for a time.

As Cascade Brook reaches its confluence with the Pemi, it gains strength and size and offers the willing hiker waterfalls, gorges, deep pools, and cascading water over granite ledges. Many of the pools hold native brook trout, but the water features alone make it worth the walk. The trailhead near the Franconia Parkway starts at "the Basin" – a popular Notch tourist attraction.

Mirror Lake

Just south of The Notch in the town of Woodstock lies Mirror Lake, off of Route 3 on Mirror Lake Road. Mirror Lake is a small beautiful kettle pond with most of its shoreline undeveloped and protected due to the efforts of the Hubbard Brook Research Foundation. It is heavily stocked with several species of trout each year and has a resident largemouth bass population as well. Despite significant ice fishing pressure, some fish do hold over. The deep hole in the lake is marked by a buoy. Access for canoes, kayaks, or paddleboards is from the public beach, which is clearly marked. What makes this lake interesting, besides the good fishing, is that it is the most studied lake of this size in the world. Due to the proximity of the Hubbard Brook Experimental Forest, scientists have monitored and

studied this lake for over 50 years. Two books have been written about it and the acid rain threat was first discovered and publicized here. For more information go to www. hubbardbrook.org.

Sky Pond

Farther south in New Hampshire, Sky Pond contains brook trout and rainbows and is located in the town of New Hampton. Found just east of the Newfound River and the lower Pemigewasset fisheries, angling on this 13-acre pond is by flyfishing only. Sky Pond is heavily stocked and is managed as a quality fishery with restrictive regulations. A friend hit this pond at the right time one spring when the larger fish were cruising the shoreline and landed 15- to 18-inch brook trout by casting to shore and retrieving beadhead nymphs. Other times he hasn't fared well, but that is not unusual on ponds with large trout. Often they are not active, resting down deeper in the water, and not accessible to fly casters.

Hunkins Pond

Hunkins Pond holds rainbows and browns and is located in the town of Sanbornton. Not far from the lower Pemigewasset fishery, this 15-acre water is accessible from Hunkins Pond Road just northeast of the village of Sanborton. Expect fish from 9 to 11 inches.

CENTRAL NEW HAMPSHIRE PLANNING CONSIDERATIONS

Nearby Hub Cities and Towns

- North Conway (www.mtwashingtonvalley.org)(www.northcountryangler.com)
- Lincoln (www.lincolnwoodstock.com)
- Franconia (www.franconianotch.org)

Easy Access Options

- In North Conway, head west half a mile on River Road, and find a parking lot on the right before the bridge over the Saco River (44.056369,-71.137235). Park there and you will find yourself about in the middle of the catch-and-release section. It is an easy walk upriver on a grassy field. To reach the water, you have to pick your way down a relatively short, but steep, rocky slope. There is a long deep run here that is stocked heavily and fish hold over and even overwinter here as well. Unless you see rising fish, it pays to fish with sink-tip or sinking lines in order to propel your flies to the bottom.
- One easy access point on the Ellis River is to park on either side of the so-called Honeymoon Covered Bridge in Jackson (44.141444,-71.186655), and follow the very short path on the east side of the bridge that leads to the water. With just a few steps, you can fish the good pools and runs both immediately upstream and downstream of the bridge.
- A convenient parking lot (44.161185,-71.676951) and a 50-foot walk will lead you to the easy-to-wade shoreline of Profile Lake in Franconia Notch. The outlet stream there can hold trout as well. Best to fish in the spring and fall when the trout can be found within casting distance.

Suggested Beginner Options

- Try below Goodrich Falls on the Ellis River. On NH 16 heading north from the intersection of Route 302, take a left on a modest unmarked road right before the bridge (44.125592,-71.188846). It will dead end at set of barriers. Park there and take the trail to the right, which will lead you to the pools below the falls. There is plenty of room for backcasts and you know the fish are there. You will be sharing this spot with other anglers but that can be a good learning experience as well, as you watch what they do.

- Try the Ellis farther upstream. This is small-stream fishing at its best. Choose a generic attractor pattern such as Hornberg or large foam ant, and walk up and down the stream making short casts to the deeper pockets, pools, and runs. Chances are good you will hook up with at least a few brook trout.
- Any of the small trout ponds in central New Hampshire are a good bet in June. Choose one, launch a small boat, and look for signs of rising fish. A Hornberg, Parachute Adams, or Royal Wulff cast a short distance from the boat should result in a strike. If nothing is visible, troll your fly line behind the boat with a Wood Special or Gray Ghost streamer.
- Most small White Mountains streams hold eager wild brook trout. Explore a little and find your own secret spot. For example, the outlet stream from Lonesome Lake (Cascade Brook) has little brookies in every small pool. This is small water and you will be dapping your fly more than casting it. The exact fly pattern doesn't really matter.

Vacation Suggestions

Weekend Getaway

- Choose a beautiful late September weekend as the leaves begin to turn, and stay in North Conway. Fish the nearby Wild, Ellis, and Saco Rivers. The fishing won't be easy for the holdover trout that have been fished to all summer but with spawning season approaching, fish will begin to move and get more aggressive again.
- Fish Lake Winnepesaukee and the myriad of surrounding lakes and ponds in May and June after the ice is out and the surface waters are still cool. Plan on trolling and some casting if surface activity is spotted. There are a number of local, small, and quaint hotels in which to stay.

One-week Vacation

- Take a week-long camping trip to the White Mountains and sample the surrounding streams. July is a good time because the fishing is still good and the biting black flies and mosquitos have tapered a bit. There are a number of campgrounds to choose from and you might want to divide your time between two or three. Some options include Lafayette Campground in Franconia Notch and any of the six campgrounds on the Kangamangus Highway, including the Covered Bridge Campground. Smaller camping areas are also tucked away, such as the camping area on the upper Saco River by the Fourth Iron Bridge, just a short walk from the parking lot.

You might want to devote one day each to fish the following:
- Wild River
- Ellis River
- Saco River
- Mad River
- Upper Pemigewasset River
- Profile and Echo Lakes

And then choose some White Mountains hikes that take you alongside any of the mountain streams or remote ponds and try fishing for wild little brookies. I heartily recommend the hike up to Lonesome Lake but there are dozens of options.

TOP: A long, deep run on the Saco River just upstream from the River Road Bridge in North Conway.
LEFT: The author wading into Profile Lake. The parking lot is off to the left just out of frame. Photo courtesy Lindsey Rustad.

Northern New Hampshire

Northern New Hampshire's Coos County offers many wonderful angling opportunities. The Androscoggin and upper Connecticut Rivers are often the main attraction for flyfishing enthusiasts. However, stillwaters such as Diamond Ponds, Back Lake, and the Connecticut Lakes should not be overlooked. Many of the region's small streams support wild brook trout. At night, you'll fall asleep listening to the mournful call of loons, the North Country's most vocal bird. During daytime outings, you'll often see yearling moose lurking along roadsides.

Fishing the Upper Connecticut River by First Connecticut Lake Dam. Photo courtesy of the Cabins at Lopstick.

ANDROSCOGGIN RIVER

The Androscoggin River (called the Andro by locals) has much to offer the flyfisher because of its diversity of water types, easy access, good hatches, and multiple fish species. It is one of the larger rivers in New England and drains a huge expanse of northern New Hampshire and western Maine as it makes its way 50 miles from its origin at the Errol Dam to the Maine border west of Bethel, before continuing on through Maine. Every drop of water from all of the Rangeley area lakes, and the famous Rapid, Magalloway, and Kennebago Rivers eventually moves through Lake Umbagog and over the Errol Dam to become the origin of the Andro.

The Andro contains a variety of salmonids including rainbow, brook, and brown trout as well as landlocked salmon. This river is stocked heavily and fish do hold over with large brown trout occasionally caught. Natural reproduction occurs in its many tributaries. This water was polluted years ago but now is vastly improved; the limiting factor now is that during the summer, the mainstem of the river does get warmer than is optimal for trout. Therefore, the best time to fish this river is from mid-May to mid-July and then again from Labor Day until water temperatures drop significantly in late fall, or when the season closes on October 15 (for waters north of Berlin). During hot early summers, the best fishing will move to the mouths of tributaries as soon as late June.

South of the town of Errol, NH 16 winds its way next to the upper Andro for miles, providing easy access. There are miles of water for wading anglers to spread out in, and crowding is never an issue.

Many anglers prefer to float this river as long as the flows are above 1,500cfs. Floating is the best option above 3,000cfs, when wading becomes difficult. The key to fishing this larger river is to look at the features right in front of you (runs, riffles, pools, eddies, boulders, etc.) and concentrate on fishing just one feature or one section – conceptually imagining it as a combination of smaller rivers, and fishing just one smaller river at a time.

The most famous hatch on the Andro is the so-called alderfly emergence that starts roughly the third week in June and continues for two weeks or so. The zebra caddis (incorrectly called alderfly) is abundant in the upper Androscoggin and during the hatch will swarm around trees and bushes that overhang the water. During calm days, the insects will leave the shelter of the trees and sometimes blunder into the water. Conversely, strong gusts of wind will blow these insects into the water and fish rise to the sudden feast.

For best results, fish your dry-fly imitation on a dead-drift in the current, particularly in broken water. Alderfly larva patterns fished slowly on the bottom using a sinking fly line can be effective, as well. Remember the alderfly at the tying bench before any trips to this region.

Each section of the Andro has unique features and regulations, so let's cover them starting from Errol Dam, and then continuing downstream.

The first section from the Errol Dam to Bragg Bay is less than a mile and is the lone flyfishing-only section on the river. The large back-eddy pool directly below the dam

The Androscoggin is floatable with a drift boat or raft. Photo courtesy Cabins at Lopstick.

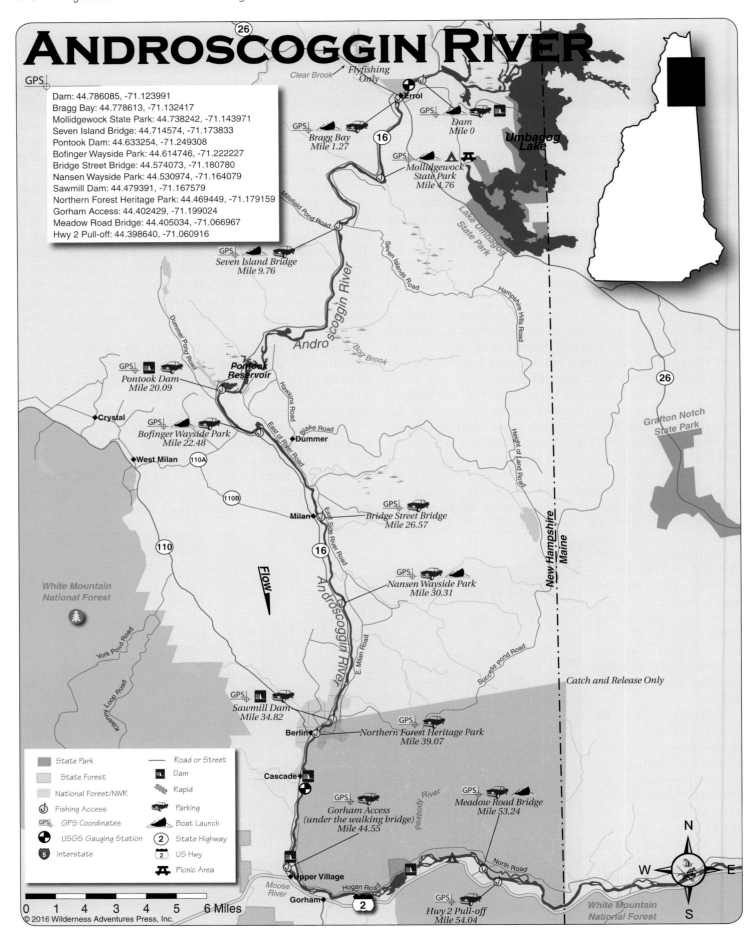

ANDROSCOGGIN RIVER

Dam: 44.786085, -71.123991
Bragg Bay: 44.778613, -71.132417
Mollidgewock State Park: 44.738242, -71.143971
Seven Island Bridge: 44.714574, -71.173833
Pontook Dam: 44.633254, -71.249308
Bofinger Wayside Park: 44.614746, -71.222227
Bridge Street Bridge: 44.574073, -71.180780
Nansen Wayside Park: 44.530974, -71.164079
Sawmill Dam: 44.479391, -71.167579
Northern Forest Heritage Park: 44.469449, -71.179159
Gorham Access: 44.402429, -71.199024
Meadow Road Bridge: 44.405034, -71.066967
Hwy 2 Pull-off: 44.398640, -71.060916

Clear Brook
Flyfishing Only
Errol
Dam Mile 0
Umbagoog Lake
Bragg Bay Mile 1.27
Mollidgewock State Park Mile 4.76
Lake Umbagog State Park
Millsfield Pond Road
Seven Island Bridge Mile 9.76
Androscoggin River
Seven Islands Road
Bog Brook
Hampshire Hills Road
Dummer Pond Road
Pontook Reservoir
Pontook Dam Mile 20.09
Crystal
Hawkins Road
Blake Road
Height of Land Road
Grafton Notch State Park
Bofinger Wayside Park Mile 22.48
East of River Road
Dummer
West Milan
110A
110B
Milan
Bridge Street Bridge Mile 26.57
East Side River Road
New Hampshire
Maine
110
White Mountain National Forest
Flow
Nansen Wayside Park Mile 30.31
Androscoggin River
E. Milan Road
Success Pond Road
Catch and Release Only
York Pond Road
Kilkenny Loop Road
Sawmill Dam Mile 34.82
Berlin
Northern Forest Heritage Park Mile 39.07
Cascade
Peabody River
Meadow Road Bridge Mile 53.24
Gorham Access (under the walking bridge) Mile 44.55
North Road
Upper Village
Moose River
Hogan Road
Gorham
Hwy 2 Pull-off Mile 54.04
White Mountain National Forest

Legend:
State Park
State Forest
National Forest/NWR
Fishing Access
GPS Coordinates
USGS Gauging Station
Interstate
Road or Street
Dam
Rapid
Parking
Boat Launch
State Highway
US Hwy
Picnic Area

N
W E
S

0 1 2 3 4 5 6 Miles
© 2016 Wilderness Adventures Press, Inc.

(44.783031,-71.129279) is best fished by canoe. My buddy, Dave, once caught a beautiful rainbow in that pool at sunset, and the sides of the fish glowed reddish-pink from a combination of its natural color and the reflection of the rose-colored sunset off the water. The rest of this section is fast water cascading over a multitude of rocks and boulders.

The next section is from Bragg Bay to Pontook Reservoir. Between the town of Errol and Mollidgewock Campground, there are more than three miles of water easily accessible from Route 16. Clear Stream, a tributary of the Androscoggin just west of town, holds good numbers of 9- to 12-inch brook trout. The confluence of Clear Stream and the main river just south of Errol can be a good spot to try.

From Mollidgewock State Campground to Seven Island Bridge is the so-called 13-mile Woods, which is a lightly developed section popular with driftboat fishers. It can also be waded, and NH 16 continues to provide access. The campground offers more than 40 sites along the river. For details regarding staying at the campground, consult www. nhstateparks.com/mollidgewock.html.

Ten miles south of Errol is the confluence of Bog Brook. This area is stocked with trout and salmon in the spring. The four-mile stretch of riffle water between Bog Brook and Pontook Reservoir offers great flyfishing for brookies,

browns, and rainbows during the alderfly hatch. The fastest water is found at Seven Island Bridge (44.714574,-71.173833) since the river pinches in here. Braided channels around islands nearby add to the fishing interest.

Immediately below Pontook Dam flows interesting riffles and runs, but the wading can be treacherous, particularly at higher flows.

Flatwater sections of the Androscoggin do not hold as many trout and salmon as the more highly oxygenated riffles. The faster runs remain cooler and offer the best flyfishing throughout the summer. If the mainstem of the river is above 65 degrees, concentrate your fishing directly downstream from any tributaries that are contributing cooler water.

The last section of the river is 20 miles long, stretches from Sawmill Dam in Berlin to the Maine border, and is the longest catch-and-release section in New England. This section is not stocked and most of the fish are wild (larger fish are possible). As the season progresses, it pays to focus on the outlets of colder feeder streams such as the Moose and Peabody Rivers.

For the entire Andro, pattern selection and fishing techniques should be dictated by how you like to fish, and what your eyes tell you, because almost anything will work at times including streamers, nymphs, dry flies, and wet flies. If you see some insect activity, match the hatch, and fishing a variety of caddis patterns on the surface is always appropriate if you have your heart set on dry-fly fishing. With the variety of baitfish and other aquatic foods including crayfish, a variety of imitations fished near the bottom may yield the largest fish. Standard nymphs such as the Hare's Ear, Pheasant Tail, and Prince Nymphs fished with a floating indicator will be effective in the long runs with moderate current.

ABOVE: The alderfly emergence starts roughly the third week in June and continues for two weeks or so. Photo courtesy Evelyn King. RIGHT: Pontook Dam.

UPPER CONNECTICUT RIVER

The upper Connecticut River is the most consistently productive fishery across every season of the year in northern New Hampshire. Because of its northern location, cold ground water, deep lakes, and bottom-release dams, it stays cold enough to support active trout all summer regardless of the outside temperatures. As such, sometimes during hot summers, it is the only game in town when it comes to coldwater species.

The upper Connecticut is stocked with brook trout and rainbows in the 9- to 11-inch range. Landlocked salmon and browns are also stocked and they do hold over. Landlocked salmon run out of several of the lakes into the river during the spring and fall and average one to two pounds and 15 to 17 inches long.

The Connecticut River's headwaters originate from Fourth Connecticut Lake, which lies near the border of the Province of Quebec, Canada. The river flows through Third Connecticut Lake and meanders south following US 3 near Deer Mountain Campground at Moose Falls. From there, it enters Second Connecticut Lake. River sections then connect the Second Connecticut Lake and First Connecticut Lake as well as First Connecticut Lake and Lake Francis. All of these waters were natural lakes and were deep and cold before dams then increased their size.

The upper section from Third to Second Connecticut Lake is a small stream fishing experience for hand-sized wild brook trout. It doesn't get fished often and requires some bushwhacking through the alders. Easiest access is from Route 3 from several logging roads that cross it. The Moose Falls stretch near Deer Mountain Campground can fish very well in the spring. Best access is near the campground: a logging road named Sophie's Lane runs parallel to it just before Third Lake and you can hike in from there.

The 2.5-mile river section between Second Connecticut Lake dam and First Connecticut Lake dam is still small, mostly pocket water with stream flows usually under 100cfs and a width of less than 20 feet. Smaller wild and stocked brook trout and landlocked salmon will take dries, nymphs, and small streamers all year in this freestone section of riffles and pools. In mid-May, usually a week or two after ice-out, larger landlocks run up from the First Connecticut Lake chasing smelt and can be caught with smelt-imitation streamers such as the Marabou Black Ghost, Marabou Gray Ghost, or even white Zonkers. In September, the larger lake salmon ascend this section again in preparation for spawning. Brightly-colored streamers with highlights of yellow are a good bet for these aggressive pre-spawn fish. This entire stretch is flyfishing only and catch and release only from the Second Connecticut dam to the upstream side of the logging bridge on Magalloway Road.

The famous Trophy Section of the Connecticut runs from First Connecticut Lake to Lake Francis. From First Connecticut Lake dam downstream to the signs on Lake Francis, it is flyfishing only with a daily limit for brook trout of two fish over 12 inches. Access the top of the trophy stretch by the First Connecticut Lake dam on US 3. There are two parking areas and a trail to the stream. This section of river flows south away from Route 3, so best access is from River Road which leads to the Lake Francis Campground. A mile down River Road toward the campground, about 200 yards before you reach the covered bridge over Perry Stream, there is a dirt road on the left which takes you within 100 yards to a small bridge over the Connecticut River, with parking and good access. There is a trail which runs from the covered bridge downstream.

The trophy section is wider with greater flows than upriver waters, but its riffles and runs are still easily waded under normal conditions. This section is heavily stocked with brook, rainbow, and brown trout, as well as landlocked salmon. This is the place for a grand slam, achieved by hooking all four species in one day. Holdover browns that weigh several pounds are not uncommon. In the spring and fall, larger landlocks move into this stretch of river from Lake Francis, at first to chase spawning smelt, and then on spawning runs of their own. By all means, fish the famous

The trophy section on the Connecticut River. Photo courtesy of the Cabins at Lopstick.

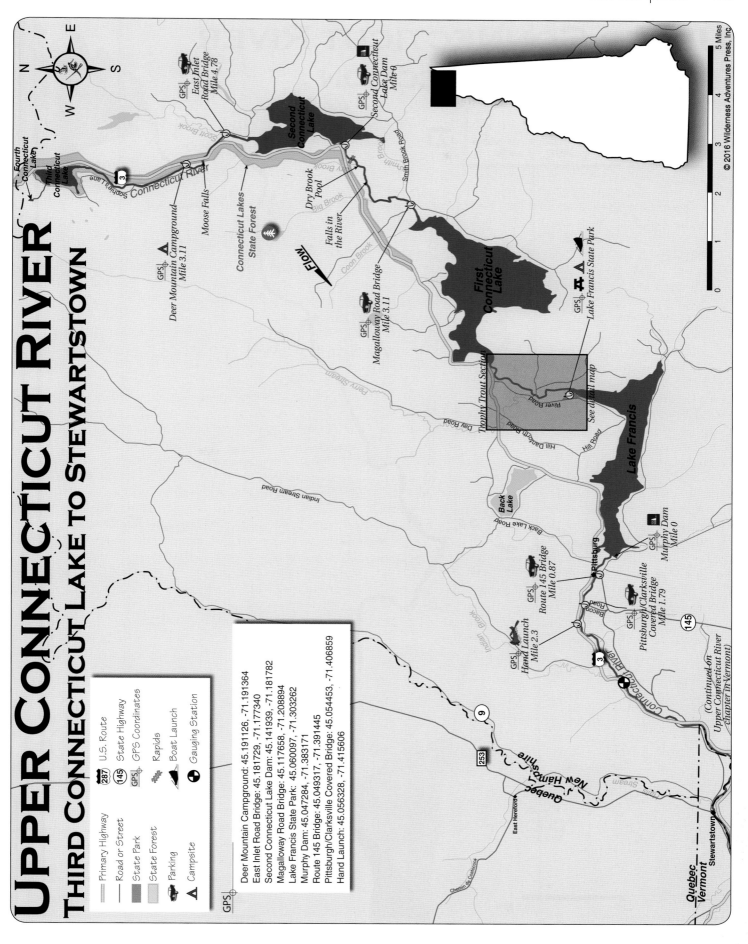

Upper Connecticut River
Third Connecticut Lake to Stewartstown

Legend:
- Primary Highway
- Road or Street
- State Park
- State Forest
- Parking
- Campsite
- (287) U.S. Route
- (145) State Highway
- GPS Coordinates
- Rapids
- Boat Launch
- Gauging Station
- GPS

Deer Mountain Campground: 45.191126, -71.191364
East Inlet Road Bridge: 45.181729, -71.177340
Second Connecticut Lake Dam: 45.141939, -71.181782
Magalloway Road Bridge: 45.117658, -71.208894
Lake Francis State Park: 45.060097, -71.303262
Murphy Dam: 45.047284, -71.383171
Route 145 Bridge: 45.049317, -71.391445
Pittsburgh/Clarksville Covered Bridge: 45.054453, -71.406859
Hand Launch: 45.056328, -71.415606

Fourth Connecticut Lake

Third Connecticut Lake

Connecticut River

Sophie's Lane

East Inlet Road Bridge Mile 4.78

Scott Brook

Second Connecticut Lake

Second Connecticut Lake Dam Mile 6

Moose Falls

Deer Mountain Campground Mile 3.11

Connecticut Lakes State Forest

Dry Brook Pool

Falls in the River

Big Brook

Smith Brook Road

Smith Brook

FLOW

Coon Brook

Magalloway Road Bridge Mile 3.11

Perry Stream

First Connecticut Lake

Lake Francis State Park

See detail map

River Road

Thorophy Trout Section

Day Road

Hill Danforth Road

Hill Road

Lake Francis

Indian Stream Road

Back Lake

Back Lake Road

Pittsburg

Murphy Dam Mile 0

Indian Brook

Hand Launch Mile 2.3

Route 145 Bridge Mile 0.87

Bacon Road

Pittsburgh/Clarksville Coverd Bridge Mile 1.79

(145)

(3)

(9)

(253)

Connecticut River

Quebec
New Hampshire

East Hereford

Chemin St-Coaticook

Quebec
Vermont

Stewartstown

(Continued on Upper Connecticut River Chapter in Vermont)

© 2016 Wilderness Adventures Press, Inc.

0   1   2   3   4   5 Miles

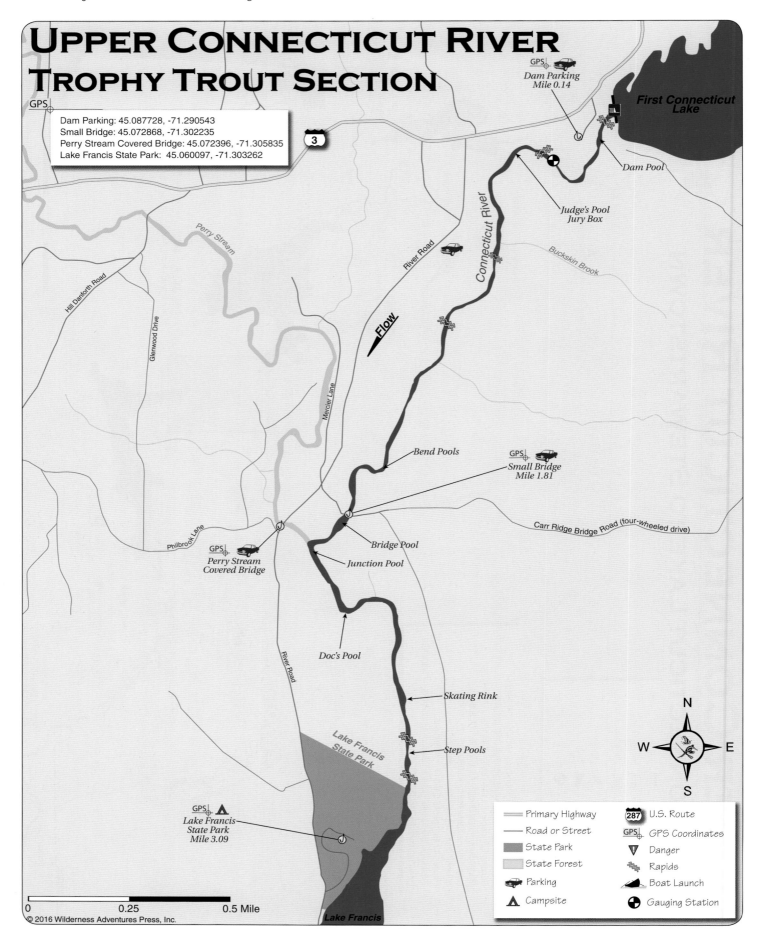

UPPER CONNECTICUT RIVER
TROPHY TROUT SECTION

GPS

Dam Parking: 45.087728, -71.290543
Small Bridge: 45.072868, -71.302235
Perry Stream Covered Bridge: 45.072396, -71.305835
Lake Francis State Park: 45.060097, -71.303262

3

GPS
Dam Parking
Mile 0.14

First Connecticut
Lake

Dam Pool

Judge's Pool
Jury Box

Perry Stream

Connecticut River

Buckskin Brook

Hill Danforth Road

Glenwood Drive

River Road

Flow

Mercier Lane

Bend Pools

GPS
Small Bridge
Mile 1.81

Carr Ridge Bridge Road (four-wheeled drive)

Phillbrook Lane

GPS
Perry Stream
Covered Bridge

Bridge Pool

Junction Pool

Doc's Pool

River Road

Skating Rink

Lake Francis
State Park

Step Pools

N
W   E
S

GPS
Lake Francis
State Park
Mile 3.09

Primary Highway	287 U.S. Route
Road or Street	GPS GPS Coordinates
State Park	Danger
State Forest	Rapids
Parking	Boat Launch
Campsite	Gauging Station

0   0.25   0.5 Mile
© 2016 Wilderness Adventures Press, Inc.

Lake Francis

pools such as the Bridge Pool, or Judges, Doc's or Junction Pools. Fish are caught there regularly on dries, nymphs, and streamers. But if you want more solitude, you can usually hike up or downstream and find less-pressured fish.

Below Lake Francis, the Connecticut River continues to be a fine fishery for over 30 miles. There are good hatches, particularly blue-winged olives and caddis, but also mixing in are sulphurs and other mid-sized mayflies. Stoneflies including yellow Sallies appear off and on during the summer.

Murphy Dam at the south end of Lake Francis not only provides flood control, but it is also the source of ice-cold water for the fish in the river below. Even on the hottest days of summer, you'll find freely-feeding browns, rainbows, and brook trout in this nutrient-rich water. Flows usually range from 300 to 600cfs. Holdover browns that weigh several pounds are caught here periodically. Even larger browns swim immediately below the dam and several over 15 pounds have been caught, though they are extremely difficult to fool. You may see the commotion as they slam a baitfish, and they may even inspect your fly, but that is usually the extent of the action. Try fishing in darkness, during bad weather, and utilizing articulated or large flies that the lunkers haven't seen. Rubbing the flies in the mud or perhaps with some fish slime (if you catch a smaller fish) in order to remove human scent is another good idea.

Access continues to be from NH 3, both near the dam and as it follows the river south. If you enjoy solitude, you will probably find it if you work your way downstream farther from the Murphy Dam, although Route 3 is never far away.

From West Stewartson downstream to Colebrook and on to the town of Columbia, the character of the river changes from a classic New England freestone with riffles, runs, and plunge pools, to having more of a winding character with deeper pools, and high muddy banks bordered by fields and corn. It is easier to float this section, although it can be waded if you pick your spots.

One nice day float is from West Stewartson to a takeout across NH 3 from a rest area. From there to Colebrook is another half-day float. The takeout is a rough dirt road and is not particularly obvious, so make sure you locate it and know what it looks like before you attempt to find it at dusk. This stretch of river can be kayaked or canoed without floating. I like to launch my kayak at the described takeout, paddle upstream a short distance, and then drift downstream casting into likely water. In midsummer, I will put in during the late afternoon, and cast streamers with nymph trailers to undercut banks and any dead-wood structure I can find, trying to fool a nice brown. When the sun is off the water, the rainbows start rising in current seams next to the high banks, and I switch to a caddis dry such as the Puterbaugh Caddis, and hook chunky rainbows that frequently jump when hooked. Every so often, I catch a brookie.

Stream Facts: Upper Connecticut River

Season
The season on the upper Connecticut runs from January 1 through October 15 (September 30 for landlocked salmon). After ice-out (around the first week of May) and for the next two weeks, larger salmon chase spawning smelt out of the lakes into the river.

After that, fishing weighted nymphs offers the highest likelihood of success until the hatches start in June. In June, the normal progression of Northeast hatches occur. After July 1, most of the activity is caddis and stoneflies. In the trophy section and continuing downstream, the fishing stays good all summer.

In September, salmon move out of the lakes again as they look for spawning areas.

Species
Mostly foot-long stocked landlocked salmon, brookies, browns, and rainbows with some holdovers. Sometimes broodstock fish weighing two to four pounds are released into the river as well. Depending on the season, larger brown trout and landlocks in the two-pound range will move into the river from the lakes.

River Flows
The dams moderate the flows, but water releases are based on a variety of factors. Sometimes during droughts, water flow will increase because southern New Hampshire interests call for more water.

Access
NH 3 is your primary access to the area. River Road runs south of Route 3 below First Connecticut Lake and provides good access as well.

Fly Patterns
All-purpose flies, such as the Hornberg, Elk Hair Caddis, and beadhead Pheasant Tail nymphs can be the best producers in early June. Flyfish the early summer caddis hatch with Elk Hair Caddis patterns as well as caddis emergers because case-making caddis are found throughout the upper river. Woolly Buggers, white, grey, or yellow Marabou Soft-hackle streamers, and bucktails can attract larger-sized holdover browns and landlocked salmon.

OTHER NORTHERN NEW HAMPSHIRE RIVERS AND STREAMS

Ammonoosuc River

The Ammonoosuc River starts at the famous Lake of the Clouds (well known but fishless) on the upper flank of Mount Washington and gathers water from other small Presidential Range streams cascading down from the lofty peaks.

Wild brook trout can be found upstream from the small town of Twin Mountain in the riffles and pocket water of the upper river near Base Station Road (on the way to Mount Washington's Cog Railroad). You can spot brook trout finning right behind the Omni Mount Washington Hotel at Bretton Woods in both the Ammonoosic and its tributary Crawford Brook.

The Ammonoosuc changes directions at the Omni Mount Washington Hotel in Bretton Woods and starts to parallel NH 302 before eventually emptying into the Connecticut River near Woodsville after a 60-mile journey.

From Bretton Woods to Twin Mountain, the angler will find frequent small dirt parking areas or camping areas with access to the river. Near NH 302, stocked rainbows can be caught and farther downstream as the river levels out, a few brown trout as well.

Beaver Brook

Beaver Brook is a small brook trout stream north of the village of Colebrook near NH 145. It flows out of the Beaver Brook Falls Natural Area and joins the Connecticut River just outside of Colebrook. Beaver Brook is stocked with brook trout in the spring.

Mohawk River

The Mohawk River flows down from Dixville Notch along NH 26 to Colebrook, where it meets the Connecticut and is stocked by the state. This water is better described as a stream than a river and flows through woods, small farms, and modest house lots. It is very visible from the road almost everywhere, and it is a simple matter to look for interesting water as you drive along, stop and fish. Try prospecting with a Hornberg (either wet or dry) or a Wood Special streamer.

The Ammonoosuc River in September, near the town of Twin Mountain.

Dead Diamond River and Swift Diamond River

The Dead Diamond and Swift Diamond Rivers meet to form the Diamond River, which then joins the Magalloway River near the Maine/NH border in Wentworth; location 10 miles northeast of village of Errol on Route 16. These are freestone rivers filled with wild brook trout, but water levels fluctuate significantly and the quality of the fishing varies from year to year and month to month. There is a USGS gauge on the Diamond and you can check on recent flows before you go.

Much of the Diamond watershed is managed for timber, recreation, and wildlife by Dartmouth College with restricted vehicle access. Public access to the Second College Grant is welcomed by foot or bike only from the entrance next to the cemetery just north of Mount Dustan General Store on Route 16.

The entrance roads are gated, restricting vehicle access to logging operators and Dartmouth employees, students, and alumni who can stay at several cabins maintained by the college. I have stayed in these cabins, and can say that it is a wonderful wilderness experience with miles of fishing options to explore.

You can also easily walk or bike to excellent freestone pocket water on the lower section of Diamond River just a half mile in from the gate to a bridge crossing the river below Diamond Gorge. If you venture farther upriver, special regulations apply in the Swift Diamond and Dead Diamond Rivers above the Gorge.

Another way to access the Swift Diamond River near Ellingwood Falls is by driving up New Greenough Pond Road, which leaves the west side of NH 16 about four miles northeast of Errol. This dirt road reaches a gate with parking at the south boundary of the Dartmouth Grant. There is excellent fishing for small wild brook trout within a mile walk of the gate.

Upper portions of the Dead Diamond River outside the Dartmouth Grant are accessible from the north via the Parmachenee Road off Route 16 in Wilson's Mills with a left onto Abbot Brook Road.

Indian Stream

Indian Stream flows down from near the Canadian border and joins the Connecticut River south of Pittsburg. Indian Stream Road off US 3 follows Indian Stream, providing access along its full length. It is heavily stocked with brook trout and its upper reaches and small tributaries hold wild brookies. Terrill Pond (flyfishing only) is found near the headwaters of Indian Stream (discussed later in this section).

Mollidgewock Brook and Bishop Brook

Mollidgewock Brook joins the Androscoggin right across

The Swift Diamond River looking up toward Ellingwood Falls. Photo courtesy David Van Wie.

the river from the Mollidgewock State Campground (44.736922,-71.142729). There are unimproved access roads, such as Moll Brook Road, and foot trails off NH 16. This remote little stream holds wild brookies. Bishop Brook is accessible upstream from Route 145 near the village of Stewartstown Hollow, or from US 3 before it enters the Connecticut River. It is paralleled by Bishop Brook Road for most of its entire length. The stream receives regular stockings of brook trout.

Perry Stream

Perry Stream is another long stream flowing from near the Canadian border. It crosses US 3 and meets the Connecticut in the trophy stretch between First Connecticut Lake and Lake Francis. The portion of Perry Stream upstream from the confluence to the bridge at Happy Corner on Route 3 is flyfishing only. Both the Perry Stream and Connecticut River are heavily stocked with brook trout. Brown trout will move up into the river from Lake Francis during times of high water. There is an excellent state campground at the head of Lake Francis, just a couple of miles from the covered bridge on River Road (see Upper Connecticut River map).

Upper Ammonoosuc River

The Upper Ammonoosuc River is a heavily stocked brook trout stream. It flows along Route 110 north of Berlin and meets the Connecticut River near Groveton. Anglers looking for a secluded experience will enjoy the upstream reaches of the Upper Ammonoosuc River and the West Branch of the Upper Ammonoosuc River, north of Berlin. The Bog Dam Road (Kilkenny Loop Road) – off of the paved York Pond Road from NH 110, offers the best access to this area, with excellent opportunities for brook trout. While you are in the area, check out the Berlin Fish Hatchery also on York Pond Road, and stare at the large trout.

Wild River

Wild River is in the southeast corner of Coos County. Its origins are in the White Mountains National Forest at remote No Ketchum Pond and it enters the Androscoggin River near Gilead, Maine. Route 113 south of Gilead provides access to the Highwater Trail on the north bank or Wild River Road on the south bank, which bring you back into New Hampshire and follows the Wild River to its headwaters. The Wild is regularly stocked with rainbows and brook trout but it is best fished after spring runoff has diminished, but before it gets too low in the summer when the fish get skittish. The river is all rocks and boulders so it is best to fish the deeper pockets and pools created by different boulders and rock formations. The confluence with the Wild and the Andro is a very popular place to fish because trout stack up there throughout the year, but I also like to fish the headwaters.

There are myriad trails that parallel small streams in the White Mountains National Forest and the Presidential Mountains, and most of these tiny waters hold populations of hand-sized native brook trout. These tributaries stay cool all summer and fish well even on the hottest days. One example is Moriah Brook, a tributary of the Wild River that joins it just upstream from the Wild River Campground. You can follow the stream's course up the mountain on the Moriah Brook Trail.

Moriah Brook is the classic New England mountain stream cascading down small waterfalls, flowing over and around large boulders, and filling up pools ranging from washtub to swimming-pool size, all carved out of solid granite by thousands of years of melted snow running down the side of the mountain. At least a couple of small brookies can be spotted finning in the gin-clear water at the bottom of every decent-sized pool. It is great fun (and a little strenuous) to hike up the river with a 3-weight and a handful of flies and enjoy a simpler kind of flyfishing, similar to tenkara fishing. Give it a try, but please, on all of these small streams, fish with barbless hooks and practice catch and release. And don't all flock to Moriah Brook because I mentioned it – there are dozens more. Find your own secret treasure.

Fishing a typical New Hampshire mountain stream. The air temperature might have been 80 degrees but the water temperature was in the upper 50s.
Photo courtesy Lindsey Rustad.

Stillwaters of Northern New Hampshire

Big and Little Diamond Ponds

Picturesque Big Diamond Pond measures 179 surface acres, while Little Diamond Pond covers 51 acres. These Stewartstown stillwaters are heavily stocked right after ice-out in mid-May. Early in the season, flyfishers have the opportunity to catch lake trout, particularly on Big Diamond's westernmost side. Fish smelt-imitating streamers, such as the Gray Ghost, at daybreak right after ice-out. The best angling for brook trout and rainbows usually starts around Memorial Day and lasts into late June. Holdover fish do well in this Coos County pond, which has a maximum depth of 117 feet.

Little Diamond runs shallower, with a maximum depth of 15 feet. Brook trout dominate stocking lists for this put-and-take water. Fishing from shore is possible, and anglers can expect fish from 9 to 14 inches (don't hesitate to keep a few). Limits are five fish or five pounds, whichever comes first. On Little Diamond, trout may be taken by flies, artificial lures, or worms. Bass and perch are also present and there are those that believe the perch are outcompeting the trout.

For access to both stillwaters, take Diamond Pond Road from the town of Kidderville on NH 26, just west of Dixville Notch. Head north to Upper Kidderville, then on to Coleman State Park and Little Diamond. Diamond Pond Road exits the park, providing access to Big Diamond. Boat launches are found off this main road. A side trip can also include flyfishing the Mohawk River (previously mentioned), which runs along Route 26 in Colebrook.

If you pass through the Notch, you can't miss the Balsams, a stunning hotel located just off the road. Currently vacant, I hope the powers that be find some way to restore this magnificent representation of the Great Hotel Era of northern New England.

Back Lake

This spring-fed 359-acre Pittsburg trout pond is two miles long and averages only seven feet deep, so the trout are accessible to fly casters everywhere. It opens to fishing on the fourth Saturday in April and the season closes on October 15. The best fishing starts in mid-May and holds through July. September can offer good fishing as well. Back Lake is heavily stocked with brook trout, rainbow trout, and brown trout. As the water warms, so does the smallmouth bass action if the trout aren't cooperating. Bring your bass poppers with you.

After ice-out, most flyfishers troll a sinking fly line with standard streamer patterns such as the Marabou Black Ghost, Gray Ghost, or Mickey Finn. As the weather warms in May, fish will cruise the shoreline looking up. Mayfly patterns to try include Parachute Adams and Klinkhammer emerger patterns. Fish early summer caddis hatches with a Deep Sparkle Pupa, Emergent Sparkle Pupa, Diving Caddis, or Elk Hair Caddis.

The greatly anticipated *Hexagenia* hatch occurs as night falls from late June to mid-July. Large Wulff or extended deerhair patterns work well at this time. Dragonfly and damselfly nymphs, scud patterns, and midges all catch fish when there is no major hatch occurring. Terrestrials, especially ants and moths, work well when mountain breezes have been blowing these insects onto the surface. Very early in the morning, fish cruise to pick off insects that fell in overnight. Beach and Spooner Roads parallel this Coos County lake. Back Lake Road provides access off Route 3. Launch from the public beach off Beach Road.

Christine Lake

Very close to the Upper Ammonoosuc River lies this tiny gem of a lake. It is surrounded by the Percy Peaks and Nash Stream State Forest. In the spring, brown trout and brook trout chase spawning smelt as they run up feeder streams, and it is then that fly rodders have the best chance to cast smelt-imitation streamers and hook up with some nice fish. Fishing and boating traffic is minimal on this water, which does have a horsepower limit. From the town of Stark take the Northside/Percy Road.

Lake Francis

Depending on when you flyfish the region, Lake Francis and the Connecticut Lakes can strike you as inviting, or as windswept and forbidding. Lake Francis is a 2,051-acre impoundment created to produce hydropower for the town of Pittsburg. It offers angling for stocked brook trout, rainbows, browns, landlocked salmon, and lake trout. Holdover fish from this stocking will reach several pounds. A boat ramp off Route 3 and Lake Francis State Park both provide boat access. The former is 1.3 miles north of Pittsburg and the latter is another five miles up the road. Trolled streamers work well in the spring and fall.

First Connecticut Lake

This is the largest of the Connecticut lakes. At 2,807 acres, First Lake provides ample elbowroom for the boating flyfisher. Three-pound lake trout are commonly taken in the spring on trolled streamers and bucktail patterns. Brook trout, rainbows, and landlocked salmon are also frequent catches. Canoeists who flyfish this big water should hug the shoreline as whitecapped waves can make for choppy going. Kayaks are a safer option. Public access is found near the lake's westernmost tip, off US 3 (visible from the road). There is also a launch for small craft across from the Cabins at Lopstick.

Second Connecticut Lake

The Second Connecticut Lake covers 1,286 acres. Common catches by streamer-trolling include lake trout and salmon, though some brook trout are also caught. Boat access is found off Route 3 on the southwestern side of the lake (find the access road 7.5 miles up from the dam on First Connecticut Lake) and a launch at the end of Camp Otter Road. Ice-out arrives around early May. Classic New England streamer patterns work well on all the lakes.

Third Connecticut Lake

Third Lake boat access is off Route 3 just south of the Canadian border. This tree-lined, undeveloped 278-acre pond is surprisingly deep at 110 feet and produces catches of rainbows and lake trout. With its location, the wind just funnels through the valley, and waves can really whip up here. A stable craft is recommended.

Big Brook Bog

Located in Pittsburg, Big Brook Bog is a 37-acre pond west of the Second Connecticut Lake. Like many other fisheries in this region, access is from Route 3. Flyfish the June through early July caddis hatch.

Pittsburg's Boundary Pond is found in the northernmost tip of the state near the Quebec border. This 17-acre pond is stocked in the spring.

Coon Brook Bog

Coon Brook Bog, a six-acre flyfishing-only pond in Pittsburg (45.141842,-71.249917) offers a more remote setting and is recommended by Lisa Savard, former owner of the Cabins at Lopstick.

Other Ponds

Clarksville Pond is a 25-acre pond in Clarksville, east of NH 145. Little Bear Brook Pond (44.831420,-71.099307) can be reached by driving north from Errol and taking the first left after Long Pond; located a mile north of Route 16 after the turn. Expect somewhat selective holdover fish in the 7- to 10-inch range in this four-acre pond. Lime Pond is 14 well-stocked acres (44.870103,- 71.490233), located in Columbia. Holden Road south of Colebrook will give you access. Trout average 9 to 11 inches. Little Millsfield Pond offers 37 acres of flyfishing-only water west of Errol. Pittsburg's 10-acre Moose Pond (45.096194,-71.381306) is well stocked by early in the season. This is one of the earliest ponds that can be reached and fished successfully in the spring. Access is gained from Moose Pond Road west of Black Lake, just off Back Lake Road.

Perry Pond is 10 acres of trout water in Pittsburg near the Third Connecticut Lake. Access is by foot trail off Perry Stream Road. More pond than lake, Saco Lake is a nine-acre water in the town of Carroll that is stocked every year. Scott Bog covers 100 acres in the town of Pittsburg. It is heavily stocked with brook trout. Access is off Route 3 north of Second Connecticut Lake on East Inlet Road. Remember that wilderness-road logging trucks have the right of way.

Terrill Pond or "West Branch Pond" is a recommended first choice among other flyfishing-only options, by local guides. It is fed by the West Branch of Indian Stream off Indian Stream Road. This 10-acre pond is stocked heavily, and holds 9- to 11-inch brookies that become fairly selective by midsummer. There is usually action to be had at the outlet of the pond, either above or below the dam. Enormous moose hoof prints are a fixture of the mud surrounding this pond that is quite close to the Canadian border.

Upper Trio Pond, located in Odell, is a remote 21-acre pond holding spunky holdover brookies. Unknown Pond is a six-acre pond located in the town of Pittsburg just west of the Second Connecticut Lake. Expect 7- to 10-inch brookies. Wright Pond, another six-acre pond in trout-rich Pittsburg can be reached via a remote access by foot trail (45.221654,-71.229905).

This bridge over the Androscoggin River offers easy access to several fishable runs.

Northern New Hampshire Planning Considerations

Nearby Hub Cities and Towns

- Pittsburg (There are two major lodges in the area. Lopstick is the area's largest lodge with 53 cabins on First Lake and Back Lake and an Orvis-endorsed fly shop. Lopstick Lodge & Cabins, Pittsburg / 800-538-6659 / www.cabinsatlopstick.com. The Tall Timber Lodge is on Back Lake and offers boat rentals, fishing gear, and a flyfishing school: www.talltimber.com. Also see www.chamberofthenorthcountry.com.)
- Colebrook: 603-237-8939 (www.chamberofthenorthcountry.com)
- Errol (www.umbagogchamber.com)

Easy Access Options

- The Bridge Pool in the Trophy Section of the Connecticut is a few steps from the car down a gentle slope to the water. While there are always holdover fish available, the closer you time your visit to the stocking truck, the easier the fishing will be.
- Below Pittsburg, US 3 closely parallels the Connecticut for miles with a number of easy access points. Choose any spot within your physical capabilities. Wading can be difficult because of the rocky bottom, but just a step or two from the bank allows you to reach trout that will rise to a dry fly from late June through August.
- Route 16 provides an easy canoe launch point to the pool below the Errol Dam, the origin of the Androscoggin River. June is a prime month to look for rising trout. Keep your craft well away from the heavier currents and the tail of the pool. There are plenty of trout in the quieter sections.
- The narrow bridge over the river about half way between Pontook Dam and the town of Errol (44.714121,-71.173868) offers an easy way down to the river with fishable runs on both sides.

Suggested Beginner Options

- Try anywhere in the Trophy Section of the Connecticut, but particularly in the named pools (see the Trophy Section Map). There is plenty of back-cast space and there will be trout within reach of even the most novice anglers. Choose a versatile fly such as the Hornberg that will fool fish whether fished dry or wet. Pick a spot where the current will do your work for you by taking your fly downstream and giving it movement.
- Book a driftboat trip on the Connecticut with a Lopstick Outfitters guide (www.cabinsatlopstick.com). He or she will offer you suggestions as to how to improve your skills, the boat puts active trout

within reach, and chances are good that you will hook at least a few fish.
- Fish the outlet of Terrill Pond, either above or below the dam (45.217500,-71.342762). Particularly early in the year it is filled with eager brookies. Take Indian Stream Road from Route 3, south of Pittsburg. About ten miles in, take the next left after East Branch Road, cross Indian Stream, and the pond will be on your left.

Vacation Suggestions

Weekend Getaway

- During July or August, when options are limited, escape to the Cabins at Lopstick and the upper Connecticut for a weekend. On Saturday, float the upper Connecticut either on your own or with a guide. This is not a tricky river to float, so if you have any experience, don't be afraid to tackle it yourself, although the guides are very good. Fish streamers (with a nymph trailer) or subsurface until fish start rising in late afternoon or evening. On Sunday wade a section of the upper river, either the trophy section below Lake Francis, or above First Connecticut Lake.

One-week Vacation

- During the month of July, stay in one of the Cabins at Lopstick or Tall Timber Lodge for a great base of operations to explore the entire area. You can fish the lake immediately in front of your cabin anytime that you want to, but I recommend the following as your primary flyfishing activities:
  - Guided float trip down the Connecticut.
  - Fish the trophy section.
  - Fish your way downstream from the Murphy Dam. Remember that this section is general law, so if you are with family members that fish but don't flyfish, they can fish with you here.
  - Try a few of the local flyfishing-only ponds. My recommendation is Terrill Pond, but you have a number to choose from. Since it is July, fish morning or evening and look for large Hex mayflies, particularly if it is still before July 15.
  - Take a small rod, a handful of flies, and explore a small stream for hand-sized wild brookies. Two good options are the Upper Ammonoosuc River and the Swift Diamond from the Greenough Pond Road gate (it is about a mile to the river). There are other alternatives as well, and the folks at either of the lodges can point you in the right direction.

Maine

Maine offers more diversity than any other New England state – diversity of geography, climate, fish species, flyfishing experience and vacation options. Part of this is due to size: 35,000 square miles of geography containing 30,000 miles of rivers and streams, 3,000 lakes and ponds, and 3,500 miles of rugged coastline. Driving from Kittery on the southern Maine border to Fort Kent near the Canadian border will take someone six hours at highway speeds if they don't hit traffic (in southern regions) or a moose (in northern locales).

This state supports a variety of ecosystems, including alpine, coastal marine, coniferous forest, trackless beaver bogs, mighty river systems (where Atlantic salmon still hold on), agricultural fields and fragmented urban and suburban neighborhoods.

The fishing is just as varied, with anglers pursuing brook trout and blue-backed trout, the brown trout and landlocked salmon; the pickerel, pike, and muskie; smallmouth and largemouth bass; and the white perch and striped bass.

Historically, water access to the public has been good, even over private lands. Maine has a tradition among the large landowners – in the past it was paper companies but now ownership is more diverse – to allow public recreation. If you can reach rivers, streams, ponds, and lakes, then you can fish them. Where landowners want to limit access, they typically place locked gates on roads passable by vehicle.

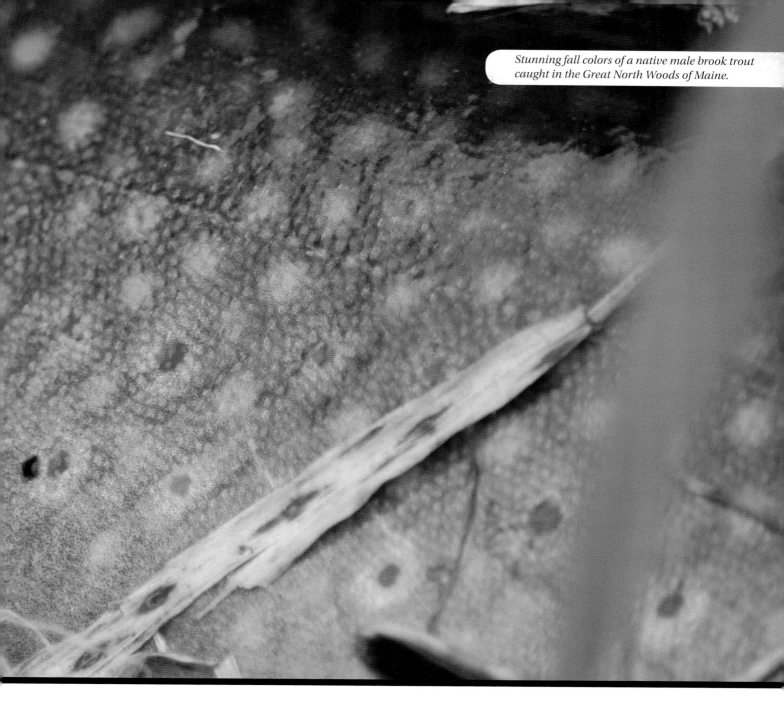

Stunning fall colors of a native male brook trout caught in the Great North Woods of Maine.

But if you walk or bike in, you can fish. Readers should treat this is as a general rule, but exceptions do exist.

Obviously, no-trespassing signs should be heeded and permission asked if uncertain. In the North Woods, visitors need to check in and pay a nominal fee. State Parks and Acadia National Park have their own unique rules and regulations.

Maine fishing regulations are quite diverse and numerous as indicated by the law book that runs pages and pages of single-spaced regulations. However, there are a few general guidelines. In the so-called southern and eastern counties – Androscoggin, Cumberland, Hancock, Kennebec, Knox, Lincoln, Oxford (south of the Androscoggin River), Penobscot, Sagadahoc, Waldo,

Washington, and York – lakes and ponds are open to fishing all year with a number of rivers having extended seasons. For other southern rivers and streams, the season runs from April 1 to September 30.

In the northern and western counties – Aroostook, Franklin, Oxford (north of the Androscoggin River), Piscataquis, and Somerset – waters are only open from April 1 to September 30 with a number of rivers and streams having special catch-and-release regulations from August 15 on to protect spawning wild fish. Extended seasons do exist on some waters to give northern county anglers some fishing options all year.

For specific locations, see the locator map on page 7. For Delorme Atlas and Gazeteer locations for hard-to-find waters, see page 191.

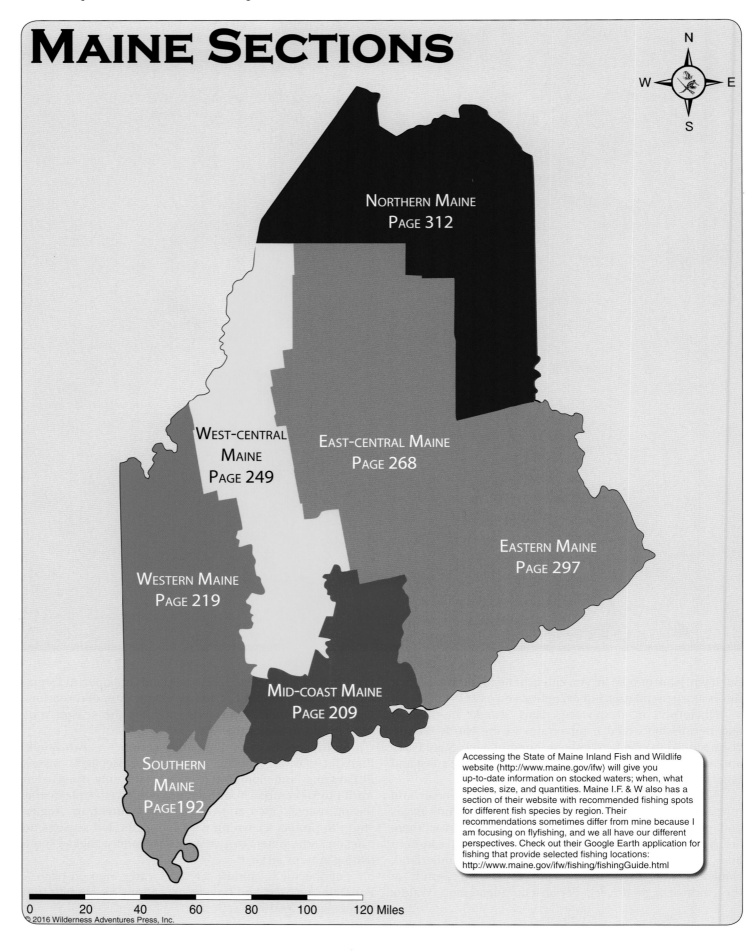

MAINE SECTIONS

NORTHERN MAINE
PAGE 312

WEST-CENTRAL
MAINE
PAGE 249

EAST-CENTRAL MAINE
PAGE 268

WESTERN MAINE
PAGE 219

EASTERN MAINE
PAGE 297

MID-COAST MAINE
PAGE 209

SOUTHERN
MAINE
PAGE192

Accessing the State of Maine Inland Fish and Wildlife website (http://www.maine.gov/ifw) will give you up-to-date information on stocked waters; when, what species, size, and quantities. Maine I.F. & W also has a section of their website with recommended fishing spots for different fish species by region. Their recommendations sometimes differ from mine because I am focusing on flyfishing, and we all have our different perspectives. Check out their Google Earth application for fishing that provide selected fishing locations: http://www.maine.gov/ifw/fishing/fishingGuide.html

0   20   40   60   80   100   120 Miles

© 2016 Wilderness Adventures Press, Inc.

Hard-to-find Fisheries in Maine

Maine is a large state with many remote waters, and in places the only avenues of travel are logging roads. Cell service can be spotty to non-existent, navigation programs unreliable, and remote campsites or cabins without electricity. That is why the Delorme Maine Atlas and Gazeteer is found in almost all sportsmen's (and women's) trucks and vehicles (including mine). On this page are Delorme Maine Atlas coordinates for selected hard-to-find Maine waters.

Fishery	Delorme coordinates	Fishery	Delorme coordinates
Alder Stream	Page 32, C 3	Little Pillsbury Pond	Page 56, D 3
Arnold Pond	Page 38, E 3	Little Wilson Hill Pond	Page 40, D 3
Baker Lake	Page 54, D 3-4	Lobster Lake	Page 49, D 3
Baxter's Matagamon Gate	Page 51, A 2	Loss Pond	Page 30, C 3
Bean Pond	Page 30, C 3	Meduxnekeag River	Page 53, A 2-4
Berry Ponds	Page 40, C 2	Moose River Bow Trip	Page 39, C 1-5
Big Reed Pond	Page 56, C 4	Mooseleuk Stream	Page 57, A 1
Bug Eye Pond	Page 38, E 3	Musquacook Stream	Page 62, D 3
Chairback Ponds	Page 42, D 1	North Pond	Page 10, B 4
China Lake	Page 13, A 3	Pierce Pond	Page 30, A 2
Cobboseecontee Stream	Page 12, C 4	Piscataquis River	Page 32, B 1
Cold Stream Falls	Page 40, D 2	Pleasant Lake	Page 52, B 4-55
Cold Stream Pond	Page 33, A 5	Prestile Stream	Page 59, B 4
Currier Ponds	Page 56, C 3	Roach Ponds	Page 42, B 1-2
Dead River, North Branch	Page 29, A 1-2	Round Pond	Page 10, B 4
Deboullie Ponds	Page 63, A 1	Sabbath Day Pond	Page 18, A 5
Dingley Ponds	Page 47, C 5	Square Lake	Page 58, E 2
Durepo Pond	Page 65, A 3	Sourdnahunk Lake	Page 50, B 3
Ellis Pond	Page 40, D 3	Spring Pond	Page 56, D 4
Glacier Lake	Page 66, C 4	Summerhaven Ponds	Page 12, B 5
Goodell Brook	Page 31, A 3	Swift River Ponds	Page 18, A 5
Hall Pond	Page 11, D 1	Tim Pond	Page 28, C 5
Hancock Pond	Page 4, B 3	Tumbledown Pond	Page 19, C 1
Horseshoe Pond	Page 40, D 3	Turner Ponds	Page 39, B 2
Hurricane Pond	Page 38, E 3	Virginia Lake	Page 10, D 5
Lake Parlin	Page 40, C 1-2	Wallagrass Lake	Page 67, D 3
Lake Matagamon	Page 57, E 1	Webb Lake	Page 19, C 2
Little Black River	Page 66, C 2	Webster Brook	Page 56, E 5
Little Enchanted Pond	Page 39, D 5	Worthley Pond	Page 11, A 1-4
Little Madawaska Stream	Page 65, B 2		

Southern Maine

Your gateway to Maine is through its southwest corner that encompasses both York and then Cumberland Counties. The drive up from the eastern United States on I-95 and US 1 will take you from the large metropolitan cities of Philadelphia, New York, and Boston; past Portsmouth and other New Hampshire cities; into the quiet, coastal communities and beaches of York, Ogunquit, and Kennebunk; and finally into the thriving city of Portland. Although more populated than other parts of Maine, and not as well known for its flyfishing, southwest Maine offers plenty of opportunities and has the advantage of being able to offer non-fishing members of your family plenty of activities.

The waterways nearest the coast provide angling for striped bass, bluefish, shad, and sea-run trout. Inland lakes, ponds, and streams hold brook trout, lake trout, landlocked salmon, and brown trout. The state maintains an aggressive hatchery stocking program, there are larger holdover fish, and wild fish remain in many rivers and streams. Bass fishing for both largemouth and smallmouth can be excellent in area rivers and lakes.

An impressive Mousam River Salmo trutta.

CROOKED RIVER

The Crooked River, named for its undulating character, stretches for 43 miles from its origins at Songo Pond, south of the village of Bethel in Albany Township near White Mountain National Forest, until it empties into Sebago Lake. Managed as a protected resource, the Crooked River provides one of the principal wild salmon and trout fisheries here in southern Maine. Vitally important to Sebago Lake, Crooked River's spawning grounds produce the bulk of the wild fish found. Because of its abundant spawning habitat, this watershed is minimally stocked in order to maintain the genetics of the native trout and salmon populations. Although fishing regulations allow fish to be kept at certain times and locations, I recommend a total catch-and-release philosophy for this water.

As a freestone river, the Crooked River usually runs high in April, settles down in May and June, can get warm and low during the summer, and then cools down and rises with the first fall rains. In the spring, fishing tends to be better from mid-May to late June, when the water warms up a bit and settles down. In the fall, fishing is dependent on significant fall rainfall.

Wild brook trout can be found throughout the river system and average 6 to 12 inches. Brook trout like moving water that contains food sources, and nearby cover in the form of deeper pockets and pools. If you find water like this, you will most likely find the trout as well. The most productive way to fish is to utilize searching patterns in order to cover a lot of water; stripping small streamers, swinging wet flies or casting dry flies like the Hornberg that can be retrieved across the surface. Then, when you find active fish, try other patterns and approaches. Standard brook trout flies work well on this river with under-the

The dam at Songo Locks.

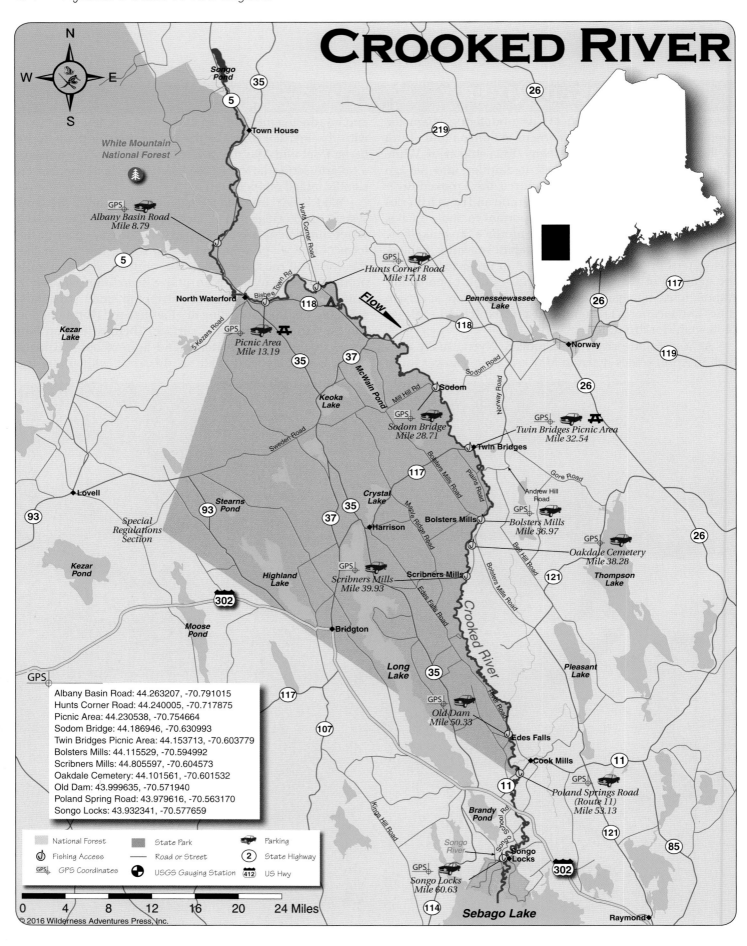

CROOKED RIVER

N
W E
S

Songo Pond
35
5
Town House
White Mountain National Forest
26
219
GPS
Albany Basin Road
Mile 8.79
5
Hunts Corner Road
GPS
Hunts Corner Road
Mile 17.18
Pennesseewassee Lake
117
26
Kezar Lake
North Waterford
Bishee Town Rd
118
Flow
118
Norway
119
GPS
Picnic Area
Mile 13.19
35
37
Sodom Road
26
McWain Pond
Keoka Lake
Mill Hill Rd.
Sodom
GPS
Sodom Bridge
Mile 28.71
Norway Road
GPS
Twin Bridges Picnic Area
Mile 32.54
Sweden Road
Twin Bridges
Gore Road
Lovell
117
Plains Road
Andrew Hill Road
93
Stearns Pond
Crystal Lake
35
GPS
Bolsters Mills Mile 36.97
93
37
Maple Ridge Road
Bolsters Mills
GPS
Oakdale Cemetery
Mile 38.28
26
Kezar Pond
Special Regulations Section
Harrison
121
Thompson Lake
Highland Lake
GPS
Scribners Mills
Mile 39.93
Scribners Mills
302
Moose Pond
Bridgton
Edes Falls Road
Crooked River
Pleasant Lake
Long Lake
35
River Road
117
GPS
Old Dam
Mile 50.33
Bolsters Mills Road
107
Edes Falls
Cook Mills
11
11
GPS
Poland Springs Road
(Route 11)
Mile 53.13
121
85

Albany Basin Road: 44.263207, -70.791015
Hunts Corner Road: 44.240005, -70.717875
Picnic Area: 44.230538, -70.754664
Sodom Bridge: 44.186946, -70.630993
Twin Bridges Picnic Area: 44.153713, -70.603779
Bolsters Mills: 44.115529, -70.594992
Scribners Mills: 44.805597, -70.604573
Oakdale Cemetery: 44.101561, -70.601532
Old Dam: 43.999635, -70.571940
Poland Spring Road: 43.979616, -70.563170
Songo Locks: 43.932341, -70.577659

Brandy Pond
Kings Hill Road
Songo School Rd
Songo River
Songo Locks
302
GPS
Songo Locks
Mile 60.63
114
Sebago Lake
Raymond

	National Forest		State Park		Parking
Fishing Access		Road or Street		2	State Highway
GPS	GPS Coordinates		USGS Gauging Station	412	US Hwy

0   4   8   12   16   20   24 Miles

© 2016 Wilderness Adventures Press, Inc.

-surface fare being the rule until hatches start occurring as the water warms. Soft-hackled flies and wingless wets can interest wild brook trout throughout the season. Also carry terrestrials, such as hoppers, crickets, and ants.

Even though the water can get low in the summer, the Crooked River lies on top of an underground aquifer and there are springs that refresh the river along its way. Even in the summer, you can find cooler spots and entering tributaries where the trout will still be active. Locals like to fish the river for brookies above and below the Twin Bridges picnic area off of ME 117 (44.153713,-70.603779). Above Twin Bridges, the river lies in Oxford County and Routes ME 118 and 35/5 parallel the river and cross it in a few places, allowing easy access. A nice picnic area lies in Waterford on ME 118 (44.230538,-70.754664). The river can change character every hundred yards, from rocky plunge pools to shallow riffles, to bend pools, to slow silty stretches, so it pays to explore.

The real draw of the Crooked River is the adult landlocked salmon ranging from 12 to 24 inches that enter from Sebago Lake in the spring and fall. This river holds a special memory for me because I caught my first wild landlocked salmon below the old mill dam at Edes Falls. He smacked a small Muddler Minnow as I dangled it in the current. I don't know who was more surprised, the fish or me. I do remember my heart threatening to leap out of my chest as I finally netted my catch after a brief but spirited tussle. Landlocked salmon fishing gets in your blood and it never leaves. There is a small park around the old dam and there is good access above and below from both sides (43.999635,-70.571940).

In the spring, when the salmon are chasing spawning smelt from Sebago Lake, the fish and anglers congregate in the pools closer to the lake for several weeks in late April or early May. The Songo Locks (43.932341,-70.577659) is near the confluence of the Songo River, the Crooked River, and Sebago Lake and is a popular and productive fishing spot to find large salmon chasing smelt. The locks were built so boats could move from Sebago to Long Lake. I watched a lucky bait fisherman haul in a salmon last year at the Songo Locks Dam that must have weighed well north of six pounds, but flyfishers also do well here. Salmon will chase smelt all the way up to ME 11, and some salmon will continue up river all the way to Bolsters Mills.

In the fall, landlocked salmon ascend the river to spawn. The spawning run is triggered by shorter days, cooler water, and most importantly, a significant rain event. It pays to time your fall fishing to coincide with rising water levels.

The Crooked River at Edes Falls.

The entire river from ME 35 in North Waterford down to ME 11 is flyfishing only, catch and release unless you hook a salmon over 26 inches. I was a participant in a landlocked-salmon-redd survey last November and we counted hundreds of redds and salmon in the sections upstream from North Waterford, so don't hesitate to fish the upper reaches of the Crooked. The redds and salmon we saw were always concentrated where the stream narrowed and provided faster water flow with a deeper holding pool nearby. The key is whether enough rain falls early enough in September to move the salmon up to the upper river before the season ends at the end of September. An extended season exists until October 15 from Bolster's Mills Bridge in the small settlement of Bolsters Mills downstream to Route 11 in Casco that offers a last change for anglers to land a trophy.

There is ample access to the Crooked at pull-off spots on roads that parallel much of the river. Some of the popular places to intercept these spawning run salmon are: Bolsters Mills (44.115529,-70.594992), a trail from the back of Oakdale Cemetery on Jesse Mill Road (44.101561,-70.601532) Scribner's Mills (44.085597,-70.604573), the riffles and pools near Cook Mills, Edes Falls Road, and River Road (Casco), the pool below the Edes Falls bridge (43.997777,-70.571948), and Mile Brook Pool (off a short dirt road from ME 11). Below the Edes Falls Bridge, the Crooked runs more slowly and putting in a canoe and drifting downstream to Route 11 (and farther) is a good strategy to cover more water than you can by wading and walking. River-mouth boat ramps on Sebago Lake near Sebago Lake State Park provide access to the lower river which is best fished by small boat, kayak, or canoe.

If the fish are fresh from the lake and haven't been fished over much, Soft Hackle Marabou Black Ghost streamers give you the best odds for success. Most of the traditional Maine streamers will be productive at times. If the fish have

seen their share of streamers, then smaller nymphs or wet flies are the ticket. Autumn Crooked River salmon are not pushovers. Sometimes fallen leaves clog the pools and it is hard to get a decent retrieve without hooking a leaf. Second, some land around good salmon pools is private or difficult to wade and getting in a good position can be difficult. Finally, climate change has made September and October warmer in southern Maine, so sometimes salmon don't really start their run until the very end of the season. Temperatures and rainfall are critical. Temperatures are always suitable by October 1, but sometimes low flows inhibit strong migrations.

Presumpscot River

While the Crooked River is managed as a wild fishery, the Presumpscot River has minimal spawning habitat and is heavily stocked to maintain the fishing.

The Presumpscot flows out of Sebago Lake and winds its way 25 miles before emptying into Casco Bay, near Portland. The name Presumpscot means "many falls" and before the construction of ten dams, this river hosted a variety of salmonid species, including the now extinct Presumpscot Jumper, a unique subspecies of salmon that sported red spots and jumped frequently when hooked.

The most popular flyfishing stretch of this river is the upper Presumpscot, the first two or three miles from Sebago Lake (see the Sebago Lake map). For most of the 20th century, the salmonid fishing in this stretch was spotty at best. Almost all of Sebago's flow was rechanneled from the Eel Weir Dam into a canal for power generation and additional dams warmed and slowed the water. All this changed in 1988 when the original river channel from Sebago Lake was rewatered with a minimum flow requirement and Maine's Department of Inland Fish and Wildlife began regular stocking. Fishing has improved dramatically.

The first mile of the upper Presumpscot runs from Sebago Lake to North Gorham Pond. This is a beautiful section with no development and clear, highly-oxygenated water flowing around and through good ole Maine granite. During the past 30 years of continuous flow, hatches of aquatic insects have increased with midges, small caddis, and mayflies dominating along with terrestrials such as inchworms, ants, and beetles. The state of Maine is justifiably proud of its restoration project and stocks this section regularly in both the spring and the fall with brookies, brown trout, and landlocked salmon at normal stocking sizes as well as large brood fish best measured in pounds. The stocked fish are of high quality – the autumn brook trout in particular have striking bright red bellies.

In addition to stocked fish, there are holdovers that

A nice upper Presumpscot landlocked salmon finds the net.

show up, particularly in the fall when some trout and salmon that have dropped down into North Gorham Pond ascend up the river looking for spawning locations. I have caught and have seen caught salmon up to five pounds in November. Some fish no doubt drop over the dam from Sebago as well. Wild smallmouth of various sizes add to the diversity.

Because Sebago is such a large lake, its waters cool slowly in the fall such that the upper Presumpscot's water stays warmer longer, which leads to tremendous fishing in October, November, and even December, when most other Maine options are frozen. Continued fall stockings (usually containing 18-inch browns) and spawning holdovers keep the fishing exciting.

This section does get heavy fishing pressure at times and the fish become educated quickly. Most success comes from nymphing. However, in the fall, the fish do get aggressive on Muddlers and other streamers.

One November day around Thanksgiving, when most of my friends had put away their flyfishing gear for the year, I caught several stocked 18-inch browns, half a dozen brook trout, and a fat five-pound landlock – all on the upper Presumpscot. My type of holiday.

The best access to the upper Presumpscot is from a large parking lot by the ME 35 bridge where it crosses the river (43.830778,-70.449215). Farther downriver, the short tailwater sections below the North Gorham Pond Dam (43.830778,-70.449215) and Dundee Pond Dam in Windham (43.779266,-70.452815), and Gambo and Mallison Dams in South Windham also hold trout and salmon in both spring and fall. Again, some of them are holdovers of impressive size. For instance, the Pleasant River is heavily stocked with brown trout and some move into the Presumpscot, where it is only a short distance upstream to the Dundee Dam tailwater. Smallmouth bass can be caught as well.

North Gorham Pond itself has prolific midge hatches after ice-out and on calm late April evenings, salmon rise to the tiny morsels. A float tube or kayak, stealth, and a selection of small flies are critical for success. The Presumpscot River runs into North Gorham Pond over a small falls, and salmonids gather at the base of the falls during certain parts of the year, so that is another spot well worth trying. The best access is by boat.

The head of tide (the farthest that the tidal influence extends upriver) on the Presumpscot is accessible by a series of trails on conservation land in Falmouth, at the site of Smelt Hill dam that was removed in 2003. Now the river tumbles down a short waterfall into Casco Bay. When conditions are right – seasonality and water temperatures – stripers and shad can be caught at the base of the falls.

The Presumpscot is open year round for fishing. There is a flyfishing-only section from the Outlet Dam at Sebago Lake to North Gorham Pond. Please refer to the Maine fishing law book or the on-line equivalent for all of the up-to-date regs.

Royal River

Try Cumberland County's Royal River as a year-round fishing option since the regulations allow it. This river does rise quickly and becomes quite muddy after a significant rain, so it's best to wait several days before fishing in such cases. The Royal offers a number of fishing options in suburban Yarmouth as it passes over several dams and becomes salt under the I-95 bridge. From Bridge Street

December fishing for sea-run browns in the Royal River.

downstream, the Royal has a short section of faster water with plunge pools, pockets, and runs that empties into a very large pool before dropping down a rocky section into the salt. There is foot access on both sides and a large parking lot (43.801326,-70.180466). The state stocks this section heavily in spring and fall with 8- to 12-inch brook and brown trout, occasionally accompanied in the fall with broodstock that are best measured in pounds and are quite fun to catch. If you look up, you can occasionally see ospreys, bald eagles, cormorants, and herons, which also vie for the stocked fish.

My experience with this part of the river is that the fish are quite moody. Try different approaches until you find one that works. On some days large bright Woolly Buggers work, other days, small Muddlers or nymphs. Most rising fish are feeding on small blue-winged olives. There are also sea-run browns. Stocked fish will enter the salt portion of the Royal River and move back into freshwater in the late autumn. I have a neighbor that catches a few big sea-runs every year. He fishes throughout the winter when conditions allow and uses large flashy flies and lures. A few fish have been caught approaching 30 inches. An all-tide boat launch provides saltwater access to the river mouth, where anglers target their efforts near the I-95 overpass.

Upstream from Bridge Street to East Elm Street, a paved trail provides further access alongside a park. This section is also stocked. Immediately downstream from the East Elm Street Dam, faster water empties into a large pool. In late May through June, try drifting small dry flies toward the noses pooking up in the foam.

Much farther upriver in New Gloucester, the cooler waters of Collyer Brook enter the Royal slightly upstream from Depot Road (43.891753,-70.277321). Fishing here for holdover browns is an option all summer, as soon as the sun leaves the water. These fish are as finicky as any spring-creek fish –a small ant pattern is one good option.

The Royal River section that flows through New Gloucester receives annual springtime stockings of brook or brown trout. Fish below the Bald Hill Bridge or Brown's Crossing in Auburn, the Route 231 bridge, or the Penny Road bridge in New Gloucester from late April through June.

Little River

Little River is a tributary of the Salmon Falls River on the New Hampshire border north of the village of Berwick and ME 9. The state stocks brook trout and browns annually.

A Little River pool under Messenger's Bridge on Long Swamp Road.

Head of tide on the Mousam.

There is easy access from the Little River Road. Downstream from the so-called Messenger's Bridge (43.318195,-70.864749) by the intersections of Little River Road, Cranberry Meadow Road, and Long Swamp Roads is a two-mile catch-and-release section with mixed pools and pocket water. Upstream from the bridge, a dirt road parallels the stream on the right side providing easy walking access. Even into early July, brook trout still rise in the deep pool under the bridge. As the season progresses, small chubs will attack your dry flies in certain sections which can be a little annoying.

Mousam River

The Mousam River (pronounced Mouse-am) begins its journey at the outflow of Mousam Lake near the village of Emery Mills. The river passes through several ponds and dams between the villages of Springvale, Sanford, and West Kennebunk. From Kennebunk, the Mousam makes a five-mile run to the Atlantic Ocean near Parsons Beach. There are three distinct sections: the upper, the midsection, and the estuary. The Mousam's upper section, between Emery Mills and the dam in Springvale, offers flyfishing opportunities for brook trout and browns. Trout measured in pounds are occasionally taken at the outlet of the Emery Mills Dam. ME 11 and 109 parallel the river and provide canoe and fishing access. The river runs more slowly and is considerably warmer through the dams and ponds of its midsection. Smallmouth bass, perch, and pickerel are abundant, and there are several canoe and boat accesses.

One block south of US 1 in Kennebunk on River Road is Rogers Pond Park (43.382023,-70.540799). The Mousam River edges the park as it tumbles quickly over a series of ledges that produces pocket water, pools, and deeper runs. Slightly downsteam, but still bordering the park, the river slides into a long quiet run that is tidal. You never know what you might catch in this section. It is stocked with brown trout and brook trout. Some of the brown trout go into the estuary and return in the fall and winter as 10- to 20-inch sea-runs (the Mousam has an extended season and can be fished legally year around). The afternoon I was there taking photos, a gentleman had just landed and released a 20-pound striper. Stripers swim right up to the river ledges in late May and stay until warming water pushes them out farther towards the ocean.

Anything could be caught near the park as the Mousam River becomes tidal – stocked browns, sea-runs, good-sized brook trout, large stripers, or shad (in June). If you want to give the shad fishing a try, throw a fly with some pink coloration. There are commercially-tied pink shad patterns, but a Wood Special streamer works just fine. When the tide is in, the best way to explore the tidal area is by boat, but when the tide is out, you can wade right down the middle of the river where it is a little shallower and cast towards the edges. Large trout can be caught in surprisingly shallow water.

Folks target sea-run browns fish in November and December. Some prefer low tide, walking down the exposed middle bar and casting to remaining water. Others try to be fishing at mid-tide when the water is shallow enough to reach the bottom and the browns are actively feeding. Another spot for sea-runs is both upstream and downstream from the ME 9 bridge, where there is a parking lot.

Striped-bass fishing in the estuary of the Mousam River has drawn flyfishers from all over New England in recent years. There are areas of flats for those who enjoy wading and stalking stripers by night. Boat access is available for fly casters who chase stripers during the day. Two miles east of the village of Wells, Route 9 leads to Parsons Beach and the mouth of the Mousam River. Canoeing the winding estuary under and upstream of the ME 9 bridge also can produce striped bass, sea-run brown trout, and shad.

Other Rivers and Streams

Branch Brook
Branch Brook in Wells is a wild-trout stream with good numbers of fish. It starts at the Sanford airport, crosses ME 109 and has plentiful access points from the bridges that cross the water or from the railroad tracks from US 1.

Kennebunk River
The upstream section of the Kennebunk River, north of the city of Kennebunkport, is a heavily stocked put-and-take brookie and brown trout fishery. The river mouth offers fishing for stripers and blues. Access is limited to boat fishing. At least a half-dozen guides operate out of the Kennebunk River if you prefer the services of a guide. There is also some striper fishing available near the mouth of the York River near York Beach.

Little Ossipee River
Little Ossipee River is a small put-and-take stream that flows east through the village of Newfield. The state manages this fishery with springtime stockings of brown, brookies, and rainbows that average 8 to 10 inches in length. The stretch between the dam west of the village of North Shapleigh and the bridge in Newfield is accessible from Mann Road. The river from Newfield to the village of Ossipee Mills also fishes well. Fishing is best in May and June before high water temperatures drive the fish to coldwater refuge areas. Caddisfly and early season mayfly patterns are effective, as well as attractor patterns such as Hornbergs and small Wulffs. The river can be floated in the early season from North Shapleigh to Ossipee Mills. Access is found on Mann Road and the take-out near the ME 5 bridge in Ossipee Mills.

Merriland River
Merriland River is primarily a put-and-take fishery, but that doesn't mean it isn't fun to fish. My favorite access point is off of Cole Hills Road in Wells (43.349345,-70.579681), and then I fish downstream. The woods are beautiful, walking is easy, and there is no development. A few minutes of walking brings you to a half-a-basketball-court-sized, dark, shady pool with a small waterfall at its head, surrounded by large hemlocks and granite ledges. This is a must-stop spot. Look for subtle rises in the foam but retrieve small nymphs or muddlers just under the surface. Wood Specials have also worked for me. Farther downstream are more rocky pools that hold fish. Try to fish it in the middle of the week or in the middle of the day to avoid the other anglers. It can get popular.

Farther downstream in Wells, at the confluence of Branch Brook, there can be some sea-run brook trout in May or June.

Big Ossipee River
The Big Ossipee River runs along ME 25 from the New Hampshire border and is known for its bass fishing more than its trout fishing. Still, good-sized browns are taken from this river every year. The state stocks brown trout in the spring and fall, brook trout in the spring. Best fishing for trout is in the spring (through June). There is canoe/kayak access below the dam at Kezar Falls, and it's a pretty river to fish during good flows. Floating from the dam to the Saco River confluence will yield double-digit numbers of smallmouth, along with occasional brown trout. Try Muddlers tied with yellow highlights.

Saco River
The Saco River is over 130 miles in length, so while its journey ends at Biddeford Pool (an estuary in York County), the river's origin is in New Hampshire and enters Maine in southern Oxford Country near the town of Fryburg. This river is best known for its thousands of canoeists and kayakers that paddle down the western Maine section every warm weekend with coolers of beer and camping equipment in order to enjoy the water, camp on the numerous sandy beaches, and party.

The Saco does get warm in the summer and most of the flyfishing is for smallmouth bass and other warmwater species. The East Limington area holds good numbers of smallmouth in the faster water and largemouth in deadwater sections. The Saco does get stocked with brown trout and some of the brownies hold over. One place to try for big browns in the fall is below Skelton Dam in Buxton. I have seen some photographs of brown taken there that got my attention. Some anglers drive the farm road on the south shore and walk out on a sandy peninsula, but there are other nearby access points.

The best trout fishing is probably in its western tributaries. The Shepards River which flows into the Saco near East Brownfield is a little known but excellent native brook trout fishery. Look for the river from ME 5/113, north of the intersection of ME 160. There are a number of access points off Main Street in Brownfield and a trail follows the south bank of the stream in some sections. The last time I fished this stream, a brook trout nailed my Mini-muddler in almost every deep bend or fallen-tree-created pool. One of my favorite access points is off Hampshire Road, near where the river crosses (43.935100,-70.927159). Fish downstream.

South River
The South River runs into the Ossipee River in Parsonsfield. But before that, it runs through the Plantation – 8,000 acres of forested land. A recent column in the Maine Sportsman suggested that this area has among the best native brook trout fishing in York County. Try exploring the logging roads in this area and fish the South River and Emerson Brook.

Collyer Brook

This is a small stream that I have fished for over 30 years and is a special place to me. It fishes well very early in the season, so it is often the first place I wet a line after winter. I seem to hook at least one trout on every visit. It runs cool all summer (a Maine state hatchery uses the spring-fed water upstream) and there are fish to be caught even in July. It is stocked regularly from different sources (school kids raise some trout and do their own stocking) but it is general law and plenty of fishermen take home fish. Still, enough brookies and brownies survive.

Although there are rumors of large holdover browns, the largest brookies and browns that I have seen have been around 14 inches. For a small stream, it has a wide variety of water types over a relatively short distance: woodland pools, rocky riffles, a good-sized natural waterfall and plunge pool, and farm-field runs with undercut banks. I use small dry flies such as an Adams in the riffles, and Wood Specials and Muddlers (with a split shot) to fish the deeper slots and pools. On summer evenings, I might sneak through a farmer's field to locate deeper pools with undercut banks, and then on my knees – invisible to the fish – toss in a grasshopper pattern.

The best approaches to Collyer Brook are at the Route 100 bridge several miles north of Gray, the Merrill Road, the Maguire Road (off the Mayall Road – 43.909954,-70.309696), and the Depot Road. Each location offers different stream features.

MAIN IMAGE: The lower Saco River at Limington Rips with early morning mist.
UPPER RIGHT: The Big Ossipee River in Kezar Falls.

Pleasant River

The Pleasant River in Windham has a fairly large catch-and-release section, is stocked well with brook trout and brown trout in both spring and fall, and is open until the end of November. The catch-and-release section runs from the ME 302 bridge to the River Road bridge. Find the dirt parking lot at the 302 bridge (43.806191,-70.410990) and look for rising fish in the large pool just below the bridge. There is also good access and fishing from Windham Center Road and the Pope Road.

The stocked brown trout seem to acclimate quickly, rise to naturals, but can be darn finicky. Early in the season, I have had success with conehead Woolly Buggers in olive or black. Later on, weighted Mini-muddlers have fooled brown trout in the faster water. Many anglers stick with dries and try for any risers that they find. Fish do not seem to holdover well because there is some poaching and the water can get pretty boney in the summer. Sometimes larger fish enter the Pleasant from the Presumpscot River – seeking thermal relief or spawning gravel – and a lucky angler is surprised by a trophy brown trout.

Willett Brook and Stevens Brook

Willett Brook in Bridgton is stocked with brown trout and some hold over for quite some time. Locals really enjoy fishing this stream. The best stretch is the faster water downstream from Sunset Park. Willett Brook's tributary, Stevens Brook is also stocked but with brook trout. The Stevens Brook Trail travels along the bank of Stevens Brook from the bridge over Depot Road in Bridgton and provides an easy way to fish the river.

Other Options

It is worth noting that many dozens (more than you might expect) of small creeks, tributaries, and streams throughout southwest Maine hold wild and holdover brook trout. The state's fishery biologists have surveyed hundreds of brooks and streams in this part of Maine, and nearly 70 percent support wild brook trout. Some of the trout were born there, others were stocked fish that moved into the smaller waters from larger ones, and still others travel up these waterways in the fall looking for spawning habitat. These small waters can be difficult to fish as they can be surrounded by brush and trees and the fish can be spooky, but after several wet summers that help survival rates, the fishing can be quite productive. Conversely a hot, dry summer can reduce numbers significantly the following year. One year, my son pulled a 14-inch brook trout from under a culvert that I would have thought was nothing but frog water.

If the angler is interested in larger quarry, from May through October is a great time to chase after stripers because they are found in relatively shallow water and spend some of their time near the surface attacking baitfish (and hopefully flies). There are countless coastal striper flyfishing options among the many saltwater marshes, beaches, rivers, inlets, islands, points, and other structure; too many to mention. Which spots fish best depends on the time of year, time of day, tides, wind direction, weather, and the vagaries of striper migration. Generally, you will find stripers around rock piles, rip-rap, jetties, breakwaters, and manmade structures such as docks, piers, or hazard markers. Always keep your eye out for active seabirds diving and squawking because that usually means stripers are nearby pushing baitfish to the surface.

Your best bet for more information is to visit local fly shops (Eldredge Bros, Breton's Bike and Fly Shop, LLBean, and Cabela's, to name a few), search local flyfishing blogs, and keep your eyes open for striper fishermen, so you can ask for information.

Dozens of small creeks, tributaries, and streams throughout southwest Maine hold wild and holdover brook trout.

SEBAGO LAKE

Sebago Lake, derived from the Native American description for "big water", spans 28,771 acres, with a maximum depth of 316 feet – the deepest New England lake – and is only a half an hour from Portland. Depending on the time of year, a variety of fish species are available to the angler. Ice-out usually means trolling or casting for landlocked salmon, Maine's official state fish, which range from two to four pounds here. The state record landlocked salmon, caught here in 1908, weighed 22 pounds, 8 ounces. Ice-out will typically start on the "Big Bay" sometime during the first 10 days of April. Often, the entire lake won't be free of ice until the end of the month. "Big Bay" is the area of Sebago extending from the mouth of the Songo and Crooked Rivers to Frye Island near the middle of Sebago Lake and the bay area along the entire western shore.

It is important to note though that winter weather has become more erratic over the last several decades. During some recent winters, Sebago Lake never completely froze and the famous Sebago Lake ice-fishing tournament had to be cancelled. Conversely, the winter of 2014/2015 was colder than average and ice-out was later than other recent years. If you are trying to time your fishing to coincide with ice-out or shortly thereafter, it is best to consult with local information sources on current ice conditions.

Shortly after ice-out, smelt, trolling anglers and flyfishers begin to stage at specific Sebago Lake river and brook mouths. These include the Crooked and Songo Rivers near Sebago Lake State Park, the Muddy River, Bachelder and Nason Brooks on the western shore, and Panther Run in Raymond on the eastern side. The biggest concentration of smelt usually occurs near the mouth of the Songo River in April, often toward the end of the month. Access is good for boat anglers at the nearby Sebago Lake State Park public boat ramp (43.916346,-70.571786). Look for State Park Road off of US 302 north of Raymond (43.942006,-70.546467).

During weekends in late April or early May, there may be dozens of boats trolling the drop-off at the mouth of the Songo River. Early in the season, the most consistent action is near shore in shallower water, or perhaps right at the edge of the first big drop-off from shore. This is where the smelt stage before spawning, and where the salmon will be found as well.

Good landlocked salmon flyfishing can also be found at the mouth of the Northwest River, just south of both Nason and Bachelder Brooks. Hundreds of hatchery brook trout (10 to 12 inches) are also stocked in the Northwest River annually. The shoal just offshore from this spot holds good numbers of spring fish. In fact, the entire western shore of the lake qualifies as a general location worth targeting. Sticky River on the lake's southern end offers shoreline access and good flyfishing opportunities.

The best approach is to troll different areas until someone feels the hard take of a salmon. Then stay in that general vicinity, either trolling or casting, because salmon typically school at this time of year. I prefer to troll from a canoe or kayak as I paddle. The activity keeps me warmer, and I find it easier to adjust speed or move towards or away from shore at different angles. Be aware of weather, wind, and wave action, however, and always wear a personal flotation device, as the water is in the low 40s.

There are myriad fly patterns to choose from and dozens of local ones such as the Senator Muskie and the Bibeau Killer. Most of the classics such as the Gray Ghost, the Mickey Finn, or Joe's Smelt work well enough, at least some of the time. Try your favorite first, and then switch until you find something that brings action. I encourage you to try the newer versions that are constructed with more lifelike materials such as marabou, rabbit fur, or even the new synthetic materials that have more flash and sparkle.

Landlocked salmon range from two to four pounds at Sebago Lake.

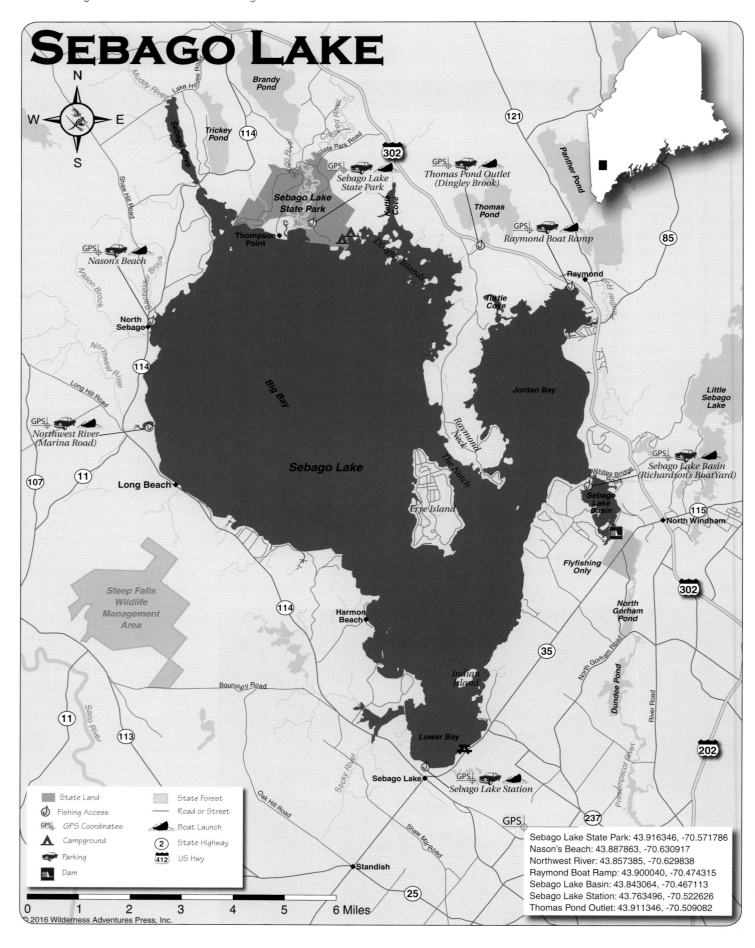

SEBAGO LAKE

N W E S

Muddy River

Lake House Road

Brandy Pond

Trickey Pond

114

Crooked River

State Park Road

GPS

302

121

Panther Pond

GPS
Thomas Pond Outlet (Dingley Brook)

Sebago Lake State Park

Sebago Lake State Park

85

Kettle Cove

Thomas Pond

GPS
Raymond Boat Ramp

Shaw Hill Road

Thompson Point

Dingley Islands

Raymond

GPS
Nason's Beach

Bachelder Brook

Nason Brook

Turtle Cove

North Sebago

114

Little Sebago Lake

Northwest River

Long Hill Road

Big Bay

Jordan Bay

GPS
Northwest River (Marina Road)

Raymond Neck

Whites Bridge Road

GPS
Sebago Lake Basin (Richardson's BoatYard)

107 11

Sebago Lake

The Notch

Sebago Lake Basin

115

North Windham

Long Beach

Frye Island

Flyfishing Only

North Gorham Pond

Steep Falls Wildlife Management Area

114

Harmon Beach

302

Saco River

11

113

Boundary Road

Indian Island

35

North Gorham Road

Dundee Pond

River Road

202

Lower Bay

Sticky River

Sebago Lake

GPS
Sebago Lake Station

Presumpscot River

Oak Hill Road

Standish

Shaw Mill Road

GPS

237

25

	State Land		State Forest
	Fishing Access		Road or Street
GPS	GPS Coordinates		Boat Launch
	Campground	2	State Highway
	Parking	412	US Hwy
	Dam		

0 1 2 3 4 5 6 Miles

© 2016 Wilderness Adventures Press, Inc.

Sebago Lake State Park: 43.916346, -70.571786
Nason's Beach: 43.887863, -70.630917
Northwest River: 43.857385, -70.629838
Raymond Boat Ramp: 43.900040, -70.474315
Sebago Lake Basin: 43.843064, -70.467113
Sebago Lake Station: 43.763496, -70.522626
Thomas Pond Outlet: 43.911346, -70.509082

In addition to this exceptional springtime landlocked-salmon fishery, anglers will find abundant numbers of lake trout in Sebago Lake. Maine lake trout are also dubbed "togue", the French Canadian word derived from the MicMac Indian word atoghwaasu. High numbers of these fish in Sebago have reduced their size from an average weight of six pounds down to just 2.5 pounds. However, lake trout from 10 to 20 pounds are not uncommon. On June 3, 1996, Kezar Falls angler William Day landed a 27.5-pound Sebago Lake togue.

To benefit both lakers and salmon, the Maine Department of Inland Fisheries and Wildlife is engaged in an ongoing effort to better manage this fishery. Flyfish early, from ice-out through May, for the best springtime results on shallows-staging togue. The sandy shoals in front of the Songo, the state park, and at Sebago Station are the best locations to try. Togue go deep in the summer – just after ice-out remains the best time to get one on a fly. Try fishing a fly tied on a jig hook with white marabou and fish it off the bottom just like you would any jig.

What about browns and brookies? Maine Department of Inland Fisheries and Wildlife records show that although Sebago produced a 19-pound, 7-ounce brown trout in the late 1950s, these waters now offer negligible brown trout fishing because only a couple of waters in the drainage are stocked. Brook trout numbers here are also spotty. Look to nearby rivers and creeks for brookies and brown trout.

As Sebago Lake waters warm, flyfishers shouldn't neglect its warmwater species – a total of 23 species swim here. As the shoreline waters warm into the upper 50s, smallmouth and largemouth bass move into the shallows for breeding activities. Top-water fishing using small poppers can be outstanding along shorelines with rocks, logs, or other structure. Turtle Cove (43.894431,-70.502178) is a favorite spot because it is more sheltered than other areas. My favorite popper for smallmouth is a small chartreuse or yellow popper (size 6 or so). In general, smaller is better as long as it still makes an audible pop or gurgle when retrieved erratically. Sebago Lake also has large pickerel that will attack your fly in the weedier areas. Fish with a heavier tippet in these areas or the pickerels' teeth will slice your leader.

To reach Sebago Lake from the Interstate, look for the sign reading "Sebago Lake West Shore" from I-95 and take Exit 44. Follow Route 114 to the west shore. Route 302 follows Sebago's northern shore and can be found near Exit 48; Route 114 will get anglers to the westernmost tributaries; and Route 35 parallels the southeastern end. Boat ramps are Northwest River (western shore), Raymond (northern shore on Jordan Bay), Sebago Lake Basin (eastern shore), Sebago Lake Station (southern shore), Sebago Lake State Park (two ramps on the northern shore), Thompson Point (northern shore near park), and Thomas Pond Outlet (aka Dingley Brook, northern shore near Dingley Islands).

Please consult with Maine's Inland Fish and Wildlife Departments fishing regulations before fishing. Also consult that same department's on-line real-time stocking report for the latest information as to which species of fish have been stocked, where, and when.

Other Stillwaters of Southwestern Maine

Adams Pond

Adams Pond, a small Bridgton pond off ME 107, generally holds 10- to 12-inch brookies but larger fish can be caught. Flyfish through the month of May and into June for the best results. This is good canoeing water, and a hand-carried boat launch is available. Adams Pond is open to open-water fishing from October 1 through November 30 but mandates use of only artificial lures, and all salmonids must be released alive at once. It is closed to open-water fishing from December 1 through March 31, and is closed to ice fishing. Carry a nymph box full of Zug Bugs, Pheasant Tails, Gold-ribbed Hare's Ears, and Prince Nymphs in sizes 10 to 14. Fish in the summertime (using a sinking line in the evening) with small size 18 to 22 dark flies to imitate a prolific species of zooplankton found in this pond that supports brookies up to three pounds on occasion.

Coffee Pond

Coffee Pond, located just off ME 11 in Casco, holds 10- to 12-inch hatchery brookies from late April into June, when the water begins to warm. Smallish Woolly Buggers catch these trout. The Wade State Fish Hatchery, located in Casco, raises landlocks for annual plantings. The public can visit the rearing station by request.

Cold Rain Pond

Cold Rain Pond lies off Tiger Hill Road in Naples and has a launch for canoes or small boats. Expect springtime brook trout from 10 to 12 inches. Fish all-purpose nymphs on this water.

Crystal Lake

I try to fish Crystal Lake (in the town of Gray) right after ice-out at least a couple of times every year. This water is stocked steadily and often with large fish. It is a smaller body of water, and a few kayak strokes from the boat launch in the southwest corner (43.922260,-70.362859) brings me to fishable water. I often see fish rising right along the edge of the retreating ice. Casting attractor patterns such as a

Micky Finn streamer or a Prince Nymph right to the edge of the ice with a slow retrieve can bring you the first fish of the season.

To reach this water, take Route 26 north out of downtown Gray and then left on North Raymond Road.

Lily Pond

Lily Pond in New Gloucester is noteworthy because it is one of the few places in Maine where you can fish for stillwater rainbows. The state stocks at least a couple hundred rainbows towards the end of May. It is a beautiful little pond, although it is very close to the Interstate, so you can hear the growl of trucks as they pass. A muddy and rutted parking lot off Snow Hill Road from Upper New Gloucester (43.984131,-70.316310) is adequate to launch a canoe, kayak, or small boat.

I have caught a number of species in Lily Pond on a fly including smallmouth bass and black crappie, but obviously, it is the rainbows that I am interested in. Subsurface, I have had luck with Wood Special streamers, but towards evening on calm days, the rainbows cruise the pond gulping midges. If you can time their rises and correctly gauge their direction and can place a small black-bodied fly carefully on the surface (I like a size 18 Puterbaugh Caddis), then you can usually hook up with a few spirited, jumping rainbows.

Little Sebago Lake

Brown trout and rainbow trout are annually planted in Little Sebago Lake, located north of North Windham. Look for trout along the shallow water shoreline just after ice-out, especially during the low-light hours of the day. A western-shore boat launch provides access to this 1,898-acre fishery. Ice-out typically arrives by late April. Fish Woolly Buggers, streamers, and large stonefly nymphs and expect catches of both trout and bass. Smallmouth and largemouth bass spawn in the shallows in late spring.

Topwater bass fishing is excellent during this time. Fly anglers can anticipate catching more bass than browns as summer commences, since trout move into the depths by Independence Day. Return here in early fall to flyfish during the extended October 1 to December catch-and-release season, which can be productive because this lake is stocked in the fall as well.

Moose Pond

For those flyfishers who enjoy casting surface poppers for lunker largemouth bass, Moose Pond comes highly recommended by the regional biologists from Maine's Inland Fish and Wildlife Department. The largemouth are large and plentiful and the scenery is terrific, with Shawnee Peak rising up next to the pond. If you have a family that doesn't fish, they can hike a very scenic trail up the back side of the mountain, while you wet a line. There is a boat ramp right off Route 302, which bisects this pond.

Range Pond Chain

Three ponds make up this watershed: Upper, Middle, and Lower. They are stocked with rainbows, brook trout, and brown trout and are also home to a variety of warmwater species including largemouth and smallmouth bass. The bottom line is that you never know what you are going to catch during the transition season between spring and early summer when water temperatures are moderate and all species of fish are fairly active. Middle Range Pond is the deepest of the three, while Upper Range Pond is shallow with a lot of pickerel water. Access points include the State Park launch and a public launch on Skellinger Road off of ME 26.

Thompson Lake

The northern border of Cumberland Country runs right down the middle of this long lake. Maine's Inland Fisheries biologists highlight this lake for its good fishing for a variety of species including landlocked salmon, lake trout, and smallmouth bass. Salmon frequent "the causeway", a section that connects the main lake with "the heath" – a separated southern pond.

Square Pond

Though Cumberland County's Sebago Lake and nearby stillwaters and streams get most of the attention, fisheries located

Perfect surface popper conditions on Moose Pond with Shawnee Peak in the background.

Boat ramp between Upper and Middle Range Pond on Range Hill Road.

in Maine's southernmost tip are also worth noting. Square Pond is famous because Robert Hodsdon's all-state brown trout record of 23.5 pounds was caught there in 1995. In fact, this entire region of the state, which includes Mousam Lake and Great East Lake, can provide good brown trout fishing. Former Maine Department of Inland Fisheries and Wildlife Director John Boland agrees, "Square Pond is probably the best brown-trout pond in Maine." Anglers should note that this fishing experience is not for everyone. Fishing can be slow, but if you want a chance at a trophy brown trout in southern Maine, this is a great option. Primary forage is landlocked alewives, so use appropriate flies along sandy shoals in June.

Square Pond is about nine miles northwest of the Sanford-Springvale area off ME 11. There is a state-owned boat launch on West Shore Drive at the southwest corner of the pond. Other access is available off Route 11 and Town Farm Road on the northern end of the lake.

Mousam Lake

Primarily managed for browns with landlocked alewives stocked as forage, Mousam Lake trout numbers are healthy and are maintained with regular stockings. Focus on the mouths of tributaries, bars, and shoals in May and June. Streamers and Buggers work well, but be prepared for hatches in early mornings and late evenings. Two easily accessible Mousam Lake boat launches are found on the southern end off ME 11 and ME 109. The Mousam River, running southeast from the big water along the main highway toward Sanford, is heavily stocked with browns and brookies. Fish this location and the lake itself April through early June.

Great East Lake

Located in the village of Acton, Great East Lake is a 1,768-acre coldwater lake. Shoreline locations are best fished just after ice-out. Browns, salmon, and lakers roam these shores early for smelt. Togue averaging two to three pounds are common and are good sport on the fly rod. Just ask any ice anglers who fish this shallow water during the winter months – many of their catches match this size. It is easily accessible from ME 109 northwest of Wilson Lake. Check special regulations for Maine and New Hampshire border waters regarding limits, open seasons, and tackle restrictions. A license from either state is valid for fishing on Great East Lake.

Kennebunk Pond

Kennebunk Pond, just west of the village of Saco and Biddeford, offers fishing for holdover brookies and browns from two to five pounds, with some eight-pounders caught on occasion. Browns run larger than brookies. There is a good population of landlocked alewives providing forage. The state annually stocks trout from 10 to 18 inches. Access is made off route 111 on Kennebunk Pond Road. Fish late April through May during low-light margins of the day. All-purpose nymphs, Marabou Muddlers, leech patterns, and wet flies will catch these fish.

In October and November, the flats near the outlet can be waded and browns up to five pounds can be caught by chucking streamers and buggers.

Spicer Pond, Warren Pond, Eli Pond, Littlefield Pond

Other ponds to try are Spicer Pond in Shapleigh (wild brook trout), Warren Pond in South Berwick (stocked rainbows), and Eli Pond in Sanford (stocked with both brookies and rainbows). Littlefield Pond in Sanford is only 19 acres but offers good largemouth, smallmouth and brook trout fishing. To catch the brook trout, fish during lower light periods tight to the bottom. Access is from the gravel Emmons Road and you can hand launch a small boat.

SOUTHWEST MAINE PLANNING CONSIDERATIONS

Hub Cities

- Ogunquit (www.ogunquit.com)
- Windham (www.sebagolakeschapter.com)
- Naples (www.sebagolakeschapter.com)
- Yarmouth/Freeport (www.yarmouthmaine.org)

Easy Access Options

- The Presumpscot River at the ME 35 Bridge in Windham (43.830777,-70.449197). Just a few steps from the dirt parking lot bring you to water's edge where a number of spots offer convenient fishing. Trout are almost always found here because it is heavily stocked, and it is open year round.

- Pineland Pond at Pineland Center, ME 231 in New Gloucester (43.902371,-70.252634). Open space with mowed grass surrounds this small pond just 50 feet from a parking lot. Fishing is good for stocked brook trout in the spring until they get fished out or the pond warms.
- Crooked River at Twin Bridges. Just park in the parking lot by the picnic area and it is a few feet to the stream's edge.
- Crooked River at Songo Locks. Can park right by the dam and a few steps take you to the mill race. Best when the smelt are running in early spring. See the detailed Crooked River description earlier in this section.
- Crystal Lake boat launch/beach. Cast from the beach or paddle out a short distance in a canoe or kayak. A good spot to try when you only have half an hour to fish.

A hardy angler fishing by the Route 35 Bridge in the dead of winter. Photo courtesy Erika Zambello.

Suggested Beginner Options

- Pineland Pond at Pineland Center, ME 231 in New Gloucester (43.902371,-70.252634). Open mowed lawn surrounds this small pond just 50 feet from a parking lot. Fishing is good for stocked brook trout in the spring until they get fished out or the pond warms. An added bonus is a good natural food casual eatery within walking distance.
- Stevens Brook Pond, Gloucester Hill Road, New Gloucester (43.957365,-70.286849). Kids Only! Small pond stocked in the spring. Usually enough space for young fly casters to practice. Check the Maine Inland Fish and Wildlife Department website for when it is stocked.

Suggested Vacation Options

Weekend Getaway

- In early November, when most other flyfishing options in Maine are closed to you, try fishing parts of two days on the Upper Presumpscot River, the Pleasant River catch-and-release section, and the Royal River downstream from Mill Street (see the detailed write-ups of these spots earlier in this section). If the weather is bad or fishing poor, you can always visit nearby Freeport and shop at L.L. Bean or the outlets. If you decide to stay in Portland, known for its fine restaurants, ocean-view hotels, and funky shops, you are only half an hour from the fishing.

One-week Vacation

- In late May, find a lake-side cottage, a hotel, or a bed-and-breakfast in the Windham or Naples area. Sample the following fishing options:
- Troll Sebago Lake for Togue and Salmon. Either hire a guide or trailer your own boat.
- Fish the Crooked River for landlocked salmon chasing smelt, either by boat or wading.
- Fish both the Upper Presumpscot and Pleasant Rivers for recently stocked fish.
- For a small stream experience, take your 3-weight and walk Collyer Brook and enjoy the simple pleasures.
- Finally, you can paddle a small boat around Little Sebago and cast poppers to prespawn smallmouth bass hunting for food in the shallows.
- During downtime, sample any number of local restaurants, and try a few of the leisure activities in the area, such as hiking up Pleasant Mountain or biking on the Sebago Lake to the Sea Trail.

Mid-coast Maine

Mid-coastal Maine encompasses Sagadahoc, Lincoln, Waldo, and Knox Counties. The lakes, ponds, and streams of this region hold salmonid flyfishing opportunities for wild brook trout, stocked brook trout, browns, and landlocked salmon. Some rivers adjacent to the coast offer angling for wild sea-run brookies, while others provide opportunities for sea-run browns and brook trout that have hatchery origins. Stripers are also abundant in certain locations from late May into October.

Mid-coastal Maine's Passagassawakeag River.

LOWER KENNEBEC RIVER

In this section we are only going to cover the lower Kennebec River up to Brunswick, which is primarily saltwater. Upstream, the river between Brunswick and the Waterville dam in central Maine, a distance of some 95 miles, is tidal. The middle sections of the river will be described in the west-central Maine section.

The huge area that is the mouth of the Kennebec River includes Merrymeeting Bay northeast of Brunswick, and the river itself as it flows past the shipyards of Bath, the Morse River, and Popham Beach. Regulations that cover saltwater species apply. For stripers, the season is from June 1 through November 30. Please check the current Maine regulations booklet for a complete listing of Kennebec River regulations. This river has a reputation for large-sized stripers and bluefish closer to the mouth. The best fishing is during June and July, when stripers up to 20 pounds migrate upriver to the Waterville Dam. Let's start in Casco Bay and work our way upriver.

The confluence of the Kennebec and Casco Bay (part of the Gulf of Maine) is located roughly at Fort Popham and Popham Beach, which is about 18 miles south of Bath on ME 209, where there is plenty of parking at the state park (43.737046,-69.797116). The shoreline from Fort Popham out to the sand bar at Woods Island is a good bet when there is a good tidal current. Popham Beach offers two miles of beautiful, sandy shoreline. The Morse River is on the backside of Popham Beach. You can reach the river's estuary by a foot trail from the state park parking area or by walking along the beach. Stripers enter these shallows at night and can provide the stalking angler good sport.

The Kennebec's strong currents below Bath require boats with strong engines. There is a boat launch in the village of North Bath upriver from US 1. It is advisable to use the services of one of the many excellent area guides for your first trip.

Merrymeeting Bay, the confluence of the Kennebec and Androscoggin Rivers located just upstream of Bath, is a treasure of tidal marshes teeming with wildlife. School-sized stripers are in abundance during June and July. There is a good launch for boats and canoes in the village of Richmond. Recently, there have been articles written about flyfishing for carp in this tidal bay. Apparently, escaped carp have naturalized in this bay and flyfishers are targeting carp that weigh more than 10 pounds. Carp are not easy to hook with a fly rod, as they are wary, difficult to fool, and fight hard when hooked.

The lower Damariscotta River (south of the town of Damariscotta) and the New Meadows River (just west of the city of Bath) are also tidal saltwater systems that have plentiful numbers of stripers during their seasons. The New Meadows River has more benign currents than the larger rivers and is a good option if you are fishing from a kayak or a smaller boat.

Stripers feed on the widest variety of foods any fish species in North America. Imitating the prevailing food source at the time is the key to success. Good searching patterns include weighted Clousers or Deceivers in chartreuse and white, blue and white, and red and white.

Sheepscot River

The Sheepscot River was once a good Atlantic salmon fishery, but is now closed to fishing for them as restoration efforts continue. This river was also a favorite of several well-known Maine flyfishing writers for decades even though they had a choice of many quality waters. Relatively

The lower Sheepscot River.

large wild brown trout rose to prolific hatches of mayflies and other bugs. Brown trout stockings in the 1950s were responsible for the brown trout population that produced fish up to seven pounds.

This small river had great fertility because of the effluent from the Palermo Rearing Station (fish hatchery). Unfortunately, the fishing has declined significantly over the last dozen years to the point that it is a middling fishery at best. Trout stocking ceased in 1997. Stricter water standards reduced the nutrients from the hatchery, and continued stocking of Atlantic Salmon smolts increased the completion against young wild brown trout. There are still brown trout to be caught but not in the numbers of yesteryear, particularly since it is not stocked. Don't let me be too discouraging however; I still see photos of some nice-sized brown trout taken from this river.

There are three distinct sections of the Sheepscot River. Starting upstream, the upper Sheepscot above Sheepscot Pond is a small stream that holds both brook trout and brown trout. A west branch of the river joins the main branch farther down in North Whitefield and it is similar to the upper river in that its overgrown waters are tough to fish and access is difficult.

A popular river section starts at the Sheepscot Pond dam and continues downstream past the Palermo Fish Hatchery for two miles to ME 105 and the village of Somerville. This section is catch and release only. Casting is done in tight quarters on this heavily overgrown stream, but there is still fair fishing for brown trout here, especially during mayfly hatches from mid-May through June. Years ago the Sheepscot was known for its strong Hendrickson hatches around Mother's Day, but they have diminished over time for reasons that are not clear. Access to this section of riffles and pools can be gained from Turner Ridge Road.

The river section downstream from Somerville to the dam at Head Tide, south of the village of Whitefield on ME 218, is popular among canoeists. The farther one progresses downstream, the more warmwater species are encountered There is a put-in access area off ME 126 near the village of North Whitefield and a take-out area at the dam.

Below the dam at Head Tide, the water is tidal. There is a small run of Atlantic salmon in the Sheepscot. Of course, it is not legal to fish for Atlantics anywhere in Maine. The pools below the natural "reversing falls" in the village of Sheepscot offer lies for migrating fish as well as upstream at the corner pools near the bridge in the village of Alna. In Sheepscot, river access is available along the east shore from the bridge and in Alna near the bridge and downstream. The months of July and August are good months to fish for feeding stripers near the mouth.

Medomak River

Medomak River is easily accessible from ME 32 north of the village of Waldoboro. The state stocks the river several times a year with brown and brook trout and manages the stretch of river from the outlet of Medomak Pond to the head of tide (the farthest the tidal influence extends upriver) for a two-trout limit, although that law might be changing, so always check the current regulations. This river warms during the summer and survival rates of the stocked trout are low, although a few fish may move into the estuary and return when the water cools. A small Muddler Minnow, weighted to keep it near the bottom, is a reasonable fly to start with in this water. To the south, the Pemaquid River also offers angling for stocked brown trout, with a few migrating into the salt and returning in the fall. Access is limited to a boat access off ME 130 north of the village of Bristol.

Ducktrap River

This small river runs from Belmont to Lincolnville and is a filled with wild (and probably native) brook trout. These trout have quite a unique color to them, perhaps best described as a greenish overlay, as you can see by the accompanying photo. This relatively undiscovered gem stays cool all summer because of its cold springs and tributaries and offers classic small-water fishing, which means lots of walking to find the pools and sheltered habitats that wild trout prefer. Better to wear hiking boots than waders.

The Ducktrap's flows fluctuate significantly based on rain events. There is a USGS gauge on this river, so you can check current flows online. It fishes fine from 10 to 60cfs,

The Ducktrap River offers classic wild brook-trout water. Photo courtesy Tim Shaw.

A beautiful Ducktrap River wild brook trout. Photo courtesy Tim Shaw.

but for most of its length, fishing is best at the lower end of that range.

Access is either from US 1 to the south or ME 52 to the north. Hike upstream or downstream from the bridges, it is all public land. You can actually hike upstream quite a ways but it is a lot of work and the fishing doesn't really improve. In the fall, if there is a significant rain event, the river near Route 1 can fish very well with streamers. Another access is via the end of Tanglewood Street (44.313236,-69.041260). The river borders Camden Hills State Park both upstream and downstream of this access point. As you prospect along the river, you can't go wrong with any small caddis imitation in black or olive. Subsurface, try a Hornberg or Baby Brook Trout streamer. Even if there is not hatch or fish rising, the natives will usually come up to any reasonably presented dry fly.

Protect this resource by practicing flyfishing only with barbless hooks, and catch and release.

St. George River

The St. George River flows nearly 30 miles from the outlet of St. George Lake in Liberty, until it reaches tidewater in Warren. It flows into and out of several water bodies on

its journey to the sea including Stevens, True, Sennebec, Round, and Seven Tree Ponds. Because of this, the lower stretches of this river are host to a variety of species including brown trout, bass, and serious numbers of white perch in the spring when they run out of the ponds to spawn. Brown trout are the primary target for most flyfishers, particularly farther upstream. Like most brown trout waters, the larger fish are found in the deeper pools in sections of the river that are hard to get to and receive less fishing pressure. The limiting factor on this river is that it can get pretty warm during hot or droughty summers and not all of the trout have access to thermal refuges. Although this picturesque river is fun to fish, in reality it is mostly a put-and-take fishery, although there is no question that holdovers are possible.

For those of you who like to float and fish from a canoe or kayak, the four-mile section between Searsmont and North Appleton comes highly recommended. For wading anglers, the outlets of all the ponds and any access from bridges are good spots to try. The outlet of Senebec Pond is a favorite of many and, thanks to the work of Trout Unlimited, the rock ramp to the pond allows the larger fish to move into the pond to find cooler water.

Anglers can catch large browns in the St. George River. Photo courtesy Tim Shaw.

Salters rarely exceed 12 inches. Photo courtesy Sea Run Brook Trout Coalition (www.searunbrookie.org).

SEA-RUN BROOK TROUT

Few people are aware of the sea-run trout fishery that exists throughout mid-coast Maine. From Damariscotta up to and including Acadia National Park, dozens of rivers, streams, and creeks offer the opportunity to catch sea-run brook trout (with the occasional rainbow and brown trout mixed in) at certain times of the year and under certain conditions. Many of the brook trout are wild; other fish were stocked in local ponds, rivers, and lakes, and made their way to saltwater environments.

Salters, as they are called, spend the winter in shoreline estuaries and bays, run up coastal rivers and streams in the early spring if there is adequate flow, return to the ocean when waters warm, and then migrate back into freshwater in the fall to spawn. Most of these waters are small, and the salters are too – they rarely exceed 12 inches. How can you tell if a small brook trout that you catch has recently been in the salt? Look for traditional markings that seem to be overlaid with a silvery sheen.

I am not going to identify specific salter waters because these are sensitive fisheries. The Maine Audubon Society is currently using volunteer anglers to conduct surveys of coastal streams to gather data on this wild trout fishery, but I hope they will be judicious with the information that they release. If you are interested in flyfishing for salters, the best approach is to drive along Route 1 or any other secondary roads within a few miles of saltwater, and when you cross any freshwater stream, stop and try a few casts. Check that the waters you want to fish are not posted. Consult a map frequently, because the coast of Maine is very jagged with fingers of saltwater that extend well inland in places. The best months are April and September. This will be small stream fishing and you will have to manage with little or no casting room. Try small streamers such as Mini-muddlers or small black Woolly Buggers and prospect in small pools or other likely holding water.

In some years and on some waters, you will probably hook a few salters, and other years, you may not. It really is a treasure hunt, and that's what makes it fun.

The Georges River Land Trust maintains several trails that parallel the river (see www.georgesriver.org). The Georges River Trout Unlimited chapter continues to do important conservation work, such as funding the replacement of culverts that block trout movement into cooler tributaries. It is also a good source of information (see www.georgesrivertu.org). They recommend stonefly nymphs, midge larva, Gold-Ribbed Hare's Ears, caddis larva, Adams (standard and parachute), Woolly Buggers, Muddler Minnows, Black-nosed Dace, and Gray Ghost streamers as year-round producers.

Megunticook River
If you find yourself in Camden, the Megunticook River offers in-town angling for stocked brook trout and a few rainbows that drop down from Megunticook Lake. This small water fishes best in the spring when water flow is good. Try fishing along Washington Street, downstream from where the river runs under the road, where the town owns a large vacant lot (44.215417,-69.076815) or find the trail that runs along the river for a short distance.

STILLWATERS OF MID-COAST MAINE

Mid-coast Maine contains numerous freshwater ponds and smaller lakes. They all have either coldwater or warmwater species that can be hooked with a fly rod. I am not going to write about each one but rather focus on those that have unique features or fisheries that make them better choices than other options. They are listed geographically from south to north.

DAMARISCOTTA LAKE

Damariscotta Lake is a 4,625-acre impoundment between the villages of Jefferson and Damariscotta Mills, just north of US 1. The lake is a mixed warm and coldwater fishery supporting thriving togue and some landlocked salmon, primarily in the colder and deeper north basin; and smallmouth bass and other warmwater species, primarily in the middle and southern section. Most of the salmonids are caught by trolling, but for fly casters this lake is not recommended for coldwater species.

However, this is an excellent lake to flyfish for smallmouth and largemouth bass, and I confidently make this claim after fishing this lake for over 40 years. The narrow profile of the lake with numerous rocky shoals, points, and islands, means that the angler can almost always find a calm spot to cast surface patterns. In the spring, once the water temperatures warm, the bass will clobber small bass or pan fish poppers in yellow, chartreuse, or orange. When in doubt, try smaller poppers, not larger. Cast towards the shallows and retrieve slowly with frequent pauses. Fishing is better in the early morning and early evening, before a sea breeze kicks up and the motor boat traffic increases.

This lake receives a run of alewives from the sea. Later in the summer, the bass feed on young alewives as they gather in massive school in the lake shallows. You can actually see the commotion as the bass trap their prey against certain structures. Small marabou streamers with grey or white wings work well at this time.

In late May, alewives migrate from Casco Bay up the saltwater Damariscotta River, into a very short section of freshwater river, where an elaborate fish ladder has been built of stone and masonry, allowing the fish to bypass the dam that creates the lake. This event is quite a spectacle in and of itself, with tens of thousands of fish quite visible as they ascend the series of obstacles with eagles, ospreys, seagulls, and even seals waiting to pick off the weak and wounded. Thousands of visitors come every year to observe and photograph the action. Drive to Damariscotta Mills and look for signs and groups of people gawking and taking photographs. Recent conservation efforts have rejuvenated this alewife run from thousands to hundreds of thousands of fish annually. For more information, go to www.damariscottamills.org.

Damariscotta Lake has public boat launches near the public beach at the state park on the lake's northern end, where there is also camping available nearby, and one on the west side of the lake about three miles north of Damariscotta Mills.

Damariscotta Lake has many islands, points and peninsulas that create great smallmouth bass habitat.

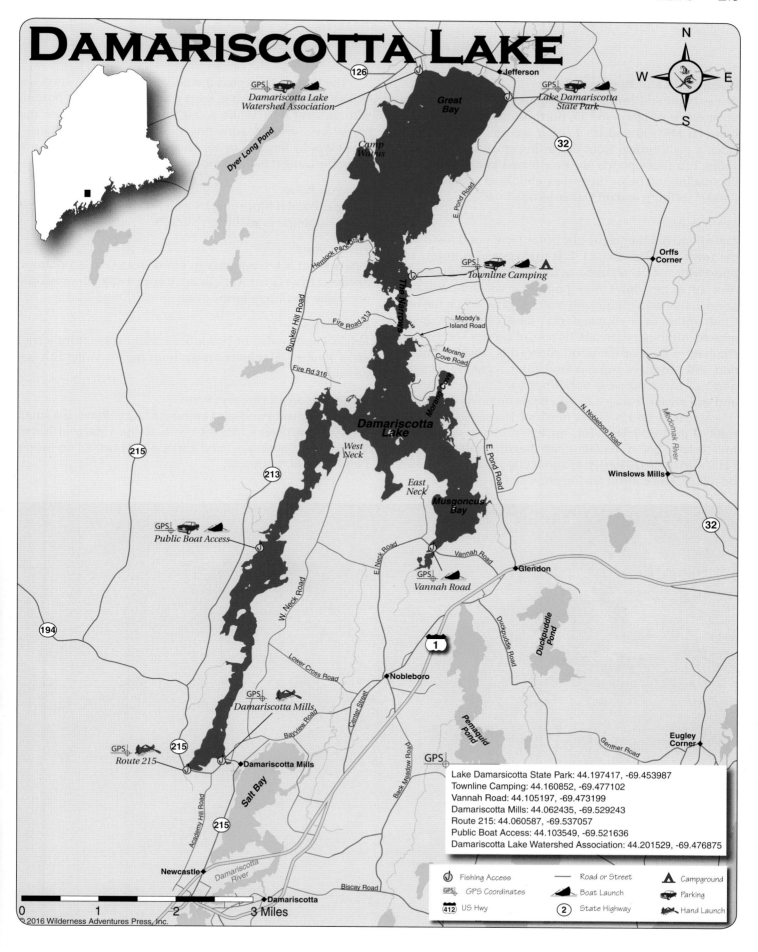

DAMARISCOTTA LAKE

N
W E
S

126
Jefferson

GPS
Damariscotta Lake
Watershed Association

GPS
Lake Damarscotta
State Park

Great
Bay

Dyer Long Pond

Camp
Walrus

32

Orffs
Corner

GPS
Townline Camping

Hemlock Park Drive

The Narrows

E. Pond Road

Moody's
Island Road

Fire Road 313

Morang
Cove Road

Bunker Hill Road

Fire Rd 316

Morang Cove

Damariscotta
Lake

West
Neck

N. Nobleboro Road

Medomak River

E. Pond Road

East
Neck

Winslows Mills

213

Musgoncus
Bay

32

GPS
Public Boat Access

E Neck Road

Vannah Road

Glendon

GPS
Vannah Road

194

W. Neck Road

Duckpuddle Road

Duckpuddle
Pond

1

Lower Cross Road

Nobleboro

Eugley
Corner

GPS
Damariscotta Mills

Center Street

Bayview Road

Genther Road

GPS
Route 215

215

Damariscotta Mills

Back Meadow Road

Pemaquid
Pond

GPS

Lake Damarsicotta State Park: 44.197417, -69.453987
Townline Camping: 44.160852, -69.477102
Vannah Road: 44.105197, -69.473199
Damariscotta Mills: 44.062435, -69.529243
Route 215: 44.060587, -69.537057
Public Boat Access: 44.103549, -69.521636
Damariscotta Lake Watershed Association: 44.201529, -69.476875

Salt Bay

215

Academy Hill Road

Newcastle

Damariscotta River

Biscay Road

Damariscotta

0   1   2   3 Miles

© 2016 Wilderness Adventures Press, Inc.

Fishing Access   Road or Street   Campground
GPS GPS Coordinates   Boat Launch   Parking
412 US Hwy   2 State Highway   Hand Launch

Biscay Pond and Pemaquid Pond

Biscay Pond and Pemaquid Pond are part of the Pemaquid River chain of lakes and lie north of the village of Bristol between ME 130 and US 1. After ice-out, it is possible to catch a good brown trout by casting streamers toward the shore, but these ponds are best fished later in the spring for smallmouth bass. There is a public boat access at Biscay Pond's northern end off Damariscotta Road.

Little Pond

Little Pond is a unique trophy brook trout pond just outside the town of Damariscotta. It is managed as a trophy trout pond with special regulations (artificial lures only, one fish over 18 inches only). This pond is a walk-in-access-only pond that hosts a unique tiny water organism that the brook trout utilize as a supplemental food source for healthy growth. Although there are dozens of canoes and rowboats chained to trees at the pond shore, it is stocked annually, and still produces three-pound trout regularly to patient anglers. There are also very impressive largemouth bass and you are encouraged to take those home if you desire.

Access is off US 1 just north of Damariscotta. Take a right after the McDonalds, on Biscay Road. After several miles, look for a woods road heading off to the left (44.033107,-69.477140). It is about 200 yards to the pond, a doable distance if you are lugging a canoe or kayak.

The best way to catch the larger trout is not a surprise. Unless you see fish rising, keep your fly close to the bottom with sinking line. While a few anglers try to imitate the small food sources with tiny flies of green and orange, small Woolly Buggers or conehead marabou streamers are probably more reliable options.

Sprague Pond

Sprague Pond (Phippsburg) is a nice walk-in pond for brook trout. Parking is available on ME 209.

Peters Pond

Peters Pond is a small walk-in pond located in Waldoboro. Access is from Gross Neck Road. It is an artificial-lures-only pond that has larger brook trout.

Kalers Pond

Kalers Pond is also in Waldoboro with access from a trail off of Route 1. Holdover brown trout means larger fish are possible.

Little Medomak (Storer) Pond

Little Medomak Pond, also known as Storer Pond, is a small brown trout fishery located north of the village of North Waldoboro. There is a hand-carried boat access on Storer Pond Road off Route 32.

Alewives moving upstream. Photo courtesy of the Damariscotta Mills Fish Ladder Restoration Project.

Little Pond brook trout. Photo courtesy Maine I.F.&W.

St. George Lake

St. George Lake is an inviting piece of water located amid hills and forests off Route 3, west of the village of Belfast in Liberty. The lake covers about 1,000 acres and has a maximum depth of 65 feet. It is a mixed cold and warmwater fishery holding landlocked salmon and brown trout as well as smallmouth bass and chain pickerel. There are camping facilities, boat rentals, and a boat launch at the state park on the lake's northern shore.

Sheepscot Pond

Sheepscot Pond, due west of St. George Lake, is a 1,200-acre impoundment that provides the flow for the Sheepscot River from the dam at the pond's south end. The pond itself supports both cold and warmwater species. In its colder depths, it holds brook trout and togue. There is a boat launch just off Route 3 at Greely Corner on the north shore.

Bowler Pond

Bowler Pond is accessible from Level Hill Road off ME 3, west of St. George Lake. It is managed as artificial lures only, no limit on bass, and a two-trout limit – minimum 12 inches and only one longer than 14 inches.

Crystal Pond

Crystal Pond in Washington is accessed from Crystal Lake Road and is stocked both spring and fall with brook trout.

Spectacle Pond

Spectacle Pond in Vasselboro has larger multiple-year classes of both brook and brown trout and a good Hex hatch that will bring these fish to the surface. Access is from a dirt road of Church Hill Road.

Sanborn Pond

Sanborn Pond holds brook trout and lies northwest of the village of Belfast on ME 137. There is a boat launch at the pond's southern end. Half Moon Pond, another small brook trout pond, is just north of Sanborn off Route 203.

Alford Lake and Megunticook Lake

Alford Lake is located off ME 235 with a public boat launch on the west shore. Megunticook Lake, north of Camden, offers boat access of ME 52. It holds browns and rainbows. The outlet stream offers decent brook trout fishing as well. Nearby is Swan Lake. Fish for brook trout in the boulder fields on the north end near the state park.

MID-COAST MAINE PLANNING CONSIDERATIONS

Nearby Hub Cities and Towns

- Damariscotta (www.damariscottaregion.com)
- Belfast (www.belfastmaine.org)

Easy Access Options

- From the town of Union, go north on ME 131 until you reach Sennebec Pond. Fish the St. George River downstream of the rock ramp outlet of Sennebec Pond (44.236708,-69.278368). The first pool is usually crowded but there is easy trail access downstream for another mile or so.
- Farther north on ME 131, take Ghent Road going east and fish the St. George River for several hundred yards on either side of the bridge (44.335673,-69.198833). If you check the online stocking report, you can time your visit shortly after the stocking truck has made a visit.

Suggested Beginner Options

- Launch a small boat from the western Damariscotta Lake boat launch and cast small bass poppers along the rocky islands and points for bass. The best times are early or late in the day when the on-shore winds tend to settle down. June is the most productive month. The boat launch road (44.103809,-69.524379) is off ME 213 about five miles north of Damariscotta Mills.
- The easy access options on the St. George River listed on this page are also good beginner spots, especially if you arrive within several weeks of the stocking truck when trout are plentiful and naïve.
- Try the Wagner Bridge Road crossing to the Medomak River after stocking occurs (44.144750,-69.415615).

Part of the Damariscotta Mills alewife fish ladder.

Vacation Suggestions

Weekend Getaway

- Spend Memorial Day weekend in the town of Damariscotta. Fish for the abundant smallmouth bass that will be in the shallows preparing to spawn. Double-digit catches during a single morning is possible. A boat with a small outboard, a canoe, and a kayak are all effective options. It is best to fish early in the morning or in the evening when waters are calm and boat traffic wanes.

  During the day, go to Damariscotta Mills at the southern end of the lake and watch the alewives on their spawning run and the plentiful predatory birds including bald eagles feeding on nature's bounty. Find the parking area (44.060030,-69.526104) and walk up the short freshwater river. The town of Damariscotta itself is delightful with interesting shops and restaurants.

One-week Vacation

- In June, put a canoe on top of the car, explore the mid-coast of Maine, and catch all of the coastal sights: quaint towns, lighthouses, beaches, and the rocky coast (my favorite is Pemiquid Point). Camden Hills State Park has hikes with tremendous views of the ocean from 1,400 feet above sea level. Eat some lobster and, of course, do a little fishing.

  Smallmouth bass will still be prowling the shallows of Damariscotta Lake. Try Little Pond for large brookies. Try a leisurely hike up the St. George and Ducktrap Rivers for browns and wild brookies. Hire a guide to take you fishing for stripers on the Kennebec or try it yourself at Popham Beach. The only downside? You will have to bring a number of fly rods, reels, and lines to handle everything from tiny wild brookies to 30-inch stripers.

Western Maine

In the 1800s, when native populations of large brook trout diminished on Long Island, New York, then the Catskills, and finally the Adirondacks, adventurous anglers discovered the giant brook trout of western Maine. The Rangeley area was producing brook trout that weighed in the double digits, the only place in the continental United States ever to do so. Railroad tracks were laid, and it became the destination for trophy-hunting anglers. The great old fishing lodges of this area hosted flyfishers from all over the country: Colonel Joseph D. Bates, Jr., flyfisher and author; Carrie Gertrude Stevens, housewife-turned-fly-dresser who designed the Gray Ghost streamer; and Herb Welch, one of the first fly tiers to fashion smelt patterns on long-shanked hooks, are part of the long list of flyfishing pioneers who sought the large brook trout and landlocked salmon of western Maine.

The Rangeley Outdoor Heritage Museum in Oquossoc is well worth visiting to see photos, artifacts, impressive mounted trout and salmon, and the history of Rangeley Lakes flyfishing. Go to www.rangeleyoutdoormuseum.org for more information.

The western Maine area contains Oxford and Franklin Counties and stretches from the White Mountain National Forest south of Bethel, west to the Mahoosic Mountains on the Maine/New Hampshire border, east to Farmington and north to Sugarloaf, the second highest peak in Maine. There are hundreds of miles of prime fishing rivers including the mighty Androscoggin, the Magalloway and Kennebago watersheds, and the entire Rangeley Lake system. Much of the water is flyfishing only. Wild brook trout and landlocked salmon up to five pounds are still caught every year by lucky anglers.

Rangeley Area Rivers

Flowing south from the Canadian Border before emptying into the Rangeley Lakes are – from west to east - the Diamond, Magalloway, Cupsuptic, and Kennebago Rivers. Three other waters, the Rangeley River, Upper Dam Outflow, and the Rapid River connect the Rangeley Lakes with each other. These waters are all covered in this section except the Diamond River that flows through New Hampshire.

MAGALLOWAY RIVER

The Magalloway River may be the most underrated wild salmonid flyfishing river in the eastern United States. I have fished this water for over 30 years and it is truly a flyfishing experience second to none because of the unspoiled setting, the quality of the fishery, and the wadeability of this smaller, more intimate water. Two lakes and a tailwater divide the river into four distinct sections and all of them (at certain times of year) hold wild landlocked salmon and native brook trout up to four pounds. The downside to this water is access; some of the sections are behind locked gates with no vehicle access, although walking or bushwhacking in is allowed. You can also stay at Bosebuck Sporting Camp and get a key to the gates.

The Magalloway begins in a bog on the Canadian border and flows 12 miles to Parmachenee Lake. Expect small stream fishing for small native brookies year round, and larger trout and salmon that run up the stream from Parmachenee in the spring to feed on smelt, sucker eggs, and emerging mayflies, and again in September to spawn. A kettle pond named Rump Pond is connected to the river, about four miles up from the lake. Access to the upper stretches of the river (best fished by canoe) is from a logging road that travels along the eastern shore (if you stay at Bosebuck and have gate access).

The pools immediately above Parmachenee Lake are well-known: Landing Pool, Little Boy Falls (sometimes called Eisenhower Falls because president Dwight D. Eisenhower fished there), and Cleveland Eddy. Access is again limited by the gates but for those of you who like to hike, it is a reasonably straightforward six-mile walk on a good logging road to reach these lower pools.

The second section of the Magalloway connects Parmachenee Lake with Aziscohos Lake. The most consistently productive spots are the outlet of Parmachenee Lake, both below and above the remains of the old wrecked wooden dam, and the confluence of the river with Aziscohos Lake. Between those two spots, the river does offer pocket water opportunities and a few good pools.

Access to this river section is easier; the lowest portion directly above Aziscohos Lake is not gated and parking is available at the so-called #10 Bridge (sometimes called the Camp 10 Bridge, 45.117333,-70.985608). It can be reached by taking the Parmachenee Road from Wilson's Mills, past Bosebuck Camps, and taking a right immediately before the locked gate. There is another access approaching from the other side from the Lincoln Pond Road to Green Top Road.

The road to the Parmachenee Lake outlet is gated but can be reached by walking upstream from the #10 Bridge or taking a 45-minute walk up from the locked gate. Allow plenty of time if you bushwhack upstream. The last time I talked to an angler who had walked the stream, he told me he saw a mother black bear and three cubs. He had to detour around them and ended up walking back on the road.

The Little Magalloway River crosses Parmachenee Road above Aziscohos Lake and can offer good fishing for brook trout, particularly

A good fish on the Magalloway River below Parmachenee Lake.

MAGALLOWAY RIVER

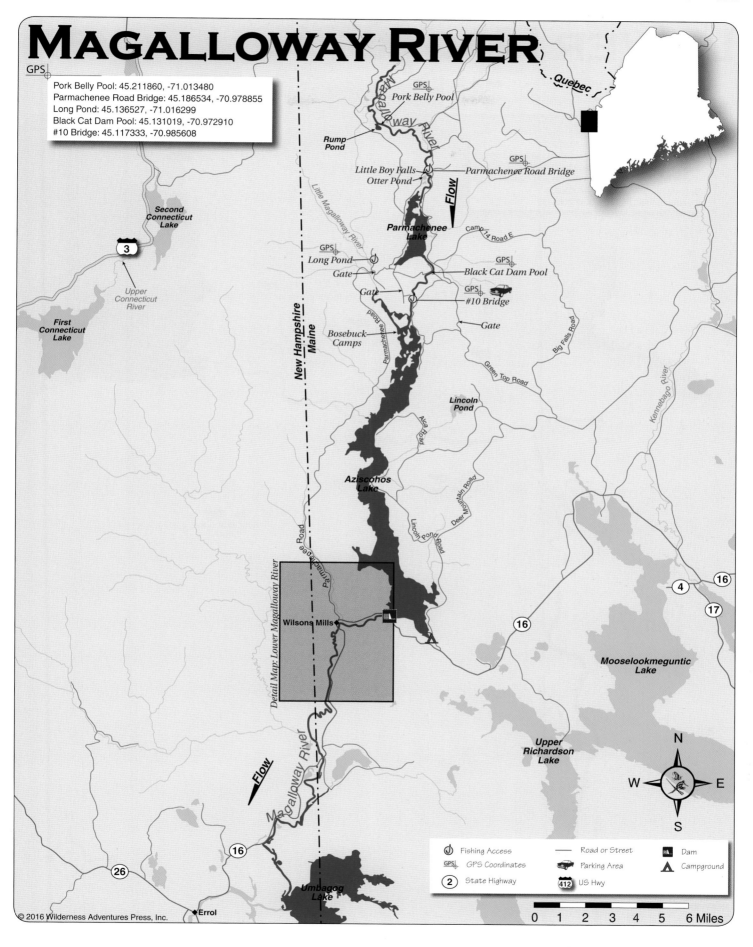

GPS

Pork Belly Pool: 45.211860, -71.013480
Parmachenee Road Bridge: 45.186534, -70.978855
Long Pond: 45.136527, -71.016299
Black Cat Dam Pool: 45.131019, -70.972910
#10 Bridge: 45.117333, -70.985608

Quebec

Pork Belly Pool

GPS

Magalloway River

Rump Pond

Little Boy Falls
Otter Pond

Parmachenee Road Bridge

GPS

Flow

Second
Connecticut
Lake

Parmachenee Lake

Camp 14 Road E

Little Magalloway River

Long Pond

Gate

Black Cat Dam Pool

GPS

Upper
Connecticut
River

Gate

GPS

#10 Bridge

Bosebuck
Camps

Gate

First
Connecticut
Lake

Parmachenee Road

Green Top Road

Big Falls Road

Kennebago River

Lincoln
Pond

New Hampshire

Maine

Alca Road

Aziscohos
Lake

Lincoln Pond Road

Deer Mountain Road

4

16

17

Detail Map: Lower Magalloway River

Wilsons Mills

16

Mooselookmeguntic
Lake

Parmachenee Road

Flow

Upper
Richardson
Lake

N

W   E

S

16

Magalloway River

26

Fishing Access

Road or Street

Dam

GPS

GPS Coordinates

Parking Area

Campground

Umbagog
Lake

Errol

2

State Highway

412

US Hwy

0   1   2   3   4   5   6 Miles

LOWER MAGALLOWAY RIVER

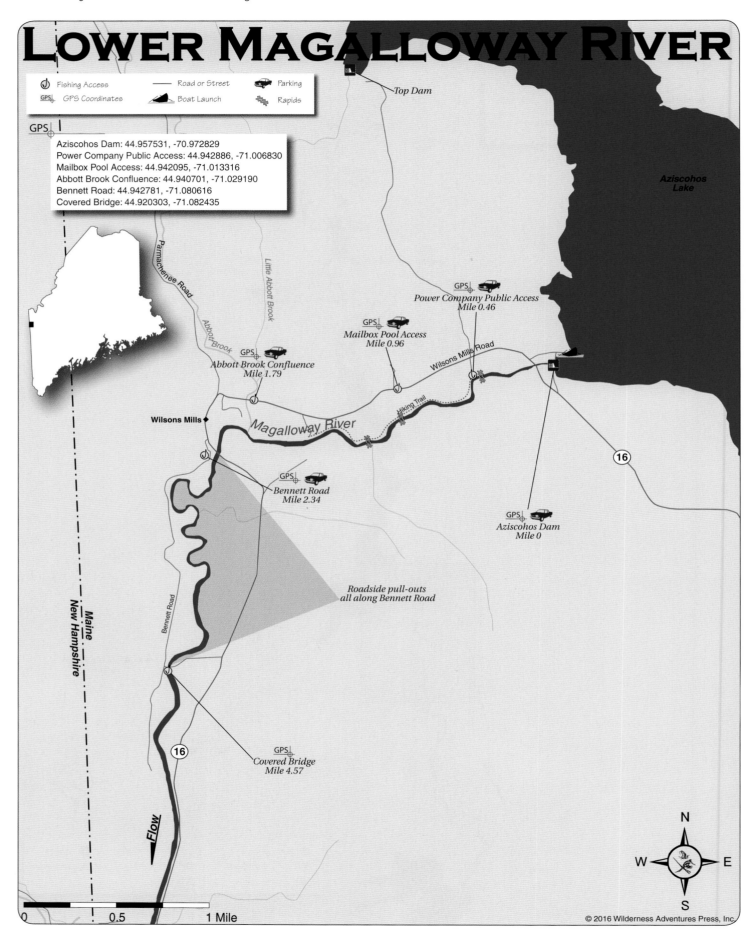

Fishing Access
GPS GPS Coordinates
Road or Street
Boat Launch
Parking
Rapids

GPS
Aziscohos Dam: 44.957531, -70.972829
Power Company Public Access: 44.942886, -71.006830
Mailbox Pool Access: 44.942095, -71.013316
Abbott Brook Confluence: 44.940701, -71.029190
Bennett Road: 44.942781, -71.080616
Covered Bridge: 44.920303, -71.082435

Top Dam

Aziscohos
Lake

Parmachenee Road

Little Abbott Brook

Abbott Brook

GPS
Power Company Public Access
Mile 0.46

GPS
Mailbox Pool Access
Mile 0.96

GPS
Abbott Brook Confluence
Mile 1.79

Wilsons Mills Road

Hiking Trail

Wilsons Mills

Magalloway River

16

GPS
Bennett Road
Mile 2.34

GPS
Aziscohos Dam
Mile 0

Roadside pull-outs
all along Bennett Road

Bennett Road

16

GPS
Covered Bridge
Mile 4.57

Maine
New Hampshire

Flow

N
W   E
S

0   0.5   1 Mile

© 2016 Wilderness Adventures Press, Inc.

The tailwater section of the Magalloway gives up some big brook trout. Photo courtesy Emily Bastian.

upstream from the road where you'll find Long Pond (for more information, see the Long Pond write-up). Access is by either an overgrown logging road that ends at the southern shore or a trail that culminates on the eastern shore (45.136527,-71.016299). The pond can be waded along one gravelly ridge that crosses the stream above the pond. You can also fish it by float tube, borrow a nearby boat, or drag a canoe in from the logging road.

Effective fly patterns to fish the Magalloway River depend on the season. Shortly after ice-out, smelt-imitation patterns are critical to catch the larger lake-dwelling salmonids that move into the river. As the fishing season progresses, sucker spawn imitations, then small mayfly imitations such as the Prince Nymph, Hare's Ear, or Copper John, and finally ants become more important. In heavily-fished pools, emergers or nymphs featuring unique colors such as pink, blue, and orange will fool jaded fish.

In the fall, larger fish again ascend the river from the lakes on their spawning run, and colorful subsurface fare such as the Wood Special, marabou streamers featuring yellow or red colors, or the traditional Mickey Finn are effective. In heavily-fished pools, nymphing or fishing small blue-winged olive imitations will tempt fished-over salmonids.

The third section of the Magalloway is a tailwater where the water flows from the bottom of the Aziscohos Dam and stays cold all summer. Trout and salmon, from a modest six inches up to five pounds stay in this section all summer.

Access is easy as ME 16 parallels the river. Several good trails run down each shoreline and a large parking area sits where the water exits the powerhouse about half a mile down the road from the dam (44.942886,-71.006830).

Several miles downstream from the dam, Route 16 crosses the Magalloway River and continues on the west shore, while Bennett Road continues along the downstream righthand shore. Even though this fourth section of the river changes character as it flows through a widening valley and slows down as it reaches Lake Umbagog, good brook trout and salmon are still present, along with big fallfish and some smallmouth bass.

The tricky part of fishing below the dam is that water flows can vary a great deal from day to day. Generally, 350cfs is ideal, and the river remains fishable up to 550cfs. Above 650cfs fishing is more difficult and wading dangerous (always check water release schedules at www. americanrivers.org). Flows drop early and late in the day, so one strategy is to fish before 9:00am and after 6:00pm.

Because the lower Magalloway is a tailwater, small blue-winged olives are predominant. Nymphing with size 16 to 20 Pheasant Tails, Prince Nymphs, or Copper Johns is the most productive way to fish here. However, some anglers do well with large articulated streamers and big stonefly imitations at dusk or later.

Stream Facts: Magalloway River

Season and Regulations
The season is April 1 to September 31, and it's flyfishing only with a slot limit until August 14. It's catch and release after August 15. Below Aziscohos Dam, it's catch and release all year with only barbless hooks allowed.

Species
Brook trout and landlocked salmon

River Flows
Below Aziscohos Dam flows range from 300 to 1,000cfs. The best fishing is below 700. Optimal fishing and easier access to all waters and wading is below 500. Flows are generally lower in the early morning and in the evening. Flows are higher on the weekend to accommodate whitewater rafters and kayakers.

Access
Below Aziscohos Dam, access is from Route 16 at the powerhouse parking lot, the so-called Mailbox Pool Trail (44.942095,-71.013316), the trail along Abbott Brook (44.940701, -71.029190) and at ME 16 bridge. A good trail parallels the river along the north bank. There are a few places where the river can be crossed during lower flows, and there is a rough trail on the south bank.

For the middle section between Aziscohos and Parmachenee Lake, park at # 10 Bridge and walk upstream. The bridge can be reached by Parmachenee Road from Route 16 (over 16 miles), or from the east on Green Top Road. You can walk the dirt road past the gate for several miles to reach the outlet of Parmachenee Lake.

The Upper part of the Mags above Parmachenee Lake is best reached by staying at Bosebuck Camps, where they can give you a key to the gate and you can drive up the west shore of the lake until you cross the river right above Little Boy (Eisenhower) Falls.

Equipment
For casting streamers on sink-tip line or full-sink line, a 6-weight rod, for nymphing use a 10-foot 4-weight, and for casting dries in skinnier water, a 3-weight is ideal.

Flies
Early in the spring, smelt imitation patterns such as the Marabou Black Ghost or Gray Ghost, and then sucker spawn patterns with pale yellow egg yarn. When hatches begin, size 14 black Puterbuagh Caddis to imitate early black stoneflies, then size 14 Hornberg, Quill Gordons, Royal Wulffs, and Parachute Adams to match spring mayflies.

In June, try brown and green drake emerger patterns or extended deerhair patterns. For subsurface fare, Baby Brook Trout, Mini-muddlers, and Wood Specials work all year. Productive nymph patterns include Prince Nymphs, Hare's Ears, and Copper Johns in copper, green, pink, and black (all with and without tungsten beadheads).

Cupsuptic River

The Cupsuptic River begins near the Canadian border as a small woodland stream and builds slowly in size during its course south towards Mooselookmeguntic Lake, although it never gets as large as its neighboring rivers, such as the Kennebago. The water varies from pocket water, plunge pools, short runs, small waterfalls and a short canyon section to larger gravel-bottom pools.

The Cupsuptic is fed by springs and bogs and stays cool all summer long. When fishing in other rivers slows down in hot weather, this river remains excellent. It has always held wild trout, although historically they grew bigger before logging and road building silted in the larger pools.

Several miles up the river from Green Top Road is a series of cataracts called Big Falls (45.083519,-70.889942). Above the falls the trout are hand-sized or smaller, although beautifully colored with yellow undersides and contrasting blue and pink spots. Immediately below the falls, the trout can run larger because in spring and fall, trout from Mooselookmeguntic Lake make their way up to the falls. The native trout of this river are a valuable resource, so be sure to pinch down your barbs and release all fish without touching them.

If you are visiting the Rangeley area with your family, the Cupsuptic River offers activities for non-fishing family members as well. Besides climbing around the Big Falls or swimming in the pool below it, other interesting water and rock formations throughout the canyon section offer photography or painting subjects. Streamside wilderness campsites are available managed by Cupsuptic Campground on Route 16 north of Oquossoc (www.cupsupticcampground.com). Rangeley Lakes Heritage Trust manages the campground (which also has campsites on the shore of Cupsuptic Lake) and the folks on site can provide you with all of the information, advice, and maps that you require.

Flyfishing on the Cupsuptic is not technical. In the summer, all you need is a 3-weight rod, a pair of hiking boots to wade along (or in) the stream, and a pill bottle of small dry or wet flies. Try small dry flies such as a Hornberg, Puterbaugh Caddis, or Adams; any small black or gray wet fly; a Mini-muddler, or a small Mickey Finn.

To reach the river, take ME 16 north from Oquossoc past the Cupsuptic Campground, and then take the first major dirt road to the right (the Morton Cutoff). Using whatever map source you prefer, find the dirt logging roads that parallel both sides of the river. The best road to Big Falls and the campsites follows the west shore of the river. From Oquossoc to the falls is about 30 minutes.

KENNEBAGO RIVER

Similar to other Rangeley area rivers, the key to Kennebago River fishing is the lakes that are part of the Kennebago watershed. Lakes provide the trout and salmon refuge from winter ice, summer heat, and continuous fishing pressure. It is the lakes, along with excellent river spawning habitat and restrictive regulations that allow native brook trout and wild landlocked salmon to grow old and sometimes quite large.

The Kennebago Lake trout and salmon move around a lot – from the lakes into the river, up and down the river, and back to the lakes again. The key to consistent fishing is to determine where the concentrations of fish are. The quality of the fishing varies from season to season and year to year depending upon the amount of rain, and when Kennebago salmonids ascend and descend the river from the lakes to feed or spawn.

The Kennebago River descends from Big Island Pond (2,149 feet) to Little Kennebago and Kennebago Lakes (1,782 feet), and then downstream to the Mooselookmeguntic confluence (1,467 feet). Each section is very different and there are actually two distinct populations of trout and salmon, with the Kennebago Lake Dam separating the two.

The lower Kennebago River below the Kennebago Lake dam offers very different types of water during its 12-mile run to its confluence with Cupsuptic Lake, including plunge pools, pocket water, boulder-strewn runs, and deep gravelly pools. Regardless of season, anglers can always find native brook trout that range up to 10 inches and immature landlock salmon parr. It is the larger migratory fish from Mooselookmeguntic Lake, however, that draw the anglers. In the spring after the water has warmed into the 50s, there is often a false spawning run and the river fills with salmon from 12 to 18 inches that stay in the river all summer. Some years it happens and some years it doesn't.

Between early August and throughout the fall, a cold rain will bring a true spawning run of larger salmon and trout. Once again this is weather dependent. In 2014 after a series of heavy rain events in early August, schools of salmonids ascended the river, and in mid-August the fishing was unbelievable, although few anglers were around to enjoy it. Sometimes large trout and salmon will overwinter in deep holes and are available to catch the following spring.

Popular access points to the lower Kennebago include the ME 16 bridge (canoes can be put in and taken out there, 44.984968,-70.786800), and the Boy Scout Road that parallels the right bank of the river until a gate blocks access. The famous Steep Bank Pool (45.009669,-70.791227) is obvious from the Boy Scout Road and classic pools can be found both above and below it. Some choose to put a canoe in and float down the river from Steep Bank Pool to the Route 16 bridge or even the lake itself. Some anglers park at the gate and walk or bike the old railroad bed beyond the gate to reach other trails that lead to the river.

The author fishing the Kennebago River above Kennebago Lake. Photo courtesy Erika Zambello.

KENNEBAGO RIVER

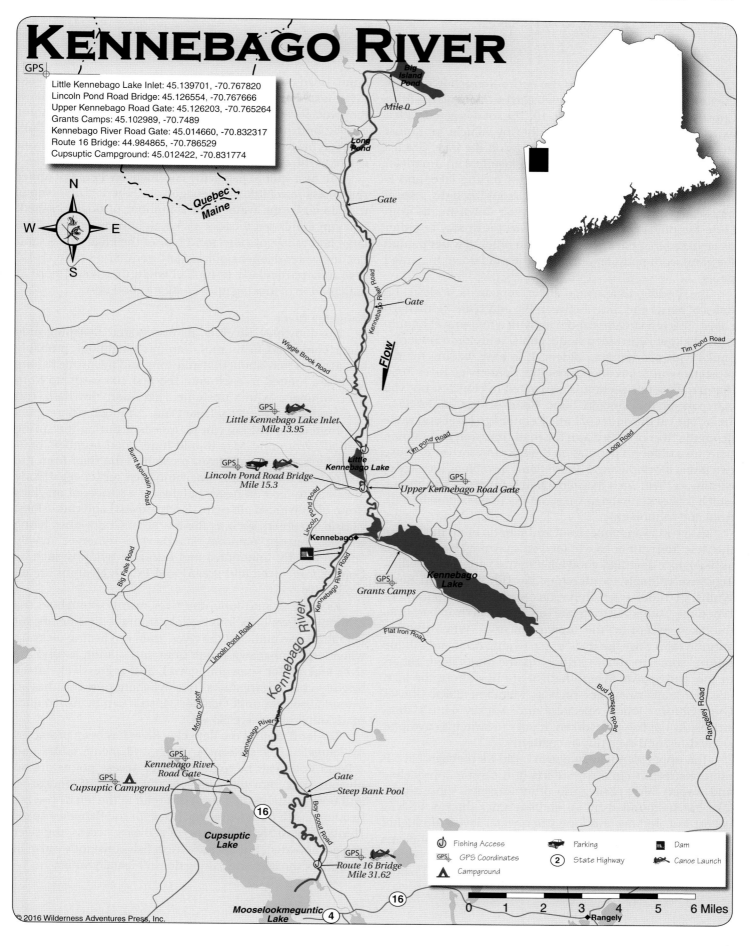

GPS

Little Kennebago Lake Inlet: 45.139701, -70.767820
Lincoln Pond Road Bridge: 45.126554, -70.767666
Upper Kennebago Road Gate: 45.126203, -70.765264
Grants Camps: 45.102989, -70.7489
Kennebago River Road Gate: 45.014660, -70.832317
Route 16 Bridge: 44.984865, -70.786529
Cupsuptic Campground: 45.012422, -70.831774

Big Island Pond

Mile 0

Long Pond

Gate

Quebec
Maine

N
W   E
S

Kennebago River Road

Gate

Flow

Wiggle Brook Road

Tim Pond Road

GPS
Little Kennebago Lake Inlet
Mile 13.95

Little Kennebago Lake

Tim Pond Road

GPS
Lincoln Pond Road Bridge
Mile 15.3

Upper Kennebago Road Gate

GPS

Loop Road

Burnt Mountain Road

Kennebago

GPS
Grants Camps

Kennebago Lake

Lincoln Pond Road

Big Falls Road

Kennebago River Road

Flat Iron Road

Bud Russell Road

Rangeley Road

Kennebago River

Morton Cutoff

Kennebago River Road

GPS
Kennebago River Road Gate

GPS
Cupsuptic Campground

Gate
Steep Bank Pool

Boy Scout Road

16

Cupsuptic Lake

GPS
Route 16 Bridge
Mile 31.62

Fishing Access

GPS GPS Coordinates

Campground

Parking

2 State Highway

Dam

Canoe Launch

16

Mooselookmeguntic Lake

4

0 1 2 3 4 5 6 Miles

Rangely

© 2016 Wilderness Adventures Press, Inc.

The main access road to the entire Kennebago area is the Kennebago River Road, which can be found across from Cupsuptic Campground on ME 16. The road is gated with a manned gatehouse. To travel farther by vehicle, you must stay at one of the two sporting camps on the lake. Grant's Kennebago Camps on Kennebago Lake offers an American plan and a number of small cottages on the lake, and is known for its food. Kennebago Camps include several housekeeping cabins on the river just downstream from Little Kennebago Lake. It is well worth it to stay at either place in order to have access to seven miles of water behind the gates, with paths leading from the road down to named pools.

The middle Kennebago River section is a short 1.5 miles of twists and turns between Big and Little Kennebago Lakes. This is a stream-sized river with a fine-gravel bottom with shallow runs, deep bend pools, and some undercut banks with overhanging alders. It is easy wading for the most part with a few deep spots. The Kennebago River Road that parallels this section is also gated to vehicles, but you can park at the Lincoln Pond Road bridge (45.126554,-70.767666) at the outlet of Little Kennebago River and wade down the river or walk down the road. The trout and salmon here are a different population than the lower river because two dams block passage. These dams also block passage of warmwater fish such as yellow perch from the lower river, which is why Kennebago Lake and the upper watershed are trout and salmon only.

In late May and June, trout and salmon enter this part of the river from either lake to feed on spawning baitfish such as blacknose dace and good hatches of a variety of mayflies. They rise willingly to attractors like Hornbergs and Royal Wulffs, or more exact imitations such as Klinkhammers. When the waters warm in late June, the fish drop back into the lakes, except for the smallest of trout. When the first autumn rains raise the river, big spawning trout and salmon return; some to move farther up the watershed, others to stay and spawn. When the fish are fresh from the lake, classic Maine streamers such as Marabou Black Ghosts, Gray Ghosts, Wood Specials, and Mickey Finn's draw strikes. As the fish get worked, it pays to switch to nymphs, small dries, and even tiny ant patterns.

The upper Kennebago above Little Kennebago Lake is more a stream than a river. Parts of it can be approached and waded fairly easily, and other stretches close to the lake are surrounded by an endless alder thicket. Fishing is best in Late May and June when water levels are higher and brook trout ascend the stream from Little Kennebago to feed on emerging insects. Easiest access is to take the Morton Cut-off from ME 16, and then a right on Lincoln Pond Road, and after you cross the Upper Kennebago River, take a left on Kennebago River Road which parallels the river. Several miles up, the road is gated against motor vehicle and bicycle traffic by the private Megantic Club, and you have to walk. However, if you make the effort, you will have the entire stream to yourself.

The best spot to fish is the confluence where the upper river flows into Little Kennebago Lake. There is an obvious trail down to the water with a number of boats stashed. You can either put a canoe or kayak in or walk out to the large and rather obvious sand bar. At the edge of the sand bar, the water deepens quickly and good-sized trout cruise that area, particularly in the fall when they stage there in anticipation of moving upriver after a good rain.

Rangeley River

The Rangeley River is an underrated flyfishing-only water compared to its more famous neighbors, probably because it is only about one mile long and the prime fishing spots are limited to each end: the first 100 yards up from its confluence with Cupsuptic Lake, and the Bath Tub Pool under the Rangeley Lake Dam. Although prime spots are limited, the fishing can be excellent during the spring and fall. From mid-May to mid-June, good numbers of 8- to 20-inch salmon and trout move into the river from the lake to feast on spawning smelt and then sucker eggs. Many then stay to feed on heavy hatches of a variety of mayflies (from blue-winged olives to March browns) and caddisflies. Classic streamers such as the Marabou Gray Ghost, along with sucker-egg patterns, standard or emerger mayfly and caddis fly imitations, and attractor nymphs such as Copper Johns (red and green) and Prince Nymphs are all productive.

As early as mid-June, the river warms enough so the salmonids drop back into the lake until the first significant fall rains raise and cool the river. Then the fishing picks up when large pre-spawn brook trout and salmon ascend the river looking for spawning gravel, and aggressively attack brightly-colored streamers. This flyfishing-only river has an extended season until October 31, so it can be fished after many other waters are closed.

The land around the Rangeley River has been protected by Rangeley Lakes Heritage Trust and picnic tables and a Porta Potty can be found on site. Access points are an obvious trail from the center of the village of Oquossoc, and from Route 16 off a short dirt road to the left as you are heading north from Oquossoc (look for the Rangeley Lakes Heritage Trust sign). Because of the easy access, the river can get crowded, but because fresh fish constantly move in and out of the lake, the fishing doesn't usually suffer.

UPPER DAM

The Mooselookmeguntic Dam ("Upper Dam") area consists of a large pool below the dam and then several hundred yards of moving water before it mingles with the water of Lower Richardson Lake. This is deep and wide water as well, so I have chosen to list it as a short river, which it resembles. Road access is off ME 16 on Upper Dam Road (44.929161,-70.909637). Park at the first closed gate that you come across (this varies by season) and walk to the dam.

For anglers who enjoy flyfishing history, this is hallowed ground because Carrie Stevens, inventor of the Gray Ghost, is reputed to have first cast her now-famous streamer in this flow, landing a 6-pound, 13-ounce brook trout in the process. The original dam was built in the 1850s to assist with log driving, and generations of anglers have stood on her stone piers and cast their Gray Ghosts in the hopes of hooking their own trophy.

A replacement dam has been under construction since 2013 and the work will continue until 2016. The new dam will be different than the old one, and it is unclear what the final impact will be on the dam pool, its currents, and the fishing. Anglers will have to be patient and let the rebuilding take its course.

Since fish are prevented from moving upstream into Mooselookmeguntic Lake via Upper Dam, mature salmonids congregate, providing a tremendous fishery throughout most of the year. Brook trout and salmon measured in pounds are a common occurrence. The fish are a mixture of wild and stocked fish because, for reasons that are unclear to me, Maine IF&W continues to stock both salmon and brook trout in the Richardson Lakes.

On the Upper Dam Pool, the area between the Mooselookmeguntic Lake Dam and a line drawn between the two cribwork piers approximately 800 yards west of the dam is flyfishing only. This water is open until the end of October and is the best October fishing option in the Rangeley area because most other area fisheries are closed. The daily limit is one landlocked salmon with a 16-inch minimum and all brook trout must be released alive immediately. No motorboats are allowed from the dam gates downstream or westerly for 150 yards. See the law book for other regulations.

Patience increases your chances of flyfishing success here. Good-sized fish are always present but conditions change constantly; fresh fish move in, hatches start and stop, and weather changes. It pays to be persistent, put your time in, and constantly try new patterns if the fish are stubborn. Eventually the fish will become active.

Flows can vary a great deal. When water flows are lower in the fall, the lower part of pool and subsequent runs can be waded and more areas become accessible. Try high-stick (Czech-style) nymphing and drop your beadhead patterns into the nooks and crannies between the rocks.

Fish are taken throughout the Upper Dam area on dry flies, nymphs, and streamers. Choose the type of fishing that you enjoy most. If you are going to fish subsurface, make sure your offerings get down near the bottom. Tungsten conehead Woolly Buggers or marabou streamers are helpful in that regard; otherwise strong currents will keep your flies too high in the water column. Try dry-dropper combinations – I like a Goddard Caddis dry (the stacked deer-hair floats well in heavy current) with a flashback Pheasant Tail or Copper John in various colors as a dropper.

This is big water so bring your best casting rod in at least a 5-weight, although a 7-weight is helpful to punch through the wind that always seems to be funneling up the river.

Casting from the southern shoreline of the Upper Dam Pool.

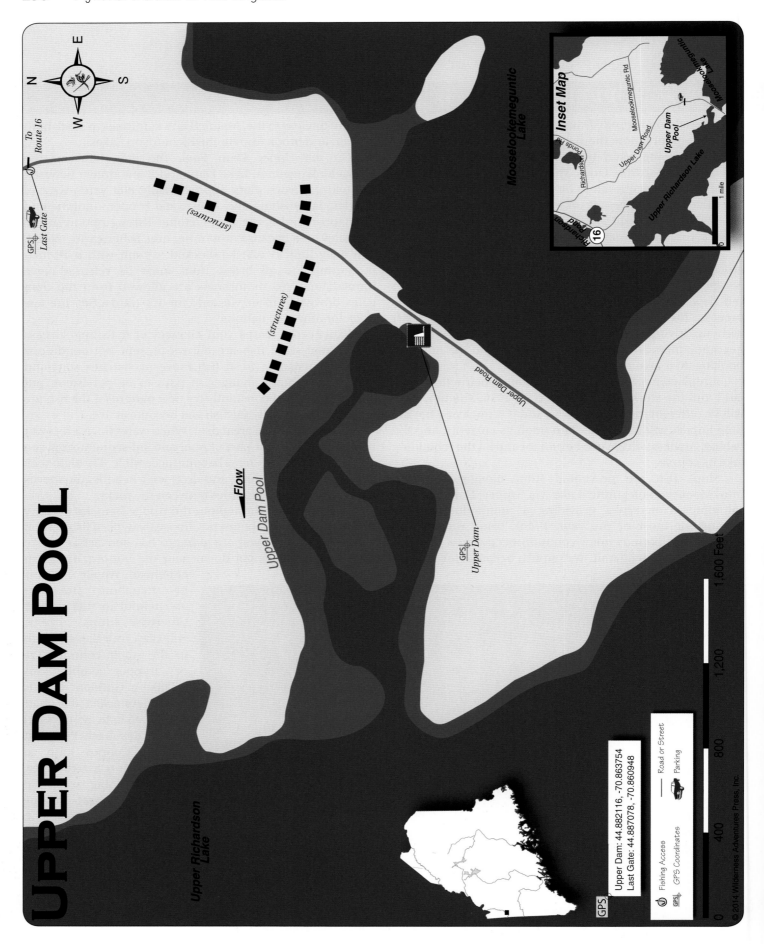

Upper Dam Pool

To Route 16

GPS
Last Gate

(structures)

(structures)

Flow

Upper Dam Pool

Upper Dam Road

GPS
Upper Dam

Upper Richardson Lake

Inset Map

Ponds Rd

Mooselookmeguntic Rd

Richardson Rd

Upper Dam Road

Richardson Road

Upper Dam Pool

Upper Richardson Lake

Mooselookmeguntic

16

1 mile

0

Mooselookemeguntic Lake

N E S W

GPS
Upper Dam: 44.882116, -70.863754
Last Gate: 44.887078, -70.860948

Fishing Access
GPS Coordinates
Road or Street
Parking

0   400   800   1,200   1,600 Feet

© 2014 Wilderness Adventures Press, Inc.

RAPID RIVER

The Rapid River is the best known river in the Rangeley area because of its reputation for growing trophy brook trout, as big as five or even six pounds. Trout are large here because:

1. They have inherited genetics from the giant Rangeley trout of yesteryear
2. Unique features like the Pond in the River that provide the fish with a thermal refuge in the summer and winter
3. Plentiful food sources
4. Restrictive regulations

The fishery is not what it once was because of the invasion of smallmouth bass and (perhaps) stocked fish, but it still gives up some very large trout every year. There are also plentiful landlocked salmon from 14 to 17 inches as well.

The Rapid River starts as the outflow of Lower Richardson Lake, and the first mile includes popular fishing spots such as the Dam Pool, Chub Pool, First Current, and Second Current, before it passes through the "Pond in the River". Below there, it continues in a series of runs and pools including the site of the former Lower Dam – the remains of which were removed in 2005 – and into Umbagog Lake on the New Hampshire border. Some spots to try on the lower river include the pocket water at Smooth Ledge, S-turn, and Devil's Hopyard rapids.

Fishing the Dam Pool is a must for many anglers. Three sluice-ways create seams for feeding fish, often visible to anglers that can dapple flies from parallel walkways. There are also several good wading spots on the north bank of the pool including near the tail. This pool is heavily fished so natural drifts and quick hook sets are mandatory.

Many of the river's 13 named pools are at least partially wadeable on the edges, but the bouldered bottom and strong flows limit the angler's options. Wading demands strong legs, wading staffs, and prudent decision making. Anglers walk the banks and then step into the water when they want to fish.

The Rapid River just below where lower dam once stood. Photo courtesy Phil Trasatti.

This is a flyfishing-only river with trout fishing restricted to catch and release, and after September 15, the Rapid is closed to fishing from the portion between the remnants of Lower Dam to the red markers near the head of Long Pool to protect spawning trout. Please dispatch any smallmouth bass that you catch.

Early in the year, streamers are the way to go. In mid-to late May (depending on the ice-out date) suckers run into the river to spawn and large trout and salmon follow them to feed on the eggs. The First and Second Current above Pond in the River is one good location to look for suckers. The best rig is to fish small light-yellow egg flies under a floating strike indicator. McFly Foam egg (yarn) in the McCheese color works great if you like to tie your own.

As the water warms, a variety of mayflies and caddis emerge. Hendricksons start hatching in late May, followed by light Cahills, and blue-winged olives (size 18) in early June. Fish the flats below Pond in the River, or the water above Lake Umbagog at dawn and dusk with long leaders and sparsely-tied imitations or emergers. Try size 14 to 18 Klinkhammers in various colors. Sometimes swinging a small wet fly can fool jaded fish.

In late June, the river is renowned for its famous alderfly hatch. These dark caddisflies swarm in the thousands along the cedar trees that line the river. Large golden stones are also fluttering around most of the spring and summer. Patterns to try include Brown Owls, Hornbergs,

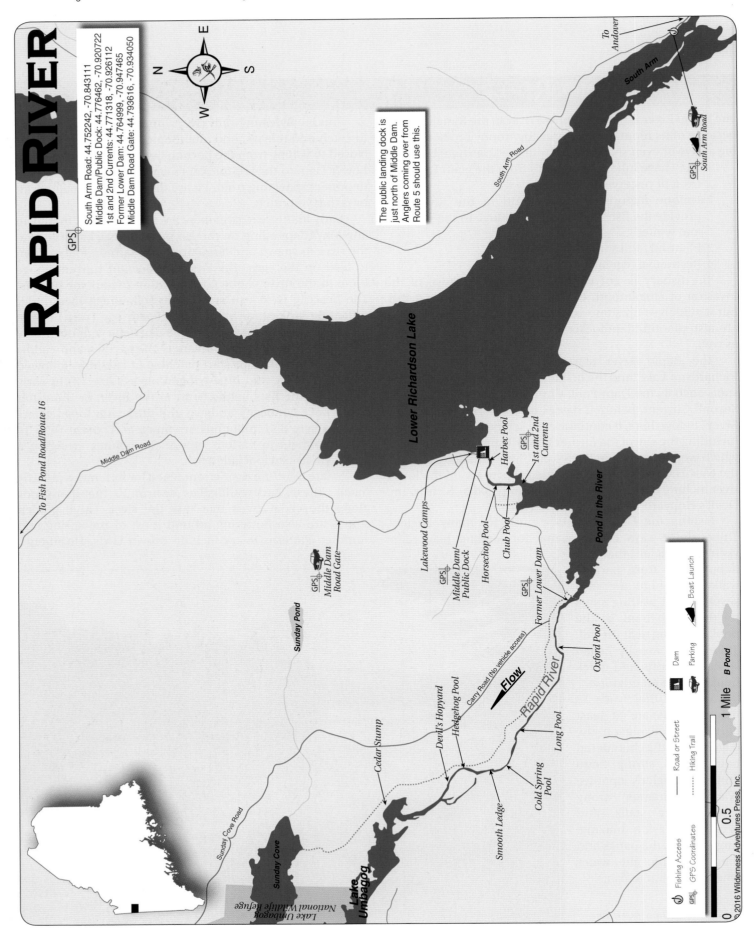

RAPID RIVER

2016 Wilderness Adventures Press, Inc.

South Arm Road: 44.752242, -70.843111
Middle Dam/Public Dock: 44.776462, -70.920722
1st and 2nd Currents: 44.771318, -70.926112
Former Lower Dam: 44.764999, -70.947465
Middle Dam Road Gate: 44.793616, -70.934050

The public landing dock is just north of Middle Dam. Anglers coming over from Route 5 should use this.

To Andover

South Arm

South Arm Road

GPS
South Arm Road

South Arm Road

To Fish Pond Road/Route 16

Lower Richardson Lake

Middle Dam Road

GPS
Middle Dam
Road Gate

Sunday Pond

Harbec Pool

GPS
1st and 2nd
Currents

Lakewood Camps

GPS
Middle Dam/
Public Dock

Horsechop Pool

Chub Pool

Pond in the River

GPS
Former Lower Dam

Oxford Pool

Cedar Stump

Devil's Hopyard

Hedgehog Pool

Carry Road (No vehicle access)

Flow

Rapid River

Long Pool

Cold Spring Pool

Smooth Ledge

Sunday Cove Road

Sunday Cove

Lake Umbagog
National Wildlife Refuge

Lake
Umbagog

B Pond

1 Mile

0   0.5

Fishing Access

GPS   GPS Coordinates

Road or Street

Hiking Trail

Dam

Parking

Boat Launch

Klinkhammers, dark caddis imitations, Goddard Caddis (with nymph droppers), Swanson's Stoneflies, and Royal Wulffs.

The larger trout also feed on sculpins, and smaller bass and trout. They are not easy to fool but the easier-to-hook salmon keep the action steady. Large articulated streamers, Double Bunnies, Zoo Cougars, or olive conehead Woolly Buggers are patterns to try if you think the fish are in a big-meal mood. Nymphs should include caddis imitations in green or olive or large stonefly nymphs.

When Rapid River temperatures reach 68 or above in July and August, brook trout migrate out of the main currents to Pond in the River. This is a thermal refuge and fishing in the pond is officially closed for those two months. When temperatures cool in the autumn, the trout return to moving water. Landlocked salmon often stay and feed in the river all summer.

Gated logging roads restrict access to the Rapid River, but you have a number of options to reach the river. The best boating option is a boat launch near the South Arm Campground (a good camping option, www.southarm. com) at the South Arm of Lower Richardson Lake that can be reached via South Arm Road north of the village of Andover and Route 120. It is about five miles by water to Middle Dam and Rapid River.

By car, if you are coming from Rangeley, take Route 16 for 20 miles, then take a left on Fish Pond Road, which leads to Middle Dam Road which ends at a locked gate and a parking area (44.793616,-70.934050). It is a relatively short and pleasant mile-long walk to the dam where you'll find a dirt road and well-worn footpaths leading to the river. Another access point is from the Sunday Cove Road farther west on ME 16 that leads to a trail along the lower river. Park at the gate and walk upstream to the lower rivers pools and runs.

As of 2016 anglers are no longer allowed to bicycle into the Rapid River from either gate.

Stream Facts: Rapid River

Season and Regulation
This water is flyfishing and barbless hooks only. It is catch and release only for brook trout and a three-fish limit (must be over 12 inches) for landlocked salmon, although I have never seen anyone keep one. The season runs from April 1 to September 30.

Species
Brook trout, landlocked salmon, and smallmouth bass

Flows
In the spring, flows are generally 1,000 to 1,200 cubic feet per second (cfs) but can go much higher during peak runoff. Summer flows are usually 800 to 1,000 but lower during droughts. In the fall, flows range from 600 to 1,000, or lower.

Access
Restricted by locked gates and requires a walk of roughly 30 minutes (or a faster bike ride) unless you are staying at one of the sporting camps or are fishing with a guide who has a gate key. To reach the gates requires a 30-minute drive on rough dirt roads.

Equipment
A fast-action 5- or 6-weight (single-handed or switch rod) with floating line and long tapered leaders for fishing dries and nymphs.

A 7-weight rod with fast-sink or sink-tip lines, good reels with smooth drags, and 2x or 3x short leaders to fish big streamers.

The wading can be difficult, so bring a good pair of waders and rubber-bottomed wading boots with studs. A wading staff and wading belt should be mandatory.

Flies
Rapid River (dark) Stimulator (size 6 to 12), alderfly imitations and stonefly imitations (size 18 to 20), blue-winged olive (size 16 to 20), Parachute Adams and caddis imitations such as Elk-hair Caddis (size 16 to 18), flying ants, Zebra Midge dropped below any of the larger dry flies. White Wulff with CDC emerger (size 22) dropper, Black Ghost and Gray Ghost (size 4 to 8), Wood Special (with nymph dropper).

Alder Stream

Access to Alder Stream, a wild brook trout stream is made northwest of Eustis off Route 27 in Alder Stream Township. June offers the best flyfishing when water levels begin to drop. Barbless hooks and a gentle release are recommended. During the consistent mayfly hatches, you'll find fly anglers stalking the holding lies in hip boots.

Carrabassett River

The Carrabassett River, near the village of Kingfield, is a beautiful freestone stream running between Sugarloaf and Reddington Mountain to the south and the Bigelow Mountain Range to the north. Snowmelt and huge chunks of ice scour the streambed in the spring and reduces its fertility. The Carrabassett is stocked by the state with brook trout, but many small streams, bogs, and beaver ponds flow into the river and many of these waters have small, wild, brook trout that are fun to catch. The stocking of both brook trout and rainbows occurs below Kingfield. Above Kingfield, only the west branch is stocked. Trout do find their way to the mainstem but fishing tends to be slow.

The south branch of the Carrabassett River is filled with small brook trout that are exquisitely-colored. They run a little larger by the Sugarloaf golf course and you can also pick up several dozen golf balls that have been shanked into the stream. Sometimes I wear a bike helmet when I fish there.

The upper section of the Carrabassett River is flyfishing only, all of the way down to where Route 146 crosses the river at East New Portland. The upper river is paralleled by an old narrow gauge railroad bed that has been converted to a walking/biking/x-country ski trail that has several parking areas. If you enjoy back-country biking, then you can bike, stop and fish, and continue biking to other promising water. The best canoe access along this water is made farther downstream on Route 16.

LEFT: The author knotting on a new fly for a client on the Rapid River.
BOTTOM: During the spring melt, huge chunks of ice scour the beds of many western Maine rivers.

ANDROSCOGGIN RIVER

The Androscoggin River enters Maine from the White Mountains of New Hampshire near the small village of Gilead. It flows east through the pulp mill villages of Rumford and Mexico, south through the cities of Lewiston and Auburn, and on to the city of Brunswick, where it enters Merrymeeting Bay. For a description of the river in New Hampshire, see the Northern New Hampshire Section. For a description of the river from Livermore Falls to Merrymeeting Bay, see the West Central Maine Section.

Years ago, the Androscoggin River was almost written off as a dead river. Pollution from the discharge of pulp mills and dams pushed this river to a fatal limit. Restoration efforts were started, however, and now the state of Maine can once again be proud of this river.

The best trout fishing on the Androscoggin is in the section from the New Hampshire border to just west of the dam in Rumford. Ten years ago, big brown and rainbow trout were caught regularly in this section and surveys of many of the tributaries showed wild rainbows and browns, indicating successful natural spawning. Today, for reasons unclear to the state fisheries biologists, natural spawning is greatly diminished, larger holdover fish are fewer, and the fishery is maintained by stocking. While the river isn't as good as it once was, anglers still fish the river regularly because of the spectacular scenery and the uncrowded conditions. Access is good with US 2 running along the river to the south and North Road paralleling the river to the north. Popular spots to fish include where tributaries enter the river such as the confluence with the Wild River and Lary Brook, and just above and below the so-called Green Bridge in Gilead (44.398319,-70.971574). As the river warms in late spring and early summer, all cooler tributary mouths including French Brook, Twitchell Brook, Peabody Brook, Whites Brook, and Chapman Brook are worth trying. All flow from the Bear Mountain Range.

Many anglers choose to float the river, which opens up more areas to fish while enjoying the river and landscape.

From Bethel to Rumford, US 2 runs along the north bank. The confluence of the Sunday River is an easily accessible location to try (44.455338,-70.801288), with the prime holes changing from year to year based on river currents. Where the Ellis River meets the Androscoggin at Rumford Point is another spot to try.

Downstream from Rumford, the Androscoggin becomes a smallmouth bass fishery, but what a fishery it is! An afternoon float down the river will usually lead to double-digit hauls of scrappy bass in the one- to three-pound range, and occasionally larger. Cast surface patterns such as bass poppers or Gartside Gurglers, subsurface patterns such as big Woolly Buggers in black, brown, or olive, or any crayfish imitation around boulders, logs, gravel bars, or other underwater obstructions, and you will likely be rewarded with a strong strike. While floating the river is the best way to cover the water, if you pick your spots, there are places that you can wade as well. Roads on both sides of the river provide access with occasional turnouts and paths to the river.

Even in downtown Mexico, the fishing can be good for stocked rainbows where the Swift River enters the Androscoggin. A parking area and a nice trail parallels the river right off of US 2 (44.556160,-70.546286). Farther up the Swift River (paralleled by ME 17) you can often see smaller trout finning in the deep but clear pools (44.642480,-70.587883). If you arrive early in the day before the swimmers, you can cast for trout all summer long.

Another spot to try is the Webb River confluence in Dixfield (44.530830,-70.459560). While the catch will be primarily smallmouth, brown trout do feed here early in the morning and in the evening and may be visible during a good hatch. Downstream from the Webb River hole, car-sized boulders give both brown trout and smallmouth a break from the current and fish hold in these locations.

A nice-sized Androscoggin River brown trout.

ANDROSCOGGIN RIVER
Lower Richardson Lake
STATE BORDER TO LIVERMORE FALLS

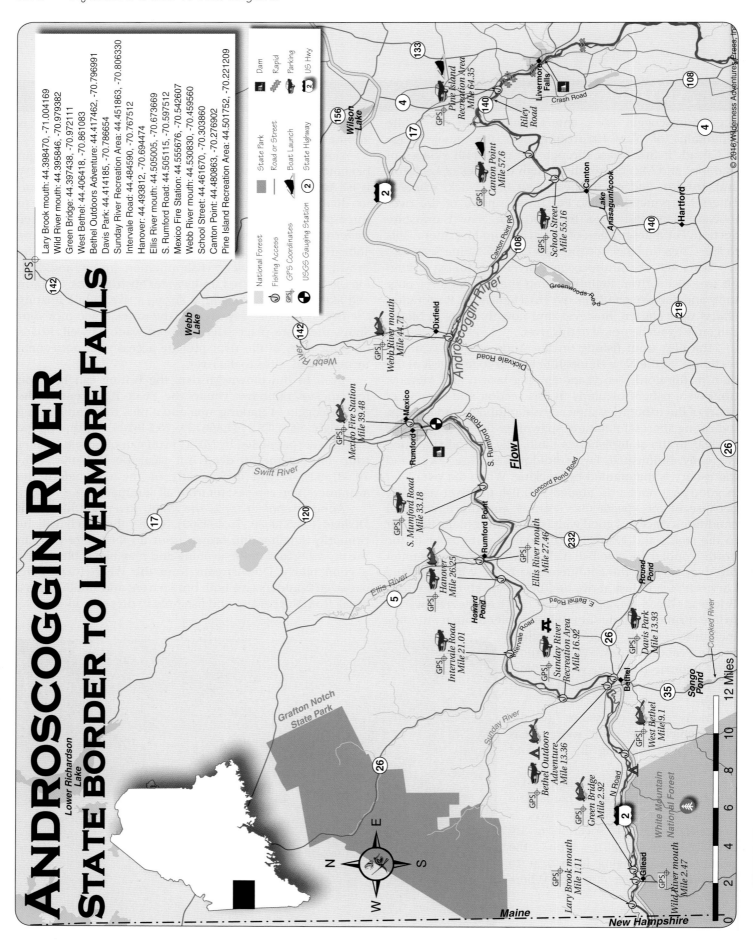

Lary Brook mouth: 44.398470, -71.004169
Wild River mouth: 44.395846, -70.979382
Green Bridge: 44.397438, -70.972111
West Bethel: 44.406418, -70.861083
Bethel Outdoors Adventure: 44.417462, -70.796991
Davis Park: 44.414185, -70.786654
Sunday River Recreation Area: 44.451863, -70.806330
Intervale Road: 44.484590, -70.767512
Hanover: 44.493812, -70.694474
Ellis River mouth: 44.505005, -70.673669
S. Rumford Road: 44.505115, -70.597512
Mexico Fire Station: 44.555676, -70.542607
Webb River mouth: 44.530830, -70.459560
School Street: 44.461670, -70.303860
Canton Point: 44.480863, -70.276902
Pine Island Recreation Area: 44.501752, -70.221209

STILLWATERS OF WESTERN MAINE

Rangeley Lake

Rangeley, a 6,000-acre lake with a depth of 150 feet, draws flyfishers pursuing landlocks and brook trout, especially after ice-out in early May. Landlocked salmon were introduced in 1873 and salmon angling is sustained by both natural reproduction and annual plantings. The brook trout are also both wild and stocked.

Originally called Oquossoc Lake (a nearby town still bears the name), this Franklin County lake offers springtime flyfishing opportunities, particularly in its many coves. Target sheltered bays near Rangeley Lake tributaries where smelt stage during their annual spawning ritual. Springtime salmon-holding locations include Greenvale Cove (at the southeastern end of the lake), Town Cove, Hunter Cove, Smith Cove (northern shore), and South Bog Cove (southwestern end of Rangeley).

Flyfish near the Greenvale Cove tributary mouths, specifically Nile Brook and Long Pond Stream. Town Cove tributaries (Hatchery and Haley Pond Brooks) draw smelt as does Hunter Cove, where Quimby Brook and Dodge Pond Stream feed into the bigger water. South Bog Cove's shoals around the South Bog Islands and near the South Bog Stream shoreline offer flyfishing opportunities as well, particularly in the fall when brook trout stage there in preparation for running up South Bog Stream to spawn.

Trolling with a floating or slow-sink fly line and traditional smelt patterns is a good way to locate fish, and then if you want to cast, try it, particularly in the first deep water closest to small streams where the smelt run. Some local salmon die-hards, eager to wet a line, paddle a canoe around and fish open water near remaining ice, casting streamers to potential fish. Ice-out can arrive between May 1 and 15, depending on the year.

Later as the water warms, trolling deeper with lead-core line at a distance of 70 feet or so behind the boat will be more effective, but always keep a fly rod rigged with a dry fly in case the water calms and you see rising fish.

Chilly springtime afternoons can be accompanied by occasional gusty winds, snow squalls, and choppy water conditions. Dress warmly and think with your head not your heart.

The scenery never disappoints. Bald Mountain, situated on Maine Public Reserve Land near the western shore, rises to 2,443 feet. Here in Maine's western mountains, the classic outdoor town of Rangeley sits at 1,800 feet on the lake's northeastern shore.

Several roads will lead you to Rangeley Lake. Maine Route 4 will take you to the town of Rangeley, while South Shore Drive provides entry to Rangeley Lake State Park. Route 17 skirts the westernmost shore. Boat ramps can be found at Town Cove off Route 4 on the northeastern shore, the mouth of Rangeley River off Routes 4 and 16 on the northwestern shore, and Rangeley State Park off South Shore Drive on the southern shore.

A late September view of Rangely Lake.

Mooselookmeguntic Lake

The largest of the Rangeley Chain of Lakes at 16,300 acres, Mooselookmeguntic offers exceptional trout and salmon fishing, drawing anglers from all over the country. No salmonid has been stocked since 1984, so these fish are truly wild and run as large as five pounds. Despite eastern shoreline development, much of the shoreline remains untouched, which adds to the fishing experience. If you enjoy camping, this lake has a number of spectacular campsites around the western shore.

It is always important to pay attention to weather conditions on the lake, as they can change in an instant and this lake can get extremely rough. Access to the lake includes the Haines Landing boat launch, which provides trailered access on the easternmost shore off Route 4 and fishing from nearby rocky shoals after the mid-May ice-out. Roads providing access include Bald Mountain Road on the eastern shore, Birches Beach Road on the southeastern shore, and Upper Dam Road on the southwestern shore.

In the spring and again in the fall, it pays to concentrate in shoreline areas around incoming streams. The confluence of Bemis Stream has a sandy shoreline that can be waded and can be accessed by the Bemis Road bridge. Some very nice brook trout stage there in September and usually several anglers are present trying to catch them. Try fishing small Woolly Buggers or wet flies right on the bottom, or unique patterns that the trout haven't seen. If fish are rising around Bemis Stream and standard dries don't work, try very small midge patterns.

The outlet for Mooselookmeguntic Lake is Upper Dam, which I have covered in the Rangeley Lake's rivers and streams section. The Rangeley River, Cupsuptic River, and Kennebago River all empty into the northern arm of this lake, which is referred to as Cupsuptic Lake and trolling in the spring and fall can be excellent for large brook trout.

Upper and Lower Richardson Lakes

The upper and lower lakes are actually one lake distinguished by two basins. Upper Richardson covers 4,200 acres, while Lower Richardson has 2,900 acres of angling. Connected by the bottleneck dubbed "the Narrows", both lakes are each roughly 100 feet deep. Maximum and mean depths are 108 feet and 44 feet, respectively. The Union Water Power Company draws water from the Richardson Lakes in the fall, lowering lake levels by several feet. The Richardson Lakes are oligotrophic waters, which mean that they lack plant nutrients and have large amounts of dissolved oxygen throughout.

The Richardson Lake's inflow is from Mooselookmeguntic Lake via Upper Dam and a number of small tributaries. Its outlet is Middle Dam, which is the origin of the Rapid River.

Brook trout, salmon, and lake trout can be caught by trolling the undeveloped shorelines. In the spring and fall, efforts should be concentrated on areas close to the mouths of any incoming tributaries.

Public boat launch sites are available on either extreme of the lakes. Mill Brook offers access on the northern shore, while South Arm does on the southern end (44.752056,-70.842063). Unrestricted vehicular access via Upper Dam Road is available to within a mile of Upper Dam Pool, the main inlet to the lakes. As with other large northern New England waters, the size of these lakes and their surrounding geography create dangerous boating conditions during days with strong north or northwest winds. One of my fishing buddies, attempting to reach Middle Dam from the South Arm during a windy day had the transom of his wood and canvas boat split from the pounding of the waves. He spent a very cold and hungry night on a remote shore before he was able to make emergency repairs from a piece of scrap wood that he found, and make it back to South Arm the next morning.

A spectacular male brook trout caught in September wading the shoreline of Mooselookmeguntic at the confluence of an incoming stream. Photo courtesy Tom Clough.

Kennebago Lake

Little shoreline development disrupts the beauty of this fishery, which rests 1,779 feet above sea level, surrounded by higher mountains. Only brook trout, brown trout, landlocked salmon and a forage base of rainbow smelt swim in this flyfishing only water (no trolling). None of the prolific perch and bass species that plague other coldwater fisheries are found here.

Unlike some of the larger lakes in the area, there can be good dry-fly fishing along the shorelines and the shallow western and eastern ends of the lake. The scene can be very picturesque, with anglers standing in classic wooden Rangeley-style boats painted green and grey and their fly lines unfurling towards pods of dimpling trout.

Ice-out varies widely, but generally arrives around the first week of May. Resident rainbow smelt run up the lake tributaries shortly thereafter and good-sized brook trout, salmon, and brown trout follow them. Brown trout exceeding five pounds have been caught during the smelt run. Smelt-imitation streamers such as the classic Nine-Three (named after the 9-pound 3-ounce salmon this fly caught when first tried), Kennebago Smelt, Grey and Black Ghost marabou streamers are all popular.

As the water warms, mid-sized black and brown mayflies and caddis emerge starting in the far western end of the lake, called "the Logans". A size 12 to 18 Red Quill, size 12 to 18 Dark Hendrickson, size 14 Hornberg, and a size 12 to 16 Parachute Adams can interest trout during these hatches.

The Brown Drake Spinner, the Brown Drake Thorax, and Quigley Green Drake Cripple (all in sizes 8 to 12) will catch brookies and salmon from mid-June through early July. Think *Hexagenia* duns by summer, a stillwater dry-fly favorite in New England. Fish a size 8 to 10 Parachute Hex but don't forget about the nymph (sizes 4 to 6), often imitated by a pattern with the interesting name of the Maple Syrup. Hexes will emerge sporadically until early August. It pays to scrutinize the water closely for emerging duns during the early morning.

By September, the Nine-Three, Gray Ghost, Kennebago Smelt, and Wood Special streamers become effective as the larger fish start staging in shallow water in preparation for their spawning runs and become aggressive.

For continued autumn surface action, fish black gnat patterns after Labor Day in sizes 14 to 20. Carry a few tiny Adams for a similar imitation. During warm and calm Indian summer days, look for a flying-ant emergence, and fish large black foam ants. Sometimes large (size 6 to 10) colorful dry flies such as Royal Wulffs, red or yellow Humpies, or orange Stimulators will bring up aggressive fish.

Kennebago Lake's season is April 1 to October 31 and is the largest flyfishing-only stillwater east of the Mississippi. Public access is available via the upper Kennebago River or by a private road open to guests at Grant's Kennebago Camps or Kennebago River Kamps. There is also limited public boat access to Kennebago Lake only administered by Grant's (call 800-633-4815 for further information).

Little Kennebago Lake

Little Kennebago Lake is not behind locked gates and is easily accessed from the Lincoln Pond Road. You can put a kayak or canoe in where the road crosses the river (45.126274,-70.767896), and then it is a short, easy paddle upstream to the lake, where a no-motorized boat law is strictly enforced. During hatches and in the evening, brook trout from 6 to 14 inches rise at the outlet, inlet, mouths of tributaries, and along certain shorelines. Despite a few camps along the east shore, it is picturesque water, particularly in the fall when the surrounding hills glow with the yellows, oranges, and reds of aspens and maples.

MAIN IMAGE: Hexagenia hatch time on Kennebago Lake. Photo courtesy Erika Zambello.
UPPER RIGHT: A Kennebago Lake Hex dun. Photo courtesy Lindsey Rustad.

Franklin County Flyfishing Only Stillwaters

Arnold Pond, Caribou Pond, South Boundary Pond, and Horseshoe Pond

The wilderness area north and west of the village of Eustis holds a number of flyfishing-only stillwaters. This region is reached by ME 16 from the village of Rangeley and then ME 27. Arnold Pond, Caribou Pond, South Boundary Pond, and Horseshoe Pond are four flyfishing-only stillwaters located on the border of the Province of Quebec near Coburn Gore and Massachusetts Gore off Route 27. The ponds are accessible from foot trails off the highway. There are primitive campsites in the area.

Blanchard Pond and Round Mountain Pond

Blanchard Pond and Round Mountain Pond are located in Alder Stream Township. The access road just north of Alder Stream Bridge is gated, and the ponds can be reached by foot trail.

Tim Pond

About 4,000 acres of this area are privately owned by the Calden families, who operate Tim Pond Wilderness Camps. Only guests of the camp can fish Tim Pond. Staying at these camps is a relaxing experience that takes you back in time to when the country was a quieter and simpler place. Contact them at www.timpond.com.

From Eustis, Tim Pond Road provides access. This pond holds plentiful numbers of wild brook trout that are in the 10- to 14-inch range with occasional larger specimens. A tremendous Hex hatch in July typically generates plenty of surface activity. Hex-imitating dry flies or the Maple Syrup wet fly will hook fish.

Little Jim Pond

Little Jim Pond is easily accessible via King and Bartlett Road north of Eustis and Route 27. There is a primitive campsite near the trail. It is well stocked and large trout are caught here.

Kamankeag Pond, Quimby Pond, Ross Pond, and Round Pond

In the Rangeley Region, Kamankeag Pond, Quimby Pond, Ross Pond, and Round Pond are found north of Rangeley Lake. Access to Kamankeag and Round is from Dodge Pond Road about three miles west of Rangeley village off Routes 16 and 4. The access road to Quimby Pond is about two miles west of Rangeley, and a hand-carried boat launch can be utilized near the pond's inlet. Quimby Pond has been a popular fishing pond for decades. It is a shallow, stocked (though there are some wild fish), flyfishing-only brookie water with a prohibition on boat motors. It has long given Maine fly rodders productive surface action in May and June. In this case, shallow means that half the pond's depth is under 10 feet with the deepest spot running 12 feet. Bottom-dredgers with smelt imitations like a Black Ghost or a Muddler Minnow or Woolly Bugger do very well early in the spring. In June, fly rodders can expect mayfly and caddis hatches, including a giant-sized caddis that is somewhat unique to the area. For this hatch, bring the largest Hornbergs that you can find or any other size-6 caddis imitation that you can find or tie.

Moxie Pond

Moxie Pond and another stillwater named Round Pond are located in Maine Public Reserve Lands east of Mooselookmeguntic Lake. They are accessible from the Appalachian Trail near ME 17 north of the city of Rumford. Spencer Pond is a short distance south of the trail. All of these ponds can be reached from logging roads off of ME 17 and ME 4. Short trails take you to the water's edge.

Beal Pond can be reached from Route 4 south of Rangeley. There is an access road near the small village of Madrid.

Shiloh Pond and McIntire Pond

On the eastern edge of Franklin County is Shiloh Pond. This flyfishing-only stillwater is accessible from Tufts Pond Road off Routes 16 and 27 north of the village of Kingfield. McIntire Pond is located in the southernmost corner of Franklin County near the village of New Sharon on Routes 2 and 27 east of the city of Farmington. Access to McIntire Pond is from Route 27 about four miles south of Sharon.

Franklin County All-tackle Stillwaters

The Maine Department of Inland Fisheries and Wildlife stocks several other Franklin County lakes and ponds with brook trout, togue, and brown trout. General fishing regulations for the majority of these stillwaters restrict the use of live bait and limit creels to two fish at least eight inches in length.

Bug Eye Pond, Otter Pond, and Hurricane Pond

There are three easily-accessible brook trout ponds in the northwest corner of Franklin County. Bug Eye Pond and Otter Pond are located near the border of Quebec off ME 27 north of Eustis. Gold Brook Road off Route 27, just north of Bug Eye Pond, provides access to Hurricane Pond in Kibby Township.

Big Indian Pond and Barnard Pond

Big Indian Pond is a more remote stillwater that lies north of Route 27 and is accessible from unimproved roads and foot trails off Gold Brook Road near Bug Eye Pond. Barnard Pond, east of Eustis, is accessible by foot trail from Tim Pond Road. There is a primitive campsite at the pond.

Little Greely Pond, Gull Pond, Dodge Pond, and Saddleback Lake

Four brook trout ponds are located east of Rangeley Lake in Dallas Plantation. Little Greely Pond, Gull Pond, and Dodge Pond are north of Rangeley and accessible from Route 16. Dodge Pond is a favorite for those with just a few hours to fish because it is on Route 16, offers plenty of angling action, and has great views of Saddleback Mountain and surrounding peaks. Loon Lake is north of Rangeley as well, and can be reached from Loon Lake Road. Saddleback Lake is accessible from Dallas Hill Road off Route 4 south of Rangeley. Saddleback Lake is stocked well and there is little fishing pressure. An added bonus of fishing there is the view of Saddleback Mountain rising just south of the pond. Boats with motors are prohibited on both Loon and Saddleback Lakes.

South (Pine Tree) Pond, Ledge Pond, and Perry Pond

Located in Sandy River Plantation in the Saddleback Mountain region, South Pond, also called Pine Tree Pond, and Ledge Pond can be reached by the Appalachian Trail off Route 4 north of the village of Madrid. Midway Pond and Rock Pond are farther north on the Trail or can be reached from a secondary trail off Dallas Hill Road south of Rangeley. Perry Pond is easily accessible from an unimproved road off Route 4 north of Madrid.

Stetson Pond and Lufkin Pond

Stetson Pond and Lufkin Pond are in the town of Phillips and can be reached from a foot trail off Route 4 near Madrid. Both ponds offer hand-carried boat launches.

Swift River Pond, Little Swift River Pond, Sabbath Day Pond, and Long Pond

Swift River Pond, Little Swift River Pond, Sabbath Day, and Long Pond are located in Township E north of the city of Rumford. These brook-trout ponds are accessible from the Appalachian Trail off of Route 17 or old logging roads from ME 17 and 4. I enjoyed a day fishing Sabbath Day Pond out of a canoe after being flown into Long Pond and taking the short hike to Sabbath Day. Some very healthy 12- to 14-inch trout took Wood Specials and Royal Wulffs. There are several float plane operators that will fly you into remote ponds and lakes (where they have stashed canoes) and the cost is less than you might think (see www.acadianseaplanes.com).

The author on Sabbath Day Pond. Photo courtesy Pete Kendall.

Beaver Pond, Varnum Pond, Wilson Pond, Podunk Pond, Webb Lake, and Staples Pond

Beaver Pond lies in Township D and has convenient access off Route 17. Varnum Pond and Wilson Pond are easily reached from ME 156 and US 2 near the village of Wilton. Podunk Pond in the town of Carthage is accessible from an unimproved road and trail off Route 2 west of Wilton. Also in this region, west of the city of Farmington are Webb Lake and Staples Pond, two stillwaters stocked with brown trout. Webb Lake, the larger of the two, is located near the village of Weld off ME 142 north of the village of Dixville. Access is from a boat launch in Mount Blue State Park. Springs on the north part of the lake attract trout as the water begins to warm and active fish can be found well into the summer. Staples Pond is found north of the village of Temple off Route 43.

Tumbledown Pond

Tumbledown Pond is a spectacular pond nestled in a depression at the very top of Tumbledown Mountain. It is a steep climb from one of several trails, but if you like combining backpacking with flyfishing then this is a hike for you. Brook trout are stocked annually, a variety of aquatic food in the pond feeds them and, because of the elevation, this pond stays cool and fishes well all summer long. Rocky ledges along the shore give shorebound anglers numerous spots to fish if they can roll cast. This is quite a popular hike these days, so if you don't want to share the pond with swimmers, dogs, and rock throwers, I suggest you hike very early in the morning, or stay later than the casual hiker. Access is from Byron Hill Road in Weld or from the town of Bryon on a good dirt road that becomes Byron Hill Road (44.729173,-70.532338).

Mount Blue Pond, Schoolhouse Pond, Pinnacle Pond, and Grindstone Pond

North of Farmington, in the town of Avon, you will find Mount Blue Pond and Schoolhouse Pond. Both stillwaters can be easily reached from unimproved roads off Route 4 between the villages of Strong and Phillips. Pinnacle Pond and Grindstone Pond are located near the village of Kingfield north of Strong off Routes 145 and 142.

Oxford County Stillwaters

Aziscohos Lake

Created after the 1910 damming of the Magalloway River, the Aziscohos Lake Dam at that time was the largest concrete dam in the world, and created the 12-mile long and narrow 6,700-acre lake. This is a great boating lake because its topography limits large waves so it can be canoed or kayaked regardless of the strength of the wind. The lake level is dropped significantly during the summer, drying most of lake shores and shallows, so hatches are minimal with the exception of midges near the inlets. Therefore, most of the fishing is by trolling, although in the spring, casting near inlets is productive as the resident wild trout and salmon follow the smelt on their spawning runs. This act can be repeated in the fall as fish stage near tributary outlets before their spawning runs. Despite the absence of hatches — other foods such as smelt, bait fish, crawfish, and other aquatic fare feed the fish and with minimal fishing pressure — salmon and trout over three pounds are fairly common.

Black Brook Cove Campground near the southern lakeshore (44.932813,-70.964440) offers campers a beautiful option with canoe rentals. It is accessible off Route 16 on the Lincoln Pond Road. There is also a trailered boat launch on the east shore slightly south of where the Magalloway River enters the lake. To find it, take the gravel Green Top Road to the Parmachenee Road. Please study maps of the area before you go, because numerous similar-looking logging roads make navigating confusing.

Parmachenee Lake

North of Aziscohos Lake is Parmachenee Lake. This remote stillwater holds brook trout and landlocked salmon. Angling is restricted to flyfishing only, casting or trolling. The roads in this region are private and gated. Access to Parmachenee Lake is by float plane, or by staying at Bosebuck Mountain Camps. You can also walk in about half a mile from a Parmachenee Road gate with a float tube. There are good hatches on this lake, although the high population of chubs that readily rise can make fishing frustrating. Salmon and trout grow because of limited fishing pressure and good food sources. The most productive areas are the inlet and outlet channels. Contact Bosebuck Mountain Camps at the north end of Aziscohos, 207-243-2925, for services and access information.

A very nice brook trout netted at Long Pond. Photo courtesy Brett Damm.

Oxford County Ponds (from north to south)

Otter Pond

Otter Pond is a small, flyfishing-only pond located just north of Parmachenee Lake (45.182048,-70.981516) that can only be reached by folks with access past the gates (or by a four-mile walk). It is a picturesque pond that holds mostly small brook trout that are difficult to catch unless there is some sort of hatch activity.

Long Pond

Long Pond is a pond-in-a-river of the Little Magalloway River and has public access, although it is restricted to flyfishing only. Access to this area is on a good dirt road off Route 16 (Parmachenee Road) in the town of Wilson's Mills. Follow the Bosebuck Camp signs, drive past the camp, cross the Little Magalloway River, and take the next left. Look for a good trail and small parking area (45.136488,-71.016285). During certain times of the year, particularly in the fall, large trout from Aziscohos Lake run up the river to Long Pond. There is a shallow gravel bar that bisects the pond and allows for easy wading, although a float tube provides access to other parts of the pond. If there are no fish rising,

try large marabou streamers or black leech patterns near the bottom. One can also reach the southwest shore of the lake via an old logging road and it is a short drag to put a canoe in the water (45.131446,-71.022252).

Brett Damm guides in this area (www.rangeleysportshop.com)

Richardson Ponds

Richardson Ponds (East and West) are ponds reached from Route 16 from Wilson's Mills. West Richardson (artificials only) can be seen from the road and it easy to put a small boat in. East Richardson (flyfishing only) requires a short hike in from the Richardson Pond Road off of Upper Dam Road. Both ponds are open through October 31. The best time for dry-fly fishing is late May through June. When rising, the trout aren't picky. A parachute or traditional Adams pattern or a Hornberg in a variety of sizes will usually suffice.

B Pond

B Pond is roughly the same size as Pond in the River on the Rapid River, and relatively close by. You can walk or bike in from Middle Dam or access from the loop road off B Hill Road. Take a left after you cross the East Cambridge River and then bear right. Take your *Maine Atlas and Gazetteer* and a GPS with you. This deep pond holds landlocked salmon and brook trout. It is easiest to fish in the spring when the fish are feeding on the surface and closer to the shorelines.

Surplus Pond
Surplus Pond is a tiny flyfishing-only stillwater located off the Appalachian Trail north of the village of Andover and Route 5. The trail can be reached from East B Hill Road and from there it is a couple mile walk in. Unlike other ponds on the A.T. in this part of Maine that require a strenuous hike, this part of the trail is fairly flat. Packing a float tube is a good option.

Speck Pond
Speck Pond lies west of Surplus Pond on the Appalachian Trail near Grafton Notch State Park off Route 26. Speck Pond is roughly 1,000 feet below the summit of Old Speck Mountain (44.563516,-70.973187) but still rests at 3,400 feet and requires a rugged hike to reach it. If you enjoy adventure and are in good shape, take a weekend and enjoy hiking the surrounding area including the difficult Mahoosuc Notch. A lean-to and tent platforms alongside the pond are managed by the Appalachian Mountain Club.

Although the shores of the pond are tree-lined, you can find spots where you can stand and cast reasonably well. The fish are aggressive if you can reach them. I once hooked a beautiful male 14-inch brook trout in this pond on a green drake imitation, and when I unhooked him, I noticed he had a five-inch salamander with blue spots down his gullet with the tail still sticking out of his mouth. Yet he still took my dry fly.

Little Ellis (Garland) Pond
Little Ellis Pond, also called Garland Pond, offers salmon and brookies and lies west of the village of Byron and Route 17. It is accessible by a trail off Andover Road. East of the city of Rumford is Howard Pond, another brook trout resource in the town of Hanover. Access is from US 2 and ME 5, west of the village of Rumford Point.

Worthley Pond and Canton (Anasagunticook) Lake
Worthley Pond and Canton Lake, also known as Lake Anasagunticook, are larger stillwaters located southeast of Rumford off ME 108 near the village of Canton. Canton Lake offers brown trout. Worthley's browns and rainbows are best found by the south-shore public access site, and up the east shoreline. Honey Run Campground rents boats and offers campers a peaceful place to spend the night. Canton Lake is an excellent smallmouth bass fishery with a limited number of brown trout in the deeper areas.

Abbott Pond, Little Concord Pond, Shagg Pond, and Washburn Pond
West of Worthley Pond are Abbott Pond, Little Concord Pond, Shagg Pond, and Washburn Pond, in the towns of Woodstock and Sumner. All are stocked with brook trout. Little Concord Pond is flyfishing only. Shagg Pond is a deeper pond and offers brookies and splake. The splake do fairly well here and can reach two to three pounds, while the brookies range from 10 to 14 inches. Abbott and Little Concord were recently chemically reclaimed to eliminate introduced fish species, and are now producing 10- to 17-inch (and occasionally larger) brook trout. Expect stocked 8- to 11-inch trout from Washburn. These ponds are accessible from Route 232 and Shagg Pond Road south of Rumford.

North Pond, South Pond, and Round Pond
North, South, and Round Ponds are connected and located near the village of Locke Mills off Route 26 east of the village of Bethel. South is the deepest and as a result holds salmon, whitefish, and togue (lake trout). North is stocked with brownies and most fish taken will be 10 to 18 inches. Round contains mostly bass.

Bryant Pond, Broken Bridge Pond, Round Pond, and Crocker Pond
Bryant Pond, also called Lake Christopher, holds brook trout as well as landlocked salmon and splake (a brook trout/lake trout hybrid). It is located east of Locke Mills off Route 26 and east of the village of Bethel. Broken Bridge Pond, Round Pond, and Crocker Pond are located south of Bethel off an access road from Route 5 and were reclaimed after trash fish were eliminated. Broken Bridge tends to hold the largest trout. Round Pond requires a one-mile walk in and was just reclaimed in late 2015. Trout Pond lies in Mason Township west of Bethel. There is an access road and trail off Route 2 in West Bethel.

Hall Pond, Big Pennesseewassee (Norway) Lake, and Little Pennesseewassee Lake (Hobbs Pond)
Hall Pond holds both brookies and brown trout and is easily reached from Route 119 and Hall Pond Road east of the village of South Paris. West of this region, in the town of Norway are two brown trout fisheries: Big Pennesseewassee Lake, also called Norway Lake, and Little Pennesseewassee Pond, known locally as Hobbs Pond. These stillwaters are accessible from Route 118 west of Norway.

Trout Pond, Virginia Lake, Cushman Pond, and Bradley Pond

West of Norway are Trout Pond and Virginia Lake in the town of Stoneham. Virginia Lake lies north of Route 5 near the village of East Stoneham. Trout Pond is south of Route 5 on a gated road. Cushman Pond, just south of Trout Pond, is more easily accessible. Take Route 5 to Slab City Road and Cushman Pond Road. Bradley Pond is reached from an unimproved road off Route 5 near the village of North Lowell. Motorboats are prohibited on Bradley Pond.

Keoka Lake, Bear Pond, and Stearns Pond

Keoka Lake and Bear Pond are accessible from Route 37 near the village of Waterford. Bear Pond holds brookies, landlocks, and togue. Keoka holds brook trout and landlocked salmon. Stearns Pond is a brown trout fishery located in the town of Sweden and can be reached off the Waterford-Sweden Road. Don't tell anyone that I told you, but Stearns Pond contains abundant small forage fish (they might be smelt or alewives) and as a result, the brown trout grow to impressive size here and can be caught by trolling or casting in relatively shallow (four to eight feet) water. The largemouth bass population in this pond is not to be missed either.

Clay Pond, Hancock Pond, Burnt Meadow Pond, and Stone Pond

There are several stillwaters found in the southwest corner of Oxford County west of Sebago Lake. Clay Pond lies south of the village of Fryeburg and is accessible via Porter Road. Motorboats are prohibited on Clay Pond. Hancock Pond is a brown trout fishery located in the town of Denmark. Burnt Meadow Pond holds brook trout and browns. It is easily reached from Route 160 south of the village of Brownfield. Stone Pond is a wild brook trout pond and is also found in Brownfield via Dugway Road, although access is difficult.

Little Clemons Pond, Stanley Pond, Chapman Pond, Colcord Pond, and Bickford Pond

Little Clemons Pond and Stanley Pond are located off Route 160 north of the village of South Hiram. For those that like to hook rainbow trout, a species not commonly found in Maine, Stanley Pond is a mixed warm and coldwater fishery that supports rainbows as well as smallmouth bass. Chapman Pond (for brookies) can be reached from a trail off Spec Pond Road north of South Hiram. Colcord Pond and Bickford Pond are both reached from Route 25 north of the village of Porter.

Beautiful West Richardson Pond.

WESTERN MAINE PLANNING CONSIDERATIONS

Nearby Hub Cities

- Bethel (www.bethelmaine.com, www.umbagogchapter.com)
- Rangeley (www.rangeleymaine.com, www.rangeleysportshop.com)
- Rumford/Mexico (www.rivervalleychamber.com)

Easy Access Options

- Route 16 crosses the lower Magalloway River in Wilson's Mills. You can park alongside Bennet Road just downstream from the bridge (44.936118,-71.034301) and it is a few steps on level ground and low grass to reach the pool below the bridge. It is also an easy wade out on even gravel. There are always trout and salmon present in this pool throughout the entire fishing season, although they can get persnickety because they get fished to every day. Try very small emergers or nymphs. A natural drift without drag and a quick hook set is critical for success.
- Steep Bank Pool on the Kennebago River is one of the best known flyfishing spots in all of western Maine, yet access is very straightforward. Take a right on the Boy Scout Road several miles north of Oquossoc on Route 16 and look for parking alongside the road (there are usually already several cars there) with the large bend pool right beside the road (45.009671,-70.791211). You do have to make your way down a set of stairs to the water, but the bottom is fine gravel and fairly even so wading is straightforward if one wants to cross the pool and fish the other side. The best fishing is in the spring and the fall when the larger trout and salmon hold in the pool as they prepare to move up or down the river to feed or spawn. The downside to this spot is it can get crowded. Best to fish very early in the morning, at lunch time, or very late. Suprisingly, sometimes Sunday afternoon is less crowded as the weekenders head back home.

Suggested Beginner Options

- The Rangeley River in Oquossoc is full of fish in May and early June, and a beginner flyfisher is usually going to hook at least a few fish. A mile north on ME 16 out of Oquoosoc, look for a Rangeley Lakes Heritage Trust sign on the left. Follow the narrow gravel-pit road and continue to bear left for a short distance until you reach the parking area and a gate. It is a quick walk down to the snowmobile bridge that crosses the river. Walk down either bank until the water becomes at least knee deep, wade out a little, and start fishing. Try whatever flyfishing option with which you feel most comfortable: small streamers, a Hornberg, or any standard nymph patterns. Watch other anglers to see what they do.
- In July and August, try the Cupsuptic River. Stop in at Cupsuptic Campground, north of Oquossoc (45.012298,-70.831481) and get directions to Big Falls. Walk upstream above the falls and cast any small dry fly such as a Hornberg, Elk Hair Caddis, or an Adams into every water pocket that has a little depth to it. Before too long, a wild brook trout will rise to your fly.
- Book a few days at Grant's Kennebago Camps on Kennebago Lake during late June. Rent one of their Rangeley Boats or bring your own canoe or kayak and fish "the Logans", a shallow, calm end of the lake that is usually full of rising fish at this time of year. All you will need is a Hornberg or Parachute Adams pattern. Another option is to fish the confluence of the lake and the Big Sag stream. Schools of small but eager brookies make for great practice in casting, hooking, playing, and landing trout.

Suggested Flyfishing Vacation Options

Weekend Getaway

- Book a weekend at any one of several sporting camps that serve the area. They are more expensive than standard lodging or camping, but you get to experience the traditional Maine Sporting Camp adventure, which is unique. And since they take care of your every need and all your meals, you can spend more of your time fishing. The quality of the fishing varies based on the season and the type of water the sporting camps are on. For river fishing in late May thru mid-June and then early September, try Bosebuck Camps on Aziscohos Lake. For June, July, and mid-September river, lake, and pond fishing, book a stay at Grants Camps on Kennebago Lake. For pond fishing in June and July, try Tim Pond Camps on Tim Pond. For a listing of all of your options, check out the Maine Sporting Camp Association website, at www.mainesportingcamps.com.
- If one has an appetite for real adventure, spend a weekend hiking up to Speck Pond in the Mahoosuc Mountains. Although fishing is included in the

activities, it is a small part. Access to Speck Pond is either over Speck Mountain, a climb of 2,700 feet and then a 1,000-foot descent to the pond (from a parking lot in Grafton Notch State Park) or through Mahoosuc Notch – a half-mile walk/crawl over and under giant boulders before ascending 1,000 feet to the pond. Access from this direction is from Berlin, New Hampshire on Success Pond Road. There is an AMC campsite by the pond but you must carry in and out all of your gear, food, and camping stuff on your back. Do not attempt this unless you are in excellent shape and have two full days. The trout in Speck Pond are not tough to fool, but it takes some effort and good roll casts to get your fly on the water away from the overgrown banks.

One-week Vacation

- Take the entire week and stay at two different sporting camps so you can experience a variety of waters. In addition to the three mentioned above in the weekend getaway section, an additional option would be Lakewood Camps (www.lakewoodcamps.com) to fish the Rapid River with perhaps a side trip to Upper Dam. A trip combining Lakewood Camps and Tim Pond Camps would provide both moving-water and stillwater experiences.

- For a less-expensive week vacation, stay at Cupsuptic Campground (www.cupsupticcampground.com) on Cupsuptic Lake and sample all of the surrounding water. The best months would be late May, June, early July, and mid- to late September. Cupsuptic Campground has remote campsites on a Cupsuptic Lake island and by Big Falls on the Cupsuptic River, if you prefer a more remote experience. During your week-long stay, you could fish the following waters, none of which would be more than 45 minutes from the campground:

  - Day 1: The Cupsuptic River
  - Day 2: The Upper Kennebago River
  - Day 3: The lower Magalloway below Aziscohos Dam
  - Day 4: The Rangeley River
  - Day 5: Upper Dam
  - Day 6: The Rapid River (this would be the longest distance and take the most time)
  - Day 7: The lower Kennebago River

Tim Pond Camps on Tim Pond.

The Kennebec River Valley with the western Maine mountains in the background.

West-central Maine including the Kennebec River

This region of Maine is dominated by the Kennebec River watershed that occupies almost 6,000 square miles in the west-central part of the state. The headwaters originate in the row of mountains on the Quebec border, then these upper tributaries combine to form the Moose River, which then flows into Moosehead Lake. The Kennebec River itself originates from two outlets at Moosehead Lake that combine at Indian Pond. Further south, several branches of the Dead River combine to form the Dead River, which meets the Kennebec at the Forks. Other tributaries join downstream. Above Waterville, the topography ranges from mountainous to hilly with the exception of the river valley itself.

The lower third of the Kennebec River's course is indicative of a coastal drainage area. It is influenced by tidal movements from Augusta – 25 miles upriver from the coast – to Merrymeeting Bay, the conclusion of its 145 mile journey. Communities along the Kennebec River include Jackman, Bingham, Anson, Madison, Norridgewock, Skowhegan, Waterville, Winslow, Augusta, Hallowell and Gardiner. Today, the major travel route for anglers is US 201 that parallels the Kennebec for much of its length, and runs north from US 1 in Topsham all the way to Jackman, and then the Canadian Border.

West-central Maine also includes other major watersheds, such as (about) 50 miles of the Androscoggin River, and the interconnected Belgrade Lakes. Numerous and varied stillwaters dot the landscape as well; from rocky mountain ponds to beaver bogs; from deep crystal-clear lakes to shallow, weedy, dam-created flowages.

This west-central Maine section is ordered as follows:

1. A detailed review of the Kennebec River (north to south)
2. A description of the Kennebec River tributaries (north to south).
3. Summary of other moving waters
4. Review of ponds and lakes (north to south)

KENNEBEC RIVER

The mighty Kennebec River has such a variety of water that describing it is the equivalent of writing about five separate rivers. In fact, this large river travels through so much of Maine that parts of it are covered in three different Maine sections of this book. The Kennebec flows from Moosehead Lake, carving a long, deep valley through the center of Maine to the Atlantic Ocean south of the city of Bath. The Kennebec's passage south is interrupted by a series of dams that have for years prevented the upriver migration of spawning fish in the lower river. On November 25, 1997, the Federal Energy Regulatory Commission (FERC) in a landmark decision, ordered the removal of Edwards Dam located on the lower Kennebec in the city of Augusta. The removal of this dam opened up a 15-mile section of river between Augusta and the village of Waterville to spawning sea-run fish. Wild Atlantic salmon, striped bass, sturgeon, shad, and rainbow smelt once again were able to return to their native spawning areas. I always marvel at catching striped bass in Waterville, which is at least a good hour at highway speeds from the ocean.

Upper Kennebec

From Moosehead Lake's East and West Outlets, the Kennebec flows through Indian Pond to a dam at the pond's southern end. This part of the river is covered in the East-central Maine section of this book. The Dead River joins the Kennebec at The Forks near US 201. During the summer months when water levels are down, this is a good area to hike into, following the river north. There are some nice runs and brook trout pools near the confluence of Cold Stream and Moxie Falls.

Middle Kennebec

The Kennebec continues south through the Wyman Lake impoundment. Wyman Dam in the village of Moscow has a coldwater release and provides good fishing downstream throughout the season. The river immediately below the dam holds larger-sized landlocks and rainbow trout, and there are good caddis hatches in June. Anglers are cautioned to watch flow levels. There is a well-marked access to the dam from Route 201 in Moscow. Downstream, there are access points near the Route 16 bridge in the village of Bingham and the Route 201A bridge in the village of Solon as well.

A multiuse trail along the east side of the river provides miles of access. Find the trail where it crosses US 201 just south of Bingham (45.041743,-69.865823). If you like to combine mountain biking and flyfishing, then this is the place to do it because the trail continues for 14.7 miles, with the first half of the distance along and over the river at the Williams Dam. The trail travels alongside some productive water as the river braids into channels, creating some good runs and a few eddy pools. One good spot to try is where Jackson Brook enters. You can fish many spots without waders from the bank, but be aware of rapidly changing water levels from dam releases.

Below Williams Dam in Solon, the Kennebec is stocked with thousands of brown trout every year and fish do hold over. There are a variety of salmonids in this section and the angler has a chance at a grand slam: rainbow, brown, brookie, and landlocked salmon. This section of river has been described as similar to Catskill waters with gently-sloping banks, braided channels, a fine-gravel bottom, clear water and gentle flows. Popular methods include nymphing the faster water under a strike indicator and casting large articulated streamers towards the banks in hope of luring a larger holdover brown trout.

The Kennebec River at the Forks off of Route 201.

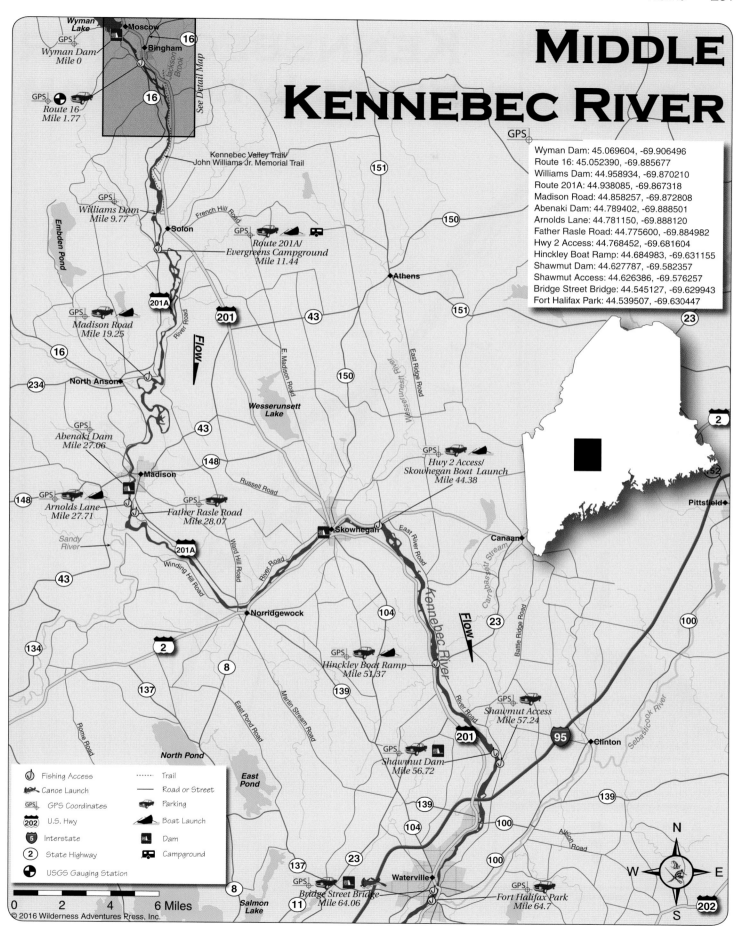

MIDDLE
KENNEBEC RIVER

GPS

Wyman Dam: 45.069604, -69.906496
Route 16: 45.052390, -69.885677
Williams Dam: 44.958934, -69.870210
Route 201A: 44.938085, -69.867318
Madison Road: 44.858257, -69.872808
Abenaki Dam: 44.789402, -69.888501
Arnolds Lane: 44.781150, -69.888120
Father Rasle Road: 44.775600, -69.884982
Hwy 2 Access: 44.768452, -69.681604
Hinckley Boat Ramp: 44.684983, -69.631155
Shawmut Dam: 44.627787, -69.582357
Shawmut Access: 44.626386, -69.576257
Bridge Street Bridge: 44.545127, -69.629943
Fort Halifax Park: 44.539507, -69.630447

Wyman Lake
Moscow
Wyman Dam Mile 0
Bingham
GPS
Route 16 Mile 1.77
Jackson Brook
See Detail Map

Kennebec Valley Trail
John Williams Jr. Memorial Trail

Embden Pond

Williams Dam Mile 9.77
Solon
French Hill Road
GPS
Route 201A/
Evergreens Campground Mile 11.44

Athens

201A
201
43
150
151

Flow

Madison Road Mile 19.25
GPS

16
234
North Anson
Wesserunsett Lake
E. Madison Road
150

43

Abenaki Dam Mile 27.06
GPS
148
Madison
Russell Road

Hwy 2 Access/
Skowhegan Boat Launch Mile 44.38
GPS

148
Arnolds Lane Mile 27.71
GPS
Father Rasle Road Mile 28.07
GPS

Sandy River

201A
43
Winding Hill Road
Ward Hill Road
River Road
Skowhegan
East River Road
Canaan
Pittsfield
2

134
2
Norridgewock
8
137
104
Flow
23
95
Clinton
100

Hinckley Boat Ramp Mile 51.37
GPS
139

Rome Road
North Pond
East Pond Road
Martin Stream Road
201
139
Shawmut Access Mile 57.24
GPS
Carrabassett Stream
Battle Ridge Road
Sebasticook River

East Pond
Shawmut Dam Mile 56.72
GPS
139
100
139

Fishing Access
Canoe Launch
GPS GPS Coordinates
202 U.S. Hwy
Interstate
2 State Highway
USGS Gauging Station

Trail
Road or Street
Parking
Boat Launch
Dam
Campground

137
23
Waterville
100
100
Albion Road

8
Salmon Lake
11
Bridge Street Bridge Mile 64.06
GPS
Fort Halifax Park Mile 64.7
GPS
202

N
W E
S

0 2 4 6 Miles
© 2016 Wilderness Adventures Press, Inc.

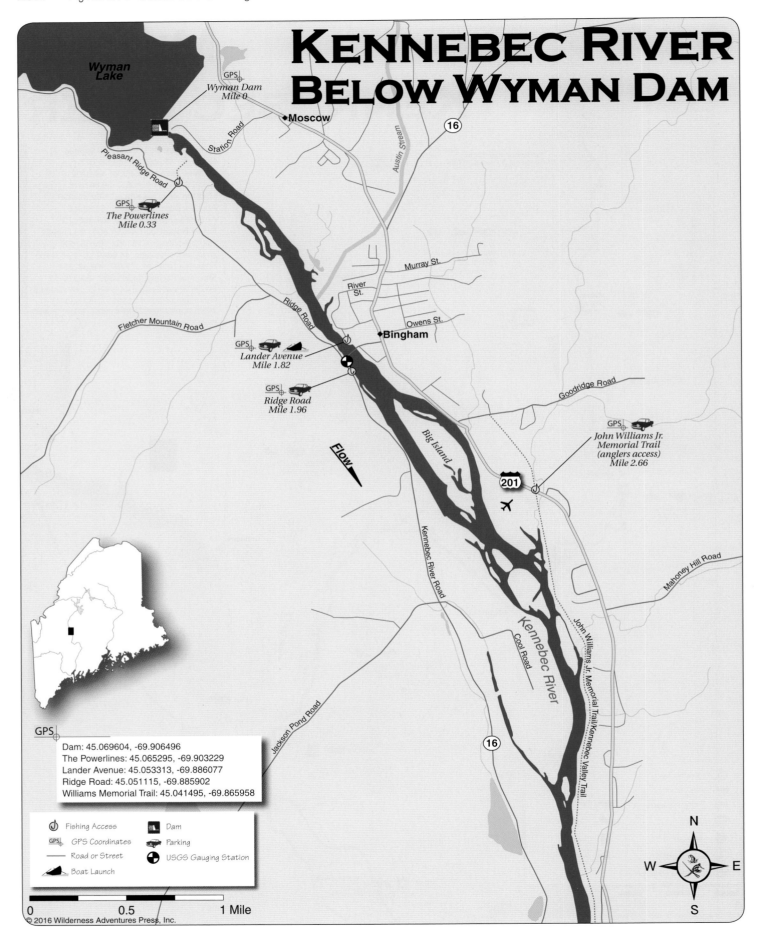

KENNEBEC RIVER
BELOW WYMAN DAM

Wyman Lake

GPS
Wyman Dam
Mile 0

◆Moscow

Station Road

Pleasant Ridge Road

GPS
The Powerlines
Mile 0.33

Fletcher Mountain Road

Ridge Road

Murray St.

River St.

Owens St.

◆Bingham

GPS
Lander Avenue
Mile 1.82

GPS
Ridge Road
Mile 1.96

Flow

Big Island

Goodridge Road

GPS
John Williams Jr.
Memorial Trail
(anglers access)
Mile 2.66

201

Kennebec River Road

Kennebec River

Cool Road

John Williams Jr. Memorial Trail/Kennebec Valley Trail

Jackson Pond Road

Mahoney Hill Road

16

16

Austin Stream

GPS
Dam: 45.069604, -69.906496
The Powerlines: 45.065295, -69.903229
Lander Avenue: 45.053313, -69.886077
Ridge Road: 45.051115, -69.885902
Williams Memorial Trail: 45.041495, -69.865958

Fishing Access   Dam
GPS Coordinates   Parking
Road or Street   USGS Gauging Station
Boat Launch

N
W   E
S

0   0.5   1 Mile
© 2016 Wilderness Adventures Press, Inc.

ABOVE: A nice Kennebec River brown trout. Photo courtesy Bob Mallard.
RIGHT: Wyman Dam during a period of low flow.

Many anglers float this part of the river because bank access is limited. You can reach the large pool below the dam from the dam itself, just north of downtown Solon. There is a private boat launch and some wading at Evergreens Campground in Solon, and then a public takeout for float trips off of Madison Road in North Anson (44.858257,-69.872808). This is an excellent facility with ample parking including reserved handicapped spots near the river. The Kennebec River flows slow enough here such that you can also launch a canoe or kayak, paddle upriver, and then fish your way back downstream.

Farther downriver is the Abenaki Dam in the town of Madison. Below this dam the Kennebec has a slightly different character with steeper banks, boulders, and greater current producing a variety of rapids, runs, pools, and riffles. Some claim that the several miles below Madison is the best wading brown trout fishery in New England. After Memorial Day, a classic New England series of hatches begin on this section including size-14 quill Gordons, Hendricksons and grannom caddis, followed by large sulphurs, then a variety of other caddis. During the fall, afternoon hatches of blue-winged olives are prolific and predictable. Due to the weed growth in this part of the river, subsurface fishing can be difficult.

Fish the Madison section via Arnolds Lane just off ME 148 on the west side of the river in Anson. After the road turns to dirt, there are several entrance points before the road ends. You can also reach this area via Father Rasle Road off US 201A on the east side of the river in Madison. You will see a small park with tables and an obvious parking spot along the road (44.775600,-69.884982). It is a bit of a scramble getting down the steep bank, but once down to water level, you can walk up and downstream.

The flatwater section of the Kennebec below the city of Skowhegan offers excellent smallmouth bass fishing and a put-and-take fishery for brown trout and salmon. Most of this river stretch is fished from boats or canoes. It is possible to wade the faster-flowing stretch upstream from a boat launch located off US 2.

On the Skowhegan section, blue-winged olive dries and nymphs will work. Fish nymphs slowly along the stream's bottom. Olive-bodied dry-fly patterns with smoky-gray wings are hard to beat for Kennebec River trout because they can imitate a variety of species. Go from sizes 14 to 18 as the season progresses. Fish June and July for the best results.

The river between Skowhegan and Shawmut Dam consists of flat but steady runs. Boat launches for this part of the Kennebec include the Skowhegan Boat Launch on Canaan Road, the River Road Boat Launch, and the

Hinckley Boat Launch on U.S. Route 201. Because of rapid changes in water levels due to dam releases, certain sections are wadable but caution is a must. Riverbank or boat fishing is the safest way to go.

The area from Skowhegan to Shawmut Dam has open fishing year round. Please check the rule book for the complete list of regulations for the middle Kennebec River. Heavily stocked, the river holds hatchery brown trout from 8 to 10 inches when first planted, and holdovers grow larger. Landlocked salmon average one to two pounds. Smallmouth bass mix with browns between Skowhegan and Shawmut Dam.

The river between Shawmut Dam and the Waterville Dam used to be the best brown trout fishing in Maine. Immediately below the dam – on both sides of the river – are clear parking areas and trails to the river (44.626386,-69.576257/ 44.627787,-69.582357). I had memorable days hooking 18-inch and bigger brown trout, as well as spunky, fat rainbows on Hendrickson and caddis imitations. Wading dangerously close to the top of my waders while tempting pods of slurping noses was exhilarating.

Unfortunately, for reasons not clear to anyone, those days are gone as the big browns are greatly diminished. Still, browns are stocked and it is a worthwhile section to fish. Hatches of spring mayflies and caddis are diminished but still present. Blue-winged olives are also active on the Shawmut area of the river where access makes bank fishing popular. Basic Elk Hair Caddis offerings also catch fish here. Go with size 14 in June, then switch to size 18 in July. Also try a range of more realistic caddis dries, from the Henryville Special to the Elk-wing Parachute Caddis. Fish

stonefly nymphs, which include the early black and early brown stonefly, as well as traditional wet flies. Streamers are effective for September bass and salmon.

Lower Kennebec

This section stretches from Waterville through Augusta to Merrymeeting Bay. In Waterville, spring fishing is good for smallmouth, landlocked salmon, and brown trout until the stripers arrive from the Gulf of Maine sometime in late May, and then smaller fish go into hiding. You can launch a small boat from the Waterville side of the river just downstream from the Bridge Steet bridge (44.545127,-69.629943). One good bank-fishing access point is right across the bridge in Winslow. Park behind the auto parts store (44.544038,-69.626672) or Dunkin Donuts and take the trail down to the rocky shoreline. A rocky ledge allows anglers to walk along the bank both upstream and downstream. In the evening, dark caddis and other bugs get trapped in the foam lines along the ledge and noses poke through the foam. You never know what you will hook; it could be a smallmouth bass, a landlocked salmon, or a brown trout. One of my favorite flies for this section is a size-16 black Puterbaugh Caddis – it floats well and imitates the numerous small dark caddis perfectly.

Just downstream from this area is another favorite river spot among local anglers: Halifax Park at the Sebasticook confluence. Anglers wading out on a gravel bar sometimes catch impressive salmonids.

Later in the spring, the stripers get into the action in the Waterville area. I once hooked a strong fish on a small Puterbaugh Caddis in the foam that I thought might be a record brown trout, until I spotted his bassy dorsal fin. It turned out to be a 26-inch striper. Yet another species that offers great sport arrives in June. Schools of shad can be found in deeper, slower water and can be tempted with shad darts, pink Woolly Buggers, or Wood Specials. If you have never flyfished for shad, read up a little on how best to locate schools and cast to them. Techniques don't vary much up and down the East Coast, so any good magazine article or blog about shad should give you the information that you need.

Farther downstream in Augusta, anglers still cast for stripers where the old Edwards Dam used to stand. The Kennebec River description below Augusta is covered in the Mid-coast section of this book.

The Kennebec Valley Multi-use Trail provides access to miles of prime fishing water.

Kennebec River Stream Facts

Fish Species
Landlocked salmon, wild brook trout, wild rainbow trout, stocked brown trout, smallmouth bass, striped bass and shad

River Characteristics
This is a large river – 200 to 300 feet wide – with islands and braided channels in spots. Water flows fluctuate widely so it is best to check flows before determining your fishing strategy. Four major tailwaters dominate the fishing on the the upper river, with other dams contributing to the fishing downstream. Below Harris Dam is the gorge, a very remote area with large brook trout and landlocked salmon. The Wyman tailwater in Bingham is an excellent rainbow trout fishery. Below Williams Dam, the water is best floated in a small watercraft, and anglers target brown trout along with other salmonids. The Abenaki tailwater is also a brown trout fishery (with brookies and landlocked salmon as well) but can be waded in many places. Farther downstream, other dams create different fisheries. Below the Waterville Dam, stripers and shad stack up at certain times of the year.

Rules and Regulations
All four tailwaters (Harris, Wyman, Williams, Abenaki) are artificials only. The upper three are open April through October while the lower one is open year round.

Tackle
Your primary weapon should be a 9-foot 5-weight rod with a floating line because that gives you the most versatility. For fishing streamers in deeper slots or pools, a 9-foot 6-weight with fast-sinking line is ideal. For dry-fly fishing under skinny conditions, a 9-foot 4-weight with 6x tippet will allow the angler to cast tiny flies to skittish trout. Any strike indicator must be big enough to float two flies and added weight on occasion.

Flies
Try sculpin and smelt patterns including some of the newer large gnarly articulated patterns for carnivorous trout. Carry patterns to match all sizes, colors, and life stages of mayflies, stoneflies, and caddis. If you are a minimalist, Hornberg, Klinkhammer, Wulff, Adams, Copper John, and Pheasant-tail nymph patterns will cover most of your bases.

Supplies
Kennebec River Outfitters (469 Lakewood Rd, Madison, ME 04950 / 207-474-2500 / www.kennebecriveroutfitters.com)

Upper Moose River
The Moose River begins near the state of Maine's western border with the Province of Quebec, west of the village of Jackman, and flows through a number of ponds and lakes before it enters Moosehead Lake. It is not a direct tributary of the Kennebec, but feeds Moosehead Lake, the origin of the Kennebec. West of Jackman and US 201, the river passes through a remote wilderness area that is accessible only by air or water from Jackman. Local sporting goods stores, flying services, and guides will be able to assist you with your plans if you have a bent towards exploration. Anglers can walk along the railroad tracks from Holeb Road to reach parts of the Moose River rarely fished and offering a true wilderness experience combined with brook trout and landlocked salmon fishing. Other popular Moose River spots include the short section of river between Attean Pond and Wood Pond (particularly the inlet after ice-out when the smelt are running), the inlet to Attean Pond (Attean Falls), Spencer Rips, and Holeb Falls.

Some anglers opt for the famous Moose River bow trip. Because of the arc the Moose River takes and the presence of nearby lakes, with one 1.5-mile portage, canoeists can take a three-day river trip and end up back where they started. This 35-mile wilderness trip starts and ends at Attean Pond. It begins with a long paddle across two lakes with the aforementioned portage in between (the only lengthy portage on the trip).

The Moose River offers decent fishing even in downtown Jackman where Route 201 crosses the river. You can scramble down the bank on either side of the bridge to fish the faster currents. Trout and salmon will move into that area in spring and fall, depending on water levels. One day I caught a number of nice brookies right under the bridge on small caddis imitations, Hornbergs, and Marabou Black Ghost streamers.

The section of the Moose River that connects Long Pond and Little Brassua Lake, as well as the stretch between Brassua Lake and Moosehead Lake (covered in the East-central Maine chapter), holds some of the most beautiful landlocked salmon and brook trout pools in central Maine. These sections of the Moose River are much more reachable than upriver, since the river runs parallel to ME 6/15 and the Canadian-American Railroad tracks.

Between Long Pond and Little Brassua, the Moose is big water with huge boulders, riffles, and long runs. One way to reach the river is from Demo/Moose River Road, off Route 6/15 that crosses the river at Long Pond Dam (45.617587,-69.967288).

Parlin Stream

Parlin Stream runs out of Lake Parlin and has a number of nice pools for a small stream that hold beautiful wild brook trout. In the fall larger trout and salmon run out of the lake to spawn. This water is open for an extended season through the end of October. If the fish are rising, try a small Parachute Adams, Hornberg, or Puterbaugh caddis. If not, try a Mini-muddler or a small wet fly. To find the stream, head north on US 201 past Lake Parlin, then take a right on Parlin Mountain Road and park where the road crosses the stream just a short distance from 201 (45.537917,-70.101085.) Parlin Stream joins Bean Brook and eventually empties into Long Pond, part of the Moose River system.

A beautiful Parlin Stream brook trout in spawning colors falls for a small caddis imitation.

Wood Stream

The section of Wood Stream from the outlet of Little Big Wood Pond to Mud Pond is filled with native brook trout, particularly in the spring and fall when bigger fish enter from connected stillwaters such as Big Wood Pond (part of the Moose River system). Best access is to take Gander Brook Road just north of Jackman off of Route 201/6.

Cold Stream

Cold Stream is a very productive brook trout stream. Expect fast action for 5- to 10-inch trout in the headwaters/mid-section. Some larger trout as you get closer to the Kennebec. Difficult to reach gravel logging roads travel in the vicinity of the west bank, near the Kennebec River. Anybody floating that section of the Kennebec should take the time to anchor and walk up the stream from the confluence. Another good option is Capital Road off of US 201 that crosses the stream farther north (45.436076,-70.036321). A crossroad just east of the Capital Road bridge allows the intrepid angler to reach even more water by following this road both north and south. Cold Stream Falls is certainly a highlight in this area that you don't want to miss.

A group of undeveloped ponds at the headwaters of Cold Stream, located between Parlin Mountain and Chase Stream has great fishing for native brook trout, and Trout Unlmited (and others) are looking to protect them with easements or purchase. Hire a local guide to take you in there and you won't be disappointed.

North Branch Dead River

The Dead River's North Branch runs from near the Canadian border to the western end of Flagstaff Lake. It holds brook trout and some landlocks and is paralleled by ME 27 and crossed by several major gravel roads, all of which provide many ways to reach the river. The North Branch is composed of both whitewater stretches and glass-flat pools. Its trout average 10 to 12 inches. While there are mayfly and caddisfly hatches, fly choice should be based upon how the angler prefers to fish. For dry-fly fishing, try a Hornberg, Puterbaugh Caddis, or a dark Quill Gordon. For subsurface fishing, a small conehead Woolly Bugger, Baby Brook Trout streamer, or a Wood Special will be effective.

South Branch Dead River

The South Branch of the Dead, flowing from Saddleback Lake to Flagstaff Lake, a distance of 25 miles, also holds both wild and stocked hand-sized brook trout. ME 16 provides entry where the river flows near the road, but when the river serpentines away from Route 16, it can also be reached by dirt roads that branch off the main drag. Try fishing both

The South Branch of the Dead in late April. This photo makes the river look bigger than it really is. It will be several more weeks before fishing picks up, even though fishing season has officially started. Photo courtesy Lindsey Rustad.

up and downstream from where tribs enter. Nash Stream is a large tributary that crosses under ME 16 and it has native brook trout as well. Downstream from the Kennebago Road crossing (45.104889,-70.525343), the river can be canoed all the way to Flagstaff Lake when water levels are good. Please don't confuse this Kennebago Road that leads to the east end of Kennebago Lake with the Kennebago River Road that leads to the west part of the lake. Fishing must be good at this bridge, based on the number of bobbers that I always see hanging from the powerlines there. The South Branch is a general-law fishery and provides a non-flyfisher with an opportunity that most Rangeley area flyfishing-only rivers do not.

The entire Route 16 route near the South Branch of the Dead is known for its plentiful moose – sightings are frequent in the mornings and evenings.

Dead River

The mainstem of the Dead River flows out of Flagstaff Lake for 20 miles before reaching the Kennebec River. The Maine Huts and Trails organization has recently completed construction of the Grand Falls Hut, and that gives angler a convenient place to stay while fishing the upper river.

Before July, the hut is not officially open, but anglers can stay there for $25 a night if they bring their own food. It is a short hike from the parking lot to the hut, and then another short hike to the water. For more information see www.mainehuts.org.

The key fishing spots are the riffles and big eddy below the Flagstaff Dam (45.222837,-70.200890) and Grand Falls, which is about six miles below the dam. Long Falls Dam Road from the town of North New Portland leads to the dam and also crosses the river, but it is at least a half-hour drive. Another route in is from Eustis via the Big Eddy Road that follows the north shore of Flagstaff Lake until it reaches Long Falls. A good gravel road exits Long Falls Dam Road before it crosses the river and leads down the downstream right bank.

The Dead is a rainbow trout fishery thanks to an illegal introduction years ago. Fish feed on smelt that tumble down from the lake, so smelt-imitation streamers are productive in the spring. Below the falls, the river continues for another 15 miles of pools and rips with any number of different salmonid species possible. Unfortunately, modest-sized smallmouth bass have also invaded the river and sometimes there is a fishy smell along the banks from bass that anglers have thrown on shore to kill. In the summer, concentrate your efforts on mouths of cool tribs or deeper pools. This is good dry-fly and nymphing water. Don't be afraid to try terrestrials such as foam ants and small grasshoppers. There are access points at Spencer Rips and Poplar Hill Falls from Lower Enchanted Road.

The mainstem of the Dead River is an extended season fishery and remains open through the month of October.

Carrabassett River

The Carrabassett River is stocked with rainbows and brookies below Kingfield (see Western Maine section).

An angler trying his luck at Grand Falls on the mainstem of the Dead River. Photo courtesy Tim Shaw.

Sandy River

Offering brown trout, Sandy River is artificials only from October 1 through 31 from the ME 145 Bridge in the village of Strong (44.802272,-70.220520) where there is a good access point by the town ballfields, downstream to the Kennebec River confluence. Holdovers suffer the rigors of winter runoff and warm summer water, with planted hatchery fish supplementing surviving stocks. Both brookies and browns are stocked from Strong downstream to Norridgewock and anglers familiar with the river catch holdover brownies. Closer to the headwaters, wild brookies can be caught. Ample access off ME 149 and 4 north of Farmington, and US 2 downstream from town makes this trout water worth trying.

This is a long river – 73 miles in length – so it would take weeks to explore it all (although it can be canoed south of Strong, just as the Abenaki tribe did historically). Before dams stopped their journey, the Sandy River enjoyed significant Atlantic salmon runs as fish came up the Kennebec and into the Sandy's headwaters to spawn in its ample gravel. Restoration efforts, most recently by planting developing salmon eggs, continue to this day.

The Sebasticook River

The Sebasticook Watershed between Pittsfield and Winslow holds plentiful wild brook trout between 6 and 12 inches, particularly in the upper reaches of the tributaries, away from the main stem of the river.

Cobbosseecontee Stream

Cobbosseecontee Stream starts below the dam that is the outlet for Cobbosseecontee Lake. The lake itself is renowned for the size of its largemouth bass that can run up to five pounds or better. Flyfish in the north basin in June with surface poppers or divers and be prepared for a lot of fun.

Anglers flyfish the stream itself below the dam off Collins Street (44.278820,-69.886745) for large brown trout. The stream and lake is stocked annually with browns and some do hold over, grow, and add inches and pounds every year. Best chance for big browns is in the early spring when the smelt are running, and late in the fall when the browns get aggressive and move around in preparation for spawning. Cobbosseecontee Stream is open to fishing all year.

LOWER ANDROSCOGGIN RIVER

From Livermore Falls down to the ocean, the lower Androscoggin is primarily a smallmouth and now growing pike fishery. There are a number of locations to launch a small boat, float a section of river, and then take out farther downstream. Access the river in Turner where there is a boat launch and work upstream between the islands. Or launch in Durham and drift downstream to Lisbon Falls. Both hand-carry and trailered-boat launches can also be found in Brunswick.

If you are targeting bass, try either the boulder field at the end of Switzerland Road in Lewiston, where Central Maine Power has a rough launch site for canoeists that want to portage around the Gulf Island Dam, or the boulder field near the Durham launch.

This section of the river also boasts Maine's newest state park, running 12 river miles from Turner downstream to Auburn on the west shore of the river. There are now several great trails, picnic areas, and parking areas to provide access to Gulf Island Pond, the impoundment above the dam at Lewiston and Auburn.

If you are targeting smallmouth, most of your favorite bass techniques will work fine. However, if you have never caught a pike on a fly, this is where you should give it a try. Pike prefer the slower water along the edges, particularly if there are weeds near some sort of drop-off. Fish large pike or saltwater streamers with lots of flash on an 8- or 9-weight and hold on. The best pike fishing is in the spring immediately after the spring run-off has subsided. If I was to fish one river location for pike, it would be upstream from the Turner boat launch. If you would like a guided trip, I recommend Matt Bickford of Maine River Guides (www.maineriverguides.com).

For detailed information about the upper Androscoggin, please see the Northern New Hampshire and the Western Maine sections.

Nezinscot River and Branches

Nezinscot River and its two branches, the East and West, flow south from the town of Sumner through the villages of Buckfield and Turner, joining the Androscoggin near Turner Center. The state stocks the Nezinscot heavily with brook and brown trout. There is convenient access to these streams along ME 117 and 140 and their side roads. Below Turner Dam (44.256282,-70.255428), the Nezinscot River offers extended season fishing and is open year round. Check the Maine IF&W Rule Book for specific regulations.

Little Androscoggin River

The Little Androscoggin River flows south and east from the village of West Paris, twisting and turning until it joins the Androscoggin in Auburn/Lewiston. The Maine Department of Inland Fisheries and Wildlife aggressively stocks both the Androscoggin and Little Androscoggin.

Maine Route 26 parallels the Little Androscoggin and offers good fishing and canoeing access. Upstream from

Angler Brian Whalen plays a good-sized brown trout caught while high-stick nymphing below the Little Androscoggin Dam off Route 26.

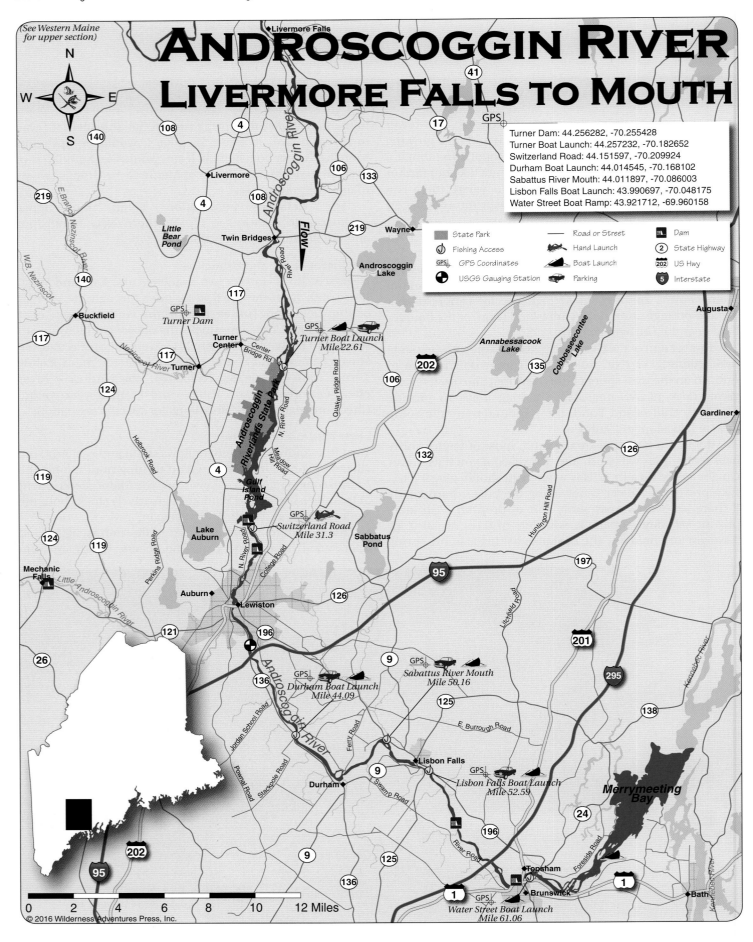

(See Western Maine for upper section)

ANDROSCOGGIN RIVER
LIVERMORE FALLS TO MOUTH

Turner Dam: 44.256282, -70.255428
Turner Boat Launch: 44.257232, -70.182652
Switzerland Road: 44.151597, -70.209924
Durham Boat Launch: 44.014545, -70.168102
Sabattus River Mouth: 44.011897, -70.086003
Lisbon Falls Boat Launch: 43.990697, -70.048175
Water Street Boat Ramp: 43.921712, -69.960158

State Park
Fishing Access
GPS Coordinates
USGS Gauging Station
Road or Street
Hand Launch
Boat Launch
Parking
Dam
State Highway
US Hwy
Interstate

Livermore Falls

Livermore

Twin Bridges

Little Bear Pond

Androscoggin Lake

Wayne

Buckford

Turner Dam

Turner Center

Turner

Center Bridge Rd

Turner Boat Launch
Mile 22.61

Annabessacook Lake

Cobbosseecontee Lake

Augusta

Gardiner

Androscoggin Riverlands State Park

Gulf Island Pond

Switzerland Road
Mile 31.3

Sabattus Pond

Lake Auburn

Mechanic Falls

Little Androscoggin River

Auburn

Lewiston

Androscoggin River

Durham Boat Launch
Mile 44.09

Sabattus River Mouth
Mile 50.16

Lisbon Falls

Lisbon Falls Boat Launch
Mile 52.59

Merrymeeting Bay

Durham

Topsham

Brunswick

Bath

Water Street Boat Launch
Mile 61.06

0   2   4   6   8   10   12 Miles

© 2016 Wilderness Adventures Press, Inc.

the ME 26 crossing, the river is only lightly stocked and wild fish are present, although the fishing is spotty. The most consistent fishing is from the dam on Route 26 just south of ME 121 (44.132879,-70.462689) and continuing downriver all the way to the Androscoggin River. Every road crossing and dam is stocked with brookies, rainbows, and brown trout. The section immediately below the ME 26 dam is a particularly good spot to fish for stocked and holdover browns and other species. I have caught both landlocked salmon and brown trout on nymphs and dry flies and even spotted humungous largemouth bass here.

There are shallow runs and a deep eddy pool just below the dam, and then some deep mysterious runs farther downstream with large boulders, timbers, and logs that look like holdover butterbelly (brown trout) water to me. Wading is workable in spots because of shallow sandbars that allow access to deeper water. Obvious trails follow both sides of the river and a few local retirees fish this water almost every day when conditions are good. Brown trout will rise to dry flies. Nymphing will also hook fish, and the best way to tempt the larger browns is with large meaty streamers on sink tip lines during periods of low light. Obvious unpaved parking areas can be found by the dam. Be careful of the luxurious stands of poison ivy growing between the parking lot and the water.

Somerset County Stillwaters (Jackman area)

Somerset County encompasses the northern region of west-central Maine and holds dozens of brook trout ponds managed by the Maine Department of Inland Fisheries and Wildlife as flyfishing-only waters. Many of these stillwaters are remote and are only accessible by all-terrain vehicles, water, air, or by foot trail. Fishing pressure for all of the waters here is low.

The village of Jackman on US 201 is the outpost for services and the access to several of the ponds located in the county's northwest corner. Jackman is not touristy and doesn't cater solely to fly fishers, but because it does supply hunters, anglers, loggers, and others who work in the woods, you will be able to find the basics of what you might need.

The following patterns are some of the local favorites. In the spring, when pond brookies start looking up, Hornbergs and red Doodles Bugs are the flies to try. Doodle Bugs have colorful bodies covered with a deerhair back. They look like nothing in nature but attract wild brookies like nobody's business. Later on in the season as hatches begin in earnest, a large grey Parachute Adam matches the emerging grey drakes. Good searching patterns when rises are scarce are the Grey Ghost steamer and Muddlers tipped with red or orange in various sizes. Try to fish on or near the bottom with sinking or sink-tip lines.

Dingley Ponds, Wounded Deer Pond, Cape Horn Pond, and Little Fish Pond

The three Dingley Ponds, Upper, Little, and Dingley are remote stillwaters located northwest of Penobscot Lake, about as far in northwest Maine as you can go without being in Canada. Wounded Deer Pond and Cape Horn Pond are in Prentiss Township south of Penobscot Lake. Old Kelly Dam Road, from Route 201/ 6, about five miles east of the Quebec border, provides access to the logging roads and trails to these ponds. As this road runs parallel to the South Branch of the Penobscot River, it also provides access to the trail leading to Little Fish Pond in Alder Brook Township.

Daymond Pond

Daymond Pond lies north of Jackman, just east of Route 201/6 in Moose River Plantation (45.695408,-70.271066). Look for a dirt road (Daymond Pond Road).

Rancourt Pond and Big Fish Pond

On the west side of Route 201/6, just north of Jackman, take a left on Holeb Road and travel several miles to an unimproved access road and trail to Rancourt Pond, a spot highly recommended by local anglers. Holeb Road is a major dirt road but the access road is very rough. I rode my mountain bike up this road rather than risking the vehicle. Big Fish Pond is a remote pond in Holeb Township. The pond lies within the jurisdiction of the Maine Indian Tribal-State Commission that regulates the fishery. Motors greater than 10 horsepower are prohibited. Access to Big Fish Pond can be made by air or by water as part of the Moose River Bow Trip from Jackman.

Baker Pond

Baker Pond is found west of Moosehead Lake in Tomhegan Township about six miles from the village of Rockwood. There is an access road off ME 6/15, where a trail to the pond can be found.

Iron Pond, Upper Enchanted Pond, and Little Enchanted Pond

Hardscrabble/Spencer Road, west from US 201 near the village of Lake Parlin (south of Jackman), provides access to the trails leading to Iron Pond in Hobbstown Township, Blakeslee Lake in T5 R6 BKP WKR west of Hobbstown

Township, and Little Enchanted Pond in Upper Enchanted Township. There is a primitive campsite at Little Enchanted Pond.

Big Berry Pond, Little Berry Pond, Snake Pond, Durgin Pond, and Cold Stream Pond

Big Berry Pond, Little Berry Pond, Snake Pond, and Durgin Pond lie in Johnson Mountain Township east of the village of Lake Parlin. Boats with motors are prohibited on Durgin Pond and Little Berry Pond. From just south of Lake Parlin, unimproved roads provide access to the ponds and adjacent primitive campsites. However, these ponds are only a short distance from the main road, and could even be biked. Cold Stream Pond lies east of Lake Parlin as well. However, the best access to this pond is south on the road (called Williams Mountain/Capital Road on the *Delorme Atlas*) that intersects Route 6/15 near the east end of Long Pond on the Moose River. Cold Stream Pond is the headwaters of Cold Stream, described earlier in this section.

Markham Pond

The road to Markham Pond is a float-tube sized pond, just south and very close to US 201. Take Markham Pond Road (45.470393,-70.065697) and you will see several camps by the pond or you can take a short walk in from Enchanted Pond Road.

Tobey Pond, Little Wilson Hill Pond, Ellis Pond, Horseshoe Pond, and Dead Stream Pond

Capitol Road, south of the Markham Pond access road off Route 201, provides access as you head east to the trails for Tobey Pond and Little Wilson Hill Pond in Johnson Mountain Township, the Dead Stream Road (45.479771, -69.969505) leading to Ellis Pond and Horseshoe Pond, and

Dead Stream Pond in West Forks Plantation. For further descriptions of this cluster of ponds and others in this area, see the East-central Maine section of this book.

Crocker Pond, Long Pond, McKenney Pond, Turner Pond, and Little Turner Pond

Frequently, the best strategy to explore remote ponds is to become familiar with one access road and explore all the nearby waters. In Jackman, the Holeb Road off of Route 201/6 north of town is a great route to a number of ponds (look for a large log yard at the entrance – 45.676928,-70.284152). Holeb is a well-maintained road and passes close by Crocker, Long, McKenney, Turner, and Little Turner Ponds. Putting in a canoe or kayak takes a minimum of effort. Keep going and you reach the Moose River. All of the ponds are remote, beautiful, and small enough to explore in a canoe or kayak. They have a variety of fishing, horsepower, and fishing season regulations so please check the law book.

Spencer Lake, Chub Pond, and Fish Pond

Another good route to explore is the Hardscabble Road (becomes Spencer Road) off from US 201 opposite of Lake Parlin. After a drive of a little over 15 miles lies Spencer Lake, and on the other side of the road is Chub Pond (45.457087,-70.304405), filled with small trout and with a small campsite. One way to Spencer Lake is through Fish Pond where you can launch a small boat. At the access point on the southeast shore of Fish Pond is a good campsite with a sandy beach. Good moose-watching possibilities are there as well.

Spencer Lake offers good brook trout fishing, particularly on the south end where Spencer Lake Dam lies (flyfishing only). Easiest access is by boat. The last time a

Ready to head out on Turner Pond, outside of Jackman.

friend of mine was there in mid-June he caught trout from 8 to 17 inches. There is an excellent campsite on the eastern shore with a sandy beach and an outhouse about five miles down the lake. It must be reserved ahead of time. A number of other ponds lie nearby, including Grace and Whipple Ponds.

The following waters are flyfishing only except for Pierce Pond, which is artificials only.

Everett Pond

Everett Pond is located in the King and Bartlett Township. The gated access road to this region is the King and Bartlett Road that can be found off of ME 27, north of Eustis (45.232357,-70.491466). The King and Bartlett area was historically accessible via the sporting camp of the same name, but it is now privately owned. Everett Pond is a float-tube sized pond, a short walk from the gate. Anglers are not discouraged from walking in, fishing, and even camping.

Butler Pond and Little Jim Pond

Butler Pond is also in the lease area, but has a good hex hatch and lots of trout in the 8- to 12-inch range. Little Jim Pond is located just outside the King and Bartlett gate so access is easy, and it offers good fishing for trout up to 18 inches.

Pierce Pond

Pierce Pond and its surrounding smaller, remote ponds is a terrific flyfishing destination. Pierce Pond is lake-sized and consists of upper, middle, and lower sections, with the upper pond connected by a narrow, short thoroughfare that allows passage of small boats. This pond holds wild brook trout and stocked landlocked salmon. What makes Pierce Pond so special is its completely natural shoreline, beautiful scenery, and the fact that it grows really large brook trout and salmon. Dozens are caught over three pounds every year. We know this because Cobb's (Sporting) Camps on lower Pierce Pond attaches a large, wide, wooden plank on the dining room wall every year and records the fishing action. Every time a lucky angler catches a fish over three pounds, their name, date, fish, and weight is recorded on the plank. By the end of the fishing season, they sometimes have to add an additional plank when they run out of space on the first one.

The season starts with anglers trolling or casting smelt-imitating streamers after ice-out when the smelt are running. The first consistent dry-fly fishing is around Memorial Day when Black Quills start emerging in consistent numbers. Later on black caddis, green drakes, and *Hexagenia* mayflies also appear in certain areas of the pond. The best dry-fly fishing is usually after dinner. I

Pierce Pond holds wild brook trout and stocked landlocked salmon. Photo courtesy John Patriquin.

am not going to lie – Pierce Pond's fishing is inconsistent. At times certain years, steady hatches bring fish to the surface and the planks in the dining room fill with big-fish statistics. Other times the flyfishing can be slow and a guest might only hook a good fish or two after several days of hard fishing. It is the good days (and the atmosphere at Cobb's) that keep you coming back.

The main access road is gated, but if you stay at Cobb's Camps or Harrison's (another sporting camp), you will have access to the entire pond system. You can also drive down to the pond with your own boat and fish for the day, but you have to be out before dark. You can also reserve one of the island camping spots (administered by Cobb's). Carry Pond Road runs north along the west side of the Kennebec River north of Bingham and provides access to logging roads and trails in this region. This is how you reach Harrison's on Pierce Pond Stream, a short walk from Pierce Pond's eastern corner. Moreover, the Appalachian Trail passes by that same corner as well and, if you hike in on the Trail, you can stay at the lean-to right on the lake. This was my introduction to Pierce Pond when I through-hiked the Trail with my wife, more years ago than I want to believe.

Kilgore Pond, Split Rock Pond, and Dixon Pond

Surrounding satellite ponds offer a variety of flyfishing experiences and are short walks down easy trails from Pierce Pond. Regulations vary, so check the Maine fishing rule book. Kilgore Pond (flyfishing only) and Grass Pond (artificials only) are known for growing large trout. Fish the bottom with black Woolly Buggers, leech imitations, or Hex nymphs (such as the Maple Syrup) on sinking line. The fishing may be slow, but on an annual basis, a few anglers catch brook trout approaching or exceeding five pounds. The very picturesque Split Rock Pond and Dixon Pond are flyfishing only and offer faster fishing, but the brook trout are smaller.

Fish Pond, Helen Pond, and High Helen Pond

From the lower Pierce Pond access point of Lindsay Cove (45.247540,-70.088640), you will find a good trail that follows the shoreline towards Cobb's. Another trail off of that takes you up Pierce Mountain to the high ponds: Fish Pond, Helen, and High Helen. These are flyfishing-only ponds that have yielded small trout with a beautiful pink coloration, probably from food sources unique to those ponds. Continuous logging activity and new logging roads that also lead towards those ponds mandate a call to Cobb's to find out the latest and best route up.

Bean Pond, Clear (Mill) Pond, and Lost Pond

Bean Pond, Clear Pond (also known as Mill Pond), and Lost Pond are located in Pleasant Ridge Plantation and are accessible from Rowe Pond Road west of Moscow. The small streams in this area such as Sandy Stream, Carrying Place Stream, and their tributaries all hold native brookies as well. Years ago, while hiking the nearby Appalachian Trail and half-famished, I caught (and ate) some beautiful trout in these streams.

Heald Pond and Spruce Pond

Heald Pond is located in the town of Caratunk north of Moscow. Take Stream Road off US 201 in Moscow to reach the pond and a nearby primitive campsite. Spruce Pond lies north of the village of North New Portland in Lexington Township. The east fork of Long Falls Dam Road will put you on the trail to the pond.

Belgrade Lakes

The seven lakes and ponds that make up the Belgrade Lakes used to be a major fishing destination for flyfishers targeting a number of species, particularly landlocked salmon. This changed when one of the lakes was illegally stocked with northern pike, which spread and decimated the fishery. However, these stillwaters still offer some angling for trout and salmon, as well as smallmouth bass, and of course,

northern pike. Great Pond, the largest of the lakes, covers 8,000 acres. It receives annual stockings of brown trout, and formerly received landlocked salmon and brookies. Larger fish are occasionally taken in the marshy, shallow area near Bog Brook at the pond's southern end. In 2015, a 16-pound brown trout was landed through the ice, and six-pounders are taken every year by a variety of angling methods. This lake is known for its large and hefty white perch population as well.

North Pond (the Belgrade lakes don't have the most creative names), located on ME 137 near the village of Smithfield, is an excellent largemouth-bass fishery. It also supports limited numbers of brown trout and northern pike. The boat launch is on the northwest corner. East Pond is primarily a warmwater fishery with some stocked brown trout that hold over and can be measured in pounds. East Pond's real claim to fame is its large smallmouth and largemouth bass. Four-pound smallies and seven-pound largemouths are caught here every year. It lies east of Smithfield and is also reachable from Route 137 with a boat launch in the southeast corner.

Salmon Lake, also called Ellis Pond and McGrath Pond, is actually one body of water joined by a narrows. This 1,000-acre stillwater is located east of Great Pond off ME 8 near the village of North Belgrade. It is a mixed warm and coldwater fishery that offers brown trout and limited landlocked salmon fishing in the early and late seasons and bass fishing in between. These waters are heavily developed and utilized, so best fishing is very early or late in the day when the boaters and swimmers are off the water.

Messalonskee Lake offers good fishing for landlocked salmon and warmwater species. It is located southwest of the village of Oakland with access areas along ME 23 and ME 11 with the boat launch in Oakland. Long Pond is located west of the village of Belgrade Lakes off ME 27. This stillwater has a maximum depth of over 100 feet and is managed by the Maine Department of Inland Fisheries and Wildlife as a landlocked salmon fishery, although pike have really taken a toll. It is stocked and there is a special catch-and-release season in October.

Androscoggin Lake

Androscoggin Lake, located off ME 106 north of Lewiston, has an excellent and well-deserved reputation for largemouth and smallmouth bass.

Basin Pond, Echo Lake, and Kimball Pond

Basin Pond supports brook trout and splake. It is located north of Androscoggin Lake in the town of Fayette and is accessible from a trail off ME 41 and Sandy River Road near the village of West Mount Vernon. Echo Lake, also called

Crotched Pond (Echo Lake sounds better), lies south of West Mount Vernon. It supports landlocked salmon, lake trout, and warmwater species. Kimball Pond, a small brook trout pond, is found in the northern section of this region near the village of Vienna off ME 41. Access is from Berry Hill Road.

Cobbosseecontee Lake

Cobbosseecontee Lake, sometimes called Cobbossee Lake, is a large stillwater covering nearly 5,000 acres located east of Augusta. It is best known as a largemouth and smallmouth bass fishery. However, the lake is heavily stocked with brooks and browns, and larger holdover brown trout up to five pounds are commonly caught.

Cochnewagon Pond

Cochnewagon Pond is a brown trout fishery located near the village of Monmouth on Route 132 north of Lewiston. The pond also offers good bass fishing in the warmer months through October.

China Lake, Threemile Pond, and Maranacook Lake

China Lake and Threemile Pond are located in eastern Kennebec County near the village of South China. Both stillwaters have convenient access and boat launch facilities off Routes 3 and 9. The southern China Lake ramp is at the intersection of those two roads.

These are mixed warmwater and coldwater fisheries supporting bass and stocked brown trout. While fishing can be good, both waters suffer from algae blooms, so best to fish early in the season. The outlet of China Lake, Outlet Stream, can be a good brook trout fishery in early spring. The outlet of Maranacook Lake in Winthrop can also yield good numbers of brook and brown trout in late April.

Auburn Lake as seen from the Route 4 boat launch.

Summerhaven Ponds

The so-called Summerhaven Ponds are a collection of tiny bodies of water between Manchester and Sidney that can offer good trout fishing. Fairbanks Pond, Gould Pond, Silver Lake, and Tyler Pond are stocked. The favorite of many flyfishers is 22-acre Tyler Pond. It has a robust smelt population that produces large trout, an artificial-lures-only regulation, and a completely undeveloped shoreline.

Auburn Lake

Auburn Lake is a public water supply covering 2,260 acres just north of the city of Auburn. This impoundment supports landlocked salmon and larger-sized togue, as well as large smallmouth bass and plentiful white perch. Fishing for landlocks and togue immediately after ice-out usually means trolling traditional streamers with a fly rod.

As the water warms, great topwater smallmouth bass action is possible with small surface poppers when the smallies move to the shoreline to make their circular nests and spawn. Male smallmouth remain to protect their eggs or newly hatched offspring and will aggressively attack anything perceived as a threat. Prime spots to try (by boat) are along Lake Shore Drive. Cast to the shoreline along Taber's Driving Range or near Townsend Brook. Anglers walking the shoreline along Spring Road and casting will also hook their fair share of the bronzebacks during the spring. Later in the year, the small rocky island located near Route 4 is situated atop a gravel and boulder field that holds large numbers of bass when they are not spawning

The lake's southern end, south of a line from the Route 4 boat launch to Pine Point on the west shore, is closed to fishing and all other water-related activities. Check law book for specific regulations. This lake is open for October and November but it is artificial lures only and catch and release for all species.

Gulf Island Pond, Pleasant Pond, Crystal Pond, and Beals Pond

Gulf Island Pond is the upstream stillwater formed by the Androscoggin River dam north of Auburn. The "pond" holds brown trout as well as warmwater species including pike. Pleasant Pond and Crystal Pond, also known as Beals Pond, are located north of the village of Turner. Crystal is stocked with brown trout and couldn't be more convenient with a small parking area right on ME 4. It is sheltered and almost always calm. Pleasant Pond supports brook trout and is found north of Turner Center off Route 117.

WEST-CENTRAL MAINE PLANNING CONSIDERATIONS

Nearby Hub Cities

- Jackman (www.jackmanregion.org)
- Kingfield (http://www.kingfieldme.org)
- Waterville (www.midmainechamber.com)

Easy Access Options

- Moose River in Jackman: Just park in the small parking area north of the US 201 bridge and walk down the obvious short paths to the water. Don't neglect to fish right under the bridge.
- Parlin Stream (outlet of Lake Parlin): Fish any small dry fly. Access is from US 201. Head north past Lake Parlin, take a right on Parlin Mountain Road and park where the road crosses the stream (just a short distance from 201). There are short trails that lead from the bridge, but you don't need to go very far – the pools immediately below and above the bridge hold trout.
- Kennebec River (below Bingham) from the Kennebec Valley Trail: This entry does require walking, but the trail is an old railroad bed so it is wide and level with no hills. A few hundred yards puts you next to the river and some fishy spots.
- Stay at Cobb's Camps at Pierce Pond and hire one of their very competent guides who will take you anywhere you want to go.

Suggested Beginner Options

- Chub Pond (one of many with the same name in Maine) is a small pond near Spencer Lake reached by a fairly long drive down Spencer Road from ME 201. It is very close to Spencer Road and a short walk brings you to pond's edge and a small campsite (45.459272,-70.302819). During late May to early July evenings, Chub Pond comes alive with rising fish. From a small boat, the only skill required is to tie a small Hornberg on and cast 10 feet.

Foliage around Jackman is breathtaking in late September.

- Take a float trip down the Moose River. This is a great trip for a beginning flyfisher to learn the basics and catch brook trout. However, you should be a knowledgeable canoeist or kayaker because there is flat-water paddling, river paddling, and portaging involved in fairly remote country. Study maps and talk to folks who have done this trip before you go.
- Parlin Brook: Fish any small dry fly on short casts to eager brookies. Access is from Route 201 heading north past Lake Parlin, take a right on Parlin Mountain Road and park where the road crosses the stream (just a short distance from 201).
- The Little Androscoggin River by the ME 26 dam offers plenty of trout after the annual stocking and they remain plentiful and catchable for quite some time. Only short casts are required and the currents create multiple hook-up opportunities where the fish almost hook themselves. The beginner can practice dry-fly fishing, streamer fishing, or nymphing.

Suggested Flyfishing Vacation Options

Weekend Getaway

- From Memorial Day to early July, pick a weekend and stay at Cobb's Pierce Pond Camps and fish Pierce Pond's evening hatch for trophy rising brook trout and salmon. Cobb's is always fully booked during the most popular times, so try to book far in advance, or you may have to settle for mid-week or less ideal times the first year. Camping on one of the islands (book with Cobb's) is another alternative.
- Late September weekend in Jackman: The foliage is spectacular and is several weeks ahead of the rest of New England, so you get to enjoy the foliage season twice. The trout and salmon are coming out of the deep holes and are available to the fly casters once again, particularly if early September rains cook and raise the streams. Try a few of the small flyfishing-only ponds and the Moose River. A good base of operations is Bishops Country Inn Motel and the Bishop's Store across the street. Both locations will take care of lodging, provisions, and food, so you can concentrate on enjoying the outdoors.

One-week Vacation

- Explore the entire Kennebec during one action-packed week in late June to early July. What a lifetime experience to fish this entire river from its origin to the ocean. An example itinerary:
  - Day 1: Wade (or float) the East and West Outlets
  - Day 2: Boat Indian Pond for bass
  - Day 3: Wade below Wyman Dam
  - Day 4: Solon section float trip
  - Day 5: Wade Madison section
  - Day 6: Wade or float the Shawmut Dam and Fairfield sections
  - Day 7: Hire a guide to fish the Kennebec for stripers below Bath.
- Canoeing or kayaking the Moose River Bow Trip in late September as the foliage turns is spectacular even if one didn't hook one fish, which of course wouldn't happen. Jackman would be the best base of operations. See the details earlier in this section.
- How about a warmwater species flyfishing vacation in June? Hire a guide to drift the lower Androscoggin for pike. Cast to the shorelines for surface bass action on Little Sebago, Cobbossocontee, or the Belgrades. Early season stripers can be caught on the lower Kennebec River, anywhere below Waterville. This part of Maine offers much more than just trout and salmon.

East-central Maine

Flyfishing opportunities abound in the huge area that is central Maine, and that represents a dilemma in how best to structure this book so it is most useful for the reader. Since most major approach roads run north-south in Maine, almost all anglers travel north on Route 6/15 to Moosehead or on Route 11 to Millinocket to begin accessing the east-central region of Maine. This section includes the waters that would best be fished from those two hubs. This includes all of Piscataquis County, a tiny slice of eastern Somerset Country, and a small western section of Penobscot County.

Since Baxter State Park is a distinct entity with unique regulations and access restrictions, I discuss its fishing possibilities in a separate heading in this section.

In 2016 President Obama designated part of the East Branch of the Penobscot River and surrounding lands as Katahdin Woods and Waters National Monument. This land, bordering the eastern boundary of Baxter State Park, was donated to the federal government by the owner, Roxanne Quimby. Better roads, new trails, and other helpful infrastructure will be built that will make this area easier to access, explore, and fish. Find the latest information and maps at https://www.nps.gov/kaww/index.htm to stay up-to-date with this new preserve.

Piscataquis County's Moosehead Lake is Maine's largest lake. It is a massive body of water, covering 74,890 acres. More than the big water itself, Moosehead Lake tributaries and nearby stillwaters offer some of the best flyfishing in the northeast. The village of Greenville, the commerce center in the area, though sparsely populated, provides a number of comfortable accommodations and dining options. Flyfishers visiting the region will enjoy Greenville; it offers spectacular views of the lake, it has its own special kind of character, and it caters to outdoor enthusiasts.

There are myriad flyfishing options in this area. Local outfitters and guides can provide excellent introductions to these trout and salmon waters. Over time, flyfishers can revisit their favorite salmon pools and trout runs with or without the angling wisdom of the natives who acquainted them with this area. Dan Legere of the Maine Fly Shop & Guide Service in Greenville (for sale as I write this) probably knows as much about flyfishing the Moosehead region as anyone. Right next to his shop is a used-book store, From Away Books and Antiques, whose proprietor, Bob, eagerly promotes the region and will provide you with excellent flyfishing maps of the area. He is an avid angler and knows the area well. Give either of them a call, or stop by if you visit.

Fishing options in this area include Moosehead Lake itself, west-shore rivers (the East and West Outlets of the Kennebec River and the Moose River), east-shore rivers (the Roach River and West Branch of the Penobscot), and myriad wilderness ponds and smaller streams. Most coldwater species are found in this region including brook trout, lake trout, and landlocked salmon. There is also some terrific smallmouth angling to be had as well. Trophy-sized fish can be caught at any time.

The view of Mount Kineo on Moosehead, as a serious autumn storm approaches.

ROACH RIVER

The Roach River seems to attract the fierce devotion of anglers. Even with all of the available water in Maine, and the Moosehead area specifically, a number of flyfishers makes sure that they come back to fish the Roach year after year. It is smaller than some rivers, yet it yields large trout and salmon as they enter the river from Moosehead Lake. There are three distinct sections of the river: the first section from First Roach Pond to the confluence with Lazy Tom Stream, the middle section with long pocket water sections and more difficult access, and the section near Moosehead Lake. Large trout and salmon (from two to four pounds) move in and out of the stream from Moosehead Lake, depending on the availability of food sources and water temperatures and flows.

In the spring, fish follow the smelt and then suckers, and stay in the stream feeding on mayflies and caddis as spring turns into summer. If the summer is cool and wet, more fish will stay in the stream all year. As the water warms, most trout and salmon will drop back into the lake. Some salmon always move upstream and take up residence directly below the First Roach Pond dam all summer, but they see a lot of fishermen and get very finicky except for very early or late in the day.

The first increased flows in mid-September from dam releases bring fresh fish into the river, and trout and salmon continue to move in until numbers are quite significant. Most of your favorite New England patterns will work in the Roach whether it be nymphs, streamers, or dry flies. Fresh fish from the lake will not be too particular, but as they see fishing pressure it pays to switch to something that they haven't seen.

Since the fish move around, it's worthwhile to prospect with a streamer or a wet fly so you can cover a lot of water. When you locate activity, try your favorite methods. I generally carry two rods, one rigged with a streamer and the other with either a nymphing rig or a dry fly.

If you fish downstream from the Dam Pool, the river reconfigures into a long run, and then opens up in the Dump Pool which is quite obvious because of the log cribworks in the pool and the rusty junk on the riverbank. Farther downstream you will find the Wardens Pool.

You can access the middle section of the river several different ways. Traveling north of Kokadjo on Lily Bay Road, take the first major dirt road which is Spencer Bay Road (45.686413,-69.429691). After a large clearcut, take another left on Roach River North Road that parallels the river on the north side. There are pull-offs periodically that have trails leading to the river. Be careful though, some paths that look like trails to the river are in fact game trails or false starts and will leave you lost.

My favorite trail to the river (45.681254,-69485447) leads directly to Spring Pool, with Corner Pool directly upstream. Although fishermen tend to concentrate on the well-known pools, there are fish to be had in the faster pocket water if the flows are moderate. Look for deeper runs along the bank or pockets behind large boulders. Wading can be difficult because of heavy growth along the banks and uneven bottom. A wading staff helps a great deal. Carry a map or use GPS so you don't get lost.

Fishing the less pressured middle section of the Roach River.

Stream Facts: Roach River

Season
From May 1 to September 30

Species
Brook trout and landlocked salmon up to four pounds

Tackle and Flies
It is most efficient to carry two fly rods. One fly rod would be a 9- or 9.5-foot 5-weight, rigged with a full-sink or sink-tip line, or sinking leader with a short leader tapering to 3x. Fish this rod when you are prospecting with a streamer. If working to rising fish, a 4-weight with a floating line and a 9-foot leader tapering to 5x will allow you to make a more delicate presentation.

If no rising fish are visible and you are prospecting, the best combination is to fish a large streamer with a smaller nymph or wet fly trailer. The guides utilize brown, green, or gray conehead Woolly Buggers or Soft-hackle Marabou streamers. The trailer can be a green or brown caddis pupa, Prince Nymph, or a soft-hackled wet fly.

For rising fish, match the hatch. Generic "close-enough" flies are usually sufficient including Puterbaugh Caddis, Parachute Adams, Hornberg, and Elk Hair Caddis.

In September, local anglers swear by a large white Wulff on the surface or an orange Woolly Bugger close to the bottom.

Flows
Generally 100 to 250cfs. Wading is difficult at 450cfs but that occurs rarely.

The river is dam-controlled which moderates the ups and downs, but the holding capacity of the First Roach Pond watershed is limited so drought can cause limited water flows.

Access
The Maine Department of Inland Fisheries and Wildlife owns corridors on either riverbank, excluding several hundred yards of land immediately below First Roach Pond. Easements are provided by the state at six access sites—three on either side of the river—that provide right-of-way foot access from Scott Paper Company logging roads. NOTE: When parking at trailheads, pull off main roads – active logging operations require open passage. Access on north side is from Roach River North Road. Access from south side is off a side road from Hardwood Valley Road. Access to the river from the dam down to the first four pools is along a dirt trail from Lily Pond Road along the north bank of the river.

A 9-foot 5-weight with a sink-tip line and 3x tippet is a great setup for streamer fishing on the Roach.

WEST BRANCH PENOBSCOT RIVER

For those anglers who value a wild Maine adventure, the West Branch of the Penobscot is a destination to add to their "bucket list". Under the shadow of Mount Katahdin as the river skirts the southern Baxter State Park boundary, fishing the West Branch can also combine whitewater floats, wildlife viewing, miles of wading, and fishing to pods of rising fish. This river is considered by some to be the best landlocked-salmon river in the country. Although this species was introduced years ago, all the fish are river-bred and grow plentiful and large under ideal water conditions and plentiful food sources. Literally tons of smelt go through the Ripogenus Dam turbines or swim up from other lakes in the system. Salmon gorge on smelt for weeks before switching over to sucker spawn and then heavy caddis hatches. Salmon over four pounds are possible and there are brook trout opportunities as well. Although the area is remote, the Golden Road and other park and logging roads provide good access to many sections.

Two river sections of the West Branch Penobscot are of interest to flyfishers. The first commences at Seboomook Dam flowing northward 25 miles to Chesuncook Lake. Access is limited and many people float the river (or move up and down in small motorized boats), camp overnight alongside, and make a weekend of it. Campsites can be found below Moosehorn Stream and are first-come first-served. Because spring run-off makes the float problematic, this is a more popular fall fishery as brook trout and landlocked salmon enter the river from Chesuncook and Lobster Lakes. Fishing is best with brightly-colored streamers including classics like the Mickey Finn. The fishing is hit or miss depending on the weather. The last time I floated this section, it was mid-September and 80 degrees, and the fishing was tough.

The second river section is the most popular with flyfishers and is the six-mile stretch from Ripogenus Dam to the Nesowadnehunk Deadwater. It begins as heavy water muscling its way through the vertical granite walls of Ripogenus Gorge. The river then emerges as a lengthy downstream glide before reaching the Nesowadnehunk Deadwater.

Dan Legere, owner of the Maine Guide Fly Shop & Guide Service in Greenville, rafts the gorge and opts for a driftboat on the lower river section. The Class I to Class IV rapids make this water best traveled by experts. I wholly recommend floating this river with a guide. It is an exhilarating experience with great fishing opportunities, and you will stay safe by being with someone experienced with the river.

To get to the West Branch, turn off I-95 at Medway and proceed to the town of Millinocket on ME 157/11. Find Golden Road (not the access road to Baxter State Park) – because Golden Road parallels the southern bank of the river upstream from the Nesowadnehunk Deadwater, most wading anglers fish this stretch. The first spot most anglers fish is Abol Bridge (45.835830,-68.966478) and Abol Campground where a road leads downstream to several productive areas. There are three large rapids in this area and fishing can be good above and below

West Branch of the Penobscot River as seen from Abol Bridge on the border of Baxter State Park. Photo courtesy Tim Shaw.

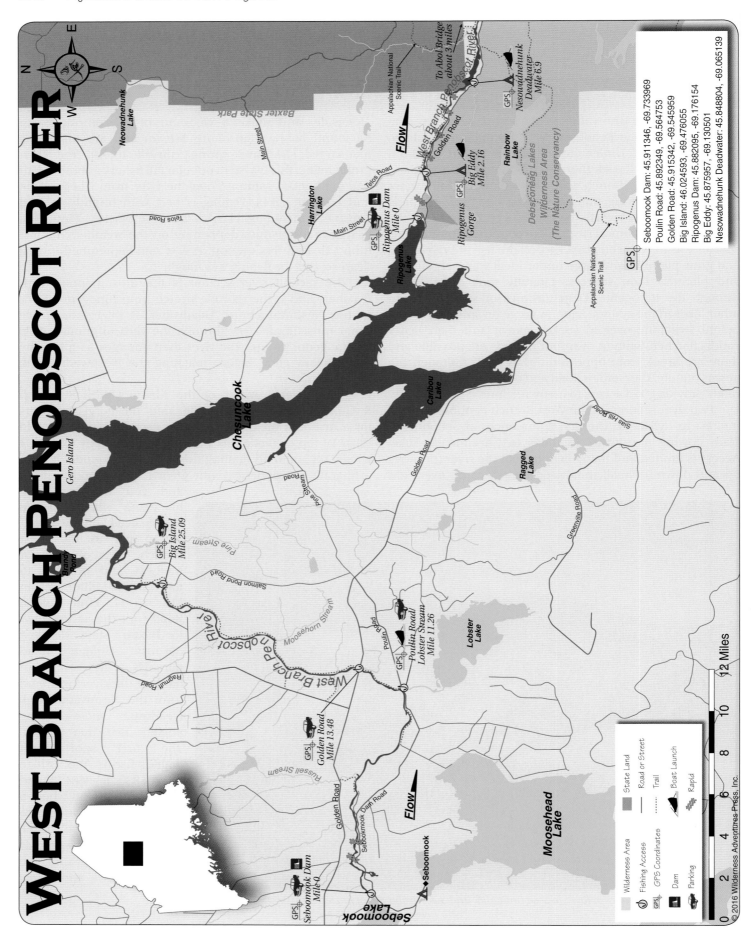

WEST BRANCH PENOBSCOT RIVER

Seboomook Dam: 45.911346, -69.733969
Poulin Road: 45.892349, -69.564753
Golden Road: 45.915342, -69.545959
Big Island: 46.024593, -69.476055
Ripogenus Dam: 45.882095, -69.176154
Big Eddy: 45.875957, -69.130501
Nesowadnehunk Deadwater: 45.848804, -69.065139

Neowadnehunk Lake

Baxter State Park

To Abol Bridge
about 3 miles

West Branch Penobscot River

Appalachian National
Scenic Trail

Flow

Golden Road

Nesowadnehunk
Deadwater
Mile 6.9
GPS

Rainbow Lake

Harrington Lake

Main Street

Telos Road

Big Eddy
Mile 2.16
GPS

Ripogenus Dam
Mile 0
GPS

Ripogenus Gorge

Debsconeag Lakes
Wilderness Area
(The Nature Conservancy)

Telos Road

Ripogenus Lake

Appalachian National
Scenic Trail

GPS

Chesuncook Lake

Caribou Lake

Ragged Lake

Stias Hill Road

Gero Island

Brandy Pond

Pine Stream

Pine Stream Road

Greenville Road

Big Island
Mile 25.09
GPS

Salmon Pond Road

Moosehorn Stream

Lobster Lake

Poulin Road

Lobster Stream
Mile 11.26
GPS

West Branch Penobscot River

Ragmuff Road

Poulin Road

Golden Road
Mile 13.48
GPS

Russell Stream

Flow

Moosehead Lake

Golden Road

Seboomook Dam Road

Seboomook

Seboomook Dam
Mile 0
GPS

Seboomook Lake

12 Miles

0   2   4   6   8   10

Legend

- Wilderness Area
- State Land
- Fishing Access
- Road or Street
- GPS Coordinates
- Trail
- Dam
- Boat Launch
- Parking
- Rapid

© 2016 Wilderness Adventures Press, Inc.

Fishing the evening hatch on the West Branch of the Penobscot River. Photo courtesy Tim Shaw.

Golden Road provides access to lesser fished pools and pocket water where the fish are less pressured (remember the road is a working logging road so be aware of large logging trucks). It pays to do a bit of scouting first to choose the best access points. Other spots to try are the Telos Bridge area (walk downstream from the small parking area there) and downstream from the visitors parking lot at Chewonki Campground.

In the spring, swinging smelt patterns such as the Black Ghost, or a local favorite, the Ripogenius Smelt are the way to go. Landlocks on this river are suckers for floating smelt imitations. These patterns are created with a foam body and mylar covering, or turkey quill, or a large parachute hackle over a long-shank hook dubbed with white and sparkle dubbing. Once the water warms in May, dry-fly patterns to try include the Dark Hendrickson (sizes 12 to 14) in June, the olive Elk Hair Caddis (sizes 14 to 16) in July, and Stimulators, including olive, yellow, and royal (sizes 8 to 10) in August. When nymphing, try the Giant Black Stone (size 6), beadhead Hare's Ear (size 12), and a beadhead caddis pupa (olive).

The West Branch is a perfect river to swing a small wet fly with an olive body. Salmon love to come up and hit the wet fly as it dangles in the current at the end of the drift.

The West Branch offers good hatches of the famous alder fly in June, the giant red sedges in late August, and golden stoneflies off and on all summer.

these spots. Walk to find interesting pools and pocket water.

Farther upstream, famous pools include Big Eddy (45.875957,-69.130501), Little Eddy, and Steep Bank Pool (not the only famous Steep Bank Pool in Maine). Fishing Big Eddy is not a wilderness experience as there are usually plenty of anglers and a campground is right there. There are schools of salmon in this very large pool, but they get fished to and can be particular. I have been frustrated there by seeing so many rising fish, but having none come to my fly. The salmon are usually feeding on one stage of some species of caddisfly, so I would bring my full assortment of larva, pupa, emergers, and adult imitations in all sizes and colors.

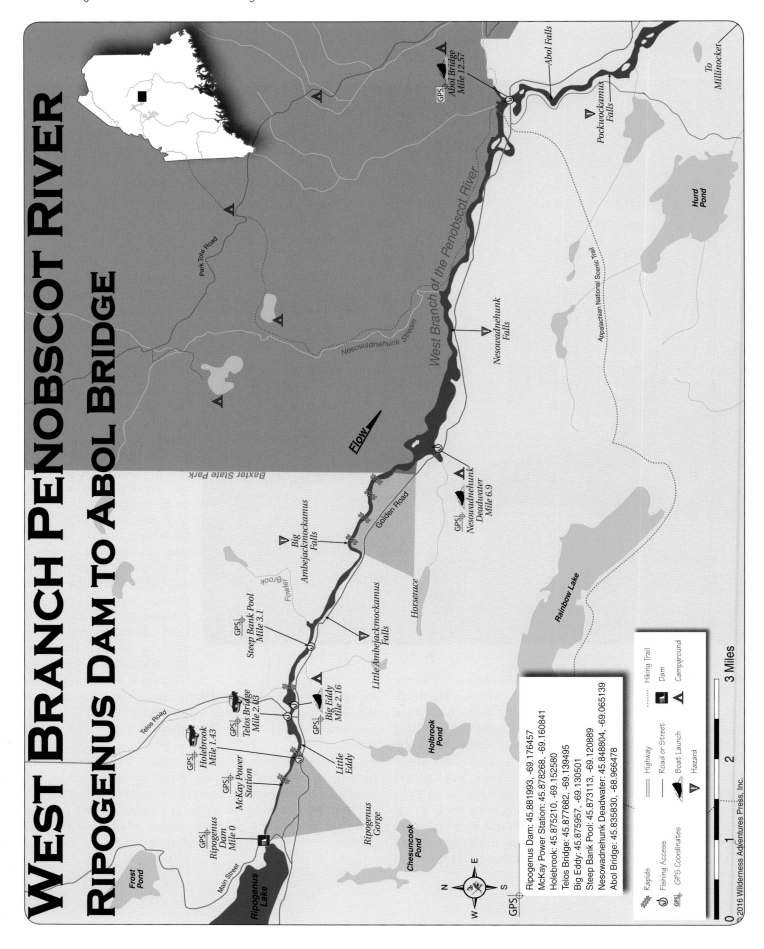

West Branch Penobscot River
Ripogenus Dam to Abol Bridge

Flow

Abol Bridge Mile 12.57

GPS

Abol Falls

To Millinocket

Pockwockamus Falls

Hurd Pond

West Branch of the Penobscot River

Nesowadnehunk Stream

Park Tote Road

Nesowadnehunk Falls

Appalachian National Scenic Trail

Baxter State Park

Golden Road

Nesowadnehunk Deadwater Mile 6.9

GPS

Rainbow Lake

Big Ambejackmockamus Falls

Fowler Brook

Steep Bank Pool Mile 3.1

GPS

Little Ambejackmockamus Falls

Horserace

Holbrook Pond

Big Eddy Mile 2.16

GPS

Telos Bridge Mile 2.03

GPS

Telos Road

Holebrook Mile 1.43

GPS

Little Eddy

McKay Power Station

GPS

Holbrook Pond

Ripogenus Gorge

Chesuncook Pond

Ripogenus Dam Mile 0

GPS

Frost Pond

Main Street

Ripogenus Lake

N E S W

GPS

Ripogenus Dam: 45.881993, -69.176457
McKay Power Station: 45.878268, -69.160841
Holebrook: 45.875210, -69.152580
Telos Bridge: 45.877682, -69.139495
Big Eddy: 45.875957, -69.130501
Steep Bank Pool: 45.873113, -69.120889
Nesowadnehunk Deadwater: 45.848804, -69.065139
Abol Bridge: 45.835830, -68.966478

Rapids
Fishing Access
GPS Coordinates
Highway
Road or Street
Boat Launch
Hazard
Hiking Trail
Dam
Campground

0   1   2   3 Miles

©2016 Wilderness Adventures Press, Inc.

EAST BRANCH PENOBSCOT RIVER

Views of Mount Katahdin, beautiful falls, and water flowing around rugged granite boulders highlight the spectacular scenery along this 40-mile river. This river is not really in the Moosehead area and could be included in the Baxter State Park write-up, but since the West Branch has just been covered, I am going to include it here.

The tailwater section starts at Lake Matagamon on the northeast border of Baxter State Park and joins with the West Branch near the small village of Medway. Matagamon is a productive brook trout, togue, and landlocked-salmon fishery. Most anglers troll but fish do rise at times – there is a good green-drake hatch in early July.

The East Branch is primarily a native brook trout fishery (up to 14 inches) and although a few hardy souls take multiday canoe trips, it is less arduous to access the river by taking rough dirt roads along the west bank from Lake Matagamon in the north or Whetstone Bridge in the south.

Some spots to try include below Lake Matagamon Dam, below Great Falls, at Spencer Rips, and the confluences of Lunksoos Stream and the Seboeis River. The area immediately below the Lake Matagamon Dam is off limits (note the red markers), but slightly below the dam is Matagamon Wilderness Campground and Cabins (www.matagamon.com) and the river on both sides (and on either side of the ME 159 bridge) fishes well in spring and fall. Sue and Joe own the campground, are very accommodating and run a top-notch operation. They can help you plan your fishing trips to all of the waters in the surrounding area.

The last time I fished the river near the campground, a large trout ate a soft-hackled Marabou Gray Ghost streamer in pretty good current and I chased him downstream 30 yards before the hook pulled out, damn it.

The upper East Branch area (above Matagamon Lake) includes a number of very lightly fished waters including Snake Pond, Fourth and Third Lakes, and the small rivers in between. Access is limited off of either Telos or Huber Road but if you don't mind exploring old logging roads, avoiding new beaver ponds, and have at least two spare tires with you, you can catch fish that have never seen a hook. One can also take a boat up Grand Matagamon Lake (Second and First Lakes combined into one when the dam was built) and up Webster Brook, another part of the headwaters. In the fall, it is worth making the 0.75-mile hike upstream from the boatable section to reach Webster Brook's so-called Grand Pitch (46.205497,-68.939449) where large trout and salmon stack up on their spawning runs. The first pool above the confluence with the lake is also well worth fishing (46.20574,-68.92336).

The Seboeis River is a major tributary and has good trout fishing in the spring, although the southern section below the steep and rocky Grand Pitch is increasingly being affected by annoying smallmouth bass. A multi-day canoe trip – putting in at the Grand Lake Road Crossing (near picturesque Shin Pond Village, 46.143018,-68.633602) and taking out at Lunksoos Camps – offers lots of fishing opportunities. The Grand Pitch must be portaged around, but there is an official campsite there and is a good base of operations to fish the Grand Pitch tailwater for its abundant brookies. Every tributary that enters the river also offers good action. If you spot a few rises, try any blue-winged olive or small mayfly imitation. Otherwise, small Baby Brook Trout, Black Ghost, or olive Woolly Bugger streamers will attract attention.

Most angler's fish attractor dry flies or caddis imitations that float well such as Wulffs, heavily-hackled Adams, or Elk Hair caddis. Nymphing works well in areas with moderate flow and even bottoms such as the tail-outs of pools. Try patterns with a hint of flash such as Zug Bugs, Flashback Pheasant Tails, Brassie's or Sim's Stones. A small Baby-brook-trout streamer sometimes attracts bigger fish.

The author fishing the East Branch near the Route 159 bridge, with Horse Mountain in the background. Photo courtesy Lindsey Rustad.

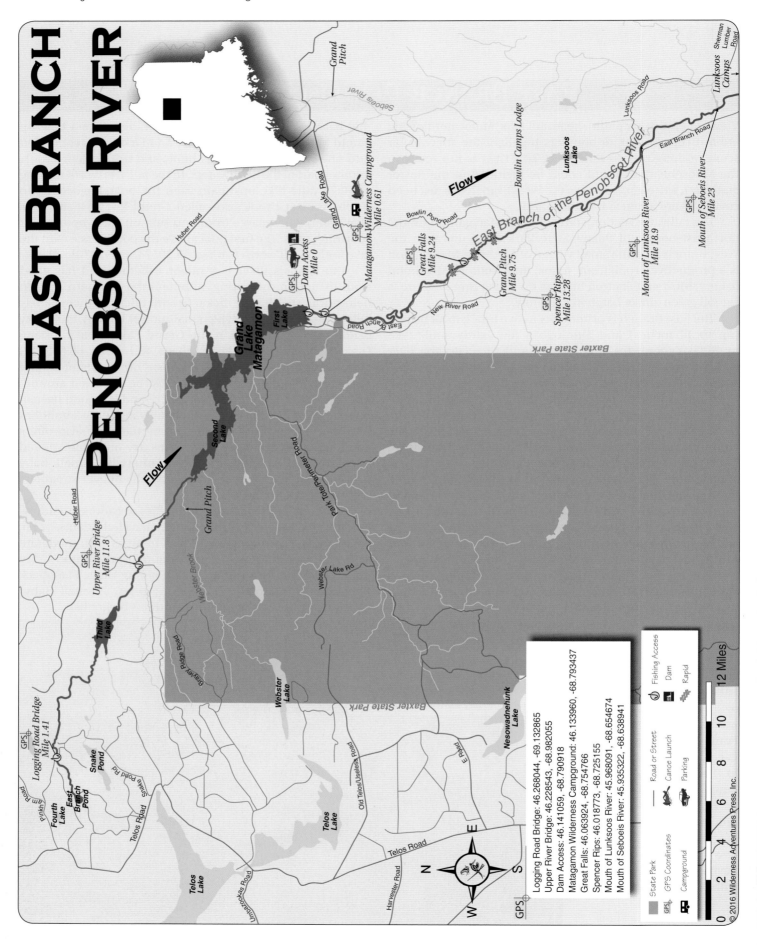

EAST BRANCH

PENOBSCOT RIVER

Grand Pitch

Seboeis River

Matagamon Wilderness Campground Mile 0.61

Grand Lake Road

Flow

Bowlin Camps Lodge

Lunksoos Lake

East Branch of the Penobscot River

East Branch Road

Lunksoos Camps

Sherman Lumber Road

Lunksoos Road

Bowlin Pond Road

Huber Road

Dam Access Mile 0

GPS

Great Falls Mile 9.24

GPS

Grand Pitch Mile 9.75

New River Road

Mouth of Lunksoos River Mile 18.9

GPS

Mouth of Seboeis River Mile 23

GPS

Spencer Rips Mile 13.28

GPS

First Lake

Grand Lake Matagamon

East Branch Road

Baxter State Park

Second Lake

Flow

Park Tote/Perimeter Road

Grand Pitch

Webster Brook

Upper River Bridge Mile 11.8

GPS

Huber Road

Webster Lake Rd

Braley Ridge Road

Third Lake

Logging Road Bridge Mile 1.41

GPS

Snake Pond

East Branch Pond

Fourth Lake

Pinky E Road

Snake Pond Rd

Telos Road

Old Telos/Useless Road

Webster Lake

Baxter State Park

Nesowadnehunk Lake

Telos Lake

E Road

Telos Lake

Telos Road

Harvester Road

Umzaooka Road

Logging Road Bridge: 46.268044, -69.132865
Upper River Bridge: 46.228543, -68.982055
Dam Access: 46.141059, -68.790918
Matagamon Wilderness Campground: 46.133960, -68.793437
Great Falls: 46.063924, -68.754766
Spencer Rips: 46.018773, -68.725155
Mouth of Lunksoos River: 45.968091, -68.654674
Mouth of Seboeis River: 45.935322, -68.638941

State Park	Road or Street	Fishing Access
GPS GPS Coordinates	Canoe Launch	Dam
Campground	Parking	Rapid

0 2 4 6 8 10 12 Miles

N E S W

© 2016 Wilderness Adventures Press, Inc.

UPPER KENNEBEC RIVER (EAST AND WEST OUTLET)

The Kennebec flows from the East and West Outlets of Moosehead Lake before carving a long, deep valley through the center of Maine. The West Outlet river section is about eight miles long and generally has sluggish flows compared to its cousin, the East Outlet. ME 15 north from the village of Greenville will take you to the headwaters, where there is a campground and hand-carried canoe put-in area. There is also access from Indian Pond. This water can be flyfished by small watercraft or on foot. West Outlet flows through a series of ponds and pools and is floatable only during periods of good water flow. There is a gravel road that parallels the river on the west bank and offers easy access for wading.

Kennebec's West Outlet season opens to fishing on April 1 and has a two trout limit. From August 16 to March 31, artificial lures only. All landlocked salmon must be released alive at once. Both outlets offer good flyfishing opportunities in October when much of the surrounding water is closed.

Pools, riffles, ample stillwater, and moderate flows provide a mixed bag of conditions, as well as game fish.

The connected ponds – Long Pond, Round Pond, and particularly Indian Pond – offer excellent smallmouth bass fishing as these fish thrive in this part of the river. Some contend that Indian Pond offers some of the best smallmouth bass fishing in the state, particularly in June, when the bass head for the shallows to spawn.

In the West Outlet section directly downstream from the dam (easily accessed from the road, 45.652348,-69.745061), anglers can anticipate 8- to 10-inch stocked brook trout along with the occasional wild fish. This river section is stocked annually by the state and is managed as a put-and-take fishery. I can attest to the fact that there are plenty of salmon in the pools below the dam as well, both in the spring and in the fall. One September, another fisherman and I landed over a dozen salmon in just a few hours. Some hardy anglers fish a few deep dead-water holes downstream from Route 15 early in the spring for very large brook trout that overwinter there.

Another access point that holds trout in the fall is Somerset Junction off of the Somerset Road that parallels the north bank.

Hooked up to a good salmon at the West Outlet.

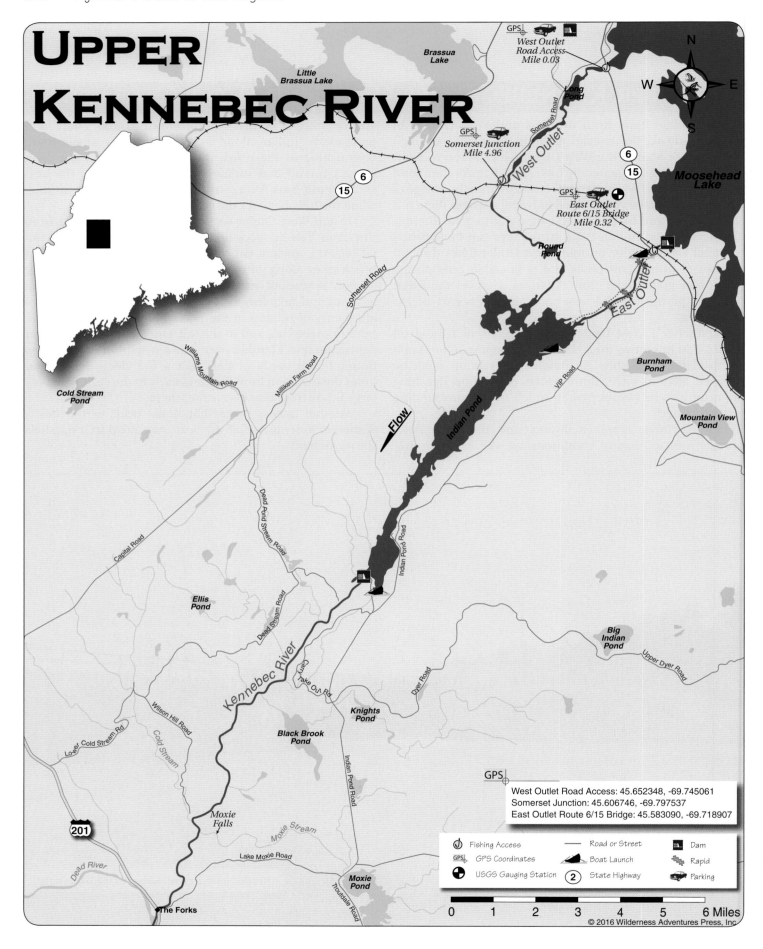

UPPER KENNEBEC RIVER

West Outlet Road Access Mile 0.03

Brassua Lake

Little Brassua Lake

Long Pond

Somerset Junction Mile 4.96

West Outlet

Moosehead Lake

6

15

6

15

East Outlet Route 6/15 Bridge Mile 0.32

Round Pond

Somerset Road

Milliken Farm Road

East Outlet

Williams Mountain Road

Cold Stream Pond

Indian Pond

Burnham Pond

VIP Road

Flow

Mountain View Pond

Capital Road

Dead Pond Stream Road

Indian Pond Road

Ellis Pond

Big Indian Pond

Upper Dyer Road

Kennebec River

Cold Stream

Carry Take Out Rd

Dyer Road

Wilson Hill Road

Knights Pond

Lower Cold Stream Rd

Black Brook Pond

Indian Pond Road

GPS

West Outlet Road Access: 45.652348, -69.745061
Somerset Junction: 45.606746, -69.797537
East Outlet Route 6/15 Bridge: 45.583090, -69.718907

201

Moxie Falls

Moxie Stream

Lake Moxie Road

Dead River

Moxie Pond

Troutdale Road

The Forks

Fishing Access
GPS Coordinates
USGS Gauging Station

Road or Street
Boat Launch
2 State Highway

Dam
Rapid
Parking

0 1 2 3 4 5 6 Miles

© 2016 Wilderness Adventures Press, Inc

The East Outlet of the Kennebec runs four miles from the dam at Moosehead Lake to Indian Pond (Moosehead is that rare lake that has two outlets, both of which empty into Indian Pond). This is a wide river with varied habitats from wide riffles to deeper runs and languid pools. Unlike other well-known fisheries with less fishable water that can get crowded, there is enough room for everyone on the East Outlet, particularly the farther you walk or bushwhack from ME 15.

The East Outlet is stocked heavily. Additionally, wild trout and salmon move down the fish ladder (or get sucked over the dam during high water) from Moosehead to the East Outlet in the spring and fall. They also will move up from Indian Pond. New arrivals are the easiest to catch. The best time to fish this water is May through July, and September and October. The dam at Moosehead is a top-release dam so the water can heat up to the point where many fish vacate the river by either moving down to Indian Pond or up to Moosehead Lake through the fish ladder. Anglers, particularly those in driftboats, do catch fish all summer. The East Outlet is open for fishing year around, and hearty anglers can do quite well through November and into December during warm spells.

There is access from both banks of the river. There are parking areas on both sides of the Route 6/15 bridge (45.583090,-69.718907). On the south bank, a good trail runs downstream to the Beach Pool and then a rough path continues farther downstream to Crib Pool. Upstream, anglers can use a dirt road to access the railroad trestle area. On the north bank, you can drive your car downstream to a mid-stream parking area and access the river from there, and walk a trail farther downstream all the way to Indian Pond. Several fabulous campsites are available along the river. Fire permits are required.

Because the East Outlet is a wide river with fish holding anywhere from bank to bank, a float trip is a great way to access unfished water or fish when the flows are high. It is a good idea to hire a guide, at least the first time as flows can change quickly, and there are Class II and Class III rapids.

Generally, anglers cast streamers in the spring and the fall and have good success nymphing with stoneflies and mayfly nymphs the rest of the year, switching to dries when they see a hatch or rising fish, particularly in the evening and in the more prominent pools.

The wild fish move around a lot on this river depending on water flow and availability of food sources. It pays to prospect with a fly that covers a lot of water and if you don't see signs of activity, move to another spot until you find active fish. Then stick around and try a variety of flies until you find what is working best that day. Stocked fish tend to stay where they are released (usually near spots where the stocking truck can access).

A cloudy day makes for good fishing weather at the dam on the East Outlet.

Stream Facts: East Outlet of the Kennebec River

Season
The East Outlet, from Moosehead Lake to the markers at Indian Pond, is open to fishing in October, and a shorter section, from the dam to the yellow markers at Beach Pool, is open to fishing year round. This is flyfishing-only, catch-and-release water. Special regulations apply to spawning areas after November 1.

Flows
The river typically flows at the 1,000 to 2,500cfs range. At the lower ranges, the river is difficult to float. At 3,000, it becomes difficult to wade, and above 5,000 difficult to driftboat effectively. Twenty-four hundredcfs is an ideal flow for both wading and drifting the river. To check the flow level, call the water line at 800-557-3569.

Species
Both wild and stocked brook trout and landlocked salmon. Most landlocked range from 14 to 18 inches. Brook trout range from 8 to 16 inches, occasionally larger.

Tackle and flies
This is a big river with long casting distances sometimes required, frequent wind, and larger fish, so a 6-weight rod with floating, sink-tip and sinking lines will cover you for most circumstances. Fish standard smelt streamers in the spring and fall. Nymphs would be black stoneflies, Copper Johns, Pheasant Tails, Zug Bugs, and Prince Nymphs. Fish caddis imitations that float well such as Puterbaugh Caddis, Goddard Caddis, and Stimulators. When in doubt, small muddlers fished on the bottom will tempt jaded fish (add weight or use beadhead if necessary).

Area Fly Shops
Wilson's (by the East Outlet) has opened the East Outlet Guide and Fly Shop.

MOOSE RIVER (BRASSUA LAKE TO MOOSEHEAD LAKE)

This section of the Moose runs three miles from Brassua Lake Dam to its mouth at Moosehead Lake near the village of Rockwood. Moderate currents, tumbling riffles, and deep pools create prime brook trout and salmon lies in this stretch. The dam's coldwater outflow from near the bottom of Brassua Lake creates good angling throughout the season in the upper mile of this flyfishing-only section. The lower two miles flow at lake level throughout the summer and are best fished by boat. Trolling is allowed below the red markers until August 16. Anglers take togue (lake trout) in this section immediately after ice-out.

The section of river immediately below the dam holds large fish that are "meat-eaters" thanks to the power turbines sending a constant chum line of chopped up smelts, yellow perch, and other baitfish into the Moose. Even when a caddis hatch brings smaller fish to the surface, the larger fish hang back and prefer to attack the rising fish. Action turns off and on, but when it is on, the Powerhouse Pool section can boil with activity. To catch the larger fish, cast large smelt or yellow perch imitation streamers into the major flows. Often, just letting the streamer drift with the current with an occasional twitch is the best way to fish. Use a strike indicator if you want to assist in detecting subtle grabs. Choose Black Ghost or Gray Ghost patterns with lots of marabou to undulate in the current.

Farther downstream, the fish are usually a little smaller and many anglers nymph, using large stoneflies as well as the usual assortment of Copper Johns, Pheasant Tails, and Prince Nymphs.

Stream Facts: Moose River

Seasons and Special Regulations
The Moose River is generally open to fishing from May 1 to September 30 with a number of special regulations. In the opinion of many, the Moose River has the most complicated and misunderstood fishing regulations in the state. Check current laws carefully in the Maine IF&W rule book for all the specifics on this highly regulated water.

Species
Brook trout, lake trout, landlocked salmon and smallmouth bass.

Flows
Generally in the 500 to 2,000cfs range. Higher flows are difficult to wade.

Access
From Route 16/5 take the dam road. There is a parking area on the south side of the dam with a toilet. A trail follows the river. You can also cross over the dam and follow a trail on the north bank. Many anglers bring a canoe to access more water. You can wade across in several areas and there are small islands from which you can fish.

To fish the Rock Pile or Gilbert Pool, park on Maynard Road on the north side of the river. To troll the lower river's flatwater section, use the Rockwood Boat Launch.

Fly Shops
Maine Guide Fly Shop, 34 Moosehead Lake Rd, Greenville / (207) 695-2266 / www.maineguideflyshop.com

As you approach the Moose River on Route 15, you will see the famous flying moose statue.

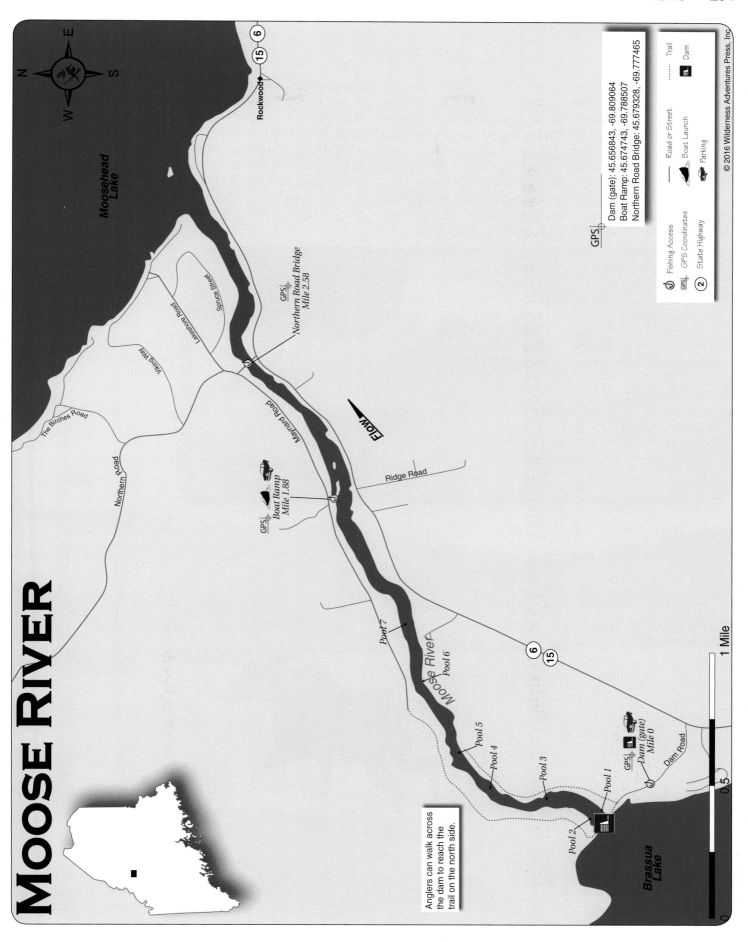

Moose River

Moosehead Lake

Rockwood

Spruce Street

Lakeshore Road

Viking Way

The Birches Road

Northern Road

Maynard Road

Northern Road Bridge
Mile 2.58

GPS

FLOW

Boat Ramp
Mile 1.88

GPS

Ridge Road

Pool 7

Moose River

Pool 6

Pool 5

Pool 4

Pool 3

Pool 1

Pool 2

GPS

Dam (gate) Mile 0

Dam Road

Brassua Lake

Anglers can walk across the dam to reach the trail on the north side.

GPS

Dam (gate): 45.656843, -69.809064
Boat Ramp: 45.674743, -69.788507
Northern Road Bridge: 45.679328, -69.777465

Fishing Access
GPS Coordinates
State Highway

Road or Street
Boat Launch
Parking

Trail
Dam

© 2016 Wilderness Adventures Press, Inc.

0.5   1 Mile

Wilson Pond Outlet

The outlet of Wilson Pond below its dam (45.456669,-69.530636) is a nice football-field-sized stretch of moving water. Both stocked and wild fish – trout and salmon – can be found there in spring and fall. Try small streamers such as a Wood Special, downsized Black Ghost, or a Baby Brook Trout. Access is just past the airport on the East Road.

Almost every small stream or brook in the Moosehead area contains wild or sometimes stocked brook trout. Access moving water from any road or trail, choose an upstream or downstream section and explore. The fish will most often be hand-sized but there are always surprises. The fishing is simple – a 6-foot 3-weight fly road with a short, relatively heavy leader (to pull out of branches) and a handful of Hornbergs, Wood Specials, Prince Nymphs, or small Muddlers should suffice. Be careful, this is wilderness and getting lost could be an overnight proposition. Don't wander away from your chosen stream and carry some form of GPS locator.

LEFT: Almost every stream in the Moosehead area contains brook trout.
BELOW: Moose!

MOOSEHEAD LAKE

This is such a large body of water that most of the fishing is done by trolling. But not exclusively. In the Lily Bay area in particular, there are good hex hatches during the summer, and on calm days you can see fish rising. It pays to be opportunistic and carry a fly rod. Still, remember that weather can change fast. I was on Moosehead one evening with flat, calm conditions, and the next morning after a weather front blew in, the lake looked like the ocean with three- or four-foot waves crashing on shore.

This lake is stocked with salmon and there is plenty of wild reproduction. Salmon range in size from 14 to 20 inches, but brook trout up to four pounds are possible.

Moosehead is also known for its togue that generally run two to four pounds, although 20-pounders live in the lake. Popular trolling spots include the area between Rockwood and Kineo. Togue can run a little bit larger if one trolls off "the toe of the boot" – a peninsula off the north side of North Bay.

Golden Road is the primary access road to a number of large lakes northwest of Moosehead including Chesuncook Lake and Lobster Lake, both part of the upper West Branch of the Penobscot River system.

Chesuncook Lake

This relatively unknown lake is the third largest body of water in Maine. It boasts a landlocked-salmon population along with lake trout and brook trout. The health of these fisheries is directly related to the health of the smelt population, which fluctuates. Most of the fishing with flies is trolling streamers behind boats and canoes. In the spring and fall, salmonids become more accessible when they chase spawning smelt or are interested in spawning themselves. The lake waters near the inlet and outlet streams such as Ragged Stream, Ripogenus Brook, Mud Brook, and Frost Brook will yield the best results.

Lobster Lake

This remote, undeveloped lake has limited access, and most folks put a small boat in at the Lobster Stream Road crossing adjacent to the West Branch (45.892579,-69.564143) and paddle up into the lake from there. This is a very picturesque lake with mountain views and good camping spots. There are large landlocked salmon to be caught by trolling a fly line but the fishing is fair at best. It is a place to go to experience the beauty of Maine and if you happen to hook a good fish, that is a bonus.

Other lakes off of Golden Road that offer good salmonid fishing include Seboomook Lake, Ragged Lake, and Harrington Lake.

Roach Ponds

A cluster of ponds – over 15 in all – lies to the east of Moosehead Lake. First Roach Pond sits in the tiny village of Kokadjo and is the source of the Roach River. There are six other interconnected Roach Ponds that stretch for 15 miles east of First Roach. First and Second Roach Ponds are the largest and the most developed with good road access and boat launches, and good populations of brook trout, lake trout, and landlocked salmon. Most anglers troll these ponds but in the spring, fish concentrate at the mouths of inlets and fly casting can be productive. In the spring and particularly the fall, fish will also concentrate right above the dam as they look for an outlet to spawn in, and can be fished to from shore.

The view of First Roach Pond from the village of Kokadjo.

MOOSEHEAD LAKE

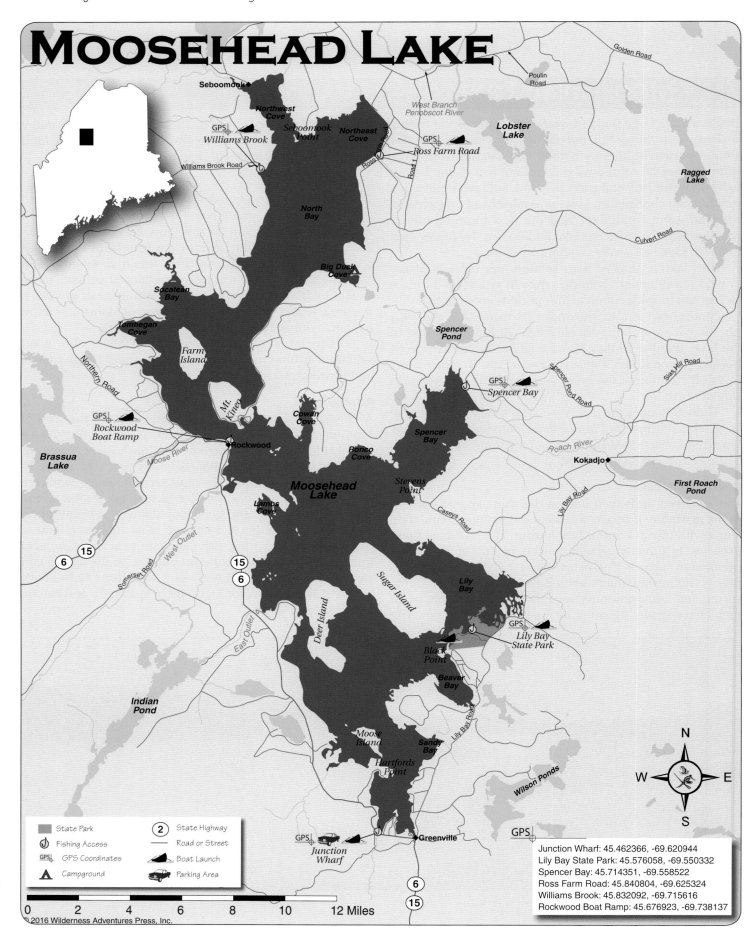

Junction Wharf: 45.462366, -69.620944
Lily Bay State Park: 45.576058, -69.550332
Spencer Bay: 45.714351, -69.558522
Ross Farm Road: 45.840804, -69.625324
Williams Brook: 45.832092, -69.715616
Rockwood Boat Ramp: 45.676923, -69.738137

Legend:
State Park
Fishing Access
GPS Coordinates
Campground
State Highway
Road or Street
Boat Launch
Parking Area

0 2 4 6 8 10 12 Miles

©2016 Wilderness Adventures Press, Inc.

Moosehead Area Remote Trout Ponds

There are dozens of ponds in the Moosehead area. Only a few are stocked, most have wild brook trout. Some have modest numbers of small trout, others have plentiful numbers of wild fish, and a few have trophies. Regulations vary. Access to most are by remote logging roads and it is easy to get lost. Wading can be difficult and limits your options. Some are best fished with a float tube while others are close enough to the road such that a small boat can be portaged in.

Safety precautions are in order. Let someone know where you are going and when you expect to be back. Cell phone reception is spotty at best. Make sure you have plenty of gas. Some logging roads – particularly if they have been recently graded – have sharp rocks that can easily give you a flat tire. Explore the ponds in one specific area so you become familiar with the access points instead of fishing one pond here and one pond there. It will save you a lot of wasted driving time and minimize the time you spend lost.

Secret Pond, Salmon Pond, Rum Pond, Indian Pond, Brown Pond, and Hedgehog Pond

Out of Greenville, take East Road which takes you to and then past the airport. This route takes you past these ponds. Secret and Salmon have good-sized fish, Rum has fast action with lots of small trout (though some up to 18 inches), Brown has 8- to 14-inch fish, and Hedgehog features fast action with smaller fish.

The ponds are a short distance away from the road, far enough so that carrying a float tube is preferable to dragging a kayak or canoe. Rum Pond has a good access road with good signage, leading to a parking lot with picnic tables (45.464018,-69.476155). Other ponds are accessed by grown-over grassy paths that you will drive by without noticing, so use GPS. Boats are available at each pond, left by local anglers, but you have to decide for yourself if it makes sense to borrow one that isn't chained to a tree. It is a good idea to arrive with your own life jackets and a paddle.

Ten Forty Pond, Bean Pond, and Rocky Pond

Also east of Moosehead Lake but north of the Roach Ponds is another cluster of remote ponds that come highly recommended for holding larger than average brook trout. Rocky is near Ripogenus Dam and is a 1.5-mile hike in (mostly uphill), but worth it if you don't mind the walk. Study your favorite map source and find Rocky Pond near the dam. Drive the dirt road towards Rocky from Golden Road until you can't proceed any farther, then hike up the hill and at the top, you will see the pond down to your left.

Ten Forty Pond and Bean Pond can be accessed off Golden Road on a logging road opposite the tip of Caribou Lake. Ten Forty (unnamed on my DeLorme Atlas) is right beside the road on the right and Bean is a little farther. As of this writing, they have blocked the road before you can reach Bean, so you have to walk the old road before looking for a hard-to-find trail to the right.

Prong Pond, First West Branch Pond, and Second West Branch Pond

A very accessible stillwater is 400-acre Prong Pond, about 15 minutes outside of Greenville up Lily Pond Road. It is stocked in the spring and offers immediate fast action. The boat launch is on the east side of the road on the north side of the pond (45.545451,-69.539577). For more information, see the chart listing ponds below. One additional note: As the water warms, this pond has many good sized white perch (in addition to smallmouth). A white marabou streamer with a conehead, jigged on sink tip line will tempt tasty white perch. First and Second West Branch Ponds also offer easy access and plentiful 6- to 12-inch trout.

Little Moose Pond and Big Moose Pond

The Little Moose Unit of Maine's Bureau of Parks and Lands sits just west of town. Little Moose Mountain lies within this area, along with several remote ponds that offer good

Often, local anglers leave their old boats at their favorite remote pond.

brook trout fishing. From the Moose Mountain Inn parking lot on ME 16/5, a ridgeline trail offers spectacular views of the Moosehead area until after about two miles it drops down to three ponds. Little Moose Pond offers fast fishing for plentiful brook trout and Big Moose Pond also fishes well. These ponds – no motorboats allowed - offer a truly wilderness experience even though they aren't very far from town. The Moose Mountain Inn is the closest lodging to the East Branch of the Kennebec, is reasonably priced, and the rooms have been recently updated.

There are another cluster of ponds west of Moosehead accessed from the Somerset Road, which is a good dirt road that goes off to the left, immediately after the West Outlet Bridge on Route ME 6/15. After 15 miles the road goes over a bridge and the next left takes you to Round and Island Ponds. In the same vicinity are Ellis, Horseshoe, Dead Stream, and others. There is a shorter access from Route 201 on the Capital Road. These ponds are all beautiful and give

you a true wilderness experience. A few of them will yield brook trout in the 12- to 18-inch range. I am not going to tell you which ones, you will have to discover that for yourself.

For Moosehead area remote ponds, fly choice is not usually critical. If fish are rising at all, Hornbergs in various sizes and colors, small Royal Wulffs, Parachute Adams, or small caddis imitations will draw strikes. If you are lucky enough to be on the water during a hatch of the larger mayflies, Wulffs in various colors or extended-body deer-hair green or yellow drakes are effective. Earlier in the season, it is hard to beat Doodle Bugs with red undersides. During summer, foam ants are a good choice in the evenings. If there are no signs of surface activity, sink-tip lines with black-nose dace imitations, Wood Specials, Woolly Buggers, leech patterns, and light Edison Tigers usually will drum up a few fish.

Here is a listing of 40 remote ponds within an hour's drive of Greenville. A few of the ponds I have listed above are not on this list.

Township	Water	Acres	Max. Depth	Avg. Depth	Fish	Gear	Min. length	Access
East Bowdoin College Grant	1st Little Lyford Pd	21	16'	5'	BKT-W	FFO	6"	T
Shawtown	1st, 2nd & 3rd West Branch Ponds	119	25'	8"	BKT-W	FFO	6"	R
East Bowdoin College Grant	2nd Little Lyford Pd	18	11'	5'	BKT-W	FFO	6"	T
West Bowdoin College Grant	Baker Pond	10			BKT-W	FFO	6"	T
Little Moose Twp. (Squaw)	Big Indian Pond	208	68'	31'	BKT-W, LKT-S	ALO	BKT-10", LKT-18"	T
Shawtown	Big Lyford Pond	152	40'	13'	BKT-W	FFO	6"	T
Little Moose Twp. (Squaw)	Big Moose Pond	91	96'	29'	BKT-W	ALO	10"	H
Little Moose Twp. (Squaw)	Big Notch Pond	12	40'	8'	BKT-W	ALO	10"	H
French Town	Bluff Pond	10	31'	15'	BKT-W	FFO	6"	H
Shawtown	Branch Pond	214	25'	7'	BKT-W	FFO	6"	R
West Bowdoin College Grant	Brown Pond	18	8'	4'	BKT-W	ALO		T
T7 R9 NWP	East Chairback Pond	46	58'	16'	BKT-W	FFO	12"	H
West Bowdoin College Grant	Fogg Pond	23	20'	10'	BKT-W	FFO	10"	H
West Bowdoin College Grant	Grassy Pond	5	7'	5'	BKT-W	FFO	6"	T
Greenville	Grenell Pond	6	18'	7'	BKT-W	NLFB	6"	T

Township	Water	Acres	Max. Depth	Avg. Depth	Fish	Gear	Min. length	Access
West Bowdoin College Grant	Hedgehog Pond	40	4'	2'	BKT-W	ALO	10"	T
West Bowdoin College Grant	Horeshoe Pond	160	35'	16'	BKT-W	FFO	6"	T
West Bowdoin College Grant	Indian Pond	70	26'	5'	BKT-W	ALO	18"	T
Little Moose Twp. (Squaw)	Little Moose Pond	25	50'	19'	BKT-W	NLFAB	6"	H
Little Moose Twp. (Squaw)	Little Notch Pond	10	21'	7'	BKT-W	ALO	10"	H
Taunton & Raynham	Long Pond	173	29'	9'	BKT-S, SMB-W	GL	BKT-6", SMB-12"	R
West Bowdoin College Grant	Mountain Brook Pond	21	11'	5'	BKT-W	FFO	8"	T
Beaver Cove Plantation	Mountain Pond	56	10'	5'	BKT-W	FFO	12"	H
Big Moose Twp. (Squaw)	Mountain View Pond	550	17'	9'	BKT-S	NLFB	6"	R
West Bowdoin College Grant	Notch Pond	10	24'	13'	BKT-W	FFO	10"	H
West Bowdoin College Grant	Pearl Pond #1	10			BKT-W	FFO	6"	T
West Bowdoin College Grant	Pearl Pond #2	8			BKT-W	FFO	6"	T
Beaver Cove Plantation	Prong Pond	427	27'	8'	BKT-S, SMB-W	GL	BKT-6", SMB-12"	R
Greenville	Rum Pond	245	77'	32'	BKT-W	ALO	6"-12" Slot	T
Greenville	Salmon Pond	12	15'	7'	BKT-W	ALO	C & R	T
Greenville	Sawyer Pond	67	23'	9'	BKT-S	GL	6"	R
Greenville	Secret Pond	14	34'	10'	BKT-W	ALO	6"-12" Slot	T
Greenville	Shadow Pond	17	38'	21'	BKT-S	NLFB	6"	R
Little Moose Twp. (Squaw)	Trout Pond	33	16'	7'	BKT-W	FFO	10"	T
West Bowdoin College Grant	Trout Pond	20	23'	6'	BKT-W	NLFB	6"	T

LEGEND

BKT=Brook trout	FFO=Flyfishing only	W=Wild
LLS=Landlocked salmon	ALO=Artificial lures only	S=Stocked
LKT=Lake trout	C&R=Catch & release	T=Trail
SMB=Smallmouth bass	H=Hike over 1/2 mile	R=Roadside
NLFB=No live fish as bait	GL=General law	

Information compiled by Maine Department of Inland Fish & Wildlife

BAXTER STATE PARK

Baxter State Park consists of over 200,000 acres of forested land around Mount Katahdin. The name Katahdin was derived from the Abenaki Indian name of Kette-Adene, translated as "greatest mountain" and was a holy place for these Native Americans. For some anglers who travel to Baxter every year, flyfishing this region also borders on a spiritual experience. Its remote location, lack of motor vehicle traffic, camping and hiking options, and the looming obelisk of Mount Katahdin in view most of the time, cannot be duplicated anywhere else in Maine or even New England, with the possible exception of New Hampshire's White Mountains. For those of you who have fished in the western United States, the experience is similar to fishing in one of the large western national parks like Yellowstone. Flyfishing in Baxter is all about fishing its remote trout ponds, although there are a few moving water options.

The most popular pond at Baxter is Chimney Pond, right at the base of the big mountain. The scenery is spectacular so I recommend hiking in to see it, but don't bother casting – there are no fish in it. There are however, over 40 ponds inside or adjacent to the park that have wild brook trout, and often, no other competing species. The ponds closest to the parking areas get fished regularly – the remote ponds, not so much.

Fishing in the park turns off and on. Many of these ponds are small and the water is very clear. During a hot, sunny day, it may seem as if the ponds are sterile because the flyfishing is so tough. However, on a humid evening after the sun is off the water, a mayfly hatch will cause the entire surface of the pond to come alive with rising and splashing fish. Ice-out can be as late as late May. The most consistent all-day fishing is mid-June to early July. In mid-summer, the fishing can still be good, but better in the early mornings and evenings.

The park authority has placed canoes in many of the ponds. Some have multiple canoes, others just one or two. Some are available as is; others are locked and require keys. There is an honor system and a $1-an-hour fee. For a listing of all of the Baxter Park ponds (including the fish they contain) and for all the specifics regarding canoes, check the website www.baxterstateparkauthority.com/outdoors/fishing.htm.

The southwest corner of the park sees most of the fishing pressure because Daicey and Kidney Ponds have rental cabins and roads leading directly to them. The park road to Daicey Pond leads to cabins that you can reserve and rent from the park. There is a campground there as well. You must bring in all of your bedding and supplies.

The fishing holds up surprisingly well despite the popularity of these ponds. Match the hatch if you see surface activity, otherwise prospect with a Hornberg on the surface or small bucktail streamers such as Baby Brook Trout or a Wood Special. Sometimes in early July there can be a good *Hexagenia* hatch and hex-nymph imitations such as a Hex Wiggle Nymph, a sparsely tied yellowish-brown Woolly Bugger, or the local Maple Syrup will be effective.

There are a cluster of ponds that can be hiked to in less than a mile from Daicey and Kidney Ponds, including flyfishing-only waters Draper, Rocky, and Lily Pad Ponds. For those interested in larger fish, try Celia Pond which can be reached by a trail on the left side of Kidney Pond.

The Matagamon Gate in the northeast corner of the park offers access to another group of ponds if you don't mind hiking a few miles. Access this entrance by following Route 159 (Grand

Chimney Pond in Baxter State Park.
Photo courtesy Five Lakes Lodge.

BAXTER STATE PARK

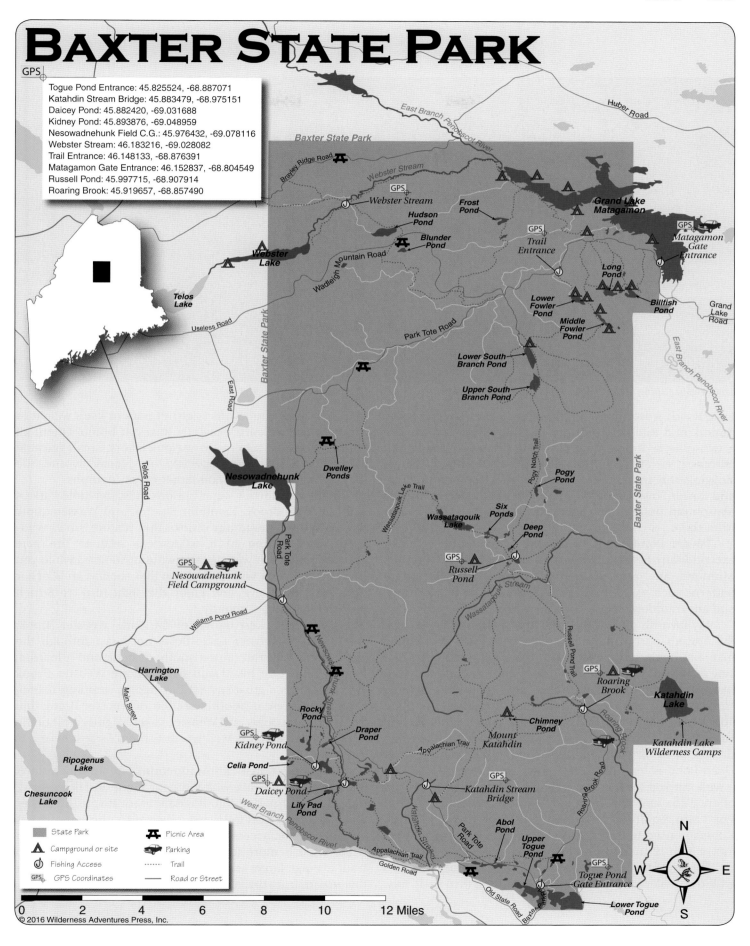

Togue Pond Entrance: 45.825524, -68.887071
Katahdin Stream Bridge: 45.883479, -68.975151
Daicey Pond: 45.882420, -69.031688
Kidney Pond: 45.893876, -69.048959
Nesowadnehunk Field C.G.: 45.976432, -69.078116
Webster Stream: 46.183216, -69.028082
Trail Entrance: 46.148133, -68.876391
Matagamon Gate Entrance: 46.152837, -68.804549
Russell Pond: 45.997715, -68.907914
Roaring Brook: 45.919657, -68.857490

Baxter State Park

Webster Stream

Frost Pond

Grand Lake Matagamon

Hudson Pond

Blunder Pond

Trail Entrance

Matagamon Gate Entrance

Webster Lake

Long Pond

Telos Lake

Lower Fowler Pond

Billfish Pond

Brayley Ridge Road

Wadleigh Mountain Road

Park Tote Road

Middle Fowler Pond

Useless Road

Lower South Branch Pond

Grand Lake Road

East Road

Upper South Branch Pond

East Branch Penobscot River

Pogy Notch Trail

Pogy Pond

Dwelley Ponds

Nesowadnehunk Lake

Wassataquoik Lake Trail

Six Ponds

Wassataquoik Lake

Deep Pond

Telos Road

Russell Pond

Park Tote Road

Nesowadnehunk Field Campground

Wassataquoik Stream

Williams Pond Road

Russell Pond Trail

Roaring Brook

Katahdin Lake

Harrington Lake

Main Street

Newsowadnehunk Stream

Rocky Pond

Chimney Pond

Katahdin Lake Wilderness Camps

Kidney Pond

Draper Pond

Mount Katahdin

Roaring Brook Road

Ripogenus Lake

Celia Pond

Appalachian Trail

Chesuncook Lake

Daicey Pond

Lily Pad Pond

Katahdin Stream Bridge

West Branch Penobscot River

Abol Pond

Upper Togue Pond

Park Tote Road

Appalachian Trail

Golden Road

Togue Pond Gate Entrance

Old State Road

Lower Togue Pond

Legend

State Park		Picnic Area	
Campground or site		Parking	
Fishing Access		Trail	
GPS Coordinates		Road or Street	

0 2 4 6 8 10 12 Miles

N W E S

Two anglers fishing Lower Fowler Pond in late September.

Lake Road) west from Patten, Maine. Lower Fowler, Long, Round, and Billfish Ponds are flyfishing only and require a two-mile or longer hike from the perimeter road (trail entrance is at 46.148133,-68.876391). Intrepid fishers slogging the muddy trails shortly after ice-out to Long and Lower Fowler Ponds may expect to land some one- or two-pound trout when casting streamers on sink-tip lines from shore.

Fowler Pond brook trout have a reputation of being exceptionally beautiful with a lot of yellow belly-coloring. Minnows are quite numerous in these ponds, so try patterns such as the Nine-three, Gray Ghost, Black Ghost, and any traditional black-nose dace imitations.

My favorite part of Baxter is the Russell Pond area in the interior part of the park which requires a seven-mile hike, but has very little fishing pressure. It makes sense to stay at Russell Pond and use it as a base of operations for hiking to other ponds. You cannot purchase anything there, so make sure you bring in adequate food and supplies. There is usually fast fishing for small trout in Russell and Deep Ponds. In early July, Russell has a good hatch of green drakes so bring your Wulffs and green-drake imitations. Deep Pond is less than a mile hike from Russell Pond on a well-marked trail. It is a great dry-fly pond because it is often calm and the trout are always accessible. Center Pond also requires a long walk, and longtime guide Wiggy Robinson used to call it "Mecca" because it was filled with lots of 8- to 12-inch trout.

For larger trout, try Six Ponds. The best fishing coincides with the peak of the black fly season – June thru early July.

Life is all about trade-offs (sigh). It pays to keep weight to a minimum, so leave heavy fly boxes at home. Often, all you need are Hornbergs in various colors, small bucktail streamers, a few Wood Specials, or a local favorite, the Maple Syrup, which imitates larger mayfly nymphs.

There are moving-water options in Baxter State Park as well. Roaring Brook, Katahdin Stream, and Wassataquoik Stream are all mountain brooks that feature small wild-brook-trout fishing in a wilderness setting. The best approach is to wet wade (wade without waders) while you boulder hop, stick with one or two flies such as an Elk Hair Caddis or Hornberg, and enjoy the sight of 6- to 8-inch brookies slashing at your fly.

In the northwest corner of the park, Webster Brook, the outlet of Webster Lake, flows northeast through the park. There is a trail on the southern bank and a lean-to. People who have hiked and fished along Webster Brook say that this is a great several-day hiking/camping/fishing adventure. There is another section of Webster Brook that flows between Telos and Webster Lakes, slightly west of the park boundary that is well worth fishing. Easiest access is by boat.

Another option is Nesowadnehunk Stream which starts at the outlet of the lake with the same name and flows for 12 miles before entering into the Penobscot River. The Baxter State Park loop road follows the river for a number of miles and offers good access. This is a larger river – about 30 feet wide – and is more fertile than other nearby streams, so trout average larger (around 10 inches). Larger trout enter this stream from the lake to spawn in the fall.

Additional Piscataquis County Notable Flyfishing Waters

Piscataquis County north and east of Moosehead and Baxter State Park encompasses large acreage. I have divided it up by southern, eastern, western/central, and northern regions since each area is separated by significant travel times. Anyone wishing to explore this area should purchase from Delorme, The Maine Atlas and Gazetteer, an essential orienteering resource for this area, and all of Maine.

Southern Piscataquis County

Southern Piscataquis County is generally considered the area around Dover-Foxcroft and Guilford and has more of an agricultural feel to it as some of the waters here border cultivated land on small farms. All of the following rivers and streams are within half an hour of each other and are stocked regularly; the Piscataquis River (both brown and brook trout) runs through town, Dunham Brook (north of town), Black Stream (ME 7 south), and Alder Stream (ME 15 south). Closer to the town of Monson, for early spring action, try Monson Pond for salmon and togue, but don't neglect nearby tiny Goodell Brook for 6- to 10-inch native brook trout. For other fishing options in this general area, see the Western Penobscot County Stillwaters section on page 292.

Eastern Piscataquis County

In eastern Piscataquis County, the Appalachian Mountain Club (AMC) has purchased several sporting camps clustered northeast of Moosehead on conservation land. They offer a chance to enjoy the outdoors under pristine conditions while staying at historic, but renovated sporting camps. In addition to hiking (I recommend walking into Gulf Hagas), and boating, there is of course fly fishing. Little Lyford Camps on Little Lyford Pond, Medawisla Lodge and Cabins on Second Roach Pond (closed for renovations in 2015), and Gorman Chairback Lodge on Long Lake offer angling for wild brook trout on a number of ponds. Lyford Camp also offers moving water fishing on the West Branch of the Pleasant River. For more detailed information and access options, go to www.outdoors.org/lodging/lodges.

Other fly-fishing only, hike-in stillwaters found east of Moosehead Lake are best reached from Route 11 southwest of Millinocket. Little Pleasant Pond and its tributary waters, the three Birch Ridge Ponds, and Fox Pond are located not far from the Appalachian Trail off Johnston Road and J-Mary Road in TA RI1 WELS. Further south, East Chairback Pond and West Chairback Pond (up to three-pound brook trout) can be reached from the Appalachian Trail a short distance from where it crosses the Katahdin Ironworks Road northwest of the village of Brownville Junction. Check in with the AMC for latest access and the availability of canoes.

Central and Western Piscataquis County

The Golden Road, north from the village of Millinocket and about nine miles west of Interstate 95, is the gateway to the remote stillwaters, rivers and streams of central and western Piscataquis Country, north of Moosehead Lake.

On the western border of Baxter State Park are several fly-fishing only waters including Nesowadnehunk Lake, also known as Sourdnahunk Lake, and Little Nesowadnehunk Lake in T5 R11 WELS. The larger lake contains lots of eight- to 14-inch trout, the smaller one has fewer fish but they are larger (up to 16 inches). Access is from East Road and Telos Road east of the Telos Checkpoint. Nesowadnehunk, or Sourdnahunk Stream, the outflow of the lakes, is a flyfishing-only tributary of the West Branch Penobscot River. These waters offer excellent brook trout fishing. When Maine I.F.&W. trap-netted these waters, they found a large number of trout in the one- to two-pound range. At that size, they still rise to dry flies but also put quite a bend in a 4-weight rod.

Northern Pisacataquis County

Northern Pisacataquis County is the large area generally north of Baxter State Park. It is part of Maine's Great North Woods and provides a true wilderness experience for those who enjoy fishing for wild trout in an unspoiled setting. There is a variety of waters that would take a lifetime to fish and certainly more than I could mention here, so let me suggest a few ways for you to explore this area.

One option is to stay at one of the sporting camps that serve this area. Immediately north of Baxter State Park is Libby Camps (www.libbycamps.com). It is one of the best known and is located off Oxbow Road on Millinocket Lake (the one north of Baxter State Park, not the one south of the town of Millinocket). They own two seaplanes and 10 remote cabins in excellent fishing locations that they fly you to. They also have 80 canoes in 30 fishing locations within 20 miles of their lodge.

Bradford Camps is another option on Munsungan Lake (www.bradfordcamps.com). They also have remote cabins and a float plane to assist you in getting to where you want to go.

If you are interested in exploring on your own, several very good gravel roads transect the area from east to west. These roads are well maintained and you can travel at a good rate of speed and cover miles quickly. The only caveat is that after a recent road grading, sharp rocks are exposed and flat tires are a common occurrence. Be prepared with spares or repair kits, and go slow. I get a flat tire every time I travel when they are grading the roads.

One access point is Ashland (due west from Presque Isle). You can travel west on American Realty Road for a short distance and then take Pinkham Road. This will take you across west Penobscot County and then all the way across northern Piscataquis County. Another option is to exit ME 11 to the tiny settlement of Oxbow (46.418793,-68.491727) and take Oxbow Road west until it intersects with Pinkham Road near Munsungan Lake. Huber Road runs north from ME 159 on the eastern border of the park, continues below Millinocket Lake, and offers a way to reach more waters above the northern park border. You will be required to stop, register, and pay a fee at checkpoints as you enter and leave the designated North Woods area on all of these roads.

Aroostook River, Millinocket Stream, Munsungan Stream
Some good moving-water options north of the park are the Aroostook River and its tributaries, Millinocket and Munsungan Stream, both near Libby's and Bradford Camps and also accessible from Oxbow Road. Munsungan Stream is the smallest of the group, and Musungan Falls and a beautiful small campground can be found on Pinkham Road, just east of the intersection with Oxbow Road (46.368308,-68.917464).

Millinocket Stream is more of a river than a stream and offers good brook trout fishing, especially away from Oxbow Road if one canoes up or downstream from the bridge at Moosehorn Crossing (46.332026,-68.781072). There is a logging road that parallels the stream upstream.

Little Pillsbury Pond and Currier Ponds

ABOVE: Fishing Munsungan Falls during late summer low flows.
LEFT: The Huber Road is a typical North Maine Woods artery.
Photo courtesy Erika Zambello

A very large blueback trout. Photo courtesy Maine I.F.&W.

Farther west from the area just described are a number of interesting ponds to fish. John Boland, the former Maine Inland Fish and Wildlife Director suggested the following ponds: Little Pillsbury Pond off of the Pinkham Road and the 47 Mile Connector, and the Currier Ponds (One through Six) that are clustered together west of Munsungan Lake.

The six stillwaters known as Currier Ponds are found off Pell & Pell Road in T9 R11 WELS. Some of these ponds produce big trout. For lodging options near these ponds, Spider Lake and others, contact Macannamac Camps (www.macannamac.com).

Big Reed Pond

If you are interested in trying a truly unique fishery, 90-acre Big Reed Pond hosts a relic from the last glacial period: the blueback trout. This is an arctic char that survives in only a few waters in Maine and nowhere else in the continental U.S., and is the same fish that fed the huge brook trout in the Rangeley area before they were exterminated in the early 1900s. Bluebacks have survived in Big Reed Pond, although it has taken quite a conservation effort. They were almost gone less than a decade ago because rainbow smelt had been illegally introduced and were out-competing them. Maine Fish and Wildlife and other conservation groups captured the remaining bluebacks and moved them to a hatchery for breeding and safe keeping. The pond was then poisoned with rotenone, and then over several years, the native blueback and brook trout were placed back in the pond. Brookies are thriving with fish that weigh several pounds caught on occasion. The blueback story is a bit more mixed with very few of these char showing up in research nets.

You can fish Big Reed Pond and catch an actual blueback trout. It is a pretty good haul to get there; at least an hour from the nearest North Woods checkpoint. South-southeast of the pond is an access road at mile marker 45 on the Pinkham Road. After crossing the pond outlet, the trailhead is in a small clearing. Reaching Big Reed Pond requires a 1.5-mile hike in from the access road. The hike itself is fascinating because the obscure trail passes through a 10,000-acre old-growth forest protected by the Maine Nature Conservancy. You will reach the pond just north of the outlet stream. The Nature Conservancy keeps a couple of canoes at the outlet and use is on a first-come first-served basis.

Big Reed Pond bluebacks are not easy to catch but the native brook trout are, so my guess is you won't get totally skunked. The regulations are obviously catch and release only.

Mooseleuk Stream

In far northern Piscataquis County lies Mooseleuk Stream, the outflow of Mooseleuk Lake in T10 R9 WELS. It is a tributary of the Aroostook River. This stream is flyfishing only and restricted to catch and release for landlocks. Chase Road and Mooseleuk Dam Road follow the river north from Pinkham Road. Little Pleasant Pond, in T10 R11 WELS, is west of Mooseleuk Lake and accessible from an extension of Jack Mountain Road. Expect fast fishing for 8- to 14-inch trout.

Brown Brook Pond

Brown Brook Pond also has lots of trout and lies in T9 R9 WELS and is reached from an access road located near the ranger station off Pinkham Road. Ragged Pond is accessible off Pell & Pell Road and Island Pond Road in T9 R10 WELS.

Coffelos Pond

To the west, Coffelos Pond is a flyfishing stillwater located in the Allagash Wilderness in T6 R11 WELS. Access is available from Telos Road, running north from Golden Road near Big Eddy Pool and the West Branch Penobscot River.

Spring Pond

To the east, Spring Pond is located in T7 R10 WELS and can be reached from an extension of Huber Road 20 miles northwest of the village of Shin Pond and Route 159. A number of other ponds can be found in the same general area but this is remote county, so be prepared.

Western Penobscot County Stillwaters

West Garland Pond

West Garland Pond is a brook trout pond located about 4.5 miles east of the village of Dexter on Route 94. There is a two-fish limit, with a minimum length of eight inches. Brookies typically run from 8 to 10 inches. Fish stonefly-, damselfly-, and dragonfly-nymph imitations. A hand-carried boat launch off Valley Avenue Road at the east end of the pond will put you on this small fishery.

Wassookeag Lake

Wassookeag Lake, in the town of Dexter, holds brookies, lake trout, and landlocked salmon. According to the Maine Department of Inland Fisheries and Wildlife, this 1,062-acre impoundment is highly oxygenated and the cold depths (to 86 feet) produce some good trout. Salmon angling is limited, despite the ongoing salmon-stocking program. Lake trout angling is particularly good. The 20-inch length, one-fish limit on togue sees four-pounders caught with regularity. Streamers catch many fish right after ice-out on the lake's rocky shallows. Two boat launches are available off Crockett and North Dexter Roads not far from downtown Dexter.

Cold Stream Pond

Cold Stream Pond, located in Enfield, holds brook trout, togue, and landlocked salmon. Please check the current regulations. Brook trout run from 8 to 12 inches. Fish beadhead Pheasant Tails, small Woolly Buggers, and dries such as Elk Hair Caddis and blue-winged olive patterns. A boat launch is available off Route 188, which runs through the village of Enfield (45.247376,-68.561717).

LEFT: New flyfishers dream of catching their first landlocked salmon. Photo courtesy Ben Rioux.
BELOW: Millinocket Stream at Moosehorn Crossing is lined with mature evergreens. Photo courtesy Erika Zambello.

Eastern-central Maine Planning Considerations

Nearby Hub Cities and Towns

- Greenville (www.mooseheadlake.org, www.maineguideflyshop)
- Millinocket (www.katahdinmaine.com)

Easy Access Options

- In Kokadjo, fish the upper Roach River. From the large parking lot at the dam on Lily Pond Road (45.671729,-69.446230), it is just a few steps to the Dam Pool. Fish hold here all year. It is a short walk down a straight and level dirt road to the next major pool, the Dump Pool, but it is a bit of scramble to get down to the water. The fish in these two pools do see more than their share of flies so for consistent success, try patterns that are somewhat unique that the trout and salmon haven't seen before. Also try fishing at first light or at dusk.
- There is a nice pool directly below the dam at the West Outlet of the Kennebec, just upstream from ME 15. Look for a small paved parking area on the left as you head north, just past the bridge over the river. The area around this pool is mowed, with stairs and an easy route over the dam so you can fish both sides.

The salmonids here are subjected to many flies, so it pays to fish something that they haven't seen before. One September day, I fished traditional streamers such as the Black Ghost and Wood Special, as well as a proven attractor dry-fly (the Royal Wulff), and didn't get as much as a look from a trout. A few very small caddis were flitting about, and when I tied on a size-18 Puterbaugh Caddis on 6x tippet, salmon and brook trout appeared as if from nowhere, and started hitting my fly with abandon. So try smaller fare, down to size 20, on lighter tippets.

- Rum Pond, just a few minutes east of Greenville on the East Road, has excellent signage showing the way in, a nice parking lot with picnic tables, and a short walk to the pond. It offers a wilderness pond for folks that are a little nervous about finding ponds with less defined access.
- The East Branch of the Penobscot River flows right through the Matagamon Wilderness Campground by ME 159 (46.134118,-68.793136). In the campground there are mowed grass surfaces right down to the river with plenty of backcast room. You don't need to wade and, despite fishing pressure, there are plenty of wild brookies in the spring and fall.

The East Outlet is a good place for beginners.

Suggested Beginner Options

- Carry a stable canoe into an accessible remote pond for an evening of fishing. I recommend Prong, Rum, Secret, and Salmon Ponds near Greenville since they are close to town, small, calm, and a very short walk from the car. Kneel in the canoe for good stability; have one person cast while one manages the canoe. Fish a small Hornberg dry fly. There is no need to cast more than 10 feet from the canoe and once your fly is on the water, keep it there. You should catch a few fish.
- You might try Millinocket Stream near Millinocket. This moving water is kind to beginners.
- Fish the East Outlet of the Kennebec at the following spot. Drive north on ME 15, cross the East Outlet, take a left and drive down the dirt road that follows the north bank of the river. After a short distance, there will be an obvious parking spot with an equally obvious trail downhill to the river (45.583282,-69.722512). It is easy to wade out a short distance or along the shore and the current here is modest. Both stocked and wild trout and salmon can be found here. Try a Hornberg here as well, either fished as a dry or retrieved just under the surface.
- Stay at Libby's or Bradford Camps. They will find you water with naïve brook trout where you can practice, and guides there can give you pointers.

Vacation Suggestions

Weekend Getaway

- Pack your float tube, your bug spray, and your hex patterns and spend a weekend in late June or early July fishing any of the remote trout ponds in this part of Maine. Consult with the local fly shop, choose

Osprey have made a huge comeback in Maine and are now quite common along the Penobscot River.

several ponds close to one another with the same road access, and have fun. There is a variety of lodging options right in Greenville, and there are many ponds within 45 minutes of town. It gets light at 4:00am and the hexes will not emerge until the evening or later, so you can cram 16 hours of fishing in during just one day.
- Stay in the Millinocket area and fish the West Branch of the Penobscot for one day and explore a few of Baxter State Park's ponds on Sunday.
- Camp at the Matagamon Wilderness Campground and fish the East Branch of the Penobscot and Grand Lake Matagamon. You can also try your luck at any of the hike-in ponds in the northeast corner of Baxter State Park, only a short car ride (and hike) away. If you plan your trip for early July, biting insects will be diminished and you might catch the green drake hatch on the lake.

One-week Vacation

- Take a solid week to explore Baxter State Park anytime in June, early July, or late September. Spend some time researching so you can camp at the campground closest to the ponds or streams that you want to fish. Reserve your spots early and figure out if you are going to rent canoes that are supplied on some of the ponds or carry a float tube in. The park is spectacular, as is the fishing. If you are physically fit, reserve one day to climb Mount Katahdin, the tallest mountain in Maine. Baxter State Park is too magnificent for your trip to be all about the fishing.
- During the latter part of September, stay in Greenville and sample all of the great rivers in the area when larger trout and salmon move into the rivers on their spawning runs. Also take the time to look up at the spectacular fall foliage that usually peaks about the third week in September. Since you will be staying a week, carefully consider the type of lodging that you prefer and that fits your budget. I usually stay on the lake at the Chalet Moosehead Lakefront Motel. Clean, basic rooms with a lake view, spacious grounds with grills, and very reasonably priced. As far as the fishing goes, consider the following six-day itinerary.
  1. Float the West Branch of the Penobscot with a guide.
  2. Explore the Roach River.
  3. Fish the West Outlet.
  4. Fish the East Outlet.
  5. Fish the Moose River.
  6. Try some local small ponds in a float tube.
  7. Fish your favorite river (or stretch of river) again.

Eastern Maine

Eastern Maine, sometimes referred to as "Downeast", is a unique part of New England. The land is still rising by ice several miles high after being compressed during the last ice age. This has yielded a fascinating topography with myriad wetland, bogs and springs, and some high points such as the hills and mountains of Mount Desert Island. Eastern Maine includes, from west to east, Penobscot, Hancock and Washington Counties.

While fishing for Atlantic salmon is now closed, efforts to restore the fishery continue. Progress is being made with dam removals on the Penobscot River, genetic studies, and new propagation techniques including in-stream egg incubation. It is my fervent hope that Atlantic salmon stocks will increase over time and fishing can be restored in my lifetime.

Downstate the other salmon rivers (the Dennys, Machias, Pleasant, and Narraguagus) are barely sustaining their meager stocks. Despite major efforts to restore the wild Atlantic salmon that started in 1948 with the creation of the Atlantic Sea-run Salmon Commission, progress has been difficult.

Today, you may find it interesting to visit the Downeast Salmon Federation's facilities/hatcheries on the Pleasant River in Columbia Falls and on the Machias River in East Machias, Maine. Depending on the time of year, you may get to see salmon smolts being raised before release and see exhibits about the latest plans for salmon and watershed restoration.

BROOK TROUT FISHING

What I say here holds true for all of eastern Maine, including Penobscot, Washington and Hancock Counties. Countless small brooks, tributary streams, ponds, and bogs hold native brook trout. The trout are usually less than 12 inches and populations fluctuate depending on drought, beaver activity, availability of good food sources, and competition from other species. I couldn't possibly list all the fisheries, and I haven't fished but a handful. Two examples are Lord Brook in the small town of Grand Falls and Cold Stream in Enfield.

The best strategy is to choose a road and explore. Small tributaries of most of the major river systems hold brookies, including tributaries of the Machias, Pleasant, and St. Croix

Rivers. A number of streams cross under ME 9, which bisects much of this section. But any road with culverts can yield a stream worth investigating. Pull off the road and explore. This type of fishing includes a fair amount of bushwhacking, and you will encounter beaver bogs, blow downs, biting insects, and other challenges. Some of the larger streams are best fished from a small canoe, but that also can include dragging your watercraft around fallen trees or bony water. Many find this type of fishing rewarding despite the bites, scratches, and exertion. The reward is a stretch of stream or perhaps a few deep holes, relatively unfished, where beautiful wild brookies rise willingly to your fly.

Mainstem Penobscot River

The mainstem of the Penobscot River begins at the confluence of the west and east branches at the town of Medway, and reaches the tidal waters in Bangor after a journey of 70 miles. Its main claim to fishing fame today is its excellent smallmouth bass fishing. The best way to experience this fishing is to float a section of river, fishing as you go. A canoeist can choose from multiple put-ins and take-outs from paved roads on both sides of the river. Under normal water flows, rips or tricky currents are minimal below Lincoln. Despite the river's proximity to several towns including Bangor, it maintains a natural character and wildlife abounds. The water quality improves every year. I floated the section of river below the town of Howland one day and thoroughly enjoyed it.

Mattawamkeag River

The Mattawamkeag River is a major tributary of the West Branch of the Penobscot River. The upper river consists of both east and west branches where the fishing can be very good for 6- to 12-inch brookies in the spring. With reasonable spring water flows, this section can be floated in a canoe.

The section between the villages of Kingman and Mattawamkeag is the most accessible and offers good fishing for brook trout and bass. An unimproved road off US 2 in Mattawamkeag follows the river on the south side and leads to the Mattawamkeag Wilderness Park where campsites are available. The river has dangerous rapids in the spring and should only be canoed by experts. From the ME 171 bridge in Reed Plantation downstream to the ME 170 bridge in Kingman, the river remains open to open-water fishing from October 1 through December 31, but is catch and release and artificials only. Pattern choices include Marabou Leeches (sizes 4 to 6, black or olive), beadhead Pheasant Tail nymphs (sizes 12 to 18), stonefly nymphs (sizes 4 to 12) and Woolly Buggers (sizes 2 to 8 in black or brown). Please check current regulations for this river, which vary by section.

Mopang Stream, Old Stream, and the Crooked River

Mopang Stream, Old Stream, and the Crooked River all hold native brookies and can be accessed off of ME 9. A small canoe can be helpful to cover more water. Best bet is to fish south from the road (your right hand side as you are heading east).

The Mattawamkeag River hosts brook trout and landlocked salmon, like this handsome specimen.

ACADIA NATIONAL PARK

Maine's only national park is very popular and is the 10th most visited national park in the United States. It is located on Mount Desert Island next to the town of Bar Harbor, about an hour's drive from Bangor, in Hancock County. While it is known for its fabulous ocean views, exposed granite peaks, carriage, hiking and biking roads, it also has a number of ponds and lakes populated by trout, salmon, and bass. Most of the waters are stocked every spring. These ponds are so picturesque and peaceful, that I enjoy every minute on the water even if the fish aren't active that day. Even though it can get crowded in the summer along the coastal routes, I guarantee that if you fish the inland ponds early or late in the day, you will leave 95 percent of the tourists behind. If you find yourself taking a family vacation to Acadia, include flyfishing as part of your itinerary, you won't regret it. Most waters are easily accessible and best fished with a small boat such as a canoe or kayak, although casting from shore can be productive in spring and fall. The waters aren't large and you don't want to mess with a boat trailer, given the tourist traffic.

There are 16 ponds within the park boundaries and nearby Mount Desert Island locations. I am going to touch on only a selected group here, but for more information, Maine Inland Fish and Wildlife Department has a pamphlet available entitled, *Go Fish Mount Desert Island* that includes all the ponds with depth maps.

Bubble Pond

Bubble Pond may be the most picturesque pond in the entire park and is worth fishing for just that reason. Bubble is a brook trout pond. Fish range from 6 to 12 inches and it is stocked both spring and fall. Access is off Park Loop Road just south of Eagle Lake.

Eagle Lake

Eagle Lake, with its deep, cold, and well-oxygenated water offers ideal habitat for brook trout, landlocked salmon, and togue. Brook trout and landlocked salmon are stocked annually and there is a self-sustaining wild lake trout population. Brookies run from 10 to 12 inches, and lakers average several pounds. Motorboats over 10 horsepower are prohibited. Trailered boat access is available at the boat launch off ME 233 on Mount Desert Island.

Jordan Pond

Jordan Pond is a popular location because the Jordan Pond House – a restaurant favored by visitors – is located on its southern shore, and because of the abundance of nearby walking trails. This pond is well-suited for freshwater gamefish. Its water is crystal clear, as translucent as any water I have seen anywhere in the United States. It is stocked annually with landlocked salmon that grow up to 20 inches. According to Maine's IF&W biologists, there is an overabundance of naturally reproducing lake trout

Evening descends on Bubble Pond in Acadia National Park.

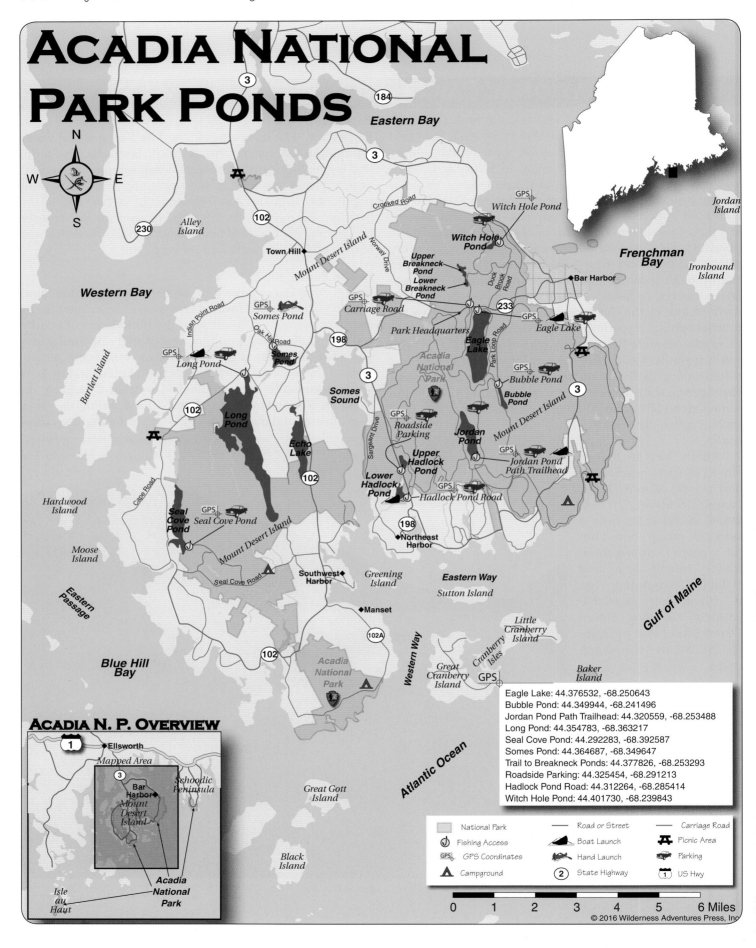

ACADIA NATIONAL PARK PONDS

Eagle Lake: 44.376532, -68.250643
Bubble Pond: 44.349944, -68.241496
Jordan Pond Path Trailhead: 44.320559, -68.253488
Long Pond: 44.354783, -68.363217
Seal Cove Pond: 44.292283, -68.392587
Somes Pond: 44.364687, -68.349647
Trail to Breakneck Ponds: 44.377826, -68.253293
Roadside Parking: 44.325454, -68.291213
Hadlock Pond Road: 44.312264, -68.285414
Witch Hole Pond: 44.401730, -68.239843

ACADIA N. P. OVERVIEW

National Park		Road or Street		Carriage Road
Fishing Access		Boat Launch		Picnic Area
GPS Coordinates		Hand Launch		Parking
Campground		State Highway		US Hwy

0 1 2 3 4 5 6 Miles

© 2016 Wilderness Adventures Press, Inc

here and you can harvest as many as you want. Early in the season, you can take lakers casting streamers, but trolling is the highest percentage play for both lakers and landlocks.

Long Pond

Long Pond is one of the larger water bodies on Mount Desert Island and holds brook trout, landlocks, smallmouth bass, and chain pickerel. There is trailered-boat access off ME 102A. It pays to target trout and salmon during spring and fall, and switch attention to smallmouth and pickerel during the warmer months.

Seal Cove Pond and Somes Pond

If you have a youngster that craves faster action, either flyfishing or spin fishing, consider Seal Cove Pond (access off Park Road) or Somes Pond (carry-in access off Route 102 and Oak Hill Road). Both water bodies hold plentiful numbers of chain pickerel up to five pounds. Nothing excites a younger fisher like the wake of a large pickerel as it knifes through the weeds to attack a surface popper or a floating lure.

Echo Lake

Echo Lake lies partly within park boundaries and offers excellent brook trout and landlocked salmon fishing. This picturesque water can be reached by ME 102 that parallels its eastern shore (look for the public boat ramp). Some of the trout are wild and the salmon can reach three or four pounds.

Breakneck Ponds

Upper and Lower Breakneck Ponds are shallow and weedy but clear ponds of about eight acres each that are stocked annually with brook trout. They are best fished with a float tube to clear yourself from the weedy shorelines. Access is a 1.5-mile walk or bike down a carriage road from the Eagle Lake entrance.

Hadlock Ponds

Upper and Lower Hadlock Ponds are each about 40 acres with maximum depths of about 40 feet. Both are stocked with brook trout. The upper pond produces somewhat larger brook trout than other area ponds – up to 17 inches. During spring and fall, trout congregate around the lower pond's inlet and outlet. There is a carry-in access to both ponds off Route 3/198.

Witch Hole Pond

Witch Hole Pond in Bar Harbor is a popular pond with anglers in the spring for its consistent brook trout action for fish up to 16 inches. Brook trout are stocked in the fall as fingerlings, so the trout act and fight like wild fish. There is walk-in access on Duck Brook Trail.

Stream Fishing

I would be remiss if I didn't mention the stream fishing in Acadia. A number have robust, fishable populations of wild brook trout with the potential for sea-run brookies in a few areas as well. I am not going to provide specific directions on how to access these streams but for those willing to explore, it is worth checking out Asticos, Breakneck, Cannon, Cromwell, Denning, Marshall (east and west branches), Fire Pond, Hadlock, Hunter's, Jordan (Stream) Kebo, Kitteredge, Little Harbor, Old Mill, Prays, Richardson (outlet of Aunt Betty Pond), Sargent, and Stanley Brooks.

The north end of Eagle Lake.

HANCOCK COUNTY STILLWATERS

Alamoosook Lake, Silver Lake, Chemo Pond, and Swetts Pond

These bass stillwaters area a short drive south or east of Bangor. Alamoosook Lake is known for its exceptional smallmouth fishing. Some spots to try are around any of the small islands, the vicinity of Randall's Bridge, and near the outlet. For access off of US 1 in East Orland, follow the signs to the Craig Brook National Fish Hatchery where a public boat launch can be found. Other good bass spots to try are Silver Lake in Bucksport, Chemo Pond off ME 9 in East Eddington, and Swetts Pond.

Alligator Lake, Duck Lake, Nicatous Lake, Green Lake, Phillips Lake, and Beech Hill Pond

Some other lakes to consider east of Bangor and Old Town are Alligator (beautiful, wild brook trout), Duck, Nicatous (all lightly developed); and Green, Phillips, and Beech Hill (known for large togue). Some of these waters have extended seasons until December 31, catch and release only. Many have restrictive regulations allowing for larger fish. Check the latest Maine IF&W regs. All of these waters have fair salmonid flyfishing early in the spring if you can fish areas where the smelt are running, such as the mouth of any stream. For example, on Green Lake fish where Great Brook enters the lake. For most of the rest of the fishing season, these waters are a warmwater species fishery unless you like to troll.

Billings (First) Pond and Fox Pond

Billings (aka First) Pond in Blue Hill is one of the area's best wild brook trout ponds, sometimes yielding brookies over a foot long. The small boat landing is located off of ME 172 in Blue Hill on a dirt road (44.355078,-68.589690), but it is a bit of a paddle to get to the main part of the pond. Fox Pond is a total catch-and-release pond that is open to fishing though the end of November. It is located in T-10 SD.

Georges Pond

Georges Pond holds brown and brook trout and is located in the town of Franklin. Brownies average from 12 to 14 inches in length. Fishing regulations for bass change during the year; please check law book for specifics. Bass will take a popping bug or meaty streamer in the summer. Boat access is available off Georges Pond Road just northwest of Flanders Pond.

Hopkins Pond

Hopkins Pond holds brookies and togue and is located in the town of Mariaville. Trout range from four to ten inches, with lake trout reaching several pounds. There is a hand-carried boat launch available on the pond's eastern side.

Long Pond

Long Pond is a brook trout and brown trout fishery located in the town of Aurora near Great Pond. Artificial lures only. All trout, landlocked salmon, and togue must be released alive at once, and there is no limit for bass. Boat launches are found off Great Pond Road on the pond's southernmost shore and near King Pond to the north.

Lily Pond

For vacationers on Deer Isle, 37-acre Lily Pond offers brook trout. This is a shallow pond and fly anglers do best with subsurface nymphs or wet flys.

Rift Pond

Located in the Great Pond Plantation near Alligator Lake, Rift Pond is stocked with brookies and browns. There is an artificial-lure-only restriction. Minimum length on brook trout is 16 inches. The minimum length on browns is 20. These regulations suggest that the trout grow large in this pond. Fish damselfly and dragonfly nymphs (sizes 4 to 8).

Toddy Ponds

The Toddy Ponds (First, Second, and Third) are three waters near Orland separated by a set of narrows. A variety of salmonids swim in these waters including landlocked salmon, togue, splake (Second), and brown trout.

Tunk Lake

Tunk Lake is a well-known trophy salmon and togue lake with fishing regulations to support that objective. Over the years the size and numbers of togue have fluctuated but recently the population has been robust. Locals like to troll the northeast shoreline from the boat launch to Birch Point. The lake does have spectacular scenery even if the fishing is slow for a visiting angler. It is easily accessible with a boat launch on ME 182 (44.609555,-68.058897)

Upper Oxhead Pond

Upper Oxhead Pond is a small trout pond that is stocked and recommended by Maine's Inland Fish and Wildlife department. Find it west of Nicatous Lake.

Narraguagus Lake

Narraguagus Lake is a decent wild brook trout water although, like many lakes, is best in the spring and later in the season when the fish are more accessible.

WASHINGTON COUNTY SMALLMOUTH BASS FISHERIES

Some folks consider Washington County the best smallmouth bass fishing area in the country. I am sure fishermen from Lake Erie or parts of Pennsylvania might disagree, but I am sure of one thing; there might be smallmouth waters equal to this part of Maine, but none surpass it. Flyfishing legend, Lefty Kreh, can fish anywhere he wants all over the world, but he still comes up to Washington County every year. Smallmouth in these watersheds will get over four pounds, and 20-fish days are a reasonable expectation.

My favorite kind of smallmouth flyfishing is working the shoreline with a small topwater popper. The take is so visual. Sometimes the popper is attacked with a savage strike, throwing water in all directions. Other times, the popper is just slowly sucked down off the surface. Smallmouth prefer smaller popper sizes – a size 4 hook is not too small – mostly in chartreuse, yellow, or orange. The preferred lake habitat of the smallmouth bass is gravel and rocks with structure such as islands, points, and drop-offs. Stay away from muddy, weedy bays and coves. Cast right to shore. Sometimes, bass are cruising within a foot of the shoreline or protecting spawning nests that are frequently next to rocks and in less than three feet of water.

After casting into the shallows, slowly, with frequent pauses, work the popper into deeper water. You will soon determine how far from shore the bass are hanging out based where the strikes come from and you can then optimize your casting. If the strikes are coming from within 20 feet of the shoreline, then concentrate your casts there. Sometimes, the bass are in deeper water. Certainly, the larger bass tend to build their nests down at greater depths.

Later in the year as the water warms, the bass move into deeper water and subsurface fare such as weighted leach or crawfish imitations are the way to go. Concentrate on drop-offs near structure, such as rocky points and islands.

Washington County lakes have a "Grand" tradition (pun intended) of guided trips for smallmouth. I recommend hiring a guide for a day just to experience a bit of history. The day consists of a guide picking you up and paddling or motoring you along one of the lakes in a traditional Grand Laker canoe. Typically one might cast towards shore or perhaps troll. Some of your catch is kept for your mid-day meal. The highlight of the day is a shore lunch on an island or similar picturesque spot where the guide prepares fresh fish filets (and other complementary fare) over an open fire.

Many places offer guided services and about 25 guides live in the small village of Grand Lake Stream alone. I heartily recommend Weatherby's Lodge as an option for a place to stay and arrange trips. Weatherby's Lodge has been a Grand Lake tradition for over 80 years. It offers lodging, meals, trips, and is a full-fledged Orvis dealer as well. Jeff McEvoy, the owner, knows the fisheries and runs a topnotch operation.

The western St. Croix drainage contains (from upstream to downstream) Upper, Middle, Lower Chain Lakes, Sysladobsis Lake, Pocumucus Lake, Junior Lake, West Grand Lake, Big Lake, Long Lake, Louis Lake, and the Grand Falls Flowage. The eastern St Croix drainage contains North Lake in New Brunswick, Canada, East Grand Lake, and Spednick Lake (sometimes referred to as the Chiputneticook Lakes). All of these lakes hold bass.

In addition to the lakes, these drainages have river sections such as the St. Croix River that offer equally good smallmouth action if you do a float in a canoe, kayak, or driftboat. There are spots to wade as well. Often, the bass will be visible as they rise to insect hatches, or later in the summer when they pound baby alewives like stripers. Fishing can be quite straightforward – casting brown or green Woolly Buggers or similar fare into holes, deeper riffles, and shoreline pockets.

I have had phenomenal fishing on the St. Croix. One hot August day, in the middle of the afternoon, while I was wading below Great Falls Dam in Princeton, I caught a bass on every cast for two hours as they slashed the surface around me, and didn't move more than 100 feet.

I would be remiss if I didn't mention the pickerel fishing as well. Most Washington County waters contain healthy numbers of pickerel that range up to 24 inches. They will be found in the areas that smallmouth are not: shallow, weedy bays. Tie on any bright streamer or surface popper, tippet that can withstand their teeth and watch pickerel come out of nowhere. Have pliers handy to unhook these toothy creatures. It is a great way to introduce a youngster to flyfishing.

Carl Hoffman with a nice Washington County smallmouth bass.
Photo courtesy of Weatherbys.

WEST GRAND LAKE

West Grand Lake and East Grand Lake are well known for their landlocked salmon angling. Ice-out arrives in early May most years and fishing usually picks up toward the end of the month. Indeed, cold, blustery weather often pervades available flyfishing early on. Nevertheless, a small number of die-hard West Grand Lake traditionalists hook up on ice-out salmon. They feed line through frozen fingertips until the warmer Memorial Day weekend. Usually, that is when angler activity begins to flourish. A word of caution to ice-out flyfishers: Some early May days find West Grand Lake seeing whitecaps charging toward boats and canoes like NFL linebackers. Falling overboard early in the season can be fatal. Simple safety precautions such as wearing lifejackets, not standing in the boat, and attaching the motor kill-switch lanyard to one's person are good ideas. Every spring, drowned boaters are found with their trouser fly open. We can all hypothesize what probably happened.

West Grand Lake is half the size of Cumberland County's Sebago Lake. Angling pressure is rarely a problem on this 14,340-acre fishery, which is still large by Maine standards and has many miles of undeveloped shoreline. The lake has several distinct sections divided by natural features such as large islands, points, and coves, and is the headwaters for Grand Lake Stream. The best boat launch is located in the village of Grand Lake Stream. This is a quaint town that is literally at the end of a paved road and is devoted almost entirely to the fishing industry.

According to the Maine Department of Inland Fisheries and Wildlife, Grand Lake Stream is primarily managed for landlocks and togue. Both game fish target smelt as a food source. Like Sebago, a healthy forage base helps keep gamefish populations thriving and feeder streams, including Oxbrook and Burroughs Brooks, hold spawning smelt come spring. Coves around the lake contain staging smelt. Whitney Cove, Dyer Cove, Kitchen Cove, Big and Little Mayberry Coves, Farm Cove, Steamboat Cove, and McLellan Cove all provide reliable salmon angling. Landlocks gather in these sheltered bays to feed on schools of forage fish. Areas

to fish close to the boat launch are Munson Island, Kitchen Point, and Dyer Point.

Most West Grand Lake flyfishers will tell you their sole objective is to catch one of the lively landlocks. However, lake trout are also targeted by a few streamer-wielding anglers, especially early on, from the first two weeks after ice-out to the end of May. Smelt-imitating streamers rule on the big lake for both landlocks and lake trout, though big stonefly nymphs and Woolly Buggers work as well. A few of the popular streamer patterns are the Red (Gray) Ghost, the Barnes Special, and the Governor Aiken.

While trolling with a fly rod and streamer patterns is the most common "flyfishing" method on West Grand Lake, fly casting is also possible. Sometimes schools of salmon will stack up in one area and it pays to stop trolling, anchor, and start casting. On calm days or in the calm areas of leeward shorelines, look for rising salmon. Mayfly and caddis hatches will bring fish to the top. The first warm days of the year may trigger the emergence of flying ants that blunder into the water and create top-water action. Any foam ant pattern of similar size to the naturals should pay dividends.

West Grand Lake's season is December 1 through October 20, although ice-out arrives in May. From October 1 to 20, fishing is by artificial lure only, and all fish caught must be released at once. For all of the regulations, refer to the Maine IF&W website.

Lake trout average two to ten pounds, while salmon typically weigh one to three pounds, occasionally more. The lake has a maximum depth of 128 feet. A passable road skirts the northwestern lakeshore that will take you to the

A nice salmon caught on West Grand Lake on a hot day. Photo courtesy of Weatherby's.

Whitney Cove boat launch and an unimproved road access to the Farm Cove boat launch.

The other lakes in this flowage are accessible from West Grand but, to avoid the long boat ride, there are other access points at Ellsmore Landing and Sysladobsis Dam.

East Grand Lake

This lake is considered one of the best landlocked salmon lakes in the state. The lake, located near Danforth, is shared with the Province of New Brunswick and covers more than 16,000 acres. Its Canadian name is Chiputneticook Lakes. The East Grand Lake region offers several lodges, camps, and services.

Big Lake

Big Lake obviously has salmon too, since Grand Lake Stream empties into it. I enjoy fishing this lake and don't usually see another angler for hours at a time.

Baskahegan Lake

Baskahegan Lake in northwest Washington County is an excellent smallmouth lake. To find this water, go north on US 1 from the Grand Lake Stream area and take a right in Brookton on Baskahegan Lake Road. Within a mile of the turn-off will be the lake's only boat launch (45.527153,-67.784573). Fishing improves the farther you move away from the launch point.

Bog Lake

Bog Lake holds brown trout and landlocked salmon. It lies north of the village of Machias on ME 192, where there is hand-carried boat access.

Meddybemps Lake

Meddybemps Lake covers well over 6,000 acres and supports both coldwater and warmwater species. It has a reputation as a fine smallmouth bass fishery. There is a boat launch in the tiny town of Meddybemps on ME 191, near the lake outflow that is the beginning of the Dennys River.

Pleasant Lake

Pleasant Lake is located south of the village of Danforth, just south of ME 6. Pleasant Lake has good smallmouth bass fishing throughout the season as well as ice-out landlocked salmon fishing. There is camping and a boat launch at the lake's north end off of Pleasant Lake Road.

Gardner Lake

Gardner Lake is a mixed warmwater and coldwater lake east of the village of East Machias. The best angling for landlocks is after ice-out in the spring. There is a boat launch near the lake's outlet at Chase Mills off Route 1.

Other lakes to try for landlocked salmon include Schoodic, Cathance, Crawford, Nash's, and Pocomoonshine (my favorite name of all of the Maine lakes).

East Monroe Pond, West Monroe Pond, and Pineo Pond

East and West Monroe Ponds are stocked and dependable fisheries for small trout, although West Monroe tends to produce the bigger fish. Pineo Pond in Deblois is open for angling all year and is another good choice. Study a map before you go because it is near a cluster of ponds. From Deblois, take ME 193 south. Find and take a left on the unpaved Hatchery Road, then a right on Schoodic Pond Road. After several miles, look for a left on a short dirt road (44.715839,-67.942119).

Simpson Pond

Simpson Pond is located in Roque Bluffs State Park and is an excellent family destination because of its wonderful scenery, abundant bird life (including bald eagles), sandy beach, hiking trails, and picnic area. This shallow pond is only a few hundred yards from the Atlantic Ocean but gives up brown and brook trout over 12 inches. It can be waded, but a kayak or small canoe will allow you to cover more water to find active fish.

A guide's Grand Laker canoe, beached at White's Island on Big Lake for a shore lunch. Photo courtesy of Weatherby's.

GRAND LAKE STREAM

Grand Lake Stream flows for three miles from the dam at the outflow of West Grand Lake down to Big Lake. It is home to one of the four native pools of landlocked salmon in the US. Landlocked salmon have been swimming in the waters of Grand Lake Stream since the last ice age. Grand Lake Stream landlocks have been stocked throughout Maine and the United States. The stream holds the occasional brook trout up to several pounds, and early spring lake trout in the lower sections from two to five pounds. But every angler visits this river to hook up with native salmon from one to three pounds, occasionally bigger.

Anglers travel to Grand Lake Stream on April 1, the traditional opening of flyfishing season, to catch their first salmon of the year. Fishing is frequently a cold affair with very high flows and water temps only slightly above freezing. Still, overwintering salmon in the large pool below the dam are worth the chill. Flyfishing is best from late May, right after the Memorial Day weekend, and throughout June. During cooler and wetter summers, fishing lasts through July, particularly in the early morning and late evening. Good angling picks up again in mid-September and is especially good in the first two weeks of October.

Salmon can be caught almost anywhere all the way down to Gould's Landing on Big Lake. The section from Big Falls to Little Falls offers the best angling under most water conditions. The most productive pools are also the most popular and flyfishers tend to congregate there. Several strategies increase success. First, fish at first light, during the middle of day, or at dark – you will find it less crowded. Second, fish the runs and pocket water between the pools. There are salmon there as well and they are less pressured. Third, don't fish standard patterns that the fish get wise to. For example, emerger patterns might be more effective than traditional dries. Nymphing with small patterns such as size 18 or 20 beadhead caddis pupae, Brassies, and Pheasant Tails catch fish. Late May through mid-July, caddis hatches should be fished with a range of selections (nymphs and dries) including bright or olive green caddis

Early autumn hook-up on Grand Lake Stream Photo courtesy of Weatherby's.

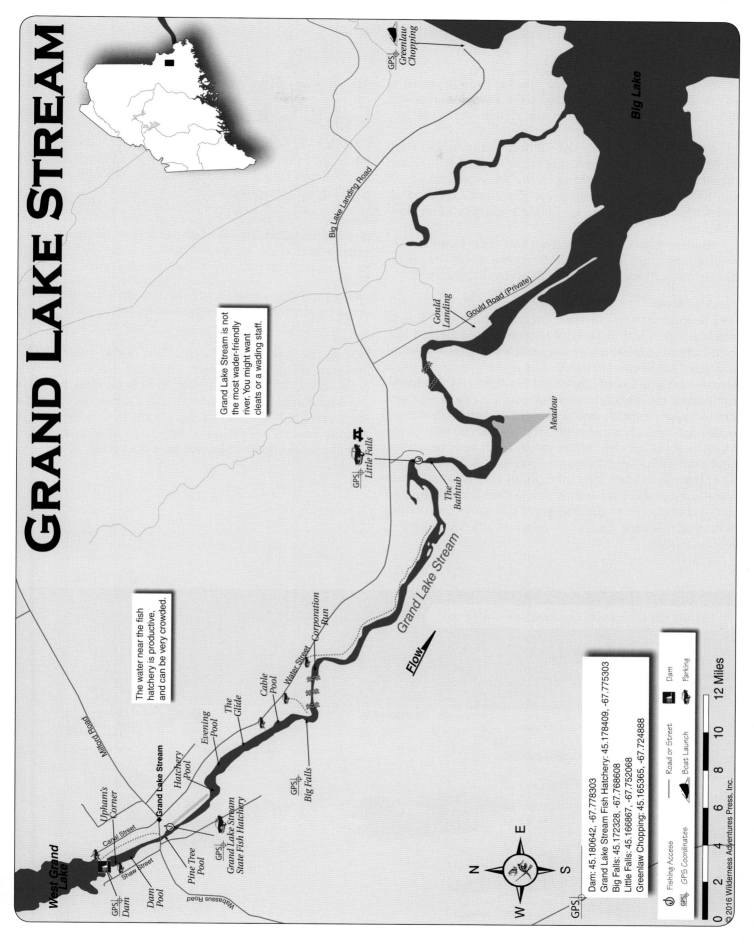

GRAND LAKE STREAM

Grand Lake Stream is not the most wader-friendly river. You might want cleats or a wading staff.

The water near the fish hatchery is productive, and can be very crowded.

Big Lake

Greenlaw Chopping

GPS

Big Lake Landing Road

Gould Landing

Gould Road (Private)

Meadow

The Bathtub

GPS | Little Falls

Grand Lake Stream

Flow ►

Corporation Run

Water Street

Cable Pool

The Glide

Evening Pool

Hatchery Pool

Grand Lake Stream

GPS | Big Falls

Upham's Corner

Milford Road

Canal Street

Shaw Street

Pine Tree Pool

GPS | Grand Lake Stream State Fish Hatchery

Wabassus Road

Dam Pool

GPS | Dam

West Grand Lake

Dam: 45.180642, -67.778303
Grand Lake Stream Fish Hatchery: 45.178409, -67.775303
Big Falls: 45.172328, -67.768608
Little Falls: 45.166867, -67.752068
Greenlaw Chopping: 45.165365, -67.724888

Fishing Access
GPS | GPS Coordinates

Road or Street
Boat Launch

Dam
Parking

N E S W

0   2   4   6   8   10   12 Miles

© 2016 Wilderness Adventures Press, Inc.

GPS

nymphs and LaFontaine's Deep Sparkle Pupa (sizes 10 to 16) in dark gray and ginger. Show the salmon something different, such as large stonefly nymph patterns in black or brown, or hot-spot nymphs.

Most standard landlocked salmon streamers will work when the fish are in the mood to chase them. A pattern not fished frequently on this stream is the Wood Special, which can be deadly, particularly if you fish in cloudy or rainy conditions. Remember to retrieve it erratically to increase its action.

Anglers can expect a gravel and rock bottom with wading opportunities available. There is a passable road on the northern riverbank that affords access to anglers.

Machias River

This flowage consists of First, Second, Third, and Fourth Machias Lakes with moving water connecting them. There is still a limited Atlantic-salmon run (closed for fishing) and pan-sized brook trout in many of its upper tributaries (New Stream and Old Stream, for example). If you do fish in the tributaries, be cognizant of what you are catching; there are juvenile Atlantic salmon present and they should be realized as quickly as possible. The primary appeal of the Machias River, though, is the smallmouth bass which are abundant throughout the entire watershed. Believe it or not, all of the smallmouth bass throughout eastern Maine were introduced and are not native. While their introduction no doubt contributed to the decline of the native brook trout fishery in this area, they are now a tremendous fishery in their own right.

Stream Facts: Grand Lake Stream

Season
From April 1 to October 20. Closed to all fishing within 150 feet of Grand Lake Stream dam. See State of Maine laws and rules for further regulations.

Species
Native and stocked landlocked salmon, some brook trout, rarely lake trout.

Flows
Expect a strong current early in the season that usually drops by May, although it is rainfall dependent.

Access
Several roads parallel the river. Most of the water can be accessed off of Water Street. There are obvious parking areas and trails down to the river. Near to the dam, access is from West Shore Drive. Walk through the hatchery parking lot to reach the famous Hatchery Pool. The bridge right in town is another access point with large salmon available just upstream and downstream from the bridge.

The Machias River from Route 1A, west of Machias, Maine.

St. Croix River

I have already covered some generalities about the St. Croix in the smallmouth bass introduction at the beginning of this Eastern Maine section. The section of the St. Croix from Spednick Lake downstream to the Grand Falls Flowage is a good option to fish in late July and August when the flyfishing is tougher on other waters. While sections are wadable, this is a perfect river to float in a kayak, canoe, or driftboat. Remember that the east bank of the St. Croix is the Canadian border. If you are a U.S. citizen, you are not allowed to exit the water on that side for any reason, even to urinate.

Stream Facts: St. Croix River

Season
From April 1 to September 30, except the section from Grand Falls Dam to Milltown Dam, which is open during October.

Species
Primarily smallmouth bass, but brook trout are found near the tributaries.

Flows
The river is dam-controlled which moderates the ups and downs due to rainfall events, and maintains reasonable flows all summer.

Access
The St. Croix River is 72 miles long and the eastern stem creates the U.S. and Canadian border for much of its length. US 1 parallels much of that distance but is not often next to the river, so side roads are required for access. Many anglers like to float this river, although many spots can be waded. Some good floats that don't include difficult rapids (rips) are Vanceboro to Little Falls, Little Falls to Loon Bay, and Loon Bay to Kelleyland on Grand Falls Flowage. For more information contact Weatherby's. Each is a day float and shuttle services are available locally.

UPPER LEFT: Come late July, think St. Croix smallies.
MAIN IMAGE: Canoeing on the St. Croix. The far shore is Canada; the photographer is standing on U.S. soil.

ST. CROIX RIVER

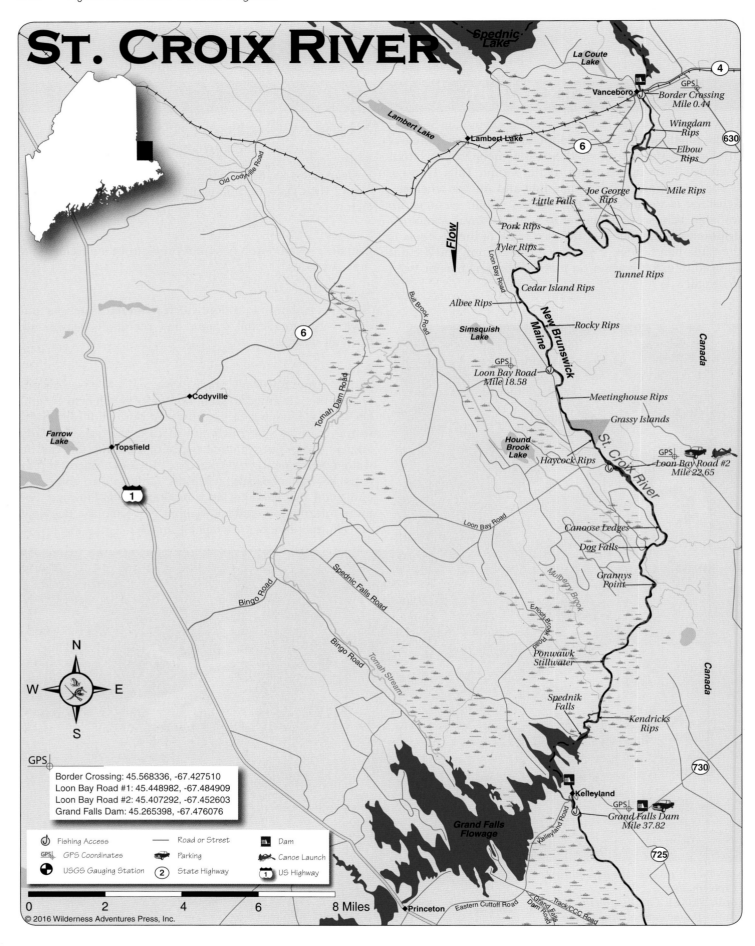

Spednic Lake

La Coute Lake

4

GPS

Vanceboro — Border Crossing Mile 0.44

630

Wingdam Rips

Elbow Rips

Mile Rips

Joe George Rips

Little Falls

Pork Rips

Tyler Rips

Tunnel Rips

Cedar Island Rips

Albee Rips

Rocky Rips

Simsquish Lake

GPS
Loon Bay Road Mile 18.58

Meetinghouse Rips

Grassy Islands

Hound Brook Lake

Haycock Rips

GPS
Loon Bay Road #2 Mile 22.65

Canoose Ledges

Dog Falls

Grannys Point

Ponwawk Stillwater

Spednik Falls

Kendricks Rips

730

Kelleyland

GPS
Grand Falls Dam Mile 37.82

Grand Falls Flowage

725

Lambert Lake

Lambert Lake

6

Old Codyville Road

Bull Brook Road

6

Tomah Dam Road

Codyville

Farrow Lake

Topsfield

1

Spednic Falls Road

Bingo Road

Bingo Road

Tomah Stream

Loon Bay Road

Mulberry Brook

Enoch Brook Road

Kelleyland Road

Grand Falls Dam Road

Track/CCC Road

Princeton

Eastern Cutoff Road

New Brunswick

Maine

Canada

Canada

St. Croix River

Flow

N
W E
S

GPS
Border Crossing: 45.568336, -67.427510
Loon Bay Road #1: 45.448982, -67.484909
Loon Bay Road #2: 45.407292, -67.452603
Grand Falls Dam: 45.265398, -67.476076

Fishing Access
GPS Coordinates
USGS Gauging Station
Road or Street
Parking
State Highway
Dam
Canoe Launch
US Highway

0 2 4 6 8 Miles

© 2016 Wilderness Adventures Press, Inc.

EASTERN MAINE PLANNING CONSIDERATIONS

Nearby Hub Cities and Towns

- Bar Harbor (www.barharborinfo.com, www.mountdesertchamber.org)
- Grand Lake Stream (www.grandlakestream.org, www.weatherbys.com)
- Machias (www.machiaschamber.org)

Easy Access Options

- Many of the ponds in Acadia National Park have car-accessible roads, parking lots, or easy-walking carriage trails that end at water's edge or darn near close to it. Most of the shorelines are firm-bottomed and you can certainly wade out a bit to reach the deeper water where the trout cruise in spring and fall.
- On Grand Lake Stream, the Hatchery Pool, and the Dam Pool are a very short walk from the road in the center of town and there are always salmon there, except for perhaps mid-summer. These pools can get crowded, so it pays to get up at first light or wait until the middle of the day. You do have to navigate down a few rocks to reach the Hatchery Pool.
- Near Princeton, Maine is the Grand Falls Dam on the St. Croix River, which can be reached by taking Route 1 south to just south of town, and then taking a left on Grand Falls Dam Road. It will change from paved to dirt after a few miles. When you reach the dam, take the road on your immediate right that will take you downhill, past the power house, and then down to the river downstream from the dam, where the road dead ends. It is just a few steps down a gradual bank and into the water where the wading is easy on a mostly gravel bottom. And best of all, the bass are plentiful.

Suggested Beginner Options

- See Grand Falls Dam under Easy Access Options. This is a great place to practice new flyfishing skills. You can wade out far enough to clear your back cast and practice line manipulation, fly presentation, hooking and playing fish. It isn't technical fishing – just cast a brown or green Woolly Bugger, retrieve steadily with a pause once and a while, and see what happens.

- Hire a registered Maine flyfishing guide to take you out to one of the Grand Lake Stream lakes. The best way to improve flyfishing knowledge and skill is to hire a guide, so you can concentrate on your fishing, while they handle everything else. Guides are usually good and patient instructors as well. Smallmouth bass are a great fish for beginners. If you are fishing on the surface, you can often see the strike and practice setting the hook as well as learn how to play and land strong fish.

Vacation Suggestions

Weekend Getaway

- Stay in one of Bar Harbor's many lodging options and explore Acadia National Park, particularly if you have never visited. Choose a spring weekend after the park opens but before school gets out. Get up early with a kayak or canoe, put in to any of the waters I described early in this section and work the shorelines. Join your family later in the morning to explore the rest of the park by car, bike, or on foot. Try to sneak out at the end of the day for more fishing.

One-week Vacation

- From mid-June to early July, stay in the Grand Lake Stream area. The town harkens back to a simpler time and visitors relax upon arrival. A number of lodging options beckon, including Weatherby's. You're weekly activities could include:
  1. Wade Grand Lake Stream for its native landlocked salmon.
  2. Fish Big Lake or West Grand Lake for smallmouth and pickerel.
  3. Float the St. Croix for river fun and more smallmouth.
  4. When you want a break from fishing, Route 1 and the Maine coast are close enough for a day trip, where you can play tourist and enjoy the coastal scenery and activities.

Northern Maine

This section encompasses the entirety of Aroostook County, the northernmost part of Maine, some six hours by car from Portland to its most northern territories. This vast county has only 11 people per square mile. Its major towns are Presque Isle, Caribou, Fort Kent, Houlton, and Madawaska. It is wilderness with moose, deer, coyote, bear, bobcat, and lynx in abundance around the Allagash and St. John Rivers. Eastern Aroostook County has a different character than the undeveloped western part, and is a land of farms, fields, woods, and small towns.

Swimming in the abundant waters are the following trout species: brook, brown, lake, splake, and the rare blueback. Warmwater species include smallmouth bass, white perch, and muskellunge. There isn't the space to cover all of the waters that hold trout, let alone other species. Brook trout swim in almost every small creek, stream, and river, at least some of the year.

An angler could explore these waters for a lifetime and never fish the same water twice. But the best reason to travel to "the county" is that even in the best fishing locations, it will never be crowded. In fact, frequently, you will have the place to yourself.

Don't forget how far north this county is from the rest of New England. In this neck of the woods, June is still a time of high water from winter run-off. Ice sometimes doesn't leave the lakes and ponds until mid-May, so don't visit too early in the year.

From big muskies to big brookies, northern Maine has a lot to offer anglers. Muskie photo courtesy Ben Rioux. Brook trout photo courtesy Red River Camps.

ALLAGASH RIVER

In the wilds of far northern Maine, the Allagash River is best traveled and fished by canoe or kayak. This designated National Wild and Scenic River offers angling for native brook trout and an opportunity to experience one of the great wilderness areas of America. The river flows through harvested timberlands and bogs. Strips of trees, intended to lessen the visual shock of clear-cuts, preserve forested views. Maine conservation organizations continue to purchase land and conservation easements to protect this remote waterway.

The best way to fish the Allagash Wilderness Waterway is as part of a multi-day float/paddling trip. Plan on several days to a week or more to fish this river thoroughly. The river runs 90 miles from Telos Lake to Allagash and features Class I and II water with falls, gentle runs, and lake sections. Most first-time canoeists are surprised at how much lake paddling is involved. Flows are moderate to gentle but strong winds can be expected on the lakes. Portaging is necessary at times. One of my favorite canoeing sayings is: "When in doubt, get out", meaning it's better to portage or walk along shore with your canoe than dumping all of your fishing gear in the river. This is a wilderness fishery, so services you may be accustomed to are not available – no coffee, food, supplies, or cell phone service.

Study the maps and carry a GPS, so you can identify important features and access points. Access points to the waterway are severely limited by regulation. A helpful primer can be found at https://www1.maine.gov/dacf/parks/get_involved/planning_and_acquisition/management_plans/docs/AWW_Final_mgt_plan_Background.pdf.

The Allagash Waterway is, however, no longer limited to extended paddling trips. If you only have three or four days, start at the Churchill Dam, which is about half-way. You can also take out at Michaud Farm instead of going all the way to the town of Allagash. Day trips are now possible thanks to access points such as Henderson Bridge and Umsaskis Thorofare.

Flyfishers with canoes – and plenty of bug dope – target river sections in June, which often proves to be the best month. It is one of nature's cruel jokes to anglers that the worse the black flies and mosquitos swarm, the better the fishing is. The reason for this is that all aquatic insects, whether they be mayflies or mosquitos, are sensitive to drying out, therefore both swarm on calm or humid days.

September is also a great month to try this trip as long as sufficient rain has kept the river system at reasonable levels. Water conditions are critical for both the kayaking/canoeing and fishing. If there has been inadequate rain, the trip involves a lot of boat dragging. Too much rain makes for a dangerous trip and tougher conditions to fish. Ideal canoeing levels are 1,000cfs; below 500, sandbars start to appear and dragging commences. For current water levels, go to http://waterdata.usgs.gov. Find out the conditions before an extended trip and be ready to make alternate plans. Different groups report very different trips based on conditions.

Trout fishing in the summer is generally poor in the mainstem because the river is too shallow and warm for brookies. If the weather has been hot, trout become less active and stack up in cold water near the tributaries. When conditions are good, expect prolific numbers of brook trout from 8 to 12 inches. Good trout run in the two-pound range, but are not common. Downstream from Allagash Falls, muskies have infiltrated the river from the St. John and pretty much wiped out the trout fishing. We should all pray that muskies don't somehow get over the falls or the entire watershed would be at risk.

If you want to fish the river for just a day or two, there are other ways to access. From Round Pond, which is connected to the Allagash River, you can access the moving water and fish upstream or down. You can stay at Jalbert Camps on Round Pond and overnight at several wilderness

You will see plenty of moose if you canoe the Allagash Wilderness Waterway.

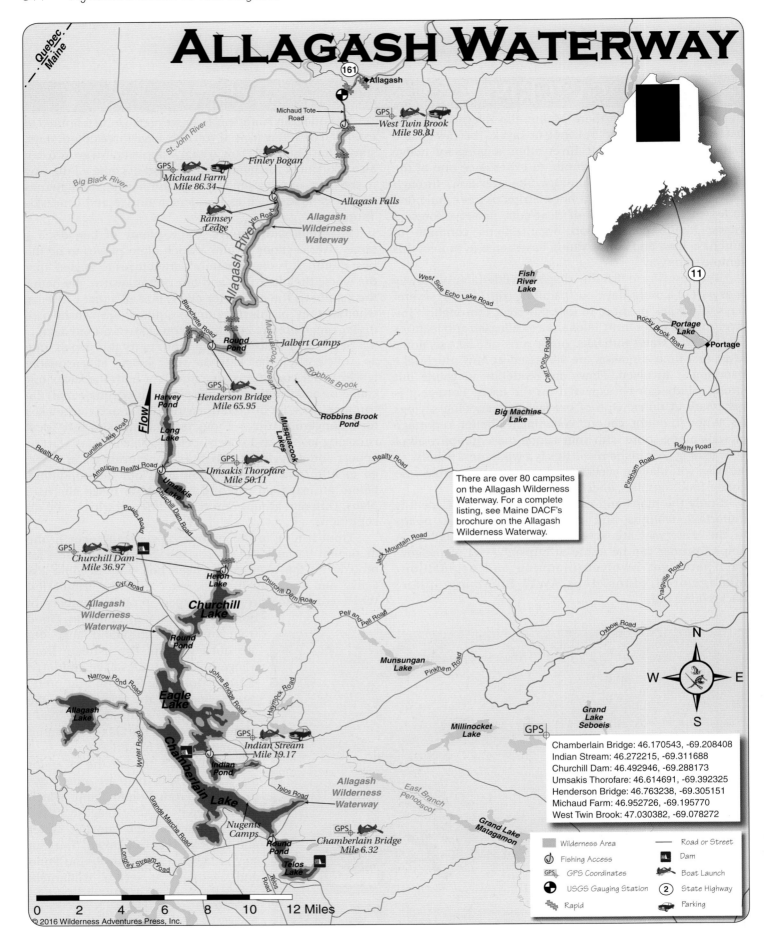

ALLAGASH WATERWAY

Chamberlain Bridge: 46.170543, -69.208408
Indian Stream: 46.272215, -69.311688
Churchill Dam: 46.492946, -69.288173
Umsakis Thorofare: 46.614691, -69.392325
Henderson Bridge: 46.763238, -69.305151
Michaud Farm: 46.952726, -69.195770
West Twin Brook: 47.030382, -69.078272

There are over 80 campsites on the Allagash Wilderness Waterway. For a complete listing, see Maine DACF's brochure on the Allagash Wilderness Waterway.

West Twin Brook
Mile 98.81

Michaud Farm
Mile 86.34

Henderson Bridge
Mile 65.95

Umsakis Thorofare
Mile 50.11

Churchill Dam
Mile 36.97

Indian Stream
Mile 19.17

Chamberlain Bridge
Mile 6.32

Legend:
- Wilderness Area
- Fishing Access
- GPS Coordinates
- USGS Gauging Station
- Rapid
- Road or Street
- Dam
- Boat Launch
- State Highway
- Parking

0 2 4 6 8 10 12 Miles

© 2016 Wilderness Adventures Press, Inc.

The starting point for many canoeing the Allagash Waterway - the Chamberlain Bridge on Telos Road (46.170543, -69.208408)

campsites as well. Another nearby authorized access point is the Henderson Bridge just upstream from Round Pond. The only other set of sporting camps on the waterway is Nugents Camps on Chamberlain Lake. Access to both camps is by boat only.

Many canoeists don't bother to fish during their river journey – even though they often bring fishing equipment. Their narrow focus on the travel, the next campsite, etc., makes for poor attention to fishing. Therefore, the fish are generally unpressured and aren't all that selective.

Numerous tributaries of the Allagash – too many to list here – are good native trout waters in their own right and well worth exploring and fishing. For example, Robbins Brook, a trib of Musquacook Stream (in turn a trib of the Allagash River) is a good springtime brookie spot. One access point is the bridge where it crosses under Rocky Brook Road, shortly before its confluence with Musquacook Stream. Logging roads that run parallel to both banks along the length of Robbins Brook provide additional entry points. Several roads cross Musquacook Stream, for those wishing to try a few casts in that water. Nearby is 20-acre, artificials-only Robbins Brook Pond, which can be fished with a float tube for native brookies. Several different logging roads end near or on this pond from different access roads. Utilize Google Earth to determine the best route for you, based on where you are coming from and the latest road conditions. American Realty Road is the main roadway into this area.

Dry-fly purists carry a range of standard patterns into the Allagash's wilderness waters, including the Mosquito (size 12 to 20), Blue-winged Olive (size 14 to 20), March Brown (size 12 to 16), Light Cahill (size 12 to 20) and Black Gnat (size 12 to 18). Olive Woolly Buggers catch some of the bigger Allagash River trout and also work in many of the region's lakes. Caddis hatches are to be relished in June, and anglers fish grasshopper patterns in July and August. Other terrestrial choices include foam or cork beetles and ants.

The Allagash River's season runs April 1 to September 30. Most of the anglers who catch the most and largest trout, camp on the large lakes shortly after ice-out and troll lures, streamers, or sewn smelt (a live-bait concoction). Maybe the best fishing on the entire waterway is at Allagash Lake and Allagash Stream. It has more restrictive regulations and no motors are allowed (including ice augers in the winter). It is also a remote place that is difficult to access, requiring either upstream canoeing or a difficult portage/shuttle to reach the headwaters.

Current angling laws, which are lengthy, are found in the Piscataquis County section of the Maine Department of Inland Fisheries and Wildlife's open-water fishing regulations. For a complete copy of regulations and reservation information for the use of the Allagash Wilderness Waterway, see the Maine Bureau of Parks and Recreation website or call 207-287-3821.

FISH RIVER SYSTEM

The Fish River watershed is one of the largest in New England, draining over 1,000 square miles, connecting eight lakes, and traveling 50 miles as it makes its way from the remote village of Portage, east across Aroostook County, and finally bending north and entering the St. John. Fortunately, Fish River Falls has so far blocked the migration of introduced muskies into the upstream watershed, so the brook trout fishing hasn't declined like it has on the St. John. Fish River has some remote areas, but it isn't really in the deep woods because ME 11 and its services are often close by.

The upper Fish River starts at Fish River Lake and connects this lake with Portage Lake. Both lakes and the medium-sized river in between hold brook trout and landlocked salmon. The river holds both species from May to early July, and then in September, particularly around the inlet and outlets of both lakes. In the summer, the water warms to the point where the fish move into the lakes. This is a remote area, and this easily wadable river will not have many anglers. Campers can find a few campsites here and there, particularly near Fish River Lake. If you want to canoe or kayak this section, you can put in at Round Pond (near Fish River Lake) and float the 10 miles to Portage Lake. For a shorter float, you can take in or take out in the middle of this section from Hewes Brook Road (48.832779, -68623477).

Access is from the small town of Portage where you can get supplies, directions, and information. From Route 11, take the gravel Rocky Brook Road – you will pass through the Fish River checkpoint on the way to the river.

The next section of the Fish River runs between Portage and St. Froid Lakes, is also fairly remote with limited intercept points (even though Route 11 is nearby), and is best fished by canoe from one of the lakes. Portage Lake is shallow and the fishing is not as good as some of the other lakes in this drainage. St. Froid Lake is cold and deep and in addition to brookies and salmon, the occasional lake trout up to five pounds ends up in the net.

The Nadeau Thoroughfare between St. Froid Lake and Eagle Lake offers excellent fishing both spring and fall. From Eagle Lake, boat over to the thoroughfare – it is easy wading. If you stay at Fish River Lodge on Eagle Lake, it is just a ten-minute paddle over to the

thoroughfare. After ice-out in late May, the salmon chase the smelt into the thoroughfare and casting smelt imitations like the Marabou Gray Ghost is very productive. Later into June, trout and salmon stay to feed on emerging insects. If no surface activity is obvious, the go-to fly is a small olive Woolly Bugger with a cone or beadhead. Otherwise, your favorite mid-size dark brown or grey mayfly pattern is probably fine.

In Eagle Lake itself (and the other Fish River lakes), the most popular way to fish with a fly rod is to troll traditional streamers such as the Gray Ghost. After ice-out, salmonids are within three feet of the surface and trolling with a floating line is fine. Later as the water warms, trolling with weight or even leadcore line to run the streamers deeper will result in better action. In the evening or during hatches (if the water is calm enough), you will see fish rising across all of Eagle Lake (and the other lakes). Then it is time to pick up your casting rod, match whatever you see on the water, and enjoy some dry-fly action.

With all of the Fish River lakes, particularly if you are in a small craft such as a canoe, be aware of weather forecasts and potential strong winds because these lakes can become rough quickly and trap you in a corner. Always bring extra food, water, and clothes in case you have to wait out a

Biologists urge anglers to keep their catch on the Fish River system. Tenley Bennett, guide and manager of the Fish River Lodge, is taking this nice brookie home. Photo courtesy Fish River Lodge.

FISH RIVER CHAIN

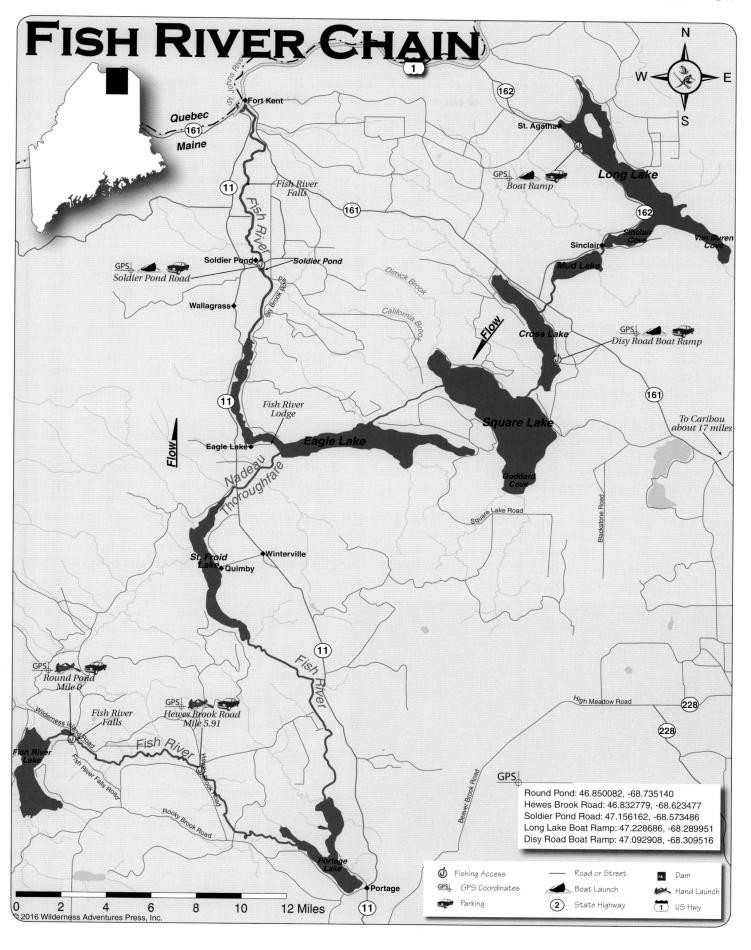

Quebec

Maine

Fort Kent

St. Johns River

161

1

162

St. Agatha

Long Lake

162

GPS
Boat Ramp

Sinclair Cove

Sinclair

Van Buren Cove

11

Fish River Falls

161

Mud Lake

Soldier Pond

Soldier Pond

GPS
Soldier Pond Road

Fish River

Sly Brook Rd

Dimick Brook

California Brook

Flow

Cross Lake

GPS
Disy Road Boat Ramp

Wallagrass

11

Fish River Lodge

Eagle Lake

Square Lake

161

To Caribou
about 17 miles

Flow

Eagle Lake

Nadeau Thoroughfare

Goddard Cove

Square Lake Road

Blackstone Road

St. Froid Lake

Winterville

Quimby

Fish River

11

High Meadow Road

228

GPS
Round Pond
Mile 0

228

Wilderness Island Road

Fish River Falls

GPS
Hewes Brook Road
Mile 5.91

Fish River Lake

Fish River

Fish River Falls Road

Hewes Brook Road

Beaver Brook Road

GPS

Rocky Brook Road

Round Pond: 46.850082, -68.735140
Hewes Brook Road: 46.832779, -68.623477
Soldier Pond Road: 47.156162, -68.573486
Long Lake Boat Ramp: 47.228686, -68.289951
Disy Road Boat Ramp: 47.092908, -68.309516

Portage Lake

Portage

11

| 0 | 2 | 4 | 6 | 8 | 10 | 12 Miles |

© 2016 Wilderness Adventures Press, Inc.

Fishing Access   Road or Street   Dam

GPS Coordinates   Boat Launch   Hand Launch

Parking   2 State Highway   1 US Hwy

sudden wind storm in an area with no other access.

The third part of the Fish River runs from Eagle Lake to Fort Kent (the confluence of the Fish and St. John Rivers). This entire section is wadeable but the easiest access is by boat. This is an easily reached section from US 161 traveling south from Fort Kent. Sly Brook Road offers a good approach to the upper river where fishing is best. Parts of the river can only be reached by crossing private property. Permission is usually given if you ask first.

One notable feature to this part of the fish river is Soldier Pond. Soldier Pond is a pond in the river, and a small road (Soldier Pond Road) off of ME 11 crosses the river here, providing good access. This section has good hatches of both green drakes and *Hexagenia* mayflies, and you can use a boat to move down the Fish River, anchoring and getting out to wade and to cast. Fish River Falls is another feature to note. Even though muskies are present in the river up to the falls and other trout and salmon anglers fish elsewhere, a good number of landlocks and large brook trout still swim in the faster current below the falls. This section down to the St. John River is open to fishing all year, and anglers catch landlocked salmon even during cold winter weather.

A side branch of the Fish River (sometimes called the lower Fish River Drainage) connects Long, Mud, Cross, Square, and Eagle Lakes. The so-called thoroughfares between these lakes offer good fishing during May, June, and September.

Long Lake is the largest and northern-most lake in this drainage but is also the most developed. It is known for its large salmon, but difficult for the fly caster because the fish are so spread out. Your best bet is trolling with the fly rod or perhaps casting smelt-imitation streamers on the south shore of Sinclair Cove or Van Buren Cove, as brooks in these locations attract spawning smelt in the spring. ME 162 runs right alongside the lake for miles, giving great views with trailered boat launches in several locations, including the village of Seymour right next to the outlet and the northwest shore (47.228686,-68.289951).

A short distance downstream from Long Lake is Mud Lake, followed by Cross Lake. Most flyfishers concentrate their efforts relative to Mud Lake and Cross Lake to the thoroughfares where the fish concentrate.

Square Lake, the next lake in the chain, is popular with fly casters for several reasons. First, it has a wide-open feel to it and, with a lightly-developed shoreline, the visuals are spectacular. Second, it has good populations of both salmon and trout. Third, the fish congregate near the brook outlets at ice-out to feed on smelt, and an angler can anchor their boat, cast towards shore, and hook up. Fourth, dry-fly activity is consistent as the water warms, with trout and salmon taking mayflies off the surface during calm evenings. Try the vicinity of Goddard Cove or the California and Dimick Brook inlets.

The best way to reach the Cross/Square Lakes thoroughfare and the mouth of Square Lake is to launch a boat at the Cross Lake Boat Ramp because it is only a five-minute motor to reach the outlet. Take ME 161 between Caribou and Fort Kent and look for the Disy Road turn-off to reach the boat ramp (47.092908,-68.309516). Be careful of the large boulders as you motor through the passageway between the two lakes. Cautionary Note: Because of the topography, this lake is exposed to a north wind that can come up in a hurry in spring and fall and create large waves and currents.

Salmonids from the entire Fish River drainage take traditional Maine fly patterns. For surface activity, fish a Hornberg (in various colors), Royal Wulff, standard or Parachute Adams, March Brown, or a Klinkhammer. Standard nymphs to imitate caddis larvae or mayfly nymphs and classic streamers such as the Gray Ghost, Black Ghost, Mickey Finn, and a Magog Smelt (including a pink version that is a local pattern) and olive, brown, and black Woolly Buggers or leech patterns should also work at times.

Regulations are not consistent across all parts of the Fish River watershed so please refer to the Maine law book for all of the specifics.

Fishing the Warden's Pool on the thoroughfare between Eagle and Square Lake. Photo courtesy Fish River Lodge.

ST. JOHN RIVER

The St. John is a mighty river, originating from the most remote area of northern Maine, forming a good portion of the Maine/New Brunswick border, then flowing through New Brunswick and eventually into the Bay of Fundy. The St. John is 418 miles and drains over 21,000 square miles, which makes it the second longest river in the eastern United States (the Susquehanna River is longer).

The 130-mile stretch of upper river that traverses northern Maine between its headwater ponds and the village of Allagash offers the adventurer and flyfisher an opportunity to canoe and fish in a truly wild area.

The St. John is what is called a "flashy" river, or river of extremes. At ice-out, blocks of ice 30 feet tall crash through the trees and scour the river channel. In contrast, on a hot summer's day, the river turns shallow and "bony", making it possible to cross by wading at almost any point. For canoeists, this means a narrow window of opportunity during moderate flows.

In general, with the permission of the lumber companies, access is good, although some of the roads run in and out of Canada. North Maine Woods, an organization of the lumber companies, controls the gated roads and manages the primitive campsites and "carry only" canoe accesses in the St. John River Wilderness Area. Their headquarters are in Ashland, where they can be reached at 207-435-6213. You can contact them for reservations into the area and for information about river conditions.

Generally, the best time to canoe or kayak the river is in May and June. By July, the river is barely passable in places, although that can change if there is a big rainstorm and you have scheduling flexibility. One common put-in for the St. John is Baker Lake. A several day trip would be a 60-mile run from the North Maine Woods Red Pine campsite to Castonia Farm campsite. Several rapids in this trip should be approached with caution and don't forget to bring appropriate clothing and bug repellent for the black flies and mosquitos.

The St. John's season runs from April 1 to September 30, and anglers are advised to refer to the Maine Department of Inland Fisheries and Wildlife regulations. The river still supports some wild brook trout in the six- to ten-inch range in its upper stretches and tributaries. However, over the past 20 years, the fishing for trout has really declined because of the invasion of the predatory muskellunge. Fish elsewhere if your sole purpose is targeting brook trout or salmon.

But if you want to catch a muskie on a fly rod, the St. John is a very good option. This is a developing fishery, particularly with a fly rod. A few guides offer muskie outings on the St. John, as the fishery continues to gain popularity among locals and tourists alike. Several boat launch points are located adjacent to towns along the river, including hard-surface boat landings for larger boats in Fort Kent, Frenchville, Madawaska, and Van Buren.

Best practice in the spring of the year (while the water is high and before the water warms too much) is to fish inlets and deeper channels and cast large, synthetic, articulated muskie flies on intermediate (slow sink) fly line on a 9- or 10-weight fly rod. Often you will be rewarded

Chris Bard of Fort Kent shows off a winter landlocked salmon caught below Fish River Falls. Photo courtesy Ben Rioux.

Jesse Jalbert with a big muskie caught in early spring on the St. John River. Photo courtesy Ben Rioux.

with a slashing strike. As the water warms, cast to structure, weed beds, and the deadwater pools that can be found throughout the river between Allagash and Van Buren. Blue and chartreuse streamers bring bites in the spring, while any combination of white, red, and orange will score in the fall. For the most thrilling action, try large deer-hair poppers retrieved quickly on the surface.

Also try Glacier Lake, connected to the St. John through the Saint Francis River. From Fort Kent, drive west on Route 205 along the north bank of the St. John River, just over the U.S. border. Baker Lake is also a good muskie trip option. I know of a group of flyfishers who make the long drive every mid-September, put in a small boat, cast to shore, and catch many hefty water wolves. In both spring and fall, muskies move into the shallows to feed and can be easily cast to.

Aroostook River

Some people who fish this river regularly say that the river is one of the most underrated wild brook trout waters in New England with trout found along most of its entire 100-plus-mile length at certain times of the year.

Like many other rivers in the county, the river runs high with run-off in late May, and the best way to fish it is in a canoe or kayak retrieving marabou or bucktail streamers, or swinging traditional wet flies in the current. In downtown Caribou below the small dam, the fish stack up at this time and the fishing can be outstanding. As waters drop in June, this river is more easily waded and hatches of mayflies and caddis make dry-fly fishing more productive. Don't give up in July though, because fishing pressure diminishes and the trout start stacking up near the mouths of cooler tributaries. Hopscotch your way from trib to trib, starting at first light with longer leaders and dry flies. Dozens of small tributaries

Playing a trout at dusk on the Aroostook River at the Oxbow boat ramp. Photo courtesy Erika Zambello.

can be found along the length of the Aroostook and trout school at their mouths as the waters warm. For example, a productive section of the Aroostook is the mouth of Little Madawaska Stream down to the confluence with Moore Brook. Access is from the North Caribou Road along the north shoreline, and South Caribou Road (ME 161) south of the river. A multitude of field and farm dirt roads lead to the river, so it is never more than a short walk to the mouth of a small creek or stream. It is private property, so be courteous.

Another section to try is between the tiny towns of Maysville and Parkhurst where Hardwood, Birch, and Richardson Brooks join the river. You can reach the river from either side utilizing Roach River Extension on the west and East Presque Isle Road on the east.

Plenty of boat launches can be found, particularly in or near the major towns of Fort Fairfield, Caribou, and Presque Isle. An excellent trailered boat launch (46.428054,-68.552643) sits just upstream from Oxbow (from ME 11 take Oxbow Road). The last time I was leaving the boat launch, it was dusk and trout were still rising within casting range.

Aroostook River trout average 6 to 12 inches with an occasional lunker hitting 16 inches. Most brownish-grey dry flies in the size-14 range will work, such as the Hornberg, March Brown, or Quill Gordon. If the fish aren't looking up, try a Hare's Ear or small Pheasant Tail.

Little Madawaska Stream

Little Madawaska is a good stream to fish in its own right with lots of wild brook trout. As the water warms, look for the trout to bunch up near spring holes or other colder water sources.

Mooseleuk Stream

Mooseleuk Stream is yet another tributary of the Aroostook River that holds numbers of wild brookies. For good paddlers, a nice fishing run is from Mooseleuk Lake to Oxbow, a distance of 19 miles. For a shorter trip start at the Pinkham Road, which halves the distance, or wade downstream from the Pinham Road and fish the spot where Chandler Brook enters.

Little Black River

The Little Black River is a very remote water that travels through forested land with very little fishing pressure. Its native brook trout are spread out up and down the river, but do congregate in the deeper pools and stream mouths as the water warms in July. Any attractor dry fly or small streamer will probably work. I am hearing rumors that muskies have worked their way into the lower portions of this stream and the trout fishing has suffered. I hope that is not the case.

Access is through the Little Black checkpoint. Take Hafey Road and then look for any good logging road off to the left that will take you towards the river. You may have to walk/bushwhack a little to get to the water. You want to fish the stretch downstream from Carrie Bogan Brook. A boat landing between Johnson and Moores Brook is a good spot to shoot for.

Machias River (Aroostook County)

Aroostook County's Machias River (and its many branches) is a different river from the Machias River of Downeast Maine, and can be found due west of Ashland. It has a good reputation as an excellent trout stream with remote stretches and excellent campsites. Trout will move from the Aroostook River into spring-fed sections of the Machias River during summer's heat.

Prestile Stream

"The County" – as it is called by many – has an eastern region that has a different geology than much of the rest of New England. Underlying some of its waters is limestone instead of granite, giving a few rivers a character closer to Pennsylvania spring creeks than Maine.

Prestile Stream is the best known of the limestone waters in the county, but is still mostly fished by local anglers. It is a relatively small stream that begins near Easton and flows for about 25 miles before crossing the Canadian border and that fishes well all year. Early in the season, brook trout can be found where they have overwintered in the deeper pools such as the Dam Pool at Mar's Hill. As the water warms the trout spread out, and most runs and riffles hold fish that are feeding on hatching insects. Due to good water chemistry and fertility, hatches including Hendricksons and blue-winged olives occur in most of the river almost all year. If you like to swing wet flies, this method works well for Prestile Stream, particularly if you choose wet fly versions of the March brown or other early season mayflies.

Since many anglers keep the fish they catch, most of the trout are under 10 inches with a few growing larger.

Prestile Stream flows through farms, fields, and small towns and an angler can reach the water from numerous farm roads, bridges, and an abandoned right-of-way from the Bangor and Aroostook Railroad. In fact, if you enjoy biking, the former railroad bed is now a well-maintained rail trail that parallels a portion of the river. You can bike along, stop at river access points, try some casts, and then move to the next spot.

Some large farms grow potatoes and broccoli along the river, so ask permission before walking through a farmer's fields. A couple of popular spots are the riffles and pools found between Westfield and Mars Hill, and the deep hole where Whitney Brook dumps into the stream. The half mile from above the Boundary Road bridge (46.449132,-67.788776) to the Canadian Border also fishes well in June and early July, particularly the faster water sections.

Three Brooks Stream

A tributary of Prestile Stream, Three Brooks Stream is a great little trout water in its own right, particularly in the summer when Prestile trout seek refuge in its cooler waters. Three Brooks has some nice pools for its size, and away from the obvious access points it is lightly fished. Any attractor fly such as a Baby Brook Trout, Mickey Finn, Hornberg, Light Cahill, Royal Wulff, or Hare's Ear nymph will usually tempt the native trout. My favorite access point is Three Brooks Bridge (46.473576,-67.850170) because from there you can work down the roughly two miles to the confluence with Prestile Stream. Take Robinson Road or Old Houlton Road from US 1 to find the bridge. The Southern Bangor and Aroostook Rail Trail and the Rideout Road both provide several other access points.

Meduxnekeag River

The Meduxnekeag River (not to be confused with the Mattawamkeag River) also benefits from the limestone substrates found in this area. To my knowledge, this is the only river or stream in the county that offers brown trout. Brookies and browns both reach respectable sizes (10 to 16 inches) in these fertile waters that produce good hatches. Many flyfishers enjoy wading this river in the evening when they can cast dry flies to rising trout.

Three different stretches of river provide good angling: The North Branch, the South Branch, and the mainstem. The North Branch flows through the village of Monticello and good fishing can be found a few miles northwest of town near West Road. The best opportunities for fly casting to small brookies is to follow the river both upstream and downstream of the bridge.

The South Branch has better access and contains a mixture of larger brookies and browns. As such, the fishing pressure is a bit heavier. The pool at the confluence of the South Branch and the mainstem of the river (near Carys Mills) is a good place to fish.

The mainstem of the Meduxnekeag begins at the outlet of Drews Lake and travels for about 20 miles before crossing into New Brunswick. The river is divided into two distinct sections by the city of Houlton. The upper river has some beautiful deep pools that hold bigger than hand-sized trout. A number of farm roads provide good access.

Foxcroft Road parallels the lower river, and farm field roads provide good access for wading or boating anglers. Some good spots are the Big Brook Outlet, Smith Brook Outlet, and the Covered Bridge Pool (46.209917,-67.800055).

DEBOULLIE MOUNTAIN REGION

The Deboullie Township is a very interesting geological area with a number of excellent ponds relatively close together that offer a variety of excellent flyfishing options. Most of the ponds are within walking distance or a short drive from each other. There isn't any river or stream fishing to speak of; you can jump across the Red River and trout are only a few inches long. This area offers abundant wildlife, scenic hikes (including one up to the summit of Deboullie Mountain), unique features such as ice caves and rock slides, and virtually no development.

If traveling to this area, take I-95 north to Exit 264, and follow ME 11 for 70 miles to Portage. Go left on West Road and follow the sign until after three miles, you can check in at North Maine Woods Gate. Then follow signs for 23 miles to the Red River and surrounding ponds. From the north, follow ME 161 from Fort Kent for 23 miles and then turn left at Chamberlain's store and find the gate a half-mile in.

While you can drive in for the day from Portage or Fort Kent on relatively good dirt roads, the best way to experience this area is to camp at one of several camping areas or stay at Red River Camps, the only alternative in the area. Fortunately, it is an excellent option. The owner, Jen Brophy, knows the entire area well (her parents owned the camp before her) and provides her guests with a quality wilderness experience with excellent food and friendly hospitality. They also have stashed canoes at all of the ponds. If you are camping in the area, you need to bring your own canoe, kayak, or float tube.

The 19 ponds offer a variety of fishing experiences including: casting to abundant but smaller native brookies, harvesting stocked fish, trying for trophy-sized trout, and even a chance to catch a blueback trout, part of a remnant population from the last ice age that are only found in a few ponds in Maine (or the world). The best way to proceed is to decide what type of fishing suits your fancy, find the ponds that provide it, and then try to hit a few of those ponds in one day. The fishing regulations vary from pond to pond and change each year, so please check the latest Maine booklet of rules and regulations.

Black Pond

Black Pond is at 1,225 feet elevation and is an artificial-lure-only fishery filled with wild brook trout, but deep enough to hold arctic char as well (which it does). It is a pretty pond with a hand-carry boat launch and is a short walk from Red River Camps. Brophy says that Black Pond fishes consistently well and holds larger trout than some of the other ponds.

Red River Camps' main lodge. The original burned down in 2009 when it was struck by lightning. Photo courtesy Red River Camps.

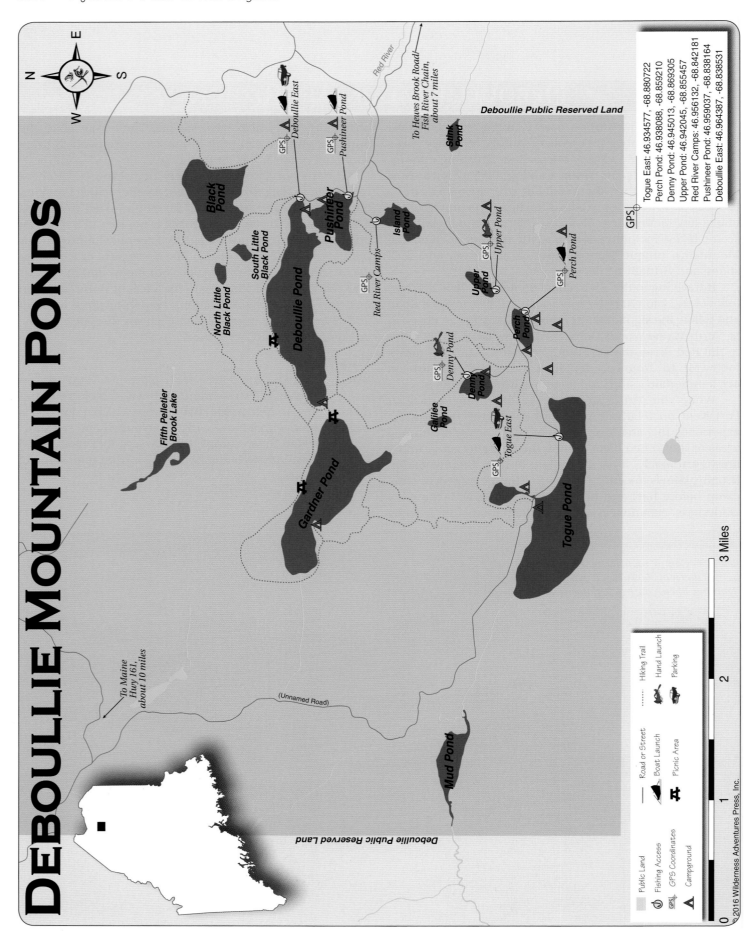

DEBOULLIE MOUNTAIN PONDS

Togue East: 46.934577, -68.880722
Perch Pond: 46.938088, -68.859210
Denny Pond: 46.945013, -68.869305
Upper Pond: 46.942045, -68.855457
Red River Camps: 46.956132, -68.842181
Pushineer Pond: 46.959037, -68.838164
Deboullie East: 46.964387, -68.838531

Deboullie Public Reserved Land

Red River

To Heues Brook Road—
Fish River Chain,
about 7 miles

Stink
Pond

Deboullie East

Pushineer Pond

GPS

GPS

Black
Pond

North Little
Black Pond

South Little
Black Pond

Pushineer
Pond

Island
Pond

Upper
Pond

GPS

Upper Pond

Perch Pond

GPS

Deboullie Pond

Red River Camps

GPS

Fifth Pelletier
Brook Lake

Perch
Pond

Denny Pond

GPS

Denny
Pond

Galilee
Pond

Gardner Pond

Togue East

GPS

Togue Pond

To Maine
Huy 161,
about 10 miles

(Unnamed Road)

Deboullie Public Reserved Land

Mud Pond

Public Land
Fishing Access
GPS GPS Coordinates
▲ Campground

Road or Street
Boat Launch
Picnic Area

Hiking Trail
Hand Launch
Parking

2016 Wilderness Adventures Press, Inc.

0   1   2   3 Miles

Little Black Ponds

It is flyfishing only on picturesque North Little Black Pond and South Little Black Pond. Access to both is by foot trail. North Little Black Pond, in particular, is overpopulated with small brook trout and is an excellent spot for beginner flyfishers. Anglers report that both ponds seem to fish either really hot or really cold; not sure why, or if that experience is actually shared by everybody. If fish are looking up, a Parachute Adams, Hornberg, or a red Doodle Bug will all attract attention. If nothing seems to be stirring on the surface, then damselfly and dragonfly nymphs are especially good as well as any black-leech-imitating streamers (sizes 8 to 10).

Crater Pond

Crater Pond is an artificial-lure-only pond with a hand-carried boat launch. Flyfish the Mosquito Emerger (sizes 14 to 20), brown and tan Woolly Worms (sizes 6 to 12), and a range of caddis pupa and larva patterns.

Deboullie Pond

Deboullie Pond, called "Deboullie Lake" on some regional maps, sits at 1,128 feet elevation and has a boat launch that will handle trailered boats. This is one of the larger waters in the area at 282 acres and almost 100 feet deep, and it grows bigger trout than other ponds. In addition to brook trout, this is one of the waters where arctic char still swim. Char are not easy to catch and, except for early spring, tend to be found in deep waters. If you want to try to hook this rare fish, fish deep with sinking line and small wet flies.

Denny Pond

Denny Pond is flyfishing only and also has a hand-carried boat launch. A 25-acre spring-hole pond that is 35 feet deep, it is full of 8- to 12-inch brook trout. An Elk Hair Caddis will do the job, though terrestrials, especially hoppers, catch trout in the summer. Two well-maintained forest campsites are located on the eastern shore. Access is by a rough dirt road.

Fifth Pelletier Brook Lake

On Fifth Pelletier Brook Lake, try olive, black, and brown caddis (sizes 12 to 16), terrestrials including beetles and inchworms, damselfly and dragonfly nymphs, and finally, cream or olive scuds (sizes 4 to 10).

Gardner Lake

Fish scuds, leech patterns, and damselfly or dragonfly nymphs on 1,134-foot Gardner Lake (listed as "Gardner Pond" on some maps). This is another deep pond (over 120 feet) that holds arctic char because of its cold waters. Gardner Lake (along with Debouillie and Black) also holds the largest trout in the area.

Galilee Pond

Galilee Pond is a spectacular flyfishing-only seven-acre pond with sheer cliffs dropping all the way to the water's edge and continuing underwater to a depth of 27 feet. Concentrate your efforts on the edges of the deep hole. Retrieve midge, dragonfly or damselfly nymphs and scud patterns to catch trout. Stop here on your way to and from Gardner Pond.

Island Pond

Cast from a canoe along the western shore of Island Pond, which is flyfishing only. The entire 32-acre, 44-foot deep pond holds trout, and similarly to other nearby ponds, caddis dries, pupae and larvae, along with damselfly and dragonfly nymphs are effective patterns here. This smaller pond will stay calmer on windy days and is a good float-tube option.

The cliffs of Galilee Pond. Photo courtesy Red River Camps.

Mud Pond

On Mud Pond, fish traditional mayfly and caddisfly patterns. Scuds fished along the pond's bottom also catch trout.

Perch Pond

Small flies work on Perch Pond, including scuds, foam or cork beetles, and mosquito drys (sizes 18 to 22). Cast and retrieve scuds slowly with sinking lines. Access is by unimproved road, with a hand-carried boat launch.

Pushineer Pond

Fish scuds, damselfly and dragonfly nymphs on Pushineer Pond, which also has a trailerable boat launch. This is another deep pond with arctic char. Several years ago, a father and son hooked a large fish (the son thought he had hooked a log). When they boated this beast that looked to be over five pounds, they didn't know what it was because it didn't look like a brook trout. They stopped at Red River Lodge where they were told that it might be the state-record arctic char. It was officially measured and weighed at 25.4 inches and 5.2 pounds – indeed a state record.

Stink Pond

Stink Pond, a 16-acre float-tube water, is five feet deep at most and flyfishing only. The limited access to this fishery diminishes angling pressure.

Togue Pond

There is a trailered boat launch on Togue Pond, and yes, it has togue (lake trout) as well as landlocked salmon. It also has several maintained wilderness campsites located on the pond's northern shore, with unimproved road access available. Search this water with sinking line and a black or olive Marabou Leech (sizes 4 to 6).

Upper Pond

Upper Pond is flyfishing only and has a hand-carried boat launch and is accessible by unimproved road.

OTHER STILLWATERS

Baskahegan Lake

County residents tell me that the best smallmouth bass lake in their area is Baskahegan Lake. Go south on US 1 from Houlton and Danforth and take a right in Brookton on Baskahegan Lake Road. Within a mile of the turn-off will be the lake's only boat launch (45.527153,-67.784573). Fishing improves the farther you move away from the launch point.

Blake Lake

Blake Lake is more pond-sized than lake and is remote (47.091217,-68.536736), found north of Eagle Lake (of the Fish River Chain) about 45 minutes down rough logging roads. Upon reaching it and launching a canoe or kayak, anglers will be rewarded with a multitude of eager wild brook trout. It has a tremendous *Hexagenia* hatch in late June and early July during the late afternoons and evenings on still, warm, and humid days. Ask the folks at Fish River Lodge for more detailed instructions and directions.

Durepo Pond in Limestone, just on the border of the Aroostook National Wildlife Refuge is well stocked and is a good stillwater flyfishing option for this part of the state.

Nadeau Lake

Nadeau Lake, which lies between Route 1A and the US/Canada boundary north of Fort Fairfield, has a unique story. From the IF&W website:

"For 30 years its bottom was dredged for a valuable liming agent, marl, that was used in regional agriculture. In 2007 I.F.&W. completed a multi-year project to restore the original water level, improve trout habitat, and remove several competing species of fishes. The chemical reclamation in 2007 was highly successful. In 2014 trout fishing was reportedly very good with trout up to 20 inches being caught.

A state-owned launch and parking area are easily accessed off Route 1A approximately 6 miles north of downtown Fort Fairfield. A concrete ramp is available for launching small watercraft and there is a large area available for shore angling as well."

Pleasant Lake

Pleasant Lake is a relatively good-sized lake for this part of Maine and can be found near the hamlet of Island Falls with easy access from US 2. It has a reputation as a fine brook trout and landlocked salmon water.

Wallagrass Lakes

First and Second Wallagrass Lakes are also prime native brook trout waters. Good locations to fish are the thoroughfare between the lakes, the outlet, and along Wallagrass Stream. Access is from the tiny town of Wallagrass on ME 11. Just north of town, take a left on Carter Brook Tote Road which will take you right to both the thoroughfare and the outlet. Near the outlet of First Lake it is possible to hand carry a small boat down to the water, allowing an angler to cover more territory.

Northern Maine Planning Considerations

Nearby Hub Cities

- Ashland (www.northmainewoods.org, townofashland.org)
- Fort Kent (www.fortkentchamber.com)
- Houlton (www.greaterhoulton.com)
- Presque Isle (www.centralaroostookchamber.org)

Easy Access Options

- Soldier Pond Road crosses the Fish River below Soldier Pond (a wider and slower part of the river). Access is easy for both wading and boating anglers from the bridge. A well-maintained boat ramp and parking area can be found immediately downstream from the bridge on the eastern shore. From Fort Kent, travel south on Route 11 for about six miles and look for Soldiers Pond on your left.
- The Aroostook River boat ramp just west of Oxbow Maine provides a parking area and an easy walk or wheelchair roll to the water's edge on pavement. Trout will often be holding right at the ramp because a large boulder to the left of the ramp creates an eddy line. A few steps around the boulder or down the bank opens up more water to fish, with no trees or bushes to bother a back cast. From ME 11, travel west on Oxbow Road, pass through the hamlet of Oxbow and then look for the boat ramp on the right (46.428070,-68.552683).
- Several good sites to reach Prestile Stream or its tributary, Three Brook Stream, within close proximity to each other are half way between Mar's Hill and Bridgewater. Take US 1 north of Bridgewater and then bear right on Old Houlton Road until it crosses the tributary. You can take a few steps down a gentle grade from the bridge to reach this productive stream. If you take a right on Robinson Road at the bridge and travel a little farther, you will reach Prestile Stream at the site of a small dam with a park on either side. It is easy to fish above the dam or below the dam on either side of the stream at this location. Travel farther on Robinson Road and then take a right on Barrett Road and you soon cross a small stream with a very short dirt track at the edge of a field that leads right to Prestile Stream.

Suggested Beginner Options

- In the Deboullie Mountain area, Jen Brophy, the owner of Red River Camps, recommends fishing Upper Little Black Pond (teeming with small brook trout), as well as Denny Pond and Birch Pond.
- Try the outlet of First Wallagrass Lake. Usually, eager brook trout will be anxious to take your offerings. Try a Hornberg or an Adams and if the fish don't appear eager to hit on the surface, try a small Gray Ghost or a Wood Special.
- State of Maine fisheries experts indicate that Little Madawaska Stream's wild trout are a good option for a beginner.
- Hire a guide from Fish River Lodge. Tenley and Wayne Bennett will improve your technique and know where best to go to catch brook trout and landlocked salmon.

Suggested Flyfishing Vacation Options

Weekend Getaway

- Spend the weekend at Red River Camps and fish the surrounding ponds. Owner Jen Brophy will help you choose the type of pond that has the fishing you are interested in – large trout, lots of small trout, blueback trout, etc. Regardless of the fishing, you will have a good wilderness experience.
- Choose any weekend from late May through June and stay at Fish River Lodge on Eagle Lake. Not only is Eagle Lake a productive lake for trolling for salmon, brook trout, and lakers, but rising fish are a distinct possibility in the evening and during hatches. The lodge is only a short paddle from the Nadeau Thoroughfare, the section of the Fish River that connects Eagle Lake and St. Froid Lake. This part of the river offers easy wading for brook trout and landlocked salmon that enter the moving water in the spring to chase smelt and feed on emerging mayflies and caddis flies. The experience will seldom be crowded. That is the beauty of fishing in Aroostock County – frequently you will have the water all to yourself.
- Fish the unique limestone streams of eastern Aroostook County. If you stay overnight anywhere between Mars Hill and Presque Isle, you won't have to travel far to try Prestile Stream and the Meduxnekeag

River. Their unique chemistry and numbers of brook trout and brown trout make for an interesting and productive weekend. The fish won't likely be large and this is not a wilderness setting, but if you enjoy pastoral settings, consistent fishing action, and the convenience of stores and services only 15 minutes away, this might be a good weekend choice.

One-week Vacation

- Canoe the Allagash Wilderness Waterway. One great information source is www.maine.gov/allagash. It has Google Map locations of all campsites with photos, printable maps, video links, rules, and fee information. You also might want to read "The Allagash Guide" by Gil Gilpatrick.
- Explore the different waters of Aroostook County. One day can be spent floating the Fish River from Eagle Lake to Fort Kent. Fishing any of the other thoroughfares from Fish River Lake to Eagle Lake could take several more days.

    Fish the Allagash River while camping at Round Pond.

    Fish the ponds of Deboullie Mountain from Red River Camps.

    Hire a guide to take you muskie fishing at Glacier Lake or the St. John River.

ABOVE: Aroostook County is an excellent place for beginners to learn to flyfish. Photo courtesy Ben Rioux. BOTTOM: An angler trying his luck right off the Oxbow boat ramp. Photo courtesy Erika Zambello.

Recommended Flies
Streamers

CONEHEAD MARABOU SOFT HACKLE

HEAD: Black conehead of various sizes and weights
WEIGHT: Two or three turns of lead wire pushed into conehead
HOOK: Size-6 4x long streamer hook
THREAD: 8/0 black Uni-thread
BODY: None
UNDERWING: Contrasting bucktail
WING: Gray, white, or green marabou hackled with fibers swept back toward the hook bend
HACKLE: A turn or two of mallard or grouse

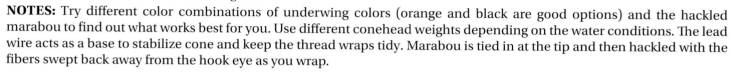

NOTES: Try different color combinations of underwing colors (orange and black are good options) and the hackled marabou to find out what works best for you. Use different conehead weights depending on the water conditions. The lead wire acts as a base to stabilize cone and keep the thread wraps tidy. Marabou is tied in at the tip and then hackled with the fibers swept back away from the hook eye as you wrap.

BEADHEAD MINIMUDDER

HOOK: Size 16 3x long nymph (Daiichi 1720 or the equivalent)
HEAD: 5/32" black tungsten bead
THREAD: 8/0 tan Uni-thread
TAIL: Mottled turkey
BODY: Gold Mylar
UNDERWING: Pearl Crystal Flash, sparse orange deer body hair
HEAD/COLLAR: Fine natural deer hair, spun and trimmed tight

WOOD SPECIAL

HOOK: Standard 4x streamer hook, sizes 4-8
THREAD: 8/0 black Uni-thread
HEAD: Black bead or cone (optional)
TAIL: Six golden pheasant tail fibers
BODY: Large diameter pink chenille with spiraled silver tinsel
RIB: Silver oval tinsel, counter wound
WING: Wood duck or dyed mallard flank feather
HACKLE: Grizzly color, but larger and "webbier" hackle than for a traditional dry fly

CRYSTAL WOOLLY BUGGER

HOOK: Tiemco 5263 (or similar streamer hook) size 6-12
THREAD: Uni-threadWhite 6/0
BEADHEAD: Spirit River brite bead or its equivalent
BODY: Chenille (Ice) or J. Fair shuck (sometimes called cactus chenille)
RIBBING: Silver wire
HACKLE: Whiting Bugger Wet Fly Hackle
TAIL: Marabou with a little Crystal Flash

TYING NOTES: Be creative about how you combine different shades of materials.

CHARLIE'S BBT HORNBERG

HOOK: Orvis Muddler hook (or any 3x long shank streamer hook size 6-10
THREAD: Black Uni-thread 6/0
TAIL: Red fibers
BODY: Silver tinsel (thin)
UNDERWING: Dyed soft-hackle tips, orange and yellow
WING: Four natural mallard flank feathers
HACKLE: Soft grizzly hen collar. Can substitute red or orange hackle.

TYING NOTES: For the underwing, the orange hackle tip is tied in above the yellow feather. The mallard feather is tied in Hornberg style, two on each side of the hook, almost completely covering the underwing, but not entirely, so that a bit of orange shows at the top and a bit of yellow shows at the bottom. Jungle cock eye optional.

Dries

PUTERBAUGH CADDIS

HOOK: Size 16, standard dry fly hook
THREAD: 8/0 black Uni-thread
BODY: 1/4-inch wide rectangle of black foam, from thorax to hook bend – not too wide or long
WING: Light tan, fine, elk hair extending slightly beyond the body
HACKLE: Ginger hackled at thorax

HORNBERG (DRY FLY VERSION)

HOOK: Size 14, standard dry fly hook
THREAD: Black 8/0 Uni-thread or similar
UNDERBODY: Silver flat tinsel
UNDERWING: Yellow and sparse; could be hen hackle or a few soft hairs
WINGS: Two barred mallard flank feathers, with the cupped sides facing inward
HACKLE: Grizzly

TYING NOTE: Coating the back edge of the mallard feathers with a thin coat of Dave's Fleximent or similar (and tapering to a point) will add to the durability of the dry fly. If you want to fish this fly as a wet fly or streamer, utilize a 4XL Daiichi model 1750 hook in size 8 or 10 and add a second layer of tinsel and more yellow underwing.

YELLOW COMPARADUN

HOOK: Standard dry fly hook, size 10-14
THREAD: Danville Flymaster 6/0 #7 orange/ yellow/brown
WING: Bleached deer hair
TAILS: Yellow Microfibetts, six fibers split 3/3
ABDOMEN: Amber rabbit dubbing, and ribbed with the tying thread
THORAX: Amber rabbit dubbing, more robust than the abdomen
HEAD: Orange/Yellow

KLINKHAMMER

HOOK: Partridge 15BN klinkhammer or 2x long nymph hook bent slightly
THREAD: 8/0 black Uni-thread
ABDOMEN: Black thread and fine black dubbing
THORAX: Peacock dubbing
WING POST: White z-lon or similar
HACKLE: Black hackle parachute style on post

TYING NOTES: Try different color combinations to imitate different insects. Pheasant tail wrapped with copper abdomen, peacock herl thorax, natural CDC wing, and brown hackle on a white z-lon post (sometimes referred to as the Adams version) is a good general mayfly imitation.

QUIGLEY GREEN DRAKE CRIPPLE

HOOK: Size 10 2x long dry fly
THREAD: 8/0 olive Uni-thread
BODY: Olive pheasant aftershaft feather (philoplume) or olive ostrich feather
THORAX: Olive dubbed rabbit ball
WING: Natural deer hair
HACKLE: Grizzly dyed olive

MIDGE

HOOK: Tiemco TMC 100 size 22
THREAD: Black 8/0 Uni-thread
EXTENDED BODY (SHUCK): Black or golden olive Montana Fly Company Midge Body Thread or similar material
WING: Gray Medallion Sheeting
HACKLE: Grizzly saddle hackle
THORAX: Peacock herl

TYING NOTES: To make the shuck, after tieing in at the middle of the hook shank, twist a 3-inch piece of Midge Body Thread or a similar material in opposite directions using your index fingers and thumbs. As you bring your fingers together, the thread will collapse and twist on itself. Tie the now-furled thread so it extends a quarter-inch over the hook bend. The rest of the fly is straightforward.

SWANSON'S STONE

HOOK: Size 8 Mustad 3665A (or any 6xl hook like the 3665A)
THREAD: Yellow
TAIL: Two Yellow goose biots
BODY: Yellow polypropelene yarn (I would split it in half or even by quarters)
UNDERWING: Reeves pheasant body feather trimmed with two notches on each side and with the tip cut out to represent legs (The feather trimming is optional. It's a problematic additional step and gets lost under the wing anyways. It looks cool but is mostly for show.)
WING: Natural Dark Brown bucktail from a white tail. Use the thicker, hollower hair from the very base near the tailbone)
HACKLE: Two or three natural brown/furnace rooster hackles or a really long saddle. You want this sucker FULL after it's wound, don't skimp.

TYING NOTES: Very few professional tiers tie and sell this fly. My first samples were tied by Deryn LaCombe and he still sells them at www.squaretails.com The key to this fly being more effective then other stonefly patterns is that it sits more naturally on the water. Don't make the body too thick. Rather than yellow polypropelene yarn, Deryn LaCombe uses Hareline rabbit dubbing, color Yellow #9. Ringneck pheasant "church" feathers are a good substitute for Reeves pheasant.

Nymphs

MAPLE SYRUP

HOOK: Size 8 or 10, Mustad 3665A or similar streamer (6X) hook
THREAD: 8/0 black Uni-thread
BODY: Tan medium chenille
TAIL: Yellow Calf Tail or soft Bucktail (tied sparse)

TYING NOTES: The Maple Syrup is meant to imitate a hex nymph and was developed by Alvin Theriault from Stacyville, Maine. This fly can also be tied using a healthy amount of lead wire beneath the chenille. If not tying in lead, make sure you double the chenille back on itself for a double layer.

PHEASANT TAIL

HOOK: TMC 100SP-BL size 14-20
THREAD: 8/0 Rusty brown
HEAD: 1/16" gold or tungsten bead
TAIL: Ringneck pheasant tail fibers
RIB: Fine copper wire
ABDOMEN: Ringneck pheasant tail fibers
BACKSTRAP: Crystal Flash
WING CASE: Green holographic Flashabou
LEGS: Ringneck pheasant tail fibers
THORAX: Peacock Herl from the eyed quill

TYING NOTES: Keep this fly thin by utilizing the same pheasant fibers for the entire fly. Other colors are worth tying, including black and olive.

SIMS STONE, HOT-SPOT VERSION

HOOK: Size 10 2x long nymph hook (Daiichi 1710 2x long or the equivalent)
THREAD: 8/0 black Uni-thread
HEAD: 1/8" black, red, or orange tungsten bead
TAIL: Black hackle tips
BODY: Black Hare's Ear dubbing
RIB: Fine copper counter wound
WING CASE: Clear Flashback or any iridescent clear plastic
LEGS: Black Hare's Ear dubbing tied on a loop or teasing out dubbing

TYING NOTES: Black tungsten bead is the standard tie, but orange or red creates a "hot spot" that attracts jaded fish or is more easily seen in off-color water. Size of bead depends on the sink rate that you want to achieve.

STOCKIE BASHER

HOOK: Jig hook, sizes 16 to 10
BEAD: Copper tungsten
THREAD: Dark brown 6/0 (140 denier)
TAILS: Medium coq de Leon
ABDOMEN: Tying thread
RIB: Small copper wire
THORAX: Light pink Ice Dubbing
HOTSPOT: Fluorescent pink 6/0 (140 denier) tying thread

COPPER JOHN, PINK

HOOK: TMC 5262, sizes 14-20
THREAD: UTC 140 brown
UNDERBODY: lead wire 0.4mm
BEAD: Gold 3.3mm
TAIL AND LEGS: Partridge or mottled hen back (some tyers like goose biot for the tail)
BODY: Pink copper wire, here UNI
WING CASE: Hemingway's Flash Back Foil – Peacock and UV glue

TYING TIPS: This fly works best for me in smaller sizes – 18 being ideal. Any flashback material can be utilized including black Thin Skin or pearl tinsel

SUCKER SPAWN

HOOK: Size 14 scud or egg hook
THREAD: 8/0 yellow Uni-thread
BODY: McFlyfoam egg yarn – McCheese color (light yellow)
TYING NOTES: Tie 1/4-inch wide strand of yarn, then loop yarn loosely back on itself to create egg shape, tie off, and trim ends. Optional: for faster sinking egg, place small bead in center of hook shank, glue and wrap to secure, loop yarn over bead both top and bottom.

Postscript

Thank you for purchasing my book. I hope that you will find it useful in discovering new favorite fishing spots. I am interested in obtaining your feedback and learning how my fishing experiences with these waters compare to your own. I am also interested in learning of any information in the book that is obsolete, needs to be updated, or is just plain wrong. If you would like to share with me any waters that you believe are worth adding to the book, I will take those ideas as well. Please e-mail me at louzambello@gmail.com. When this book is updated and reprinted, I will incorporate your information in the new version.

To read my blog and keep up to date with what I am doing, visit my website, www.mainelyflyfishing.com, or check my facebook page. For hundreds of additional photos of the waters described in this book, also see my website. For videos of some of the locations described in this book, search YouTube for "mainelyflyfishing" videos.

This book, "Flyfishers Guide to New England" is primarily a where-to-go book. My previously published book, "Flyfishing Northern New England's Seasons: How to fish ice-out, hatch season, summer, the fall spawning run, and winter" is a companion book that is a how-to primer to maximize your success on the waters described here. If you haven't read it, I think that you will enjoy it and find it useful.

Index